T0401352

# Knowledge Management Initiatives and Strategies in Small and Medium Enterprises

Andrea Bencsik
*Széchenyi István University, Hungary & J. Selye University, Slovakia*

A volume in the Advances in Logistics,
Operations, and Management Science (ALOMS)
Book Series

www.igi-global.com

Published in the United States of America by
IGI Global
Business Science Reference (an imprint of IGI Global)
701 E. Chocolate Avenue
Hershey PA, USA 17033
Tel: 717-533-8845
Fax: 717-533-8661
E-mail: cust@igi-global.com
Web site: http://www.igi-global.com

 Library of Congress Cataloging-in-Publication Data

Library of Congress Cataloging-in-Publication Data

Names: Bencsik, Andrea, editor.
Title: Knowledge management initiatives and strategies in small and medium
 enterprises / Andrea Bencsik, editor.
Description: Hershey : Business Science Reference, 2016. | Series: Advances
 in logistics, operations, and management science | Includes
 bibliographical references and index.
Identifiers: LCCN 2016037430| ISBN 9781522516422 (hardcover) | ISBN
 9781522516439 (ebook)
Subjects: LCSH: Knowledge management. | Small business. | Organizational
 learning.
Classification: LCC HD30.2 .K63746 2016 | DDC 658.4/038--dc23 LC record available at https://lccn.loc.gov/2016037430

This book is published in the IGI Global book series Advances in Logistics, Operations, and Management Science (ALOMS) (ISSN: 2327-350X; eISSN: 2327-3518)

British Cataloguing in Publication Data
A Cataloguing in Publication record for this book is available from the British Library.

For electronic access to this publication, please contact: eresources@igi-global.com.

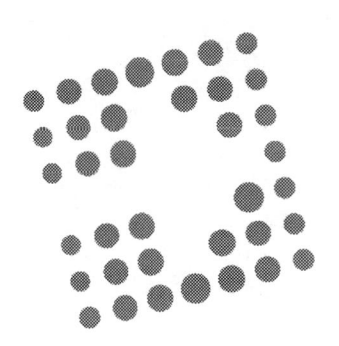

# Advances in Logistics, Operations, and Management Science (ALOMS) Book Series

John Wang
*Montclair State University, USA*

ISSN: 2327-350X
EISSN: 2327-3518

## MISSION

Operations research and management science continue to influence business processes, administration, and management information systems, particularly in covering the application methods for decision-making processes. New case studies and applications on management science, operations management, social sciences, and other behavioral sciences have been incorporated into business and organizations real-world objectives.

The **Advances in Logistics, Operations, and Management Science** (ALOMS) Book Series provides a collection of reference publications on the current trends, applications, theories, and practices in the management science field. Providing relevant and current research, this series and its individual publications would be useful for academics, researchers, scholars, and practitioners interested in improving decision making models and business functions.

## COVERAGE

- Information Management
- Marketing engineering
- Production management
- Risk Management
- Services management
- Finance
- Political Science
- Computing and information technologies
- Decision analysis and decision support
- Operations Management

IGI Global is currently accepting manuscripts for publication within this series. To submit a proposal for a volume in this series, please contact our Acquisition Editors at Acquisitions@igi-global.com or visit: http://www.igi-global.com/publish/.

# Titles in this Series

*For a list of additional titles in this series, please visit: www.igi-global.com*

*Optimum Decision Making in Asset Management*
María Carmen Carnero (University of Castilla – La Mancha, Spain) and Vicente González-Prida (University of Seville, Spain)
Business Science Reference • copyright 2017 • 523pp • H/C (ISBN: 9781522506515) • US $215.00 (our price)

*Green Supply Chain Management for Sustainable Business Practice*
Mehmood Khan (Abu Dhabi University, UAE) Matloub Hussain (Abu Dhabi University, UAE) and Mian M. Ajmal (Abu Dhabi University, UAE)
Business Science Reference • copyright 2017 • 330pp • H/C (ISBN: 9781522506355) • US $185.00 (our price)

*Multinational Enterprise Management Strategies in Developing Countries*
Mohammad Ayub Khan (Tecnológico de Monterrey, Mexico)
Business Science Reference • copyright 2016 • 490pp • H/C (ISBN: 9781522502760) • US $200.00 (our price)

*Strategic Management of Sustainable Manufacturing Operations*
Rameshwar Dubey (Symbiosis International University, India) and Angappa Gunasekaran (University of Massachuesetts, Dartmouth, USA)
Business Science Reference • copyright 2016 • 419pp • H/C (ISBN: 9781522503507) • US $215.00 (our price)

*Handbook of Research on Global Fashion Management and Merchandising*
Alessandra Vecchi (London College of Fashion, U.K.) and Chitra Buckley (London College of Fashion, U.K.)
Business Science Reference • copyright 2016 • 862pp • H/C (ISBN: 9781522501107) • US $335.00 (our price)

*Handbook of Research on Managerial Strategies for Achieving Optimal Performance in Industrial Processes*
Giner Alor-Hernández (Instituto Tecnológico de Orizaba, Mexico) Cuauhtémoc Sánchez-Ramírez (Instituto Tecnológico de Orizaba, Mexico) and Jorge Luis García-Alcaraz (Universidad Autónoma de Ciudad Juárez, Mexico)
Business Science Reference • copyright 2016 • 674pp • H/C (ISBN: 9781522501305) • US $365.00 (our price)

*Supply Chain Strategies and the Engineer-to-Order Approach*
Richard Addo-Tenkorang (University of Vaasa, Finland) Jussi Kantola (University of Vaasa, Finland) Petri Helo (University of Vaasa, Finland) and Ahm Shamsuzzoha (Sultan Qaboos University, Oman)
Business Science Reference • copyright 2016 • 283pp • H/C (ISBN: 9781522500216) • US $200.00 (our price)

*Optimal Inventory Control and Management Techniques*
Mandeep Mittal (Amity School of Engineering and Technology, India) and Nita H. Shah (Gujarat University, India)
Business Science Reference • copyright 2016 • 406pp • H/C (ISBN: 9781466698888) • US $170.00 (our price)

www.igi-global.com

701 E. Chocolate Ave., Hershey, PA 17033
Order online at www.igi-global.com or call 717-533-8845 x100
To place a standing order for titles released in this series, contact: cust@igi-global.com
Mon-Fri 8:00 am - 5:00 pm (est) or fax 24 hours a day 717-533-8661

# List of Reviewers

Helena de Almeida, *University of Algarve, Portugal*
Karoly Balaton, *University of Miskolc, Hungary*
Gyorgy Bogel, *CEU Business School, Hungary*
Monika Brezinova, *University of South Bohemia in České Bedějovice, Czech Republic*
Sara Csillag, *Budapest Business School, Hungary & University of Applied Sciences, Hungary*
Silvia Fernandes, *University of Algarve, Potugal*
Janos Fustos, *Metropolitan State University of Denver, USA*
Darja Holatova, *University of South Bohemia in České Bedějovice, Czech Republic*
Osaze Ijiekhuamhen, *Federal University of Petroleum Resources Effurun, Nigeria*
Libena Kantnerova, *University of South Bohemia in České Bedějovice, Czech Republic*
Ferenc Kiss, *Metropolitan University of Budapest, Hungary*
Gabor Klimko, *Corvinus University of Budapest, Hungary*
Bernardo Meyer, *Federal University of Santa Catarina, Brazil*
Saturday Omeluzor, *Federal University of Petroleum Resources Effurun, Nigeria*
Bernadett Oszene Samu, *Jedlik Anyos Engineering Industry & Informatics High School, Hungary*
Laszlo Pitlik, *Szent István University, Hungary*
Jozsef Poor, *Szent Istvan University, Hungary*
Emeric Solymossy, *Western Illinois University, USA*
Radka Vanickova, *Institute of Technology and Economics in Czech Budejovice, Czech Republic*
Sarka Zapletalova, *Silesian University in Opava, Czech Republic & School of Business Administration in Karviná, Czech Republic*
Jarmila Zimmermannova, *Moravian University College Olomouc, Czech Republic*

# Table of Contents

**Section 1**
**Theoretical Basics of a Knowledge Management System and Its Connection with
Enterprises'/Companies' Processes**

# Detailed Table of Contents

## Section 1
## Theoretical Basics of a Knowledge Management System and Its Connection with Enterprises'/Companies' Processes

**Chapter 1**
Knowledge Management and Its Approaches: Basics of Developing Company Knowledge
Management Systems ............................................................................................................................ 1
  *Anikó Balogh, Central European University, Hungary*

This chapter briefly covers the basics and definitions of knowledge and knowledge management, the connection between KM and communication, its Hungarian and international development and tendencies in the past years and the so called KM generations. The chapter's goal is to show how and why the support and appreciation of knowledge (which almost exists since the beginning of humankind) developed into a system. Successful management of companies using KM systems bring to the surface a new breed of organization operating models operating with intelligent solutions, which are manifold, may be structured in a variable way, and are specifically unique in the light of these knowledge-intensive services.

**Chapter 2**
Decision Maker in the Global Village: Thinking Together ................................................................. 25
  *Jolán Velencei, Óbuda University, Hungary*
  *Zoltán Baracskai, Babeş-Bolyai University, Romania*

The Nobel Memorial Prize in Economics has been awarded twice so far to researchers in the area of decision making. In 1978 to Herbert Simon "for his pioneering research into the decision-making process within economic organizations" and in 2002 to Daniel Kahneman "for having integrated insights from psychological research into economic science, especially concerning human judgment and decision-making under uncertainty". In spite of this, in business schools and schools of economics courses in decision making focus on decision tools of applied operations research. There are, however, newer views that have not yet made their ways into the decision curricula. Therefore the authors argue that in the Global Village the decision taker's role is wearing off while the decision maker's role is changing. Now, that a great deal of knowledge is available freely and free of charge, a new possibility is opening up for a new type of thinking together. In this Chapter the authors take a closer look at this thinking together.

This chapter reveals the prospect of organizational learning; organizational learning and networks; organizational learning, organizational innovation, and transformational leadership; organizational learning, absorptive capacity, open innovation, and information technology (IT); organizational learning and training; organizational learning capability (OLC) and enterprise resource planning (ERP); and learning organization. Organizational learning is an important method by which organizations develop, enhance, and manage knowledge within their organizational functions and improve their efficiency by making better use of the wide range of skills of their employees. Regarding organizational learning, organizations improve the ability to respond to various business situations and enhance competitive performance through generating new knowledge. The chapter argues that encouraging organizational learning has the potential to improve organizational performance and gain sustainable competitive advantage in the workplace.

# Chapter 4

Successful business operation depends on several factors. Among these factors knowledge management and innovation are extremely important business areas. The aim of this theoretical study is to introduce how these two models work together and how their relationship reinforces the chance for success. Relying on secondary data analysis and literature review, the authors prove that the classical innovation model can be a part of this relationship together with the organizational innovation where the human resource comes to focus. The logic of system building of knowledge management emphasizes that the path leads from the attainment of innovation knowledge to the evaluation of utilization. This study reviews the steps of the two business models and highlights the most important relationships in a new model linking the appropriate phases. The second part of this paper shows the connection between frugal innovation and knowledge management, and their theoretical significance and practical adaptability.

# Chapter 5

Building up a knowledge management system is a commonly arising challenge in managing organizations. Leaders need to change their leadership style in order for their organization to be successful, in accordance with the requirements of building and operating a knowledge management system. The aim of this chapter is to sketch the necessity of the change and the right leaders' behavior. The author shows the relationships residing in the background of the elements that are in close connection with the suitable leadership style: EQ, competence, organizational culture, trust, communication, and employees' commitment and satisfaction. During this chapter readers will be led logically across the connections of the above-mentioned elements and, at the end, a figure summarizing the connections closes the chapter.

## Chapter 6

*Erzsébet Noszkay, Budapest Metropolitan University, Hungary*

This chapter focuses on the presentation of the interrelationship between corporate strategy and the KM system, how could requirements and tasks related to the latter be derived from the former and not separately and for its own sake but to facilitate the implementation of the strategy. It contemplates system approach and KM operating as a system. A fundamental methodological belief of the author is that a KM system adapted to a corporate strategy necessitates harmonizing along various dimensions. In view of the focal points of a corporate strategy and on the ground of an actual knowledge map, determination of new competencies and knowledge elements are necessitated by the strategy to be implemented. This could be followed by the elaboration of a KM strategy whose main dimensions are: human resource allocation (People dimension); inclusion of KM into the expediently reengineered new corporate processes (Process dimension); and the deployment of information technologies that are adequate for the processes and ultimately with the specific knowledge demand (Technology dimension).

### Section 2
### Best Practice (Models, Methods, Tools)

## Chapter 7

*Erzsébet Noszkay, Budapest Metropolitan University, Hungary*

This chapter focuses on an experience based presentation of the parameters that determine organizational culture, and the impact that basic interrelationships among such parametric factors exercise on the elaboration of KM; the timing and the sort of KM structure, configuration that is feasible to make KM an approved and successful management function within a corporate structure; the possibility and the proper timing of the elaboration of KM through corporate strategic approach i.e. starting from above (decision of the senior management), and the efficiency of a solution initiated from below (by the members of the organization). This chapter will describe some practice-proven solutions, such as: the application of the problem solution method named action research that could be expedient in the implementation of KM in certain cases, and times and situations where the application of the "sandwich method" could be expedient. Also, this chapter describes knowledge transfer experiences that facilitate the recognition of the "capillary model", its substance and scope of utilization.

## Chapter 8

*Giulia Bruno, Politecnico di Torino, Italy*

An important issue present in the most of manufacturing systems, and become worse in SMEs, is the systematic management of the huge amount of unstructured information generated about products, from their design to their disposal. The aim of this chapter is to define a framework to manage such kind of data, overcoming the actual issues of the meaningless and the unstructured nature of generated information. To this aim, a knowledge management platform is proposed, both to store product information with semantic enrichment and to retrieve product information by means of a new similarity index. Such platform is based on the one hand on a non-relational data management system and on the other hand on a set of manufacturing ontologies. An example of the potentiality of the proposed framework is shown in the domain of telecommunication filter manufacturing.

## Chapter 9

*Adam Pawliczek, Technical University of Ostrava, Czech Republic & Moravian University College Olomouc, Czech Republic*
*Miroslav Rössler, Moravian University College Olomouc, Czech Republic*

The chapter deals with knowledge management principles and their implication to knowledge in management represented by contemporary sophisticated management tools and systems. The most important management branches and methods, tools and systems, generally considered as very helpful for professional business operating, are presented. Further research results of management tools knowledge in contemporary enterprises are presented impacting the need of education and knowledge transfer in management responsible positions. The need of management knowledge for the competitiveness of enterprises is accented. Business and competitive intelligence as media for competitiveness are introduced. In the last part of the chapter, a model of the knowledge management system applicable in SMEs is suggested. The purpose of the chapter is to make the reader familiar with some of the most important management tools, methods and systems and suggest principles for an easy and effective knowledge management system in the enterprise.

## Chapter 10

*Tamás Bognár, Széchenyi István University, Hungary*
*Irma Rácz, Széchenyi István University, Hungary*

This chapter provides a survey of methods, utilizing the human capital that helps on one hand identify the talents or the shortage of it; specify the developmental dynamics of a skill or competence, and gives help to the prognosis of successful assessment forms by following the development progress. The authors intend to suggest best practices that provide to find and complete the best possible mission for SMEs and employees as well by taking into consideration the progressive tools of knowledge management. The chapter introduces the methods of measuring talent and capability existence or shortage, the measurement possibilities of hidden potentials and the utilization of these among SMEs' routine. Authors pay special attention to the employees maturing progress on higher levels of working experience where the talent possibly manifests as utilized knowledge. Methods will be introduced that provide this manifestation to give best practices to assessment for a better prediction.

## Chapter 11

*Marcello Chedid, University of Aveiro, Portugal*
*Leonor Teixeira, University of Aveiro, Portugal*

Software development organization (SDO) is a kind of knowledge-intensive business and their large majority is small and medium enterprise (SME) facing similar challenges of large ones. The diversity and complexity of the SDO environment makes knowledge the fundamental element in the software development process, which strengthens the importance of an effective knowledge management process. The software development process involves multidisciplinary teams, and the various working meetings that occur during a project are conducive to generate and share a lot of knowledge, in particular tacit knowledge. The use of a knowledge management process that enables to manage tacit knowledge will define the difference between a good SDO performance and the best SDO performance. This chapter aims to present an exploratory study based on literature review, with the aim of identifying the main challenge of knowledge management in the SDO context. The authors also aim to address some new research directions.

## Section 3
## Practical Experience (Research Results and Case Studies)

### Chapter 12

*Balzhan Orazbayeva, Münster University of Applied Sciences (MUAS), Germany*
*Thomas Baaken, Münster University of Applied Sciences (MUAS), Germany*

The following chapter is dedicated to knowledge management, whereby the focus is on the transfer of relevant knowledge in an intercultural team. The purpose of this study was to empirically examine, how an intercultural team deals with the cultural diversity of its members and how it influences the knowledge transfer. The research object was the intercultural team of the research institute Science-to-Business Marketing Research Centre at the Münster University of Applied Sciences (MUAS) in Germany. Ten guided interviews were conducted with ten employees of ten different nationalities. As the investigation has shown, the processes of knowledge transfer within the team of the research centre are not standardized. The actual transfer of knowledge occurs between team members on a personal level during intercultural communication in a setting of provided framework conditions. The team's cultural diversity is able not only to transfer but also to generate new knowledge. Intercultural competence in a provided framework is the crucial factor for successful cross-cultural knowledge transfer.

### Chapter 13

*Nora Obermayer, University of Pannonia, Hungary*
*Anikó Csepregi, University of Pannonia, Hungary*
*Edit Kővári, University of Pannonia, Hungary*

This chapter introduces the possible differences revealed of the applied methods in knowledge sharing based on generational differences. In addition the chapter investigates the relationship of knowledge sharing to competences, emotional intelligence and social media tools and presents research that were carried out between 2006-2015. The aim of this part is to enable companies, especially SMEs to learn from these research outcomes and develop strategies to trigger knowledge sharing among different generations regarding the vital competences, emotional intelligence and social media tools.

# Chapter 14

In this chapter a summary of the role family businesses play in the economy will be presented along with one of the main issues of family businesses in Hungary that is succession. Innovation as one of the most important factors of successful family businesses and the organizational culture supporting innovation will also be analysed. Some of the most relevant findings of a research study conducted in Hungary in 2015 will be given. The most significant components of knowledge sharing in SMEs especially in family businesses have been identified. The research results are based on over 300 questionnaires. The following questions have been answered: 1) What is the most decisive factor of choosing between cooperation and competition? 2) Is it possible that family businesses are able to respond to changes and as a result are they innovative? and 3) Is the organizational culture necessary for tacit knowledge sharing present in family businesses?

# Chapter 15

Personal knowledge is the construction of the individual. It is the context of factual knowledge and experience. Collective work, thinking, writing requires adaptation, adjustment, coordination. The VID SME Group demonstrates the significance of collective knowledge, as the group is dominated by diversity, manifold ordering, but also by the maintenance and coordination of plurality. The present paper provides the framework and the praxis of the plural management of collective knowledge, hence allowing for the attainment of the approach and thinking lying therein. Following an overview of the background of the adopted systemic, pluralistic approach, the paper gives insight into the VID Group's systemically, corporally-corporately and textually ordered architecture, into its management and control praxes of collective knowledge, but it also presents the business group's principles, tasks, networks, its functional ordering and connections.

This abstract deals with mentoring as one of the most popular forms of knowledge-sharing nowadays. On one hand the authors give a theoretical introduction about the protocol, the types, and the participants and about the realization of mentoring; while on the other hand some results of a complex research are also shown. The research was carried out with the participation of Hungarian companies and employees, both in qualitative and in quantitative way. Although the researches cannot be considered representative, the authors of the chapter reckon that a clear view can be obtained about the Hungarian mentoring practice. In light of the results it can be stated that the respondents basically consider this form of knowledge-sharing useful, which provides a good base and support for the operation of a consistent knowledge-management system and mentoring should represent positive values and practice in this process.

Innovation is transformed in an encompassing domain where different types of actors are connected and interrelated. Nevertheless, academic science often feels threatened by the new emerging institutional paradigm characterized by the economic exploitation of public research results. This chapter explores university-firm relations and tensions, discussing the increased relevance of knowledge transfer. The ideas of Ludwik Fleck, intellectual precursor of Social Studies of S&T, contribute to the understanding of the difficulties of communication between different collectives, their styles of thought and the importance of 'marginal individuals' in connecting different institutional spheres. Based on a qualitative approach to the case study of a Portuguese university attempting to create bridges with the business world, the text illustrates differences between the 'academic science' and the firm, the recent institutionalization of commercialization of research, and findings for policy-making and management of knowledge transfer activities.

# Foreword

In the twenty-first century, there are less and fewer projects and solutions, which are lineal and simple. Nowadays not just our ordinary life, but also the economy is more complex, where the changing of the relation of the enterprises and the interior processes of the companies are much faster than before. Owing to the technological developments space and time have shrunk to a degree that humanity has never seen before. Globalization presents new challenges for us every day. Moreover, ideas previous held as unshakeable were made useless and inadequate. The question is how the SMEs can develop in this kind of environment which is constantly changing and accelerating. This book offers various answers for this question by examining comprehensively the topic of knowledge management and point it out how important is the role of knowledge management for small and medium scale enterprises.

It is well-known that they could not compete with the multinational companies pertaining to aspects such as capital, size, and transnational roles and relations, but knowledge management could be a resource for increasing their competitive edge. Those SMEs could survive and develop which are able to adjust to the constantly changing environment and react properly to new challenges. This is an area where knowledge management could help SMEs. It generates the knowledge of the people. It also makes the human and the institutional synergies in the company stronger and supports the development of the SMEs. Besides these, it can also facilitate the capability for responding to the changes in the environment. The knowledge management requires us to encounter continuously with ourselves and our environment. It can also contribute to the self-knowledge regarding the enterprise, motivates the changes and supports a proactive approach.

The book introduces not only the basic definitions of knowledge management but also its different aspects such as innovation, HR, process-organization, strategy, logistics and alike by demonstrating how they could affect for SMEs. Furthermore, this work also deals with the importance of those different approaches which can offer useful information for both legislative and operative levels. The authors of the fine studies compiled into this volume point out that the knowledge management could make SMEs more successful. The tools of the knowledge management could also assist to find common values and interests, and makes stronger the enterprises in a long-term. The open-mindedness for acquiring new knowledge effectively and quickly as well as the implementation of that is vital for development. This current work also emphasizes the human factor by demonstrating how it would be possible to reach a better result from a personnel, a team, and integrate it into business, firms and companies that may function as an incentive to the development. By doing so knowledge-management can make companies more successful and their employees contented and pleased. It is a characteristic of knowledge that by sharing it, the person who possessed it before will also benefit from its distribution. The book provides information about how the share of knowledge facilitates the interest of any company and throws light on the necessity of development and integration of the knowledge through a mentoring process.

I wholeheartedly recommend this book to the academic world – both for professors and students – since it could be used as a concise handbook for university students, which transfers structured material and it was written in a practice-orientated approach in mind. Moreover, I also hope that the executives of the economic sphere will also find this book interesting for the aforementioned reasons as well as useful since it fills a gap that has been lacking for years. By reading the pages of this well-crafted work, it is my sincere hope that the readers shall find useful and valuable thoughts in it that can be implemented in their companies and respective enterprises.

*Barnabas Kovacs*
*Ministry of Foreign Affairs in Hungary, Hungary*

**Barnabás Kovács** *received both his law degree and also his degree in economics (international relations) in 1995. He spent several semesters in an international environment, for example in Austria, Germany, Spain, and Russia. After these experiences, he chooses the Mediterranean area again, and he got his degree at Academy of Diplomacy in Madrid. During this time he also started to work in the Ministry of Foreign Affairs in Hungary at the Department of Parliamentary Affairs, where, by 2000, he became the head officer. He worked as a professor in several Hungarian higher education institution, and also as a leader counsel of Magyar Telecom Nyrt. From 2009 he continued his carreer in Károli Gáspár University, where he was in charge as a strategic director. In 2015 he was appointed to be the consul general of Hungary in Barcelona with a diplomatic rank of an ambassador.*

# Foreword

Even in ancient times, information was a staple of daily interaction in social, economic, and political settings. Individuals conversed at home and outdoors, in the marketplace and in work settings. They would exchange ideas about past events, present activities, and future scenarios. In organizations, large, and small, teams and groups interacted on the basis of both solid news and informal gossip. Government agencies and military establishments relied on messengers who would bring updates on political leanings and troop locations.

However, it was not until after World War II, that information has become 'the flight map' for both individuals and organizations to navigate in a complex world of technical progress, political upheavals, and changing social customs. While data in the form of census-taking by governments and record-keeping by companies occurred earlier, the collection, storage, and retrieval of economic and business information did not happen until the 1950s when computer hardware and software made their appearance.

In his pioneering book a half-century ago, 'The Production and Distribution of Knowledge in the U.S.', by Fritz Machlup (1962), noted that millions of data bits were now yielding much more than 'mere information'. Studying diverse industries and occupations he observed that knowledge has become a resource for professionals and for business organizations.

Knowledge management became an established discipline after the publication of Nonaka's 1991 and 1994 articles in which he dealt with types of knowledge (explicit and implicit); levels of knowledge (individual and organizational); and the promotion of organizational learning. The field of KM or knowledge management now constitutes a range of processes and practices whose common feature is the goal of generating value from knowledge. The field of KM currently encompasses many organizational functions ranging from technical research to human resources, from intellectual property use to strategic planning.

The current volume, ably edited by Dr. Andrea Bencsik of Hungary, supplements as well as complements previous books by other authors published by IGI Global. Dealing with the various aspects of knowledge management, especially in the setting of small to medium size establishments, the contributions offer descriptive details, analytical insights, and lessons learned. The various chapters, 17 in all, focus on a wide variety of topics that encompass many managerial activities and organizational processes. The geographical settings include Thailand, Germany, Hungary, Slovakia, Czech Republic, Romania, Italy and Portugal.

The various contributors deal with a range of topics, but the focus is on both explicit and implicit knowledge, that is 'knowing about' and 'knowing how.' The sharing of knowledge among members of teams and divisions of organizations is rightly emphasized. Both problems and solutions need exposure in order to advance the well-being of firms. Knowledge is seen as a resource, as a capital, and as one that can accumulate and yield ideas for current and future action in a competitive landscape. Small and medium organizations must harness the knowledge of employees and become "learning entities." Good practices need to be emulated until further refinements are made. KM is seen as a link that holds together effective governance, corporate goals, and daily activities.

The authors focus on specific activities at the level of the organizations. Coverage here ranges from family-run businesses in Hungary to state-operated enterprises in Brazil. KM plays a major role in proper logistics; indeed, supply chain management is as much a conceptual undertaking as it is the physical arrangement for transport and storage. KM plays a major role in today's world of instant and constant telecommunication—with organizations emphasizing both internal dealings among departments or divisions and interaction with suppliers and customers. In a world of complexity and cost-cutting, frugal innovation should be the preferred mode of operation.

The writers look at broader implications of KM with emphasis on system building, organizational response to challenges, bridge-building to government agencies, academic institutes, and private sector participants. Thinking and acting in a spirit of collaboration is recommended; today's rivals can become tomorrow's partners. 'Decisions in the global village' means thinking and acting together, soliciting input from above and below, creating an interface in both directions.

The knowledge needs of firms are likely to expand in the coming years. The acquisition, development, and management of knowledge are fundamental to the growth of firms.

Chapters in this book manage to delve into the above facets and offer useful insights and lessons.

*Andrew C. Gross*
*Cleveland State University, USA*

**Andrew Gross** *has served on the faculty of Cleveland State University since 1968. He was also a visiting professor at various universities in Australia, Canada, and Hungary. In 1989 and in 1992 he was a Senior Fulbright Scholar in his native Hungary. Earlier he was a consultant to the Science Council of Canada and other organizations, both profit and non-profit. He worked in industry as an engineer and was the first employee and later a Board of Directors member of a major market research organization. He is the lead or co-author of four books, fifteen monographs, and over 100 refereed journal articles in management, marketing, economics, and environmental studies. He serves on various editorial boards and is active in various associations and community organizations.*

## REFERENCES

Machlup, F. (1962). *The Production and Distribution of Knowledge in the United States*. Princeton, NJ: Princeton University Press.

Nonaka, I. (1991). The Knowledge-Creating Company. *Harvard Business Review*, *11-12*, 96–104.

Nonaka, I. (1994). A Dynamic Theory of Organizational Knowledge Creation. *Organization Science*, *2*, 14–37.

# Preface

In the past two decades, studying, education and human resources (HR) developments have become determinative factors in the area of HR management. People not only talk about the revaluation of roles in relation to studying and knowledge, but these expressions also mean much more than previously. Addressing studying at a relatively high level has become a strategic question, as well as a dominant source of competitiveness at the same time.

Why do studying and knowledge have a strategic role? The origins of this issue come from a very simple connection. For the most part, knowledge – especially non-formalized (tacit) knowledge – is acquired and accumulated over a long period of time inside any organization and this type of knowledge can be copied and adapted, albeit with more difficulties, than any other types of sources (Davenport & Prusak, 2001; Sveiby, 2001; Prahalad & Hamel, 1990). The aforementioned two features ensure that knowledge should be a source of long-term competitiveness from the viewpoint of strategy. Through knowledge accumulation and stocking, in terms of an input, companies can realize a long-term competitive factor in relation to the other companies. This is why the adaptation of a knowledge management system (KMS) is spreading widely among company systems. It is not only true in terms of a theoretical focus, but also in the practical life of companies as well. A committed expert perceives with pleasure that companies and organizations handle the operation of a KMS in a natural way as part of their strategies. Multinational companies create new positions for knowledge management (KM) experts and leaders in their hierarchy at a higher and higher level. Several case studies confirm that there are advantages and profit opportunities for companies that have focused their attention on human capital.

While multinational and other large companies deliver KM processes as a part of their everyday operations, small- and medium-sized enterprises (SMEs) feel disadvantaged because of the lack of sources and chances. That said, research has shown that SMEs can also be competitive and enjoy advantages similar to larger competitors, provided that they identify gaps in the market in which they can exploit the distinctiveness of their culture, leadership style and workplace atmosphere. This book was created by the authors because they wished to prove the existence of a way of thinking, which discloses the possibilities for adapting a KMS within SMEs. The ensuing chapters provide every reader with the help and experience needed to build and operate a KMS in this particular enterprise context.

## THE CHALLENGES

At the level of the national economy, there are two basic strategies in the competitive market. Firstly, there is the conventional strategy known as the 'cost-competing strategy', which aims to produce and serve at the lowest cost (Csath, 2008). The other, which was created by the European Union, is an 'economic growth strategy' founded on the basis of knowledge. This strategy is based on the idea that knowledge value added is also a resource, which can be maintained for a long time. International research shows that knowledge, innovation and creativity are needed to sustain development, while the economy can become too volatile and vulnerable due to the cost reduction strategy.

How do these two strategies appear within companies?

The answer is based on Porter's classical strategy model, which separates three basic strategies (Porter, 1980). In Porter's strategies, the two above-mentioned strategic directions can be identified. In the case of companies, 'low-cost leadership' is the same as the 'cost-competing strategy' in the case of the national economy. 'Differentiation strategy' and 'focused strategy' often go hand in hand with knowledge-based strategies. In this case, the source of competitive advantages can be knowledge capital. Against the background of differentiation and focused strategies, knowledge capital as a precondition appears to be closely connected with the role of education and training.

The question is, do Hungarian SMEs have any knowledge-based strategies? If the answer is yes, what kind of HR policy supports these features? Our book investigates this special segment from different aspects in different cultures and economic environments. This segment does not typically focus on investigations, although their significant role in knowledge-based sectors is well-known within the international literature. The actors in this segment are characterized by very different ways of thinking, attitudes and features in the global market economy. The challenge is meaningful because HR management and the activities of leaders, which support studying and training, concentrate on the so-called soft features (they are difficult to measure), such as quality of leadership and expected personal characters of employees. Whether it is possible to estimate them is disputed among professionals, primarily because they cannot be expressed numerically.

## SEARCHING FOR A SOLUTION

Education and training – as a function of HR management - have a specific role in the realization of knowledge-based strategies. Within companies, education and training appear to be a necessity, although they can sometimes be realized only in an implicit form.

According to the classical definition of knowledge capital, three core types have been differentiated: customer capital, structural capital and intellectual capital.

These three types of capital have become interlocked hierarchically and formed a value chain. At the bottom, there is structural capital, which is a foundation stone of human capital. It makes a connection in the direction of customer capital.

Previous research projects have led to the construction of a theoretical model, which incorporate the most important factors that are significant in the learning processes of SMEs. Two different study types are to be found. On the one hand, knowledge and information can be acquired from the outside environment. Typical examples are connections with higher education, professional organizations, chambers etc. On the other hand, there is an acutely different form that uses the internal resources of companies, namely, team and individual learning. These two categories are built on knowledge sharing, knowledge transfer and knowledge multiplying, which can be developed by teamwork, mentor systems and spontaneous collaborations (practical community). Within the SME sector, there is a requirement for such companies to operate an organization or to create and adopt a KMS successfully by applying one of the above-mentioned knowledge-based strategies.

From the viewpoint of a knowledge-based economy, there is an important criterion: companies should be able to meet the challenges of the future. In a traditional context, studying, training and education – meaning the acquisition of acquire internal knowledge – fall into the background in the case of SMEs for the time being. In a wider sense, studying – which also encompasses the viewpoint of KM – in the SME sector is in a good state. Proper interpersonal relationships and a democratic leadership style – which is based on the small organizational size of SMEs - promote knowledge sharing and knowledge creation, which is a new paradigm of modern economic life.

Out of the two different types, strategic types of studying - as mentioned above - can be completed by two additional ones. There are organizations where none of their strategies is characteristic. The opposite type for SMEs is where both studying types – traditional- and external- based – are involved. Additionally, there are some SMEs where only a KM-based strategy is used, while there are other SMEs where only the internal studying type is characteristic.

Overall, researchers can say that SMEs have deficiencies in the view of traditional education and teaching, but they also have competitive advantages in the area of informal knowledge transfer, knowledge sharing and knowledge creation. Indeed, it is worth exploiting the advantages and use them against their competitors, which are large or multinational companies. Readers can see that many strategic questions come to mind in connection with learning, studying, knowledge and KMSs. The upcoming book chapters highlight the different sides of these questions. In these chapters, the authors guide the readers through the necessary theoretical basis and explore important areas, such as effective methods, tools, conditions of the learning organization, a suitable culture and IT systems. Previous research findings and examples from practical experience can be read in the chapters about the relationships between a KMS and the different professional areas of companies.

## ORGANIZATION OF THE BOOK

The book is organized into three main parts, which are in turn divided into 17 chapters. These chapters present the possibilities for SMEs, both theoretically and practically, from different viewpoints. A brief description of each is to be found below:

### Theoretical Basics of a KMS and the Connection with Enterprises'/Companies' Processes

Chapter 1: This chapter briefly covers the basics and definitions of knowledge and KM, the connection between KM and communication, recent developments and trends in Hungary and internationally, and the so-called KM generations. The chapter's goal is to show how and why the support and appreciation of knowledge (which has existed virtually since the beginning of humankind) developed into a system. The successful management of companies using KM systems foreground new types of organizational operating models using intelligent solutions, which are manifold, may be structured in variable ways and are specifically unique in the light of these knowledge-intensive services.

Chapter 2: The Nobel Memorial Prize in Economic Sciences has been awarded twice so far to researchers in the area of decision-making. In spite of this, courses on decision-making in business schools and schools of economics focus on the decision tools found within applied operations research. James March argues that, within organizations, decisions simply happen, as opposed to people making them. Authors argue that, within the global village, the decision taker's role is wearing off, while the decision maker's role is changing. Given that a great deal of knowledge is freely available, a new possibility is opening up for a new type of thinking together. In this chapter, the authors take a closer look at thinking together.

Chapter 3: This chapter explores the prospect of organizational learning and its connections with other processes of an enterprise; these include: organizational learning and networks, organizational innovation and transformational leadership, absorptive capacity, open innovation and information technology, organizational learning and training, organizational learning capability and enterprise resource planning. Organizational learning is an important method by which organizations develop, enhance and manage knowledge within their organizational functions, as well as improve their efficiency by making better use of the wide range of skills of their employees. Regarding organizational learning, organizations improve the ability to respond to various business situations and enhance competitive performance through generating new knowledge. This chapter argues that encouraging organizational learning has the potential to improve organizational performance and gain sustainable competitive advantage in the workplace.

Chapter 4: The aim of this theoretical study is to show how KMS and innovation models work together and how their relationship reinforces the chances for success. Relying on a secondary data analysis and a literature review, the authors prove that the classical innovation model can be a part of this relationship, together with organizational innovation in which HR comes to focus. The logic of KM system building emphasizes that the path leads from the attainment of innovation knowledge to the evaluation of utilization. This study reviews the steps of the two business models and highlights the most important relationships in a new model linking the appropriate phases. The second part of this chapter shows the connection between frugal innovation and KM, as well as their theoretical significance and practical adaptability.

Chapter 5: Building up a KMS is a common challenge in managing organizations. Leaders need to change their leadership style in order for their organization to be successful in line with the requirements of building and operating a KMS. The aim of this chapter is to highlight the necessity for the change and the appropriate behaviour of leaders. The author shows the relationships residing in the background of those elements that are in close connection with a suitable leadership style: EQ, competence, organizational culture, trust, communication, and employees' commitment and satisfaction. In the course of this chapter, readers will be guided logically through the connections of the above-mentioned elements, with a figure summarizing the connections closing the chapter.

Chapter 6: This chapter focuses on the presentation of the interrelationship between corporate strategy and the KMS, as well as consider whether the requirements and tasks related to the latter may be derived from the former, and not separately and for its own sake, in order to facilitate the implementation of the strategy. It contemplates the system approach and KM operating as a system. A fundamental methodological belief of the authors is that a KMS, which is adapted to a corporate strategy, necessitates harmonization with various dimensions. In view of the focal points of a corporate strategy, and on the ground of an actual knowledge map, determination of new competencies and knowledge elements are necessitated by the strategy to be implemented. This could be followed by the elaboration of a KM strategy whose main dimensions are as follows: HR allocation (people dimension), inclusion of KM into the expediently re-engineered new corporate processes (process dimension), and the deployment of information technologies, which are adequate for the processes and ultimately meet the specific knowledge demand (technology dimension).

## Best Practice (Models, Methods and Tools)

Chapter 7: This chapter focuses on an experience-based presentation of the parameters that determine organizational culture, as well as the impact that basic interrelationships among such parametric factors exercise on the elaboration of KM. Also considered are the timing and the nature of the KM structure, whether the configuration is feasible enough to allow for KM to be an approved and successful management function within a corporate structure, the possibility and the proper timing of the elaboration of KM through a corporate strategic approach, i.e., starting from above (decision of the senior management), and the efficiency of a solution initiated from below (by the members of the organization). This chapter will describe some practice-proven solutions, such as the application of the problem-solution method known as action research, which could be expedient in the implementation of KM in certain cases, as well as those times and situations where the application of the 'sandwich method' could be expedient. In addition, this chapter describes knowledge transfer experiences that facilitate the recognition of the 'capillary model', its substance and scope of utilization.

Chapter 8: The aim of this chapter is to define a framework in which to manage those kinds of data need to overcome the actual issues of the meaningless and the unstructured nature of generated information. To this end, a KM platform is proposed, both to store product information with semantic enrichment and to retrieve product information by means of a new similarity index. Such a platform is based on a non-relational data management system on the one hand, and on a set of manufacturing ontologies on the other hand. An example of the potentiality of the proposed framework is shown in the context of telecommunication filter manufacturing.

Chapter 9: This chapter deals with KM principles and their implication for knowledge in management, as represented by contemporary sophisticated management tools and systems. Further research results are presented concerning management tool knowledge within contemporary enterprises in terms of the impact on the need for education and knowledge transfer in responsible management positions. In the last part of this chapter, a model of a KMS applicable to SMEs is suggested. The purpose of the chapter is to make the reader familiar with some of the most important management tools, methods and systems, as well as suggest principles for a simple and effective KMS in the enterprise.

Chapter 10: This chapter provides a survey of methods, utilizing the human capital that helps to either identify the talents or the shortage of it, specify the developmental dynamics of a skill or competence, and support the prognosis of successful assessment forms by following development progress. The authors suggest best practices that seek to find and complete the best possible mission for SMEs and employees, as well as taking into consideration the progressive tools of KM. The chapter introduces the methods of measuring talent and capability existence or shortage, the measurement possibilities of hidden potentials and the utilization of these within SMEs' routine. The authors pay special attention to employees' maturation progress at higher levels of working experience, where the talent possibly manifests itself as utilized knowledge. Methods will be introduced that offer the best practices for assessment with a better predictability.

Chapter 11: A software development organization (SDO) is a kind of business based on a knowledge-intensive process, where knowledge is the raw material and the intellectual capital constitutes the major asset. That said, what is the KM challenge in an SDO? The current environment of SDOs is one of increasing diversity and complexity in software development projects. Due to this environment, the software development process involves multidisciplinary teams, given that an individual member of a team can no longer be expected to have all the necessary knowledge. Based on the literature review, the authors aim to identify the best practices for achieving the most effective response to this challenge.

## Practical Experience (Research Results and Case Studies)

Chapter 12: The chapter is dedicated to KM, with the focus on the transfer of relevant knowledge in an intercultural team. The purpose of this study was to empirically examine how an intercultural team deals with the cultural diversity of its members and how it influences knowledge transfer. The research object was the intercultural team of the research institute Science-to-Business Marketing Research Centre at the Münster University of Applied Sciences (MUAS) in Germany. Ten guided interviews were conducted with 10 employees of 10 different nationalities. As the investigation has shown, the processes of knowledge transfer within the team at MUAS are not standardized. The team's cultural diversity not only enables the transfer but also the generation of new knowledge. Intercultural competence in a provided framework is the crucial factor for successful cross-cultural knowledge transfer.

Chapter 13: This chapter introduces the possible differences revealed by the applied methods in knowledge sharing based on generational differences. In addition, the chapter investigates the relationship between knowledge sharing and competencies, emotional intelligence and social media tools, as well as presents the outcomes of research carried out between 2006 and 2015. The aim of this chapter is to enable companies, especially SMEs, to learn from these research outcomes and develop strategies to activate knowledge sharing among different generations regarding vital competencies, emotional intelligence and social media tools.

Chapter 14: In this chapter, a summary of the role that family businesses play in the economy will be presented, along with one of the main issues faced by family businesses in Hungary, namely, succession. Innovation as one of the most important factors behind successful family businesses and organizational cultures in this context that support innovation will also be analysed. Some of the most relevant findings of a research study conducted in Hungary in 2015 will be given. The most significant components of knowledge sharing in SMEs, especially in family businesses, have been identified. The research results are based on over 300 questionnaires. The following questions have been answered:

- What is the most decisive factor of choosing between cooperation and competition?
- Is it possible that family businesses are able to respond to changes and are they innovative as a result?
- Is the organizational culture necessary for tacit knowledge sharing present in family businesses?

Chapter 15: Personal knowledge is the construction of the individual. It is the context of factual knowledge and experience. This chapter provides the framework and praxis of the plural management of collective knowledge, which facilitates the attainment of the approach and thinking that are found therein. Following an overview of the adopted systemic, pluralistic approach, the chapter then gives an insight into the VID Group's systemically, corporally, corporately and textually ordered architecture for the management and control praxes of collective knowledge, as well as presents the business group's principles, tasks, networks, their functional ordering and connections.

Chapter 16: This chapter deals with mentoring as one of the most popular forms of knowledge sharing nowadays. On the one hand, the authors present a theoretical introduction to the protocol, the types, and the participants involved in mentoring, as well as its realization. On the other hand, some results from a complex research project are also presented. The research was carried out with the participation of Hungarian companies and employees, in both a qualitative and a quantitative way. In light of the results, it can be stated that the respondents essentially consider this form of knowledge sharing to be useful because it provides a good basis and support for the operation of a consistent KMS, while mentoring should represent positive values and practice in this process

Chapter 17: This chapter explores the relations and tensions between academia and business in the course of discussing the increased relevance of knowledge transfer. The ideas of Ludwik Fleck, the intellectual precursor of the social studies of science and technology, contribute to the understanding of the difficulties in communication between different collectives, their styles of thought and the importance of 'marginal individuals' when connecting different institutional spheres. Based on a qualitative approach to the case study of a Portuguese university, which attempted to build bridges with the business world, the chapter illustrates the differences between 'academic science' and the business world, the recent institutionalization of commercialized research, and the implications for policy-making and the management of knowledge transfer activities.

*Andrea Bencsik*
*Széchenyi István University, Hungary & J. Selye University, Slovakia*

## REFERENCES

Csath, M. (2008). *Globalizációs végjáték*. Budapest: Kairosz Kiadó.

Davenport, T., & Prusak, L. (2001). *Tudásmenedzsment*. Budapest: Kossuth Kiadó.

Porter, M. E. (1980). *Competitive strategy*. New York: The Free Press.

Prahalad, C. K., & Hamel, G. (1990). The Core Competence of the Corporation. *Harvard Business Review, 3,* 81–92.

Sveiby, K. E. (2001). *Szervezetek új gazdagsága: a menedzselt tudás*. Budapest, KJK- Kerszöv Jogi és Üzleti Kiadó Kft.

# Acknowledgment

First, the editor would like to thank each one of the authors for their contributions. My sincere gratitude goes to the chapter's authors who contributed their time and expertise to this book.

Second, the editor wishes to acknowledge the valuable contributions of the reviewers regarding the improvement of quality, coherence, and content presentation of chapters. Most of the authors also served as referees; I highly appreciate their double task.

*Andrea Bencsik*
*Széchnyi István University, Hungary & J. Selye University, Slovakia*

# Theoretical Basics of a Knowledge Management System and Its Connection with Enterprises'/Companies' Processes

# Chapter 1
# Knowledge Management and Its Approaches:
## Basics of Developing Company Knowledge Management Systems

**Anikó Balogh**
*Central European University, Hungary*

## ABSTRACT

*This chapter briefly covers the basics and definitions of knowledge and knowledge management, the connection between KM and communication, its Hungarian and international development and tendencies in the past years and the so called KM generations. The chapter's goal is to show how and why the support and appreciation of knowledge (which almost exists since the beginning of humankind) developed into a system. Successful management of companies using KM systems bring to the surface a new breed of organization operating models operating with intelligent solutions, which are manifold, may be structured in a variable way, and are specifically unique in the light of these knowledge-intensive services.*

## INTRODUCTION

Within the era of information society and knowledge economy knowledge plays an important part besides the traditional production factors, thus knowledge management (KM) becomes a key issue. One of the basic aims of knowledge management is to increase organizational efficiency.

This chapter outlines the history of knowledge management summing up the most important works on the subject providing the literature basis for the whole book. Thus it gives an overview of the main narratives and models on the subject of information, information society and knowledge management. It also focuses on the international development history of KM.

Finally the chapter discusses the role of KM in small and medium-sized enterprises, summarizes the main points of knowledge management and enterprises and suggests solutions and models to follow based on case studies.

DOI: 10.4018/978-1-5225-1642-2.ch001

## Information Society

The notion of information society dates back to the 1930s when Austrian-born economist Fritz Machlup (1962) published his book *The Production and Distribution of Knowledge in the United States*. With this work he established the new field of information economics. The transformation to a knowledge economy has become even more significant especially after the spreading of the internet. The next important author is Peter Drucker (1969) who claimed that there is a transition from a material goods based economy to knowledge based one. Marc Porat (1977) defines a primary and a secondary sector of the information economy. Porat uses the total value added by the primary and secondary information sector to the GNP as an indicator for the information economy. Based on these indicators, the information society has been defined by as a society where more than half of the GNP is produced and more than half of the employees are active in the information economy. (Deutsch, 1983)

## Digital Economy

The concept of a digital economy emerged in the last decade of the 20th century. According to Nicholas Negroponte's (1996) allegory, society changes from processing atoms to processing bits. In Richard Barbrook's (1999) definition, digital economy is characterized by the emergence of new technologies (computer networks) and new types of workers (the digital artisans), which is strongly similar to the notion of Drucker's knowledge worker (Drucker, 1993).

The definition of knowledge is connected to the definition of data, information, wisdom and different types of knowledge. This subdivision is also referred to as the hierarchy of wisdom. This hierarchy is one of the few models that are accepted by information and knowledge related literature. Its basic assumption is that we can create information from data, knowledge from information (including explicit and tacit knowledge) and wisdom from knowledge.

Data is only a denuded value; it doesn't have any information value by itself. It becomes information, once it gets a meaning in some interpretation. Knowledge is the information's interpreted and subjective form. Wisdom is proven knowledge that comes from experience and from drawing conclusions with the help of from self-knowledge and empathy.

The previous definitions are applied on the individual level, but knowledge also has an interpretation that is connected to an organization. The most valuable knowledge creates value for organizations, but this knowledge is also "in the possession" of these individuals. Its exploration is one of the most important tasks of the organizations.

## BACKGROUND: DATA, INFORMATION, KNOWLEDGE

To sum up the notion on knowledge several literatures may be used. These works all go back to the basics and differentiation between data, information and knowledge. Ternes, (2011) sums up the development of information to data as follows. According to Gill's (2001) knowledge pyramid in Ternes (2011) (Figure 1) which is based on Luzwick's (1999) "classic information hierarchy" there is data on the first level. Data consists of numbers and text, but it does not have a meaning on its own. Nevertheless data is the starting point of the intellectual property of an organization. On the next level of the pyramid the application and use of data comes into the picture. Data becomes information. Information is necessary to

*Figure 1. The knowledge pyramid*
*(Gill, 2001) Source: Edited by the Author, 2016*

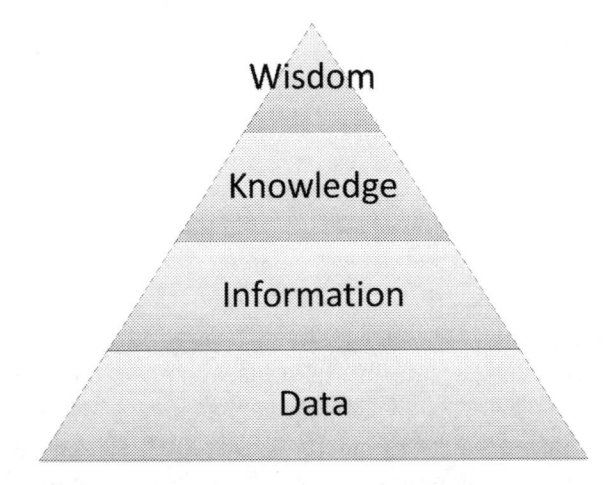

create and formalize knowledge. Nonaka defines information as "data or messages having recognizable context and order that are capable of adding, restructuring, yielding, or becoming knowledge (Nonaka, 1994; Gill, 2001).

Knowledge appears on the third level of the information pyramid. Knowledge is a high-value form of information or intellectual content possessing meaningful context that usually originates from and is applied in the minds of people (Fahey & Prusak, 1998). The possession and use of knowledge is an important asset in organizational knowledge management, as the appropriate application of knowledge is a considerable competitive advantage.

On the top of the pyramid there is wisdom. Wisdom is "knowledge that has been incorporated into the core fabric of individual, group, organizational, and or societal activities" (Vance, 1997). Some researchers believe that wisdom may be the next step in the evolution of human intellectual growth (Curley and Kivowitz, 2001).

## KNOWLEDGE MANAGEMENT

### Definition

Knowledge Management (KM) as a discipline appeared in the 90s. Several definitions were born to describe it. This chapter will focus on the definition of knowledge management and summarizes some of the theories, methodologies and models of knowledge management developed to describe the different aspects of knowledge management processes by different authors.

The Hungarian Scientific Academy's (HSA) Management and Organization Science Committee's Knowledge Management Subcommittee defined knowledge management as follows: "Knowledge management (KM) is a process (management subsystem) and a culture, during which knowledge capital's exploring, gathering, creating, tracking, retention, sharing is a constant enrichment is integrally treated and is supported with information technology. Its goal is the increase of the organization's added value creation, the enhancement of its innovation potential and its key concept is synergy." (Noszkay, 2012).

Drucker (1993), who also introduced the concept of knowledge worker, later described knowledge management as a strategic resource which is a major competitive advantage. Most literature refers to this aspect.

## Explicit and Tacit Knowledge

Most of knowledge management literature is based on the definition of Mihály Polányi the Hungarian-born philosopher's (1964) tacit (hidden) and explicit (expressible) knowledge. The majority of knowledge management literature deals with fundamental questions of tacit and explicit knowledge. This differentiation of tacit and explicit knowledge later became the main source for further research. Polányi explicates tacit knowledge (tacit knowing or tacit knowledge) in his main work Personal Knowledge. Hereinafter, he continued to examine tacit knowledge in several of his works, but the notion's definition remained unclear. "There are some things that we know, but we cannot express." he writes (Polányi, 1966).

Explicit knowledge according to Stankosky and Baldanza (2000) is knowledge that has been captured and can be articulated in tangible form. Explicit knowledge is codifiable, may be extracted, shared and used by others. It may take several forms like books, catalogs, directories, manuals, briefings, spreadsheets, web sites, and various other digital or physical forms.

Tacit knowledge is difficult to describe and transfer, it is neither easily visible nor expressed. It is highly personal, is hard to formalize (unlike explicit knowledge) thus not easy to communicate or share. Tacit knowledge is deeply rooted in an individual's actions, experience and ideas.

The difference between the two kinds of knowledges is the possibility to transfer them between individuals. Tacit knowledge is difficult to transfer and requires trust and personal contact. Further literature mostly focuses on how this tacit knowledge may be transferred.

## Knowledge Management Models

### Nonaka and Takeuchi's Knowledge Transfer Model

Nonaka and Takeuchi (1995), two leading Japanese business experts focused on tacit and explicit knowledge transfer, as one of the basic issues of KM nowadays is the institutionalization of personal knowledge transfer within an organization. They point out that Western and Eastern cultures have a different notion about these two types of knowledge. Western managers focus on explicit knowledge, which is stored in in manuals and procedures. The Japanese, on the other hand, focus on tacit knowledge learned only by experience, communicated indirectly, through metaphors and analogies. This is the key to their success as they learned how to transform tacit into explicit knowledge. This difference has its roots in Zen Buddhism. Their knowledge spiral (Figure 2) or the so-called SECI model shows how tacit knowledge becomes explicit knowledge.

The figure shows a circular procedure during knowledge flows between the different levels of organization (O) and also between individuals (I) and groups (G). It is imperative that all four phases must be satisfied to accomplish successful knowledge transfer within the organization. These steps form a circle, which is an escalating spiral. During this process the knowledge of the participants also increases, thus a learning progress takes place.

*Figure 2. The knowledge spiral*
*(Nonaka & Takeuchi, 1995) Source: Edited by the Author, 2016*

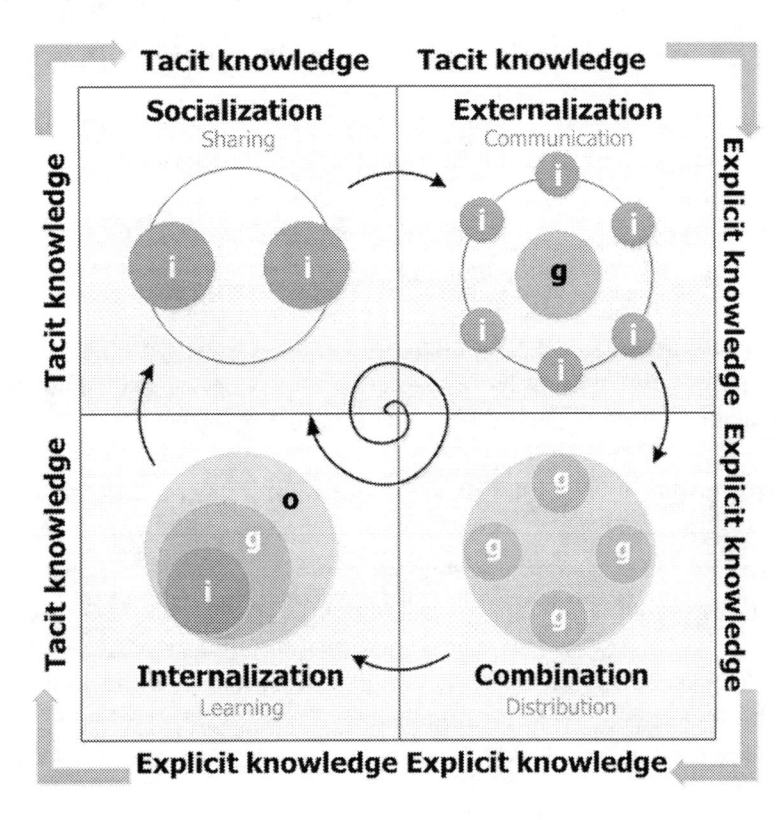

Nonaka and Takeuchi also introduce the concept of '*ba*' which is a Japanese word for the context of knowledge sharing. The word literally means 'time and place' as it may be a physical or virtual space where knowledge is shared. Based on the knowledge spiral *ba* also has four types:

1. **Originating:** Socialization, individual face-to-face knowledge sharing e.g. apprenticeship, talking to customers.
2. **Dialoging:** Externalization, collective face-to-face knowledge sharing e.g. quality control.
3. **Systemizing:** Combination, collective virtual knowledge sharing e.g. translating corporate vision to everyday concepts.
4. **Exercising**: Internalization, individual virtual knowledge sharing e.g. training programs.

## Karl Wiig's KM Model

in Wiig's (1993) approach knowledge management is a framework including all activities needed for the overview, management and utilization of the organization's knowledge assets and the conditions to create them. He highlights the following principle: in order for knowledge to be useful and valuable, it must be organized. Knowledge should be organized differently depending on what the knowledge will be used for. Some useful dimensions in the Wiigs KM model described by Dalkir (2011) are:

1.  **Completeness:** Completeness refers to the amount of important knowledge which is available from a given source. Sources may vary from the individual's intellect to databases. First it needs to be established that knowledge is available. In case all information available on the subject is accessible but its existence is unknown, then this knowledge cannot be used.
2.  **Connectedness:** Connectedness refers to the relationships between different knowledge objects. Most knowledge objects are related to each other. The more connected a knowledge base is, the more consistent is the content, so its value is higher.
3.  **Congruency:** A knowledge base is supposed to be congruent when all the facts, concepts, perspectives, values, judgments, and relative links between the objects are consistent. Most knowledge content does not reach this idealistic state.
4.  **Perspective and Purpose:** Perspective and purpose is a phenomenon assisting to know something but from a particular point of view, or for a specific purpose. Most of the knowledge is organized using these dual dimensions of perspective and purpose.

## Probst, Romhardt, and Raub's Building Blocks of Knowledge Management

As mentioned before knowledge is an important asset within the organization.

To manage and describe knowledge within an institution the notion of Knowledge Lifecycle was introduced. The knowledge lifecycle approach suggests that in order to take full advantage of organizational knowledge, companies must manage their intellectual property rights as a living entity with a definite life span (Probst, Raub, & Romhardt, 2000).

Based on this model, the building blocks of knowledge management which act while interacting with each other are the following, see Figure 3:

*Figure 3. Building blocks of knowledge management*
*(Probst, Raub & Romhardt, 2000) Source: Edited by the Author, 2016*

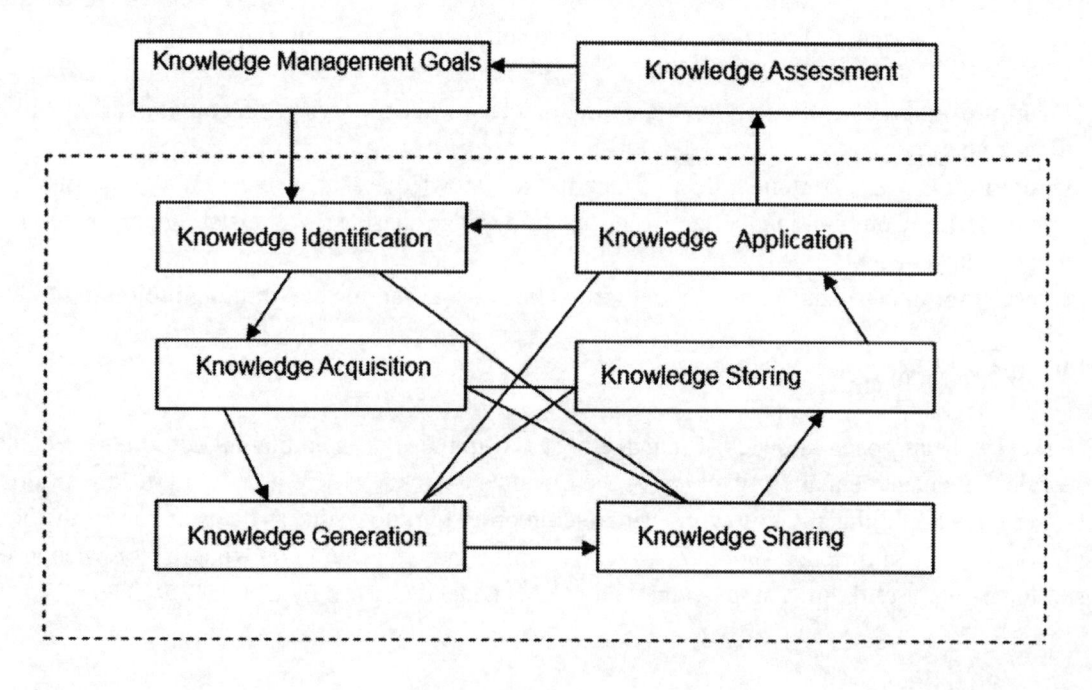

1. **Identification of Knowledge:** Before any further investment into knowledge capital, knowledge already existing within the organization needs to be pinpointed. To achieve this knowledge transparency several tools may be used, e.g. knowledge maps. Nevertheless technical solutions are not enough; the human aspect also needs to be taken into consideration. If an organization dedicates itself to the introduction of strategic knowledge management tools, it may be useful if independent experts, analysts carry out the identification and mapping of existing knowledge by using various methods e.g. interviews and questionnaires. Results of the survey are published in the organization and raise the awareness of the employees that during the procedure of knowledge sharing which tools are used to store data and how they should be used.

2. **Acquisition of Knowledge:** Organizational knowledge partially exists already within the organization, partly drawn in from the outside. New employees come from teachers who bring their professionalism, their experience from other institutions. Knowledge may also be purchased in the form of standards, literature and software.

3. **Improvement of Knowledge:** During institutional co-operation projects professional contacts also develop and improve. Research and development work is being conducted especially in universities, knowledge centers. Employees take part in trainings, further professional studies are conducted. The idea of Lifelong Learning is also one of the official programs of the European Union since 2007.

4. **Sharing of Knowledge:** Knowledge sharing is the process where individuals jointly exchange their tacit and explicit knowledge and create new knowledge. Sharing is vital for knowledge organizations as it is the sign for the atmosphere of social interactions in the organizations.

5. **Preservation of Knowledge:** The interwoven processes listed above are to ensure the efficiency and preservation of storage media. Pieces of information which may be categorized, e.g. addresses, phone numbers, contacts, schedules, are necessary to codify and capture and store on surfaces that are both easy to handle and also provide safe keeping, meaning data protection figuratively, but also in the physical sense. Physically data backups must be prepared. These backups may not even be stored physically at the same place to avoid data loss in case of a potential natural disaster, e.g. not to be lost in fire. On the other hand, compliance with data protection rules is important, especially in the case of personal data. Only authorized personnel, such as human resources or finance employees should have access to others' home addresses, telephone numbers or bank account data.

6. **Consumption of Knowledge:** This is the main goal of knowledge management. Information must be stored in user-friendly, easily searchable, manageable systems, which stakeholders have easy access to.

## Evaluation of Knowledge

There are several methods to assess and evaluate existing knowledge within the organization such as the Kaplan-Norton (1996) Balanced Scorecard or Sveiby's (1997) Intangible Assets method. Companies often use these methods to somehow quantify the benefits of knowledge management.

As we could see the different actions are connect to, build on and influence each other. These activities appear in all organizations that apply knowledge management (KM) approaches on purpose or only in some aspects.

## Burlton's Knowledge Lifecycle Model

Burlton's (2001) theory also defines different actions during the process of knowledge management within the organization. Based on the Probst, Raub and Romhardt model he focuses on the use of intellectual property (IP) within the organization's knowledge lifecycle. He divides the knowledge lifecycle into six phases:

1.  **Knowledge Creation:** As there already information within the organization, the first task is to capture and codify knowledge. Here the model refers to the Nonaka-Takeuchi model of "grabbing" tacit knowledge from the minds' of the employees and transforming it into tangible form.
2.  **Knowledge Storage:** After knowledge is created and grasped it should be stored in such a way that later it should be easily and reliably accessible. Many technologies exist for storing knowledge, e.g. wikis, websites, e-learning systems, different documentations, intranets, thus it is an important asset for companies to identify and apply those solutions which suit their purposes best.
3.  **Knowledge Discovery:** The next step is closely connected to the previous one, namely finding the knowledge already stored in the system. It may sound a bit trivial, but sometimes it is a serious difficulty to identify the exact piece of information which is needed in that particular moment and situation. To achieve this purpose several information technology tools are also used, like data mining, artificial intelligence, business analytics, knowledge mapping and social media search engines. In case knowledge is not codified yet, discovery also means to find the person who may be of assistance, who owns the tacit knowledge another person needs.
4.  **Knowledge Acquisition:** The difference between knowledge creation and knowledge acquisition is that in the first case knowledge either does not exist, the actors create it from data and information, or it is already there, but the users have to mine it out of the company's collective knowledge. In case of knowledge acquisition the users have to gain physical or intellectual access to knowledge. Some examples are: buying licenses of intellectual property rights, hiring new employees who already have the desired knowledge, acquiring databases.
5.  **Knowledge Use:** Burlton believes that if knowledge is used appropriately it significantly increases organizational efficiency and effectiveness while improving the possibility of a positive return on investment (ROI). This notion is similar to Drucker's idea mentioned above, who considered knowledge management as a strategic resource, which is a major competitive advantage.
6.  **Learning:** During the learning phase explicit knowledge is refreshed, internalized and made tacit again, hence the lifecycle starts again. Nevertheless learning is most important both for the individuals to grow intellectually and for the organization to document its knowledge in the form of best practices, handbooks, tutorials.

This methodology is similar to Sveiby's personality and technology centered approach, but personalization gets a strong emphasis here, as only one pillar corresponds with technology. As a matter of fact it matches with Sveiby's opinion who considered human factor key in his later works.

## Sveiby's Personalization and Codification Strategy

Sveiby (1996) uses two approaches. One of them focuses on the person, the other on the technology. Based on this methodology Hansen et al (1999) identify personalization and codification knowledge management strategy. In personalization strategy knowledge is linked to people, knowledge transfer happens in person, while codification strategy is assisted by information technology tools. A successful strategy as always is a mixture of the two attitudes. In personalization strategy knowledge is associated with an individual, its transfer happens in person, while codification strategy uses technology and IT devices. The most successful strategy (as usual) is the combination of these two strategies. Based on this approach Sveiby later introduced an assessment system of organizational values called the Intangible Assets Monitor.

## Sveiby's Intangible Assets Monitor

Sveiby (1997) introduced the notion of intangible assets. Intangible assets are those invisible values within a company which make up a significant "invisible equity" which make up the value of a firm. As a contradiction to tangible, financial net book values, intangible assets lay within the minds of the employees of the company. Sveiby divides intangible assets into three categories:

1. **Individual Competences:** Sveiby considers people as the only true agents in business. All physical products and intangible relations are the result of human activities. Competences are owned only by the employees of the organization. He also stresses that employees are voluntary members of the organization, meaning if they leave the company, their skills and competences are also lost for the organization.
2. **External Structures:** Relationships with customers and suppliers, brand names, trademarks and reputation, goodwill of the firm are external structures. These values may change over time, and are difficult to grasp. Difficult, because there are no exact metrics to measure them.
3. **Internal Structures:** These correlate with more tangible systems, documents, information within the company, e.g. patents, concepts, models, and computer and administrative systems. The internal structure and the people together constitute what is generally considered as the organization.

These models all add a different approach to the understanding of the various features of KM procedures and assessments.

## KNOWLEDGE MANAGEMENT'S INTERNATIONAL AND NATIONAL DEVELOPMENT HISTORY

The description of KM's first three generations is based on Anklam's work (2002). Its Hungarian development history is the same as the international experience Noszkay (2012). Anklam's subdivision is improved and completed by KM's fourth and fifth generation (Figure 4).

## Generations of Knowledge Management

- **First Generation:** The first generation's main feature is that it mainly focuses on knowledge production technology and it perceives knowledge as a product. The first generation used documents to collect and catalogue written and published materials such a way that they could be accessed when there is a need for them. "Getting the right information to the right people at the right time

*Figure 4. Knowledge management's generations*
*(Noszkay, 2012)*

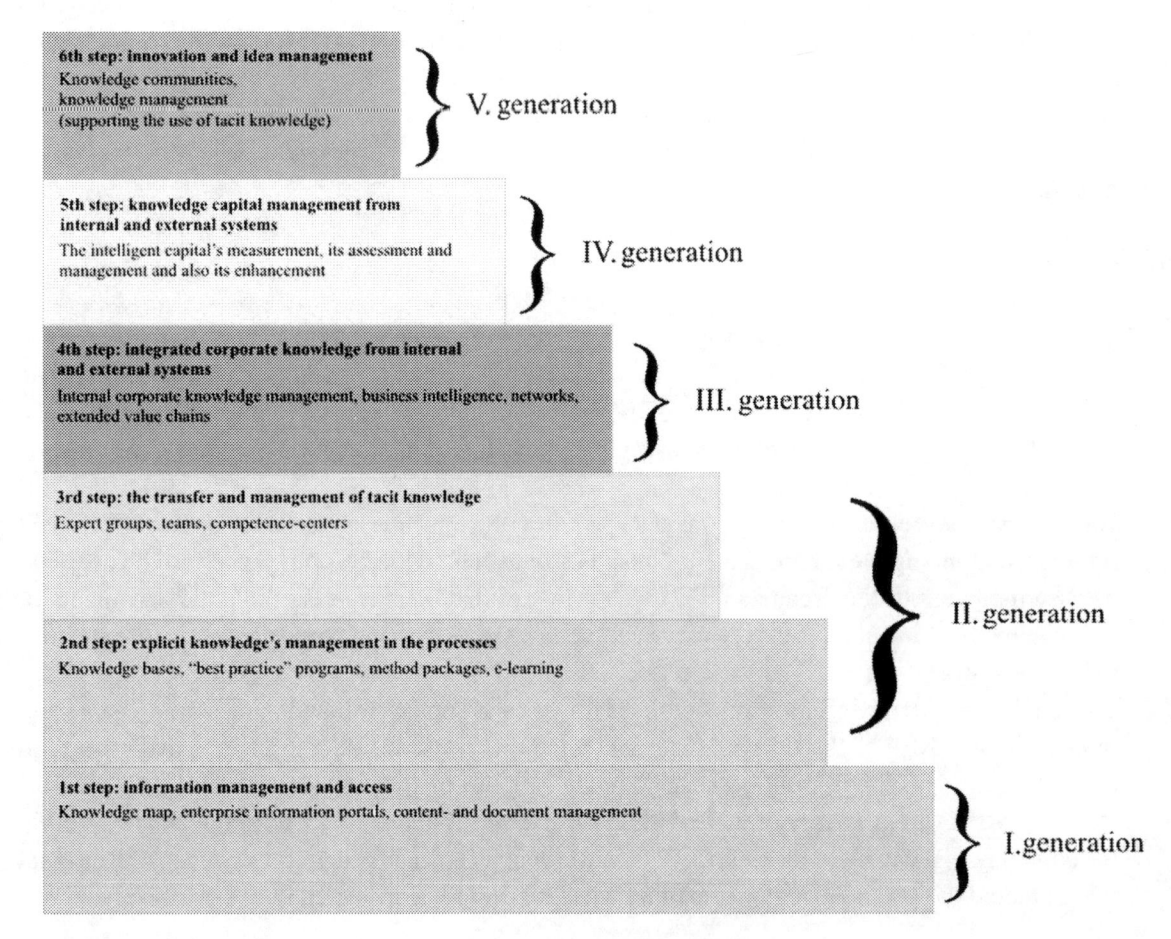

in a form they can use and a context that will help them succeed." (Anklam, 2002). The solutions for knowledge utilization are to be solved by information technologies. Due to its nature, these solutions cannot be applied successfully for tacit knowledge.

- **Second Generation:** The second generation realizes the difference between explicit and tacit knowledge and the importance of their management. It was acknowledged that knowledge cannot be easily transcript, most of what is essential knowledge is buried in people's minds' and work practices and can only be transferred through structured and regular interactions. The importance of leadership assisting knowledge sharing's, construction of organizational culture and human resource management supporting these goals grew significantly. Measurement problems of knowledge capital's value appeared in the second generation. E-learning came in the picture here as a tool for knowledge integration within an organization.

- **Third Generation:** In the third generation knowledge goes beyond the product and it appears as a network. It takes into account the explosion of people's ability to work in networks: engaging in constant conversations and shared learning with multiple stakeholders within the organization. These networks are in constant motion, they change and this flexibility also contributes to their adaptability. Its types can be business clusters, tender consortia, university knowledge centers, SMEs' clusters.

- **Fourth Generation:** In the fourth generation, knowledge is displayed as a measurable, intellectual capital factor. Declaring knowledge as a capital factor, the fourth generation also brought a paradigm shift: the analysis of knowledge factor's added value creation, knowledge capital's distinction from other capital factors, and value measurement was also needed. This resulted in the appearance of the notion known as a knowledge-based organization.
- **Fifth Generation:** Knowledge management's fifth generation has brought the formation of knowledge communities and it has also raised the awareness of knowledge management. Hidden tacit knowledge is explored. Web 2.0. based social platforms (Facebook, LinkedIn, etc.) make this process happen.

## THE IMPROVEMENT OF KNOWLEDGE MANAGEMENT PROJECTS

Knowledge management projects have developed during these generations described above. Noszkay (2013) classifies knowledge management projects' main issues and characteristics that are in context with the knowledge management generations the following way:

- **Level 1: Information Transfer:**In the first generation, information management and information access were the methods used most often. The most common improvement was the portal, which enabled content and document management. Organization portals enabled information flow for the employees within the organization.
- **Level 2: Making Explicit Knowledge Available:**The goal of the second level is the recording and recycling of the organization's explicit knowledge. The most typical method for this is the use of e-learning systems, which is thence widespread. The use of e-learning systems enables continuous training of the organization's employees, which helps them in their Lifelong Learning quest due to constantly changing professional requirements.

E-learning, distance learning and also electronic learning were described broadly and also briefly by Kovács (2008). Electronic learning is: "Any training or learning that relies on electronic technology or tools from the CD ROM to computer-assisted learning to video conferences to satellite-transmitted courses and virtual educational networks… e-learning's narrow sense only recognizes trainings as electronic learning that were organized or operated through a network."

Companies can apply e-learning on different levels. Hídvégi (2003) characterizes these layers in the following:

- **First Layer:** Learning through information. Simple information websites, where the student can easily find what he/she is looking for. Read, watch, and listen! Basic information transfer it is an ideal solution at the introduction of a new product, or communication business strategy. Simple web lectures, information source web pages, where the learner can easily and simply find, what (s)he is looking for
- **Second Layer:** Learning with interaction. Learning of basic skills for new applications, simple procedures and tasks. Try that, practice it! Here the fundamental abilities belong to the new appli-

cations and the plain procedures, tasks. Entry level for example CBT (Computer Based Training) or WBT (Web Based Training) with simulations

- **Third Layer:** Learning with cooperation. For example chat, teams, online contact with the instructor. Discuss it; practice it together with other ones! Cooperation techniques, like chat, teams, keeping on-line contact with the instructor. They help for the listeners to learn from their common experiences in groups. We may assign collective tasks. Intelligent technologies, like the use of application sharing can be introduced.
- **Fourth Layer:** Learning with teamwork. This method can be used on advanced levels, but not with basic knowledge transfer. Blended learning and mixed education also belongs here. The classroom and the instructor appear finally. In the e-learning model this method could be used with really advanced level abilities, not during beginner's knowledge transfer. So the time decreases, which a student has to spend apart from the office, and students optimally allocated expensive classroom education and equipment.
- **Level 3: The Transfer of Tacit Knowledge:** In organizations, the goal of the above mentioned knowledge conversion process is knowledge sharing and the support of the forums assisting this process. Professional knowledge communities and corporate competency centers are created for specific tasks, thus they fully support this process.
- **Level 4: Integrated Corporate Knowledge:** On the fourth level almost all of the organizations' knowledge management project levels have background IT support. The following IT systems can be found in these solutions:
  - Case-based systems,
  - Neural networks,
  - Genetic algorithms,
  - Fuzzy systems,
  - Text mining,
  - Expert systems.

Because of the improvement of business intelligence (from business perspective it is very valuable to translate raw data to information assisting decision making) text mining mentioned above is particularly important.

- **Level 5: Measurement of Knowledge Capital:** In a knowledge-based organization value creation is based on intangible resources, opposite to ordinary companies, where value creation is basically finance related. The institutionalization of knowledge management processes brought to surface the measurement of knowledge capital: Boda (2008) and Stocker (2010) examined measurement possibilities of knowledge capital. They have complemented Sveiby's (1997) original figure the following way (Figure 5).

From Sveiby and Boda, Stocker (2010) distributes knowledge organizations' assets into visible and invisible property and distinguishes traditional value creation from stakeholder value creation. Knowledge organizations' value creation with traditional perception may be negative as well, according to the new approach, according to the interpretation of the stakeholder's value, it is positive. Stakeholder values are material or immaterial values that were created for different stakeholders and they can be at least partly monetarized. These soft values also need to be highlighted for knowledge organizations' stakeholders.

*Figure 5. Knowledge organizations' visible and invisible assets (Boda, 2008)*

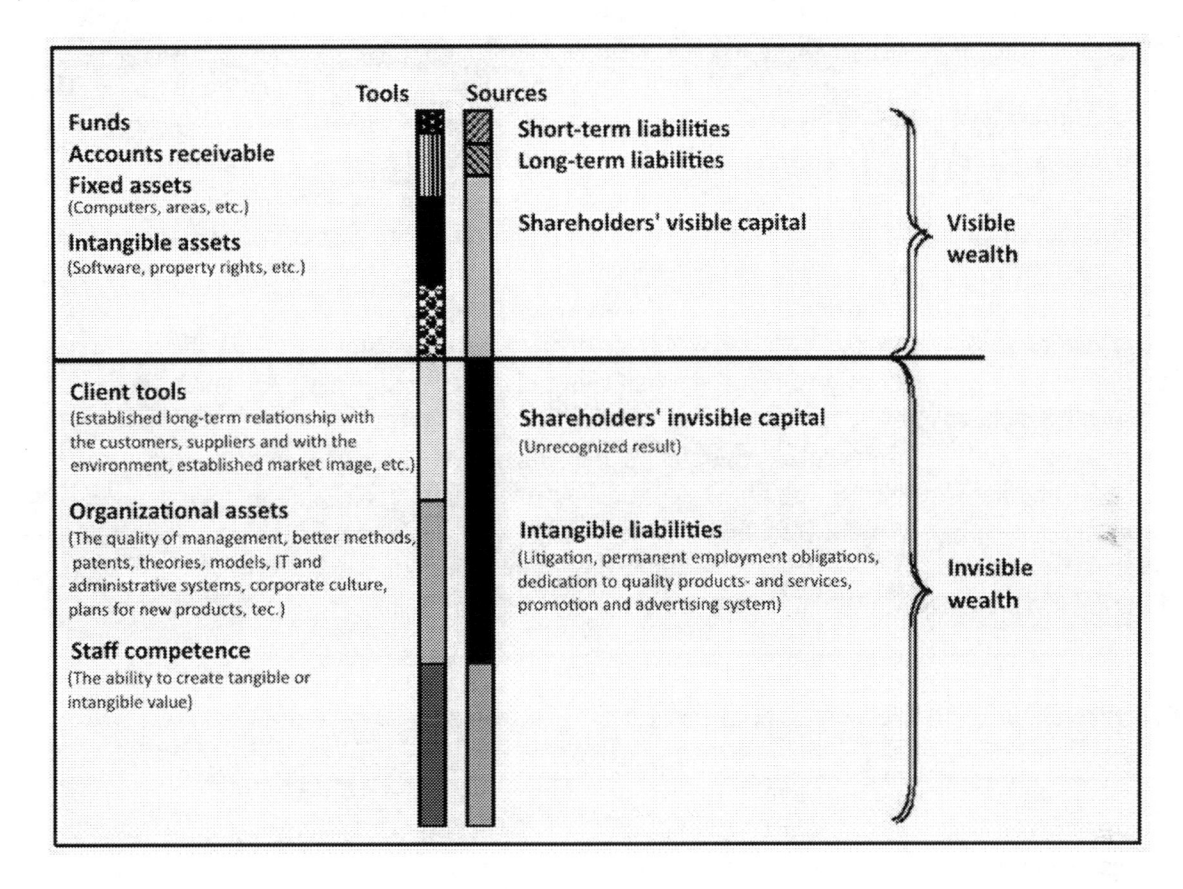

## KNOWLEDGE MANAGEMENT IN SMALL AND MEDIUM-SIZED ENTERPRISES

The literature examining knowledge management in small and medium-sized enterprises (SMEs) is naturally based on the core works on KM experts in general. Nevertheless further issues are dealt with specific to such organizations. The literature was limited by the shortage of studies in this particular business sector.

The empirical analysis of Yew Wong and Aspinwall (2005) introduced critical success factors (CSFs) for adopting knowledge management in SMEs. They found that that management leadership and support proved to be the most critical factor, while measurement was the least. Their study also emphasized technology being only a tool in this process.

Fletcher and Prashantham (2011) showed that knowledge is key to make more formal decisions during the internalization process of SMEs. SMEs used formal planned events to share knowledge and to codify tacit knowledge into explicit. Another advantage of KM for SMEs is to utilize learning and knowledge sharing to develop new market-specific knowledge (Akerman, 2014).

Several researchers used the Structural Equation Modelling (SEM) to test the plausibility of their developed model. Saini (2014) set up a model framework for measuring an organization's KM capability and its effect on innovation strategies. KM practices enhanced the quality of administering quality care to their customers and employees with low development cost and increased the innovation in SMEs by reducing efforts of duplicate research and development. These practices also improved customer relations, provided flexibility in production and innovation, thus increasing the number of markets.

McAdam et al (2010) developed and tested a model of innovation implementation in SMEs. Their study results connected the effects of leadership, people and culture on innovation implementation with Total Quality Management/Continuous Improvement (TQM/CI) and process developments.

Cegarra-Navarro and Sánchez-Polo, (2011) found that knowledge retention and knowledge transfer let the organization to have an 'organizational memory' by organizing important knowledge on demand.

As this chapter will show further, knowledge management and storage systems play an important role in the KM activities of organizations. These systems include IT-based solutions to support operational knowledge retrieval and storage (Alavi & Leidner, 1999). Knowledge storage allows the organization to build an organizational memory, that is internal knowledge collected (Chang & Cho, 2008; Cegarra-Navarro & Sánchez-Polo, 2011)

Floyde et al (2013) observed the process of the implementation of knowledge management systems and e-learning for SMEs. They also found that for capturing, retaining and sharing tacit knowledge e-learning proved to be a useful tool for employees.

Perez-Soltero et al (2015) describe in detail the procedure of introducing a KM system in a Mexican SME. Their model may be used further for the target group of this book.

## KNOWLEDGE MANAGEMENT SYSTEMS

Knowledge management as a system differs so far from everything in its modes and institutionalized solutions, which is completed with IT and background IT support. The ultimate goal of Knowledge Management is to improve organizational effectiveness by implementing such tools which enhance the ability to share what the participants already know.

During organizational implementation of knowledge management equal attention should be paid to processes, technical solutions and finally to management of human factors. For balanced development these three dimensions need to be taken into account (Bencsik, 2013).

In connection with the presentation of knowledge management systems technical dimensions are scrutinized in more detail. In this case, the expression "system" does not only refer to IT solutions, but also as a summary of all processes mentioned above. Within the notion of knowledge sharing the main goal of ICT technologies is the connection of parties concerned (Bencsik, 2013). These ICT solutions may help in the exploration, sharing, dissemination and application of knowledge's.

According to Frost (2014) knowledge management systems refer to any kind of IT system that stores and retrieves knowledge, improves collaboration, locates knowledge sources, mines repositories for hidden knowledge, captures and uses knowledge, or in some other way enhances the KM process. He argues that this explanation seems vague, but this is due to the fact that there is no consensus as to what comprises a knowledge management system.

James Robertson (2007) goes as far as to argue that organizations should not even think in terms of knowledge management systems. He argues that KM, though enhanced by technology, is not a technology discipline, and thinking in terms of knowledge management systems leads to unrealistic expectations. Instead, the focus should be determining the functionality of the IT systems that are required for the specific activities and initiatives within the firm.

In this chapter based on Ternes's (2001) summary the author describes two models which contain both IT and human factors. These models are Stankosky Four Pillar Knowledge Management Framework Model and Wieneke-Price KMF model.

## The Stankosky Four Pillar Knowledge Management Framework Model

According to Stankosky and Baldanza's (2000) approach there are four pillars of knowledge management: leadership, organization, technology and learning (Figure 6). The unity of these factors ensures the success of knowledge management within the organization.

1. **Leadership:** Without the support of leaders KM will not fulfill its goal. Organization leaders should provide policies for KM activities and in general encourage knowledge sharing.
2. **Organization:** Successful KM is about methodically implementing and managing organizational change. Besides the importance of IT, KM applications focus more on the human factor.
3. **Technology:** Provides the actual infrastructure, IT systems, and processes needed by other segments of the KM framework to achieve chosen goals and objectives. In early KM systems IT played the main role within the organization.
4. **Learning:** Successful KM frameworks require well trained employees capable of exploiting all aspects of the four KM pillars. Therefore to attain a competent workforce, organizations should

*Figure 6. The Stankosky four pillar knowledge management framework model*
*(Stankosky, Baldanza, 2000)*

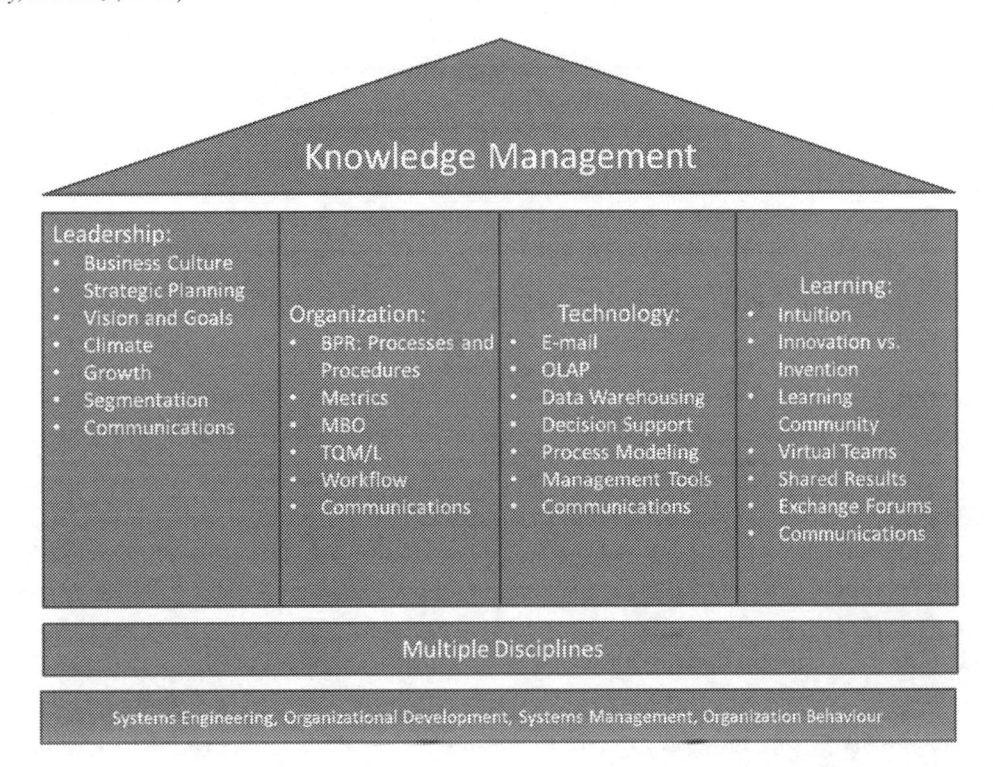

consider putting special emphasis on identifying, recording, expressing, and institutionalizing company learning procedures.

These four pillars represent various components considered essential to implementing a successful knowledge management framework (KMF). Successful KMFs meet user expectations and needs based on organizational goals, objectives, and result in an acceptable return on investment (ROI). All of these pillars are important. Their greatest impact is achieved when they are incorporated both horizontally and vertically within the organization. Calabrese also determined that the four pillars of the Stankosky framework represent a mix of cross-dimensional skills, know-how and disciplines.

## Wieneke-Price KMF Model

The General Motors (GM) KM framework model (Figure 7) also known as the Wieneke-Price KM Framework applies a taxonomy-based approach to define attributes, behaviors, and competencies they believe constitute successful KM frameworks (Wieneke & Price, 2003). Primary objectives of the Wieneke-Price KMF model include comprehensive knowledge uptake, quick retrieval, unlimited sharing, and the utilization of essential organizational knowledge assets within the organization. This model also focuses on the mechanisms, like technologies, processes, and procedures of capturing and deploying knowledge assets.

Eight KM-related subject form the core of the Wieneke-Price (2003) KM framework. The main goal of this framework is to transform organizations into "learning appreciative" cultures. The following aspects make up this framework:

1.  **Knowledge Arenas:** General categories of intellectual assets considered necessary to achieve organizational effectiveness. The notion of knowledge area is a theoretical basis of knowledge related issues comprised of primary and secondary product knowledge, manufacturing processes, enterprise business processes, customer loyalty and value knowledge, external-to-internal knowledge, and metaknowledge,

2.  **Knowledge Capital:** Refers to potential tacit knowledge, which is stored in human minds in the form of personal experience, explicit knowledge e.g. documentations, handbooks, internal (corporate) knowledge, and external knowledge sources e.g. customers, suppliers, partners, existing within and outside of a company.

3.  **Knowledge-Based Learning Processes:** These are tools for discovering and applying what employees already know, identifying and accomplishing what they don't yet know or understand, and creating newly discovered knowledge

4.  **Enterprise-Wide Infrastructure:** Focuses more on the metrics and technical features and approaches within the organization. It concludes several disciplines, e.g. Implementing reward systems, fielding IT infrastructures, software systems and training and education.

5.  **Knowledge Area Benchmarking:** Provides examples for organizations to map its explicit knowledge. To achieve this, a common framework and taxonomies should be defined to improve classification of knowledge assets.

6.  **Knowledge Area Content Management:** As a follow up to the previous point, content management is one of the most important actions of this model. It is based on definitions and ontologies described above. They introduce the notion of knowledge nuggets, which are relevant, easily un-

*Figure 7. The Wieneke-Price KM framework*
*(Wieneke-Price, 2003)*

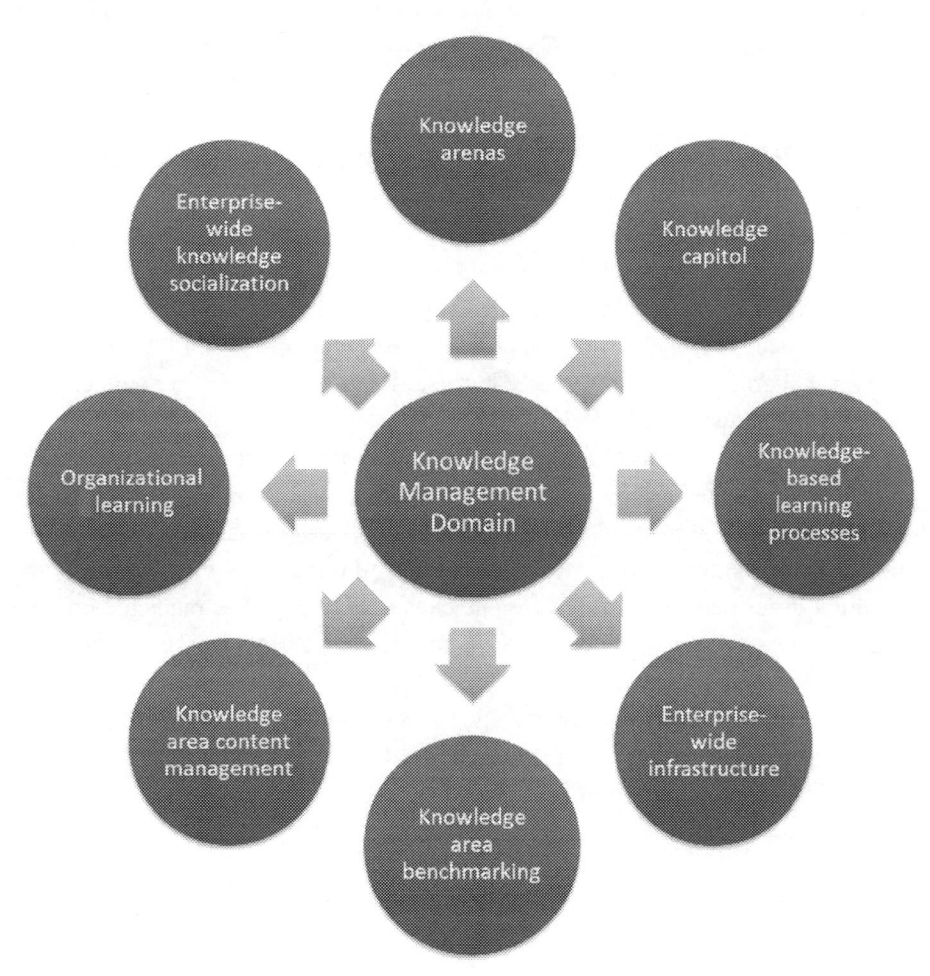

derstood parcels of knowledge that are readily applied, shared, managed, or re-used (Wieneke & Price, 2003).

7. **Organizational Learning:** Is made up the following disciplines: personal mastery, shared vision, systems thinking, mental models, team learning, human information processing and business strategy.

8. **Enterprise-Wide Knowledge Socialization:** Organizational behavior aspects make up this discipline. Knowledge socialization activities occur during this procedure, e.g. familiarization with the environment. It usually occurs when a new employee enters the organization.

As we can see these KM models cover similar procedures, thus having significant resemblances with each other. They differ in the explanation of these procedures and on the importance of the ratio of the different areas and disciplines of KM. E.g. Stankosky's model places more emphasis on the importance of the role technical and IT solutions play within KM processes, while the Wieneke-Price model puts more importance on the human factor, organizational behavior and learning.

The human factor in fact plays an important part in the KM process. in the final part of this chapter the author describes some aspects of learning which adds value, brings tacit knowledge into surface and serves as a tool in the operation of functional and successful KM companies.

## SOLUTIONS AND RECOMMENDATIONS

### How to Build a Knowledge Management System for SMEs

The case studies and models introduced above present both theoretical and practical approaches to the development of KM systems. For the target group's (SME leaders and employees) purposes a more practical approach is suitable. Based on Perez-Soltero et al's model this chapter suggests the following procedure for SME's to follow:

This practical model provides a useful approach to SMEs in the initial phase of developing a KM solution. The Seafile system used is a server-based file storing and sharing software, similar to Dropbox or Google drive, but free and open source. Nevertheless as the authors above pointed out technical and IT solutions are necessary but only act as a tool for successful knowledge management.

The methodology described serves the different phases of knowledge management. The first and second stage, identifying and analyzing the area of interest and defining process activities correlates with identification of knowledge according to the Probst, Romhardt and Raub's (2000) Building Blocks of Knowledge Management model. The third stage, developing and implementing a KMS equals to preservation of knowledge. The fourth stage can also be found in Kaplan-Norton's (1996) Balanced Scorecard or Sveiby's (1997) Intangible Assets model.

*Table 1. Methodology for the implementation of a process-based KMS area of interest*

| Stages of The Methodology | Objective | Tools |
|---|---|---|
| 1. Identify and analyze the area of interest | Determine the area of interest and perform KM analysis of this and identify the important processes of the same. | • Initial meetings<br>• Documentary information<br>• Format comparison chart areas<br>• Interviews and quiz |
| 2. Define process activities | Define the activities required for each major process area of interest. | • Interviews<br>• Format array of activities |
| 3. Develop and implement an KMS | Studying KM processes to manage knowledge of the processes of the area of study | • Meetings<br>• Interviews<br>• Knowledge mapping<br>• Existing documents<br>• Quizzes<br>• KM software (Seafile in their case, a document sharing system)<br>• E-learning |
| 4. Validate the KMS | Check the validity of the KMS in the area of interest | • Interview<br>• Comparison table<br>• Summary table of documental information |

(Perez-Soltero, 2015)

As a final summary and advice to SME's planning to implement knowledge management procedures Bencsik and Juhász (2012) suggest that it must be based on high intellectual capital, a typical strategic path and organizational learning. They also found that knowledge based companies support autonomy, risk assumption and strong organizational network.

## The Relationship of Knowledge Management and e-Learning

Based on Stankosy's model this chapter would like to focus on more in this last aspect namely learning, which may act as a possible facilitator of organizational knowledge uptake. Learning is crucial within the organization to sustain and maintain the utilization of knowledge and keep up the knowledge lifecycle. Therefore the last part of this chapter will cover some aspects of the connection of learning and knowledge management. As online learning is gaining more and more part within organizational learning, e-learning will be discussed in more detail.

Intelligent adult training, which follows contemporary expectations, that is, the realization of planned process of lifelong learning is unimaginable without knowledge management. Companies already handle these issues together within their training plans. Pure knowledge transfer is hardly possible in business without knowledge sharing and knowledge integration. All these factors unavoidably result in new knowledge combinations, which add value on the one hand to new products, on the other hand to new, acquirable knowledge products representing a higher level of the development spiral. This knowledge integration demand should not be followed but assisted by education.

The valuable developments of e-learning companies are very impressive according to analyst observations. Really good e-learning curriculum development is very labor intensive. So if the organization intends to produce a development beyond textbook adaptation, based on the linear logic of thinking patterns, they must face the fact that they could get results from only the best team, a group of teachers and experts, whose commitment and interest is vital. It is not simple, since the majority of teachers are not really motivated to change. To unlearn the old and traditional educational methods (lecture – textbook - traditional assessment methods) requires an entirely new approach. It can clearly be seen that not everyone is capable to this shift, concerning the development of e-learning materials in particular.

Reasonable use can only be effective with very serious foundation and preparatory work. In addition it must not be forgotten that the quality of e-learning requires an entirely different philosophy as traditional training. The emphasis shifts from teaching to learning; the student becomes the main protagonist of the acquisition process, opposite to traditional teacher-centered training. Content development (and not only the operation) can only be done as teamwork. Professional e-learning solutions may exclusively be developed and operated with such a complex set of conditions of which only a single element is missing, the whole system is doomed to failure.

There are also other important aspects: e-learning is not the solution to every situation, only a bonus, and a technical tool. There are several forms of training, where the use of e-learning is simply inadequate as personal relationship between teacher and student is crucial. Quick and cost-effective e-learning solutions will not either weaken the quality of education, respectively, nor the amount of content to be mastered is reduced. Such an infrastructure is available – tailored to the desirable requirements -, which allows for targeted use. There are such training situations where efficient operation is only possible through network-based systems like intranet and internet, for example when it is imperative to ensure the monitoring of student progress, a relatively instant student - teacher interaction, and a mechanism for consultation.

## CONCLUSION

## New Roles and Tasks for New Procedures

During the construction of organizational knowledge management structures while introducing information systems, managers have to review the strategy, processes, job descriptions, roles and documentations. New jobs, tasks are created that should be managed continuously on an institutional level. The prerequisite of initiating such a development is a thoughtful strategic plan, which will define the place and role of new e-learning services within the framework of the purposes, the objective and subjective criteria. Organizational strategy should be established to determine the design, implementation, and details of the operation.

Defining the objectives of knowledge management is essential for the organization. Management must be aware that knowledge management processes can only be successful if there is a clear edge detail about what they want to achieve, and these points are given managerial support. Strategy development, skills mapping and preservation are of the most typical of these goals.

The main goal of knowledge management is enhancing organizational effectiveness. These situations occur in all types of organizations e.g. employees leave due to changing their workplace or superannuation. In these cases it is imperative to store and transfer the employee's knowledge so that it would not be lost for the organization.

Customized knowledge management solutions and services play an increasing part in the business sector. Knowledge management tools can be the method of attraction and may prevent the dropout of employees. Technical and IT solutions, like e-learning management systems, have an essential function, while digital competence development and use also play a key part. In the coming years knowledge-based economy will become the engine of economic development. This process is not easy and requires a lot of work from the institutions to adapt to these changes, but the final result is worth the effort.

## REFERENCES

Akerman, N. (2014). An international learning typology: Strategies and outcomes for internationalizing firms. *Baltic Journal of Management*, *9*(4), 382–402. doi:10.1108/BJM-12-2013-0176

Alavi, M., & Leidner, D. E. (1999). Knowledge management systems: Issues, challenges, and benefits. *Communications of the AIS*, *1*(2es), 1.

Anklam, P. (2002). Knowledge Management. The Collaboration Thread. *Bulletin of the American Society for Information Science and Technology*, *28*(6), 8–11. doi:10.1002/bult.254

Barbrook, R. (1995). *Media Freedom: The Contradictions of Communication in the Age of Modernity*. Macmillan.

Barbrook, R. (2007). *Imaginary Futures: From Thinking Machines to the Global Village*. London: Pluto Press.

Bencsik, A. (2013). *Best practice a tudásmenedzsment rendszer kiépítésében*. Bungay: Longman Addison Wesley.

Bencsik, A., & Juhász, T. (2012). Chance of Success at Hungarian Small and Medium Sized Enterprises. *Problems of Management in the 21st Century, 5,* 16-30.

Boda, G. (2008). *A tudástőke mérési módszerei és használhatóságuk. CEO Magazin, 9(3).* Appendix.

Burlton, R. (2001). *Business process management; profiting from process; Principles of process management.* Indianapolis: Pearson Education-SAMS Publishing.

Cegarra-Navarro, J. G., & Sánchez-Polo, M. T. (2011). Influence of the open-mindedness culture on organizational memory: An empirical investigation of Spanish SMEs. *International Journal of Human Resource Management, 22*(1), 1–18. doi:10.1080/09585192.2011.538963

Chang, D. R., & Cho, H. (2008). Organizational memory influences new product success. *Journal of Business Research, 61*(1), 13–23. doi:10.1016/j.jbusres.2006.05.005

Curley, K., & Kivowitz, B. (2001). *The manager's pocket guide to knowledge management and organizational learning.* Los Angeles: HRD Press.

Dalkir, K. (2011). *Knowledge Management in Theory and Practice.* Cambridge, MA: The MIT Press.

Davenport, T. H., & Prusak, L. (1998). *Working Knowledge. Managing What Your Organization Knows.* Boston, MA: Harvard Business School Press.

Deutsch, K. (1983). Soziale und politische Aspekte der Informationsgesellschaft. In Die Zukunft der Informationsgesellschaft (pp. 68-88). Frankfurt/Main: Haag & Herchen.

Drucker, P. (1993). *Post-Capitalist Society.* New York: Harper Business.

Drucker, P. F. (1992). *The Age of Discontinuity: Guidelines to Our Changing Society.* New Brunswick: Transaction Publishers.

Fahey, L., & Prusak, L. (1998). The eleven deadliest sins of knowledge management. *California Management Review, 40*(3), 265–276. doi:10.2307/41165954

Fletcher, M., & Prashantham, S. (2011). Knowledge assimilation processes of rapidly internationalising firms: Longitudinal case studies of Scottish SMEs. *Journal of Small Business and Enterprise Development, 18*(3), 475–501. doi:10.1108/14626001111155673

Floyde, A., Lawson, G., Shalloe, S., Eastgate, R., & D'Cruz, M. (2013). The design and implementation of knowledge management systems and e-learning for improved occupational health and safety in small to medium sized enterprises. *Safety Science, 60,* 69–76. doi:10.1016/j.ssci.2013.06.012

Frost, A. (2014). *Knowledge Management Systems.* Retrieved March 29, 2016, from http://www.knowledge-management-tools.net/knowledge-management-systems.html

Hansen, M. T., Nohria, N., & Tierney, T. (1999). What's Your Strategy For Managing Knowledge? *Harvard Business Review, 77*(2), 106–116.

Hídvégi, P. (2003). E-learning megoldások. In J. Mayer & P. Singer (Eds.), *A tanulás kora.* Országos Közoktatási Intézet.

Kaplan, R. S., & David, P. (1996). Linking the Balanced Scorecard to Strategy. *California Management Review, 39*(1), 53–79. doi:10.2307/41165876

Kovács, I. (2008). A hagyományostól eltérő tanulási-tanítási formák. In L. Szabados (Ed.), *Pedagógia és/vagy andragógia Jászberény* (pp. 219–237). Szent István Egyetem Alkalmazott Bölcsészeti Kar.

Luzwick, P. (1999). *What's a pound of your information worth? Constructs for collaboration and consistency.* Unpublished white paper. Author.

Machlup, F. (1962). *The Production and Distribution of Knowledge in the United States.* Princeton University Press.

McAdam, R., Moffett, S., Hazlett, S. A., & Shevlin, M. (2010). Developing a model of innovation implementation for UK SMEs: A path analysis and explanatory case analysis. *International Small Business Journal, 28*(3), 195–215. doi:10.1177/0266242609360610

Negroponte, N. (1996). *Being Digital.* New York: Vintage.

Nonaka, I., & Takeuchi, H. (1995). *The Knowledge-Creating Company.* Oxford: Oxford University Press.

Noszkay, E. (2012). *Tudásmenedzsment ... és ahogyan fejlődik.* Budapest: Poziteam.

Noszkay, E. (2013). *A rendszerszemléletű tudásmenedzsment.* Pearson.

Perez-Soltero, A., Zavala-Guerrero, A. G., Barcelo-Valenzuela, M., Sanchez-Schmitz, G., & Meroño-Cerdan, A. L. (2015). A Methodology for the Development and Implementation of Knowledge Management Strategy in a Mexican SME Trading Company. *The IUP Journal of Knowledge Management, 13*(2), 25–44.

Polányi, M. (1962). Tacit Knowing. Its Bearing on Some Problems of Philosophy. *Reviews of Modern Physics, 34*(4), 601–616. doi:10.1103/RevModPhys.34.601

Polanyi, M. (1964). *Personal Knowledge. Towards A Post-Critical Philosophy.* London: Routledge & Kegan Paul Ltd.

Polányi, M. (1966). *The Tacit Dimension.* Garden City, NY: Doubleday & Co.

Porat, M. U. (1977). *The Information Economy: Definition and Measurement.* Retrieved March 29, 2016 from http://eric.ed.gov/?id=ED142205

Probst, G., Romhardt, K., & Raub, S. (2000). *Managing Knowledge. Building Blocks For Success.* New York: John Wiley & Sons.

Robertson, J. (2007). *There are no "KM systems".* Retrieved March 29, 2016 from http://www.steptwo.com.au/papers/cmb_kmsystems/

Saini, R. (2013). Model development for key enablers in the implementation of knowledge management. *IUP Journal of Knowledge Management, 11*(2), 46.

Stankosky, M., & Baldanza, C. (2000). *A systems approach to engineering a knowledge management system.* White paper. The George Washington University.

Stocker, M. (2010). *Tudásszervezetek értékteremtésének anomáliái*. Tudásmenedzsment Workshop. Budapest: Budapesti Kommunikációs Főiskola.

Sveiby, K. E. (1996). Transfer of knowledge and the information processing professions. *European Management Journal, 14*(4), 379–388. doi:10.1016/0263-2373(96)00025-4

Sveiby, K. E. (1997). *The new organizational wealth: Managing & measuring knowledge-based assets*. San Francisco: Berrett-Koehler Publishers.

Ternes, C. D. (2011). *Confirming the Stankosky Knowledge Management Framework*. The George Washington University.

Wieneke, S., & Phlypo-Price, K. (2003). *The knowledge management domain – a knowledge management approach to knowledge management*. White paper. General Motors Corporation.

Wiig, K. M. (1993). *Knowledge Management Foundations. Thinking About Thinking-How People and Organizations Create, Represent, and Use Knowledge*. Arlington: Schema Press.

Yew Wong, K., & Aspinwall, E. (2005). An empirical study of the important factors for knowledge-management adoption in the SME sector. *Journal of Knowledge Management, 9*(3), 64–82. doi:10.1108/13673270510602773

## KEY TERMS AND DEFINITIONS

**Data:** Raw facts and figures without interpretation.

**E-Learning:** Learning which is conducted by means of an electronic (online) medium.

**Explicit Knowledge:** Knowledge which is easy to express, codify and transfer between individuals opposed to tacit knowledge.

**Generations of Knowledge Management:** Phases of the evolution of knowledge management related to the development of technical solutions, focusing on different actors within this procedure. The process covers decades of the 20th and 21th century.

**Information:** Meaningful piece of knowledge that is based on data and has some added value for the user.

**Intellectual Property:** Another expression for tacit knowledge, existing in the minds of people.

**Knowledge:** Intellectual content originating from one person's mind used by another individual.

**Knowledge Codification Models:** Models describing different aspects, notions and theories of knowledge management usually explaining the view of a specific author.

**Knowledge Lifecycle:** The process of managing knowledge within the organization, which includes the creating, capturing, storing, sharing and utilizing knowledge.

**Knowledge Management:** The procedure of defining, decoding, describing, using, transferring, storing and codifying knowledge within the organization. It is considered to be a major asset, competitive advantage and added value in the information society.

**Knowledge Management Systems:** Technical, mostly information technology based applications to serve the knowledge management procedure.

**Tacit Knowledge:** Knowledge beyond words. Tacit knowledge is difficult to express and transfer verbally. It is mostly handed over by apprenticeship, learning by doing within a tutor-master relationship.

**Tangible and Intangible Assets:** Values within a company either measurable by metrics and financial results (tangible), or difficult to measure, hidden within the skills, competences of the employees, the human capital of the company (intangible).

# Chapter 2
# Decision Maker in the Global Village:
## Thinking Together

**Jolán Velencei**
*Óbuda University, Hungary*

**Zoltán Baracskai**
*Babeş-Bolyai University, Romania*

## ABSTRACT

*The Nobel Memorial Prize in Economics has been awarded twice so far to researchers in the area of decision making. In 1978 to Herbert Simon "for his pioneering research into the decision-making process within economic organizations" and in 2002 to Daniel Kahneman "for having integrated insights from psychological research into economic science, especially concerning human judgment and decision-making under uncertainty". In spite of this, in business schools and schools of economics courses in decision making focus on decision tools of applied operations research. There are, however, newer views that have not yet made their ways into the decision curricula. Therefore the authors argue that in the Global Village the decision taker's role is wearing off while the decision maker's role is changing. Now, that a great deal of knowledge is available freely and free of charge, a new possibility is opening up for a new type of thinking together. In this Chapter the authors take a closer look at this thinking together.*

## DEMARCATION

The following is one of the authors' favorite stories, Wittgenstein's Poker, a confession by Karl Popper about the philosophical greats.

*In the beginning of the 1946-47 academic year, I was invited by the secretary of the Moral Sciences Club... Wittgenstein, who was seated near the fireplace and playing with a poker, provocatively stated the question. "State one example of a moral rule." To which I replied, "Not to threaten visiting lecturers with pokers." To this, Wittgenstein abruptly left... After Wittgenstein had left, a pleasant philosophical debate ensued, to which Bertrand Russell was a member (Popper, 1998, p. 112).*

DOI: 10.4018/978-1-5225-1642-2.ch002

While this is a story, it demonstrates very well how great thoughts are formed. Even the greatest minds are merely human. What distinguishes them is that different thoughts come to great mind than to the mediocre ones when looking at something – in our case at a decision problem. The following passages might also contain thoughts that will prompt some to threaten the authors with a red-hot poker. Also, the authors are not among those who would proclaim 'all has been written; one should simply read more.' Even if it has been written, it is surely not written like this. So let us look at the discipline of decision making in a different light than the positivists would do. We could argue that positivists are not 'made that way', but in a way that is not true, for they were born into the values and culture of an age. If all their teachers were positivists, then the only thing they could have learned from them about the world was that the future is predictable based upon the past. They could not have had different teachers, for positivists never let into their midst those they did not understand – or, at least, they labelled such things unscientific. To address this situation, we outline what one of the reviewers of an earlier version of this chapter called a 'Catch 22': giving up science in order to include the soft components and improving decisions. We tackle this 'Catch 22' exploring the demarcation problem, then the changing identity of the decision maker, within this paying special attention to the development of aspiration levels to arrive at an answer in a variant of Unended Quest (Popper, 1998) which we contextualize in an ecological sense ('ecological' here refers to a complexity level 7 of Boulding's 11-level model, see Boulding, 1985. pp. 9-30).

Human and social disciplines will never give up their effort to be looked upon as sciences. According to Karl Popper (1998) it is well known that the problem of induction comes from the mistaken solution of demarcation. From the positivistic belief that what separates science from pseudoscience is the scientific method, and induction is what shall lead to true, or rather, verifiable knowledge. This attitude and approach often puts the practitioners of soft disciplines, such as those of decision-making, into an uncomfortable position. This is made stranger by the fact that there are anti-positivists who understand this and so do not consider positivists charlatans, but rarely do you find the opposite. Here and now, the authors will outline a new demarcation.

*The trouble was that man isn't suited to this kind of scientific objective study. Objects of scientific study are supposed to hold still. They're supposed to follow the laws of cause and effect in such a way that a given cause will always have a given effect, over and over again. Man doesn't do this. Not even savages (Pirsig, 1991, p. 72).*

The purpose of demarcation is not to draw a line between science and metaphysics, but rather to separate science from pseudoscience. Everything that could be said for and against science would strike back like a boomerang. Only those who know tradition back to front can be true revolutionaries in science, for without the background knowledge of the era of puzzle solving, one constantly ends up with pseudo-problems. Stories of those with incomplete background knowledge trying to discover the Americas are dime a dozen. This is because they are imagining a problem that already has an accepted solution within the base of knowledge in the field.

The "invisible establishment" of science does not wish to separate hard and soft sciences. When it comes to financing research, practitioners of soft disciplines wish to be held in the same lot as those of hard disciplines. However, when it comes to the evaluation of researcher performance, soft discipline practitioners protest against being in that same lot. To understand more easily, let us look at the field of economics. Thomas Sedlacek (2013) says Samulson's text reads like a physics book. Everything is clear-cut: behold the mechanical machine that is Economics. It is not the task, nor the scope of the authors to scrutinize the entirety of numeration. The trap lies in the fact that many things in economics can be expressed through the lens of money, which is measurable. The movement of money, however, happens in a world so complex that it is beyond determinism. The practitioners and charmers of decision making also often fall into this trap when looking at decisions of economics and business. Perhaps it is time to think about a Demarcation 2.0, which would separate the hard and soft disciplines.

More and more thinkers, either out of enlightenment or necessity, try to wriggle out of mono-disciplinarily. Over time, disciplines have become specialized. Today, more than eight thousand disciplines can be named. It is impossible to try to solve a problem within the framework of any single discipline, but this does not mean that any discipline can be selected at will. Decision-making does not do us the favor of formulating its problems within one discipline.

There is a strong separation of disciplines, which is accepted, but never became popular. The labels of Sciences and Humanities suggest that certain disciplines are contained within science, but others are left out. There are sciences (physics and chemistry for example) and then there is philosophy. From these, one can craft philosophies of science (the philosophy of physics, the philosophy of chemistry), but it is foolish to try and create a science of philosophy (the physics of philosophy, the chemistry of philosophy). There is knowledge (disciplines) that can be taught and learned. Decision-making is one of them. The sciences can be turned into disciplines, but this does not work the other way around. One cannot make decision making into decision science. At the heart of soft disciplines lies the definition of the conceptual framework and model. Here the recognition of problems and the tentative search for their solutions are not repeatable. It is simply not possible to conduct the same experiment under the same conditions.

The study of decision-making is beyond its teething problems, when it was imagined that algorithms, that is rigid sequences of operations, would remove all doubt. Applied operation research sets applied research aside, and develops useful algorithms, which optimize well-structured operations. Business schools and Schools of Economics prefer using models and methods. Referring to Thomas Sedlacek (2013), just because we can describe how something operates does not mean we understand the connections.

The authors do not wish to punish its readers by listing the mistakes and fallacies of the materials adopted in schools in the past half century. They would merely like to point out that decision-making has made four serious and numerous pointless attempts. What is more, decision-making never truly became a discipline in its own right. These attempts did not happen chronologically, but were parallel in time.

1. The Multiple Criteria Decision Making method is an offshoot of operation research focusing on the allocation of scarce resources, and so only focused on a small fraction of decision-making. The authors prefer to call this Decision Making 1.0.
2. The theory of bounded rationality is the offshoot of cognitive psychology, which aimed at clearing up the idea of rationality. The authors view this as Decision Making 2.0.
3. Game Theory models human reasoning in situations where there are two people at least as smart as John von Neumann. The authors refer to this as Decision Making 3.0.
4. The Expert System is the child of artificial intelligence, which introduced modeling based on the "if... then" rules. The authors wish to refer to this as Decision Making 4.0.

Today everybody see an age of bounty, and bear witness to the largest expansion of available choices in history. "Consume more!" is the slogan of this age. Never mind if you cannot afford it, someone is there to help, "because you're worth it". Decision is no longer an option, it is a necessity. Pathfinding, the concept, which the authors prefer to describe finding acceptable solutions to decisions in unknown territory in the complex multitudes, is sometimes attractive, but sometimes repulsive. If a lot of paths present themselves to us, we feel we can finally realize ourselves, do as we wish, and become who we want to be. Sheena Iyengar (2010) writes many examples of the suffering in over-abundance.

As Herbert Simon (1997) predicted decades ago, abundance of knowledge breeds deficit of attention. Attention is a scarce resource, it is only available to us in finite amounts, and so we are in competition for it. Today's twenty-somethings grew up with the Internet, and have gotten used to freedom and freely accessible knowledge. As Chris Anderson (2010) writes, if we had to pay for something before and no longer have to pay for it now, we often believe that it is due to a decrease in quality. But if we never had to pay for something, we never think about it this way. Nicholas Carr (2010) predicts that we will know a little about a lot of things, and so our knowledge will be shallow. The abundance of knowledge has not increased our cognitive capacity; we are still only able to retain as many cognitive schemas as in previous centuries.

Marshall McLuhan (McLuhan, Powers, 1989) introduced the concept of the Global Village. This concept refers to a world interconnected by an electronic nervous system, making it part of our popular culture before it actually happened.

The authors would divide the soft and hard disciplines along the lines of Demarcation 2.0, and would endeavor to outline Decision Making 5.0, which describes the attitudes and approaches of the decision makers of the Global Village in light of their identity, their changing expectations, their never ending quest for suitable paths, and their ecology, context and interconnectedness.

## THE IDENTITY OF THE DECISION MAKER

The following is one of the authors' favorite stories about Noblesse Oblige. When someone is accepted into the ranks of Doctors of Philosophy, it is not fitting to exalt, nor to belittle the sufferings upon the path leading to their initiation. It is, however, fitting to tell them: 'Noblesse Oblige'. What are the un-written rules that oblige one in such a rank? The authors received the following sentiments from their own teachers in the last century:

1. One does not drive a car, but calls a taxi.
2. One does not use paper tissues, but carries a steam-pressed rag in their jacket pocket.
3. One does not order anything at the usual coffee house, for the waiter knows what to bring and when.
4. One does not search for disciples; disciples flock at the door.

*The logic of appropriateness is tied to the concept of identity. An identity is a conception of self, organized into rules for matching action to situations. When Don Quixote says 'I know who I am", he claims a self that is organized around the identity of 'knight-errant'. When an executive is en-joined to 'act like a decision maker', he or she is encouraged to apply a logic of appropriateness to a conception of an identity (March, 1994. p. 61).*

But what kind of rules should be followed by someone who does not have such a strongly defined identity as Don Quixote? What can a decision maker do when they are seeking a path that is un-trodden?

If they seek advice from a professional advisor, the danger is that the advisor might 'have an axe to grind' and recommend something out of their own toolkit.

*To say that individuals and organizations follow rules and identities, however, is not to say their behavior is always easily predicted. Rule-based behavior is freighted with uncertainty. Situations, identities, and rules can all be ambiguous. Decision makers' use processes of recognition to classify situations; they use processes of self-awareness to clarify identities; they use processes of search and recall to match appropriate rules to situations and identities. The processes are easily recognized as standard instruments of intelligent human behavior (March, 1994, p. 61).*

Circumscribing and labeling certain activities within an organization can give us footholds in creating our identity. The rules of conduct can be fixed and tied to our identity, creating contracts and job descriptions. Hoping for rewards and fearing punishment, we tend to adhere to these rules. Adherence to rules is based on the logic of appropriateness, strengthening the legitimacy and authority of decision makers. The formation and expression of our identity requires that others see us, as we would like to see ourselves. Organizations would rather delegate tried and tested, standardized rules than delegate the power to make decisions. Sooner or later, decision makers become rule executors. They do not even have to ask for the rules; they are regularly inundated with them.

A rule-based behavior person will rather rigorously and industriously follow a well-worn path in small, sure steps. 'Never tread off the beaten path' is the rule. This motto can even sound reassuring. An organization, however, must sometimes tread off the beaten path, and must sometimes jump over a chasm without knowing how far the other side is or what awaits there.

The world is headed in a direction where a decision maker relinquishes decisions in favor of rigidly constructed algorithms. Over-regulation is always a sign of distrust. Organizations are getting weirder. Many speak of the obsolescence of hierarchies, but we are more familiar with hierarchies than with other structures. Decision-making is not a well-defined activity, but rather part of the workflow. Decision makers readily accept identities whose rules are easy to follow, and organizations even reward this behavior. They are even willing to make some sacrifices to ensure they do not breach the identity expected of them. They are less likely to accept attitudes that would question previous rules, preferring instead those that reinforce them. When someone accepts a path offered by a handbook written by others, then all they need to know is that a lot of people bought that handbook. Of course, it is important to choose which advisor to listen to. Even if they all peddle the same things. Yesterday it was 'lean and mean', today it is 'database management'. Rule-based behavior people are easy to replace. The fashionable slogan that an optimized organization is lean and mean is mirrored by the use of such expressions as cost reduction, outsourcing and downsizing. To be honest, lean does sound better than fat. However, drawing on Henry Mintzberg (1998), the fact that the word 'mean' has become a virtue is a sad sign of our times.

Who is it that the decision maker will be attached to? - asks Charles Handy (2002). Will it be the minimalist, virtual organization? Or suburban communities? Or the dwindling family? Is a personal network able to replace the above? If adherence to the standardized rules of an organization is irreconcilable with our personal identity, it will harm our dignity, and we might rebel against it.

Those who do not feel trust towards one another can only function if there are precise rules for everything. Today, we see over-managed and under-led organizations sprouting. This can be explained by the fact that management is a necessity; leadership is not. Without the well-defined processes of production and finance, an organization cannot function. It can, however, function without path-finding.

Over-managed and under-led organizations favor "doing well" instead of "doing good". If we examine modern organizations, we can see both "doing well" (the 'how') and "doing good" (the 'what') appear. As Peter Drucker's (2003) now famous saying goes: "Management is doing things right; leadership is doing the right things."

Organizations are seeking to find the balance between rule-based behavior and trust-based behavior. Trust-based behavior means that people are allowed to have a vision of a suitable path, which can only be described vaguely. It is difficult to understand why organizations falter so much in finding this balance; the completion of tasks require the following of standardized rules, whereas decisions are based upon trust. As simple as that sounds, we can witness so many digressions.

Most people, instead of making decisions, follow prescribed rules. This makes their work and its results controllable and measurable. If they do a little more, they get a little reward. They are comfortable in lukewarm water. The authors have often spoken of the difficulties of those having to do such drudgery, but feedback shows that there is no reason to feel sorry for them, for they like it and prefer the security it provides.

The bustle of running from one meeting to the next, from a workshop to a work lunch, and then being late for the next all create the illusion that they want to do something here and now. It is worthwhile to ask what they are working on. All this running around, the inundation of emails and the swarms of

Sometimes *NoNos* can spin up a lot of anxiety and anger to fuel a flurry of useless activity that creates what Kotter (Kotter & Rathgeber, 2005) calls "a false sense of urgency."

The Decision Making 5.0 approach accepts that decisions "happen", but no reasoning can be validated. Here and now it is the authors' viewpoint that in the age of abundance, half a century of decision making experience and footholds cannot help those who think, nor those who would wish to avoid thinking.

## THE EVOLUTION OF ASPIRATION LEVELS

Another favorite of the authors springs from the pen of Mark Twain.

*A chaplain said grace, and Tom was about to fall to, for hunger had long been constitutional with him, but was interrupted by my lord the Earl of Berkeley, who fastened a napkin about his neck; for the great post of Diaperers to the Prince of Wales was hereditary in this nobleman's family. Tom's cupbearer was present, and forestalled all his attempts to help himself to wine (Twain: The Prince and the Pauper).*

Many have seen but few have given thought to the fact that there are those who buy blue cars and those who buy white, or that there are those who are in love with a blond and others a brunette partner. In fact, many have seen people buying first a blue, then a white car, and first be in love with a blond and then a brunette. If there were expectations that hold forever true for anything, then we would only want cars of the same color and partners of the same hair. Thank goodness there are no such enduring expectations, and indeed the world would be a sorry place if it were only Twain's cupbearer allowed to pour to everyone everywhere. Expectations change and vary. They change as the renewal processes are validated. Often a decision maker will make a given decision because their hunch tells them that is the best path. Hunches cannot be verbalized. (Dörfler & Ackermann, 2012) They are more comparable to a leap in the dark: we cast data aside and rely on intuition. Can a decision made in a blink be as good as a decision based on planning and long thought? According to Malcolm Gladwell (2008) it can. The grasping of the main points can often lead to better results than careful (over)analysis of details. The recognition of the whole is an abductive leap in reasoning that cannot be properly verbalized. Every day, all of us rely on our hunches, which is just as amazing as when "it all comes together" in the head of an experienced doctor or mechanic. It is easy to accept that this requires experience. A decision maker is often hindered in occasionally reviewing their successful past expectations by their strong faith in their perceived knowledge. A new and unknown decision situation is also viewed through a lens of overconfidence, and they are unable to create new expectations (Kahneman, 2011). Once we find a suitable path that satisfies our verbalized expectations, we may also think of expectations that we were unable to verbalize before the finding of the path.

We tend to remember the stories woven from our past experiences (or even not our own experiences), and so they have a much larger influence on our expectations than the actual event itself. When we recall the past, we do not browse through experiences, we browse through memories of experiences. Our remembering self creates our expectations, and so actually makes the decision as well. When our expectations are not fulfilled, we start wondering what else we should have paid attention to. We fool ourselves into thinking we can find the cause of the fault. When a decision is made and the organization is successful, it is easy to name the decision maker. In fact, there will be several eager candidates who will willingly retrospectively take on the role of decision maker. It is a mistake, however, to think that in these cases it was the decision of one person that brought success. It is similarly a mistake to think that one person is to blame if an organization is unsuccessful. It is worthwhile to point out that in cases like this, no one is lining up to retrospectively assume the role of decision maker. In these cases, the person who loses the battle of pointing fingers will be named "guilty". After a faulty decision, it is often a desperate situation when the decision maker is judged not according to how they acted, but according to the undesired result of the decision. This is called output bias. Most often the "guilty" decision maker is kept in the organization, but their decisions are over-regulated and their expectations are prescribed to them. Everything becomes subject to bureaucracy, meaning the formation of expectations is replaced by step-by-step rigidity. The decision maker loses courage and wants to play it safe, which is impossible. The process of decision-making is drawn out so long that the competition can take advantage of the lag, and the preparation of a decision becomes more expensive than it should be. The worse a given outcome is, the greater the bias and distortion of the subsequent judgments. If decision makers anticipate that the judgment of their decisions will be in the spotlight, they will look for bureaucratic solutions. The patient might still die, but after the investigation, no one can blame the doctor. We are prone to overestimate our knowledge and underestimate the role of chance. Overconfidence is fueled by the illusion of post hoc reasoning and its certainty. Through thinking together (Pyrko et al., 2015), conclusions may be drawn from past decisions without falling into the illusion of certainty or trap of hindsight. Decisions are not made in regular intervals, but when something takes form in the decision maker's head.

There are several positions, points of view and varied knowledge in an organization, but these are usually in different places within it. Successful operation, however, requires that everyone do what they know how to do, and no one should interfere, neither from above, below nor the side. Decision-making and knowledge are often separated. We must learn to live together with the fact that there is no up or down. The decision makers of an organization must be prepared to understand that sovereignty is not destroyed, simply limited. Based on Charles Handy (2002), subsidiarity can be defined as reverse delegation, leaving all decisions that can be made locally local. Handy suggests that people have a moral right not to be interfered with. A section or department of a company is not just a part, but a community in its own right, with the possibility to delegate tasks to the center, for example to integrate something that was developed into the whole. Central leadership gives enough freedom to the departments for them to be sovereign. The point is that hierarchies are not completely negated, but restructured in a way where knowledge does not necessarily have to flow from the top down. This is an entanglement of freedom and loyalty; strange for those living and thinking in hierarchies. It originates in the idea that "knowledge" cannot fool "position", or vice versa. The question is not how you can regulate this contradiction, but how you can live with it peacefully.

The principle of subsidiarity (Handy, 2002) says that smaller, local communities can retain as much freedom and independence as they are already (and still) able to function with; no more, no less.

Two defining elements give rise to expectations in the 'then and there':

- **Paradigm**: Different expectations are borne by people who view the world through the lens of Extremistan (Taleb, 2007) than by those who view it through that of Mediocristan.
- **Fashion Trend**: Just as there are fashionable trends in shoes and furniture, there are fashionable teachings as well (Appadurai, 1996). Expectations are indeed influenced by the fashion-able status of a given toolkit.

Most organizations today effect change through single-loop learning, and are eager to pass on most operations to machines. 'Mechanized' or computerized and automated processes are fragile, how-ever, as unexpected events can harm them. If after the validation of standardized indicators an organization changes its values and/or strategy, and then relinquishes validation to machines once more, sooner or later, it will become fragile again, as it is still not prepared for improbable events. A smaller number of organizations are able to effect change through double-loop learning. These organizations also validate processes that are not automated, meaning the cases where humans make sense of operations. After human validation of operational processes the organization can change its conceptual model, making it more robust. Let us look at the ability to effect change through triple-loop learning, where an organiza-tion might be capable of a paradigm shift, maybe even making it antifragile in the end. If the title of Nobel-laureate Daniel Kahneman's book (2011) contains the work "thinking", then perhaps it is fair to snatch decision making from the clutches of the 'numerati'. The authors believe that the process of learning beckons for a new paradigm, which will present new questions. The age of knowledge abun-dance poses questions that cannot be answered through old paradigms. One of these new questions is: how are expectations formed?

Sometimes it is fashionable to solve disorder through systematic changes and reforms. More often than not, leadership will decide to initiate reform, but how and what is to be reformed is decided by the experts of a given process. These experts can be from within the organization, but more and more, external reform algorithms from the consultants of one behemoth audit company or another are favored. The expectations of the desire for order are easily defined. "Faster, better, cheaper" than others is a rose-tinted dream, but if one's dream is competition, it can often turn into a night-mare.

Starting in the sixties, tool-makers poured out one requisite after another. But requisites for what exactly? One could say for a wide range of problems. The problem hardly lies in the fact that consul-tants make money, but in the fact that services rendered through their knowledge are not in line with the magnitude of their fees. Big audit companies increase the reliability of projects through their legitimi-zation, and become standards. Decision Making 5.0 accepts that the expectations of a decision maker in the Global Village are not prefixed, but are constantly formed on the go as they sense the decision situations and possible paths.

# THE UNENDING QUEST OF PATHFINDING

Another favorite tale of the authors is from Plato.

*And I, Meno, like what I am saying. Some things I have said of which I am not altogether confident. But that we shall be better and braver and less helpless if we think that we ought to enquire, than we should have been if we indulged in the idle fancy that there was no knowing and no use in seeking to know what we do not know;-that is a theme upon which I am ready to fight, in word and deed, to the utmost of my power (Plato).*

The stories of success create the feeling that we have understood the past and can predict the future. Good luck, however, seems to be neglected. Business literature fills our shelves with books about the rise and/or fall of organizations. These stories systematically exaggerate the effect of a decision maker's personal qualities on outcomes. It is easy to fall into this trap. We hold talent, foolishness and will more important than luck, because they satisfy our need and desire for control; luck cannot be controlled. The higher a role luck plays, the more significance we attribute to the decision maker. Fortune works in mysterious ways, and so we cannot say much about the thinking and cleverness of a decision maker based upon the success of an organization. However, these stories are still touching, for they carry the simple message and explanation of success and failure. They feed the illusion of understanding, and completely neglect the defining power of luck.

It is up to random chance or luck in what way or order we meet somebody's behavioral patterns. If we come to know them as successful, we tend to notice their good attributes, and tend to forgive or neglect the bad ones. Thanks to the halo effect we simplify our expectations, and create attractive narratives which embellish them with an aura of invincibility. We assume that their future decisions will also be successful. Of course, the opposite can also be true. After a failure we expect and predict subsequent failures. The illusion of understanding can lead to erroneous thinking, and this affects our future expectations. Our personal experiences of the pain of failures and the joy of successes are easier to recall than the stories of others. The availability heuristic spurs successful decision makers to relax their expectations, while unsuccessful ones to pay attention to too many. The size of success according to Daniel Kahneman (2011) is not dependent on the size of talent but the size of luck. Drawing from Kahneman, the formula is as follows: "Success = talent + luck; Great Success = a little more talent + a lot of luck".

If someone searches for a path while knowing the outcome, then they have nothing to search for. Innovative organizations exchange the strategic plans of karaoke organizations (Ridderstråle & Nordström, 2005) for strategic thinking. What we do not know cannot be deduced from what we know. Roger Martin (2009) illustrates the filtering of knowledge with the knowledge funnel. The knowledge funnel has three different phases: mystery, heuristic and algorithm. The mystery stage comprises exploration of the problem, and then transitions to the heuristic stage, where a 'rule of thumb' is generated to narrow work down to a more manageable size. In the algorithm stage the general rule of thumb (heuristic) is converted to a fixed formula, and that takes the problem from complexity to simplicity. Explicitly or implicitly, organizations focused on reliability deny them-selves the possibilities that their design thinking, reliability and validation balancing counterparts enjoy.

Based on Hubert L. Dreyfus and Stuart E. Dreyfus (1986), the process of decision-making is a process of reasoning. But the mind is not the same as the brain. Instead of using brain re-search, the results of cognitive psychology should be used. Based on Herbert Simon (1997), if we find an objectionless (not the best) solution, we choose it and make a decision.

A new path does not have a past, and so it is only with a blurry vision of the future that a decision maker can search for it. Finding a path is a matter of good luck and patience. When we are browsing on the Internet and click on a page for the first time, we cannot know if we will like it or not. Is it the comparison of what we see with our expectations? Of course not! As soon as we find the first objectionable thing, we exit and click on the next page. At the same time, we do not even think of finding the best one, because it is impossible to know all the possible paths. Decision makers rely on their hunches, and their expectations are formed as they are browsing and discovering paths. All of a sudden they find a path that they can say they have no objection to. The concept of intuitive rationality expresses this opportunistic, adaptive searching process. In the seventies, Nobel-laureate economist Herbert A. Simon was the one who realized that in our decisions we cannot search for the best and most optimal path, because it is impossible to find all of them. Even though some decades have passed since then, there are still organizations that try to spur their decision makers to do so. The sequences of pathfinding are partially based on verbalized expectations, and partially on luck. First I see the whole, then accept it or reject it, without explaining the details. Decisions are therefore also dependent on the order of discovering possible paths. In organizations where decision processes are regulated by rigid algorithms, decision makers become used to having their expectations prescribed to them. They focus on working "well." They are dependent on the expectations of others, and so their fitness weakens. If, after a long time, they start pathfinding on their own, they will be unable to verbalize what they are actually looking for, and will become unfit for making decisions. They will mimic the behavioral patterns of others, and will spend their free time in karaoke bars, practicing to be able to sing other's songs "well".

Today, innovative organizations are seeking their paths in Experience Networks (Prahalad & Ramaswamy, 2003), where everyone attaches their own experience to a trial version. Do not pay attention to the masses, for they look right through us! Pay attention to those who care, who are curious and who are passionately talking about us. This will spread news of our organization. Experience based pathfinding has two key elements. First of all, pathfinding does not occur in the Product Space or Solution Space, but rather the Experience Space. Second, required expertise will not be found in supply chains and networks, but in Experience Networks. Elegant solutions lead us from meeting consumer demands to enchanting consumers. Instead of asking what they need, we enchant them with an attractive product. Contemporaries of Da Vinci's were using some form of non finito, which means unfinished, but his specific painting technique was called sfumato, which basically means smoky or blurry. Art pieces create an illusion of unfinished incompleteness, and leave it up to our imagination to augment it, to search for whats, whys and hows. This is what silence is in music, what a dramatic pause is in a play. (May, 2006) These are the rules which can change other rules and can spur us to multiple interpretations. The more an artist wishes to precisely define the object of their piece, the less real it will seem to its viewers.

Elegant solutions draw attention, for they have something missing that everyone can add themselves and are unusually, brilliantly simple. Simplification means taking away all that is unnecessary to let the necessary shine through.

We can only expect far-reaching change in an organization from decision makers who venture on paths where others do not. They are spurred by passion and curiosity, and they are more focused on doing "what" than doing "how". From this arises "doing good", a dynamic quality, which then leads to "doing well", which is a static quality. The order is irreversible. If this is the order, then it should be the order of pathfinding as well. Once we know what we will do, it will become easier to define how we will do it. Doing "what" cannot be extrapolated from the past when we are successful nor when we are not. Not long ago, the demand for landline phones was larger than the supply. Some decision makers thought that through the expansion of supply. Paradise would come, and consumers would flock. They started digging miles of cables into the ground. It was unimaginable for them that other paths may exist. Then suddenly, out of the blue, mobile phones appeared. These decision makers behaved as Bertrand Russell's turkey.

*The turkey found that, on his first morning at the turkey farm, that he was fed at 9 a.m.. Being a good inductionist turkey he did not jump to conclusions. He waited until he collected a large number of observations that he was fed at 9 a.m. and made these observations under a wide range of circumstances ... Each day he added another observation statement to his list. Finally he was satisfied that he had collected a number of observation statements to inductively infer that "I am always fed at 9 a.m. ". However on the morning of Christmas Eve he was not fed but instead had his throat cut (Chalmers, 1982, p.14).*

This path was unimaginable for the turkey. The "black swan" is also a metaphor for paths that are unimaginable based upon prior experience. But just because we have only seen white swans until now, we cannot say with certainty that there are no black ones. Nassim Nicholas Taleb (2007), in his book The Black Swan, tells us how we fool ourselves when we think we know more than we can know. Taleb is interested in the unimaginable, the consequences of which are unpredictable. Once they have happened, we find explanations for them. Based on Taleb, we will find decision makers who tread on unimaginable paths in Extremistan. The unusual "weirdness" and unpredictability of this land will frighten most decision makers, as they tend to live in Mediocristan. We look for paths through the lens of the Gauss-curve in Mediocristan, as averages and their scatterings are understood by it. People thinking in mediocrity will ask the question whether the scatterings of today can become an average of tomorrow.

Even Google admits that 80% of its new products fail. Instead of despair and collapse, they are actually happy about these failures, because they bear testament to the "fail fast, fail often" bravery of trying new paths. Sports are about certainty either. If there were a penalty for missing the basket, nobody would give it another throw after a while. Decision makers can prepare for failure in several ways.

What is the opposite of a person or organization that is fragile? If you ask most people this question, they will likely say "robust" or "resilient". But philosopher Nassim Nicholas Taleb would say that is not the right answer. He argues that if fragile items break when exposed to stress, something that is the opposite of fragile would not simply not break (thus staying the same) when put under pressure; rather, it should actually get stronger. We do not really have a word to describe such a person or organization, so Taleb created one: antifragile.

Those who are afraid of unknown paths have the Sword of Damocles swinging above their head. "I hope nothing unexpected happens!", they pray, and peer uneasily above their heads. They are fragile and easily injured. If a fragile item breaks due to some event, then the opposite of this fragility based on the ideas of Nassim Nicholas Taleb (2012) is not only that it does not break, nor that is stays the same, but will in fact become stronger. Taleb makes a good case that anti-fragility is para-mount is today fast-changing world. If we want to differentiate ourselves from others and want to hold our own in all areas of life, it is no longer enough to just be flexible and stand up from any blow, seeking new paths. We must become anti-fragile, become stronger and more determined every time we set out on a new path. Like Google, many accept that the survival of a few failures can make the search for new paths faster and easier. Persistent decision makers are like the mythological phoenix. They are vulnerable, but they come back to life, again and again. A series of failures, however, can leave them dejected. Failure-tolerant decision makers, however, are anti-fragile. They are like the mythological hydra.

In an organization, the expectations of a decision maker are about creating products and/or services that the competition does not offer yet. If the previous decision bore bad luck, then the formation of their expectations will focus on "how" the decision should be made instead of "which path should I take". More energy is wasted on conforming to bureaucratic decision processes than on finding possible paths. Perhaps only tattoos are final decisions. There is life after failure. Ships will also stray off course if they are caught in a storm.

Decision Making 5.0 accepts that unexpected events in the Global Village are unforeseen; they cannot be predicted from neither a little nor a lot of data.

## The Ecology of Pathfinding

Another favorite parable of the authors is about the single-minded specialist who cannot come to know many things. Steve Jobs famously said Picasso had a saying – 'good artists copy; great artists steal' – and we have always been shameless about stealing great ideas. Part of what made the Macintosh great was that the people working on it were musicians, poets, and artists, and zoologists, and historians. They also happened to be the best computer scientists in the world. They've always tried to stand at the crossroads of liberal arts and technology.

It is easy to realize that a master-apprentice relationship needs a milieu, such as the agora or a coffee house. Where there is resistance to this, the world grinds to a halt and drowns in tradition. These are closed provincial milieus, where everyone is forced to work for permanence. When the first coffee houses opened, no one knew what these places could be good for. It is said that everything, from conception to death, can happen in a coffee house. The atmosphere of rejuvenation and innovation can still be found in coffee houses today. Creative people sit there, with a latté, mineral water, a Macbook and some scraps of paper. Two or three people are discussing something. But in organizations, at a water cooler or in a kitchenette, we rarely find someone peacefully sipping coffee and lost in thought. More and more places require the protection of creative people, the revival and smooth sustaining of innovative atmospheres. The point is to have a place for thinking and pondering somewhere among the necessary everyday tasks that ensure daily production.

"Maybe" is the most important word of our time. If we knew everything for certain, we would have to live our lives in constant fear of stepping off the right path. Nothing allows us to jump to the conclusion that the success or failure of placing a given path in a given context will determine the results of future paths in future contexts.

There is an imbalance between thinking and calculation. As if the only job of a decision maker was to "play by the numbers". Nothing is more natural for them than to adopt the spirit of the age and focus on the flood of data. They hang on to the cliché that numbers do not lie. This statement is deeply ingrained in everyone. Data management tools (SAP, Oracle or even Excel) can encourage decision makers to think they can predict the future more and more precisely. Many believe that with the growing amount of data, they are able to better predict the outcomes of their decisions, and can monitor uncontrollable events. They deny the role of luck and chance. This is the illusion of understanding, the over-exaggerated trust in data. Decision makers may succumb to this illusory world, and instead of pathfinders, they become calculating agents. And if everyone is lost in numbers, we may soon end up in a "scheming society".

Business processes where events only have one outcome and the algorithm of execution is well-established can be automated with data management tools. This creation of order, however, consumes a lot of energy and presupposes permanence. Processes where events may have multiple unknown outcomes require conducting and constant intervention. For a lot of people, this is equal to disorder. A data management tool, even if it is a smart gadget, is not enough for success. Success requires smart, thinking people.

Many have tried to describe the process of decision-making. No one has properly succeeded, so it is still up to humans to use the knowledge they need when they need it, then and there. One cannot make decisions based on the few steps described by decision algorithms. The thinking of a decision maker is an internal monologue whose building blocks are meaningful symbols. They are not comprised of data, nor do they operate according to the laws of mathematical logic. The thinking of decision makers cannot be codified and modeled. There is no place for a tool that neglects or lacks the conviction and intention of a decision maker. Despite all this, many still believe that with the management of the flood of data, decision makers can be replaced. Just a click of a button, and we already see the path. Hard data, however, often turns out to be based on soft signals.

Today, some organizations are adjusting their views, and are beginning to think that they can be the winners of thinking together. If everyone closed themselves off, the Internet would lose its essence and significance an. It seems we can only share on the Internet what we want to sell. Perhaps this is what company giants are spurring us to do as well, since all we see are the aggressive approaches of agents in e-form. With the free availability of knowledge, their reliability diminishes. Uncertain knowledge is not defined by true or false, but by whether or not it is useful for us, whether we are able to place it in our current context. How we define and so find new knowledge for ourselves and others influences our pathfinding.

So what can we see when we type in a well-known concept? Take for example "knowledge sharing". About 6-7 million hits. The first hit is not a surprise either. It is a Wiki article. Somewhere on the list you can find Michael Polányi, the only one actually worth finding. Well, a decision making practitioner who googles a concept will know more than they can learn from the first few hits. For a student or a bored pensioner, this knowledge may still be useful. It seems Wiki does a great service to students and pensioners everywhere. And there is nothing wrong with that. The problem is that we have to know a lot to have reasonable number of hits and to find the novelty we are looking for among them, without knowing if it exists at all. This is when we usually say the search engine is not smart enough. It would seem that an up-to-date practitioner is smarter, for they would immediately tell you what to look at and what to skip. No search engine is capable of that. We can say that search engines are not smart enough. The winner of the search engine market will be the one who takes reasoning from physics to metaphysics. Where we stand now, "seek the guru" (alá 'Cherhez la Femme') will still yield more than browsing the Internet. This is not completely accurate, for if we know a lot, we can start tinkering with search engines. Perhaps we could even teach it to search as a practitioner would. Experiences mined from learning paths may help even more. Someone who grew up with AI, that is has seen or tinkered with Prolog and/or Lisp programs, will find problems in that area, and will search for requisites there. Those who grew up on databases will find problems in that area, and will search for requisites there. Those who grew up on cognitive psychology will, of course, find problems in that area, and will search for requisites there.

Decision support software is better if it stays silent and "thinks" more than it talks. It is a misconception to think it is better if it gives more data. Pathfinding is made easier by learning, the bringing together of new elements of knowledge and experience with the old. A decision maker will never be able to learn millions of pieces of data.

In the 1990s, decision support software was focused on developing AI. The database based systems that appeared were the first decision support tools that did not wish to replace the decision maker. One of its advantages was that not everything had to be reduced to numbers, as decision makers think in concepts, not numbers. In pathfinding, they connect these concepts, that is, expectations, with a few thousand "if... then" rules. Knowledge-based Systems (KBS) have two components: a shell, and the knowledge database. The knowledge base embodies the symbolic representation of knowledge, describing practitioner knowledge with concepts connected by "if... then" rules. With the help of software such as the DoctuS KBS (Baracskai et al. 2005, 2007, 2014; Velencei et al. 2015a, 2015b), the viable expectations used during pathfinding can be "extracted" from the "head" of an experienced practitioner. "Viable" in this case refers to the fact that in reality, of the expectations verbalized by a decision maker, only few are actually defining. Which these would be are usually a mystery to the practitioner themselves. Using these relevant points and the "if... then" rules connecting them, past decisions can be analyzed and beginners can also learn from them. "Experience mining" can be useful in decision situations that are similar to ones we have faced in the past. With original decisions, where new paths have to be found and created, statistics cannot be the only tool of the decision maker, but nor can AI. Human reasoning is irreplaceable. Yet somehow we seem to trust an "objective" support system more, even though it is in no way objective. Human reasoning lies in the background here, too.

When do you need a coach? When the decision maker is "strong" enough to admit that they have a lack of knowledge. It is not a sign of weakness if a decision maker asks for a coach. Quite the opposite; only a truly strong practitioner is able to declare that they have different duties than to follow the newest business guru knowledge all the time. Decision makers simply will not be sitting at conferences where the new concepts and ideas of business are introduced. While gurus reap most of the credit when big ideas take flight, it is the coach who is able to select from the armada of fresh ideas and place it into the decision maker's context. These ideas and knowledge pop up here and there, and were usable knowledge somewhere, but it is the business gurus who create new concepts and new context to make them famous. "Talk funny, make money!" is often said about those who are giving decision makers tips from the ringside. Exactly right, but if the coaches know "where to punch", then it is not wasted money. They do the work that would have been troublesome for the decision maker. The job of the coach is not to replace the decision maker, but a decision maker will definitely make a different decision after the coach has placed fresh knowledge into their context. This knowledge placed in context can perhaps help with pathfinding.

Decision Making 5.0 accepts that in the Global Village, discovering the cognitive patters of the decision maker requires a master's workshop which supports thinking together.

## APPLICATION

The domain of validity for a given conception may be found only once we have exceeded it. The conception of Decision Making 5.0 was observed by the authors in an EU financed project entitled "Improving the sustainable growth of family businesses involving multiple generations in the Austrian-Hungarian border region" (SUCCEED (L00177)). The project's objectives were to offer assistance in making the ownership or leadership change in family businesses in the Austrian-Hungarian border region smoother and to prepare multi-generational enterprises for handover to the next generation, thus ensuring sustainable operation for the enterprise even after changes in ownership and/or leadership. With these viewpoints in mind, we wished to improve the competitiveness of small enterprises and their exchange of experience on generational transition and the sustainable development of enterprises in the regions along the borders. Through the training and the experience exchange they received in the project, the younger generation of owners can prepare to lead the enterprise and to adequately tackle arising problems. It could improve the sustainability of a small family enterprise if the future leader carries out their training and later works in their profession in the enterprise, as the descendant becomes acquainted with the company's internal relations and business culture.

Upon generational exchange, the desired heir will often dazzle with ideas of change, and this will often make them frightening. The retiring leader of the family enterprise, the "elder", the employees and even the heir realize sooner or later that the new leader will not be the same as the old. They do not have to be the same, but then what should they be? This is an unending pathfinding quest, where Decision Making 5.0 can be of help. In the workshops led by the authors, the following six dilemmas of family business generational change in the Global Village were examined:

1. Prediction vs. vision
2. Replaceable vs. irreplaceable
3. Persuasion vs. netocracy
4. Status quo vs. untrodden path
5. Reliability vs. innovative milieu
6. Growth vs. flexibility

Our plans for future research include elaborating further the Decision Making 5.0 framework, and also examining the usability of Doctus as a tool in this conceptual framework. This means that we plan to write more about application cases and also do further work (both research and development) on the Doctus tool, to 'put it in the cloud', make it more accessible through combining it with collaborative situated online learning approaches and simplifying the use.

*Everyone seemed to be guided by an 'objective', scientific view of life that told each person that their essential self is their evolved material body. Ideas and societies are the components of brains, not the other way around. No two brains can merge physically, and therefore no two people can ever really communicate except ...[for] sending messages back and forth (Pirsig, 1991, p. 30).*

In light of this, the authors themselves were not objective either when they studied the attitudes of "elders" and "heirs" with regards to their identity, their expectations, their unending pathfinding and its ecology.

## REFERENCES

Anderson, C. (2010). *Free: The Future of a Radical Price*. New York, NY: Random House.

Appadurai, A. (1996). *Modernity at Large. Cultural Dimensions of Globalization*. Minneapolis, MN: University of Minnesota Press.

Baracskai, Z., Dörfler, V., & Velencei, J. (2007). The ES Could Probably Know More - But Man Would Not Make Better Business Decisions. VIPSI 2007, Bled, Slovenia.

Baracskai Z., & Velencei J. (2015). Smart or Wise. *Svarog, Naučno-stručni časopis, 10*(1), 29-32.

Baracskai, Z., Velencei, J., & Dörfler, V. (2005). Reductive Reasoning, *Montenegrin. Journal of Economics, 1*(1), 59–66.

Baracskai, Z., Velencei, J., Dörfler, V., & Szendrey, J. (2014). The Tunnel of Doctus KBS The Deeper You Get the Darker It Is. In *Proceedings of the 2nd International OFEL Conference on Governance, Management and Entrepreneurship* (vol. 2, pp. 397-407). Dubrovnik, Croatia: Governance Research and Development Center

Boulding, K. E. (1985). *The World as a Total System*. Beverly Hills, CA: Sage Publications.

Carr, N. (2010). *The Shallows: What the Internet Is Doing to Our Brains*. New York, NY: Norton & Company.

Chalmers, A. (1982). *What is this thing Called Science?* Queensland, Australia: University of Queensland Press.

Dörfler, V., & Ackermann, F. (2012). Understanding Intuition: The Case for Two Forms of Intuition. *Management Learning, 43*(5), 545–564. doi:10.1177/1350507611434686

Dreyfus, H. L., & Dreyfus, S. E. (1986). *Mind over Machine. The Power of Human Intuition and Expertise in the era of Computer*. London, UK: Macmillan Publishers.

Drucker, P. (2003). *The Essential Drucker by Peter F. Drucker*. New York, NY: Regan Books.

Gladwell, M. (2007). *Blink: The Power of Thinking Without Thinking*. Boston, MA: Little, Brown and Company.

Handy, C. (2002). *Empty Raincoat. Making Sense of the Future*. New York, NY: Random House.

Iyengar, S. (2010). *The Art of Choosing*. New York, NY: Hachette Book Group.

Kahneman, D. (2011). *Thinking, Fast and Slow*. New York, NY: Farrar, Straus and Giroux.

Kotter, J., & Rathgeber, H. (2005). *Our Iceberg Is Melting: Changing and Succeeding Under Any Conditions*. New York, NY: St. Martin's Press.

March, J. G. (1994). *A Primer on Decision Making: How Decisions Happen*. New York, NY: Free Press.

Martin, R. L. (2009). *The Design of Business: Why Design Thinking is the Next Competitive Ad-vantage*. Cambridge, MA: Harvard University Press.

May, M. E. (2006). *The Elegant Solution: Toyota's Formula for Mastering Innovation*. New York, NY: Free Press.

McLuhan, M., & Powers, B. (1989). *The Global Village: Transformations in World Life and Media in the 21st Century*. Oxford, UK: Oxford University Press.

Mintzberg, H., Ahlstrand, B., & Lampel, J. (1998). *Strategy Safari: A Guided Tour through the Wilds of Strategic Managament*. New York, NY: Free Press.

Pirsig, R. (1991). *LILA: An Inquiry into Morals*. New York, NY: Bantam Book.

Popper, K. (1998). *Unended Quest: An Intellectual Autobiography*. Chicago, IL: Carus Publishing Company.

Prahalad, C. K., & Ramaswamy, V. (2003). *The New Frontier of Experience Innovation*. Retrieved January 29, 2016, from http://sloanreview.mit.edu/article/the-new-frontier-of-experience-innovation/

Pyrko, I., Dörfler, V., & Eden, C. (2015). Thinking Together: Making Communities of Practice Work. Academy of Management Best Paper Proceedings, 2015(1).

Ridderstråle, J., & Nordström, K. A. (2005). *Karaoke Capitalism Management for mankind*. Harlow, UK: Pearson Education Limited.

Sedlacek, T. (2013). *Economics of Good and Evil: The Quest for Economic Meaning from Gilgamesh to Wall Street*. Oxford, UK: Oxford University Press.

Simon, H. (1997). *Models of Bounded Rationality*. Cambridge, MA: MIT Press.

Taleb, N. N. (2007). *The Black Swan: The Impact of the Highly Improbable*. New York, NY: Random House.

Taleb, N. N. (2012). *Antifragile: Things That Gain from Disorder*. London, UK: Penguin Books.

Velencei, J., Baracskai, Z., & Dörfler, V. (2015a, May). Supporting the Competent Practitioner: Transdisciplinary Coaching with Knowledge-Based Expert System. *MakeLearn, 2015*, 27–29.

Velencei, J., Dörfler, V., Baracskai, Z., & Szendrey, J. (2015b). Prelude for Experience Mining (Re-)Using Relevant Experience for Smart Decision Support. *International OFEL Conference on Governance, Management and Entrepreneurship*.

## KEY TERMS AND DEFINITIONS

**DoctuS Knowledge-Based System:** Modelling of practitioner knowledge with concepts connected by "if... then" rules.

**Human Reasoning:** During the preparation of a decision, the decision maker examines choices and possible paths through the lens of their expectations, and these can be described through "if...then" rules.

**Luck:** Being in the right place at the right time.

**Master-Apprentice Model:** The transmission of the tacit knowledge of the master to the apprentice through observation.

**Pathfinding:** When a decision maker examines individual solutions to a decision dilemma and keeps going until they find one that they have no objection to.

**Rule-Based Behavior:** Behavior based on the logic of appropriateness, which can strengthen a decision maker's legitimacy and authenticity.

**Shallow Knowledge:** The abundance of knowledge has led to the fragmentation of attention, leading us to know a little about a lot of different areas.

# Chapter 3
# Organizational Learning:
## Advanced Issues and Trends

**Kijpokin Kasemsap**
*Suan Sunandha Rajabhat University, Thailand*

## ABSTRACT

*This chapter reveals the prospect of organizational learning; organizational learning and networks; organizational learning, organizational innovation, and transformational leadership; organizational learning, absorptive capacity, open innovation, and information technology (IT); organizational learning and training; organizational learning capability (OLC) and enterprise resource planning (ERP); and learning organization. Organizational learning is an important method by which organizations develop, enhance, and manage knowledge within their organizational functions and improve their efficiency by making better use of the wide range of skills of their employees. Regarding organizational learning, organizations improve the ability to respond to various business situations and enhance competitive performance through generating new knowledge. The chapter argues that encouraging organizational learning has the potential to improve organizational performance and gain sustainable competitive advantage in the workplace.*

## INTRODUCTION

Despite the interest in issues of knowing and learning in the global strategy field, there has been limited mutual engagement and interaction between the fields of global strategy and organizational learning (Hotho, Lyles, & Easterby-Smith, 2015). Organizational learning with an appropriate leadership style is the important strategy for small and medium enterprises (SMEs) toward achieving innovation, high performance, and competitiveness (Vargas, 2015). Organizational learning is a type of learning and an important area of research that is concerned about the way organizations learn, therefore, increase their competitiveness, innovation, and efficiency (Abel, 2015). Organizational learning has the positive relationship with innovation capability (Salim & Sulaiman, 2011) and intellectual capital (Naghi, Gholamrez, Mehdi, Reza, & Majid, 2010).

DOI: 10.4018/978-1-5225-1642-2.ch003

The radical economic, social, and cultural changes experienced by the labor market within recent decades have emphasized the crucial role of learning process in individual's career development and organization's success (Manuti, Pastore, Scardigno, Giancaspro, & Morciano, 2015). Lazarová et al. (2013) indicated that the interest in organizational learning is brought about by new insights into the behavior of an organization from which the continued learning is expected. Organizational learning by team management is the main factor in the competitive global market which results with the competitive advantage (Serinkan, Enli, Akcit, & Kiziloglu, 2014). Organizations must have the easily accessible knowledge management (KM) system across the organization toward promoting organizational learning (Demirel, Arzova, Ardic, & Bas, 2013).

Organizational learning is essential in the rapidly changing environments, through seeking the new knowledge and the effective utilization of existing knowledge, in order to deliver the innovative capability in modern organizations (Dayaram & Fung, 2014). García-Morales et al. (2012) indicated that the development of new abilities and knowledge and the increase in the organization's capability enable organizational learning. Organizational learning can significantly improve family firms' ability to counter by stimulating entrepreneurship (Zahra, 2012). Organizational learning partially mediates the relationship between entrepreneurial orientation and organizational performance and fully mediates the relationship between learning orientation and organizational performance (Real, Roldán, & Leal, 2014). Learning orientation significantly affects both innovativeness and organizational performance (Garrido & Camarero, 2010).

This chapter aims to bridge the gap in the literature on the thorough literature consolidation of organizational learning. The extensive literature of organizational learning provides a contribution to practitioners and researchers by revealing the advanced issues and trends with organizational learning in order to maximize the impact of organizational learning in the workplace.

## BACKGROUND

The concepts of learning, knowledge, and information relate to one another in such a way that information acts as a meaningful input that generates the learning processes and constitutes the basis for acquiring knowledge (Lloria & Moreno-Luzon, 2014). Knowledge is the strategic asset that firms can utilize to build their competitive advantage (Chung, Yang, & Huang, 2015). Economic growth is stimulated through learning (Piazza, 2010). Learning can be enhanced through an iterative process of action and reflection as skill repertoires are exercised through a wide variety of experiences and contexts (Beenen & Goodman, 2014).

Talent management is an organization's attempts to recruit, keep, and train the most gifted and highest quality staff members that they can find, afford, and hire (Kasemsap, 2016a). Through talent management program in the workplace, learning can be maintained for a significant amount of time even in the presence of competition toward sustainable competitive advantage. Learning is the process of creating knowledge (Moreno-Luzon & Lloria, 2008) and is an important factor in an organization because it enables the creation of sustainable competitive advantage (Nwankpa & Roumani, 2014). Regarding organizational learning, knowledge sharing is associated with innovation performance (Aizpurúa, Saldaña, & Saldaña, 2011).

Organizational learning is a process of change in action that produces knowledge (Merad, Dechy, & Marcel, 2014) through either the exploratory or exploitative approach (Kim & Atuahene-Gima, 2010).

Exploratory learning refers to the acquisition and learning of information and knowledge from outside current customer and competitor boundaries, and often involves experimentation and risk-prone projects (Kim & Atuahene-Gima, 2010). Exploitative learning involves the acquisition and use of market information and knowledge within current customer and competitor boundaries (Levitt & March, 1988). Organizational learning consists of an array of subprocesses, such as knowledge acquisition, knowledge sharing, and knowledge utilization (Nevis, DiBella, & Gould, 1995).

Organizational learning seeks to create, acquire, and transfer knowledge within company in order to reflect new knowledge and insight (Santos, 2014). Increasing attention is paid to organizational learning, with the success of contemporary organizations strongly contingent on their ability to learn and grow (Za, Spagnoletti, & North-Samardzic, 2014). The work of learning and development (L&D) professionals is instrumental to organizational learning (Waight, 2015). Training professionals are required to broaden their idea of where learning can occur (Kim, Kim, & Bilir, 2014). Informal workplace learning takes an important role in human resource development (HRD) practice and research, as it contributes to organizations' adaptability and competitiveness (Froehlich, Segers, & van den Bossche, 2014).

## ADVANCED ISSUES AND TRENDS WITH ORGANIZATIONAL LEARNING

This section emphasizes the prospect of organizational learning; organizational learning and networks; organizational learning, organizational innovation, and transformational leadership; organizational learning, absorptive capacity, open innovation, and IT; organizational learning and training; OLC and ERP; and learning organization.

### Prospect of Organizational Learning

Learning is a fundamental requirement for the sustained existence of organizations (Kim, 1993), allowing them to obtain knowledge assets through human resource management (HRM)-related training and development programs that provide an opportunity for sustainable competitive advantage (Lee, Lee, & Kang, 2005). The importance of learning concerning quality comes from the fact that learning is the necessary prerequisite of knowledge as well as maturity (Chouseinoglou, Iren, Karagoz, & Bilgen, 2013). As the key elements of organizational learning, adaptability and KM are critical to organizational success as a result of a fundamental shift toward the knowledge economy (Schlosser, Templer, & Ghanam, 2006).

In a business context, organizational learning is viewed as a significant process that expands the organization's ability to accomplish the effective actions by improving its performance and results (Chiva & Alegre, 2009). Organizational learning is an emergent property that depends not only on individual learning, but also on the pattern of interactions among the learning of all individuals (Avnet, 2015). Organizational learning can be characterized as the continuous cycle of action and reflection (Carroll & Edmondson, 2002) and requires the useful tools to promote information distribution, knowledge acquisition, and knowledge organization in order to improve organizational learning (Abel, 2015). The capacity to learn is considered as a major approach of an organization's effectiveness and its potential to grow (Birenbaum, Kimron, & Shilton, 2011).

Organizational learning is a dynamic process toward creating knowledge and transferring it where it is needed (Kane & Alavi, 2007) and emphasizes the continually changing nature of a project-based company (Koskinen, 2012). Organizational learning represents a firm's efforts to manage the intellectual and social capital of individuals in order to realize the firm's potential for innovation (Yu, Dong, Shen, Khalifa, & Hao, 2013) and contributes to the internalization and application of external knowledge for organizational innovation (Zhou, Yim, & Tse, 2005). By importing new knowledge, the learning practices increase the technological and administrative variances in modern organizations (Yu et al., 2013).

Organizations will be more successful at learning from past experience if they create and promote the learning capacity for deep reflection on the whole system dynamics, which can lead to the fundamental change (Argyris & Schön, 1996). Organizations require the systematic approach to the lessons learned where learning through past experiences involves organizational processes, systems, and practices (Duffield & Whitty, 2015). Insistence on past traditions and quick fixes to the existing strategies may inhibit more powerful patterns of organizational learning (Sujan, 2015). Popper and Lipshitz (1998) indicated that organizations have a wide range of learning processes at their disposal, which may be internal (e.g., audits and adverse event reviews) as well as external (e.g., feedback from the regulator).

Efficiency-centered business model design is realized by reducing transaction uncertainty, information asymmetry, and transaction complexity among employees (Zott & Amit, 2007). Efficiency-centered business model design improves the level of information sharing (Hu, 2014). Peltier et al. (2006) indicated that data sharing is an organization learning mechanism that is contingent on how well information is disseminated, interpreted, and altered. Data sharing has a prominent position in organizational learning and data quality (Peltier, Zahay, & Lehmann, 2013). Reducing transaction uncertainty among employees means that employees are required to enhance information sharing because uncertainty establishes organizational information needs (Li & Lin, 2006).

The roles of organizational learning and leadership are critical in making KM initiatives successfully embraced in the workplace (Saito, 2012). Managers can enhance organizational learning through the perspectives of commitment to learning, tolerance for failure, and commitment to the workforce (Taylor, Templeton, & Baker, 2010). Firms can acquire knowledge from external sources, such as hiring new employees who have worked for competitors or from industrial networks which allow the firms to gain the advanced knowledge of other firms (Lyles, 2014). Learner's job experience and perceived management support for learning have a positive effect on the relationship between autonomy and learning outcomes (Cappetta & Paolino, 2015).

Organizational learning positively affects export intensity (Bengtsson, 2004). Exporting is recognized as a process of learning and knowledge accumulation during which the company identifies and exploits opportunities abroad (Brouthers, Nakos, Hadjimarcou, & Brouthers, 2009). Exporting plays a crucial role in the strategies of SMEs (Golovko & Valentini, 2011). Exporting is the simple internationalization initiative utilized by SMEs (Fernandez-Mesa & Alegre, 2015). Exporting can be effectively executed with a less resource-laden approach as compared with alternative foreign market entry modes (Morgan, Katsikeas, & Vorhies, 2012) and has been utilized as an agent of SMEs' overall performance (Stoian, Rialp, & Rialp, 2011). Regarding organizational learning in SMEs, knowledge renewal and exploitation regarding foreign markets may increase exports (Balabanis, Theodosiou, & Katsikea, 2004) because firms that effectively learn from their experience are able to export faster and with fewer mistakes. A manager with entrepreneurial orientation is capable of creating a learning organization (Wang, 2008). An organization with high capacity to learn exceeds export performance (Villar, Alegre, & Pla-Barber, 2014).

In the 1990s, cleaner production was considered as a promising concept for improving the environmental performance of firms with significant potential for cost effectiveness (Baas, 2007). In the following years, cleaner production-related implementation efforts were pursued by international organizations, national governments, universities, consultancies, foundations, business associations, and numerous firms (Baas, 2007). Regarding the actor-network theory, organizational learning entails the altered and different behavior on the part of actors, leading to the alterations in the ways in which individual behavior is interconnected (Blomme, 2015). Practical adaptation of cleaner production efforts requires the innovative behavior at different organizational levels, such as the acquisition of new knowledge, collaborative actions, and decision making by managers in modern organizations (Montalvo, 2006).

Sustainability is defined as the continued development without significant deterioration of the environment and depletion of natural resources on which human well-being depends (Kasemsap, 2016c). Organizational learning is identified as a method to promote sustainability by institutionalizing new thinking (Lozano, 2014). Organizational learning is a main requirement for the important change toward sustainability, which is easy to indicate once it occurs, but more difficult to address while it is in process (Lozano, 2013). Blended learning method and supply networks are the valuable dissemination approaches to stimulating the implementation of cleaner production through organizational learning in small firms (van Hoof, 2014).

## Organizational Learning and Networks

Organized learning facilitates the development and extension of network learning (Erkelens, van den Hooff, Huysman, & Vlaar, 2015). The interpersonal network structure of an organization directly influences the diffusion and recombination of notions and can facilitate or obstruct organizational learning (Schilling & Fang, 2014). Because information sharing helps firms acquire, integrate, and store knowledge gathered from outside or from networks, organizational learning can be enhanced by information sharing (Liu, Xu, & Hu, 2010). The formal and informal learning can take place within different types of learning networks that draw on internal resources as well as on the collaboration with external entities (Melo & Beck, 2015).

As organizational members learn and gain knowledge, they organize the existing network positions or create new ones to improve organizational learning (Laperrière & Spence, 2015). Effective collaboration among employees is critical for organizational learning (Chen, Tjosvold, Zhao, Ning, & Fu, 2011). Organizations can learn within interorganizational networks (Knight, 2002). Networks gather the information and knowledge of different firms to ensure that firms meet diverse information and knowledge needs (Uzzi, 1997). Networks boost cooperation and communication among firms, leading to information flow and knowledge transfer (Dyer & Singh, 1998). Organizations can learn through the interaction with other organizations to improve their structures, processes, and performance (Knight, 2002).

## Organizational Learning, Organizational Innovation, and Transformational Leadership

Organizational innovation is the process of translating an idea or invention into products or services that create organizational value (Kasemsap, 2015a). Organizational innovation, KM, and strategic orientation have the positive relationship with organizational performance (Kasemsap, 2014a). Transformational leadership, empowerment, and innovation support positively lead to organizational innovation (Kasemsap, 2014b). Support for innovation has a positive relationship on organizational learning and organizational innovation (Hsiao, Chang, & Chen, 2014). Organizations utilize knowledge and organizational innovation as the organizational resources for producing high-technology products and services in order to obtain sustainable competitive advantage in modern organizations (Kasemsap, 2016b). Organizational learning affects perceived organizational financial performance through the full mediation of organizational innovation (Yu, Fang, & Ling, 2009).

The ways in which organizations compete include their abilities to develop competence, perspectives of working, and leadership (Döös, Johansson, & Wilhelmson, 2015). Transformational leadership can be defined as the style of leadership that increases the consciousness of collective interest among organizational members and helps them achieve their collective goals (García-Morales et al., 2012). Transformational leadership builds teams and provides them with the support for the processes of organizational change and organizational learning (Bass, 1999). Transformational leadership allows organizations to learn through experimentation, exploration, and communication (Menguc, Auh, & Shih, 2007).

Many perspectives of transformational leadership (e.g., behavior, management training, and support received from external organizations), are relevant for organizational innovation (Gumusluoglu & İlsev, 2009). Transformational leadership can indirectly affect organizational innovation through the communication process (Tushman & Nadler, 1986) and the process of organizational knowledge creation (Nonaka & Takeuchi, 1995). Organizational learning significantly supports creativity (Yli-Renko, Autio, & Sapienza, 2001), inspires new ideas (Damanpour, 1991), increases ability to apply these ideas (Damanpour, 1991), favors organizational intelligence, and establishes a background for orientation to organizational innovation (García-Morales et al., 2012).

## Organizational Learning, Absorptive Capacity, Open Innovation, and Information Technology

Absorptive capacity is defined as an organization's ability to recognize the value of external information, assimilate it, and apply it to commercial perspectives (Cohen & Levinthal, 1990). Absorptive capacity is an important example of organizational learning that involves an organization's relationship with the new external knowledge (Sun & Anderson, 2010). Learning processes enable firms to utilize technical knowledge in an effective manner that creates the higher absorptive capacity (Lichtenthaler, 2009). Learning facilitates the behavioral change that promotes capacity absorption and usage toward improved performance (Slater & Narver, 1995).

Absorptive capacity is an important determinant for developing a company's innovativeness (Cepeda-Carrion, Cegarra-Navarro, & Jimenez-Jimenez, 2012) and can enable business performance from a company's network relationships (Hughes, Morgan, Ireland, & Hughes, 2014). Gaining an understanding about how technology can be organized to promote organizational learning is the important approach to improving organizational practices (Wang, 2012). The increasing utilization of social media at work offers organizations new opportunities for employee's learning on the job (van Puijenbroek, Poell, Kroon, & Timmerman, 2014). Social media enables the creation of knowledge value chain to customize information and delivery for a technological business growth (Kasemsap, 2014c).

One of the most important enablers of absorptive capacity is IT (Roberts, Galluch, Dinger, & Grover, 2012), and IT is considered as a catalyst of organizational learning (Tippins & Sohi, 2003) and innovation (Xue, Ray, & Sambamurthy, 2012). IT plays a significant role in strengthening the organizational learning processes that occur in knowledge alliances and networks (Dong & Yang, 2015). Organizational learning effectiveness mediates the relationship between knowledge creation capabilities and organizational creativity (Chung, Liang, Peng, & Chen, 2014). Standard IT interfaces significantly facilitate the mutual knowledge creation with supply chain partners (Malhotra, Gosain, & El Sawy, 2007). IT applications support knowledge sharing between a focal firm and its customers or distribution channel partners (Saraf, Langdon, & Gosain, 2007).

As researchers have begun to understand innovation activities as an array of knowledge exchanges and spillovers (Tsai & Ghoshal, 1998), a more dynamic conception of innovation is required to capture how knowledge can be acquired from external sources, such as knowledge alliances and networks (Hoang & Rothaermel, 2005). Many studies have been conducted regarding the growing relevance of external sources of innovation rather than a reliance on internal research and development (R&D), resulting in the notion of open innovation (Chesbrough, 2006). Open innovation describes the situation in which many innovative firms have shifted to an open model for their activities, using a wide range of external knowledge sources to help them achieve their goals (Dong & Yang, 2015).

Because open innovation is essentially externally oriented learning processes that occur by reusing the existing elements of knowledge (March, 1991), absorptive capacity theory is a powerful perspective through which to understand how the firm can generate innovation and build competitiveness by working with external partners and assimilating knowledge spillovers. Because firms do not automatically adopt the value of open innovation, their absorptive capacity becomes critical in enabling them to benefit from the external sources of knowledge (Schilling, 2012). The degree to which a firm can obtain desirable outcomes from its open innovation activities depends on how it carries out externally oriented organizational learning processes and thus on its absorptive capacity (Dong & Yang, 2015).

## Organizational Learning and Training

Training improves organizational performance by creating the effective workforce with extensive knowledge and skills (Ballesteros, de Saá, & Domínguez, 2012). Training plays an essential role in enhancing human capital and organizational knowledge (Subramaniam & Youndt, 2005). Organizational knowledge refers to the way knowledge is distributed and shared among members of an organization; it is manifested in unique routines and knowledge bases, and represents more than the sum of individual learning (Dodgson, 1993). The adoption of a learning oriented training enhances performances through its positive effect on organizational learning (Aragón, Jiménez, & Valle, 2014). Perception of learning, trainee reactions, and occupational satisfaction have the positive relationship with perceived training transfer (Kasemsap, 2014d). Training transfer is crucial for workplace effectiveness (Chiaburu, van Dam, & Hutchins, 2010).

Training is an important tool to promote employees' learning capabilities, both their competencies to learn and their motivation to learn (Chen & Huang, 2009); to provide a common language and shared vision that facilitate communication among employees and, therefore, the transfer and dissemination of individual knowledge within the firm (Fong, Ooi, Tan, & Lee, 2011); and to create a learning-oriented culture (Jaw & Liu, 2003). Training is positively correlated with organizational learning processes (Chen & Huang, 2009), knowledge transfer (Fong et al., 2011), and the development of positive learning attitudes (Jaw & Liu, 2003).

Training and development investments of an organization affect its innovative performance by promoting various learning practices (Sung & Choi, 2014). Organizational learning requires multi-skills training (Camps & Luna-Aroca, 2012) because utilizing multi-skill training, the firm can enhance employees' flexibility and broaden their understanding with innovative skills (Nonaka & Takeuchi, 1995). Organizational learning can help personnel improve skills and knowledge and provide opportunities to find out the effective perspectives of teamwork (Carroll & Edmondson, 2002). Since teamwork is crucial for organizational learning (Gagné, 2009), training should be team-based (Cabrera & Cabrera, 2005).

## Organizational Learning Capability and Enterprise Resource Planning

Organizational learning capability (OLC) can be defined as the organizational and managerial characteristics that facilitate the organizational learning process and allow an organization to learn (Tohidi, Seyedaliakbar, & Mandegari, 2012). OLC refers to the ability of an organization to implement the proper management practices, structure, procedures, and policies that facilitate organizational learning (Goh, 2003) and is the capacity to generate ideas moving beyond multiple organizational boundaries through specific management practices (Farsani, Bidmeshgipour, Habibi, & Rashidi, 2012). Lee et al. (2013) stated that OLC plays the important role in the adoption and use of new technologies. Organizations create OLC by facilitating the organizational learning process and allowing an organization to learn (Nwankpa & Roumani, 2014).

Enterprise resource planning (ERP) is a software-driven business management system that integrates the perspectives of business, planning, manufacturing, sales, and marketing (Kasemsap, 2015b). ERP system usage captures the extent to which users utilize the installed ERP functionalities (Jones, Zmud, & Thomas, 2008). Employees faced with the newly transformed processes created by ERP systems can be overwhelmed to the extent that they limit the use of the ERP system (Nwankpa & Roumani, 2014). Bradford and Florin (2003) indicated that after the deployment of an ERP package, organizations need to apply suitable organizational learning to enhance the opportunities of realizing the ERP system benefits.

OLC and innovation performance should be enhanced by managers in order to boost the positive relationship between entrepreneurial orientation and organizational performance (Alegre & Chiva, 2013). Jerez-Gomez et al. (2005) indicated that OLC should be able to create, acquire, and transfer new knowledge as well as modify the existing behavior to reflect new knowledge with a view to improve organizational performance. As ERP system implementations create the new learning curve (Amoako-Gyampah & Salam, 2004), promoting learning is essential for modern organizations. Mathematically, organizational learning process can be described as a search for better paths on the learning curve whose nodes are humans and machines (Fioretti, 2007). By having an effective OLC, organizations should facilitate the effective utilization of their ERP systems (Nwankpa & Roumani, 2014). Organizations with strong OLC have the effective ERP training programs regarding information systems implementation (Noe, 2002) and such training programs can create the higher user satisfaction (Cho, 2007).

## Learning Organization

Senge (1990) provided five disciplines for working in learning organizations that are based on the organizational learning theory (i.e., shared vision, team learning, personal mastery, mental models, and systems thinking). Learning organization is the environment that promotes both individual and team learning capabilities (Davis & Lopuch, 2016) and is recognized as a necessary strategy in order to enhance the large-scale improvement (Opfer, Pedder, & Lavicza, 2011). The ethical healthiness of an organization is an essential condition to achieve a comprehensive learning process in learning organizations on both technical and human levels (Bañón-Gomis, 2015).

Learning organization concepts, embraced by a growing number of organizations throughout the world, are strategies for competing in the dynamic economic environments (Lopuch & Davis, 2014).

Learning organization has been identified as an innovative practice essential for global businesses to not only effectively compete in today's dynamic environment, but also to achieve and maintain a sustainable competitive advantage toward increasing organizational performance (Calhoun & Douglas, 2015).

Organizational learning has become a focal point for organizations to quickly adapt to the global markets and dynamic economies (Holt, Beard, & Lee, 2013). The organizational learning culture has a positive impact on employee's job satisfaction (Sabir & Kalyar, 2013) and the motivation to transfer learning (Egan, Yong, & Bartlett, 2004). Learning motivation positively leads to learning transfer (Kasemsap, 2013). In the context of information systems, semantic learning organization is an emerging concept that extends the notion of the learning organization in a semantic dimension (Sicilia & Lytras, 2005). Organizational support and learning flow have direct effects on learning transfer and learners' satisfaction, while learning flow mediates organizational support and learners' satisfaction (Joo, Lim, & Park, 2011).

Learning organization is an organization in which learning activities are mediated and enhanced through a shared representation of knowledge of the domain and context of the organization (Abel, 2015). Learning organization promotes the perspectives of electronic learning (e-learning), organizational learning, and KM regarding the utilization of open communication, shared support, and collaboration (Kasemsap, 2016c). The organization's e-learning processes can support the development of dynamic capabilities (Costello & McNaughton, 2016). Jiao et al. (2010) indicated that dynamic capabilities involve four major dimensions (i.e., environmental sensing capabilities, renewal capabilities, technological capabilities, and organizational flexibility capabilities).

## FUTURE RESEARCH DIRECTIONS

The classification of the extensive literature in the domains of organizational learning will provide the potential opportunities for future research. Intellectual capital is the collective knowledge of the individuals in an organization. Human capital management (HCM) is an approach to employee staffing that perceives people as assets (human capital) whose current value can be measured and whose future value can be enhanced through organizational investment in the modern workforce. Organizations that embed the practices of human capital and competency across a range of human resource management activities effectively create and develop a boundary spanning culture connecting with various organizational disciplines in the global knowledge economy (Kasemsap, 2016d). Communities of practice (CoPs) help promote a growing cycle of knowledge sharing activities that allow for the members to regularly meet, reflect, and evolve in the KM environment (Kasemsap, 2016e). Cultural influences are changing dramatically, as organizational cultures are no longer dependent on local resources to formulate their characteristic tastes, preferences, and organizational behavior (Kasemsap, 2015c). An examination of linkages among organizational learning, intellectual capital, HCM, CoPs, and cross-cultural organizational behavior would seem to be viable for future research efforts.

## CONCLUSION

This chapter highlighted the prospect of organizational learning; organizational learning and networks; organizational learning, organizational innovation, and transformational leadership; organizational learning, absorptive capacity, open innovation, and IT; organizational learning and training; OLC and ERP; and learning organization. Within business, learning is a conscious attempt on the part of organizations to improve productivity, effectiveness, and innovativeness in the uncertain economic and technological market conditions. Organizational learning enables more effective responses to the dynamic environments. Effective organizational learning is associated with the increased information sharing and communication in the knowledge economy.

Organizational learning involves social interactions among many individuals toward leading to the well-informed decision making. Thus, an organizational learning culture that learns and adapts as part of working practices is essential in the workplace. Organizational learning is positively related to networks, organizational innovation, open innovation, transformational leadership, absorptive capacity, IT, and training. The ability to learn is an important competitive advantage for modern organizations. Organizations that are able to create the new knowledge, to retain that knowledge, and to transfer it throughout organizations are more productive and more likely to prosper than their counterparts that are less adept at organizational learning.

Regarding organizational learning strategy, organizations need to create, capture, transfer, and mobilize knowledge, through human resource-related training and development program, before it can be effectively utilized. Organizational learning is necessary for modern organizations that seek to serve suppliers and customers, increase business performance, strengthen competitiveness, and achieve continuous success in the knowledge economy. Therefore, it is essential for modern organizations to encourage their organizational learning and develop a strategic plan to regularly check their practical advancements toward satisfying customer requirements. Encouraging organizational learning has the potential to improve organizational performance and gain sustainable competitive advantage in the workplace.

## REFERENCES

Abel, M. H. (2015). Knowledge map-based web platform to facilitate organizational learning return of experiences. *Computers in Human Behavior*, *51*, 960–966. doi:10.1016/j.chb.2014.10.012

Aizpurúa, L. I., Saldaña, P. E. Z., & Saldaña, A. Z. (2011). Learning for sharing: An empirical analysis of organizational learning and knowledge sharing. *The International Entrepreneurship and Management Journal*, *7*(4), 509–518. doi:10.1007/s11365-011-0206-z

Alegre, J., & Chiva, R. (2013). Linking entrepreneurial orientation and firm performance: The role of organizational learning capability and innovation performance. *Journal of Small Business Management*, *51*(4), 491–507. doi:10.1111/jsbm.12005

Amoako-Gyampah, K., & Salam, A. F. (2004). An extension of the technology acceptance model in an ERP implementation environment. *Information & Management*, *41*(6), 731–745. doi:10.1016/j.im.2003.08.010

Aragón, M. I. B., Jiménez, D. J., & Valle, R. S. (2014). Training and performance: The mediating role of organizational learning. *BRQ Business Research Quarterly*, *17*(3), 161–173. doi:10.1016/j.cede.2013.05.003

Argyris, C., & Schön, D. A. (1996). *Organisational learning II: Theory, method and practice*. Reading, MA: Addison–Wesley.

Avnet, M. S. (2015). A network-based approach to organizational culture and learning in system safety. *Procedia Computer Science, 44*, 588–598. doi:10.1016/j.procs.2015.03.061

Baas, L. (2007). To make zero emissions technologies and strategies become a reality, the lessons learned of cleaner production dissemination have to be known. *Journal of Cleaner Production, 15*(13/14), 1205–1216. doi:10.1016/j.jclepro.2006.07.017

Balabanis, G., Theodosiou, M., & Katsikea, E. (2004). Export marketing: Developments and a research agenda. *International Marketing Review, 21*(4/5), 353–377. doi:10.1108/02651330410547081

Ballesteros, J. L., de Saá, P., & Domínguez, C. (2012). The role of organizational culture and HRM on training success: Evidence from the Canarian restaurant industry. *International Journal of Human Resource Management, 23*(15), 3225–3242. doi:10.1080/09585192.2011.637071

Bañón-Gomis, A. J. (2015). Ethical healthiness: A key factor in building learning organizations. In D. Palmer (Ed.), Handbook of research on business ethics and corporate responsibilities (pp. 356–372). Hershey, PA: IGI Global. doi:10.4018/978-1-4666-7476-9.ch017

Bass, B. M. (1999). Two decades of research and development in transformational leadership. *European Journal of Work and Organizational Psychology, 8*(1), 9–32. doi:10.1080/135943299398410

Beenen, G., & Goodman, P. S. (2014). Too little of a good thing? How organizational learning contracts can refocus B-schools on the business of learning. *The International Journal of Management Education, 12*(3), 248–259. doi:10.1016/j.ijme.2014.05.011

Bengtsson, L. (2004). Explaining born globals: An organisational learning perspective on the internationalisation process. *International Journal of Globalisation and Small Business, 1*(1), 28–41. doi:10.1504/IJGSB.2004.005616

Birenbaum, M., Kimron, H., & Shilton, H. (2011). Nested contexts that shape assessment for learning: School-based professional learning community and classroom culture. *Studies in Educational Evaluation, 37*(1), 35–48. doi:10.1016/j.stueduc.2011.04.001

Blomme, R. J. (2015). Self-organization as a perspective for organizational learning: A new role for learning practitioners. In P. Ordoñez de Pablos, L. Turró, R. Tennyson, & J. Zhao (Eds.), *Knowledge management for competitive advantage during economic crisis* (pp. 56–68). Hershey, PA: IGI Global. doi:10.4018/978-1-4666-6457-9.ch004

Bradford, M., & Florin, J. (2003). Examining the role of innovation diffusion factors on the implementation success of enterprise resource planning systems. *International Journal of Accounting Information Systems, 4*(3), 205–225. doi:10.1016/S1467-0895(03)00026-5

Brouthers, L. E., Nakos, G., Hadjimarcou, J., & Brouthers, K. D. (2009). Key success factors for successful export performance for small firms. *Journal of International Marketing, 17*(3), 21–38. doi:10.1509/jimk.17.3.21

Cabrera, E., & Cabrera, A. (2005). Fostering knowledge sharing through people management practices. *International Journal of Human Resource Management, 16*(5), 720–735. doi:10.1080/09585190500083020

Calhoun, J., & Douglas, A. (2015). An analysis of hospitality and tourism research: Learning organization's (LO) influence on sustainability practices. In A. Camillo (Ed.), Handbook of research on global hospitality and tourism management (pp. 359–381). Hershey, PA: IGI Global. doi:10.4018/978-1-4666-8606-9.ch019

Camps, J., & Luna-Aroca, R. (2012). A matter of learning: How human resources affect organizational performance. *British Journal of Management, 23*(1), 1–21. doi:10.1111/j.1467-8551.2010.00714.x

Cappetta, R., & Paolino, C. (2015). Is it always worth waiting? The effect of autonomy-supportive teaching on short-term and long-term learning outcomes. *British Journal of Management, 26*(1), 93–108. doi:10.1111/1467-8551.12065

Carroll, J. S., & Edmondson, A. C. (2002). Leading organisational learning in health care. *Quality & Safety in Health Care, 11*(1), 51–56. doi:10.1136/qhc.11.1.51

Cepeda-Carrion, G., Cegarra-Navarro, J. G., & Jimenez-Jimenez, D. (2012). The effect of absorptive capacity on innovativeness: Context and information systems capability as catalysts. *British Journal of Management, 23*(1), 110–129. doi:10.1111/j.1467-8551.2010.00725.x

Chen, C. J., & Huang, J. W. (2009). Strategic human resource practices and innovation performance: The mediating role of knowledge management capacity. *Journal of Business Research, 62*(1), 104–114. doi:10.1016/j.jbusres.2007.11.016

Chen, G., Tjosvold, D., Zhao, H., Ning, N., & Fu, Y. (2011). Constructive controversy for learning and team effectiveness in China. *Asia Pacific Journal of Human Resources, 49*(1), 88–104. doi:10.1177/1038411110391708

Chesbrough, H. (2006). *Open business models: How to thrive in the new innovation landscape*. Boston, MA: Harvard Business School Press.

Chiaburu, D. S., van Dam, K., & Hutchins, H. M. (2010). Social support in the workplace and training transfer: A longitudinal analysis. *International Journal of Selection and Assessment, 18*(2), 187–200. doi:10.1111/j.1468-2389.2010.00500.x

Chiva, R., & Alegre, J. (2009). Organizational learning capability and job satisfaction: An empirical assessment in the ceramic tile industry. *British Journal of Management, 20*(3), 323–340. doi:10.1111/j.1467-8551.2008.00586.x

Cho, V. (2007). A study of the impact of organizational learning on information system effectiveness. *International Journal of Business and Information, 2*(1), 127–158.

Chouseinoglou, O., Iren, D., Karagoz, N. A., & Bilgen, S. (2013). AiOLoS: A model for assessing organizational learning in software development organizations. *Information and Software Technology, 55*(11), 1904–1924. doi:10.1016/j.infsof.2013.05.004

Chung, H. F. L., Yang, Z., & Huang, P. H. (2015). How does organizational learning matter in strategic business performance? The contingency role of guanxi networking. *Journal of Business Research, 68*(6), 1216–1224. doi:10.1016/j.jbusres.2014.11.016

Chung, T. R., Liang, T., Peng, C., & Chen, D. (2014). How knowledge creation capabilities lead to competitive advantage. In M. Chilton & J. Bloodgood (Eds.), *Knowledge management and competitive advantage: Issues and potential solutions* (pp. 36–52). Hershey, PA: IGI Global. doi:10.4018/978-1-4666-4679-7.ch003

Cohen, W. M., & Levinthal, D. A. (1990). Absorptive capacity: A new perspective on learning and innovation. *Administrative Science Quarterly, 35*(1), 128–152. doi:10.2307/2393553

Costello, J. T., & McNaughton, R. B. (2016). Can dynamic capabilities be developed using workplace e-learning processes? *Knowledge and Process Management, 23*(1), 73–87. doi:10.1002/kpm.1500

Damanpour, F. (1991). Organizational innovation: A meta-analysis of effects of determinants and moderators. *Academy of Management Journal, 34*(3), 555–590. doi:10.2307/256406

Davis, D. C., & Lopuch, V. S. (2016). Learning organizations: Connections between diversity and innovation. In J. Prescott (Ed.), *Handbook of research on race, gender, and the fight for equality* (pp. 267–297). Hershey, PA: IGI Global. doi:10.4018/978-1-5225-0047-6.ch012

Dayaram, K., & Fung, L. (2014). Organizational learning in the Philippines: How do team and individual learning contribute? *Asia Pacific Journal of Human Resources, 52*(4), 420–442. doi:10.1111/1744-7941.12039

Demirel, Y., Arzova, B., Ardic, K., & Bas, T. (2013). Organizational learning on coopetition strategy: An exploratory research on a Turkish private banks credit card application. *Procedia: Social and Behavioral Sciences, 99*, 902–910. doi:10.1016/j.sbspro.2013.10.563

Dodgson, M. (1993). Organizational learning: A review of some literatures. *Organization Studies, 14*(3), 375–394. doi:10.1177/017084069301400303

Dong, J. Q., & Yang, C. H. (2015). Information technology and organizational learning in knowledge alliances and networks: Evidence from U.S. pharmaceutical industry. *Information & Management, 52*(1), 111–122. doi:10.1016/j.im.2014.10.010

Döös, M., Johansson, P., & Wilhelmson, L. (2015). Organizational learning as an analogy to individual learning? A case of augmented interaction intensity. *Vocations and Learning, 8*(1), 55–73. doi:10.1007/s12186-014-9125-9

Duffield, S., & Whitty, S. J. (2015). Developing a systemic lessons learned knowledge model for organisational learning through projects. *International Journal of Project Management, 33*(2), 311–324. doi:10.1016/j.ijproman.2014.07.004

Dyer, J. H., & Singh, H. (1998). The relational view: Cooperative strategy and sources of interorganizational competitive advantage. *Academy of Management Review, 23*(4), 660–679. doi:10.2307/259056

Egan, T. M., Yong, B., & Bartlett, K. R. (2004). The effects of organizational learning culture and job satisfaction on motivation to transfer learning and turnover intention. *Human Resource Development Quarterly, 15*(3), 279–301. doi:10.1002/hrdq.1104

Erkelens, R., van den Hooff, B., Huysman, M., & Vlaar, P. (2015). Learning from locally embedded knowledge: Facilitating organizational learning in geographically dispersed settings. *Global Strategy Journal, 5*(2), 177–197. doi:10.1002/gsj.1092

Farsani, J. J., Bidmeshgipour, M., Habibi, M., & Rashidi, M. M. (2012). Intellectual capital and organizational learning capability in Iranian active companies of petrochemical industry. *Procedia: Social and Behavioral Sciences, 62*, 1297–1302. doi:10.1016/j.sbspro.2012.09.222

Fernandez-Mesa, A., & Alegre, J. (2015). Entrepreneurial orientation and export intensity: Examining the interplay of organizational learning and innovation. *International Business Review, 24*(1), 148–156. doi:10.1016/j.ibusrev.2014.07.004

Fioretti, G. (2007). A connectionist model of the organizational learning curve. *Computational & Mathematical Organization Theory, 13*(1), 1–16. doi:10.1007/s10588-006-9003-6

Fong, C. Y., Ooi, K. B., Tan, B. I., Lee, V. H., & Yee-Loong Chong, A. (2011). HRM practices and knowledge sharing: An empirical study. *International Journal of Manpower, 32*(5/6), 704–723. doi:10.1108/01437721111158288

Froehlich, D., Segers, M., & van den Bossche, P. (2014). Informal workplace learning in Austrian banks: The influence of learning approach, leadership style, and organizational learning culture on managers' learning outcomes. *Human Resource Development Quarterly, 25*(1), 29–57. doi:10.1002/hrdq.21173

Gagné, M. (2009). A model of knowledge-sharing motivation. *Human Resource Management, 48*(4), 571–589. doi:10.1002/hrm.20298

García-Morales, V. J., Jiménez-Barrionuevo, M. M., & Gutiérrez-Gutiérrez, L. (2012). Transformational leadership influence on organizational performance through organizational learning and innovation. *Journal of Business Research, 65*(7), 1040–1050. doi:10.1016/j.jbusres.2011.03.005

Garrido, M. J., & Camarero, C. (2010). Assessing the impact of organizational learning and innovation on performance in cultural organizations. *International Journal of Nonprofit and Voluntary Sector Marketing, 15*(3), 215–232.

Goh, S. C. (2003). Improving organizational learning capability: Lessons from two case studies. *The Learning Organization, 10*(4), 216–227. doi:10.1108/09696470310476981

Golovko, E., & Valentini, G. (2011). Exploring the complementarity between innovation and export for SMEs growth. *Journal of International Business Studies, 42*(3), 362–380. doi:10.1057/jibs.2011.2

Gumusluoglu, L., & İlsev, A. (2009). Transformational leadership, creativity, and organizational innovation. *Journal of Business Research, 62*(4), 461–473. doi:10.1016/j.jbusres.2007.07.032

Hoang, H., & Rothaermel, F. T. (2005). The effect of general and partner-specific alliance experience of joint R&D project performance. *Academy of Management Journal, 48*(2), 332–345. doi:10.5465/AMJ.2005.16928417

Holt, L., Beard, J., & Lee, D. S. (2013). Use of information technology in organizational learning: Effective practices of award-winning organizations. In V. Bryan & V. Wang (Eds.), *Technology use and research approaches for community education and professional development* (pp. 24–39). Hershey, PA: IGI Global. doi:10.4018/978-1-4666-2955-4.ch002

Hotho, J. J., Lyles, M. A., & Easterby-Smith, M. (2015). The mutual impact of global strategy and organizational learning: Current themes and future directions. *Global Strategy Journal*, 5(2), 85–112. doi:10.1002/gsj.1097

Hsiao, H. C., Chang, J. C., & Chen, S. C. (2014). The influence of support for innovation on organizational innovation: Taking organizational learning as a mediator. *The Asia-Pacific Education Researcher*, 23(3), 463–472. doi:10.1007/s40299-013-0121-x

Hu, B. (2014). Linking business models with technological innovation performance through organizational learning. *European Management Journal*, 32(4), 587–595. doi:10.1016/j.emj.2013.10.009

Hughes, M., Morgan, R. E., Ireland, R. D., & Hughes, P. (2014). Social capital and learning advantages: A problem of absorptive capacity. *Strategic Entrepreneurship Journal*, 8(3), 214–233. doi:10.1002/sej.1162

Jaw, B. S., & Liu, W. (2003). Promoting organizational learning and self-renewal in Taiwanese companies: The role of HRM. *Human Resource Management*, 42(3), 223–241. doi:10.1002/hrm.10082

Jerez-Gomez, P., Cespedes-Lorente, J., & Valle-Cabrera, R. (2005). Organizational learning capability: A proposal of measurement. *Journal of Business Research*, 58(6), 715–725. doi:10.1016/j.jbusres.2003.11.002

Jiao, H., Wei, J., & Cui, Y. (2010). An empirical study on paths to develop dynamic capabilities: From the perspectives of entrepreneurial orientation and organizational learning. *Frontiers of Business Research in China*, 4(1), 47–72. doi:10.1007/s11782-010-0003-5

Jones, M. C., Zmud, R. W., & Thomas, D. C. (2008). ERP in practice: A snapshot of post-installation perception and behaviors. *Communications of the Association for Information Systems*, 23(1), 437–462.

Joo, Y. J., Lim, K. Y., & Park, S. Y. (2011). Investigating the structural relationships among organisational support, learning flow, learners' satisfaction and learning transfer in corporate e-learning. *British Journal of Educational Technology*, 42(6), 973–984. doi:10.1111/j.1467-8535.2010.01116.x

Kane, G. G., & Alavi, M. (2007). Information technology and organizational learning: An investigation of exploration and exploitation processes. *Organization Science*, 18(5), 796–812. doi:10.1287/orsc.1070.0286

Kasemsap, K. (2013). Practical framework: Creation of causal model of job involvement, career commitment, learning motivation, and learning transfer. *International Journal of the Computer, the Internet and Management*, 21(1), 29–35.

Kasemsap, K. (2014a). Strategic innovation management: An integrative framework and causal model of knowledge management, strategic orientation, organizational innovation, and organizational performance. In P. Ordóñez de Pablos & R. Tennyson (Eds.), *Strategic approaches for human capital management and development in a turbulent economy* (pp. 102–116). Hershey, PA: IGI Global. doi:10.4018/978-1-4666-4530-1.ch007

Kasemsap, K. (2014b). Developing a unified framework and a causal model of transformational leadership, empowerment, innovation support, and organizational innovation. In N. Erbe (Ed.), *Approaches to managing organizational diversity and innovation* (pp. 280–303). Hershey, PA: IGI Global. doi:10.4018/978-1-4666-6006-9.ch014

Kasemsap, K. (2014c). The role of social media in the knowledge-based organizations. In I. Lee (Ed.), *Integrating social media into business practice, applications, management, and models* (pp. 254–275). Hershey, PA: IGI Global. doi:10.4018/978-1-4666-6182-0.ch013

Kasemsap, K. (2014d). Constructing a unified framework and a causal model of occupational satisfaction, trainee reactions, perception of learning, and perceived training transfer. In S. Hai-Jew (Ed.), *Remote workforce training: Effective technologies and strategies* (pp. 28–52). Hershey, PA: IGI Global. doi:10.4018/978-1-4666-5137-1.ch003

Kasemsap, K. (2015a). The roles of international entrepreneurship and organizational innovation in SMEs. In L. Carmo Farinha, J. Ferreira, H. Smith, & S. Bagchi-Sen (Eds.), *Handbook of research on global competitive advantage through innovation and entrepreneurship* (pp. 410–438). Hershey, PA: IGI Global. doi:10.4018/978-1-4666-8348-8.ch024

Kasemsap, K. (2015b). Implementing enterprise resource planning. In M. Khosrow-Pour (Ed.), *Encyclopedia of information science and technology* (3rd ed.; pp. 798–807). Hershey, PA: IGI Global. doi:10.4018/978-1-4666-5888-2.ch076

Kasemsap, K. (2015c). The role of cultural dynamics in the digital age. In B. Christiansen & J. Koeman (Eds.), *Nationalism, cultural indoctrination, and economic prosperity in the digital age* (pp. 295–312). Hershey, PA: IGI Global. doi:10.4018/978-1-4666-7492-9.ch014

Kasemsap, K. (2016a). Promoting leadership development and talent management in modern organizations. In U. Aung & P. Ordoñez de Pablos (Eds.), *Managerial strategies and practice in the Asian business sector* (pp. 238–266). Hershey, PA: IGI Global. doi:10.4018/978-1-4666-9758-4.ch013

Kasemsap, K. (2016b). The roles of knowledge management and organizational innovation in global business. In G. Jamil, J. Poças-Rascão, F. Ribeiro, & A. Malheiro da Silva (Eds.), *Handbook of research on information architecture and management in modern organizations* (pp. 130–153). Hershey, PA: IGI Global. doi:10.4018/978-1-4666-8637-3.ch006

Kasemsap, K. (2016c). The roles of e-learning, organizational learning, and knowledge management in the learning organizations. In E. Railean, G. Walker, A. Elçi, & L. Jackson (Eds.), *Handbook of research on applied learning theory and design in modern education* (pp. 786–816). Hershey, PA: IGI Global. doi:10.4018/978-1-4666-9634-1.ch039

Kasemsap, K. (2016d). Analyzing the roles of human capital and competency in global business. In S. Sen, A. Bhattacharya, & R. Sen (Eds.), *International perspectives on socio-economic development in the era of globalization* (pp. 1–29). Hershey, PA: IGI Global. doi:10.4018/978-1-4666-9908-3.ch001

Kasemsap, K. (2016e). Utilizing communities of practice to facilitate knowledge sharing in the digital age. In S. Buckley, G. Majewski, & A. Giannakopoulos (Eds.), *Organizational knowledge facilitation through communities of practice in emerging markets* (pp. 198–224). Hershey, PA: IGI Global. doi:10.4018/978-1-5225-0013-1.ch011

Kim, D. D. (1993). The link between individual and organizational learning. *MIT Sloan Management Review*, *35*(1), 37–50.

Kim, M. K., Kim, S. M., & Bilir, M. K. (2014). Investigation of the dimensions of workplace learning environments (WLEs): Development of the WLE measure. *Performance Improvement Quarterly*, *27*(2), 35–57. doi:10.1002/piq.21170

Kim, N., & Atuahene-Gima, K. (2010). Using exploratory and exploitative market learning for new product development. *Product Development & Management Association*, *27*(4), 519–536. doi:10.1111/j.1540-5885.2010.00733.x

Knight, L. (2002). Network learning: Exploring learning by interorganizational networks. *Human Relations*, *55*(4), 427–454. doi:10.1177/0018726702554003

Koskinen, K. U. (2012). Organizational learning in project-based companies: A process thinking approach. *Project Management Journal*, *43*(3), 40–49. doi:10.1002/pmj.21266

Laperrière, A., & Spence, M. (2015). Enacting international opportunities: The role of organizational learning in knowledge-intensive business services. *Journal of International Entrepreneurship*, *13*(3), 212–241. doi:10.1007/s10843-015-0151-y

Lazarová, B., Pol, M., Hloušková, L., Novotný, P., & Sedláček, M. (2013). Support for organizational learning in Czech basic schools. *Procedia: Social and Behavioral Sciences*, *93*, 302–307. doi:10.1016/j.sbspro.2013.09.194

Lee, C. C., Lin, S. P., Yang, S. L., Tsou, M. Y., & Chang, K. Y. (2013). Evaluating the influence of perceived organizational learning capability on user acceptance of information technology among operating room nurse staff. *Acta Anaesthesiologica Taiwanica*, *51*(1), 22–27. doi:10.1016/j.aat.2013.03.013

Lee, K. C., Lee, S., & Kang, I. W. (2005). KMPI: Measuring knowledge management performance. *Information & Management*, *42*(3), 469–482. doi:10.1016/j.im.2004.02.003

Levitt, B., & March, J. G. (1988). Organizational learning. *Annual Review of Sociology*, *14*(1), 319–340. doi:10.1146/annurev.so.14.080188.001535

Li, S., & Lin, B. (2006). Accessing information sharing and information quality in supply chain management. *Decision Support Systems*, *42*(3), 1641–1656. doi:10.1016/j.dss.2006.02.011

Lichtenthaler, U. (2009). Absorptive capacity, environmental turbulence, and the complementarity of organizational learning processes. *Academy of Management Journal*, *52*(4), 822–846. doi:10.5465/AMJ.2009.43670902

Liu, X., Xu, G., & Hu, B. (2010). Relational embeddedness, exploratory learning and firm technological innovation performance. *International Journal of Technology, Policy and Management*, *10*(4), 343–359. doi:10.1504/IJTPM.2010.036921

Lloria, M. B., & Moreno-Luzon, M. D. (2014). Organizational learning: Proposal of an integrative scale and research instrument. *Journal of Business Research, 67*(5), 692–697. doi:10.1016/j.jbusres.2013.11.029

Lopuch, V. S., & Davis, D. C. (2014). The role and value of diversity to learning organizations and innovation. In N. Erbe (Ed.), Approaches to managing organizational diversity and innovation (pp. 213–236). Hershey, PA: IGI Global. doi:10.4018/978-1-4666-6006-9.ch011

Lozano, R. (2013). Are companies planning their organisational changes for corporate sustainability? An analysis of three case studies on resistance to change and their strategies to overcome it. *Corporate Social Responsibility and Environmental Management, 20*(5), 275–295. doi:10.1002/csr.1290

Lozano, R. (2014). Creativity and organizational learning as means to foster sustainability. *Sustainable Development, 22*(3), 205–216. doi:10.1002/sd.540

Lyles, M. A. (2014). Organizational learning, knowledge creation, problem formulation and innovation in messy problems. *European Management Journal, 32*(1), 132–136. doi:10.1016/j.emj.2013.05.003

Malhotra, A., Gosain, S., & El Sawy, O. A. (2007). Leveraging standard electronic business interfaces to enable adaptive supply chain partnerships. *Information Systems Research, 18*(3), 260–279. doi:10.1287/isre.1070.0132

Manuti, A., Pastore, S., Scardigno, A. F., Giancaspro, M. L., & Morciano, D. (2015). Formal and informal learning in the workplace: A research review. *International Journal of Training and Development, 19*(1), 1–17. doi:10.1111/ijtd.12044

March, J. G. (1991). Exploration and exploitation in organizational learning. *Organization Science, 2*(1), 71–87. doi:10.1287/orsc.2.1.71

Melo, S., & Beck, M. (2015). Intra and interorganizational learning networks and the implementation of quality improvement initiatives: The case of a Portuguese teaching hospital. *Human Resource Development Quarterly, 26*(2), 155–183. doi:10.1002/hrdq.21207

Menguc, B., Auh, S., & Shih, E. (2007). Transformational leadership and market orientation: Implications for the implementation of competitive strategies and business unit performance. *Journal of Business Research, 60*(4), 314–321. doi:10.1016/j.jbusres.2006.12.008

Merad, M., Dechy, N., & Marcel, F. (2014). A pragmatic way of achieving highly sustainable organisation: Governance and organisational learning in action in the public French sector. *Safety Science, 69*, 18–28. doi:10.1016/j.ssci.2014.01.002

Montalvo, C. (2006). What triggers change and innovation? *Technovation, 26*(3), 312–323. doi:10.1016/j.technovation.2004.09.003

Moreno-Luzon, M. D., & Lloria, M. B. (2008). The role of non-structural and informal mechanisms of integration and coordination as forces in knowledge creation. *British Journal of Management, 19*(3), 250–276. doi:10.1111/j.1467-8551.2007.00544.x

Morgan, N. A., Katsikeas, C. S., & Vorhies, D. W. (2012). Export marketing strategy implementation, export marketing capabilities, and export venture performance. *Journal of the Academy of Marketing Science, 40*(2), 271–289. doi:10.1007/s11747-011-0275-0

Naghi, A. A., Gholamrez, J., Mehdi, A. S., Reza, H., & Majid, R. (2010). Increasing the intellectual capital in organization: Examining the role of organizational learning. *European Journal of Social Sciences, 14*(1/2), 98–112.

Nevis, E. C., DiBella, A. J., & Gould, J. M. (1995). Understanding organizations as learning systems. *MIT Sloan Management Review, 36*(2), 73–85.

Noe, R. A. (2002). *Employee training and development*. New York, NY: McGraw–Hill.

Nonaka, I., & Takeuchi, H. (1995). *The knowledge-creating company: How Japanese companies create the dynamics of innovation*. New York, NY: Oxford University Press.

Nwankpa, J., & Roumani, Y. (2014). Understanding the link between organizational learning capability and ERP system usage: An empirical examination. *Computers in Human Behavior, 33*, 224–234. doi:10.1016/j.chb.2014.01.030

Opfer, V. D., Pedder, D., & Lavicza, Z. (2011). The influence of school orientation to learning on teachers' professional learning change. *School Effectiveness and School Improvement, 22*(2), 193–214. doi:10.1080/09243453.2011.572078

Peltier, J. W., Schibrowsky, J. A., Schultz, D. E., & Zahay, D. (2006). Interactive IMC: The relational-transactional continuum and the synergistic use of customer data. *Journal of Advertising Research, 46*(2), 146–159. doi:10.2501/S0021849906060193

Peltier, J. W., Zahay, D., & Lehmann, D. R. (2013). Organizational learning and CRM success: A model for linking organizational practices, customer data quality, and performance. *Journal of Interactive Marketing, 27*(1), 1–13. doi:10.1016/j.intmar.2012.05.001

Piazza, R. (2010). The learning region between pedagogy and economy. *European Journal of Education, 45*(3), 402–418. doi:10.1111/j.1465-3435.2010.01437.x

Popper, M., & Lipshitz, R. (1998). Organizational learning mechanisms: A structural and cultural approach to organizational learning. *The Journal of Applied Behavioral Science, 34*(2), 161–179. doi:10.1177/0021886398342003

Real, J. C., Roldán, J. L., & Leal, A. (2014). From entrepreneurial orientation and learning orientation to business performance: Analysing the mediating role of organizational learning and the moderating effects of organizational size. *British Journal of Management, 25*(2), 186–208. doi:10.1111/j.1467-8551.2012.00848.x

Roberts, N., Galluch, P. S., Dinger, M., & Grover, V. (2012). Absorptive capacity and information systems research: Review, synthesis and directions for future research. *Management Information Systems Quarterly, 36*(2), 625–648.

Sabir, H. M., & Kalyar, M. N. (2013). Firm's innovativeness and employee job satisfaction: The role of organizational learning culture. *Interdisciplinary Journal of Contemporary Research in Business, 4*(9), 670–686.

Saito, M. (2012). Managing knowledge for enhancing the participants through organizational learning and leadership. In *Organizational learning and knowledge: Concepts, methodologies, tools and applications* (pp. 1749–1759). Hershey, PA: IGI Global. doi:10.4018/978-1-60960-783-8.ch507

Salim, I., & Sulaiman, M. (2011). Organizational learning, innovation and performance: A study of Malaysian small and medium sized enterprises. *International Journal of Business and Management*, 6(12), 118–126. doi:10.5539/ijbm.v6n12p118

Santos, N. (2014). Organizational learning and Web 2.0 technologies: Improving the planning and organization of a software development process. In M. Cruz-Cunha, F. Moreira, & J. Varajão (Eds.), *Handbook of research on enterprise 2.0: Technological, social, and organizational dimensions* (pp. 512–528). Hershey, PA: IGI Global. doi:10.4018/978-1-4666-4373-4.ch027

Saraf, N., Langdon, C. S., & Gosain, S. (2007). IS application capabilities and relational value in interfirm partnerships. *Information Systems Research*, 18(3), 320–339. doi:10.1287/isre.1070.0133

Schilling, M. A. (2012). *Strategic management of technological innovation*. New York, NY: McGraw–Hill.

Schilling, M. A., & Fang, C. (2014). When hubs forget, lie, and play favorites: Interpersonal network structure, information distortion, and organizational learning. *Strategic Management Journal*, 35(7), 974–994. doi:10.1002/smj.2142

Schlosser, F., Templer, A., & Ghanam, D. (2006). How human resource outsourcing affects organizational learning in the knowledge economy. *Journal of Labor Research*, 27(3), 291–303. doi:10.1007/s12122-006-1024-x

Senge, P. (1990). *The fifth discipline: The art and practice of the learning organization*. New York, NY: Doubleday.

Serinkan, C., Enli, P., Akcit, V., & Kiziloglu, M. (2014). Evaluation of knowledge level of cargo companies about their organizational learning and team management: An empirical research in cargo companies in Turkey. *Procedia: Social and Behavioral Sciences*, 116, 4170–4174. doi:10.1016/j.sbspro.2014.01.911

Sicilia, M. A., & Lytras, M. D. (2005). The semantic learning organization. *The Learning Organization*, 12(5), 402–410. doi:10.1108/09696470510611375

Slater, S. F., & Narver, J. C. (1995). Market orientation and the learning organization. *Journal of Marketing*, 59(3), 63–74. doi:10.2307/1252120

Stoian, M. C., Rialp, A., & Rialp, J. (2011). Export performance under the microscope: A glance through Spanish lenses. *International Business Review*, 20(2), 117–135. doi:10.1016/j.ibusrev.2010.07.002

Subramaniam, M., & Youndt, M. A. (2005). The influence of intellectual capital on the types of innovative capabilities. *Academy of Management Journal*, 48(3), 450–463. doi:10.5465/AMJ.2005.17407911

Sujan, M. (2015). An organisation without a memory: A qualitative study of hospital staff perceptions on reporting and organisational learning for patient safety. *Reliability Engineering & System Safety*, 144, 45–52. doi:10.1016/j.ress.2015.07.011

Sun, P. Y. T., & Anderson, M. H. (2010). An examination of the relationship between absorptive capacity and organizational learning, and a proposed integration. *International Journal of Management Reviews*, *12*(2), 130–150. doi:10.1111/j.1468-2370.2008.00256.x

Sung, S. Y., & Choi, J. N. (2014). Do organizations spend wisely on employees? Effects of training and development investments on learning and innovation in organizations. *Journal of Organizational Behavior*, *35*(3), 393–412. doi:10.1002/job.1897

Taylor, G. S., Templeton, G. F., & Baker, L. T. (2010). Factors influencing the success of organizational learning implementation: A policy facet perspective. *International Journal of Management Reviews*, *12*(4), 353–364. doi:10.1111/j.1468-2370.2009.00268.x

Tippins, M. J., & Sohi, R. S. (2003). IT competency and firm performance: Is organizational learning a missing link? *Strategic Management Journal*, *24*(8), 745–761. doi:10.1002/smj.337

Tohidi, H., Seyedaliakbar, S. M., & Mandegari, M. (2012). Organizational learning measurement and the effect on firm innovation. *Journal of Enterprise Information Management*, *25*(3), 219–245. doi:10.1108/17410391211224390

Tsai, W., & Ghoshal, S. (1998). Social capital and value creation: The role of intrafirm networks. *Academy of Management Journal*, *41*(4), 464–476. doi:10.2307/257085

Tushman, M. L., & Nadler, D. A. (1986). Organizing for innovation. *California Management Review*, *28*(3), 74–92. doi:10.2307/41165203

Uzzi, B. (1997). Social structure and competition in interfirm networks: The paradox of embeddedness. *Administrative Science Quarterly*, *42*(1), 35–67. doi:10.2307/2393808

van Hoof, B. (2014). Organizational learning in cleaner production among Mexican supply networks. *Journal of Cleaner Production*, *64*, 115–124. doi:10.1016/j.jclepro.2013.07.041

van Puijenbroek, T., Poell, R. F., Kroon, B., & Timmerman, V. (2014). The effect of social media use on work-related learning. *Journal of Computer Assisted Learning*, *30*(2), 159–172. doi:10.1111/jcal.12037

Vargas, M. I. R. (2015). Determinant factors for small business to achieve innovation, high performance and competitiveness: Organizational learning and leadership style. *Procedia: Social and Behavioral Sciences*, *169*, 43–52. doi:10.1016/j.sbspro.2015.01.284

Villar, C., Alegre, J., & Pla-Barber, J. (2014). Exploring the role of knowledge management practices on exports: A dynamic capabilities view. *International Business Review*, *23*(1), 38–44. doi:10.1016/j.ibusrev.2013.08.008

Waight, C. L. (2015). Learning during the integration phase of mergers and acquisitions: Perspectives from learning and development professionals. *Performance Improvement Quarterly*, *28*(1), 7–26. doi:10.1002/piq.21184

Wang, C. L. (2008). Entrepreneurial orientation, learning orientation, and firm performance. *Entrepreneurship Theory and Practice*, *32*(4), 635–657. doi:10.1111/j.1540-6520.2008.00246.x

Wang, J. (2012). Organizational learning and technology. In V. Wang (Ed.), *Technology and its impact on educational leadership: Innovation and change* (pp. 217–233). Hershey, PA: IGI Global. doi:10.4018/978-1-4666-0062-1.ch017

Xue, L., Ray, G., & Sambamurthy, V. (2012). Efficiency or innovation: How do industry environments moderate the effects of firms' IT asset portfolios? *Management Information Systems Quarterly*, *36*(2), 509–528.

Yli-Renko, H., Autio, E., & Sapienza, H. J. (2001). Social capital, knowledge acquisition, and knowledge exploitation in young technology-based firms. *Strategic Management Journal*, *22*(6/7), 587–613. doi:10.1002/smj.183

Yu, H., Fang, L., & Ling, W. (2009). An empirical study on the construct and effective mechanism of organizational learning. *Frontiers of Business Research in China*, *3*(2), 242–270. doi:10.1007/s11782-009-0013-3

Yu, Y., Dong, X. Y., Shen, K. N., Khalifa, M., & Hao, J. X. (2013). Strategies, technologies, and organizational learning for developing organizational innovativeness in emerging economies. *Journal of Business Research*, *66*(12), 2507–2514. doi:10.1016/j.jbusres.2013.05.042

Za, S., Spagnoletti, P., & North-Samardzic, A. (2014). Organisational learning as an emerging process: The generative role of digital tools in informal learning practices. *British Journal of Educational Technology*, *45*(6), 1023–1035. doi:10.1111/bjet.12211

Zahra, S. A. (2012). Organizational learning and entrepreneurship in family firms: Exploring the moderating effect of ownership and cohesion. *Small Business Economics*, *38*(1), 51–65. doi:10.1007/s11187-010-9266-7

Zhou, K. Z., Yim, C. K., & Tse, D. K. (2005). The effects of strategic orientations on technology- and market-based breakthrough innovations. *Journal of Marketing*, *69*(2), 42–60. doi:10.1509/jmkg.69.2.42.60756

Zott, C., & Amit, R. (2007). Business model design and the performance of entrepreneurial firms. *Organization Science*, *18*(2), 181–199. doi:10.1287/orsc.1060.0232

## ADDITIONAL READING

Bell, J. E., Bradley, R. V., Fugate, B. S., & Hazen, B. T. (2014). Logistics information system evaluation: Assessing external technology integration and supporting organizational learning. *Journal of Business Logistics*, *35*(4), 338–358. doi:10.1111/jbl.12075

Berends, H., & Antonacopoulou, E. (2014). Time and organizational learning: A review and agenda for future research. *International Journal of Management Reviews*, *16*(4), 437–453. doi:10.1111/ijmr.12029

Berson, Y., Da'as, R., & Waldman, D. A. (2015). How do leaders and their teams bring about organizational learning and outcomes? *Personnel Psychology*, *68*(1), 79–108. doi:10.1111/peps.12071

Boone, S. (2014). Using organizational learning to increase operational and conceptual mental models within professional learning communities. *Journal of Psychological Issues in Organizational Culture*, *5*(3), 85–99. doi:10.1002/jpoc.21152

Borrás, S., & Højlund, S. (2015). Evaluation and policy learning: The learners' perspective. *European Journal of Political Research*, *54*(1), 99–120. doi:10.1111/1475-6765.12076

Brettel, M., & Rottenberger, J. D. (2013). Examining the link between entrepreneurial orientation and learning processes in small and medium-sized enterprises. *Journal of Small Business Management*, *51*(4), 471–490. doi:10.1111/jsbm.12002

Cai, L., Hughes, M., & Yin, M. (2014). The relationship between resource acquisition methods and firm performance in Chinese new ventures: The intermediate effect of learning capability. *Journal of Small Business Management*, *52*(3), 365–389. doi:10.1111/jsbm.12039

Chen, H., Li, Y., & Liu, Y. (2015). Dual capabilities and organizational learning in new product market performance. *Industrial Marketing Management*, *46*, 204–213. doi:10.1016/j.indmarman.2015.02.031

Chiva, R., Ghauri, P., & Alegre, J. (2014). Organizational learning, innovation and internationalization: A complex system model. *British Journal of Management*, *25*(4), 687–705. doi:10.1111/1467-8551.12026

Cho, S. H., Song, J. H., Yun, S. C., & Lee, C. K. (2013). How the organizational learning process mediates the impact of strategic human resource management practices on performance in Korean organizations. *Performance Improvement Quarterly*, *25*(4), 23–42. doi:10.1002/piq.21127

Chronéer, D., & Backlund, F. (2015). A holistic view on learning in project-based organizations. *Project Management Journal*, *46*(3), 61–74. doi:10.1002/pmj.21503

Cinar, F., & Eren, E. (2015). Organizational learning capacity impact on sustainable innovation: The case of public hospitals. *Procedia: Social and Behavioral Sciences*, *181*, 251–260. doi:10.1016/j.sbspro.2015.04.886

Coghlan, D., Shani, A. B., & Roth, J. (2016). Institutionalizing insider action research initiatives in organizations: The role of learning mechanisms. *Systemic Practice and Action Research*, *29*(2), 83–95. doi:10.1007/s11213-015-9358-z

Dieleman, H. (2013). Organizational learning for resilient cities, through realizing eco-cultural innovations. *Journal of Cleaner Production*, *50*, 171–180. doi:10.1016/j.jclepro.2012.11.027

Evans, S. D., & Kivell, N. (2015). The transformation team: An enabling structure for organizational learning in action. *Journal of Community Psychology*, *43*(6), 760–777. doi:10.1002/jcop.21756

Kurland, H., & Hasson-Gilad, D. R. (2015). Organizational learning and extra effort: The mediating effect of job satisfaction. *Teaching and Teacher Education*, *49*, 56–67. doi:10.1016/j.tate.2015.02.010

Lee, J., Zo, H., & Lee, H. (2014). Smart learning adoption in employees and HRD managers. *British Journal of Educational Technology*, *45*(6), 1082–1096. doi:10.1111/bjet.12210

Lim, D. H., Yoon, S. W., & Park, S. (2013). Integrating learning outcome typologies for HRD: Review and current status. *New Horizons in Adult Education and Human Resource Development*, *25*(2), 33–48. doi:10.1002/nha.20015

Marabelli, M., & Newell, S. (2014). Knowing, power and materiality: A critical review and reconceptualization of absorptive capacity. *International Journal of Management Reviews*, *16*(4), 479–499. doi:10.1111/ijmr.12031

Mena, J. A., & Chabowski, B. R. (2015). The role of organizational learning in stakeholder marketing. *Journal of the Academy of Marketing Science*, *43*(4), 429–452. doi:10.1007/s11747-015-0442-9

Nadolska, A., & Barkema, H. G. (2014). Good learners: How top management teams affect the success and frequency of acquisitions. *Strategic Management Journal*, *35*(10), 1483–1507. doi:10.1002/smj.2172

Ravenscroft, A., Schmidt, A., Cook, J., & Bradley, C. (2012). Designing social media for informal learning and knowledge maturing in the digital workplace. *Journal of Computer Assisted Learning*, *28*(3), 235–249. doi:10.1111/j.1365-2729.2012.00485.x

van Rooij, S. W., & Merkebu, J. (2015). Measuring the business impact of employee learning: A view from the professional services sector. *Human Resource Development Quarterly*, *26*(3), 275–297. doi:10.1002/hrdq.21211

Walker, C. (2014). Organizational learning: The role of third party auditors in building compliance and enforcement capability. *International Journal of Auditing*, *18*(3), 213–222. doi:10.1111/ijau.12026

Wei, Z., Yi, Y., & Guo, H. (2014). Organizational learning ambidexterity, strategic flexibility, and new product development. *Journal of Product Innovation Management*, *31*(4), 832–847. doi:10.1111/jpim.12126

Yeo, R. K., & Marquardt, M. J. (2015). (Re) interpreting action, learning, and experience: Integrating action learning and experiential learning for HRD. *Human Resource Development Quarterly*, *26*(1), 81–107. doi:10.1002/hrdq.21199

## KEY TERMS AND DEFINITIONS

**Enterprise Resource Planning:** The accounting-oriented software system used for identifying and planning the resource requirement of an enterprise.

**Information Technology:** The set of tools, processes, and associated equipment employed to collect, process, and present the information.

**Knowledge Management:** The strategies and processes designed to identify, capture, and share an organization's intellectual assets to enhance organizational performance.

**Learning:** The measurable and relatively permanent change in behavior through experience, instruction, and study.

**Learning Organization:** The organization that obtains knowledge in order to survive in the rapidly changing environments.

**Organizational Learning:** The organization-wide continuous process that enhances its collective ability to accept, make sense of, and respond to the internal and external changes.

**Training:** The organized activity aimed at informing instructions to improve the recipient's performance.

**Transformational Leadership:** The style of leadership in which the organizational leader identifies the required change and creates a vision to guide the change through inspiration.

# Chapter 4
# Relationship between Knowledge Management and Innovation

**Andrea Bencsik**
*Széchenyi István University, Hungary*

**Bálint Filep**
*Széchenyi István University, Hungary*

## ABSTRACT

*Successful business operation depends on several factors. Among these factors knowledge management and innovation are extremely important business areas. The aim of this theoretical study is to introduce how these two models work together and how their relationship reinforces the chance for success. Relying on secondary data analysis and literature review, the authors prove that the classical innovation model can be a part of this relationship together with the organizational innovation where the human resource comes to focus. The logic of system building of knowledge management emphasizes that the path leads from the attainment of innovation knowledge to the evaluation of utilization. This study reviews the steps of the two business models and highlights the most important relationships in a new model linking the appropriate phases. The second part of this paper shows the connection between frugal innovation and knowledge management, and their theoretical significance and practical adaptability.*

## INTRODUCTION

In the changing business environment, in terms of adaptability and remaining competitive, development and operation of knowledge management systems have become extremely important factors. They have a significant role in such business processes which seek synergies between data, information processing capability of IT, and creative and innovative capabilities of people (Nonaka et al., 2014).

Knowledge management is not a new phenomenon if it means managing existing knowledge. Partly, it may include some tasks of human resources, or even the exchange of experience between employees. It is a concept and methodology that is applicable in many different fields of business activities.

Nowadays, economies and also societies are being transformed. Values that were previously unknown and considered elusive, come to the front (Olšovská et. al, 2015) which includes organizational knowledge.

DOI: 10.4018/978-1-5225-1642-2.ch004

Therefore, the age of information society leads to knowledge society and knowledge-based economy. Unique knowledge, its development and reuse are the competitive advantages that allow a company to maintain its market position (Davila, 2012).

Companies of the 21ˢᵗ century must take into consideration that their often expensively acquired knowledge should be utilized in time, otherwise it can disappear. This is why continuous innovation is crucial nowadays. It is supported by the fact that, while in 1990 the development of a new car model took 6 years, today it needs only 2 years. Another example could be that the vast majority of Hewlett-Packard´s revenues come from products that did not exist a year ago. Knowledge management and innovation, these two categories that define a company's success, are inseparable.

## THE IMPORTANCE OF KNOWLEDGE

Companies are being challenged by the world market and economy, including the fierce competition caused by globalization, and the rapidly and unpredictably changing external and internal environment. Changes, that often turn up and vary, must be managed and not only experienced (Olšovská et.al, 2015). However, this is impossible without the existence of adequate resources.

Knowledge is individual. It develops during practice and experience, and this process is non-transferable. There is a great need for human resources with excellent skills in the harsh market competition; thanks to their individual competencies, they make companies unique and competitive. Therefore, in order to obtain and maintain human resources with high and/or special skills, it is crucial that the management supports their staff's continuous development, their knowledge transfer, and the update of their ideas and innovation skills. If these criteria are applied to business operations as a whole without any problem, the issues of knowledge sharing can be the management's challenges. This is supported by the development of a knowledge management system which, besides knowledge sharing, requires the implementation of further steps.

### Knowledge Sharing as a Critical Issue

The development of organizational knowledge sharing practice, which is an important part of knowledge management, is a significant challenge for managers. The competitiveness of organizations, and sometimes even their survival, lies in shared knowledge. If this knowledge is not able to flow properly in an organization, and people do not share it with others, then new solutions, ideas and innovations may disappear. Task of the management is to make the employees able and willing to share their knowledge with other colleagues. For the sake of the cause, corporate culture has to be restructured, and atmosphere must be supportive in which employees know that sharing their knowledge will not have any drawbacks, rather it will help to achieve the common goals (Mura et. al, 2016).

Why do not employees share their knowledge?

- With knowledge sharing an employee will become worthless.
- Competition leads to knowledge retention.
- There is no receiver.
- There is no time and energy.
- They do not know what to share.

In addition, many other causes of non-distribution of knowledge, which can be different in national and corporate cultures, exist (Tomka & Bőgel, 2014).

Besides knowledge utilization and sharing information, there is a strong need for information and knowledge that can be linked to innovation. The relationship between these two business models and their significance will be discussed in detail later.

## Knowledge Management and Competitive Corporate

On corporate level the relationship between performance and innovation reinforces the fact that competitiveness is an innovation struggle. Adaptable companies can be successful if they are able to guarantee continuous learning and knowledge preservation and transmission with an appropriate organizational structure (flatter hierarchy, networks) and the tolerance of intercultural elements. Large and multinational companies are in an advantageous situation in comparison with SMEs since they can predominate in the market thanks to their prosperous technical and technological know-how, to financial opportunities. Based on the authors' observations and researches, smaller companies are able to compete with larger ones in the field of knowledge management as a result of their flexibility, family- and trust-oriented culture, and human-oriented behaviour of their employees. Evidence shows that the competition is equalized and the winner is the company that understands the logic of knowledge management systems and moves forward in the process of realization earlier and more professionally.

The main obstacle of the innovation ability of European companies is not the low level of R+D expenditure, but the predominance of workplaces that are unable to ensure a prosperous innovation environment (Arundel & Colecchia, 2006). According to this definition, the background factors that are rooted in the culture determine the success of innovation activity. Many researches focusing on the system building of knowledge management (in theory and in practice) came to the same conclusion that the culture has a determining importance. The relationship of these thoughts will be explained in this section.

The presentation of this logic starts with the pyramid of competitive corporation, Figure 1 shows.

*Figure 1. Pyramid of a competitive corporate*
*(Lengyel, 2004)*

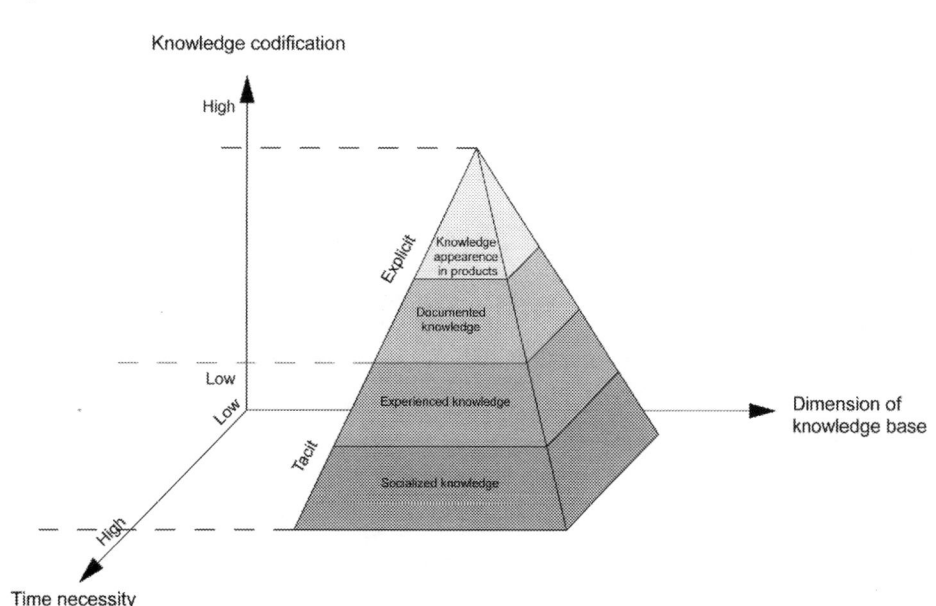

The interpretation of each category is discussed in the following section.

The base is the *socialized knowledge* that means the conformance of corporate culture. Not all corporate culture is able to support the success of a company. The most important parameters will be discussed in more details later in this study.

*Experimental knowledge* is tacit knowledge and inner processes, experts' competences, informal coordination belong to this category. All these categories are intangible, and appropriate application requires personal participation and experiments.

*Documented knowledge* is explicit and is made up of easily and well-documented knowledge elements, so it is easily accessible to anyone further on (e.g. project documentations, handbooks, researches and consumer expectations, etc.).

*Knowledge represented in the product* is among the objectives of companies and means technology, products, service packages, and innovation that can be fully capitalized (Boutellier et al., 2009).

The overview of this pyramid proves that culture is the common base which is a critical factor in case of innovation and knowledge management. Culture ensures the creation of further decisions about utilization of knowledge (experimental and documented) for the management. This leads to the final version of innovative ideas (knowledge represented in the product) that could not be produced without the transmission of knowledge, cooperative thinking, continuous development, learning, and teamwork.

## RELATIONSHIP BETWEEN INNOVATION AND KNOWLEDGE MANAGEMENT

### Innovation

The definition and organizational importance of innovation became popular as a result of J. A. Schumpeter's work (1980). The definition was developed over the past few years and today it is at the focus of attention. Among the many available definitions, the authors have devised one which refers to the relationship with the above-mentioned knowledge management system.

Innovation is equal to new technology, new management styles, new markets, new raw materials, new products, a new production management, and, instead of the foregoing human–machine relationship, the interfering human–human relationship and the evaluation of feedback results. An innovation system is a continuous and significant development and a regulated system in which the 'system' together with its limitations and estimated efficiency is able to receive, absorb, and realize innovation (Bucsy, 1976).

According to Peter Drucker, innovation is …a purposeful and focused effort to change the economic or social opportunities of a business. (Drucker, 2003).

The concept of innovation is linked to the concept of value chain management, according to Michael Porter. The main point of his model is that a company can meet consumers' needs effectively if the main activities are supported by activities that help in the production process. Innovation is such a supporting activity (Porter, 1980).

Innovation should be realized via cooperation. The most significant elements of economic corporations' effective function and the spread of innovation are the education of population, the accumulated professional knowledge, and experience. The principal sectors of our days (informatics, biotechnology, automation) call attention to the change of values occurring in the global economy. Currently, the real value is an intellectual product rather than raw materials and human physical work (Filep, 2008).

However, everyday business practice focuses on tangible solutions such as machines, equipment, processes, methods, and patent design connected to other products when companies think about innovation. The definition clearly states the importance of innovative solutions supporting the development of business operation and preferring human resource and its relationship system. This is a precondition of the emergence of product and service development. The authors think similarly about knowledge management based on the review of system building.

Innovation is based on people's knowledge, ideas, and thoughts. Similarly, knowledge management is based on the systematization of knowledge. Both areas have the same starting point that is human resource and his/her knowledge. In addition to human capital, another important trend appears in management, and this is the innovative corporate culture, the concept of an innovative company (Bencsik, 2015; George et al., 2014).

## Basic Models of Innovation

In the development of innovation models five generations can be distinguished. Among these models, the authors highlight the one which has become popular in recent years since system approach, complexity, and the relationship with a knowledge management system can be shown.

The most developed model of innovation is shown in Figure 2.

In the fifth generation model of innovation the new element consists in informatics tools which play an important role in the quality and the speed of planning. The aspects of production are taken into consideration during the process of planning to reduce significant expenses. The model is complex and knowledge-driven, which includes the strategic business management in a system-oriented approach. Strategic partner relationships are extremely important, especially the relationship with suppliers.

*Figure 2. The fifth generation model of innovation*
*(Rothwell, 1994)*

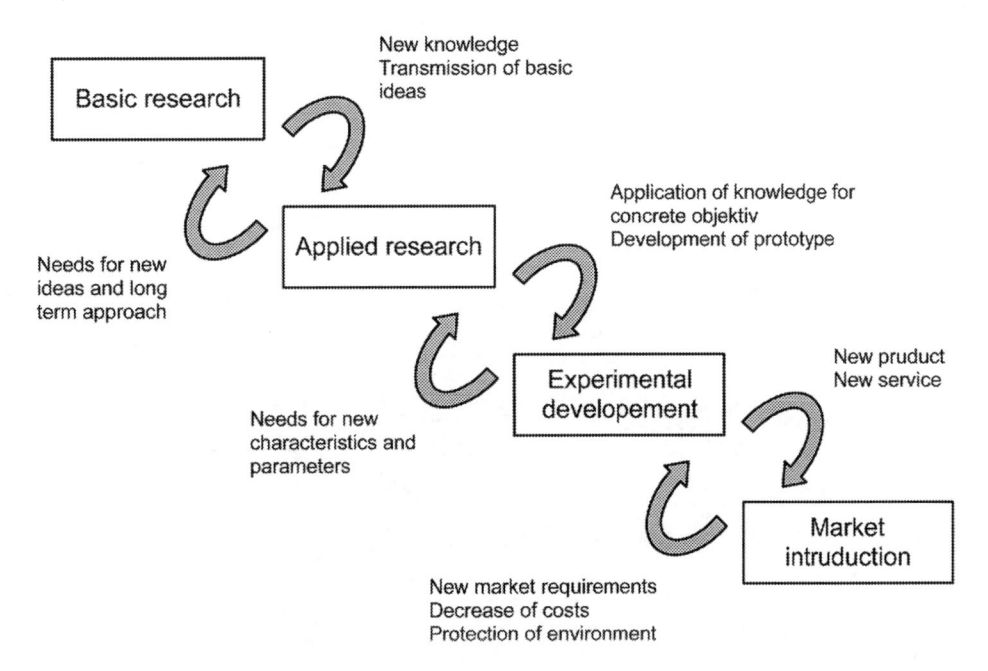

Companies regularly employ consultative and analysing services, have a close relationship with end-consumers, take attention of modelling R+D simulation, build horizontal relationships in researches and create cooperation with development groups, and focus on quality (Bucsy, 1976).

## Knowledge Management

The authors do not want to discuss the basic definition of knowledge management and its connections with the different business fields. In order to understand these connections, the authors provide a definition as a reminder, which is a clear evidence for the relationship of knowledge management with innovation.

The knowledge management is a business model that uses the knowledge as corporate property to achieve competitive advantage. It is a management tool that supports identifying, evaluating, utilizing, creating, increasing, protecting, transmitting, and applying intellectual capital of the company in an integrated way (Davenport & Prusak, 2001).

## A Knowledge Management System Model

Probst's and his fellow workers´ model is one of the most famous. It explains the stages of the operation of the business system in eight steps (Probst et al., 2006). The logic is shown in Figure 3.

*Figure 3. Probst´s model*
*(Probst et al., 2006)*

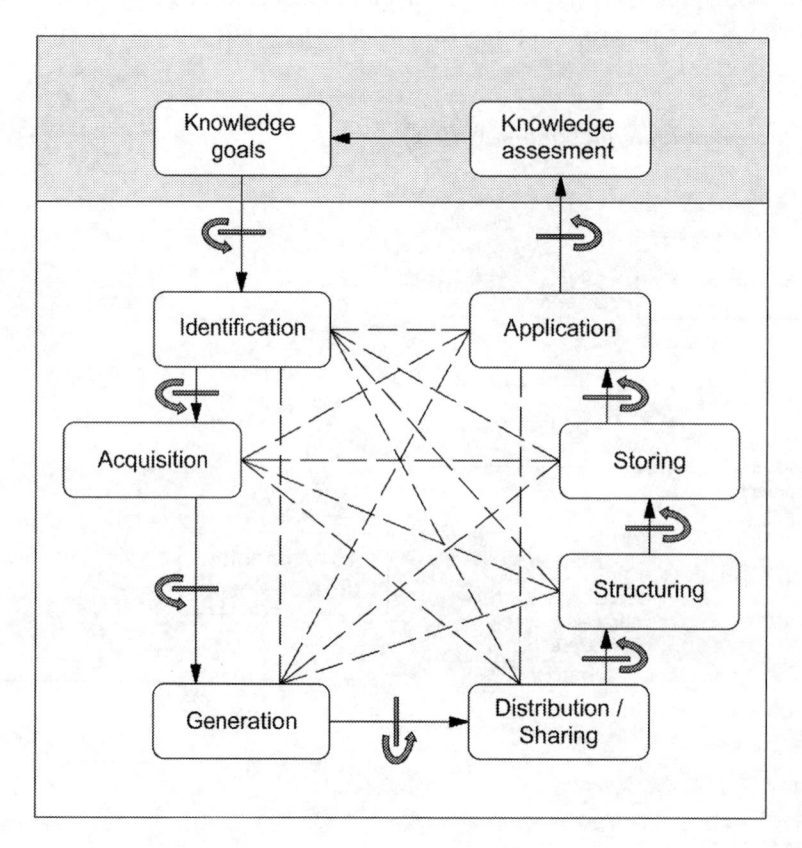

The common elements (the fifth generation model of innovation and the logic of Probst's model) introduced in the definitions can be identified in visual models, too, in the following way:

- **Strategic Thinking:** System approach.
- **Human–Human Relationship:** Network building.
- **Intellectual Skills:** Development.
- **Knowledge Transmission:** Knowledge network – feedback.

As a result of the above-mentioned ideas, the relationship between the steps of knowledge management and innovation is summarized in Table 1.

The connection between the steps of the models can be seen in Figure 4.

In order to highlight the relationship, the researchers used the logic of the basic innovation model (for the simpler perspicuity and demonstration) since, with the help of this model, those imperfections that the modern models aimed at eliminating can be improved by the feedback of knowledge management elements. In the case of the most developed innovation model, the same relationships are to be identified.

In the case of organizational innovation, when the innovation effort is aimed at the creation of a new business model, the contents of 'prototype and product development' boxes should be replaced by such activities as human resource development and business model development.

## Organizational Characteristics Supporting Cooperation between Innovation and KM

### Why is Organizational Culture Important?

Organizational culture is largely influenced by the employees' behaviour, their attitude to work, the management, colleagues, values, innovation, and participation in innovation activities (Mura & Rózsa, 2013). Culture may increase or freeze creativity, collaboration, knowledge sharing, namely the innovation

*Table 1. The relationship between the steps of knowledge management and innovation*

| The Steps of Knowledge Management System | The Steps of Innovation Process |
|---|---|
| Culture of learning organization. | Human related culture, ensuring absorption. |
| Knowledge goals. | Research focus. |
| Knowledge identification. | Labour force assigning to tasks. |
| Knowledge acquisition. | Collecting information. |
| Knowledge generation. | Finding of innovative ideas. |
| Knowledge sharing. | Development of innovative ideas. |
| External knowledge transfer. | Network building. |
| Knowledge utilization. | Development of prototype. |
| Knowledge preservation. | Usage of knowing how, invention, intellectual products. |
| Knowledge assessment. | Market feedback. |
| New circle…. | |

*Figure 4. Relationship of innovation and knowledge management models*
*(authors' construction)*

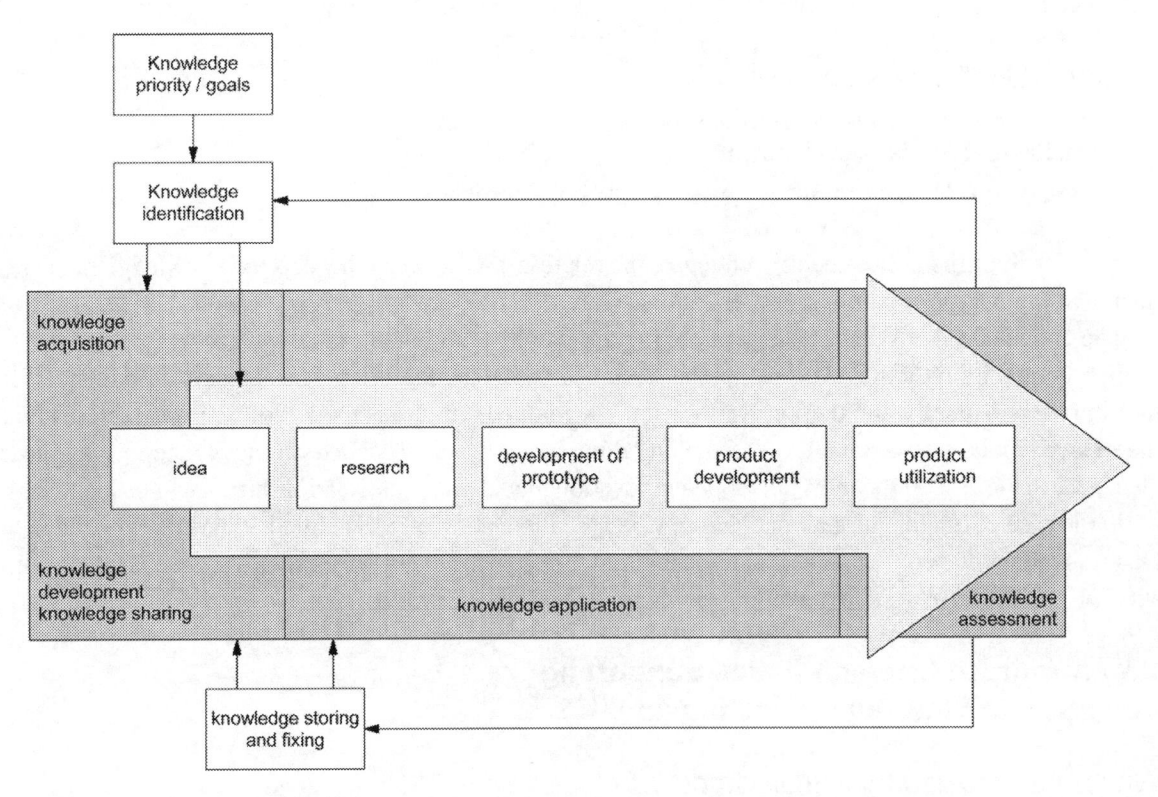

process. According to Stephen Shapiro (2011), innovation culture is the primary source of competitive advantage of businesses and it pays off. (....) If employees adopt this approach, innovation becomes part of their lives. This ensures that all human capital is used with appropriate effort in order to produce the values from the company.

## Organizational Characteristics that Support Innovation

Stephen Shapiro (2011) collected the most important managerial tasks in order to achieve innovation culture, and the results of innovation are based on the success of their implementation. Essential characteristics of the innovative organizational culture are:

- Creating a shared vision and to achieve a common goal.
- Development of internal communication.
- Involving employees in important decisions and plans.
- Job enlargement.
- Supportive managerial style.
- Continuous improvement as a common organizational value.
- Promoting teamwork.
- Knowledge sharing (Shapiro, 2011).

The characteristics of an innovation-friendly organizational culture are very similar to the expectations of learning organizational culture that enable the functioning of the system of knowledge management.

## Learning Organization that Supports Knowledge Management System Building

Learning organizations are responsible for the quick and flexible operation of a knowledge management system. The main characteristics of these organizations are: a flexible organizational structure, shared vision, team learning, collective organizational culture, self-management ability, and innovation ability (Senge, 1998). In a learning organization most of the employees are highly skilled and educated, their main task is to transform information into knowledge, and in their work their competencies are used at the highest level (e.g. Microsoft and Google). Therefore, these companies also acknowledge the principle of "shared knowledge is power." Their resources will not run out because they share their knowledge (Nonaka et al., 2014; Sveiby, 2001).

Human resources are the main resource of learning organizations, and their cooperation is the key to success. Proper communication is essential, and cooperation with partners is particularly important. If an organization accepts these principles, it can become a knowledge-based organization and it can be able to convert its employees' knowledge into a competitive advantage. Knowledge management and innovation, based on the organizational culture, can be connected (Lyles, 2014).

This culture is different in the different countries, in the USA, in the EU, and in Asia. The bases of the European Union's purpose, which is the sustainable economic growth, are research & development, innovation, wide usage of information and communication technology, the growth of competitiveness, and building on an education-based economy. This objective, linked to the philosophy of lifelong learning, stresses the coordinated development of instruction and education, keeping in view the importance of the evolving conditions of science, research & development, innovation and IT human resources. As a result, in the EU universities are in the main focus, they are learning organizations, and they cooperate with industries because the main goal is the good degree, innovation with students and professors. Building a knowledge management system at universities is crucial in the future of the EU (Filep, 2008).

A wide range of innovative solutions are known in international practice, but in this paper authors present an alternative that is almost unknown in Hungary and it provides a corporate vision.

## Common Elements and Connections of Supporting Cultures

Stephen Shapiro (2011) collected the main management tasks to achieve innovation culture and other expectations that characterize culture. Both the organizational characteristics and the elements of culture are similar to the characteristics of the learning company (Senge, 1998). This fact is reinforced by Ross's (2009) primary research results.

He found that 38% of the questioned employees answered that culture influences the success of innovation. Beyond this category, management styles and characteristics were also mentioned as an important factor [the research used the questions developed by Golman (2003)].

The Hay Group (2008) collected six characteristics of a culture that cause an excellent innovation. Relying on the answers of employees, these characteristics are:

- Clear objectives.
- Flexibility.

- Responsibility – self-determination.
- Teamwork.
- Clear definition of expectations.
- Acknowledgement.

The authors summarize the main characteristics of learning organization based on Senge's (1998) and Garvin's (1993) researches in Table 2.

Garvin (1993) put emphasis on the creation of knowledge, while Senge (1998) and his co-authors focus on individual and collective development, learning and predominance of individual objectives. Even though the wording of the two models is different, the same expectations are highlighted from the substantive contents. Culture supporting knowledge management is a condition of developing a knowledge management system and requires the rethinking of companies' strategic objectives.

Table 3 summarizes and compares all the preconditions that were defined by the above-mentioned researchers and that are related to culture supporting knowledge management and culture supporting innovation.

Table 3 proves that culture is a precondition and the operation of innovation and knowledge management systems are inseparable. Another precondition of success resulting from their connection is a good strategy. This enables companies to treat innovation and knowledge management either as separate business models or as strategic objectives defined as common expectation. Learning companies can choose among six strategies on the basis of their mechanism of operation (King, 2001).

An analysis of the opportunities highlights that the first four strategies prepare the operation of a knowledge management system, the fifth one prefers the knowledge management strategy, and the last one completes innovation (Thakor, 2013):

- Developing the infrastructure of information system.
- Management of know-how.
- Stimulus of private learning.
- Strategy of total organizational learning.

*Table 2. Parameters supporting the culture of knowledge management system building*

| Culture is Supporting KM (Garvin) | Characteristics of Learning Organization | Culture is Supporting KM (Senge) |
|---|---|---|
| | Change | Common Vision |
| Systematic problem solving, learning from private experiences. | Decision making based on participation. | Principle of personal management. |
| Experiment. | Rotation, flexibility. | System thinking or system approach, personal management. |
| | A culture based on support and trust. | |
| | Continuous development, training, innovation. | |
| Learning from others' experiences. | Flat hierarchy. | Collective learning, system approach. |
| Dissemination of knowledge. | Adaptability, external–internal openness. | Mental samples, collective learning, system approach. |

*Table 3. Comparison of corporate culture supporting innovation and KM*

| Culture is Supporting KM (Garvin) | Culture is Supporting Innovation (Shapiro) – Characteristics Supporting Learning Organization | Culture is Supporting KM (Senge) |
|---|---|---|
| | **Creation of Shared Vision and Attainment of Common Objectives - Change** | **Common Vision** |
| Systematic problem solving, learning from private experiences. | Participation of employees in important .decisions and plans - Decision making based on participation. | Principle of personal management. |
| Experiment. | Extension of occupation - Rotation, flexibility. | System thinking or system approach, personal management. |
| | Change of management style from command to supporting style - Culture based on support and trust. | |
| | Continuous development as common corporate value - Continuous development, training, innovation. | |
| Learning from others' experiences. | Supporting team work - Flat hierarchy. | Collective learning, system approach. |
| | Development of internal communication. | |
| Dissemination of knowledge. | Transmission of knowledge - Adaptability, external – internal openness. | Mental samples, collective learning, system approach. |

- Management based on knowledge (knowledge management).
- Innovation.

The main characteristics of these strategies are summarized in Table 4.

## New Factors of Success, Possible Solutions

The aim of knowledge management is to capture individual and organizational knowledge and use them to create value for the company. An important element of knowledge management is sufficient to suggest tools to fulfil the gap between existing knowledge and necessary knowledge. The authors know that companies can go outside their range accidentally in the process of knowledge management (attainment, development, transmission, and utilization of knowledge) and innovation. Nowadays this is not only an opportunity, but the main condition of success. Getting new solutions has become simpler, faster, and cheaper which influences the companies' market position (Tiwari & Herstatt, 2012a). The introduced relationships are completed with such external opportunities that mean new innovative solutions, and attainment and transmission of knowledge at the same time. The latest international examples are notable evidences for such successes as open innovation, crowdsourcing or inverse/barefooted/frugal innovation. The external knowledge attainment motivates companies to find faster and cheaper innovation solutions (Rylková, 2013).

Nowadays, the number of initiatives and endeavours coming from the marriage of open innovation and knowledge management has been increasing (interesting experiments are to be found in Hungary, too. For example, the open innovation project of accredited clusters).

The relationship between the new opportunities and knowledge management model that serves the objective of attaining and transmitting of knowledge can be seen in Figure 5, where the previously in-

*Table 4. Strategies of learning organizations*

| | Infrastruc-ture of Information System | Intellectual Property | Individual Learning | Total Organizational Knowledge | Knowledge Management | Innovation |
|---|---|---|---|---|---|---|
| **Principle** | Help of management. | Company's assets. | Improving the standard. | Preparation for future changes. | Efficiency of collective knowledge. | Development of creativity. |
| **Focus of intention** | Data, information. | Marketable intellectual assets. | More valuable human capital. | Social capital. | Improvement of competences. | New products and procedures. |
| **Objective** | Maintenance of managerial decisions. | Profitability. | Higher level of human capital. | Collective perfection. | Extension and transmission of competences. | Profit from the new ideas. |
| **Methods** | Attainment, storage, application and development of data and information. | Selling licenses. | Different trainings. | Team work, development of organization and quality. | Dissemination of the best methods. | Brain-storming. |
| **Measurement of efficiency** | Spread of information application. | Extra profit. | Advance-ment of participants. | Decrease of cycles and costs, improving the quality. | Improvement in the quality of decisions. | Extra profit from the new products. |
| **Type of organizational culture** | High tech computing. | The ability of making profit. | Thirst for knowledge. | Preparation for changes. | Universal tendency to transmit knowledge. | Environment stimulating creativity. |

(Rylková, 2013)

troduced innovation–knowledge management models are completed with the relationships outside the company. These new opportunities mean brand new solutions and drive creativity that often stays in the background (Hámosi & Szabó, 2012).

The authors integrated the two models, where the connections with the performing steps are shown, and such methods and opportunities of utilization that contribute to the success of both models (Figure 5).

After a brief presentation of the relationship between innovation and knowledge management system, this paper reveals how to exploit the opportunities in corporate life as a result of a combination of knowledge management and frugal innovation, and how to implement the two factors which determine the success of a company effectively.

## Symbiosis of Innovation and Knowledge Management System

Common elements of an innovation process and knowledge management system based on the definitions and the models (see the 5th generation innovation model and the features of Probst et al. (2006) logic) are described in the Table 1.

It is clear that these two factors of success work in close interaction with creative days of corporate life. However, according to the classical concept of innovation and thinking, research and development, innovative solutions do not mean reality for many organizations, as financial difficulties often make the realization of new ideas difficult (Govindarajan & Trimble, 2012).

*Figure 5. Completed model of innovation and knowledge management system*
*(authors' construction)*

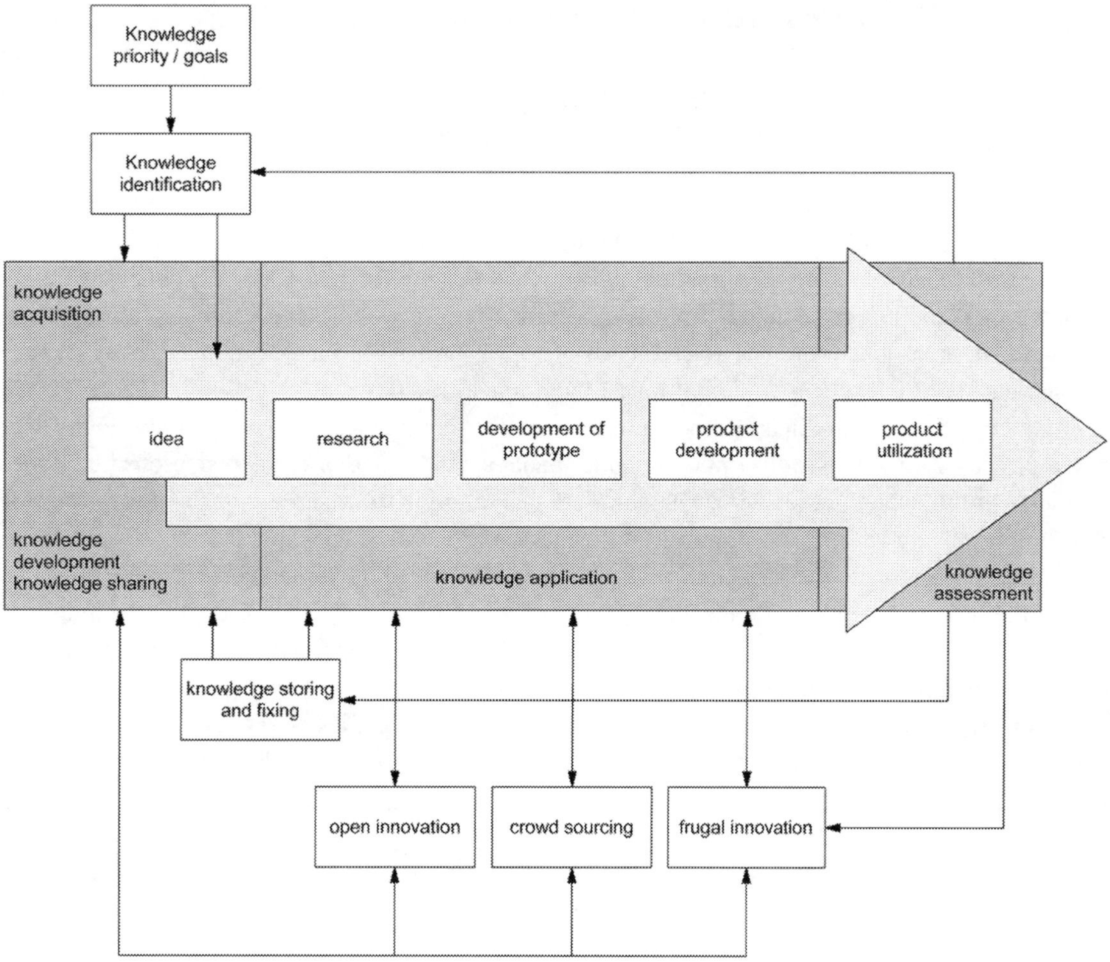

The following section illustrates an opposed way of thinking about innovation which puts innovation in a new light.

## FRUGAL INNOVATION

Cost-effective management, sustainable development, and reduction of the negative effects of globalization are the most serious challenges that businesses have to face nowadays. Companies do everything to match successful operation with sustainable growth. Recently, in the area of innovation a new trend, which has helped several large companies in the eastern world to become successful, has emerged. This new area of innovation, that is a completely different approach, is frugal (thrifty) innovation. The concept is less known in our country; foreign experts use several different names as well (green, Asian or jugaad innovation) (Agarwal-Brem, 2012; Balkrishna, 2013; Basu et al, 2013; Hartly, 2014).

Frugal innovation is the implementation of a new business strategy that enables companies to create much more business and social values while saving resources. The world's leading factories, like Renault, Siemens, and Unilever, use this type of innovation strategy (Eagar et al., 2011).

Frugal innovation and strategy originate from India, where businesses had low budget from the very beginning. It could be said that this new kind of approach was founded by necessity, and this approach helped India to become a dominant player in the global market (Tiwari & Herstatt, 2012c).

A slogan which characterizes this innovative strategy could be 'more from less'. It allows to manufacture products that are both qualitative and yet affordable. Frugal innovation is not only a new strategy. It is a brand-new and flexible way of thinking, by which companies are aware of the limitations of resources; they are able to grow sustainably and continuously though. It is an excellent strategy in developing markets such as India, Africa, China, and Brazil. Nevertheless, it can be applied very well in crisis-ridden areas where there is a need for affordable quality (Radjou & Prabhu, 2013). Frugal innovation treats poor markets as an opportunity rather than as aid targets.

This strategy has been applied by more and more western companies, because cost-conscious operation is a priority for them as well. Environmental management is one of the expectations of ´modern´ consumers, and they are looking for such solutions. Recycling is flourishing. Frugal innovation offers such solutions during product development of businesses (Pansera & Richard, 2014).

Businesses operating in western countries were the world's leading companies, because they always launched the newest, the most expensive, and the best quality products. The process was complicated and expensive. Over time, growth began to slow down more and more, and the latest developments did not result in breakthroughs either.

In contrast, in underdeveloped and developing countries, companies began their operations in the simplest possible way; they always wanted to meet the current consumer needs. This strategy is applied in India ('jugaad'), Brazil ('gambiarra'), China ('Zizhu Chuangxin'), and Kenya (called 'JuA kali'). English counterpart of the strategy could be 'do it and fix it'; eventually, it was named frugal (Bhatti, 2012).

Large western companies began to use Tata Motors' strategy. Tata Motors is one of India's largest companies. It produces 'stripped' products, they offer their products in small packages and they develop newer and newer solutions (Gardiner, 2013).

The role of frugal innovation is the creation of cheaper, but qualitative products, including services as well. Low cost does not mean cheap technology; it often requires the latest technologies and knowledge as well.

Precise understanding of the concept of frugal innovation is important because it may be identified as cheap and poor quality products. Successful frugal innovation does not only mean cheaper products. (Singh et al., 2012). The essence of the new approach is presented below.

## Frugal Innovation: 'Jugaad' Way of Thinking

It does not only mean that with fewer resources we add more value to our customers. This solution means a new business strategy and an entirely new way of thinking. Basically, it is difficult for companies to develop and implement a new strategy, but in this case even employees have to understand and accept the idea since they all must work together to achieve their goals. This can only be achieved if everyone is involved in the creation and implementation of the strategy. The term jugaad comes from India, and its uniform meaning has not developed yet. Experts characterize it with three words: modest, flexible, and receptive (Radjou et al., 2012).

Need for continuous innovation is a major challenge for companies worldwide. In many cases, cost-effectiveness limits traditional innovation, since research and development is an expensive process (time, infrastructure, human resources, capital, etc.). A lot of money has to be spent on research; since more money is invested in it, more inventions can be achieved.

However, capital investment did not recover at the same rate as it was expected by western companies (especially in electronics, computer science, health care, and automotive industries, which are really 'innovation-demanding' industries). It points to the fact that money does not solve all problems, and is unable to offer solutions for every task (Banerjee, 2013).

Based on the above, a new trend is being emerged in R&D and innovation. Innovation process has to be organized frugally, flexibly, and receptively. It should have an 'out of the box' thinking. In recent years, western countries have started to observe the efforts in India, Brazil, and China, which, despite being flexible and frugal, resulted in sensational innovations in the emerging markets (Heeks et al., 2014).

They discovered that behind frugal innovation there is an entrepreneurial spirit that can be observed in Argentina, Costa Rica, Kenya, Mexico, the Philippines, in the above-mentioned and other developing countries (Gomes, 2013). ´Jugaad´ entrepreneurs are flexible, frugal, adaptable, receptive, empathic, and passionate. Frugal thinking and innovation do not offer development opportunities only to the emerging markets, but also to those western economies that are struggling with recession and budget cuts (Santander, 2013). Several books have been published about the frugal innovation which is flourishing in the emerging markets (Govindarajan & Trimble, 2012; Radjou et al., 2012). According to the authors, 'jugaad' means clever improvisation. Studies and interviews of Navi Radjou are extremely popular (Radjou, 2014). He has become a real expert in this field. Together with the co-authors of his book (Radjou et al., 2012) he writes about western companies which are able to introduce frugal innovation in their own organizational structure and culture. This trend is likely to accelerate in the future (Schumpeter, 2012).

In the next part some solutions and ideas will be presented that have already been implemented and used in practice, and which began to "conquer the world" and fundamentally questioned the previous innovation trends.

## Frugal Innovation in Practice

´Frugal´ ideas spread from east to west. Companies with limited resources and budget have few opportunities for development.

Tata Motors developed one of the world's cheapest car in 2009, Tata Nano, which had become a symbol even before the first item was finished. The Tata Group-India's best-known company–named this product as an 'incarnate revolution'. This product was the foretaste of frugal innovation which, with its price of $2,000, made new car purchases available in India and China. According to Schumpeter, Tata Nano did not change the world, but frugal innovation will do (Schumpeter, 2012).

General Electric invented an ECG (electrocardiographs) machine that is affordable and simple. They ship not only to India and China but to Europe and America as well. It is portable and thus it can be used anywhere. Walmart created its 'small mart stores' in Argentina, Brazil, and Mexico to be able to compete (Tiwari & Herstatt, 2012b).

The Indian Mahindra & Mahindra provides small tractors to American hobby farmers. Vivian Fonseca contributed to the development of an SMS system, which sends a message to poor and elderly diabetic patients to assist them in controlling their disease (Mandal, 2014; Radjou et al., 2012). Jane Chen-the

CEO of Embrace-sells low-cost infant warmer for premature and low birth-weight babies in India and some emerging markets (Routson, 2011).

## Struggling by Savings

It is a general concern in western countries that this strategy destroys the markets based on the existing expensive technology. Why would someone buy a $10,000 product if the same company sells a little simpler machine for $1,000? According to some experts, this attitude is too pessimistic.

The world does not change completely. There will always be a group of customers who search for high-tech, luxury or unique products.

Information about the new business strategy started to spread around the world in the first months of 2013. Using the process, companies will be able to cut costs and other 'unnecessary' procedures. Frugal innovation builds upon the fact that limited resources involve a potential for growth (Zeschky et al., 2014).

Eco-conscious experts call it 'green innovation'. Unilever, which produces health and welfare products, applies this strategy. Paul Polman, the CEO of Unilever, recognized that by 2030 two planets would be needed if we continue the current pace of consumption to serve our resource requirements. He aims to double the company´s revenue by 2020, while environmental pollution is reduced by 50% (Radjou & Prabhu, 2013).

The company´s frugal innovation developments were small packaged soap and shampoo products developed for cost-conscious customers.

Western companies need to change their mentality to Jugaad thinking in order to have the strategy successful. This includes the development of creative thinking and innovative ideas, which is the fastest solution to the problems. The CEO of Nissan-Renault, Carlos Ghosn, said that: 'In the west, if we run into major problems and resources are few, we usually give it up (too) easily. The main point of Jugaad is to never give up!' (Chan, 2013).

Three key elements of frugal innovation are affordability, understanding customer needs, and supply chain makeover.

In the east price is a very important factor in customer decision making in contrast to western countries. The new type of thinking requires a change in the supply chain, as processes have to be adapted to new arrangements. Following a few steps is not enough. Operation has to be considered and should be organized flexibly in order to respond to various needs. Companies focusing on these three areas can be successful in emerging markets (Mukerjee, 2012).

## Jagaad Thinking in Hungarian Environment

The following case study is an example of a real domestic company which can attract attention of executives with a similar way of thinking. Presenting a potential partner should be the starting point.

## Mahindra and Mahindra Group, as a Potential Partner

Mahindra & Mahindra was set up as a steel trading company in 1945 in India. It joined automotive industry in 1947. It expanded into manufacturing and selling its iconic vehicle, Willys Jeep. It was divided into several branches in order to meet customer needs. The company follows a unique business model, so called entrepreneurial independence. There are already more than 180,000 employees, and it operates nearly in 100 countries. It operates in 18 key industries including automotive and farming industries. Today, it is the world's largest tractor manufacturer due to a significant increase in sales volumes. The company structure allows each business unit to develop its own vision and at the same time to take advantage of the potential impact of group synergies. Due to diversity, the company is able to maximally satisfy customers' wide range of needs. Mahindra & Mahindra has an alternative way of thinking, which means that problems are solved in a completely new approach (using less resources and entering into such markets that have seemed inaccessible so far).

Mahindra defines itself as a business with a conscience. The company tries to serve and positively influence people and community. Production processes are becoming 'greener', and M&M tries to act as a good employer (Kamp, 2012).

Their main motivation is to offer the very best to their customers every day. Mahindra´s mission is to replace traditional way of thinking with innovative attitude, and using all their resources. Their aim is to change the lives of communities around the world. Their products and services improve their customers´ standard of living, and their serious business behaviour positively affects the lives of communities (employment, education). As a sustainable enterprise, they use green technology, and their awareness appears also in their products, services, and production processes.

Commitment to sustainability is based on (social, economic and environmental) core competencies. Customers´ demands have priority; in this way they can produce creative solutions. Respect applies equally to everyone. Appreciation to employees and partners is just as important as to customers. Quality and proficiency make it possible to produce products and services that could mean a solution in emerging markets. Social responsibility is clearly apparent in the company's mission and corporate culture, and it is seen as the main competence. Their core values are in accordance with their objectives and vision, which is exemplary for all business organizations (Mahindra & Mahindra Group, 2014).

Mahindra has been present in the Northern American market with selling tractors since 1994. In less than two decades, the company has become one of the top three tractor manufacturing companies in the United States. One of its main signals was when in 2013 tractor sales in the region increased by almost 40%. The secret of their success is mainly their excellent leadership and strategy, as well as their mentality. Their aim is–still with frugal solutions-to produce products that are valuable and qualitative. Cheapness is not equal to poor quality, and frugal solutions are not extreme cuts. The company is very proud of its success in 2013, but they do not lean back, they constantly think about new solutions to be successful in the future as well (Mahindra Group USA, 2014).

The presentation of Mahindra & Mahindra emphasizes that the company has a long history with great experience. With its value and customer focus, frugal way of thinking, and innovative approach, it could become one of the leading organizations of the world in nearly 70 years. Its presence is significant both in the automotive and agricultural sectors. Demand for its products and services is growing.

## Dropping Orders and Their Solutions

The current problem of the examined Hungarian company (with automotive industry-related activities) – the number of continuously dropping orders, a shrinking customer base – urges the involvement of a potential new partner and the possibility of entering the eastern markets. Traditions are important at this company. They build on the past and their strategy is based on that. Currently, they have partners also in the eastern region, but their main customer base is to be found in Europe and in the west. With their products they are the first and second round suppliers in the market. Both economic events and the tightening of legal requirements in recent years have resulted in decreasing operating profits. There have been several attempts to reverse the process, unfortunately with no success. The currently expected main result might have similar results as in the previous year.

However, the management is open and willing to change and find new opportunities. This strategy corresponds to building new partnerships with companies such as the above described Mahindra group. The main goal of this Hungarian company has always been the production of high value-added products. This approach has to be continued also in this new strategy. The company's management has to be excellent as well, because good leadership is the basis for success. One of the most important steps is to focus on the stakeholders, as in eastern cultures people and knowledge are the most valuable resources. At this point frugal thinking meets again the expectations of knowledge management.

Frugal way of thinking is based on simplicity. This innovative approach teaches employees to listen to their instincts, rely on their knowledge and skills, which are also important features of the eastern culture. Common use of knowledge can create a solution-oriented environment in which more new ideas, innovative solutions are to be achieved. Blue-collar workers are the company's real engines, because production would not work without them. It is important that they should also understand the essence of the new strategy, and adopt the company's vision and goals. Then business development may begin. Finally, a value and quality focused operation may develop, based on trust and respect, and in accordance with the expectations of the earlier mentioned knowledge and innovation culture.

This is a long process with person-centred thinking, because, if the change does not start with the basics, the strategy will not be successful. Lean organization, as a rational, simplified, and minimalist approach to doing business, combined with a frugal way of thinking and a culture which prefers knowledge sharing, can work wonders.

Figure 6 shows a viable business model which is meant to reverse the current downward operation by applying a frugal way of thinking. Joining a business organization can be a possible way. However, search for partners and further successful cooperation depend on a number of other conditions.

## CONCLUSION

The creation, utilization, development, and transmission of knowledge are basic elements of companies and the whole economy. The theoretical and the practical approach of innovation and innovation processes have changed significantly in the last few years (this is proved by the third edition of Oslo Handbook, which was published in 2005 with the cooperation of experts from 30 countries). New approaches, broader definitions, mutual relationships with other organizational processes are really important factors. No wonder if the successful development of knowledge management and cultural elements supporting operation emerge in connection with innovation. Access to open information in the process of innovation means the attainment and transmission of knowledge. Innovative cooperation requires cooperation with other companies and organizations, and goes hand in hand with the acquisition of knowledge.

Well-qualified, flexible graduates with language knowledge are the most important factor to enterprises. Infrastructure and money are not the only ones. Innovations and the most famous spinoff companies are born in the USA, but in the globalised word all is changing from day to day (Filep, 2008).

The authors have highlighted that the development of knowledge management and the success of innovation link up profoundly. A receptive corporate culture enables the realization of these two areas at

*Figure 6. A new business model*
(authors' construction)

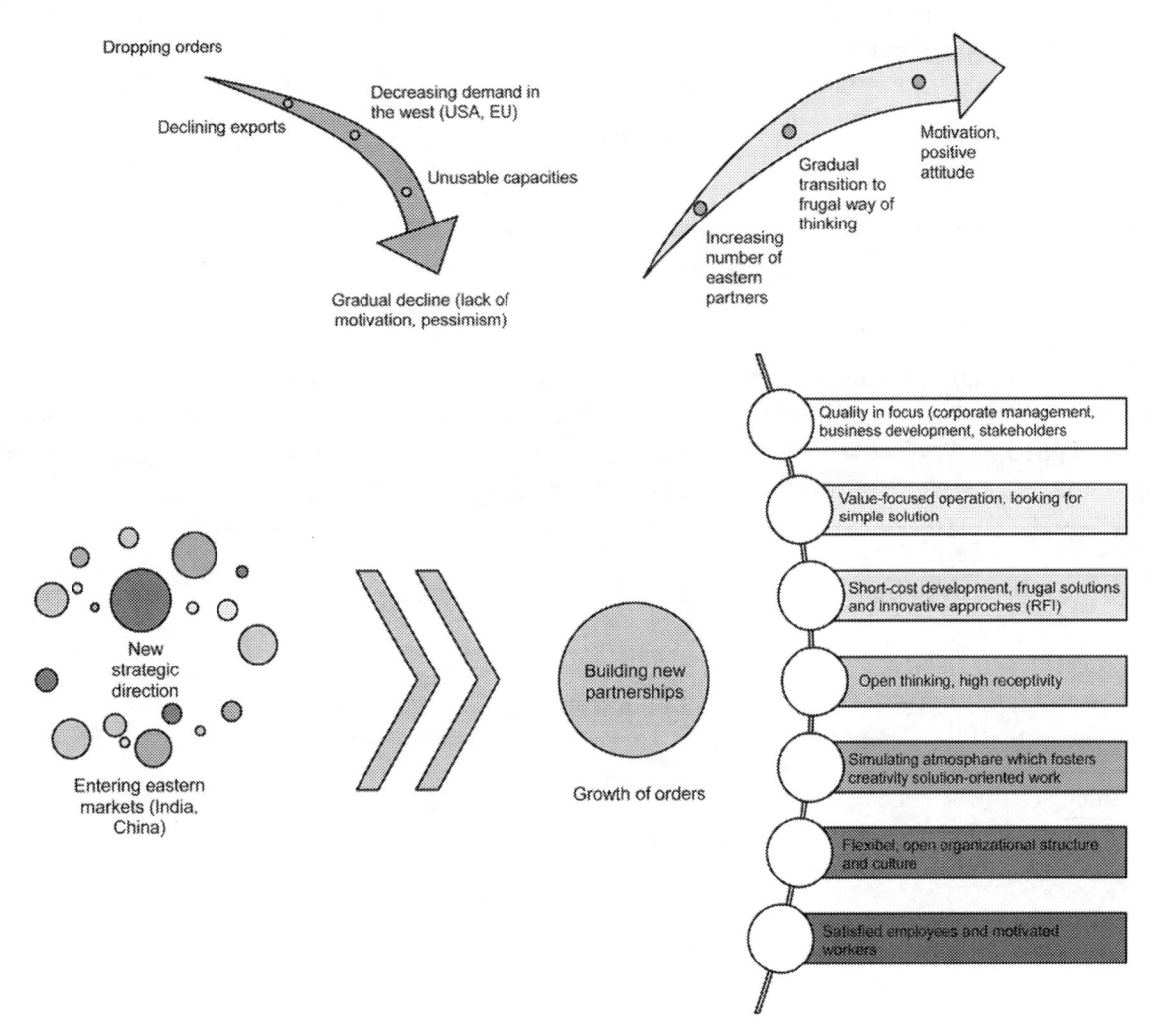

an organizational level. Qualitative change can be obtained in the efficiency of organizational operation by taking into consideration the relationship between the introduced models and conscious attention.

Frugal way of thinking and innovation come from the east and came to America across Europe. Companies with a long history and a good corporate reputation have also adapted this method, because they saw the possibility of sustainable development, the key to the efficient and economical operation. At the same time, they managed to produce high value-added products with fewer resources in order to reduce prices. More and more people can get the products of these companies. They trust companies more, and social responsibility is improving as well. In addition, even harmful environmental impacts have been reduced, because companies introduce more and more eco-friendly solutions. This innovative approach results in a win-win situation if it is used wisely and carefully. It is not advisable to confuse this method with radical reduction of costs or with innovation at the expense of quality. The essence of frugal innovation is to build a new, open, and flexible way of thinking in order to reveal human knowledge and creativity, hereby to develop unique and economical solutions.

The method is closely related to the operating logic of knowledge management system, since innovation and knowledge provide unique and sometimes ground-breaking results, and in both cases creating the right organizational culture is a requirement.

In the eastern region, values and ways of thinking which emphasize humans, relationships, knowledge and creativity, can fit also in the mentality of Hungarian companies. This mentality values human resource, and is aware that an organization can be developed only by human capital, and innovations and new solutions can be created only in this way. Personal development, development of skills and competencies are essential. In this way employees not only develop, but can become motivated, because they can satisfy one of their main demands: their need for self-realization. Investment in human resources, which is similar to the logic of a knowledge management system, is a success key in the process of frugal innovation.

Frugal innovation in a few years has become a mature business model opposing traditions. The number of its followers has been growing. In Hungary it can be applied mainly in companies with adequate knowledge base and which are open to novelties, but they are not able to compete with the huge demand for resources needed by research and development and traditional and continuous innovation.

# REFERENCES

Agarwal, N., & Brem, A. (2012). Frugal and reverse innovation - Literature overview and case study insights from a German MNC in India and China. In *Proceedings of Engineering, Technology and Innovation (ICE),18th International ICE Conference*. Munich, Germany: IEEE.

Arundel, A., Colecchia, A., & Wyckoff, A. (2006). Rethinking science and technology indicators for innovation policy in the 21st century. In L. Earl & F. Gault (Eds.), *Innovation and Impacts: The Next Decade* (pp. 167–198). Cheltenham: Edward Elgar.

Balkrishna, C. R. (2013). How disruptive is frugal? *Technology in Society*, *35*(1), 65–73. doi:10.1016/j.techsoc.2013.03.003

Banerjee, P. M. (2013). *The 'Frugal' in Frugal Innovation. Evolution of Innovation Management: Trends in an International Context*. London: Palgrave Macmillan.

Basu, R., Preeta, M. B., & Sweeny, E. G. (2013). Frugal Innovation. *Core Competencies to Address Global Sustainability Journal of Management for Global Sustainability*, *1*(2), 63–82. doi:10.13185/JM2013.01204

Bencsik, A. (2015). *A tudásmenedzsment elmélete és gyakorlata*. Budapest: Akadémiai Kiadó.

Bhatti, Y. A. (2012). *What is Frugal, What is Innovation? Towards a Theory of Frugal Innovation*. Retrieved May 02, 2014, from http://ssrn.com/abstract=2005910

Boutellier, R., Gassmann, O., & Zedtwitz, M. (2009). Managing Global Innovation. *R & D Management*, *3*(2), 225–226.

Bucsy, L. (1976). *Az innovációk rendszere és a vállalati fejlődés*. Budapest: Közgazdasági és Jogi Könyvkiadó.

Chan, K. (2013). *Frugal Innovation: A Groundbreaking Business Strategy.* Retrieved from http://www.onedesk.com/2013/04/frugal-innovation-a-groundbreaking-business-strategy/

Davenport, T. H., & Prusak, L. (2001). *Tudásmenedzsment.* Budapest: Kossuth Kiadó.

Davila, T., Epstein, M., & Shelton, R. (2012). *Making Innovation Work: How to Manage It, Measure It, and Profit from It.* Pearson FT Press.

Drucker, P. (2003). Az innováció lehetőségei. *Harvard Business Manager, 5-6,* 28–34.

Eagar, R., van Oene, F., Boulton, Ch., Roos, D., & Dekeyseret, C. (2011). The Future of Innovation Management: The Next 10 Years. London: Arthur D. Little.

Filep, B. (2008). The economic regional cooperation and management of Universities and in particular the Széchenyi István University. In *Proceedings of Integrating perspectives on performance management.* Prague: University of Economics.

Gardiner, B. (2013). Jugaad' innovation: the businesses getting creative in the face of scarcity. *The Guardian.* Retrieved September 12, 2014, from http://www.theguardian.com/sustainable-business/jugaad-innovation-business-creativity-scarcity

Garvin, D. A. (1993). Building a learning organization. *Harvard Business Review, 71*(4), 78–91. PMID:10127041

George, G., McGahan, A. M., & Prabhu, J. (2012). Innovation for Inclusive Growth: Towards a Theoretical Framework and a Research Agenda. *Journal of Management Studies, 49*(4), 661–683. doi:10.1111/j.1467-6486.2012.01048.x

Goleman. (2003). *A természetes vezető.* Budapest: Vince Kiadó.

Gomes, L. (2013). IBM's 'Frugal Innovation' Takes Root in Africa - Combining high and low tech, IBM's famous R&D lab tackles the challenges of a rapidly urbanizing continent. *Operations, Information & Technology Global Business Africa, 3.* Retrieved from https://www.gsb.stanford.edu/insights/ibms-frugal-innovation-takes-root-africa

Govindarajan, V., & Trimble, C. (2012). *Reverse Innovation: Create Far from Home, Win Everywhere.* Boston: Harvard Business Review Press.

Govindarajan, V., & Trimble, C. (2014). Reverse Innovation. *Management International Review, 54*(2), 277–282.

Hámosi, B., & Szabó, K. (Eds.). (2012). *Innovációs verseny - esélyek és korlátok.* Budapest: Aula Kiadó.

Hartley, J. (2014). New development: Eight and a half propositions to stimulate frugal innovation. *Public Money & Management, 34*(3), 227–232. doi:10.1080/09540962.2014.908034

Hay Group. (2008). *Making the leap: Encouraging innovation.* Retrieved March 24, 2014, from http://www.haygroup.com/downloads/au/au_icm_innovation_low_res.pdf

Heeks, R., Foster, Ch., & Nugroho, Y. (2014). New models of inclusive innovation for development. *Innovation and Development, 4*(2), 175–185. doi:10.1080/2157930X.2014.928982

Kamp, B. (2012). Reverse innovation: inversing the international product life cycle model and lead market theory [Innovación inversa: invirtiendo el modelo internacional de ciclo de vida del producto y la teoría del mercado líder]. *Boletín de estudios económicos, 207*(6-7), 481.

King, W. (2001). *Strategies for creating a learning organization Korszerű Vezetés 10.* Budapest: BME-OMIKK.

Lengyel, B. (2004). A tudásteremtés lokalitása: hallgatólagos tudás és helyi tudástranszfer. *Tér és Társadalom, 18*(2), 51-71.

Lyles, M. A. (2014). Organizational Learning, knowledge creation, problem formulation and innovation in messy problems. *European Management Journal, 32*(1), 132–136. doi:10.1016/j.emj.2013.05.003

Mahindra & Mahindra Ltd. (2014). *The Mahindra Group.* Retrieved February 11, 2014, from http://www.mahindra.com/Who-We-Are

Mahindra Group USA. (2014). *Mahindra USA.* Retrieved October 14, 2014, from http://mahindrausa.com/news/mahindra-usa-celebrates-20-years-growth-north-america

Mandal, S. (2014). Frugal Innovations for Global Health — Perspectives for Students. *IEEE Pulse, 5*(1), 11–13.

Mukerjee, K. (2012). Frugal innovation: The key to penetrating emerging markets. *Ivey Business Journal.* Retrieved September 20, 2014, from http://iveybusinessjournal.com/uncategorized/frugal-innovation-the-key-to-penetrating-emerging-markets#.VE4P5hZCw5A

Mura, L., & Rózsa, Z. (2013). The Impact of Networking on the Innovation Performance of SMEs. In *Proceedings of MSED The 7th International Days of Statistics and Economics.* Praha: University of Economics.

Mura, L., Žuľová, J., & Madleňák, A. (2016). Strategic management and management of personnel costs: Employing young people in the Slovak Republic. *Problems and Perspectives in Management, 14*(1), 79–84.

Nonaka, I., Kodama, M., Hirose, A., & Kohlbacher, F. (2014). Dynamic fractal organizations for promoting knowledge-based transformation – A new paradigm for organizational theory. *European Management Journal, 32*(1), 137–146. doi:10.1016/j.emj.2013.02.003

Olšovská, A., Mura, L., & Švec, M. (2015). The most recent legislative changes and their impact on interest by enterprises in agency employment: What is next in human resource management? *Problems and Perspectives in Management, 13*(3), 47–54.

Pansera, M., & Richard, O. (2014). Eco-Innovation at the 'Bottom of the Pyramid'. In Collaboration for Sustainability and Innovation: A Role For Sustainability Driven by the Global South? (pp. 293-313). Springer.

Porter, M. (1980). Competitive Strategy. New York: The Free Press.

Probst, G., Raub, S., & Romhardt, K. (2006). *Wissen Managen Wie Unternehmen ihre wertvollste Ressource optimal nutzen.* Wiesbaden: Gabler GmbH.

Radjou, N. (2014). *NaviRadjou*. Retrieved October 10, 2014, from http://naviradjou.com/

Radjou, N., & Prabhu, J. (2013). *Frugal Innovation: A New Business Paradigm*. Instead Knowledge. Retrieved May 15, 2014, from http://knowledge.insead.edu/innovation/frugal-innovation-a-new-business-paradigm-2375

Radjou, N., Prabhu, J., & Ahuja, S. (2012). *Jugaad Innovation: Think Frugal, Be Flexible, Generate Breakthrough Growth*. San Francisco: Jossey-Bass.

Ross, A. (2009). Nice Work If You Can Get It: Life and Labor in Precarious Times. New York: New York University Press.

Rothwell, R. (1994). Towards the Fifth-generation Innovation Process. *International Marketing Review*, *11*(1), 7–31. doi:10.1108/02651339410057491

Routson, J. (2011). Embracing a Way to Change the World. *Entrepreneurship, Health Care, Social Innovation, 5*(1). Retrieved from https://www.gsb.stanford.edu/insights/embracing-way-change-world

Rylková, Ž. (2013). Innovative Business and the Czech Republic. In *Proceedings of the 11th International Conference Liberec Economic Forum.*Liberec: Technical University of Liberec.

Santander, C. (2013). *Frugal forward-thinking*. Santander Corporate & Commercial. Retrieved October 07, 2014,from http://www.santandercb.co.uk/knowledge-hub/frugal-forward-thinking

Schumpeter, J. A. (1980). *A gazdasági fejlődés elmélete*. Budapest: Közgazdasági és Jogi Könyvkiadó.

Schumpeter, J. A. (2012): Asian innovation. *The Economist*. Retrieved September 03, 2014, from http://www.economist.com/node/21551028

Senge, P. (1998). *5. alapelv. A tanuló szervezet kialakításának elmélete és gyakorlata*. Budapest HVG Rt.

Shapiro, S. (2011). *Best Practices Are Stupid: 40 Ways to Out-Innovate the Competition*. London: Portfolio Penguin.

Shapiro, S. (2013). *Innovation for Innovators*. Retrieved December 12, 2014, from http://stephenshapiro.com/speaking/

Shapiro, S. (2014). *Innovation Philosophies*. Retrieved February 13, 2015, from www.stephenshapiro.com

Singh, S., Gambhir, A., Sotiropoulos, A., & Duckworth, S. (2012). *Frugal Innovation: Learning from Social Enterpreneurs in India*. Serco Institute. Retrieved April 22, 2014, from http://www.serco.com/Images/FrugalInnovation_tcm3-39462.pdf

Sveiby, K. (2001). *Szervezetek új gazdasága: a menedzselt tudás*. Budapest: Kjk - Kerszöv Jogi és Üzleti Kiadó Kft.

Thakor, A. (2013). *Innovation and Growth – What Do We Know?* Singapore: Word Scientific Publishing. doi:10.1142/8115

Tiwari, R., & Herstatt, C. (2012a). *Open global innovation networks as enablers of frugal innovation: Propositions based on evidence from India*. Hamburg, Germany: Hamburg University of Technology, Technology and Innovation Management, Working Paper 72.

Tiwari, R., & Herstatt, C. (2012b). *India - a lead market for frugal innovations? Extending the lead market theory to emerging economies*. TIM/TUHH Working Paper 67.

Tiwari, R. & Herstatt, C. (2012c). Frugal Innovation: A Global Networks' Perspective; Die Unternehmung. *Swiss Journal of Business Research and Practice, 66*(3), 245-274.

Tomka, J., & Bőgel, G. (2014). *Megéri jónak lenni? – A Biblia és a menedzsment II*. Budapest: Nemzeti Tankönyvkiadó.

Zeschky, M. B., Winterhalter, S., & Gassmann, O. (2014). From Cost to Frugal and Reverse Innovation. *Mapping the Field and Implications for Global Competitiveness Research-Technology Management, 57*(4), 20–27.

## KEY TERMS AND DEFINITIONS

**Business Model:** A business model describes the rationale of how an organization creates, delivers, and captures value in economic, social, cultural or other contexts. The model includes the components and functions of the business.

**Frugal Innovation:** Frugal innovation is a wholly new mind-set, a flexible approach that perceives resource, does not constrain challenges but a growth opportunity.

**Innovation Model:** Innovation model shows a process according to a new idea of product development, organization or business model, development.

**Knowledge Sharing:** People help each other by using their own individual knowledge. As a result of this process, individual knowledge can rise to an organizational level.

**Learning Organization:** It is a special organizational form and culture which is a precondition of a knowledge management system building and operation. In this organization people learn continuously and use their knowledge collectively to achieve their common goals.

**Open Innovation:** Open innovation is a trendy term. It is about building a system where ideas flow openly from your customers, employees and other stakeholders. This system allows companies to capture ideas collaboratively, leading to sustained innovation.

**Organizational Culture:** Organizational culture is the collective behaviour and common values of people within an organization and the meanings behind their actions.

# Chapter 5

# Appropriate Leadership Style in Knowledge Management System (KMS) Building

**Andrea Bencsik**
*J. Selye University, Slovakia*

## ABSTRACT

*Building up a knowledge management system is a commonly arising challenge in managing organizations. Leaders need to change their leadership style in order for their organization to be successful, in accordance with the requirements of building and operating a knowledge management system. The aim of this chapter is to sketch the necessity of the change and the right leaders' behavior. The author shows the relationships residing in the background of the elements that are in close connection with the suitable leadership style: EQ, competence, organizational culture, trust, communication, and employees' commitment and satisfaction. During this chapter readers will be led logically across the connections of the above-mentioned elements and, at the end, a figure summarizing the connections closes the chapter.*

## INTRODUCTION

For a long time, the knowledge management literature has been examining the creation, retention, transfer, and utilization of knowledge capital in order to ensure the competitiveness of the organization. The question of how and to whom organizational knowledge may be linked, and how this type of knowledge may be transferred, has also been the focus of researchers for a long time.

The professional literature (Argote & Ingram, 2000) defines knowledge transfer as the spreading of knowledge among individuals and groups within an organization, and this pursuit forms the basis of corporate competitiveness. At the same time, organizations have to face numerous tasks and difficulties when knowledge transfers take place among employees – especially when a new task is to be learned (Letmathe, Schweitzer, & Zielinsk, 2011).

The methods for transferring knowledge, which is the most critical step in the building and operating of a knowledge management system, must fit with the corporate and national culture; otherwise the whole process may fail. From the point of view of knowledge management, the most important elements

DOI: 10.4018/978-1-5225-1642-2.ch005

of an organizational culture are trust, communication, and learning. An unsuitable organizational culture hinders knowledge sharing/transfer (Delong & Lee, 2007). One of the most difficult managerial tasks is to decide whether the culture is suitable for attaining and receiving the necessary new knowledge.

According to Davenport and Prusak (2001), effective knowledge transfer within a company is mostly hindered by the lack of trust between management and employees. One of the reasons for this mistrust is the power distance between management and their workers; as a result, employees often do not see their leaders as partners in their work (Bakacsi et al., 2000). This often causes employees to try to retain their knowledge monopoly, and, consequently, their status (Fehér, 2002; Bőgel, 2005). In many cases, this hinders the proper transfer of knowledge within the company.

What is required from managers/leaders? How should they think and behave? How should they change in order to build a knowledge management system grounded in a successful change in the organizational culture? Which culture and leadership style will support collaboration on behalf of the operation of a knowledge management system, and especially knowledge sharing? The limits of this chapter do not allow us to discuss all the preconditions and activities; therefore, the author stresses only two important factors: leadership style expectations and the leader's behavior.

The chapter highlights the most important requirements that form the bases of economic conditions nowadays. Top management is required to realize the activities of knowledge preservation, knowledge utilization, and to create a learning organizational culture in order to operate a KM system.

What kind of leadership, behavior, attitude, and motivation are needed to reach these goals?

## BACKGROUND

## Connection between Knowledge Management and Leadership

Research results have verified (Bencsik, 2005) that people perform at their maximum if their commitment is high, if they feel the task is their own. This helps employees to reach individual goals beyond the organizational ones. For this to be a reality, a background organizational culture is needed (learning organization) that is based on confidence, helpfulness, trust, and attention.

On the basis of all these, successful competitiveness can be continuously upheld only by the development of affection and by the leaders' and employees' commitment. In order to achieve this, ensuring the flexibility of company operations is essential, and within the organization a motivational atmosphere should dominate that aligns the creativity of workers with the production of qualitative products and services. Consequently it is plainly conceivable that human attitudes influence the qualitative and quantitative properties of work; namely, the management of human resources is one of the basic pillars of successful company operations.

If a company wants to be successful in operating its KM system, managers have to endeavor to change leadership style. For example, they have to clearly know employees' demands, because if they are attentive to these demands and endeavor to satisfy them, managers will get back more initiative, commitment, and good work from their employees (Peale, 1997).

To create a picture of an organization that is acceptable to the market, its rivals, and the outside world, it is worth thinking over an idea expressed by the leader of Volvo, the car company: So that a business should appear to be well-managed to the outside world, first, the inside of the organization has to be put in order (Carlstedt, 1997).

With the traditional approach and hierarchical way of thinking, a reactive leadership style concentrates on the 'hard' problems first; for example, low quality and efficiency, etc. The managers try to handle the symptoms. A leader's task is to find the real causes of the problems, but the background of these problems are often 'soft' factors – human problems. These factors cannot be characterized by measurable parameters, but they have a critical influence on measurable 'hard' factors and, consequently, on the organizational results. Hard problems cannot be swept aside because they are the indicators of the real, 'soft' problems. This relates to dealing with people in another way; managers' way of thinking has to be approached using different methods.

Leaders who think creatively deal with 'hard' and 'soft' problems in a balanced way. Their problem-oriented way of thinking will turn to solution-oriented results. Leaders know how important collaboration is and their behavior influences people and people's activities. Leaders try to shape a common vision that reinforces unity, collaboration, and identification with organizational aims (Oakley & Krug, 1997). Such behavioral patterns fit the process of realizing a learning organizational culture, trust, and teamwork ideally.

A community at a workplace has great experience, knowledge, wisdom, creative force, and energy. An enlightened leader knows the suitable questions to ask in order to reach the decisive features. If a company wants to be a successful, the leaders have to know their employees' demands. The kind of leadership is needed that takes past experience into consideration, but that does not have preconceptions and preconditions shaped by the old style. Table 1, highlights two extreme leadership styles (Oakley & Krug, 1997).

What is the difference between the two styles? A decisive factor is consciousness, which can be seen from a comparison of the above noted characteristics. Leaders have to understand the principles that concern the organization and its people and leadership.

The principles are:

- The most important factors to organizational success are people. An enlightened leader creates an environment and culture in a workplace that frees people's creativity and energy. The possibilities

*Table 1. Characteristics of the two extreme leaderships type*

| Reactive Leader | Proactive Leader |
|---|---|
| • Feels the need to have all his or her own answers. | • Has no ego-driven need to have all the answers. |
| • Is telling-oriented. | • Is listening-oriented. |
| • Makes all the decisions personally. | • Empowers other people to make decisions. |
| • Pushes the organization to achieve results. | • Pulls the organization toward a vision. |
| • Analyses, analyses, analyses. | • Generates lasting commitment. |
| • Creates sporadic motivation. | • Is open-minded. |
| • Is highly opinionated. | • Teaches the importance of personal responsibility. |
| • Teaches subordinates to expect direction. | • Models personal responsibility. |
| • Is in a self-protection mode. | • Knows relaxing control yields results. |
| • Is afraid of losing control. | • Focuses on building on strengths. |
| • Focuses on finding and fixing problems. | • Teaches how to learn from mistakes. |
| • Is quick to fire those that fail. | |

(Author construction on the basis of Oakley & Krug, 1997)

are in harmony with people's wish to contribute to the success of the organization and this motivates them. This characterizes a learning organization;

- People do not like being told what to do, but they work with pleasure to realize their own ideas. (Colleagues have their own goals and visions and they work willingly to realize them.);
- Employees resist others' ideas and conceptions. An enlightened leader is self-confident enough that he/she does not want to claim every solution for him/herself. (Communication, trust.);
- If people feel that they get every necessary support, they do everything to help colleagues who help them in turn. If demands and wishes are satisfied, colleagues help and serve the organization that has supported them. For a proactive leader, people are important and he/she supports their personal development to help them reach their goals. (Commitment, satisfaction.);
- In a community there are great powers. The organizational members are enthusiastic; they have the initiative, ability, and willingness to create something. If they have a common aim that is treated as their own the synergy enables them to do perform outstandingly. But it also operates in reverse. (The power of teamwork.)

A change of leadership brings a chance to create a learning organization and the change can be realized with minimal confusion within an organization. In this situation, human resources play a key role. Therefore, it is worth highlighting what conditions are needed to use human knowledge at the highest levels by managers. If the learning organization is working, the necessary criteria are valid, and the organizational culture and leadership have to be balanced.

There are many groups and perspectives with respect to culture and leadership from which the best solution can be selected. To go over them in detail is not in the focus of this chapter, but in the following section the connections between culture and leadership will be shown.

## The Culture and Group Operation

This chapter summarizes the connection between organizational culture and group operation.

In modern organizations a typical unit is a group. Since the group is made up of individuals, their knowledge and the result of their learning ability are summed up in the outcome of the group's performance. Namely, the group's performance will be more than the simple mathematical sum of each individual person's knowledge. In reference to this, collective learning means, on the one hand, the learning individuals acquire, and, on the other hand, the preservation, development, and transfer of the knowledge acquired as a consequence of the common work of the whole group (Hedlund & Österberg, 2013). Consequently, for the sake of the organizations being able to continuously develop and learn, researchers have to suppose that the people and groups working in these organizations are also able to do the same (Barakonyi & Lorange, 2000).

Since in learning organizations team learning serves to achieve a team goal, both the individuals and the team are ready to tolerate some uncertainty. As the team goal is connected to the tasks being distributed in the group, collective learning contributes to the development of organizational capacity and in a given case to the execution of successful change management.

The collective work in organizational life should be supported by the operating organizational culture. Let us have a look at what the properties are that characterize groups within a learning organization. Whether the communities differ from other groups within an organization?

Collective learning works on the basis of high-level teamwork, collaboration, and collective thinking. The expectations of the groups are:

- Professional (intellectual) erudition.
- Emotional intelligence.
- Elaboration and predominance of competences.
- Learning ability.
- Knowledge transfer, predominance of the knowledge management aspect.

The groups that are able to perform the above-mentioned expectations within the organization are not definitely among the formal and regulated frames of working teams. Organizational groups taking the opportunity to learn and share knowledge are those professional communities that take shape (or can be generated) spontaneously or in a regulated manner in an organization. These groups support the dissemination of knowledge about management's point of view. Their task is to support organizational work during the implementation period of change; first of all, in that case, if the goal of the metamorphosis is to turn into a learning organization or to disseminate knowledge of management's point of view.

Who can be considered an actual member of communities of practice and how do these groups evolve within an organization? A professional team is a group of the sort of people who have common interests or those who are actively working on a project with the same target; perhaps they have similar hobbies and they are able to deepen their knowledge in such a way that they continuously collaborate with each other in a given professional field.

These teams are of great importance in the formation of a good corporate spirit and organizational culture, which plays a significant role in learning and in overcoming resistance against changes. The team members, the so-called knowledge workers, have to find their position at every level of the organizational hierarchy. They have great importance in the field of knowledge acquisition, knowledge sharing, knowledge keeping, knowledge development, and collective and organizational learning/forgetting and innovation.

Consequently, any informal and formal group that takes shape within the organizational frame is to be viewed as a community of practice whose goal is learning, knowledge sharing, knowledge spreading, knowledge keeping, and development of knowledge. It is important that their operation is characterized by the harmony of organizational and individual goals. Readers have to take into consideration that all those team processes are characteristic of the operation and formation of these groups, which are characteristic also of any other group that was formed to solve a given task or to execute a project. These phases can be separated from each other, both emotionally and work wise, from the first meeting to the when the work is completed.

According to a classic interpretation, human resource management deals with the selection of persons, motivation systems and tools, wage systems, the quality development of human resources, the development of education and organizational culture, etc. In accordance with the formulation, the question and necessity of the management of individual knowledge does not belong to the task of human management. Rightly, the questions, 'where does this subject matter fit in and whose task is it to handle this subject?' arise at this point. Do researchers have to deal with the questions of acquisition, spreading, keeping/storing, maximum utilization of competitive knowledge, which is inseparable from human resources at the highest managerial level, or does responsibility have to be delegated? Whoever is in the decision-making situation in the organizational hierarchy is responsible for building up and setting in action knowledge management, it cannot work with an autocratic leadership style that does not support the organizational culture. It is true that organizational culture – similarly to leadership style – is a 'soft' category; nevertheless, it permeates and determines the 'hard' elements of the organization, namely, the applied management methods and tools, and through this the strategy, structure, managerial decision-making and directing systems, etc. Finally, it determines the competitiveness of the organization.

## How does Leadership Style and Communication Influence the Building of a Knowledge Management System?

One of the main influential factors that makes possible (or impossible) the success of the organizational operation is leadership style. What kind of leadership style may support an organizational operation? If we consider the well-known model of any researcher, one thing is for sure, we have to seek the direction of the democratic scale. Of course, in the course of determining the leadership style, there is no absolute truth in either extreme. Mostly, a predominance of the principles of transformer management brings real success. The expectation in this field lies with the democratic/laissez-faire leadership style that supports the group operation. Within this leadership style, the socio-emotional and interpersonal skills come to the fore against the intellectual and entrepreneurial skills appearing in the feature-theory grouping (Barakonyi & Lorange, 2000).

If the learning organizational criteria and the requirements of the knowledge management principles, the implementation steps, and the expectations of the organizational culture are put in pairs, it can be confidently declared that the knowledge of management, which meets the requirements of all of these, creates a possibility to manage knowledge in an organization. What kind of managerial knowledge is needed for this?

Competence is outweighed in successful managerial work by practical knowledge or intelligence in itself. Those leadership features, such as empathy, independence, initiative skills, reliability, etc., are more important in the judgment of top managers than the qualification of possessing material knowledge. If we look at the features of emotional intelligence, we can discover numerous analogies with features describing the satisfaction of human resources, which classify the susceptibility for knowledge management that ensures the competitive operation of an undertaking. Most of the emergent features come under the category of 'soft', which highlights that human-centered leadership attitudes come to the fore. Those managers who are in a position of power who are not able to tune into this are unable to make a success of their company.

Communication also has great importance with respect to whether leaders are able to realize a human-centered leadership style. People can broadcast their own ideas, opinion, desires, etc. and can receive messages arriving from others by means of communication. If researchers investigate this subject properly, a wealth of experience would support the conclusion that, what a leader can lose (and thereby what the whole organization can lose), if managers cannot communicate in an intelligent manner is a great deal.

What does intelligent mean? A number of factors influence communication, for example circumstances, attitudes, the different noises, restrict or make impossible the reception and processing of messages. What are the most frequent obstacles? Filters can block out information. This method can be useful since it saves the organization from having to process unnecessary information that would make organizational life unmanageable. The filter defends, on the one hand, and hinders on the other. What determines how much damage it causes next to its defensive function? People's **culture** is the determining factor, but, of course, knowledge, information, and experience also play a role.

## MAIN FOCUS OF THE CHAPTER

## What Features Are Needed to Change Leadership Style?

### The Relationship between Learning, Culture, and Knowledge

The implementation of criteria of a learning organization means the requirements of a knowledge management system. In this case, organizational members, individuals and groups, are open to acquiring new skills, to continuous renewal and learning (double-loop and the deutero learning are of significance from the point of view of learning (Argyris & Schön, 1978)). Such an organizational atmosphere supports the success of knowledge sharing, which means that everyone aims to transmit his/her knowledge, to share it with colleagues and the other members of the organization for the sake of the collective goals. This fact separately contributes to the fact that people will be able to work and produce the expected results in the framework of a balanced organizational operation on a higher level of knowledge.

If the performance is higher, not only in quantity, but also in quality, it is to be seen in the efficiency of the enterprise, since it will make it possible to produce more modern, higher quality, more marketable products and services in competitive organizational conditions.

The establishment of conditions of knowledge within the company – first of all, innovative knowledge – is beyond the operation of a learning organization, such as the grounded internal knowledge base that is the condition for permanent development and renewal. As well as the organizational atmosphere (culture) that establishes creativity, the conditions of continuous learning handle the requirement on a strategic level to the employee's satisfaction, thus a reliable quality and competitive performance of the work are ensured by putting the right person in the right place.

### The Relationship between Culture and Satisfaction

It can be stated, together with the heading 'self-management', which appears among the operating conditions of a learning organizational culture, that people, in such organizational conditions, who get a chance to accomplish their own goals, perform higher quality work by harmonizing their own imagination with the organizational goals, something that is a determining factor of employee satisfaction at the same time. On the other hand, qualitative products influence customer satisfaction as a consequence of competitive operations.

Examining the activities of enterprises with regard to quality, researchers face two kinds of problems:

- Failures adjustable by the employee, which arises if the employee has all the three criteria of self-control:
  - Knows what his/her task is.
  - Knows what he/she is doing now.
  - Is able to control his/her activity.

These criteria are only the conditions of self-control: they do not mean self-control has automatically been achieved. For self-control to be achieved an employee needs to possess the appropriate approach and responsibilities, and also know and want to use these tools.

- System failures, namely, the failures that are influenced by the management of the enterprise, occur if one or more of the criteria of self-control are not fulfilled. This indicates imperfection in creating the conditions for self-control by management, if the employees do not know the expectations, the mode of actions, and the possible tools, and if they do not get feedback on their performances and the appropriate support, either physically or in terms of human resources.

In the case of striving for quality work (the competitiveness criterion), it is about the change of management's point of view, achieving long-term thinking. This brings about a new 'lifestyle', a modified behavior and a new emphasis on the life of the enterprises. This means that the increase in general effectiveness and value creation comes to the fore instead of permanent cost minimization over a short-term period. Enterprises want to produce at a cheaper and cheaper price, they try to offer more and more to meet customer needs. But these companies do not want to give more or something else that the customers want. This way of thinking is to be seen as a concept and a program wherein the implementation and the 'steps' of change have the same significance as the result itself. This is a permanent learning process, meaning the formation of a learning organization that supports continuous quality improvement.

## The Connections between Satisfaction and Emotional Intelligence (EQ)

If people look at the characteristics of EQ, they find many similarities, on the one hand, in the aspect of expected management competences and, on the other hand, in relation to the operation of the learning organization and group. Goleman mentions 25 factors (Goleman, 1997) that characterize human features. He classified them into five groups. Each of them can be measured objectively.

The five groups are:

- Self-knowledge.
- Self-control.
- Motivation.
- Empathy.
- Social sense.

The key element of successful groups is emotional intelligence, but the groups with high emotional intelligence are not simply just groups of people with high emotional intelligence. To have high EQ in a group, we have to define norms that can be the basis of mutual confidence and group-spirit, and the members need to feel the supporting power of the group. If these conditions are unfulfilled, there is still a chance of cooperation and participation, although the team would not be able to operate at optimal effectiveness.

This is something that has been confirmed by literatures: groups are more creative and productive if a high level of participation, cooperation, and mutual contribution evolves among members. To achieve this, the presence of three basic conditions is required:

- The mutual confidence of the members.
- The feeling of belonging to the group.
- The feeling of the supporting-power of the group.

Behind these conditions there are deep emotions. Confidence, the feeling of togetherness, the feeling of supporting-power, forms an environment where the emotions are handled excellently, so it is useful for the group to improve their emotional intelligence. Emotions should be intentionally brought to the surface. Researchers have to understand how they can influence teamwork through organizational work (Goleman, 2002).

Organizations have to rethink whether they need emotionally mature managers, emotionally intelligent groups, and whether they are ready to devote time and energy on it. But the advantages that come from the emotionally intelligent staff and managers for the individual and also for the enterprise are worth the effort. In the context of continuously sharpening competition, emotional intelligence at the organizational level is a key factor in survival.

## Satisfaction and EQ Based Knowledge Management System Building

Employee satisfaction research primarily comes to the foreground nowadays in order for companies to be able to check off specifications or requirements in the context of quality system audits concerning this issue. The quality aspect is a much explored factor that makes competitiveness increase and is determined by the employees' satisfaction; however, the judgment of human resources, from this point of view, must not get stuck at the level of achievable quality audits.

The transformation from any kind of organization to a learning organization does not always run smoothly. But if the transformation is paired with an enlightened leadership style, leadership competencies at the expected level, with the right level of emotional intelligence, and also keeping in mind employee satisfaction, then there is a bigger chance for retaining or generating organizational competitiveness. If we still assign to all this the quality requirements of an organizational culture explained at the beginning of this study, we get a full picture of the system of connections that lays the foundation for the chance to reach the individual and organizational wishes. Hereby, it is the most important guarantee of the thirst for knowledge, which is a precondition for learning, development, purposeful leadership behavior, and satisfaction.

There are a lot of models that show a possible way to operate a knowledge management system in a company. Among them, this way of thinking uses one of the most popular models, the Probst style model (Probst et al, (2006) summarizes the main element of a knowledge management system building in 8 steps; they are: knowledge goals, knowledge identification, knowledge acquisition, knowledge development, knowledge distribution, knowledge preservation, knowledge use, knowledge measurement).

The factors that primarily influence employee satisfaction – the focus here will be on those factors that characterize emotional intelligence – and their relationship with the elements of a knowledge management system can be seen in Table 2. The factors relevant to emotional intelligence and their meaning are those characteristics that are chosen from the 25 elements grouped by Goleman. In the second column, one of the five main groups can be read. Thereafter, the expected emotional competence appears, then the elements of knowledge management system.

## The Relationship between Leadership Style, Emotional Intelligence, and Competence

Leadership style is such a basic influential factor that either supports or, to the contrary, makes impossible the success of an organizational operation. Therefore, a change of leadership style is often needed

*Table 2. Satisfaction - EQ - Characteristics of emotional competence and the relationship of knowledge management elements*

| Features of Satisfaction | Description of Satisfaction Features | Description of EQ Features | Features of EQ | Group of EQ features | Managerial Emotional Competence | Components of Knowledge Management System |
|---|---|---|---|---|---|---|
| Setting an objective | • Identification with the organizational goals.<br>• Acceptance without conditions. | Sense for common work on behalf of common goals. | Cooperation. | Social skills. | Social competence | Defining knowledge goals. |
| Empathy | • Group interactions.<br>• Relationship of leaders and employees.<br>• Treatment of people.<br>• Problem solving.<br>• Conflict handling. | • Recognition of emotions and their effects.<br>• Sense for dissolving discrepancies. | • Emotional consciousness.<br>• Conflict handling. | • Self-conscious-ness.<br>• Social skills. | • Individual competence<br>• Social competence | Knowledge identification. |
| Learning | • Possibility to access knowledge.<br>• Assurance of continuous development. | • Readiness for grabbing possibilities.<br>• Creativity.<br>• Openness to new ideas. | • Initiative skill.<br>• Innovation. | • Motivation.<br>• Self-regulation. | Individual competence | • Knowledge acquisition.<br>• Knowledge development. |
| Mutual collegial supports | • Transfer of cognitions and experiences.<br>• Learning from colleagues and leaders. | • Sense for creating harmony in the group.<br>• Sense for common work on behalf of common goals.<br>• Looking after useful contacts.<br>• Sense and ambition for others development. | • Team-spirit.<br>• Co-operation.<br>• Networking.<br>• Others' development. | • Social skills.<br>• Empathy. | Social competence | Knowledge sharing/ distribution. |
| Admission | Performance motivation in which dependence the performance can change. | Inducement for reaching notability. | Performance-motivation. | Motivation. | Individual competence. | • Knowledge sharing.<br>• Support. |
| Commitment | • Subordinating individual goals to organizational goals.<br>• Forgiveness of failures.<br>• Practice of abilities.<br>• Applicability of knowledge. | Alignment with the goals of team or organization. | Commitment. | Motivation. | Individual competence. | • Individual and team learning.<br>• Knowledge use/ utilization. |
| Confidence | • Sincere.<br>• Open.<br>• Fearless atmosphere.<br>• Natural communication.<br>• Information flow without barriers. | Sense and ambition for changing notion. | Communication. | Social skills. | Social competence. | • Knowledge sharing/distribution.<br>• Knowledge use/ utilization. |
| Responsibility acceptance | • Self-contained decision ability.<br>• The formation of the possibility of it on behalf of management.<br>• Consciousness of work, consideration of decision results. | Taking responsibility related to our own performance. | Conscientiousness | Self-regulation. | Individual competence. | Knowledge preservation. |
| Work conditions | • Physical conditions.<br>• Perfection of technique.<br>• Infrastructural provision. | • Trust in success despite of obstacles and failures.<br>• Sincerity and truthfulness. | • Optimism.<br>• Reliability. | • Motivation.<br>• Self-regulation. | Individual competence. | • Knowledge storing.<br>• Preservation. |
| Acceptance | • Utilization of creativity, taking into consideration the ideas.<br>• Suggestions. | • Creativity.<br>• Being open against new ideas. | Innovation. | Self-regulation. | Individual competence. | Leadership support. |
| Performance assessment | • Expectation – possibility.<br>• Harmony of conditions.<br>• High level of work process organization. | • Giving inspiration to individuals and teams and their management.<br>• Knowledge of our strengths and barriers. | • Management.<br>• Exact self-estimation. | • Social skills.<br>• Self-consciousness. | • Social competence.<br>• Individual competence. | • Knowledge supervision.<br>• Assessment.<br>•Measurement. |

(author construction)

that carries with it the expectation that an enlightened leadership attitude should be combined with a high level of emotional intelligence (Bencsik, 2003). If people look at the characteristics of emotional intelligence, they can find numerous analogies with the characteristics of human resources during working. The possibilities and aptitudes have to be considered for the judgment of the relationship between leadership style and employee competencies. The starting point is the organizational human resources management strategy, which contributes to the formation of a knowledge-based economy with the assurance of a knowledge-based organizational operation.

At this phase, the challenge management faces has to be mentioned, which is very often in focus nowadays and is very important for HR managers and leaders as well. It is the problems of intergenerational management. In the literature, there are a growing number of scientific papers that choose some part of the issue of the generational problems as their focal point. This demonstrates that managers are not thinking in an entirely new way when they try to analyze the tensions that originate from the collision of different age groups.

It is common knowledge that an organization is at its healthiest when several generations are represented, allowing their advantages and disadvantages to prevail and their approaches, experiences, and new ideas interact. In those working groups where there is only one generation – which nowadays can be observed at a growing number of organizations – serious distortions arise (it is characteristic of many large organizations to express a preference for the younger generation, based on their flexibility, dynamism, IT skills, and ability to work long and hard hours. In these cases, so strong does the phenomena of peer influence become that the group members convince each other of the rightness of their actions, leaving no room for doubt or for questions about the decisions they make.

Two young generations (generation Y, which was born between 1980 and 1995, and generation Z, which refers to people born after 1996) demand a completely different type of leadership behavior than the older generations, concerning the use of tools and the organizational culture, presenting a great challenge for management. To have the competences that help in the handling of differences and conflicts between these two generations leaders', EQ is an indispensable condition. Individual differences have to be dealt with, and according to these, individual careers plans should be mapped out. At the same time, it is important to assist self-managed knowledge sharing, in which the young adults can learn from each other. The diversity of knowledge and both strong and weak formal and informal relations stabilize and make working in a group and in a network in the company more interesting and effective. To form a community from different age groups that collaborate, the first step (the leader's task) is a selection process of new co-workers.

According to a survey (Gáthy, 2004), people utilize no more than 50% of their abilities when working. It is a great wastage in every organization's life. The selection has to be preceded by such a working phase, which determines the workplace profiles with the help of a field of work analysis that describes step-by-step the necessary knowledge level for filling the given sphere of activity, the necessary and expected abilities, competencies, the possibilities that assure motivation, etc. This gives a basis for the selection process of a wanted colleague by drafting expectations, defining the standpoints of selection and the determination of the applied technology support. People can say, relating to persons, that they are 'containers' of competence, applied cognitions, 'do-knowledge', know-how and 'be-knowledge'. This renders it possible that a given person could do quality work. This competence can be obtained and made perfect by learning.

Many kinds of assemblies in the literature can be found regarding leadership competences. Based on these, a model is shown (Table 3), which was put together by SHL (Goleman, 2003) as the basis for comparison. From the elements of the model, those elements can be easily selected that can be brought into connection with the recited EQ characteristics.

The above written EQ characteristics (see Table 2), when compared with those competencies that are expected from the successful leaders of an undertaking, referenced in Table 4, there is an analogy of personality features. In relation to Table 5, leadership competences appear to fulfill the personal and social competences recited in Table 4.

In the spirit of all these, people can state that EQ is an organic part of leadership competence (personal and social too), without which managerial work could not be successful. Enlightened relationships are needed so that the leader is able to guide and manage the organization and the organizational groups that are under his/her supervision, which can enforce all of his/her competences at the highest possible level and, at the same time, will be able to enforce the principles of knowledge management.

*Table 3. The model of leadership competencies developed by SHL*

| Field | Competence | Definition |
|---|---|---|
| Leadership abilities | Management | Motivates others for reaching the organizational goals and create conditions on behalf of this. |
| | Planning and organization | Organizes the activities and resources, plans programs and controls their execution. |
| | Aspiration for quality | Keeps in view the goals and quality. Does everything for observance of quality and quantity specifications. |
| | Persuasion | It is able to influence, convince others and make an impression on people: their opinion is generally accepted. |
| Professional abilities | Professional knowledge | He/she is competent in the professional relationship of the work and attends continuously to the preservation of the level of technical skills. |
| | Problem solving | He/she analyses and takes problems into elements. He/she brings in a rational verdict based on significant information. |
| | Verbal communication | He/she speaks clearly and fluently to certain persons or groups too. |
| | Written communication | He/she writes clearly and briefly and adjusts the grammatical construction, style and language of text to the reader. |
| Entrepreneur abilities | Business consciousness | He/she understands and applies the commercial and financial principles: the viewpoints of costs, benefits and markets. |
| | Creativity and innovation | He/she has a new and creative idea in connection with the job and susceptible to query traditional conceptions. |
| | Readiness for action | He/she is ready for decision making. He/she is an initiator, man if action. |
| | Strategic sense | He/she handles businesses with a wide intellectual horizon and considers long-term effects and wider relationships. |
| Personality features | Social sense | He/she is sensitive and good at social relations. He/she respects others and works well together with others. |
| | Flexibility | He/she accommodates successfully to the changeable requirements and conditions. |
| | Tolerance | He/she works effectively amid obstacles or in a tense situation. He/she preserves calmness and evenness. |
| | Motivation | He/she works hard and enthusiastically for reaching goals. He/she wants to be successful in career. |

(Goleman, 2003)

*Table 4. Relations between EQ and leaders' competencies*

| EQ | Competence |
|---|---|
| Motivation | Motivation |
| Empathy | Collective sense |
| Social sense | |
| Self-recognition | Tolerance, flexibility |
| Self-control | Tolerance |

(authors' construction)

*Table 5. The relationship between knowledge management elements and leadership competences*

| Leadership Competencies | | | | | |
|---|---|---|---|---|---|
| Knowledge Management Elements | EQ Characteristics | Emotional Competences (Personality Features) | Leadership Abilities | Professional Abilities | Entrepreneur Abilities |
| Definition of knowledge goals | Co-operation. | • Social competence.<br>• Social sense. | • Management<br>• Planning, organization.<br>• Conviction.<br>• Aspiration for quality. | • Knowledge. | • Business conscious-ness. |
| Knowledge identification | • Emotional consciousness<br>• Conflict handling. | • Individual and social competence.<br>• Flexibility. | | •Knowledge.<br>• Problem solving. | • Business conscious-ness.<br>• Strategic sense. |
| Knowledge acquisition | Initiative skill. | • Individual competence.<br>• Motivation. | Management. | •Knowledge,<br>•Communication. | • Strategic sense.<br>• Ready for act. |
| Knowledge development | Innovation. | • Individual competence.<br>• Self-regulation tolerance. | • Management.<br>• Conviction. | Knowledge. | Creativity. |
| Knowledge distribution | • Team spirit,<br>• Co-operation networking.<br>• Developing others. | • Individual and social competence.<br>• Social sense.<br>• Motivation.<br>• Empathy. | Conviction. | • Knowledge.<br>• Communication. | • Creativity.<br>• Strategic sense. |
| Knowledge utilization | • Commitment.<br>• Communication. | • Individual and social competence.<br>• Social sense.<br>• Motivation. | • Management<br>• Aspiration for quality | • Knowledge.<br>• Problem solving. | • Creativity<br>• Strategic sense. |
| Knowledge keeping | • Conscientiousness.<br>• Optimism.<br>• Self-regulation.<br>• Motivation | • Individual competence.<br>• Tolerance and motivation. | Aspiration for quality. | Knowledge. | |
| Knowledge supervision and assessment | • Management.<br>• Exact self-assessment. | • Individual and social competence.<br>• Social skill.<br>• Self-consciousness.<br>• Self-regulation. | Aspiration for quality. | Knowledge. | • Strategic sense.<br>• Ready to act.<br>• Business conscious-ness. |

(authors' construction)

The following Table 5 summarizes those ideas with regard to knowledge management elements and leadership competences on behalf of competitiveness.

## SOLUTIONS AND RECOMMENDATIONS

### Change of Leadership Style

The guiding principles presented up to this point lead us to the recognition that three important elements emerge – amid numerous expectations – regarding the expectations of a leader:

- To have the required competencies.
- On the basis of this, to build an organizational culture that supports knowledge management.
- The enforcement of a leadership style that ensures its continuous and successful operation and supports teamwork.

The common platform of highlighted factors can be seen most of all through the success of EQ. If the effect of this succeeds with due emphasis among competences, the leader-employee relationship will also proceed at a sufficient level (good, excellent, etc.). This means that people feel good in the organization, and this is evident beyond their performance and the quality of their work in their organizational commitment; namely, people make good use of their knowledge within the organization. They share their knowledge voluntarily and willingly, and they do not wish to validate it among other organizational frames. This process shows a close correlation with the other highlighted elements, since if the teamwork operates well and the leader supports it, the collective knowledge grows more efficiently. Employees feel much more that they belong to each other, their self-esteem develops and they can also estimate each other better. If they get any possibility for individual or collective learning, their knowledge level will increase and they will better understand and like their work, which goes hand in hand with an increased desire to learn. It will ensure continuous learning and development.

One more idea belongs to the answers to the questions raised at the beginning of the study. Most of the mentioned characteristics (EQ, personality features, culture, etc.) indicate that a human centered leadership attitude is at the fore. Managers in a position of power who are not able to get tuned into this will not be able to make a success of their firm.

It is necessary to draw up, with respect to those requirements, a summary that assists companies in acquiring knowledge fast and professionally, and to spread and share knowledge within the organization.

Tasks that leaders have to do:

- Drawing up a strategy, concentrate most of all on the human resources.
- Sphere of activity, collecting and describing competences, and the development of a wage-system.
- Recruiting: the selection taking into consideration the departmental requirements and the drafted competences.
- The right person to the right place – an analysis of the discrepancies, compensation, education, training (internal benchmarking, best practice, change management, organizational development).
- Observation of the operation, performance evaluation.
- Career planning, personnel development, knowledge utilization.

- Knowledge sharing, building up supporting systems, organizational culture.
- Learning teams, building and operating communities of practice.
- Change of leadership style, further training, EQ development.

In other words, in order to turn knowledge into organizational power the management with power has to obtain such knowledge that it can put in place the transformational leading principles that form cooperating teams. Drawing up a human-centered strategy, which includes the transformation of the motivation system, continuous learning, assurance of training possibilities, the forming of a collective view, and exact collective goals will be necessary. In the course of successful management roles – building upon Mintzberg's principles (2009) – the negotiator, information, and resource allocator roles come into prominence. At the point of a leadership style change, first of all, the direction, democratic, liaison-centered, coaching styles and management by objective also play important roles.

## Employees' Satisfaction

The importance of human resources, which is a keeper of organizational knowledge, needs to be evaluated at a higher level than earlier. In connection with employee satisfaction, researchers have created different groups. Only some important categories are stressed to illustrate the connection between employee satisfaction and organizational competitiveness. The background and an ability to work are ensured by learning, learning organization, and knowledge management systems.

The following list summarizes the factors (without completeness) that influence most of all the level of employee satisfaction and its connection with the steps of a knowledge management system.

- **Setting Purposes**: Identifying with organizational purposes, to accept them without reservation (determine knowledge purposes).
- **Empathy (Sensitivity):** Collective interactions, relationship between leaders and employees, to handle colleagues, to solve problems, to handle conflicts (knowledge identifying).
- **Learning:** Possibility to reach knowledge, ensure a continuous development (knowledge acquiring, knowledge development).
- **Mutual Support Between Colleagues:** Knowledge, experience sharing, learning from colleagues, from leaders (knowledge sharing).
- **Acknowledgement:** Efficiency of a motivation system, the performance can be changeable (knowledge sharing and supporting).
- **Commitment:** To subordinate personal aims to organizational aims and to connect them to each other more and more, to forgive mistakes, to practice abilities, to use knowledge (personal and collective learning, knowledge utilization).
- **Trust:** Sincere, open, fear free atmosphere, natural communication, obstacle free information flow (knowledge dissemination/transfer, knowledge utilization).
- **Taking Responsibility**: Independent decisive ability and to establish possibilities to use them, evaluation of the results of decisions (knowledge preservation).
- **Working Conditions:** Physical fundamentals, technical perfection, supplying tools (knowledge storing, knowledge preservation).
- **Acceptance:** Utilization of creativity, to respect ideas, proposals (leaders supporting, knowledge control).

- **Performance Appraisal:** Expectation – possibility, harmony among conditions, work and process organization at a high level (knowledge control, evaluation).

Management has a possibility to mobilize organizational reserves, to undertake measures using strategic planning, to implement organizational changes and management techniques, in order to move the organization to the direction of competitiveness. To accomplish this, management can use information from benchmarks, the results of satisfaction surveys, and they can use organizational culture as a basis. According to a survey that was conducted at the end of 2000, which aimed to explore connections between used competitive strategies and competitiveness, most leaders were focused on acquiring a qualitative labor force to preserve a good position in the international market.

In the course of conducting an estimate of organizational competitiveness, more than half of the interviewed managers classified as a hard determinant factor the necessity of a well-skilled labor force. Further important features were flexibility and reliability, which managers signified as important factors in keeping the labor force, strengthening commitment of colleagues, and keeping the human resources at a high level (Simonyi, 2004). In this, an organization should react flexibly and in advance of environmental changes, and it should produce the ability to continuously learn and embrace a willingness to change. This means a transition to a learning organization, which cannot be realized with dissatisfied, resistant colleagues who cannot identify themselves with the organizational aims.

Organizational learning means conflicts and debates within the environment. A learning organization is able to change, and during this process it is able to be competitive at the same time. As learning means moving – that is, changing – a learning organization should predict the changes and their consequences in advance. In this way, it is able to attain competitive advantages through its previous plans. On the basis of this idea, a learning organization has two different qualitative grades:

- A passive and reactive learning organization that reacts only to spontaneous changes.
- A proactive and preceding learning organization that defines the environmental changes in advance and initiates the suitable strategy in advance.

According to a survey, 78% of leaders think that knowledge, as a resource, contributes to 60–100% of the most important processes of the company. But they do not use about 50% of employees' knowledge. This means that most employees are employed in an unsuitable position – they work in unsuitable areas, which are not in harmony with their knowledge and professional skills. Leaders have to think about how they can manage their professional human resources better. A feature of employees' satisfaction is that a colleague is in the right position in an organization, if he/she can, or has the possibility to accomplish self-actualization (Mura et. al, 2016).

Leaders have to be closer to the way of thinking that says that a condition of competitiveness is employee satisfaction, and that satisfied employees' willingness to learn and change can contribute to the possibility that the knowledge can be utilized and distributed in the organization at a higher level. To accept this thinking, we have to turn back to the eight elements of the Probst model (for which satisfaction is a precondition).

These elements have a logical order and leaders have to know the steps to building a KM system. Theoretical knowledge and interactions among colleagues (communication) create real knowledge, which can be utilized by an organization in order to be competitive. A chance to reach personal and organizational desires is the most important guarantee of the pursuit of knowledge, which is a precondition of learning and satisfaction at the same time. To sum up, the elements of the Probst model are:

- **Determination of Knowledge Goals:**
  - **Normative Goals:** To create an organizational culture, a joyful workplace and atmosphere that supports the competitiveness.
  - **Strategic Goals:** The existing organizational knowledge helps to realize the strategic goals and with this knowledge we can work out a new, competitive strategy on a higher level.
  - **Operational Goals:** They support the application the knowledge management, if the normative and strategic goals are concrete enough (make sure that normative and strategic knowledge goals will be translated into action).
- **Knowledge Identification:** View of the internal abilities and possessed knowledge. The once applied and experienced things do not have to be discovered again and again. It is suitable to do a comparison with the environment, to use a benchmark, and the organizational memory has a significant role to play in calling on previous experience.
- **Knowledge Acquisition:** It means to learn from competitors, rivalries, stakeholders, buying know-how, unknown knowledge integration, and to apply every cultured method of knowledge acquisition (dishonest tools, which are important from the perspective of competition, but cannot be made consistent with employee satisfaction, do not belong to this step of the KM system – for example, company acquisition, stealing knowledge, industrial espionage, etc.).
- **Knowledge Development:** New abilities and ideas develop more effective technology and the collection of new knowledge (obstacles and supporting elements, which are in close correlation with employee satisfaction, have to be identified). It is a direct factor that influences competitiveness.
- **Knowledge Distribution:** Separated knowledge has to be integrated into the whole organization. Who, what, when, how, has to be known (it is a prerequisite of satisfaction and a result at the same time; its base is communication and a knowledge sharing organizational culture in each case).
- **Knowledge Use:** Possessing knowledge does not bring a result, but to use it does. This is in connection with an ability to acquire knowledge, with willingness to learn and change, which is in interaction with satisfaction. To realize this step, the previous phase must be accomplished (this is also true in the case of internal and external knowledge).
- **Knowledge Preservation:** Knowledge does not exist forever. In preserving and in forgetting knowledge the organizational memory plays a significant role. This is very important as well from the point of view of the creation of a balance between learning/forgetting, knowledge losing processes, and fluctuations. People who join an organization bring with them their knowledge. This can be anticipated from the development of knowledge bases, knowledge stores. With the increase of satisfaction, the chance to preserve work forces and knowledge will grow (through knowledge maps, knowledge catalogues).
- **Knowledge Measurement:** In estimating competitiveness, the indexes have significant roles to play, which are suitable for measuring normative, strategic, and operational goals. At the stage of determining the knowledge goals, the evaluation of success has to be fixed (market conditions, competitors, sales, etc.).

These elements have to be handled from a systemic point of view and it is very important to review the connections between them.

People must remember that the traditional measurable and calculable indexes that are used to estimate competitiveness can verify the real value of a company only in part, because the value of human resources is an invisible category on the balance sheet report of a company. But to miss it when conducting a performance estimation is incorrect because the real value of a company is in its employees' heads. This invisible capital is valueless without human resource. Companies should take this into consideration from a uniform viewpoint when estimating competitiveness – Scandinavian countries have taken these steps. They prepare tables before their balance sheet reports in which human resource values are represented (Boda, 2003). This table is a part of a surveillance system that contains immaterial capital. It has been worked out by Sveiby (2001). It measures the efficiency, renewal, and stability of the three elements (customer, knowledge, organizational) of immaterial capital. These measurements are very important, especially with respect to knowledge companies where the rate of material capital decreases (for example, software, high-tech, designer, training, etc. companies). The BSC method is often used for this measurement.

Author has prepared a figure (see Figure 1) that shows the relationships among the following characteristics of a company, which were shown above in detail:

- Learning – culture – knowledge.
- Culture – satisfaction – quality.

*Figure 1. The role of employee satisfaction in the organizational competitiveness*
*(authors' construction)*

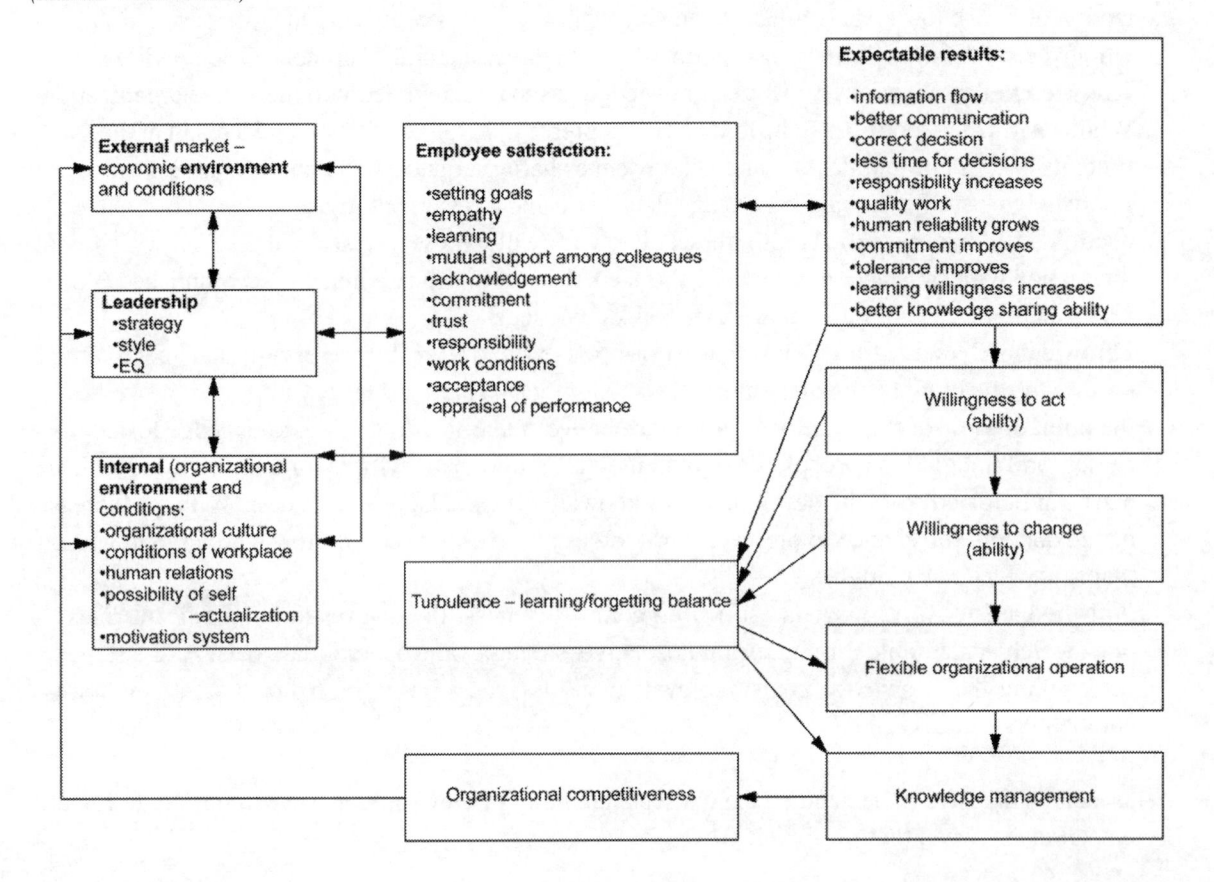

- Satisfaction and emotional intelligence (EQ).
- Satisfaction – EQ – knowledge management.
- Leadership – emotional intelligence – competence.

On the basis of the Figure 1 and the above shown connections, readers see that the success of a knowledge management system depends on leadership style, attitude, and behavior – all of which are in close connection with the listed characteristics.

## CONCLUSION

The goal of this chapter was to show the possibility of building a knowledge management system on the basis of a symbiosis among such organizational features as communication, leadership style, EQ, competence, satisfaction, and learning culture. The preconditions for a knowledge management system are a learning organizational culture and a well-operated IT system, which establishes the realization of the Probst model elements. The cultural environment is indispensable in building and operating knowledge management systems, which are a precondition for successful business management in international markets.

According to the logic of this study, readers can follow the exploration of connections among many management methods, tools, and their infiltration in the logic of building a knowledge management system. These methods have been used as independent possibilities for a long time in the areas of business management, but in this study we have shown that the relations had not been revealed earlier. Outlined below are the relationships needed in order to successfully build a knowledge management system.

Creating a learning organization culture and a knowledge management system can be summarized in the following essential section.

- **Preconditions:**
  - The characteristics of the Senge-style learning organizational culture model (personal mastery, systems thinking, mental models, building shared vision, team learning).
  - IT system building.
- **Tasks and Points of View to Lead Change on Behalf of Creating a Learning Organization:**
  - To organize team work in consideration of abilities of personal and organizational learning/forgetting, of predominance of teams' characters, of personal and collective EQ level.
  - Necessity and function of professional communities.
  - Relations among team characters and team development.
  - Stages of knowledge management cycle and the necessary team characters to realize them.
  - Relations within the knowledge management cycle and the required team efficiency model.
  - Teams' contribution to operating a knowledge management system.
  - Connection between organizational learning and knowledge management system.
  - Connections between strategy and human centered leadership elements.
  - To create a competence matrix.
  - Success of organizational memory during a change process.
  - Connections between processes of change management and becoming a learning organization.

- **Expectations for Leaders' Behavior and Activities:** In order to find connections and to handle them among the following areas on behalf of leading a change management process on the basis of the logic of the project, the following is required:
  - Leadership style – emotional intelligence – competence.
  - Satisfaction – EQ – knowledge management.
  - Satisfaction and emotional intelligence (EQ).
  - Learning – culture – knowledge.
  - Culture – satisfaction – quality.
  - Extreme leadership.
  - Satisfaction – EQ – connections among the features of emotional competencies and KM system elements.
  - Importance of employees' satisfaction in organizational competitiveness.
  - Connections among knowledge management system elements and leadership competences.

Readers can see that the relationships are multiple, which is natural and accepted at the level of top management. If leaders who have to manage a change process use the logic of our study and keep in mind the main principles and relations during their intervention that were shown above, they can realize greater success.

# REFERENCES

Argote, L., & Ingram, P. (2000). Knowledge Transfer: A Basis for Competitive Advantage in Firms. *Organizational Behavior and Human Decision Processes*, 82(1), 150–169. doi:10.1006/obhd.2000.2893

Argyris, C., & Schön, D. A. (1978). *Organizational Learning, A Theory of Action Perspective*. Boston: Addison-Westley.

Bakacsi, G., Bokor, A., Császár, C., Gelei, A., Kováts, K., & Takács, S. (2000). *Stratégiai emberi erőforrás menedzsment*. Budapest: KJK-Kerszöv Jogi és Üzleti Kiadó Kft.

Barakonyi, K., & Lorange, P. (2000). *Stratégiai menedzsment*. Budapest: KJK.

Bencsik, A. (2003). Csoportfejlődés és csoportszerepek érvényesülése a tanulószervezetben. *Matrix (Stuttgart, Germany)*, 4, 13–27.

Bencsik, A. (2005). Dolgozói elégedettség - a szervezeti versenyképességet befolyásoló tényező. *Vezetéstudomány*, 6, 41–47.

Boda, G. (2003). A láthatatlan tőkét is lehet és kell mérni. *Menedzsment Fórum*. Retrieved from www. mfor.hu

Bőgel, G. (2005). Tudás, pénz, hatalom I.-II. *CEO*, 6(1-2), 8-15, 27-33.

Carlstedt, G. (1997). Quotation. In E. Oakley & D. Krug (Eds.), *Korszerű változásmenedzselés*. Budapest: Bagolyvár Könyvkiadó.

Consulting, I. Q. (2003). *Versenyképesség az Európai Unióban – A vezetők által közvetlenül befolyásolható szervezeti dimenziók 9.* Retrieved from www.iqconsulting.hu

Cummings, T., & Worley, Ch. (2013). *Organization Development and Change.* Singapore: Cengage Learning.

Davenport, T. H., & Prusak, L. (2001). *Tudásmenedzsment.* Budapest: Kossuth Kiadó.

De Long, D. W., & Fahey, L. (2000). Diagnosing Cultural Barriers to Knowledge Management. *The Academy of Management Executive, 14,* 113–127. doi:10.5465/AME.2000.3979820

Fehér, P. (2002). Tudásmenedzsment: Problémák és Veszélyek. *Vezetéstudomány, 34*(4), 36–45.

Gáthy, A. (2004). Egyetemisták ismeretszintje a fenntartható fejlődés fogalomköréről. *Acta Agraria Debreceniensies, 13,* 232–241.

Goleman, D. (1995). *Emotional Intelligence: Why it can matter more than IQ.* New York: Bantam.

Goleman, D. (1997). *Érzelmi intelligencia.* Budapest: Háttér Kiadó.

Goleman, D. (2002). *Érzelmi intelligencia a munkahelyen.* Budapest: SHL Edge 2000. Kft.

Goleman, D. (2003). *A természetes vezető.* Budapest: Vince Kiadó.

Hedlund, E., & Österberg, J. (2013). Team Training, Team Learning, Leadership and Psychology Safety: A Study of Team Training and Team Learning Behavior during a Swedish Military Staff Exercise. *Sociology Mind, 3*(1), 89-98. Retrieved from http://www.scirp.org/journal

Letmathe, L., Scweitzer, M., & Zielinski, M. (2011). How to Learn New Tasks: Shop Floor Performance Effects of Knowledge Transfer and Performance Feedback. *Journal of Operations Management, 30*(3), 221–236. doi:10.1016/j.jom.2011.11.001

Minzberg, H. (2009). *Managing.* Oakland, CA: Berrett-Koehler Publishers.

Mura, L., Žuľová, J., & Madleňák, A. (2016). Strategic management and management of personnel costs: Employing young people in the Slovak Republic. *Problems and Perspectives in Management, 14*(1), 79–84.

Oakley, E., & Krug, D. (1997). *Korszerű változásmenedzselés.* Budapest: Bagolyvár Könyvkiadó.

Olšovská, A., Mura, L., & Švec, M. (2015). The most recent legislative changes and their impact on interest by enterprises in agency employment: What is next in human resource management? *Problems and Perspectives in Management, 13*(3), 47–54.

Probst, G. (1998). Practical Knowledge Management: A Model that Works. *Prism, 2,* 17–29.

Probst, G., Raub, S., & Romhardt, K. (2006). *Wissen Managen, Wie Unternehmen ihre wertvollste Ressource optimal nutzen.* Wiesbaden: Gabler GmbH.

Simonyi, Á. (2004). Jóléti politika a munkahelyeken és a munkaadók társadalmi felelőssége. *Esély, 1,* 26-37. Retrieved from http://www.esely.org/kiadvanyok/2004_1/SIMONYI.pdf

Snowdon, B., & Stonehouse, G. (2006). Competitiveness in a globalised world: Michael Porter on the microeconomic foundations of the competitiveness of nations, regions, and firms. *Journal of International Business Studies*, *37*(2), 163–175. doi:10.1057/palgrave.jibs.8400190

Sveiby, K. E. (2001). *Szervezetek új gazdagsága: a menedzselt tudás*. Budapest: KJK-KERSZÖV Jogi és Üzleti Kiadó Kft.

United Nations. (2014). *World Investment Report, Investing in the SDGs: An Action Plan*. New York: United Nations.

## KEY TERMS AND DEFINITIONS

**Communities of Practice:** Communities of practice are formed by people who engage in a process of collective learning, working on similar problems, they do and learn how to do something better as they interact regularly.

**Competence:** Knowledge and skills that enable a person (or an organization, or teams) to act effectively, successfully in a job or in a situation.

**EQ:** Emotional intelligence is the area of cognitive ability involving traits and social skills that facilitate interpersonal behaviour.

**Knowledge Management:** It is a concept in which an organization consciously and comprehensively gathers, organizes, shares, preserves, assesses and analyses its knowledge in terms of resources, documents, and people's skills, etc.

**Leadership:** It is a method/style with which leaders help themselves and others to do the right things. Leaders set direction, build an inspiring vision, and create something new.

**Learning Organization:** It is a special organizational form and culture which is a precondition of a knowledge management system building and operation. In this organization people learn continuously and use their knowledge collectively to achieve their common goals.

**Organizational Culture:** It is a system of shared assumptions, attitudes, values and beliefs which characterizes people's behaviour in organizations.

**Satisfaction:** It is a feeling of happiness or pleasure because employees' circumstances in their workplaces are great, their jobs are useful, interesting, their community is helpful and their compensations are fair.

**Teamwork:** It is generally understood as the willingness of a group of people to work together to achieve a common goal or to solve a common problem.

# Chapter 6
# Correlations of Company Strategy and KM

**Erzsébet Noszkay**
*Budapest Metropolitan University, Hungary*

## ABSTRACT

*This chapter focuses on the presentation of the interrelationship between corporate strategy and the KM system, how could requirements and tasks related to the latter be derived from the former and not separately and for its own sake but to facilitate the implementation of the strategy. It contemplates system approach and KM operating as a system. A fundamental methodological belief of the author is that a KM system adapted to a corporate strategy necessitates harmonizing along various dimensions. In view of the focal points of a corporate strategy and on the ground of an actual knowledge map, determination of new competencies and knowledge elements are necessitated by the strategy to be implemented. This could be followed by the elaboration of a KM strategy whose main dimensions are: human resource allocation (People dimension); inclusion of KM into the expediently reengineered new corporate processes (Process dimension); and the deployment of information technologies that are adequate for the processes and ultimately with the specific knowledge demand (Technology dimension).*

## INTRODUCTION

In the past 15 to 18 years, publications, articles in scientific magazines and scientific books discussing various aspects of knowledge management are published more and more frequently. Knowledge management's popularity and its regular usage in everyday practice are obviously interrelated with the blistering development of information technologies, even if its capabilities in "unwrapping" tacit knowledge could be deemed rather restricted. This blistering development of information technology exercises permanent development "coercion" on all areas of innovation; knowledge handling was institutionalized and has become knowledge management by now – irrespective of the size of undertakings. In practice, institutionalization calls for substantial methodological developments in view of the fact that one of the "secrets" of successful management including knowledge management lays in being methodical itself.

The first and overly significant station of this innovative development took place around the turn of the millennia when knowledge as a resource has already been built into business acumen, however, its interrelationship with and connection to strategic corporate planning was missing.

DOI: 10.4018/978-1-5225-1642-2.ch006

The organizations did not have a knowledge management strategy, and sophisticated methods and principles for managing corporate knowledge were even less elaborated. However, during the years after the turn of the millennia, in parallel with the growing awareness of the importance of knowledge as a strategic resource, knowledge management functions started to differentiate. A significant station of the handling, management and maturity of corporate knowledge was the appearance of the flow principle, which was soon followed by strategic recognition of knowledge and its management, and its interconnection with corporate strategy shortly afterwards. Although the number of methodologies and draft solutions aimed at organically interlinking corporate strategy and KM strategy or at "deriving" KM strategy from corporate strategy is low – no wonder: this is a very complicated issue –the frequency of such enforcements is increasing. This chapter attempts to offer a possible theoretical-methodological solution for this problem.

## BACKGROUND

As it has already been mentioned in the Introduction, researchers started to deal according to its merit with knowledge as a resource worthwhile economizing, at around the turn of the millennia. Strategic contemplations given to KM came to the limelight concurrently with the above concept. It has become essential that this delicate and intangible resource could be planned and managed by a managing body also from the strategic aspect. The more an organization knows, the more possibilities open up for combining various new knowledge elements into new knowledge complexes and therefore even more new possibilities open up, for instance new products and services could be developed. However, it matters what is known by an organization and to what extent. External knowledge elements (knowledge of partners, suppliers, other external parties, competitors, etc.) and internal knowledge elements (explicit and tacit knowledge of employees, knowledge intrinsic in various documents), knowledge of the organization in its entirety – of course, not only the knowledge to be found in the organizational memory but a synergic ability made up of individual and group knowledge elements which is able to compose partial knowledge elements into combinative knowledge complexes – when built into the products are able produce added value. This needs a sort of foresight, strategic view, since an organization is unable to properly recognize what it knows and what it does not. In fact, tacit knowledge to be found in the heads of the members of an organization, which forms the most valuable part of internal knowledge, is not necessarily identical with or does not overlap the knowledge covering competences required by the job description. Therefore, there are good chances that a competition between firms that from all other aspects are identical will be won by that one that could better and faster activate knowledge factors of critical importance from the aspect of competition, and utilize them in the interest of corporate objectives. Some of the researchers have already recognized this issue, i.e. that there is a need for a sort of overview and foresight for having access to the appropriately knowledgeable employee if and when they or their knowledge is needed (Davenport, 1997).

In order to describe the problem with the possible best accuracy, researches raised terminology questions, too, which enforce us that before proceeding further we would clarify on the basis of Zack (Zack, 2000) what are knowledge strategy, strategic knowledge management and KM strategy, and what are the differences among them. Knowledge strategy is elaborated in recognition of knowledge as a resource, in the interest of putting it into the center. Strategic knowledge management means the collection and handling of key knowledge complexes that are of importance and/or key significance from the aspect of strategy elaboration; meanwhile knowledge management strategy determines the key areas and methods, i.e. the aims and means of knowledge management.

At the beginning, knowledge strategy was in the center. This is perfectly understandable, since the first task that had to be solved was to find a solution that grants reputation in its merit for KM within corporate operation, moreover to include it among management functions and rank it in accordance with its significance.

The closer this issue was scrutinized, the more the relevant concepts became differentiated. Preparedness for knowledge management was deemed to be of determining importance by many. Strategies were structured from this aspect. For instance, according to the categorization by Zack (Zack, 1999), on the basis of knowledge elaborateness, a given firm will be able to apply different strategies. To this end three sorts of knowledge are differentiated:

The so-called basic knowledge, i.e. the minimum knowledge that is at least necessary for a firm to be apt for acting in a given industry. (This knowledge content, however, is insufficient for successfully struggling in the competition on the long run.)

The so-called "developed knowledge" is a knowledge content that enables the organization to viably participate in a competition within a given industry. In this case the quality of the knowledge level of the organization is similar to that of its competitors. The advantage that a competitive firm might enjoy is in general related to the different knowledge contents that in a given situation distinguish it from its competitors. (These differences in knowledge contents give a chance for this firm to apply so-called distinguishing corporate strategy.)

And finally, the highest level is the so-called innovative knowledge; attributably to this, a given firm could fill market leading position within an industry, distinguish itself from its competitors in terms of quality. Firms in the possession of such knowledge are able even to exercise influence on the given industry because they operate with certain competitive factors based expressly on their advantages.

When it comes to comparison between two firms armed with knowledge contents of the same level, one of them could come ahead of the other by way of applying traditional competitive factors (e.g. costs, prices). Thus we distinguish innovative, leading, viably competitive, retardant and endangered firms. A disadvantage of this categorization is that it is based on well perceivable and utilized knowledge elements whilst the firms' developments and latest innovations exploiting tacit knowledge complexes are not perceived or even could mean potential threat.

As regards strategy, there are certain approaches that contemplate the structure of a KM strategy applied, on the basis of the sources wherefrom knowledge is obtained (for instance Zack, 1999; Krogh, Roos & Slocum, 1994, etc.). Basically, sources of knowledge could be external and internal knowledge contents or some sort of their combination. It is not a coincidence that – in the interest of acquiring external knowledge – various strategic alliances are established in the interest of obtaining mutual advantages and of knowledge exchange. There are, of course, situations where the knowledge in the possession of the organization is appropriate (or even more than necessary) for granting advantage in a competitive situation. In the case of such firms it happens frequently that such superfluous knowledge not directly improving the firm's competitive position is sold to others incurring knowledge deficit, which again ensures competitive advantage for the seller. Exploitation and/or extension of the existing internal knowledge elements are not mutually exclusive. Moreover, so-called innovators are in ideal cases able to maintain the equilibrium between these two approaches and the main resource they can rely on is organizational learning. (Lam, 2004; Schienstock, 2009) So-called innovator undertakings extend their knowledge by utilizing all possible sources, they implement so-called aggressive strategy. The underlying reason is that the demand for the knowledge contents of the undertaking exceeds the volume necessary for preserving current competitive position (knowledge appetite) and therefore aggressive strategy is necessary. (These firms run turbulent technologies often with knowledge demanding technologies, or are firms involved in the delivery of knowledge demanding services. A practice frequently followed by these firms is that they utilize also Open Innovation models in order to obtain new knowledge and innovative concepts as fast as possible.)

Their opponents are those firms that follow conservative strategies, i.e. they rely on their existing knowledge contents and strive to make use of them to the largest possible extent.

The above KM strategies represent the two extremes.

Hansen, Nohria, and Tierney (1999) use a more tangible categorization which takes us closer to the nature of KM strategies. They distinguish two crystal clearly different strategies. One is based rather on the tacit knowledge possessed by experts; the other is based on explicit and easily accessible knowledge that can be easily supported by information technology.

Since it has been soon proven that in everyday practice none of the strategies can be observed "crystal-cleanly", fundamentally the so-called mixed strategies are deemed to be expedient. This concept can be found in the literature. (The gap closing between them, their advantages and disadvantages are discussed for instance by Aidemark, 2009).

The next perception was the understanding that a decisive factor in the success of KM strategy is its "approximation" to corporate strategy. When this perception first appeared in the philosophies, it was similar to corporate strategic approaches. One of the notable systematizations was published by Truch, and Bridger (2002) wherein Miles, and Snow, (1978) discussed corporate strategies and distinguished the following types of firms:

- **Repetitive:** No change;
- **Expanding:** Slow incremental changes;
- **Changing:** Fast incremental change;
- **Discontinuous:** Discontinuous predictable change;
- **Surprising:** Discontinuous predictable change.

*Table 1. Two different types of KM strategies*

| Personalization Strategy | | Codification Strategy |
|---|---|---|
| Creative, precise expertise; individual experiences are presented by experts | **Competitive strategy** | Reuse of codified knowledge contents with the help of reliable high quality information systems |
| **Experts** | **Economic Model** | **Re-Usability** |
| Face-to-face relationship | **KM strategy** | Human-to-document relationship |
| Modest investments Personal information exchange | **IT role** | Significant investments Easy accessibility |
| Experienced experts Taylor-shaped training Reward for personal knowledge transfer | **Human resources** | New graduates Reward for the use of knowledge warehouses |

Source: Hansen, Nohria, & Tierney, (1999)

Truch and Bridger (2002), in parallel with the above structure, specified types of firms that follow practically analogue KM strategies, whose suitability has been confirmed by a research. Let us see the following:

- **Prospectors:** Members of the organization are given possibilities to explore new ideas and novelties for the organization. This is supported by expert networks (eventually knowledge communities and/or expert teams) and easily accessible knowledge warehouses. KM strategy is closely interrelated with corporate strategy.
- **Analyzers:** Appropriate enforcements are dedicated to obtaining and utilizing tacit and explicit knowledge. Organizational culture supports learning (action learning, too) and the access to information. It strives to harmonize KM strategy with the corporate strategy.
- **Defenders**: They strive to collect as much information and knowledge as possible. They deem knowledge collection to be the basis of knowledge management but are unable to utilize same to its merit despite the fact that they rely on expert networks as well as on knowledge warehouses.
- **Reactors:** They concentrate on the existing knowledge and skills of their employees and deem information supply to be of fundamental importance. They are scarcely characterized by cooperation; they prefer directives; meanwhile they are able to relatively quickly react to changes in circumstances; however, they do not belong to the scope of really successful firms.

Some more KM classifications could be mentioned, however, essentially they are not about methodological issues related to KM strategies but rather about their features and the roles and different weights of various sorts of knowledge elements (tacit and explicit).

Nowadays researches and specifically consultants' approaches focus on the methodological concerns of KM strategy. In this context there are two distinctly significant factors:

- How and through what methodological steps could KM-related demands of the corporate strategy be satisfied, in other words, how could corporate strategy be converted to tasks to be solved or to project steps within KM strategy – this is the first;
- Implementation that follows the elaboration of KM strategy is a process that should reasonably be contemplated as a change management project that therefore could successfully be implemented in a planned manner, step by step. The question is, how could this be organized as an appropriately scheduled change management project – this is the second.

In the last period of time, this novel approach has in its entirety been most successfully systematized by Barnes and Milton (2015). This work elaborated a methodology on the basis of consultant experiences, and can be utilized as a manual.

Hereinafter we are going to focus on the main elements of knowledge management system approach concept. Meanwhile observations and experiences obtained from our own advisory expertise, which is applicable for the enrichment of this complicated scope of issues from various aspects will be handled as decisive factors worthwhile contemplating.

# INTERRELATIONSHIP BETWEEN CORPORATE STRATEGY AND KM STRATEGY

## Laying Ground for KM Strategy

Our investigations in the matter suggest that the firms were for a long while unable to find in between corporate strategy and KM strategy the means that in addition to the field of theory could make the problem manageable in terms of methodology. Given the fact that knowledge is intangible, it may grow and develop independently and this could relatively "independently" (since such growth and development may happen not necessarily within the organizational frameworks) be utilized for the given firm. Later – after knowledge started to gain reputation as a resource – it has become obvious that production and reproduction of and retrieval of knowledge differ from the rest of resources. Consequently, knowledge should be economized in a different manner if we would like to put it at the service of corporate objectives. To this end we should find instruments that would on the one hand enable us to map the knowledge demand stemming from corporate strategic objectives, and on the other hand help in the exploration not only of knowledge that "obviously" (explicitly) exists for the organization but the "hidden" (tacit) knowledge as well in order that losses that could stem from unutilized or even missing knowledge resources could be avoided.

The above problem – together with other KM-related issues – is on the agenda of the KM Working Committee of the Hungarian Academy of Sciences (it has approx. 60 members: developers, researchers, university lecturers, advisors, corporate users) for almost 11 years. We deal with the processing of observations related to corporate KM strategies (the author herself was involved as a consultant in the elaboration of several KM strategies, in action researches in the frames of specific situations, in experiments), and with the processing of the experiences of other developers-advisors, and with lessons learned from research projects, furthermore with the integration of various research statements and observations.

Last time (between 2012 and 2015) almost 40 knowledge demanding firms were reviewed with the semi-structured interview method, in due consideration of the following aspects (for more detail see. Noszkay & Balogh, 2015):

- What is the organization's strategy like and how does KM strategy fit to that;
- Is there a knowledge map and if yes in what manner is it elaborated an updated;
- How are supporting KM processes built into business processes;
- How do business processes and organizational memory operate;
- How are human factor and organizational culture connected to KM strategy;
- How knowledge efficiency and the results are measured (knowledge management "thermometer").

We learned that nowadays many of these organizations strongly relying on knowledge, work in due consideration of the model that the KM Working Committee of the Academy strived to popularize some years prior to this review, making good use of its national and international possibilities.

Hereinafter we would like to present the model composed as a result of our many-year work, together with our methodological developments; we collate them with other similar experiences and methodological results.

## The Model of Interrelationship between Corporate Strategy and KM Strategy

A fundamental criterion that should be considered in the course of the elaboration of KM strategy is that it should fit to the corporate strategy; however, it is also important that the conditions necessary for its implementation should be ensured afterwards. The following steps are inevitable:

- First of all a planner team is needed that will elaborate KM strategy and then controls the change management process (implements the KM development project);
- This team – by using the result indices of a BSC (Balanced Scorecard) aimed at breaking down the corporate strategic plan – will elaborate and enforce the training and development strategic objectives in respect of the knowledge necessary for the creation of competencies, as well as the main and inevitable conditions and actions for their future implementation;
- It controls execution and provides monitoring assistance (such as elaboration of a project plan, organization of implementing teams, etc.)
- Elaborates the aims that should be achieved on the short run; and measures the results achieved;
- Maintains successful communication in the interest of the achievement of the objectives (e.g. communicates part objectives achieved, etc.);
- Contributes to institutionalization of changes necessitated by the implementation of the strategy.

Most important interrelations between corporate strategy and KM strategy and the relevant tasks are summarized on Figure 1.

*Figure 1. Interrelations between corporate strategy and KM strategy*
*(Noszkay, 2013)*

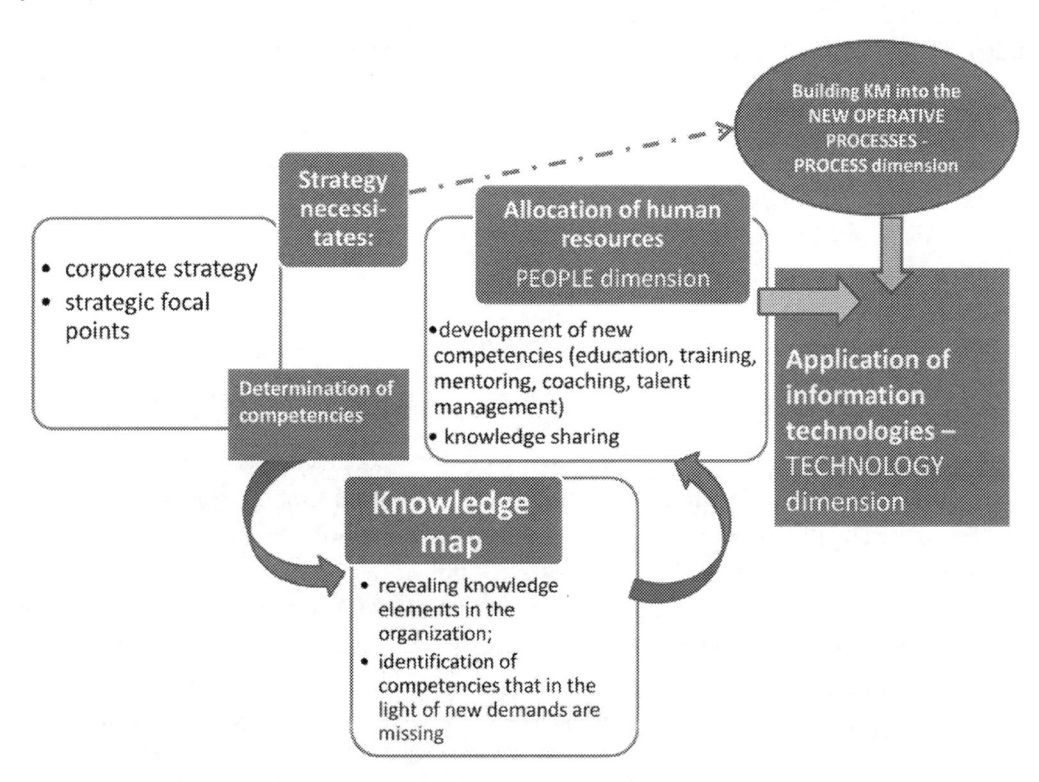

The elaboration of the KM strategy, as it can be seen from the above Figure, should reasonably start from the corporate strategy. Main steps are as follows:

- In due consideration of the focal points of the corporate strategy, those competencies are specified that are inevitable for the implementation of a successful strategy;
- Afterwards these are collated with the organizational knowledge map in order to identify those missing competences that will be necessary for the future implementation of the strategy;
- This is followed by the elaboration of those dimensions of KM strategy (people, process, technology) that form the basis of a change management project aimed at the implementation of the KM strategy. Such as:
  - Among the necessary competences, the development of the PEOPLE dimension, i.e. human resources is reasonable (education, training, mentoring, coaching, talent management, etc.). If the human resources could not be solved by way of the development of internal human resources, then new employees should be recruited. This point covers also more dynamic knowledge support and knowledge sharing, moreover, highly developed solutions for economizing knowledge as a capital element;
  - In parallel with the PEOPLE dimension, the so-called PROCESS dimension of KM should be developed, i.e. the operative elements of the KM system – which are adequate with the given process –should be built into new (or redesigned) processes fitting to the strategic requirements;
  - This is followed by the determination of the TECHNOLOGY dimension, i.e. the information technology necessary for supporting the knowledge of the human resources is specified and procured and their expedient utilization is ensured.

What we observed in the matter is that by now the majority of undertakings experienced that it is not worthwhile to start creating a KM system "for its own sake"; it should rather be fitted into a strategic vision. In the context of everyday practice this means that whatever KM sub-system has been selected for starting a development, there is an underlying concept there and – at their majority – an attempt to enforce system approach. Our latest research conducted in the scope of knowledge demanding service providers, unambiguously reflected this statement. Hereinafter we are going to discuss the content factors (sub-systems) of the dimensions of strategic planning.

Preliminarily please note that certain firms engaged in KM consulting apply similar flowcharts that are usually embedded in a wider context. We are inclined to agree with the flowchart published by GREENES Consulting (http://www.greenesconsulting.com/services/list-services/km-assessment-strategy-development), primarily because among the main factors of KM strategy, they deem structure and culture to be equally decisive. (In the course of our latest researches or consulting practices it has been unambiguously experienced that it is necessary to take into consideration impacts on or in between structure and culture, mainly in the interest of the success of the KM strategy.)

The model applied by GREENES Consulting deserves our attention for another good reason. When the elaboration and implementation of a KM strategy – linked to and harmonized with the corporate strategy – is modeled as a cycle, this ensures the continuity of the development of corporate knowledge management phased along planning periods (which therefore could be measured together with other Balanced Scorecard indices).

In the following part let us discuss the main factors of the planning of a KM strategy, in more detail.

# MAIN CONTENT FACTORS AND METHODOLOGICAL NECESSITIES OF THE PLANNING OF A KM STRATEGY

## Mapping Organizational Knowledge and Appraisal of New Competence Demands

Mapping of changes in and demands for KM necessitated by the corporate strategy is the first task.

The gap between competences intrinsic in the strategic demand and those competences that can be found within the firm should be evaluated in respect of each job and/or position and separately for the key employees and for their supporting staff. (This will be followed by the determination of KM demands to be built into the business processes, and finally by the determination of IT development demands.)

Demand for the development of new competences necessitated by the strategy should reasonably be determined on the basis of their collation with the exiting competences. Thus the expedient and viable solution is the elaboration of a knowledge map, if not yet exists. (Obviously, afterwards the knowledge map should regularly be updated because an obsolete knowledge map is invaluable.)

## Knowledge Map and Its Elaboration

Organizations apply various solutions for storing information, however, in order that information could be converted to knowledge, the knowledgeable person should be known. From the aspect of knowledge utilization it is of high significance that the person capable of solving a problem could be found, and the corporate knowledge map serves for that, it simplifies search.

Knowledge map improves the efficiency of knowledge catalogue; enables visualization of knowledge content and graphical depiction of experiences, in other words knowledge map is the imaging of a network of concepts by way of presenting the concepts and their interrelationships. This is a map of expertise and experiences accumulated within the organization. It "presents" experts by their respective knowledge, i.e. reveals who knows what within the undertaking and how that person could be contacted. It points out information moreover various knowledge elements without revealing their contents, and in the form of a list or chart determines the location of information within the undertaking, as well as the path and the method of access. In fact, the knowledge map is a description of elements of the knowledge catalogue with metadata. It specifies the properties of each information source (for instance location, author, date of creation, etc.).

Meanwhile, the knowledge map might entail corporate policy tensions because it may happen that the position or job description of a given employee does not reflect his/her professional knowledge. As opposed to knowledge map, an organizational map presents the formal structure of reporting obligations.

There are several ways for creating a knowledge map.

- The first and simplest knowledge map can be approached from the persons. Knowledge and competences of all persons are clarified and captured in a searchable data base. The method can be either the completion of a questionnaire or an interview. Its popular name is the "corporate golden pages".
- The second method pays attention to the knowledge flow within the undertaking, and shares its characteristics with the field of sociometry. Its man principle is that those knowledge owners should be found (owners of key knowledge elements) who are of decisive importance from the as-

pect of the achievement of the corporate goals, and therefore they are most frequently approached for assistance. If this solution is opted for then the knowledge of all persons must not be assessed, which would be a rather time consuming process; only the "key persons" should be approached. In the course of the elaboration of the map some people are asked about to whom they turn to for help, afterwards these persons are approached and are asked the same question, thus the knowledge flow throughout the undertaking is discovered in a "cascade". A disadvantage of this method is that it may happen that some people who possess relevant knowledge could be absent from the map if they do not or just rarely participate in the knowledge flow (e.g. they are too modest or least sociable, etc.). An advantage of this method is that only those knowledge owners are mapped who share their knowledge, and arrives at a sort of evaluation of their knowledge.

- The third method is the most complicated but could be very useful. Knowledge owners are determined by approaching them from the processes. Firstly we should select a concept or process where the knowledge necessary to it would be modeled. Then the knowledge necessary for this concept or the existing knowledge is disassembled until we arrive at the level of knowledge elements that cannot be disassembled further. At the end of the paths shown on the knowledge map, i.e. at the knowledge elements can the knowledge owners be found? The usability of a map is greatly facilitated by visualization. For this purpose we could create "knowledge galaxies" and thus knowledge map can be presented as a graph. Finally, the "knowledge galaxy" will contain all knowledge elements belonging to the concept to be modeled as well as the relevant persons. An advantage of this method is that we are able to identify knowledge deficits, too, and in the graph we could indicate not only the location of the knowledge owners, since there are certain software products that can store personal profiles that contain more detailed information and image that could be of assistance when a searcher wishes to contact the person searched.

Components of the knowledge map are drafted on Figure 2. Where the "paths" of the knowledge map terminate, there can the knowledge owners and their contact data be found.

Advantages of a knowledge map are the following:

- Reduction of the search time,
- Identification of knowledge deficits;
- Discovery and utilization of knowledge elements within the organization that are appropriate for exploiting future possibilities;

In summary: support for knowledge sharing process through a simplified retrieval of data.

The index word, the keyword or the attribute inseparable from the keyword are dependent upon taxonomy. As we proceed step by step on the knowledge map, the knowledge deficit related to taxonomies become obvious, which serves for the development, fine-tuning and modification of knowledge map.

- Possible knowledge deficits can be various (Szeghegyi, 2010), for instance: concept deficit, contact deficit and applicability deficit.
  - Concept deficit means the existence of an index word that cannot be defined or described, i.e. other keyword could be imagined.
  - In the case of contact deficit, the operation, the interaction cannot be defined, that is the absence of known or unknown inseparable attributes and their interrelations could be imagined.

*Figure 2. Components of a knowledge map*
*(source: Velencei, 2007)*

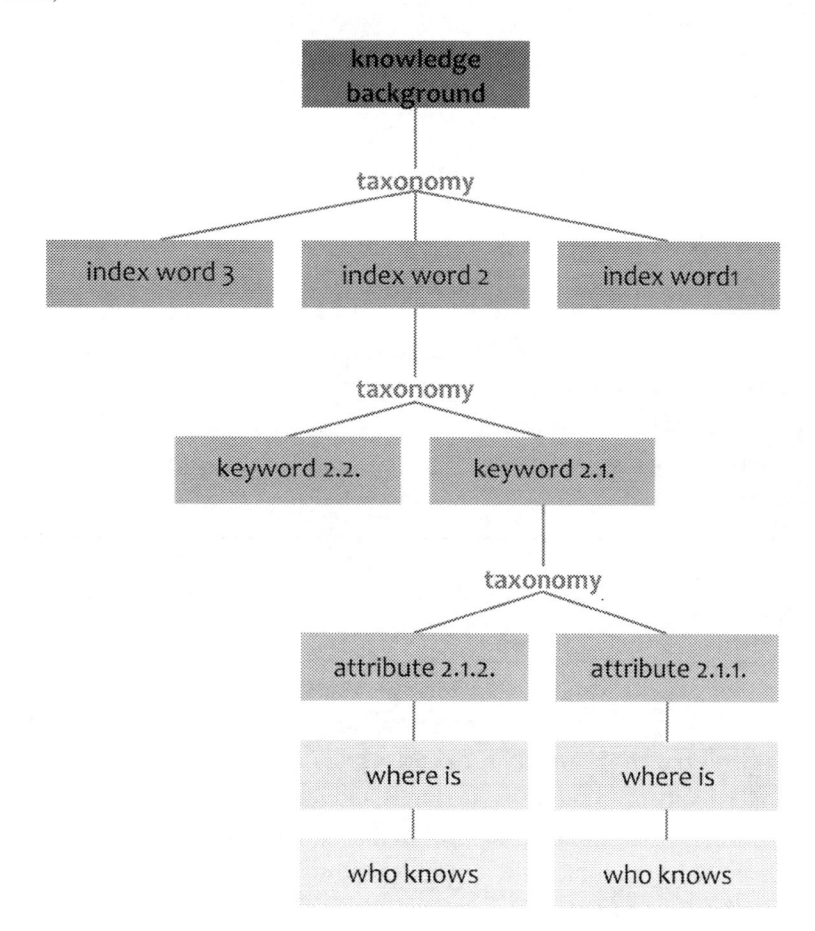

- ○ Applicability deficit means vision deficit, unknown applicability domain, deficits stemming from the existence of known or unknown attributes, or from their interactions, operation or classification.

Although knowledge maps could be created in various ways, the intrinsic difficulties are almost always identical. A knowledge map is always in close relationship with the method of its elaboration, which may intrinsically determine the "quality" and reliability of the map. The organizational culture and the recognition of knowledge sharing exercise significant impact on mapping.

The creation of a map may conflict with the subordination relationships, since in the course of mapping it can easily be revealed that the knowledge of certain employees supersedes that of a boss.

It should therefore be stated that the mapping of knowledge, the elaboration of a knowledge map can be a very useful knowledge management function, since – with the help of appropriate browsing engines – the knowledge that is actually needed by the organization could easily be found and accessed, meanwhile the members in an organization obtain practical experiences about a situation wherein the so-called organizational knowledge is for them, and assists in their work.

It is important to know that no map believed to be most perfect one could be deemed as "finalized". It is worthwhile to constantly build, develop and update it because it will yield value and therefore it forms part of the strategic and operative KM.

In summary of the above, in the process of creating a knowledge map the following steps are of fundamental importance: which the accessible knowledge resources are, where the nodes, communities are, who the users are, where the paths, cycles of knowledge exchange are, furthermore what knowledge deficits are in the system.

A fundamental issue is the clarification of the location of knowledge along the following dimensions: expertise, skill, experience.

And finally, one should assess the location and the form of the explicit knowledge. (Documents, regulations, methodologies, case studies, technical descriptions, etc., i.e. everything should be mapped including those processes wherein implicit knowledge "settles" on the product and produces added values, new products, technologies, services, etc.)

This should be followed by a more detailed elaboration of further dimensions that are necessitated by the strategy.

## PEOPLE DIMENSION

When the configuration of a knowledge management system is contemplated, one should focus on the development of the competences fitting the strategy and on the demand for the recruitment and/or retention of the best staff (with the enforcement of the principle of long-term employment relationship). In the course of all steps the appropriate means, methods and techniques are applied in close relationship with a special logic. The determination of the most important tasks is similar to the concept of Bencsik (2015) who meanwhile paid attention to the steps of the Probst model (1998). Therefore:

- Knowledge priorities (necessary competences) should be identified and built into the HR strategy, and harmonized with HR activities (information, communication paths, persuasion, etc.);
- Existing and missing knowledge elements, competences should be identified with the help of a knowledge map; competence matrix, mind mapping, best practice, benchmarking, etc.
- Missing knowledge should be acquired, possibilities found and support ensured (recruitment – selection), organizational development,
- Training system should be developed for the improvement of existing but incomplete knowledge and competences; career plans, talent management, organizational „vacuum", etc.
- Various knowledge sharing solutions should be started and knowledge culture configured (means: master-student, mentoring, quality circles, knowledge exchange, knowledge-café, other informal techniques, knowledge communities, expert groups, etc.)
- Management of human problems and conflicts stemming from knowledge utilization, maintenance of the student organization, AAR, retrospect, storytelling, etc.
- Knowledge fixing – running IT systems (in progress), LLL, configuration and operation of organizational memory, etc.
- Knowledge assessment continuously in all jobs; inclusion in the product, service; cost/benefit analyses, etc.

Identification of knowledge priorities and knowledge targets, and their derivation from the corporate strategy and the KM strategy gives an advance indication for HR about the necessary activities. If human-focused approach and preference for knowledge strategies will be given room within the strategy, then the objectives of the HR strategy should also be in compliance with expectations. To this end the communication channels and methods should appropriately be selected and applied.

Knowledge identification presupposes familiarity with external knowledge situation. Elaboration of knowledge maps, competence matrices and mind map is inevitable, whilst assessment of external situation and best practice could be supported by benchmarking instruments.

Knowledge acquisition, as one of the components, shall mean the acquisition of missing knowledge. A possible method for that is first of all development of the knowledge and competence of the intramural staff. In general, a properly operating firm lays primary emphasis on that. Only if the result of knowledge identification undoubtedly suggests that there is a need for an external coworker, then turn those firms that highly esteem their key persons toward the labor market. If a new coworker is needed, the means of recruitment and selection should expediently correspond to the desirable expectations. Obviously, the knowledge supplied by the external coworker would just moderately support our objectives if the selection was inadequate, if we do not arrange for the amalgamation of the knowledge of the new coworker and the knowledge existing at the undertaking. The appropriate means should be ensured by the PEOPLE dimension.

In order that an undertaking could successfully implement its strategy, knowledge should constantly be developed on the personal as well as on the organizational level. This necessitates the application of appropriate means, conscious redesign of the training system in its entirety in correspondence with the KM strategy, furthermore continuous renewal of knowledge communities and professional groups, harmonization of the talent management programs with the strategic and actual objectives. Obviously, newer and newer possibilities and tasks are in our focus in the areas of knowledge exploitation, commitment or contact management aimed at boosting confidence.

Knowledge development calls for teamwork, collective thinking; forming and operation of knowledge communities and professional groups, expert teams; organization of training possibilities and seminars and the elaboration of the necessary syllabi.

Attention should be paid to the career plans in order that coworkers specifically the key persons could foresee development or promotion possibility; moreover, key persons and coworkers with outstanding skills and knowledge should enjoy special support granted by talent management. Further means of knowledge development and competence improvement could be the contemplation and application of the possibility of e.g. job enrichment or rotation, mentoring young talents, networking with scientific organizations.

The most crucial element of the PEOPLE dimension is knowledge sharing and the transfer of tacit knowledge. In order that solutions could be implemented in practice and become part of the everyday culture, professionalism is needed in the application of necessary methods and techniques, such as the selection of a mentor from among suitable persons with appropriate means, design of the work order, arranging for the conditions necessary for knowledge transfer, implementation of motivation systems, etc. Establishment of knowledge and professional communities (see in more detail e.g. Noszkay, 2013) and expert groups and running them appropriately are of outstanding significance from professional and cultural aspects. The necessity of the lessons learned through experience must be emphasized, e.g. processing the lessons learned from a project, making the results available for other members of the organization.

## INCLUSION OF KNOWLEDGE IN THE ORGANIZATIONAL PROCESSES: PROCESS DIMENSION

The process dimension covers the successive phases of knowledge management, application developments and applications (partial application phases). Such as:

- **Knowledge Market:** One should determine who needs what and who could offer what, and appropriately cooperating pairs / teams should be interconnected.
- **Knowledge Brokers:** Persons are needed who could pair knowledge "owners" with the owners of knowledge demanding processes.
- **Peer Assist**: Before a team would start a task, it should expediently "visit" another experienced team (organizational unit) and examine their methods, in order that methods that are available within or even outside the organization should not be reinvented or not to make the same mistake that others have made. In addition, through such co-operations the network capital of the firm (or an individual) can be increased.
- **AAR = After-Action Review:** Making use of the possibility of collecting experiences quickly and informally after the finalization of the task / project. Key questions are:
  ○ What was planned?
  ○ What happened really?
  ○ What is the reason behind the difference?
  ○ What lessons can be used in the future?
- **Answers Given to the Above Questions and Their Recording:** Specifically if such records will be easily available for the members of the organization – can be useful, e.g. for managing similar situations or projects, for avoiding the same mistakes, for reusing success factors, etc.
- **Case Studies, Project Closing Reports:** Written, structures project / action report consisting of approx. 1000 words, for a wider community (mostly members of the organization).
- **Rewarding Knowledge Sharing:** Either built into the remuneration system or moral rewards "only" – experience obtained so far suggests that a combination is the most efficient.
- **Inter-Projects Learning and the Best Practice:** Sharing best practice with each other.
- **Exit-Interview**: Preservation, retention of the knowledge of people leaving or retiring, or at least saving their knowledge on elementary level.
- **Knowledge-Audit:** Measuring the maturity of the organization's knowledge management, identification of the existing and missing knowledge, discovery of the forms of knowledge flow (and its barriers) – in the case of a comprehensive organization development project this must be the first step. It may frequently include development actions, too, since it forms part of a complex process.
- **Interconnections with Other HR Sub-Systems:** In harmony with the discussion in the foregoing point, knowledge management related objectives and intentions should appear in every subsystem. Management of the knowledge capital is an absolute must, but performance management is essential and decisive, too; issues like 360° evaluation, selection, distinguished treatment for "key persons" (knowledge workers), career management, talent management, remuneration, etc.
- **Links to External Knowledge Sharing Systems:** There are certain issues where the creation of a "totally" closed own knowledge management system is not worthwhile. Possibilities can be found in the environment and should be integrated in accordance with the organization's objectives.

- **Inclusion of External Knowledge:** Knowledge relevant to the objectives of the "undertaking" but to be found outside the organization (e.g. critiques, articles, audience's opinion) can be reached with various means. It is worthwhile contemplating the methods of their extraction: data mining methods, community forums, utilization of Crowdsourcing in respect of innovative enforcements, etc.
- **Knowledge and Training Center:** A "cultic" place for knowledge transfer. Such center can play decisive role in changing the culture of knowledge management. The Knowledge and Training Center houses for:
  - Competence based trainings (seminars, workshops...);
  - Knowledge transfer events (organized, spontaneous);
  - Traditional knowledge warehouses (library, archives...);
  - Access to web2 forums, etc.

## TECHNOLOGY DIMENSION: INFORMATION TECHNOLOGIES CORRESPONDING TO THE DEMANDS OF PROCESSES

The technology dimension covers information technologies that support knowledge collection, transfer, sharing and use. The main planning principle is that information technologies should fit to the demands of the previous dimensions.

The knowledge treasure created with the use of various technology solutions yields added value for the organization in the course of its usage. This is why systems easing the use and utilization of knowledge and information play important role (e.g. professional knowledge warehouses, databases, document management, easily searchable automated systems). Knowledge sharing is inevitable instrument for teamwork systems, and for the use of intranet and corporate portals which make available for a given team the results that are necessary for their work (such result is e.g. a report generated by an analytic system). The flow management systems ensure scheduled supply of knowledge for knowledge-intensive activities, meanwhile such systems follow the context-relatedness of knowledge and thereby efficiently facilitate decision making. Also, these systems can be decisive as regards e-learning systems, specifically in the frames of organizational learning.

Information technology mostly plays intermediary or assistant role in the discovery, sharing, distribution and application of knowledge, however sometimes it can play key role. A great choice of information technology solutions supporting knowledge management is available, which is illustrated on Figure 3. Without claiming completeness let us review the main information technologies that could be utilized as proper means for supporting successful implementation of knowledge management strategy.

### Technologies Assisting in the Identification of an Individual Knowledge Element (Knowledge Sources)

If a knowledge element is deemed to be a (codified) object, then it can be stored in a document warehouse (database), data warehouse or content management system. If a knowledge element can be accessed via its medium then a system describing the knowledge and competence of the members of the organization ("yellow pages") can be used.

*Figure 3. Various information technologies – according to the features of their utilization*
*(source: Bencsik, A, .Boda, Gy., Klimkó, G., Kő, A. & Noszkay, E., 2010)*

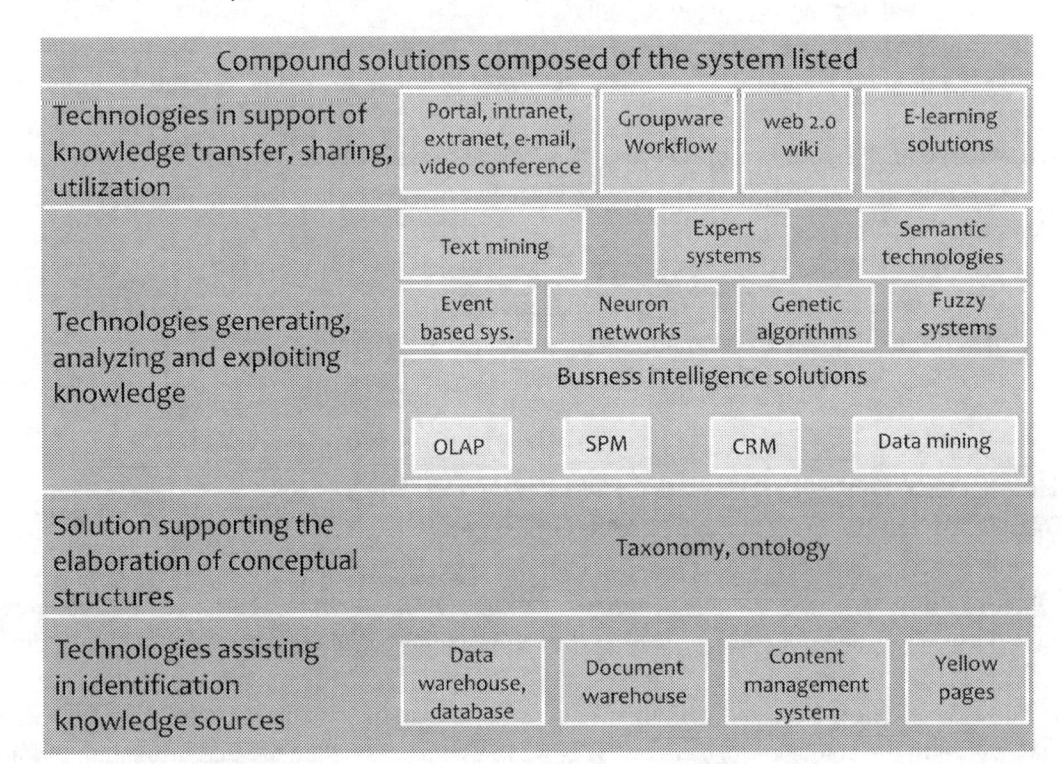

It is essential that a unified concept structure is configured within the organization in the interest of the consistent operation of knowledge management. In order that we could analyze and handle knowledge management problems actually emerging, the elaboration of a sort of "knowledge warehouse" can be useful. Such "knowledge warehouse" is in general an ontological data warehouse, document warehouse or content management system for capturing and preliminarily processing data and facts. The data warehouses, document warehouses or content management systems ensure input necessary for the running of the processes and knowledge retrieval, and ensure the basis necessary for the analyzing end exploiting systems. From the aspect of the interpretation and search of an individual knowledge element, the technologies facilitating categorization and classification are of decisive importance. Knowledge elements or their media could be classified or in other words organized into a graph structure by using either taxonomy or ontology. Taxonomy systematically classifies or categorizes knowledge elements, meanwhile ontology describe the conceptual structure of a given area in the context of knowledge management.

In the case of any structure aimed at facilitating inquiries, fundamental questions are its depth and complexity. Over-regulating causes loss of information and delineates usability, meanwhile less structured solutions are inapt for further use (for instance the next systems cannot manage them). In the case of opting for ontology, highlighting and using seed terms is expedient.

## KNOWLEDGE GENERATING, ANALYZING, AND EXPLOITING TECHNOLOGIES

Among the systems supporting the analysis and exploitation of knowledge resources one can find the business intelligence solutions that include modern forms of data storage, real time data retrieval, analytics, forecasting and data mining processes. These systems support managerial decision making (so-called OLAP solutions), assists in the evaluation of the organizational performance (strategic performance management solutions), or enables the execution of a specific knowledge-intensive task. OLAP solutions are information systems for senior managers, which ensure quick data access for the users, through slices of multidimensional views. Multidimensionality in this context means that different users may view data in different form and detail. With the help of strategic performance management systems, the user has a comprehensive picture on the performance of the undertaking, and this is supported by strategic maps, flowcharts and other imaging techniques. From among these solutions, data mining offers serious possibilities. This is a procedure aimed at discovering earlier unknown features and interrelationships primarily for the exploitation of business advantages. Data mining relies on the tools and means of statistics and artificial intelligence. Results received are most frequently the following: discovery of interrelationships, classification, grouping, forecasts, ranking. Its area of application is wide, it can provide useful help in the prevention of IT abuses, in trade (e.g. examination of linked goods), in telecommunication (e.g. investigation of audience measurement figures), and for banks and insurers (e.g. in the analysis of the habits of customers) and in several other areas (see Cser & Fajszi, 2004; Kő, 2007).

### Compound Systems

The solutions above rarely appear in isolation; in general we see compound systems that cover several part-processes of the knowledge management life cycle and utilize each other's advantages. Such a compound system can be an ontology-based document warehouse that contains teamwork and workflow components and expert system, too, and here should data mining solutions be mentioned since they utilize various models (statistical and artificial intelligence models).

## SOLUTION AND RECOMMENDATIONS

It could be deemed to be an important aspect that in the case of SMEs the KM strategy should be elaborated according to incrementalist logic. Why? The attribute "incrementalist" signalizes that this is not an entirely planned process, but rather a strategy formed step-by-step always making use of feedbacks. And "logic" signalizes that there is a concept in the process of changes, but could just restrictedly enforced in view of the complicated situations. The underlying reason is that in the case of SMEs the "matured" and in all respect "streamlined" systematized operation is still missing. The attribute "incrementalist" indicates that the target is continuously rectified and re-specified. Another reason for selecting this solution is that scheduling and prioritizing can be better handled in order to:

- Clarify our intention to make changes, for the members of the organization;
- Improve sense of comfort;
- Obtain support and agreement;

- Recruit people, select and train them;
- Overcome any habitual or managerial resistance;
- Respond to environmental changes;
- Satisfy technological and information demands;
- Convince intelligent opponents;
- Engage appropriate expert in strategy elaboration sub-systems; collect and make use of their ideas and obtain their support for the implementation project.

It would be impossible to "set right" all that in a given moment. Thus if we understand that the management in itself is unable to solve everything, it should enter into compromises (specifically if the most conservative opponent is / are the owner / owners of the SME). Therefore, at the beginning just general targets are set thereby letting room for creativity and avoiding the possibility of rigid opposition. This way ensures large latitude for ideas coming from below, and the persons concerned are just herded to the right direction, and "final" solution could be selected "as late as possible". Another reason for doing so is that inappropriate alternatives could be rejected in time and without severe risk. The essence is not that that future should be precisely calculated but rather that potent and realistic steps would be initiated along the most probable events. Then the cases of high urgency are settled, meanwhile a long-term vision is drafted and the events and results are continuously responded: successful versions are retained and adverse factors are eliminated. In fact, this is a dynamic process that creates and strengthens the culture of strategic view and planning and lays solid ground for the integration of the KM function into the corporate systems and processes.

In this context it is worthwhile considering that a KM strategy can only in that case be successful (and this is true irrespective of the size of the firm) if it serves the target of the organization. Importantly, KM strategy and its dimensions, i.e. people, process and technology would be harmonized, aligned and leveled. And then there is a durable chance for making knowledge management a live and organic function within the structure of the undertaking.

This demand is well reflected by the figure in the Appendix, which gives a hint about KM strategies that along the individual dimensions could with good probability and realistically be imagined on various maturity levels of the corporate and the corresponding strategic development.

## REFERENCES

Aidemark, J. E. (2009). Knowledge Management Paradoxes. *Electronic Journal of Knowledge Management*, *7*(1), 1–10.

Barnes, S., & Milton, N. (2015). *Designing a Successful KM Strategy: A Guide for the Knowledge Management Professional*. Medford, NJ: Information Today Inc.

Bencsik, A., Boda, G., Klimkó, G, Kő, A., & Noszkay, E. (2010). Tudásmenedzsment. In Menedzsment tanácsadási kézikönyv. Budapest, Hungary: Akadémiai Kiadó.

Bencsik, A. (2015). *A tudásmenedzsment elmélete és gyakorlata*. Budapest, Hungary: Akadémiai Kiadó.

Chesbrourg, H., Vanhaverbeke, W., & West, J. (Eds.). (2014). *New frontiers in Open Innovation*. Oxford University Press. doi:10.1093/acprof:oso/9780199682461.001.0001

Cser, L., & Fajszi, B. (2004). *Üzleti tudás az adatok mélyén – Adatbányászat alkalmazói szemmel.* Budapest, Hungary: BMGE GTK Információ- és Tudásmenedzsment Tanszék.

Davenport, T. H. (1997). If only HP knew what HP knows…. *Perspectives on Business Innovation, 1,* 20–25.

Hansen, M. T., Nohria, N., & Tierney, T. (1999). What's your strategy for managing knowledge. *Harvard Business Review, 77*(2), 109–122. PMID:10387767

Kő, A. (2007). Üzleti intelligencia, in Döntéstámogató rendszerek. Panem Gazdaságinformatika sorozat. Budapest, Hungary: Panem Kiadó.

Krogh, G., Roos, J., & Slocum, K. (1994). An essay on Corporate Epistemology. Strategic Management Journal, 15, 53-72. doi:10.1002/smj.4250151005

Lam, A. (2004). Organizational innovation. In J. Fagerberg, D. Mowery, & R. R. Nelson (Eds.), *The Oxford Handbook of Innovation.* Oxford, UK: Oxford University Press.

Miles, R. E., & Snow, C. C. (1978). Organisational Strategy, Structure and Process. New York: McGraw-Hill.

Noszkay, E. (2013). A rendszerszemléletű tudásmenedzsment. Pearson Publishing.

Noszkay, E. (2013). *Tudásmenedzsment – módszertani megközelítésben.* Paper presented at Vezetéstudományi Konferencia "Vezetésésszervezetek Taylor után 102 évvel", Szeged, Hungary

Noszkay, E., & Balogh, A. (2015). Tudásigényes vállalatok és tudásigényes szolgáltatások működési jellegzetességeik tükrében. In B. Norbert & P. Szabolcs (Eds.), *Tudásteremtés és -alkalmazás a modern társadalomban Tanulmánykötet* (pp. 146–157). Szegedi Tudományegyetem.

Schienstock, G. (2009). *Organisational Innovations: Some Reflections on the Concept.* Research Unit for Technology, Science and Innovation Studies (TaSTI) University of Tampere IAREG Working Paper 1.2.

Szeghegyi, Á. (2010). *Tudásmenedzsment.* Óbudai Egyetem.

Truch, E., & Bridger, D. (2002). The importance of strategic fit in Knowledge Management. In *Proceedings of the 10th European Conference on Information Systems: Information Systems and the Future of the Digital Economy.*

Zack, M. H. (1999). Developing a Knowledge Strategy. *California Management Review, 41*(3), 125–145. doi:10.2307/41166000

Zack, M. H. (2000). Developing a Knowledge Strategy: Epilogue. In N. Bontis & C. W. Choo (Eds.), *The Strategic Management of Intellectual Capital and Organisational Knowledge: A Collection of Readings.* Oxford University Press.

## KEY TERMS AND DEFINITIONS

**Balanced ScoreCard-Assisted Learning-Development:** A method for determining the appropriate development of an organization for implementing its strategy (Its elements and means: expedient training of the coworkers, conscious design of the age pyramid, accessible knowledge bases, motivation and promotion system, development of new competences, etc.)

**Incrementalist KM Strategy for Small and Medium Enterprises (SMEs):** In view of the fact that in the case of these undertakings systematized operation is not yet matured although work could be carried out in a planned manner, the KM strategic objectives could with good chances be implemented in accordance with the logics of change management if such objectives are continuously corrected and/or reformulated.

**Knowledge Management Strategy:** This determines the target areas, methods i.e. objectives and means for the management of knowledge contents; a basic criteria is that this should be fitted to the corporate strategy; meanwhile the conditions, dimensions of its execution – namely People, Process, Technology, Structure and Culture – are also essential.

**Knowledge Map:** This is the visualization of a concept network that presents its components and their interrelationships. Its aim is to discover the expertise and experiences aggregated within the organization, and to make them easily available.

**Knowledge Strategy:** It is aimed at the recognition of knowledge as a strategic resource and is elaborated in the interest of putting knowledge into the centre.

**Knowledge Warehouse:** This is basically a complex of data warehouses, document warehouses and content management systems, which in general is aimed at the capturing and pre-processing of data and facts. Its aim is to utilize IT background support for ensuring the knowledge content input necessary for the running of processes, furthermore for ensuring the knowledge base necessary for the analyzer and exploiter systems.

**Strategic Knowledge Management:** It means the collection and management of so-called key-knowledge contents that are important from the aspect of strategy elaboration.

## APPENDIX 1

Other authors recommend the elaboration and implementation of KM strategy on the basis of factors similar to ours. For instance Barnes, S. - Milton, N. in their manual published in 2015 one can find the following basic principles for the elaboration of a KM strategy:

1. "KM implementation needs to be organization-led; tied to organization strategy and to specific organization issues
2. KM needs to be delivered where the critical knowledge lies, and where the high value decisions are made
3. KM implementation needs to be treated as a behavior change program
4. The endgame will be to introduce a complete management framework for KM
5. This framework will need to be embedded into the organization structures
6. The framework will need to include governance if it is to be sustainable
7. The framework will be structured, rather than emergent
8. A KM implementation should be a staged process, with regular decision points
9. A KM implementation should contain a piloting stage
10. A KM implementation should be run by an implementation team, reporting to a cross-organizational steering group (Barnes, S. - Milton, N. (2015, pp 23.)."

## APPENDIX 2

*Figure 4. KM assessment strategy development*
*(source: GREENES Consulting, 2015 http://www.greenesconsulting.com/services/list-services/km-assessment-strategy-development (downloaded on 29.01.2015)*

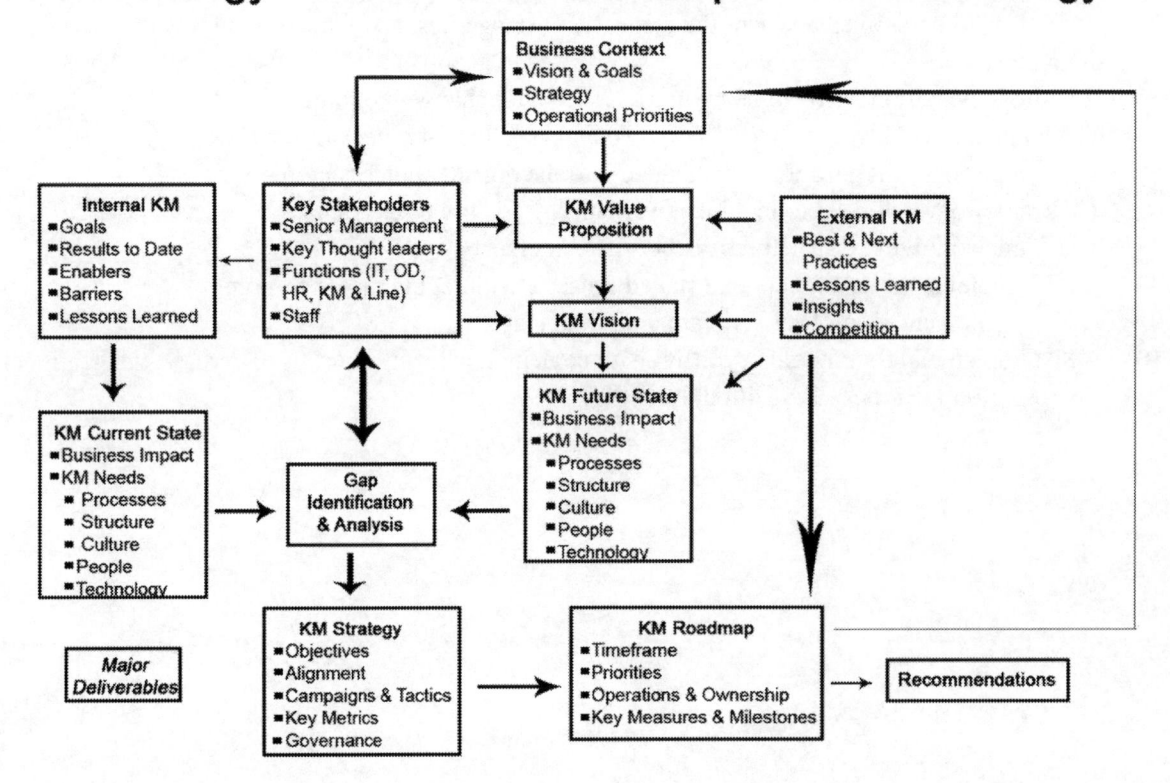

# APPENDIX 3

*Figure 5. KM assessment towards knowledge management maturity*
*(source: WIKI) https://wiki.smu.edu.sg/is101_2008/Knowledge_management (downloaded on 12.02.2015)*

| | STRATEGY | PEOPLE | PROCESS | TECHNOLOGY | |
|---|---|---|---|---|---|
| LEVEL 5- Knowledge Centric | Business Strategy is continuously adjusted to reflect organizational learning from knowledge management | A culture exists that encourages free flow of knowledge throughout the enterprise | Communities of Practice are formally linked | Corporate I/T infrastructure integrates knowledge management both internal and external to the organization | Here's the direction you move toward |
| LEVEL 4- Knowledge Managed | KM strategy is defined with leadership accountability and sufficient resources to begin having significant impact on results | There is a broad-based competency in KM across the company. Formal organizations for supporting KM emerge | KM processes, practices, and measurement are formalized and integrated with core business activities | Corporate Portals, Groupware, etc. enable cross-enterprise creation, sharing, and reuse to accelerate business results | |
| LEVEL 3- Knowledge Enabled | KM strategy is defined as part of the business strategy but no leadership (e.g., CKO) accountability is assigned | Rewards are in place to encourage creation, sharing and reuse of knowledge; Learning becomes a cultural norm | KM processes are integrated into business processes and knowledge is imbedded in business processes | Data Warehouse and Document Management technologies are in place to support knowledge capture, sharing, and reuse | Here's what you typically do first |
| LEVEL 2- Knowledge Aware | Leadership recognition of the importance of KM relative to business but has not yet incorporated it into its strategy | People are aware of limited KM capabilities, however there is no perceived leadership commitment to KM | Limited processes exist for KM (Tacit and Explicit) knowledge is available, but difficult to access | Basic KM enablers are present (e.g. e-mail) | Here's where most organizations are today |
| LEVEL 1- Knowledge Chaotic | Corporate strategy is focused internally and knowledge has no impact on the corporate direction | People within the company are resistant to change and routinely hoard knowledge | No process exists for creating, sharing and applying knowledge | KM enabling technology is not present | |

# Best Practice (Models, Methods, Tools)

# Chapter 7
# Best Practice Model Tools and Methods for Developing KM Systems

**Erzsébet Noszkay**
*Budapest Metropolitan University, Hungary*

## ABSTRACT

*This chapter focuses on an experience based presentation of the parameters that determine organizational culture, and the impact that basic interrelationships among such parametric factors exercise on the elaboration of KM; the timing and the sort of KM structure, configuration that is feasible to make KM an approved and successful management function within a corporate structure; the possibility and the proper timing of the elaboration of KM through corporate strategic approach i.e. starting from above (decision of the senior management), and the efficiency of a solution initiated from below (by the members of the organization). This chapter will describe some practice-proven solutions, such as: the application of the problem solution method named action research that could be expedient in the implementation of KM in certain cases, and times and situations where the application of the "sandwich method" could be expedient. Also, this chapter describes knowledge transfer experiences that facilitate the recognition of the "capillary model", its substance and scope of utilization.*

## INTRODUCTION

Works aimed at the description and explanation of the history of KM to various extents but surely give account on the initial uncertainty which is no wonder since knowledge even in its explicit form is a thing that can hardly be explored. A question that emerged at the beginning was the explanation of the difference between "simple" information and knowledge. In general: what is important and valuable (e.g. storable) knowledge and what is not. Another dilemma encountered at the beginning was, how to start configuring KM where knowledge handling has not been anteceded by like enforcements, moreover, where in correspondence with the perception of some managers in important position, knowledge is not really reputed, and desire for learning and knowing could not or could just hardly be found within the organizational culture. In view of the above the question must be raised: how did and how does it

DOI: 10.4018/978-1-5225-1642-2.ch007

happen that organizations scarce in knowledge culture would sooner or later at some level open up for KM. Well, the underlying reason is that organizations are not homogenous, there is always a member in the organization who is more receptive to new concepts than others are. And, of course, researchers, lecturers of the discipline and various application developers (consultants, IT developers, etc.) have discovered more and more possibilities related to KM, which is boosted by the fact that the renewal of various products and services and the production of added value could be achieved by "assembling" knowledge contents. The elaboration of this chapter was inspired by the understanding that there is a problem even today, namely that no matter how much people within the organization acknowledge the necessity the KM implementation if the solution is approached erroneously. Ranges of experiences full of failures and successes have proven that the time when and the approach with which KM is implemented do matter, since the human factor without commitment may exercise unfavorable impact and pose hindrances. In addition, the nature of certain parameters of the organizational culture can be substantial. This work wishes to be of assistance in the problem solution by way of presenting some proven models and methods that could successfully be applied in the course of implementing KM and integrating it into the operation of the organization.

## BACKGROUND

As it has been mentioned in the Introduction, adaption of KM by an undertaking never was and is not a simple task, and difficulties could be encountered even today. SMEs others than knowledge intensive enterprises and knowledge demanding service providers or enterprises that follow the sharing economy models gaining more room in economic life, encounter much more problems than larger firms, and are more hesitant in starting the adaption of KM or investing into knowledge capital. If some failed applications interfere with the process, this could result in a break for years. This is why it is not all the same in what way we start adapting and configuring KM.

It would be interesting – specifically for users, in the interest of avoiding possible failures – to have a look on the developments made by the concepts and methods related to the configuration of the KM function. Although there are several possibilities, pitfalls may be encountered if those possibilities are implemented without justifying their usability and evaluating the advantages and disadvantages of their application.

The first attempts and scientific works scrutinized rather the application principles, the failure and success factors, and not or justly slightly the methodological issues. For instance Davenport and Prusak listed nine factors related to the successful adaption of KM:

- *A knowledge-oriented culture.*
- *Technical and organizational infrastructure.*
- *Senior management support.*
- *A link to economic and industry value.*
- *A modicum of process orientation.*
- *Clarity of vision and language.*
- *Non trivial motivational aids.*
- *Some level of knowledge structure.*
- *Multiple channel of knowledge transfer. (Davenport & Prusak, 1998, p. 153)*

One year later, Skyrme and Amidon (1999) listed their success factors that essentially were the same but were less, only seven. It should be deemed to be progressive that from among the success factors special emphasis was given to vision, and that there is a need for some sort of forerunner advocating KM, also, proper organization and information technology are deemed to be important.

There are some others who deem the failure factors to be avoided to be decisive. According to Lucier and Torsilieri (1997) such factors emerge when targets are not sufficiently concrete, the strategic corporate objectives are not considered, the KM program is not adequate with the organization or with the pace of changes, senior managerial support is missing or just casual (not active enough, not continuous).

After a while more and more KM experts came to the conclusion that theories – no matter how true they are – by themselves are not sufficient, some sort of systematicness, methodicalness are also needed. This was the time when the so-called KM maturity models have been born that necessitated a sort of consciousness and together with that a structured approach in the introduction and adaption of KM. A basic deficiency of the mechanic application of structured approach is that it does not take explicit human factor into account, it rather builds on the mechanistic model of an organization.

The aim of the maturity models:

- On the one hand they should review the operation of the KM system actually in existence, and help in its development;
- On the other hand they should make the introduction of knowledge management and related activities and processes apt for being planned, in the course of introduction being regulated, controlled and eventually measured by the management.

The elaboration of a maturity model measures and determines the activities of KM initiatives along certain factors. There are activity models (see for instance Know-Net Esprit) that have been developed further, and try to determine or even improve and evaluate an undertaking's internal knowledge.

The ripening of maturity model can be useful also because it posts a vision for the members of the undertaking as regards KM function. The existence of a precisely worded vision could according to several authors contribute to the success of a KM initiative.

During the last two-three decades several models have been developed. The most characteristic investigation means are questionnaires and interviews (sometimes workshops). On the basis of the results, the organizations are in general classified on one level out of five or eight, wherein first level means that knowledge management activity is not present in the organization and the highest level means that knowledge management has become part of everyday practice. Some characteristics are common for all models. These are the following (Klimkó & Tóth, 2007):

- The development of a single entity is described with the help of few levels;
- Levels are fully systematized, start from an initial level and arrive at the uppermost level;
- During maturing no level can be leaped;
- Each level can be characterized by some criteria;
- In order to achieve a level, the entity should comply with the criteria set thereto.

The majority of the knowledge management maturity models have been elaborated by developer and consultant firms motivated by the demand for KM developments. Most of the maturity models can on the basis of their properties be classified in two groups.

- The first include Capability Maturity Models (CMM). These typically examine several parameters. One characteristic example is Siemens KMMM® maturity model developed by Siemens AG in 2002 which is structured along the following factors:
  - Analyzer model (its components are: strategy, structure, environment, leadership, personnel, technology, processes, cooperation, organizational culture);
  - Developer model provides information concerning evolvement and development. (Organizations are classified in five categories according to their processes: initial, repeated, defined, managed, optimizing);
  - Evaluation model that by way of utilizing the above factors can assist in the evaluation of the results.
- Now, the concept behind the maturity models belonging to the other category is that on the basis of various characteristics, areas could be specified in order to determine the position of the organization on its way to become knowledge centered. (Auditing on the basis of characteristics attracts the attention of many. From among the most exciting ones the work of Antonova, A. (2009) and Gourova, E., (2009) and their colleagues should be highlighted. The models mentioned above specify tasks for each area and the categorization is based on tasks completed by the firm. A well-known model is the model of KPMG that has been elaborated in 1999 (Knowledge Journey model) that examines the undertakings on the basis of four criteria (for instance in this model the tasks specified within the content criteria are the elaboration of a knowledge map or the measuring of the intellectual capital):
  - People;
  - Processes;
  - Content;
  - Technology.

All in all, the chief advantage of the maturity models is that they post a vision for the members of the enterprise regarding the configuration of the KM function. The vision itself could contribute to the success of a KM initiative, furthermore, the concept itself requests that the techniques applied in the course of the KM development are worded accurately thereby enabling a sort of planning. However, this as a method applying structured approach considers human factor just tangentially, the underlying concept is "mechanistic" and builds on the machine-like model of an organization.

In summary it can be observed that attempts aimed at the adaption of KM in the organization are various, meanwhile experts unambiguously consented that the need for knowledge management is not for its own sake and its successful introduction is expected to produce competitive advantage and added value, therefore in the course of the implementation and operation of the KM function, the enterprise's management should by all means participate actively. Obviously, the costs dedicated to the implementation and operation of the KM function should be recovered from the profit stemming from the functioning of KM. This, however, could be probable if KM function is introduced not with the eventuality characterizing a campaign, but in a procedure managed like a project, in due consideration of the corporate features.

The literature does not offer an exclusive and righteous way to the introduction of the KM function.

However, it is a general experience that those who have ever taken part in the adaption of KM systems to various organizations should agree with the trio of authors Krogh, Ichijo and Nonaka who deem five factors to be of great importance. Namely:

- Formulate knowledge vision,
- Manage conversations,
- Mobilize knowledge activists,
- Create the right context for knowledge creation,
- Globalize local knowledge (for more details see von Krogh, Ichijo & Nonaka 2000).

When at an enterprise or organization the possibilities of the implementation of a good and useful knowledge management system are contemplated, the commitment of the management is of great importance. Degree of support and commitment can be various. It is by all means of great significance that the senior management is really committed but that in itself is not enough. A research team led by the Knowledge Management Working Committee of the Hungarian Academy of Sciences scrutinized the everyday operation and by making good use of experts' help scrutinized the application developments in practice, i.e. best practice solutions (in due consideration of the properties of the organizations as quasi assumptions). Thus in the frames of consultancy assignments awarded to us by certain SMEs (applying knowledge intensive technologies, providing knowledge or media services, and/or applying state-of-the-art machinery industry technology) belonging to 10 different industries, we have modeled and tried out ways for "adopting" knowledge management and in this context the introduction of KM for facilitating developments::

- Implementation started from above as part of the corporate strategy (with decision made by and the participation of senior managers);
- Implementation started from below (by members of the organization; not based on senior managerial decisions);
- Implementation started from the middle, with support from middle managers.

## BEST PRACTICE MODELS

## Implementation Started from Above (With Decisions Made by and Participation of Senior Managers) Aimed at Serving the Corporate Strategy

If one opts for implementation started from above, the operation of the organization as a regulated system should be deemed as a condition of overall importance. Any kind of uncertainty (e.g. corporate and/or strategic vision is missing or vague, processes or the entire corporate operation is not or not sufficiently regulated, etc.) precludes chances for successful solutions. In addition, properly functional application developments listed hereunder are necessary for making the efficiency and successfulness of KM introduction more favorable[1]. Such as:

- Systems enabling management of and access to information (e.g. library, other common document storages, etc.);
- E-Learning systems, expert teams for managing explicit knowledge intrinsic in the workflows (e.g. education, processing of project experiences, etc.);
- Competence centers;
- Elaboration of business models, clusters, etc.

Even if support from the above conditions and application developments exists, our experiences suggest that only those enterprises – mostly bigger ones (or appropriately regulated medium size enterprises) – are able to achieve success, where knowledge, learning, cooperation and trust are deemed as values of the corporate culture and the so-called power distance is not big. In other words: in the absence of a corporate structure favoring KM, there are few chances for successfully configuring KM as a system.

## Implementation Started Also from Below

Excellent and successful result can be achieved with the method starting KM implementation from above wherein members of the organization recognizing the significance of KM assist in the implementation of KM with their own and active initiatives, often in the context of so-called integrating developments (knowledge communities, expert teams, etc.). A promising best practice is the so-called "sandwich method".

If this method is applied, KM implementation can be started from two ends: from above (that is with senior managerial support and as a part of the corporate vision) and from below that is with the assistance of knowledge communities organized alongside semiformal solutions. These latter ones can on the one hand be peculiar "catalyzers" of the program, and on the other hand they can from the human factor side deliver the "critical mass[2]" that is indispensable for the commitment of the organizational participants for knowledge management, for the evolvement of an organization saturated with knowledge culture, and consequently for the success of the KM program.

A special approach applied by the "sandwich method" is the implementation started from the middle. This is an interesting situation wherein the initiative is primarily started not from below, although "embryonic knowledge communities" that have been grown from below and in fact existed but were completely hidden for the management until then will appear after the launching of the program.

In the case of implementation started from the middle, the initiatives are launched by leader(s) possessing managerial competencies (but not belonging to the top management). (These persons are those who were typified by Skyrme and Amidon (1999) among the success factors of KM's adaption as champions of the topic.) In general these "champions" are people who are incited by some external changes and believe that without renewal based on up-to-date knowledge, the organization's market position can be improved only with declining probability.

Experiences suggest that from among the approaches described above, the "sandwich method", i.e. implementation started from the middle can be successful in certain corporate situations. Hereinafter we are going to discuss in more detail those organizational setups when its application can be suggested on the basis of experiences obtained so far.

Let us have a look on the „sandwich-method" – from the aspect of organizational situations.

First of all a general feature should be stated, namely that the "sandwich-method" is worthwhile for considerations in the case of organizations that decisively need knowledge and are forced to change quickly[3]. Why?! In general these are the organizations where several members of the organization and/ or the management itself would with great probability recognize: almost the sole "righteous" way to the renewal of the organization is when the added value is produced with the involvement of a critical mass of innovators and integrators. And what is more, there is no other feasible case! The underlying reason is that the demand for the active utilization of knowledge is so large everywhere – practically in each sector (but overly in knowledge demanding sectors) – that such demand cannot be satisfied exclusively by laboratories or R+D units, but the situation rather calls for the participation of (critical) masses, in many cases for the involvement of external participants (e.g. with the help of an "Open Innovation Model").

The following comparative table illustrates that "launching" the development of a knowledge management system does not totally lack probability where the top management neither really grants support for nor "prohibits" the same. In certain cases this is exactly the "sandwich method" that approaches from the middle and therefore is able to create the organizational culture that is necessary for breakthrough and that is demanded by competing organizational units initiating sub-projects as they see each other's achievements in the area of knowledge management development.

On the basis of the above comparative table it can be perceived that the "sandwich-method" has better chances with those firms that are knowledge demanding or that in view of the need for quick renewal are "coerced" to make use of all knowledge of merit.

From among the versions, the "approach from the middle" method is the most complicated and ambiguous, and therefore it needs much attention and is the most risky one, because, despite voluminous intellectual investments it might end in failure, since – specifically at the time of the initial starting steps – there could be more opponents than "true believers".

However, when successfully applied, this method can result in the most astonishing "twirl", provided that the critical mass could be engaged as a result of the aggregate impact exercised by knowledge communities[4] spontaneously organizing themselves within the organization. Obviously, if this condition is met then the processes (flowing for a long time in the informal sphere and therefore hardly identifiable) that consequently would start will be practically irreversible and offer one single "real" output for the organization's management: to step on the edge and implement and adapt KM in the real world.

The power that the head (guru) of a knowledge community (who in the case of SMEs can be for instance a reputed one from among the blue collar workers, a "crafter") has over the participants is restricted, however, he/she determines the direction where a knowledge community proceeds, helps the operation, although by virtue of his/her job he/she may not direct people or call them to account. Therefore the application of the "sandwich-method" started from the middle needs at least one or two supporting leaders from the side of the organization (champions), whose role is basically semiformal but even so a role that provides framework and support, i.e. a "sponsoring" role.

Members of a knowledge community consciously strive to engage other experts and mobilize internal and external resources. This is a sort of "networking". (The significance of the informal networks from the aspect of spread of knowledge through cooperation is highlighted by Liebowitz (2012) in several

*Table 1. Types of application of the "sandwich-method" – according to the situation where they can appear*

| Approach from Above and From Below | Approach from the Middle |
|---|---|
| Startup enterprise (e.g. subsidiary, limited liability company engaged in strategic business branch, etc.); or enterprises striving to achieve quick success on the long run as well as competitive results through change management, or to keep pace with the market and be competitive on the market of enterprises applying turbulent and knowledge demanding technologies; | With great probability among those – sometimes very conservative and knowledge demanding – organizations where competitiveness has "tumbled down" which remained unnoticed by top management but not by second management line; |
| Top managers and line managers are equally aware of the ability of knowledge to produce values and the values intrinsic therein; | Some key persons and/or gurus have already noticed that there is no other chance to set ourselves loose but by escaping forward, towards the direction of the value adding possibilities offered by KM applications; |
| Strong commitment on all levels as regards the adaption of KM. | There are initiatives that could lay ground for a KM system (e.g. knowledge communities, expert teams, etc.) |

(source: Noszkay, 2010)

books that integrate the unanimous experiences of several researchers and professionals.) Obviously, an important task of a knowledge community resulting from mutual cooperation is to arrange for structured documentation (in certain cases to build a system) of knowledge contents that attributable to the community's enforcements were integrated, and make available same for others.

The underlying cause of this phenomenon is the accelerating progress in the 21st century in consequence of which knowledge half-life shortens (obsolescence accelerates). Therefore, in the context of knowledge acquisition, "freshness" has become a basic requirement, which entails, which must entail that today the knowledge contents of knowledge owners and not necessarily the knowledge content owned by professional researchers are dominant in the course of combining knowledge contents and wording new knowledge elements.

Now let us have a look on the theoretical, methodological background of the "sandwich-method".

Certain conditions are necessary for the "approach from the middle" solution. The "sandwich-method", the solution that approaches from the middle is a model and meanwhile a method whose implementation is by far the most difficult and which is the riskiest of all. The main intrinsic risk stems from the fact that its initiator is not completely disguised. As it has already been mentioned, following an eventual failure, the initiating member of the organization's management puts his/her livelihood at risk.

On the other hand it is risky because the initiator is known and therefore it is impossible for spontaneous communities in the course of their formation to preserve their "informal" character at least until they solidify, and in such case, in an embryonic phase, they should confront serious resistance. Therefore, it is not a coincidence that the "approach from the middle" method could be successful with good probability only in the presence of a scheme of important conditions.

Let us have a closer look on some of these conditions.

It is a must that – at least initially – consciously organized so-called communities of practice are created on an elementary level, and that the nature of the organizational culture is ascertained (whether knowledge is supported or not really rewarded). The most important characteristic of a community of practice is that it functions as a network.

It cannot be emphasized enough that from among the kinds of communities of practice, the one named knowledge community could expediently be established when commitment for knowledge demand and knowledge sharing is favorable, the name and the reputation of the guru is able to keep the community together, and at the same time, the problem to be solved is "in the air" although not yet articulated, meanwhile the commitment of the members of the community is favorable, and they have several good ideas. In the course of the organization of a community, the guru is frequently (but not "statutorily") assisted by one or more community coordinators and some experts of key importance. The members of the community making good use of "loose relationships" are able to help each other. It works even if the scope of participants is relatively large and people have relatively few possibilities to meet each other personally, since the main communication means of a knowledge community are virtual; examples are the internet and the web 2.0 technology.

The situation in the case of communities of practice (Wenger, E. & Snyder, W., 2000) is totally different. Such communities could reasonably be established if the organization's aims are clear and the functional area is unambiguously defined, because thus a common identity can be established, learning and actions gain expedient meaning, and possibilities inherent in the ideas could better be utilized. The resulting community is grounded on mutual respect and trust, thus members are encouraged to raise more difficult questions and be more creative, which will strengthen the feeling of belonging together. Through their actions and activities and through combining new knowledge elements, the communities of practice

*Table 2. Compare knowledge communities and communities of practice*

| | Knowledge Community | Communities of Practice |
|---|---|---|
| Goals | Goals are not clear, but important:<br>• Learning support/learning;<br>• Systematization of knowledge;<br>• and documents; | Clear professional (and other) goals:<br>• Creating value for the organization;<br>• Keeping of talents (key members);<br>• Exploring new strategic opportunities<br>• Research/innovation;<br>• Best practice communities |
| Preparedness of members | • The „guru" creates conditions, unbalanced community, stands not only of the „qualified ones";<br>• Multidisciplinary; | Professional bests ("guru") and "key members"; |
| Content of members | Mixed, cooperative (even with the competitors); | Within organization and/or strongly ties to its goals; |
| The institutional „legitimacy" and boundaries of the community | • The „insiders" business;<br>• „Limitless" networking;<br>• „Invisible" for the organization(s) | • Acknowledgedly and consciously profitable;<br>• „Formally" dual bounded;<br>• Blurred boundaries, parts of a „partly" informal organization. |
| Cohesive force | • Professional and value based commitment<br>• Passion and interest | • Professional -, and value based commitment,<br>• Problem solving,<br>• Actions;<br>• Professional passion and interest |
| Operational methods | Experimental, social network | • Supporting;<br>• Transmitting best practice;<br>• Knowledge management;<br>• Innovative social network. |

(source: Based on the work of Van Aalst, 2003)

will produce added value in the interest of the enterprise, meanwhile the appropriate frames and styles call for joint enforcement and special control. In the course of communication personal meetings play important role, but live contacts with other communities (for instance aided by web 2.0 technologies, interfaces etc.) are also important.

Steps necessary for creating a community of practice:

- A community coordinator, a guru must exist; he/she should bear the burden of technical solutions and determine the targets;
- It must be certain that the achievement of these targets will produce value for the organization ("flavored" with the professional and value-focused commitment and professional passion of the participants, etc.);
- The organizational culture should be audited from the aspect of knowledge management, i.e. the basic properties of the organizational culture (with special regard to the relationship of the participants to knowledge itself) should be known;
- Areas within knowledge management which could be configured easily should be ascertained (e.g. mentoring program, e-learning-aided instructions for new employees, etc.) and their development "sponsored" by senior managers be started;
- Action research and the "discovery" of existing communities – informal small knowledge islands – by way of introducing capillary methods (they will be discussed later as subheading "supporting models and techniques"), implementation of connections between them; sharing of the methods facilitating cooperation;

- Knowledge communities should be put to operation in as many areas as possible (it is important that in each of them must be at least an expert and a guru);
- Knowledge communities should be operated on the appropriate level (regular personal meetings between the "core" and the "active team" are extremely important) and the adequate IT supporting system (web 2.0, Facebook, etc.) or other not very much "fixed" interface (e.g. SharePoint[5]) should be selected, made available and used;
- Agreement should be achieved with a larger scope of entities (e.g. peripheral participants in a conference, other external entities) regarding conventional events, where "chief characters" are present either on-line or – preferably – in person;
- Creation of further communities should be facilitated (within the organization, in order to achieve the critical mass);
- Increase of the communities should be encouraged and enabled;
- When a knowledge community has already achieved its target, it is often able to "produce" a community of practice (which afterwards could evolve to an expert team) or when it is unable to work on the achievement of its original target (for whatever reason, e.g. the guru left, etc.), the community should be terminated.

Experiences (obtained from several firms) concerning successful utilization of knowledge management application developments have confirmed the methodological steps described above and helped their "crystallization". As regards models and partial methods applied in the course of the methodological steps, it should be emphasized that in the frames of KM implementation with the "sandwich method", important success factors are the capillary model considered as a novel model of knowledge conversion, and a partial method namely action research, which could play role in the establishment and operation of knowledge communities.

Important supporting models and techniques are the following.

The capillary model, a model that reflects the real complexity of knowledge conversion, and a concept that would form our future consciousness has been born in an organizational situation when and where consultants and internal experts thought that the time available for the development of a KM system is insufficient. For reasons of serious technological changes, new situations and problems calling for knowledge integration (in order to avoid menacing crisis situation, the organizations were forced to accelerate the modernization of the portfolio of goods and services, produce more variable added value and high quality) the adaption of a KM function has become an issue of vital importance for the organizations. In order to achieve these aims, KM developers should contemplate various possibilities wherein KM adaption could be started simultaneously, in such manner, with such human resources, schedule and development possibilities that could prevent any eventual failure that would entail the "collapse" of knowledge utilization (e.g. knowledge integration into a product, knowledge combination with a new service, etc.) and the collapse of the developer community (communities), and that would emit some annoying communication message and therefore place the success of the enterprise's modernization program at risk.

This is why experts assigned with the task of KM adaption utilized the following solutions (that later proved to be successful):

- On the one hand those rudimentary knowledge communities were sought within the organization that were neglected by the management but where certain creative coworkers – for the sake of their own professional development, sometimes on a hobby level, mostly within the network of a small external community – participated in researches and/or development or were involved in discussions over technical concepts, models, methods or ideas;

- On the other hand simultaneously in several areas, support was ensured for starting knowledge communities (sometimes with the assistance of certain external partners engaged) where gurus or "guruish" experts could be found.

Astonishingly, the events started a "snowball effect". This inevitably led to comprehension that clarified the following:

- Knowledge conversion must not necessarily be operated linearly (as it has been described by the Nonaka, I. and Takeuchi, H. (1995) model);
- Knowledge and its conversion follow totally different rules when a new paradigm or a knowledge element based on a new paradigm is in the making.[6]

A complex and non-linear knowledge conversion can be better expressed and described with the so-called "capillary model" (which is an analogy of "capillary phenomenon"). The analogy has been discovered[7] and described on the basis of simple observations. As it has been explained above, organizational islands, nods and communities susceptible and sensitive to knowledge management had to be sought, in order that the team of knowledge management experts as the initiators and sponsors of knowledge management could through the capillaries transfer the appropriate solution and thus ensure knowledge management development and arrange for the factors and conditions necessary for development. Naturally, the addressees and the content of such transfer depends upon the nods, since it can be the transfer of knowledge content, best practice solution, or means necessary for the configuration of a knowledge community or an expert team, as well as interfaces and instructions concerning their use (see for instance wiki technologies) or eventually other additional comprehension necessary for problem solution.

Meanwhile, however, capillarity has another important property, namely that the "porous medium" (see the soil particles in the example) does matter, since it decisively influences the transfer (i.e. the height of the water in the example). This criterion can be observed in the organizational culture, since this is the medium that – with its invisible and/or hardly visible capillary vessels (hidden network) – plays important role in the transfer of knowledge elements and in the shaping of an uncustomary culture that better utilizes knowledge. It is worthwhile mentioning that this latter perception boosted a concept and later a practical solution, namely that from the aspect of the adaption of a knowledge management system the potentially positive partial features from among the characteristics of the given organizational culture should expediently be managed consciously as "capillarity factors", meanwhile the missing characteristics should be considered as "utilizable", so-called "green way" factors.

In respect of the application of the capillary method an empiric observation is interesting and deserves our attention (and is worth to be utilized), namely that those enterprises run successful knowledge management systems and programs, which do not strive to "directly" change the organizational culture to be found in the given organization, but rather adapt knowledge management in correspondence with such culture (for more detail see McDermott, R. & O'Dell, C., 2001).

This empiric observation is important for two reasons:

- One decisive fact is that knowledge (specifically its tacit part) is very delicate and concealing thing. If we start the process with the redesign of the culture, then it is not sure that we will reach the tacit fields of knowledge, since they are located not necessarily at the points where we intervene with the organizational culture. Therefore it may happen that our intervention will have adverse impact, i.e. the tacit knowledge will become more concealed. Meanwhile, if in the course of our action we "map" the segments of the culture and consciously apply the rules of the capillary model, then we may believe that the culture will develop and change at a pace corresponding to the speed of capillarity achievable in the given "medium".

- Another reason is that in the case of an organization that (as this can be ascertained in the course of KM audit) is not yet prepared for the adaption of knowledge management (attributable not to knowledge shortages but rather to unfavorable organizational culture), it is more expedient to apply information technology-aided approach started from above, which assists the organizational participants in their work and therefore is apt for creating trust. Thus the adaption of KM must not encounter strong resistance that otherwise can be experienced in the case of the "forced" establishment of a knowledge community, and the culture of utilization of knowledge infiltrating from below through capillaries will "in a natural way" reshape a formerly absolutely rigid structure and make it "arable" from the KM aspect.

Action research is a solution applicable to the sandwich method, with approach from the middle.

Within KM development the application of action research can be a useful partial method. As it is well known, action research was founded by Lewin, (1946)[8], and was primarily developed for solving societal (minority) problems, and has been extended to cover education and training (John Elliot (1991) and later applied in the field of organizational development. Action research concentrates on the solution of practical problems emerging in specific areas. It differs from general researches as its subject matters are not external developments and events but rather the acting participants and the ensuing events and results. Its aims are self-analysis and self-development; there is no fixed hypothesis at the beginning and there is no specific end; only the development concept and the development demand are worded specifically. Therefore the research process is the development process itself as it is illustrated on Figure 1.

Continuous analysis and control after the closure of each phase (as the original demand / concept is ascertained), properly enable us to check whether we do proceed towards the target set, to draw conclusions

*Figure 1. Hegelian spiral of action research*
*Source: Varga, K. (1988)*

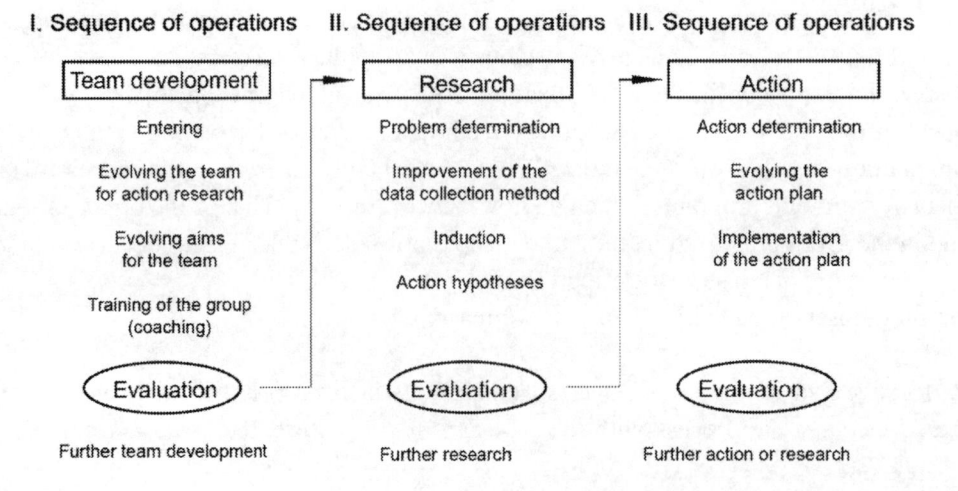

and to draft solutions that could be utilized by others. An intervening act will become action research if the process is consciously documented, which could later be analyzed and utilized in the interest of improved development, understanding and solution. The emphasis is laid not on the creation of knowledge but on the intervention. In fact this is the reason why one should expediently opt for action research method in the course of configuring KM, because it helps to successfully implement knowledge management with the sandwich method by way of approaching from the middle, or even with senior managerial support, and making good use of the integration of energies and creative knowledge elements of knowledge communities and expert teams built from below, and to avoid risks described in the foregoing.

Today we may say with confidence that the "planning downward from above" is not the only desirable way for implementing knowledge management, but in several situations – sometimes "under coercion" – KM system implementation successes could be achieved by conscious "champions" who build upon the objectivity of the "capillary model" and create conditions with the "sandwich method" approaching from the middle or from below.

Within the scope of certain organizations the investigation of the organizational culture, which serves knowledge management audit aspects, could be used as an additional instrument.

## SOLUTIONS AND RECOMMENDATIONS

The best practice solutions described in this chapter are proven and could be good-heartedly recommended for utilization, always in consideration of the characteristics of the given organizational situation.

Successful introduction and spread of KM depends upon several critical factors. These factors have already been dealt with by several authors in international literature. The first work of Wong (2005) should by all means be mentioned, where 11 factors are named (Management Leadership and Support, Culture, Information technology, Strategy and Purpose, Measurement, Organizational Infrastructure, Processes and Activities, Motivational Aids, Resources, Training and Education, Human Resource Management). Later together with a coauthor (Wong & Aspinwall, 2005) in addition to the factors in question all those authors were listed who have already described those factors. Thus in this context altogether 70 authors are referenced. An interesting issue worthwhile mentioning is that from among the critical factors most of the authors dealt with Management Leadership and Support which supports the experimental fact that without the active participation of the management bodies there are no chances for the introduction of knowledge management.

According to Sedighi and Zand (2012) eight critical factors are of decisive importance, two External, Environmental Factors and six Internal, i.e. Organizational Factors, and these factors were divided to partial factors.

In the course of our KM advisory assignments and research works similar critical factors were experienced and summarized, which we should discuss hereinafter in more detail. (We should like to mention that the factors in question appear much more vaguely than would be sufficient for their exact categorization as it is discussed by e.g. Sedighi and Zand (2012). For instance:

- **Natural Resistance Against Changes:** An organization could not survive if certain reflexes would not respond to any deviation from usual course of practice, in order to maintain stability and predictability. However, resistance to any changes – in excess of a certain level – would hinder improvements. Safeguarding the daily routine can impede innovation and testing new things. It is for sure that a knowledge management project will encounter significant resistance. If this is handled as a natural reaction, then defensive energies could be activated and turned to positive direction. It is worthwhile to connect certain change processes with each other. If for instance in the course of changing locations new spaces are dedicated to supporting knowledge sharing, then the intentions aimed at swapping cultures can more easily be presented.

- **Lack of the Active and Exemplary Conduct by Senior Management:** The key role of the senior management has been discussed in the previous points. If the management just takes notice of KM enforcements or grants insubstantial support – or in fact impedes them – then serious problems will be encountered. A solution could be a properly scheduled training where the managers would not only understand the essence, significance and real benefits of KM but their commitment could improve, too.

- Another problem could be faced if prior to the implementation of KM analyses are not conducted and contingency plan is not elaborated. On the basis of experiences obtained in respect of process reengineering projects and implementation of KM systems, the following risks could be encountered (among others):

  - Organizations are able to mobilize unbelievable energies in order to preserve status quo. Redesign of the organizational culture is in general an extremely hard task. In the course of reengineering the culture of knowledge economizing we should be prepared for resistance if the members of the organization are not aware of the advantages of KM and meanwhile should perceive the burden of additional enforcements entailed by KM implementation.

  - **Disturbances in the Operation of the Project Team in the Absence of a "Champion":** KM projects need at least one committed person who very much believes in knowledge management and continuously does his/her best for the success of the program. The project team working with him/her arranges for the complex method of approach and for common wisdom. The champion and the composition of the project team are important success factors. In the case of a project of such volume it is worthwhile to start the team with a team-building training and later to hold evaluation meetings that deal exclusively with the operation and with the solution of problems, if any. Engagement of employees only in the decision making is insufficient. There are at least two arguments in support of the possible more intensive engagement of coworkers. On the one hand the basic philosophy of KM is based on joint thinking and knowledge sharing, i.e. we must believe that the more we are the wiser we are. On the other hand, if persons concerned are left out from the creative and decision making processes, their commitment will be weaker and therefore in the course of the implementation we would encounter resistance and passivity. As the features of the program have it, in the course of the decision making process there would be possibilities for testing the methods to be implemented and the common work areas, which at the same time is a practical way for engaging persons concerned.

  - **Communication Operates Improperly:** Improper communication is the most frequently mentioned cause behind failed projects. Even so, during the process the information is frequently retained with reference to the confusion that would be caused by uncertainties prematurely disseminated among persons concerned. This pitfall must be avoided: retention of information or revealing partial information will start adverse processes; rumors will spread and the attitude of the persons concerned will be impaired. An elaborate communication plan is needed and the stakeholders should continuously be informed on the status of the project.

- ○ Impetuous steps will lead to failure (or to unachievable aims), and disappointment will paralyze the process. Redesigning culture through knowledge management is a slow process. Way of thinking or attitude cannot be changed overnight; patience and persistence are needed. We should proceed step by step, tolerate failures and should not be flustered. We should proceed along plans and the process should continuously be checked and plans be modified if necessary.

- ○ **Strained Atmosphere of Confidence:** Confidence is an important component of the program. "Dissemination" of own knowledge presupposes trust; the disseminator believes that other will do the same and knowledge sharing will worth on the long run. Reengineering projects never work without trust. Cultural changes delivered by KM projects should be well grounded with credible communication and consistent behavioral patterns. Trust is a slowly growing and extremely fragile component of the project. New culture is closer to coworkers characterized by modern comprehension, quasi favors them: certain fields within KM are closely linked to web 2.0 applications, i.e. to the most modern information technology. The younger generation might be more familiar with this latter, although an important target group of the project is the more experienced peer group that assisted in the launching of this specialization. Should they be left out, the program will achieve just partial successes.

- ○ **Conformists (Typically the Elderly) May Be Frustrated:** Leaving customary routines behind may be inconvenient; coming out of the comfort zone may entail frustration. Those with less risk appetite will find themselves in hard situation following the changes. They need more patience and tailor made treatment.

- ○ Intramural competition and the distrustful atmosphere of individualism hinders "opening up" to each other. In a culture where rivalry is strong and individual interests precede the community's interests, the cooperative attitude can hardly be popularized. Several industries are characterized by knowledge intensity where the personal competitive advantage is based on own knowledge. The risk that not everybody will join the new intellectual habit is there.

- ○ **Envy:** A withdrawing force can be for moderate persons that they do not want to attract the attention of envious colleagues; they do not want to vaunt.

- ○ **Lack of Time and/or the Insufficient Timeframe:** Knowledge sharing requests excess enforcements from the members of the organization. Into our everyday work we should include an activity to which no time was dedicated earlier. If someone is in arrears with his daily work, he/she could hardly be persuaded to systematize and share his/her knowledge. All of the members of the organization should be made aware that these enforcements are investments with high interest return which will yield for them as well as for the rest of the members of the organization. Everybody should be able to take time for implementing KM and be involved therein; furthermore the organization should ensure dedicated timeframes for these tasks (trainings, events of knowledge communities…).

- ○ **Permanent Uncertainty Caused by the Global Economy:** This could be perceived indirectly and it is not at all sure that this would exercise negative impact on KM. Sometimes it is easier to acknowledge that high quality work and cooperative conduct are unavoidable when times are hard; the necessity of changes can more easily be accepted.

- ○ **Existing Technologies are Incompatible with New IT systems (Alternative IT Standards, Macintosh, Microsoft, etc.):** Parallelism should be eliminated, but adherence to old proven systems must not impede the introduction of novelties. New system elements should be examined from technical, IT and user aspects.

- ○ **Uncertainties Regarding Functions and Scopes of Responsibility:** Tasks, responsibilities and scopes of authorities should clearly be separated in project management as well as in the KM system. All concerned persons must know what to expect and from whom, as well as their personal role in the specific tasks.
- ○ **Unexpected Costs are Incurred:** The implementation of a KM system does not necessitate the purchase of terribly expensive solutions. Starting with the establishment of knowledge communities and/or expert teams can be an easier way, and tasks could be solved through the enhancement of the creative and innovative capabilities of the organization. It may happen, however, that the implementation of certain initiatives entails unexpected costs. In such case it would not be advantageous if a community incentive otherwise deserving support would fail due to lack of financing. In the course of the elaboration of the budget it is worthwhile to allocate a buffer ("contingency budget") in order to help the achievement of the targets with flexible financial management.

- If the size of the investment is in proportion with the development of KM, then voluminous failure can be excluded. Of course, the length of the return period is dubious… On the one hand, there are lots of outputs without directly influencing the results. On the other hand susceptibility and willingness can fundamentally influence the velocity of changes. In summary, the risks and difficulties drafted above can be avoided through properly planned operation and incremental steps, and therefore the largest risks can be managed.

# REFERENCES

Antonova, A., & Gourova, E. (2009). Business Patterns for Knowledge audit implementation within SMEs. 14th EuroPLoP, Irsee, Germany.

Davenport, T. H., & Prusak, L. (1998). *Working Knowledge*. Boston: Harvard Business School Press.

Dvans, M., Dalkir, K., & Bidian, C. (2014). Holistic View of the Knowledge Life Cycle: The Knowledge Management Cycle (KMC). *Model Electronic Journal of Knowledge Management, 12*(2), 148.

Elliott, J. (1991). Action research educational. Open University Press.

Foucault, M. (1971). *L'Ordre du discours*. Paris: Gallimard.

Gourova, E., Antonova, A., & Todorova, Y. (2009). Knowledge audit concepts, processes and practice. *WSEAS Transactions on Business and Economics, 6*(12), 605 – 619.

Klimkó, G., & Tóth, R. (2007). Tudásmenedzsment az üzleti stratégia szolgálatában. *Vezetéstudományi szemle, 38*(7-8), 6-10.

Krogh, G., & Nonaka, I. (2000). Enabling Knowledge Creation. Oxford University Press. doi:10.1093/acprof:oso/9780195126167.001.0001

Lewin, K. (1946). Action Research and Minority Problems. *Journal of Social Issues*, (3).

Liebowicz, J. (2012). *Knowledge Management Handbook: Collaboration and Social Networking*. CRC Press. doi:10.1201/b12285

Lucier, C. E., & Torsilieri, J. D. (1997). *Why Knowledge Programs Fail: A CEO's Guide to Managing Learning*. Strategy & Business.

Mcdermott, R., & O'dell, C. (2001). Overcoming cultural barriers to sharing knowledge. *Journal of Knowledge Management*, 5(1), 76–85. doi:10.1108/13673270110384428

Nonaka, I., & Takeuchi, H. (1995). *The Knowledge-Creating Company: How Japanese Companies Create the Dynamics of Innovation*. New York: Oxford University Press.

Noszkay, E. (2013). A rendszerszemléletű tudásmenedzsment. Pearson.

Noszkay, E., & Balogh, A. (2015). Operational Characteristics of Knowledge-Intensive Service Companies and Knowledge-Intensive Business Services (KIBS). In Tudásteremtés és - alkalmazás a modern társadalomban. Tanulmánykötet.

Sedighi, M., & Zand, F. (2012). Knowledge Management: Review of the Critical Success Factors and Development of a Conceptual Classification Model. *10th International Conference on ICT and Knowledge Engineering*. doi:10.1109/ICTKE.2012.6408553

Skyrme, D., & Amidon, D. (1998). The Knowledge Agenda. In J. W. Cortada & J. A. Woods (Eds.), *The Knowledge Management Yearbook 1999-2000*. Boston: Butterworth-Heinemann.

Van Aalst, H. F. (2003). Networking in Society. Organisations and Education. In *Networks of Innovation for Schools and Systems*. Paris: OECD.

Varga, K. (1988). *Az emberi és szervezeti erőforrás fejlesztése*. Budapest: Akadémiai Kiadó.

Wenger, E., & Snyder, W. (2000, January-February). Communities of Practice: The Organizational Frontier. *Harvard Business Review*.

Wong, K. Y. (2005). Critical success factors for implementing knowledge management in small and medium enterprises. *Industrial Management & Data Systems*, 105(3), 261–279. doi:10.1108/02635570510590101

Wong, K. Y., & Aspinwall, E. (2005). An empirical study of the important factors for knowledge-management adoption in the SME sector. *Journal of Knowledge Management*, 9(3), 64–82. doi:10.1108/13673270510602773

## KEY TERMS AND DEFINITIONS

**Community of Practice:** A group of people interested in or showing a passion for or attempting to solve the same thing or similar problems and who improve their knowledge of the specific area through continuous cooperation. It has two types: knowledge community and expert teams.

**Guru:** An experienced and credible polymath, professional expert who attributably to his/her reputation, values and charismatic personality, and to his/her skills in appreciating others' knowledge and to his/her ability to lead people from behind, will be able to be a leader, a "spiritual father" of a community of practice.

**KM Implementation from Above:** Implementation takes place when initiated and supported by the top management. Any kind of uncertainty (e.g. corporate and/or strategic vision is missing or vague, processes or the entire corporate operation is not or not sufficiently regulated, etc.), or an organizational structure disfavoring KM (knowledge, learning and cooperation are not deemed to be values, trust is missing the so-called power distance is too big) preclude chances for successful solutions.

**KM Implemented Also from Below:** This is an organizational process where members of the organization becoming aware of the significance of KM start or contribute to the implementation of KM all by themselves, with their active initiatives, sometimes through certain communities (e.g. knowledge communities, expert teams, etc.).

**KM Maturity Model:** Its aim and essence lay in the possibility of quasi measuring on the basis of various characteristics in order to determine the position of the organization on its way to become knowledge centered. Examinations focus on human, procedural, content and technological dimensions. Another type of the models approaches from the process side. This latter is mostly applied in software and system developments. The product of the KM maturity models is the determination of a clear and unambiguous vision for the KM developments foreseen by the organization.

**Sandwich Method:** This is a method of KM implementation where the organization's several hierarchical levels initiate KM implementation. A special case is when the initiative starts from the level second to the top managerial one, which will be supported by strength of the KM communities established on the lower hierarchical levels and will produce a critical value that is necessary for the implementation of KM.

**Topic:** This is a motif several times revisited and expressed mostly in the form of an analogy. In view of the discursive fermentation of discourses (see e.g. Foucault (1971)), topics may with good chances play important role or enforce their structural-generative function in the drafting of new knowledge contents. (In view of the fact that topics and combinatorics represent two complementary aspects of creative procedures – combinatorics and its rules are "empty" without topics and topics in the absence of the mobilizing power of combinatorics are just "static building blocks".)

## ENDNOTES

[1] Siemens is one of those that possesses a properly operating KM system with the involvement of top managers. A supporting component of KM is a web 2.0 technology, named Technoweb. Technoweb in fact ensures a platform for people within an organization to find each other and by way of establishing communities they could share, build and develop the knowledge of individuals and the organization. This instrument offers solution for several problems that should be faced by most of the enterprises, for instance the transfer of the knowledge stored in the heads (tacit knowledge), streamlined flow of information within the organization (in between organizational units, across barriers built by hierarchy and geographical distance), awareness of the corporate knowledge capital. According to a survey conducted by McKinsey in 2007, employees acquire most pieces of information necessary for their work from each other and mostly during the time spent in the canteen or the coffee-room. Technoweb makes use of this instance in such manner that ensures a possibility for the people to interact with each other within a safe framework system, and share with each other their knowledge contents of whatever sort, related to or independent of their work. It can mostly be attributed to the communication and the employees' freedom of relatively high degree

and the collaboration therefrom stemming that Siemens ranks 4th in Hay's „Best Companies for Leadership".

In addition to the possibility that anybody can start a community in whatever topic thereby building and sharing knowledge, another important element of Technoweb is the so-called „Urgent request". This means that anyone in the enterprise who encountered a question or problem that he/she cannot solve, simple posts it on Technoweb (or addresses the question to a community familiar with the topic), and the answer will arrive within some hours from anywhere on Earth. The querier can evaluate the response according to its usability. Finally, within 1 or 2 days almost any problem can be solved on the basis of answers received. Technoweb proved to be expressly useful in discussions over innovative ideas.

In summary, Technoweb has three main advantages: (1) Colleagues possessing special knowledge can be connected, organization unit and country borders notwithstanding. (2) It is difficult to keep pace with continuous developments. Technoweb keeps knowledge updated and eliminates this difficulty. (3) Each and every employee has the possibility to ask expert teams.

From the business aspect, its main advantage is increased efficiency and the consequential cost decrease. Time dedicated to information research shortened and information could be made available at zero cost; meanwhile collective knowledge and content generation improves innovative skills and capacities.

[2]    A concept that originates from physics and says that for the production of certain results a specific (in general: significant) volume of means is needed and simultaneously with the achievement of that volume, successfulness improves significantly. Thus activities "on a basic level" not achieving the critical volume and the excess activities are in synergic relation with and intensify the impacts of each other. Therefore the "critical mass" in societal context means that when sufficient number of people experience, think of or create something, then beyond a certain point the impact exercised on the rest of the members of this group will increase exponentially. That is, the critical mass is a mass of people that in comparison with the entire mass is relatively small but sufficiently big to produce changes in the entire mass, and to efficiently increase the "vibration level" of the entire mass. In general these are people who do not cocoon themselves or are afraid, but they rather assume the intrinsic risk and are ready to take challenges that would strengthen their more and more credible self, they are open-minded, like learning and self-development.

[3]    A research conducted among knowledge intensive firms was finalized in 2015 (see Noszkay & Balogh, 2015). The research covered several firms providing IT services. In the course of our survey it has been experienced that apart from one exception, all firms applied the sandwich method for the efficient implementation and the wide scope application of KM.

[4]    In is important to note that there are many who identify knowledge communities with interest communities. Although there are lots of similarities, there are important differences between these two groups. An interest community is organized to reconcile, discuss information and concepts related to a given topic and to achieve the common goals of participants and stakeholders. In knowledge communities – in agreement with their true nature – participants are not delegated but join voluntarily, and they form thoughts in their mind with long term perspective, and without specific objective. Although it is an organized group, its leader ("guru") has no power, he/she plays a sort of steering and coordinating role. Beyond similarities mentioned above, an important difference is

that the members of the knowledge community share knowledge, the interest communities share information. One may say that interest communities do not create but just use knowledge.

5  The SharePoint Server (SPS) program developed by a Microsoft, can be excellently used in functions related to knowledge management. In order to support the efficient operation of organizations, the information technology system should develop five areas (unified communication, business intelligence, corporate content management, team work, searches). These together form a uniform business platform and if they support each other and the intra-organizational information flow, then huge business possibilities can be realized. Main areas where SPS supports efficiency are the following: Posting (there are several levels: group website, intranet, internet portal), Community knowledge sharing, Content management, Searches, Decision making, Development platform.

6  This concept says that our era (characterized by acceleration, when the half-life of disciplines has shortened) is the era when tacit knowledge "wishes" to bubble up to the top. Obviously, old and well proven (scientific, natural, societal, technical, economical) paradigms or customary problem solutions are not valid any more. This exercises impact on all level globally. In this situation reflecting permanent transitions, all scientific researchers and developers seek the possibility and realization of "something new", the sole option that we have is the mobilization of hiding tacit knowledge contents of as many layers as possible. This is why knowledge communities as well as discourses that assist ideas in their free flowing came to being. (Foucault, M. (1971)). Wherever and whenever any brand new thing (whose purpose might not be clear) is in the making, the discourse within the community must be let to "whirl" and where the texts start to densify there one can find a constellation, a "location" where tacit knowledge wishes to become explicit, special nods (topics) are waiting for being "worded".

7  Capillarity is often referred to by physics, chemistry or biology. Through pores in between laminas or soil particles, etc. at small distance from each other, liquids do not settle as they do in communicating vessels but attributably to capillarity, the water can find its way above groundwater level. Those thin tubes where capillarity happens are called capillary vessels. In capillarity the porous medium, for instance soil with its tiny system of gaps, also plays its role. Pores and capillary vessels in the soil are of various sizes, therefore the elevation of the capillary liquid cannot be calculated on the basis of the size of soil particles.

8  The concept of action research was founded by Lewin who in alteration of the researches focusing on scientific results, emphasized the importance of researches that are consciously aimed at the shaping of practice. Research is not separated from its application, but rather is based on the idea that all researches are in the meantime interventions into a section of reality, therefore the emphasis is laid on the comprehension of the consequences of such intervention. Research is understood as an action involving the researcher as well as the subjects. Lewin proposed the utilization of action research in the field of sociology, since this could be a tractable form of the examination of a societal system and in the meantime an attempt to change the system. The objective of the traditional social science is to discover the interrelationships within societal systems (and the knowledge contents stemming therefrom are on the long run very useful for those who wish to achieve any sort of changes). Meanwhile action research strives to understand and concurrently solve problems intrinsic in societal systems. In Hungary action research was adapted first by Károly Varga (1988) with the aim of improving the efficiency of intervention in the frames of Organization Development (OD).

# Chapter 8
# Product Knowledge Management in Small Manufacturing Enterprises

**Giulia Bruno**
*Politecnico di Torino, Italy*

## ABSTRACT

*An important issue present in the most of manufacturing systems, and become worse in SMEs, is the systematic management of the huge amount of unstructured information generated about products, from their design to their disposal. The aim of this chapter is to define a framework to manage such kind of data, overcoming the actual issues of the meaningless and the unstructured nature of generated information. To this aim, a knowledge management platform is proposed, both to store product information with semantic enrichment and to retrieve product information by means of a new similarity index. Such platform is based on the one hand on a non-relational data management system and on the other hand on a set of manufacturing ontologies. An example of the potentiality of the proposed framework is shown in the domain of telecommunication filter manufacturing.*

## INTRODUCTION

Today, embedded technology, real time collaboration, intelligence and connectivity are enabling the evolution to a seamless and agile manufacturing ecosystem, giving origin to the fourth industrial revolution. In such globalized and interconnected system, information is considered as an important production factor as capital, human resources and material (Sandkuhl, 2009). Enterprises have acquired various tools that support them to imagine, design and manufacture their products (Laroche et al. 2012). However, with knowledge and know-how contained inside different systems, it is very difficult to find the right information. The percentage of knowledge available in a structured and reusable format is very low in companies (less than 5%) and the rest is either unstructured or resides in people minds (Rasmus, 2002). Furthermore, Lynn et al. (2000) found that a storage and retrieval systems for technological information is a key factor that impact a team's ability to acquire and use knowledge to reduce cycle time and improve the probability of success. Thus, now the main challenge is no longer to guarantee the existence of the

DOI: 10.4018/978-1-5225-1642-2.ch008

information, but rather to find and provide the right information on time for a given purpose (Nadoveza & Kiritsis, 2014).

Having at disposal a huge amount of data coming from heterogeneous systems, the task of finding the right information is very difficult: studies revealed that 39% of all business executives spend more than 2 hours per day in searching for the right information (Delphi Group, 2002). Furthermore, even if digital systems are used daily to design, develop, produce, deliver and support products, the wide range of systems used has created the landscape of "isolated islands of information" where information is locked in different repositories making it difficult to share (Madenas et al. 2014). Among these systems, Enterprise Resource Planning (ERP) is a general framework for information processing, due to its ability to process and organize transactions, and build decision support applications on them (Caplinskas et al. 2012; Lupeikiene et al. 2014). However, ERP systems often lack flexibility and are not used by small enterprises.

In recent years, various forms of virtual collaboration have grown, in which the organisations try to exploit the facilities of the network to achieve higher utilisation of their resources (Jardim-Goncalves et al. 2014). The big idea is that this scenario will allow a self-controlling production process, in which production reacts autonomously to changes or faults and takes appropriate measures. This will bring systems engineering, production IT, and business systems to a new level – leveraging business benefits from an increasingly integrated product lifecycle management (PLM).

The aim of this chapter is to propose a method to organize the data available in manufacturing enterprises thus transforming data in information, and then structuring it in order to allow its easier finding and reuse, overcoming the actual issues of the meaningless and the unstructured nature of generated information. To this aim, a knowledge management platform is proposed, which is based on the one hand on a non-relational data management system and on the other hand on a set of manufacturing ontologies. The modular structure of the proposed framework allow its easy extension depending on the specific industrial domain. The use of the ontologies also allow the exploitation of a new similarity index to compute the similarity among products. The potentiality of the approach is shown in a case study.

## BACKGROUND

In the digital economy, knowledge becomes the primary raw material. The initial challenge in moving towards organizational smartness is to know where to find information and how to reuse it (Filos 2006). The management of a product from inception to disposal has strategic value for a given company in the networked economy and PLM is considered to be the 21st century paradigm for product development (Borsato, 2014). This has only been possible due to extensive use of IT infrastructure and technology to exchange information, which enables companies to explore external possibilities like partnering with suppliers and co-developers (Subrahmanian et al. 2005). Yet, the full potential of positive network externalities has not been reached, for there is the lack of interoperability and difficulties with the adoption of such technologies by small and medium enterprises, which form the supplier base in fundamental production sectors.

The amount of information flow has consistently increased in the past few years, due to product complexity and multi-disciplinary work. Historically, PLM has been about breaking the silos between engineering, manufacturing, sales and marketing, service and support. A key aspect of the fourth industrial revolution is that it will allow the use of the entire product lifecycle information during the manufacturing of products, so that they can be integrated and made available for exchange and retrieval

(Westkämper, 2000). Existing PLM systems require that product information is strictly structured accordingly to a model. However, product information produced and exchanged are almost unstructured (David & Rowe, 2015). Data format heterogeneity, limited content structure and informational richness makes it difficult to extract the information necessary for efficient classification and retrieval (Liu et al. 2008). PLM software allows the centralized management of product data but they require a huge manual effort to store data and activate the retrieval function (Tough & Moss, 2003).

The use of ontologies is important to define a set of well formalized and commonly agreed terms from a specific domain (Liao et al. 2015). Several works in literature addressed the definition of knowledge capture and management tools based on ontological models. Former works addressed the early stages, i.e., the design and manufacturing phases (Guerra-Zubiaga & Young, 2008; Fiorentini et al. 2007; Young et al. 2007; Lu et al. 2008; Baxter et al. 2008; Baxter et al. 2009; Antonelli et al. 2013; Bruno et al. 2014; Premkumar et al. 2014), while more recently works addressed the later stages, i.e., the maintenance and sustainability (Borsato, 2014; Igba et al. 2015). More specifically, Guerra-Zubiaga and Young (2008) approached how to capture information and knowledge interactions to support process planning within a manufacturing facility, Fiorentini et al. (2007) addressed the development of an assembly model to allow the interoperability between software platforms, Young et al. (2007) highlighted the importance of sharing manufacturing information to support decision making, Lu et al. (2008) proposed an ontology to eliminate confusion of semantic concepts in the ship-building industry, Baxter et al. (2008) focused on requirement management by developing a framework to help ensuring that the right requirements are met and thus customer satisfaction can be increased, Baxter et al. (2009) proposed a framework to capture and reuse the design and manufacturing knowledge to support product development in a collaborative enterprise context, Antonelli et al. (2013) proposed an high level ontology for product lifecycle management, Premkumar et al. (2014) proposed a knowledge management system specific for laminated composites to support the transfer of information among different software tools, and Bruno et al. (2014) described a semantic platform to manage product design information. More recently, Borsato (2014) defined a framework to capture data of the disposal phase of products, to allow the retrieval of information about the parts that have a high potential recycling, while Igba et al. (2015) proposed an approach to optimise product performance by using knowledge and experience gained during in-service to show how in-service knowledge can be captured and reused for the design and manufacture stages of the product lifecycle.

Beyond the semantic enrichment, another problem is the design of a storage system able to manage the dramatic mass of data generated. Due to the unstructured nature of generated information, relational data management systems are not the best way for data storage. In fact, the more complex the collection of information is, the more levels of hierarchy and cross relationships, the less possible it is to represent it within the simple table structures (Bloor, 2003). Particularly, storing and representing data structures fairly common in manufacturing, such as working sequences and bill of materials, can be very difficult. In this context, the adoption of non-relational (NoSQL) databases can significantly improve the performance of PLM systems. Handling massive amounts of data is much easier and faster with NoSQL databases, especially for the query processing. NoSQL databases have more relaxed modeling constraints, which may benefit both the application developer and the end-user analysts when their interactive analyses are not throttled by the need to cast each query in terms of a relational table-based environment (Loshin, 2013). Different NoSQL frameworks are optimized for different types of analyses. For example, one emerging model is the graph database, in which a graph abstraction is implemented to embed both semantics and connectivity within its structure (Sadalage & Fowler, 2013). Although there are some best solutions of NoSQL, few publications have mentioned the use of NoSQL for CPS. For example, NoSQL databases were used to record historical monitoring of intelligent buildings (Ma & Sun, 2013) and smart buildings (Popovici & Privat, 2015), to store data for home energy management applications (Chen et al. 2014), and to manage heterogeneous personal data coming from disparate sources (Ren et al. 2014).

Previous works on semantic PLM did not address the problem of populating the ontologies, i.e., how real data can be inserted as instances of the entities of the ontology. This is a big issue, since it is unreasonable to think that user inserts manually in the system all the data related to a product, and the definition of automatic procedures is difficult due to the unstructured nature of data. Furthermore, for these applications, it is not clear how the historical data can be stored in the system, and how the data stored can be effectively reused in the decision making processes. Successful organisations in the digital economy need to consistently create new knowledge, disseminate it and quickly embody it in new products (Filos, 2006). Particularly in manufacturing, knowledge management systems have to organize data accordingly to a semantic schema tailored to the specific product, and allow their easy retrieval throughout the whole product lifecycle. To solve these issues, this work focuses on the definition of a framework which does not involve the implementation of a new data capture system, because it is able to automatically read documents containing product information. It also highlights the importance of the user-centred ontologies, i.e., containing terms of interest to retrieve information for people working in the product lifecycle, as opposed to product-centred ontologies, which include low level information and are designed to support the interoperability among systems.

To date, no manufacturing knowledge management system has investigated the exploitation of NoSQL databases. This chapter will provide an example of the application of NoSQL databases, particularly the graph-based databases, to store both ontologies and product data to support ubiquitous manufacturing.

Once data have been stored in a database, the search and reuse of them is another critical issue.

Despite the improvements in the state of the art literature, knowledge management dealing with the classification of previous knowledge lacks in companies, especially SMEs (Efthymiou et al. 2015). Some approaches were proposed to capture the similarity between products especially when the Group technology was introduced, i.e., a manufacturing technique in which parts having similarities in geometry, manufacturing process and/or functions are manufactured in one location (a manufacturing cell) using a small number of machines or processes (Kalpakjian & Schmid, 2013). Examples of such methods are the Opitz coding schema (Opitz, 1970) and the Production Flow Analysis (PFA, Burbidge 1996). In Opitz, parts are categorized based on significant attributes such as dimensions, type of material, tolerance, operations required, basic shapes, surface finishing etc. and assigned a code which is a string of numerical digits that store information about the part. In PFA, parts are divided based on processing requirements, operational sequences and operational time of the parts on the machines. However, such methods are not used in small manufacturing enterprises, where similarity identification between new and past products relied almost exclusively on the memory and the experience of experts, thus being a time-consuming process. Furthermore, by using Opitz or PFA, it is not possible to quantify the similarity between two products, because they do not provide a distance function between product families.

On the contrary, a great number of similarity measures exist in literature and are applied in different contexts, but most of them present the limitation of being applicable only to numerical attributes (Liao et al. 1998; Efthymiou et al. 2015) or to compute string similarity based on edit-distance functions without taking into account the meaning of the words (Bouzid et al. 2013). Since here the aim is to compute a semantic similarity, an approach widely used in bioinformatics is adopted, which computes the functional similarity between genes in bioinformatics, which exploits the hierarchical tree of concepts represented by the ontology (Teng et al. 2013).

## KNOWLEDGE MANAGEMENT FRAMEWORK

The proposed framework aims at following the product during its whole lifecycle to derive a virtual representation of it, as shown in Figure 1. Particularly, during the design phase, the requirements and specification files are analyzed to extract the characteristic associated to the product, together with the bill of material (BOM) files from which the list of components is derived. In the manufacturing phase, the working sequence is analyzed to identify the processing and assembly operations that are executed to produce the product. In the maintenance phase the failure reports are analyzed to discover the failures reported by the users after the purchase of the product. Finally, in the recycling phase, the procedure to recycle the product and its components are also stored.

In this way, the virtual representation of the product is continuously enriched with additional information, which are at disposal to be analysed. The aim of this representation is to structure and link all the information related to a product in order to derive new knowledge, e.g., the correlations between the occurrence of a failure and the presence of a component, or between the requirement of a precise functional characteristic and the usage of a specific manufacturing process.

The framework to support the management of the virtual product is composed by three layers as shown in Figure 2, i.e., a user layer, a platform layer and a data layer. The user layer is represented by the product lifecycle, in which different kinds of information regarding the product are generated in different places and in different times. This unstructured information is send to the platform to be semantically enriched and stored in the database. The user layer also includes people asking for complex queries to retrieve data.

*Figure 1. Management of a real product and its virtual representation during the product lifecycle*

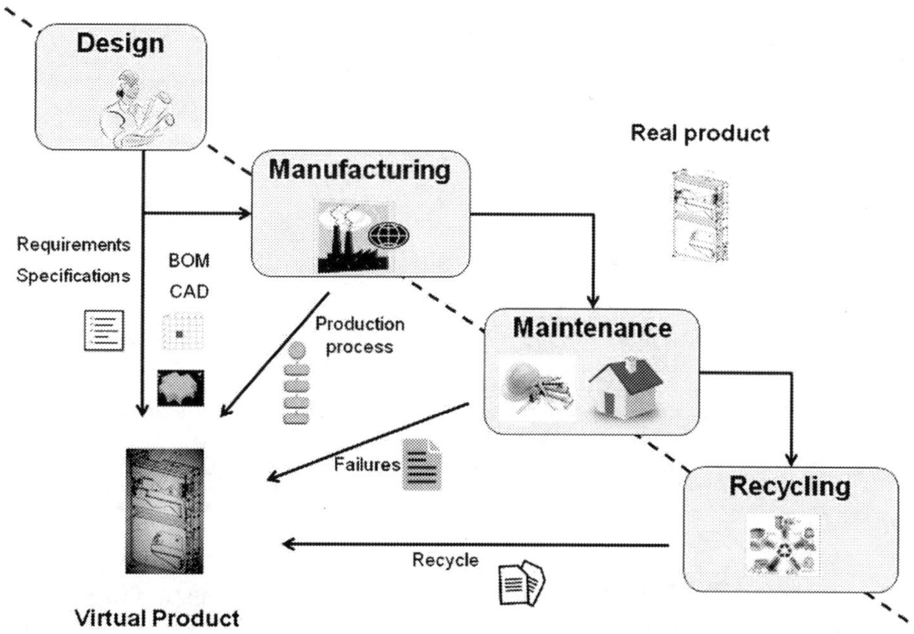

*Figure 2. Semantic framework for knowledge management*

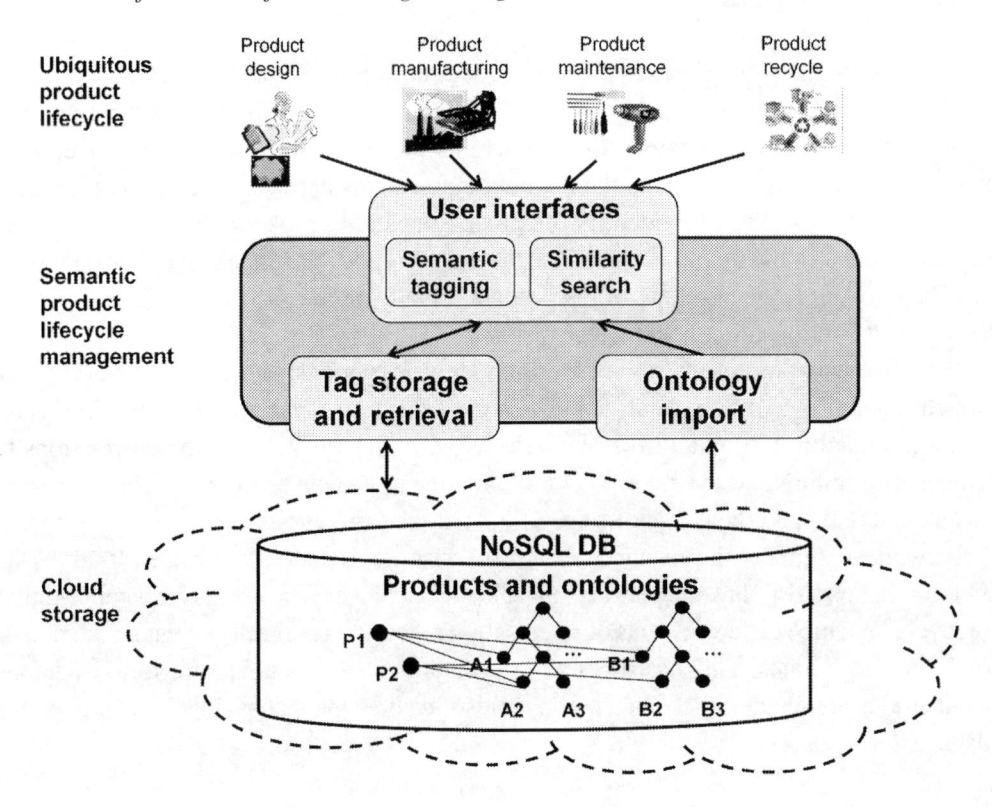

The proposed platform has a twofold scope:

1.  Store product information by means of the semantic tagging and
2.  Retrieve advanced information by means of the similarity search.

To this aim, it is composed by three main building blocks. The first block is a set of user interfaces, which analyses the input information and recall the semantic tagging or the similarity search functionalities. The ontology import block reads the ontologies stored in the database and make them available for the semantic tagging or the similarity search. The tag storage and retrieval block manages the interaction with the non-relational database to insert and retrieve data associated to products.

Finally, the data layer is the cloud storage system, to grant the access to data from anywhere and anytime. This storage system is the form of a non-relational database, particularly a graph-based database, due to its suitably to store ontology structures and connections between entities. The following paragraphs give the details of the three layers.

## User Layer

The users of the platform are of two kinds: the ones that generate information (uploading users) and the ones that ask for information (searching users). They span all the product lifecycle and they can be situated in different places and access the platform anytime, also simultaneously.

Depending on their roles, the uploading users produce different kinds of information, and different interfaces are implemented to upload different kind of data in the platform. It can be noticed that the user has not to be a real person, it can be any entity that generates information regarding a product. For example, in ubiquitous manufacturing, usually products are identified by a Radio Frequency Identification (RFID), and the machine that executes an operation on the product can directly record the data regarding the operation executed. In this way, during the manufacturing of the product, the information regarding the processes executed can be uploaded both by a human operator or by an intelligent machine. All the unstructured information generated is upload in the platform to be semantically enriched and stored in the database.

The searching users are the ones that want to retrieve information about previous products based on some similarity criteria (e.g., a product design manager, who wants to know if previous products similar to the new one had reported specific failures).

## Platform Layer

Both the functionalities of the proposed platform, i.e., the information storage and the information retrieval, are based on a set of ontologies. During the information storage, the ontologies are used to associate tags to a product, during the information retrieval, they are used to compute the semantic similarity between two products. The tagging process is similar to the ones used in other applications (e.g., Google, Facebook), but differently from them, here the user is able to define its own ontologies and exploit them during the process. For each product lifecycle phase, several ontologies can be defined. The choose of the ontologies strongly depends on the industrial domain and the kind of queries people are interesting in doing. Thus, in this section the ontologies are described in a general manner, to make clear their usage independently from the domain. In the Case study section, where an application scenario is discussed, an example of different kinds of ontologies used in the domain of telecommunication filter manufacturing are shown. The platform is developed in Java, which supports two open source libraries: Apache Lucene (http://lucene.apache.org/) for text analysis and Neo4j (http://neo4j.com) for the non-relational database interaction.

### Semantic Tagging

The sequence diagram for the semantic tagging is shown in Figure 3, accordingly to the UML Sequence diagram formalism (Fowler & Scott 2000). The Uploading user accesses the User interface to upload information and requires to upload a specific type of data through the *request_upload (P,T,F)* function. The meaning of the parameters is the following: *P* is the identifier of the product, *T* is the type of document to analyse (e.g., a BOM file, a working log, a failure report), and *F* is the URL or location identifier of the document.

The User interface turns the request to the Semantic tagging system, which based on the type of document *T*, requests the corresponding ontology to the Ontology import system through the *request_onto(T)* function. For example, if a BOM file is uploaded, the component ontology is retrieved, if a working log is uploaded, the manufacturing process ontology is retrieved, if a failure report is uploaded, the failure ontology is retrieved. Once the ontology (*O*) has been imported, the Semantic tagging proceeds to analyse the document, and search for the terms of the ontology inside the document (*Tags[]*). At the

*Figure 3. Sequence diagram of the semantic tagging procedure*

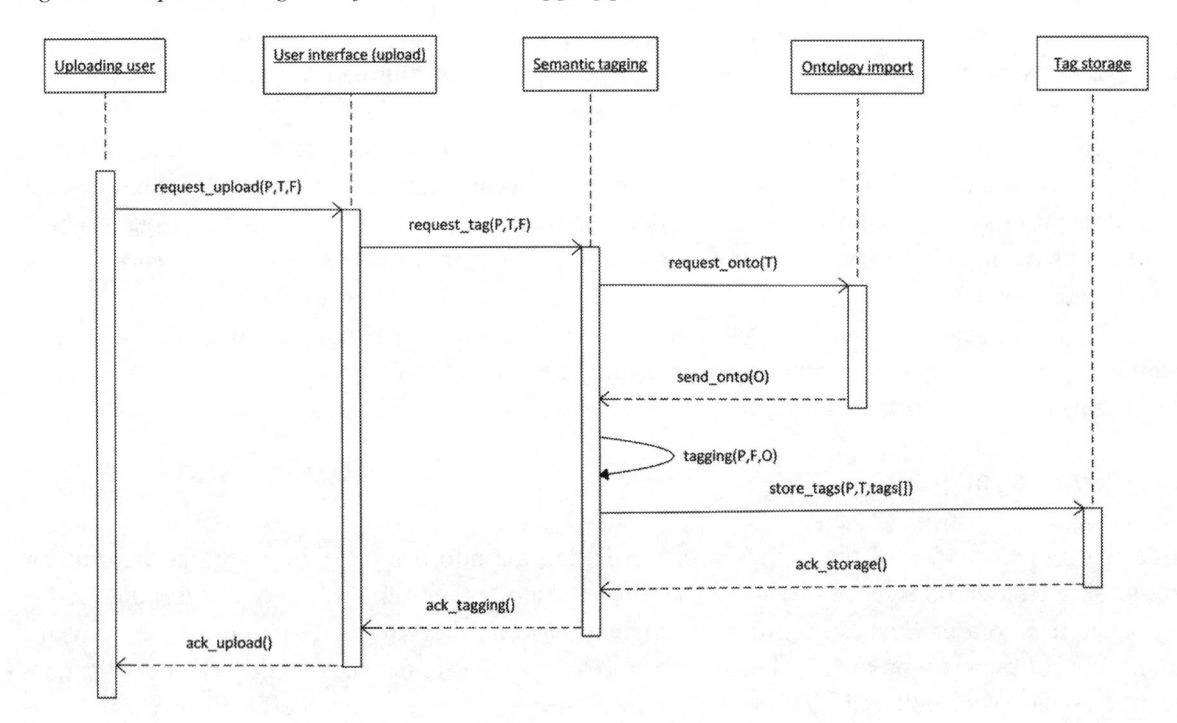

end, the tags were stored in the non-relational database by means of the Tag Storage system through the *store_tags (P,Tags[])* function. Finally, an acknowledgment of the storage completion is send to the User.

## Similarity Search

The organization of data accordingly to the proposed framework allows the computation of a semantic similarity index between products. The UML Sequence diagram of the similarity search is shown in Figure 4. The Searching user accesses the User interface to retrieve the products similar to a product ($P$) according to one or more similarity criteria ($K[]$), through the *request_search(P,K[])* function. In the current system the similarity criteria are the following:

1. Component similarity,
2. Manufacturing process similarity, and
3. Failure similarity, depending on which aspect the similarity among product has to be computed.

The User interface turns the request to the Similarity search system, which based on the similarity criteria selected requests the corresponding ontologies to the Ontology import system ($O[]$). Once the ontologies has been received, the Similarity search requires to the Tag retrieval system to return the list of products similar to product $P$ basing the similarity computation on the ontologies $O[]$, through the *request_sim_products(P,O[])* function. Due to the complexity of the *compute_similarity()* function, its detailed explanation is reported in the following section. At the end, the list of similar products $S[]$ is shown to the User.

*Figure 4. Sequence diagram of the similarity search procedure*

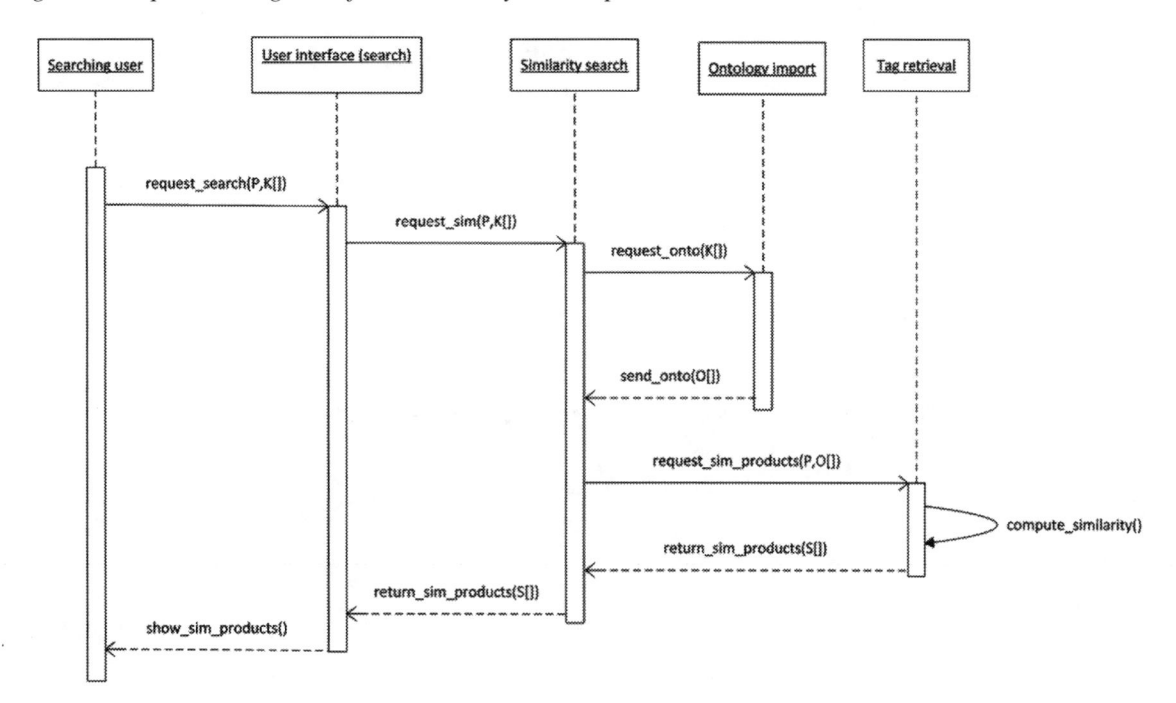

## Data Layer

The data layer is organized in a non-relational database, particularly a graph database (Sadalage & Fowler 2013). This kind of databases stores data in the form of graphs, where a graphs is composed of nodes and relationships, either of which may have properties (i.e., attributes). Nodes represent entities (i.e., concepts) and relationships (which may be directed) connect pairs of nodes. One of the strengths of a graph database lies in its ability to encode patterns of connected nodes and relationships: a single node or relationship typically encodes very little information, but a pattern of nodes and relationships can encode arbitrarily complex ideas. In the proposed framework, the Neo4j graph database (Neo4j Manual 2015) is used. Cypher is the declarative query language used for Neo4j, similar to the SQL language for relational databases. In Cypher, clauses and keywords (eg, MATCH, WHERE, DELETE) are used to combine the patterns and specify the desired queries.

During the semantic tagging procedure, data are stored in Neo4j in a graph form (see Figure 5 for a graphical example). Each ontology is stored as a set of nodes representing concepts and a set of "Is_A" relationships connecting nodes. Each product is stored as a node. Each tagging between a product and an ontology concept is stored as a specific relationship (e.g., the tag of a product with an element of the component ontology is represented by the "Has_Component" relationship).

An example of the Cypher syntax for the creation of two nodes of an ontology, the creation of a product, and its tagging with one of the concepts of the ontology is reported in the following.

CREATE (x:Component { id:"A0",name: "filter" }) // creation of component A0 referred as x
CREATE (y:Component { id:"A1",name: "plate" }) // creation of component A1 referred as y
CREATE (y)-[:Is_A]->(x) // creation of relationship Is_A between A1 and A0
CREATE (z:Product { id:"P1",name: "XX" }) // creation of product P1 referred as z

*Figure 5. Example of data stored in the graph database*

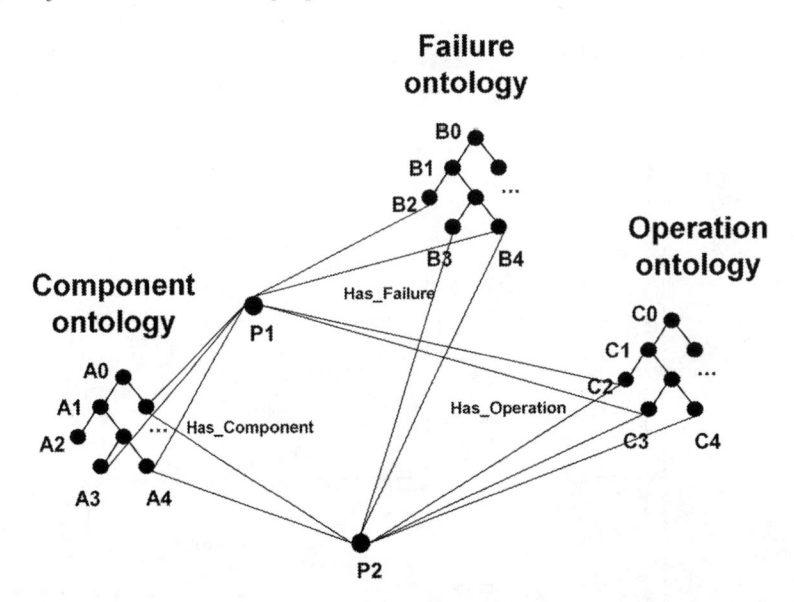

CREATE (z)-[:Has_Component]->(y) // creation of relationship Has_Component between P1 and A1

The retrieval of data in Neo4j is by defining matching patterns by means of the MATCH statement. For example, the query to retrieve all the components of product P1 is the following:

MATCH (p:Product)-[:Has_component]->(c:Component)

WHERE p.id ="P1"

RETURN c

In order to grant scalability, reliability and high performance at relatively low costs, the database will be stored in a cloud storage system instead of a dedicated infrastructure. The cloud storage is not further developed since a lot of providers are available and can be selected based on company requirements (Wang et al. 2010).

## SIMILARITY INDEX

The similarity computation is based on the portion of overlapping sub-graph of ontology existing between two products (Bruno 2015a). Since the importance of the nodes is not equal, but it depends on the number of descendants (more descendant a node has, less informative it is), the overlaps between graphs is computed by weighting the nodes by their information content.

The explanation of the exploited similarity index between two products can be done through an example. Let a sample ontology be the one represented in Figure 6. Three products are associated to some entities of the ontology, i.e., $P_1$ is associated to entities $C_1$ and $C_4$, $P_2$ to $C_2$, $C_3$ and $C_4$, and $P_3$ to $C_3$ and $C_4$, as shown in Figure 6. By using this information, a product can be represented as a sub-graph of each ontology. The product sub-graph is defined as the graph composed by each node of the ontology associated to the product and all its antecedents. The middle part of Figure 6 shows the three sub-graphs ($G_1$, $G_2$ and $G_3$), corresponding to the three sample products ($P_1$, $P_2$ and $P_3$, respectively). The intersection (or overlap) between two sub-graphs, $G_1$ and $G_2$, indicated as $G_1 \cap G_2$, is given by the maximum sub-graph shared by the two product-graphs (shown in the lower part of Figure 6).

*Figure 6. Graphs representing three products and the overlaps between them*

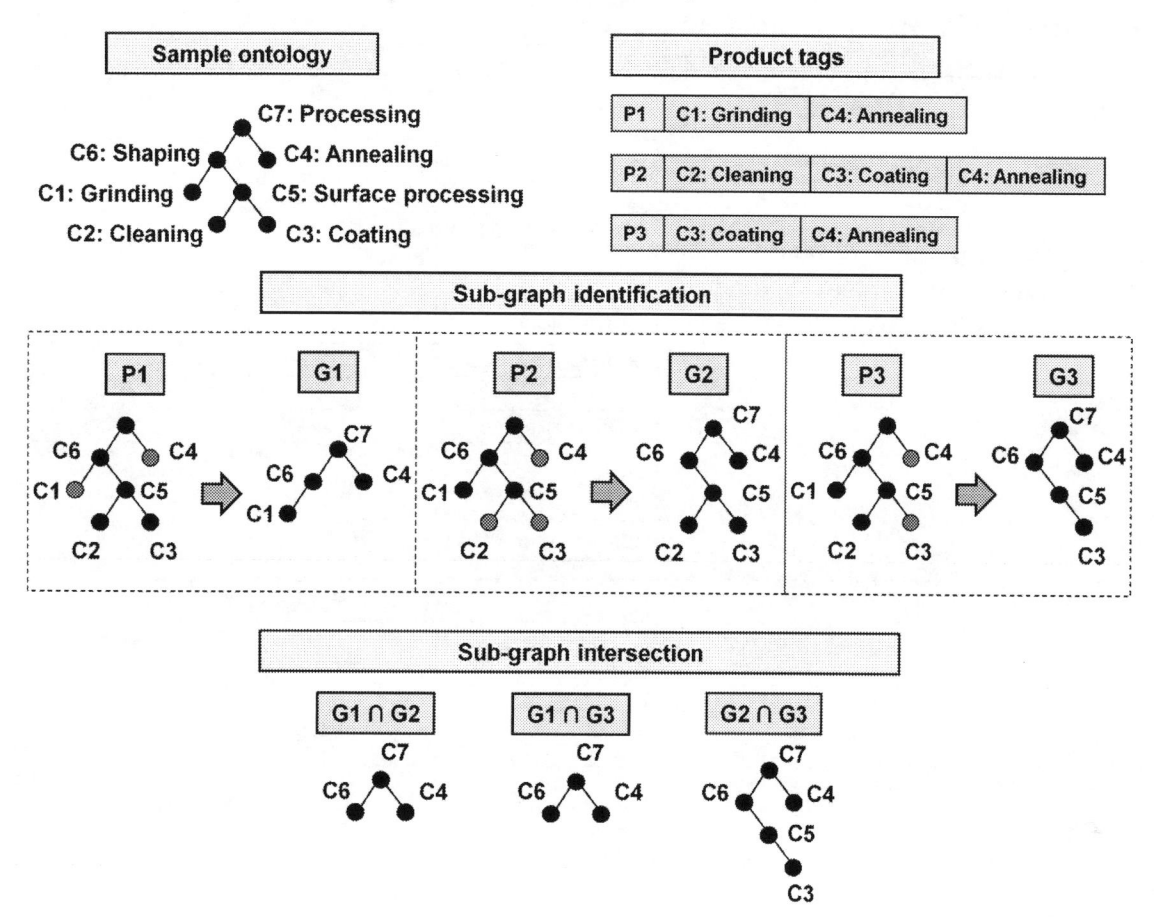

In order to evaluate the similarity between two sub-graphs, since the importance of the nodes is not equal, the concept of Information Content (IC) was introduced. Following the formulation of the structural IC approach (Seco et al. 2004), the information content of each class of an ontology can be computed depending on the number of its descendants in the ontology structure. Under this approach, the IC of class c is defined as follows:

$$IC(c) = 1 - \frac{\log(Desc(c) + 1)}{\log(Tot)},$$

where *Desc(c)* is the number of descendants of *c*, and *Tot* is the number of classes in the ontology. Figure 7 shows the computation of IC for each class of the sample ontology. It can be noticed that the information content is maximum (equal to 1) for the leaf nodes, and it is minimum for the root node (equal to 0). For the intermediate nodes, the IC value is higher for nodes with few descendants (e.g., IC of $C_5$ is higher than IC of $C_6$).

*Figure 7. Computation of the Information Content (IC) of each class in the sample ontology and the similarity index (SI) for each couple of products*

**Sample ontology**

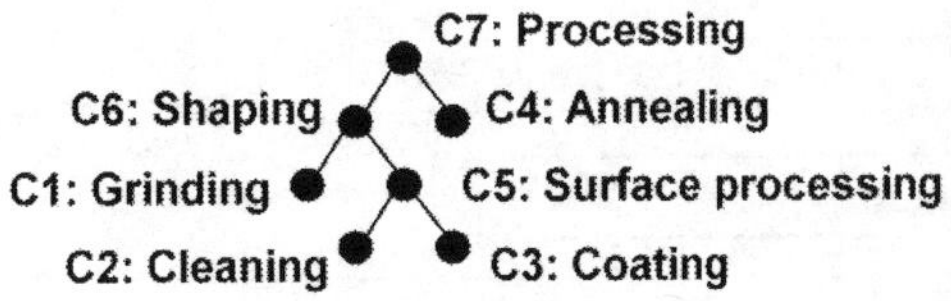

C7: Processing

C6: Shaping    C4: Annealing

C1: Grinding    C5: Surface processing

C2: Cleaning    C3: Coating

**IC computation**

| Class | Desc (C) | Log (Desc(C)+1) | Log(Desc(C)+1) /Log(Tot) | IC |
|---|---|---|---|---|
| C1: Grinding | 0 | 0 | 0 | 1 |
| C2: Cleaning | 0 | 0 | 0 | 1 |
| C3: Coating | 0 | 0 | 0 | 1 |
| C4: Annealing | 0 | 0 | 0 | 1 |
| C5: Surface processing | 2 | 0,45 | 0,53 | 0,47 |
| C6: Shaping | 4 | 0,70 | 0,82 | 0,18 |
| C7: Processing | 6 | 0,85 | 1 | 0 |

**Similarity matrix**

| | P1 | P2 | P3 |
|---|---|---|---|
| **P1** | 1 | (0+0,18+1)/ (0+0,18+1+1)= 0,541 | (0+0,18+1)/ (0+0,18+1+1)= 0,541 |
| **P2** | (0+0,18+1)/ (0+0,18+1+0,47+1+1) = 0,323 | 1 | (0+0,18+1+0,47+1)/ (0+0,18+1+0,47+1+1) = 0,73 |
| **P3** | (0+0,18+1)/ (0+0,18+1+0,47+1) = 0,445 | (0+0,18+1+0,47+1)/ (0+0,18+1+0,47+1) =1 | 1 |

The final similarity measure between two products $P_a$ and $P_b$ is given by the sum of the IC of the nodes of the sub-graph intersection ($G_a \cap G_b$) over the sum of the IC of the nodes in the graph of $G_a$. The complete formula of the semantic similarity index (SI) is the following:

$$SI(P_a, P_b) = \frac{\sum_{c_i \in (G_a \cap G_b)} IC(c_i)}{\sum_{c_j \in (G_a)} IC(c_j)}$$

Figure 7. illustrates the computation of the similarity index between each couple of the example products. The highest similarity is $Sim(P_3, P_2)$, equal to 1, since the product-graph corresponding to $P_3$ is completely contained in the product graph of $P_2$. The lowest similarity is $Sim(P_2, P_1)$, equal to 0,323, since the overlaps between $P_2$ and $P_1$ is of only three nodes, and only one of them is a leaf.

It can be noticed that this similarity is not a symmetric measure. In fact, $Sim(P_a, P_b) \neq Sim(P_b, P_a)$, due to the different values of the denominator. This chose was made because, when searching the products similar to a given product, a product which includes all the elements of the given product has the highest similarity without considering the fact that it has additional nodes. On the contrary, if a product contains few nodes than the given one, it doesn't have the highest similarity.

## APPLICATION SCENARIO

The scenario considered for the application of the proposed framework is the production of a telecommunication filter unit, a variant of the radio frequency (RF) filter family, a technical drawing of which is depicted in Figure 8. The filter is designed by an Italian company, it is produced by a Romanian company, and then it is sold by another Italian company, which also records the user complaints. The lifecycle covered thus include three phases: design, manufacturing and maintenance. Each phase is done in a different place by different people, and generates different documents that constitute the product information. The information have to be structured and linked together in order to derive new knowledge.

The following sections describes the ontologies defined for this scenario as well as the procedures executed for the semantic tagging and the similarity search.

### Ontologies for Filter Manufacturing

For each phase of the product lifecycle, it is possible to define a set of ontologies. In the present case, three ontologies were defined, one for each lifecycle phase. The ontologies were based on the analysis of the documents exchanged and the information to be retrieved by the actors involved in the three phases of the filter lifecycle. Particularly, three kinds of documents were considered: the bill of materials of the filters produced in the design phase, the working sequences containing the processes executed in the manufacturing phase, and the descriptions of product failures recorded in the maintenance phase.

The component ontology is the hierarchy of components that are used to produce a filter, shown in Figure 9. This ontology derives from the analysis of existing filters, and it is specific for this application scenario. The process ontology is the hierarchy of the manufacturing operations that can be executed. Since a lot of literature is available for manufacturing processes, the terminology defined by Groover

*Figure 8. Drawing of the telecommunication filter*

(2007) is taken as a reference. The detailed description of the definition of the ontology based on this terminology can be found in (Bruno, 2015b; Bruno et al. 2015), and a portion of it is reported in Figure 10 and Figure 11. The failure ontology classifies the failures causing filter malfunctions reported by the users. Its representation is shown in Figure 12. Also this ontology is specific for the current application scenario. These three ontologies were stored in the graph database, as described in the previous section.

## Semantic Tagging

The database was populated by uploading different information derived from various lifecycle phases and by performing the semantic tagging. An example of the BOM file and the working sequence file produced during the product design and the product manufacturing is reported in Figure 13. The failure

*Figure 9. Component ontology for the telecommunication filter*

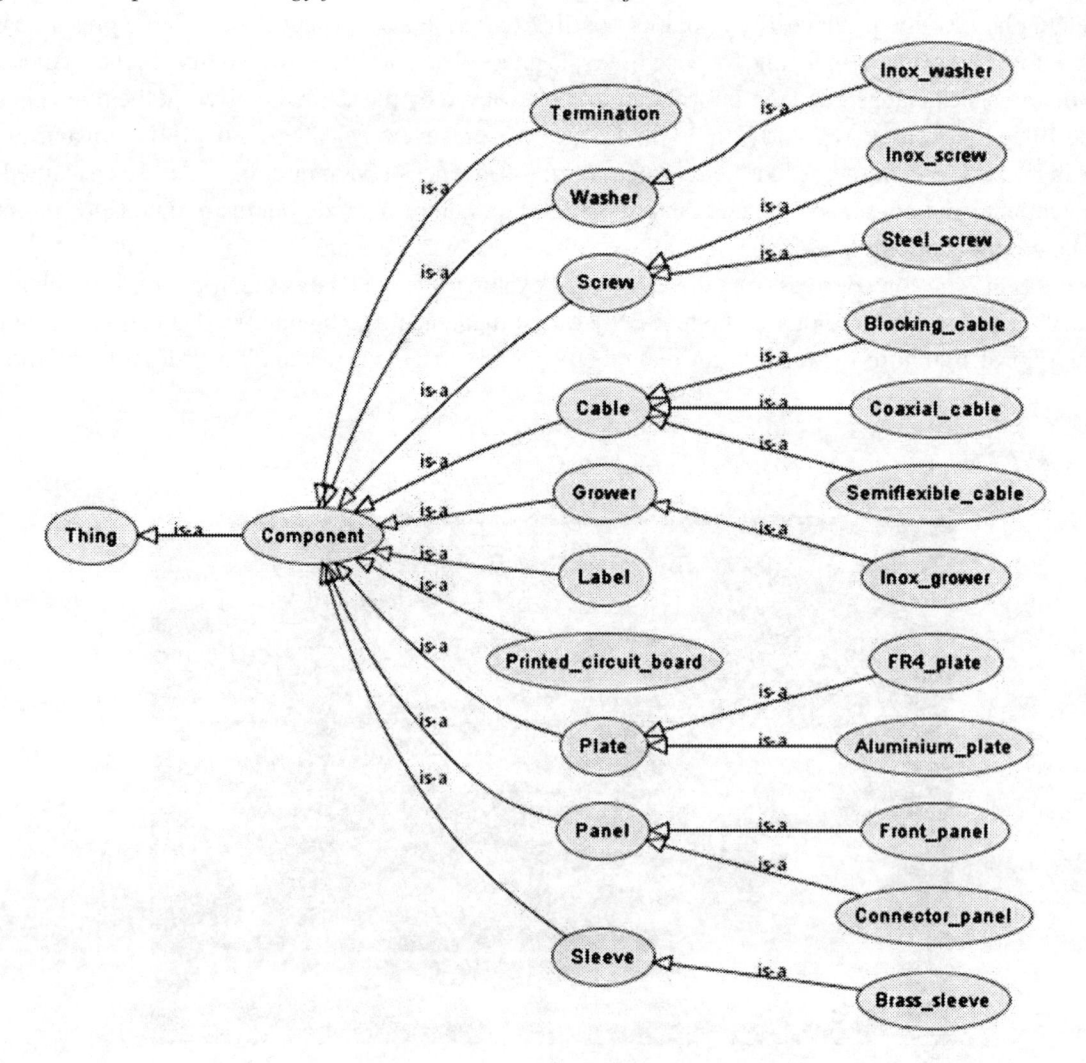

*Figure 10. First four levels of the Process ontology (Processing operation)*

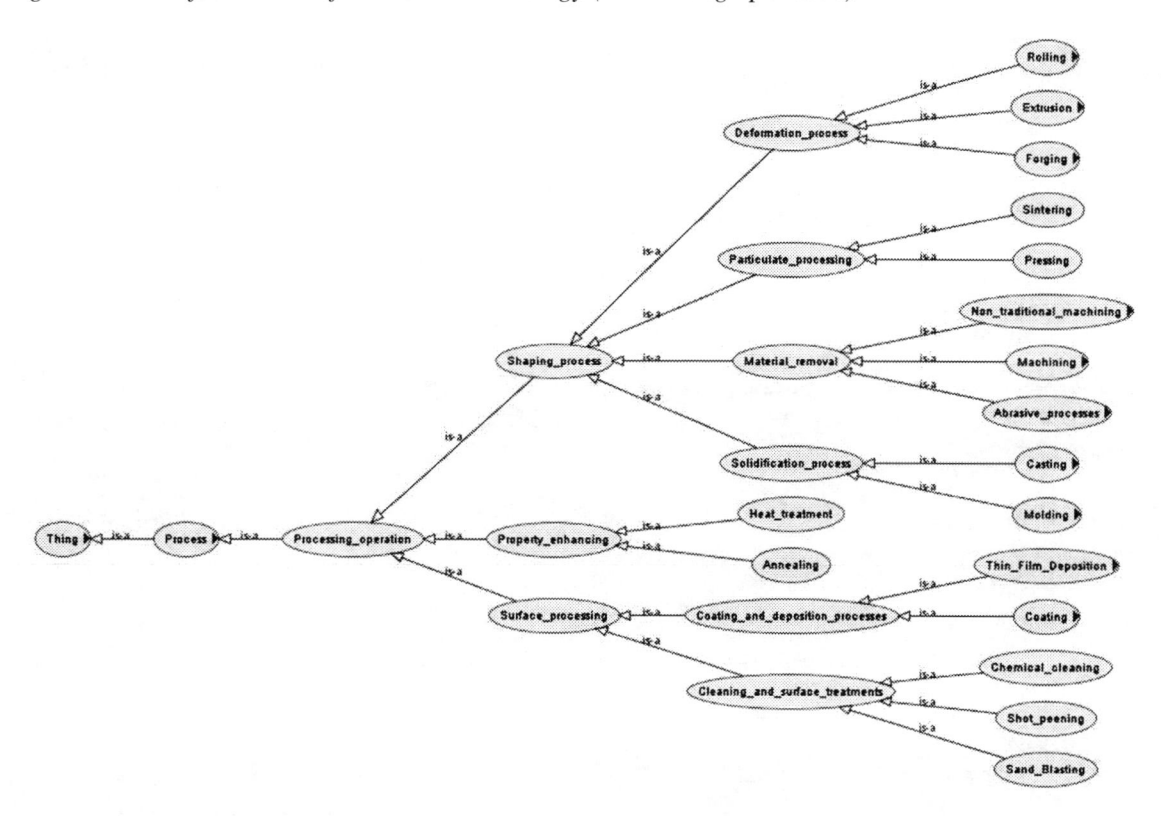

*Figure 11. First four levels of the Process ontology (Assembly operation)*

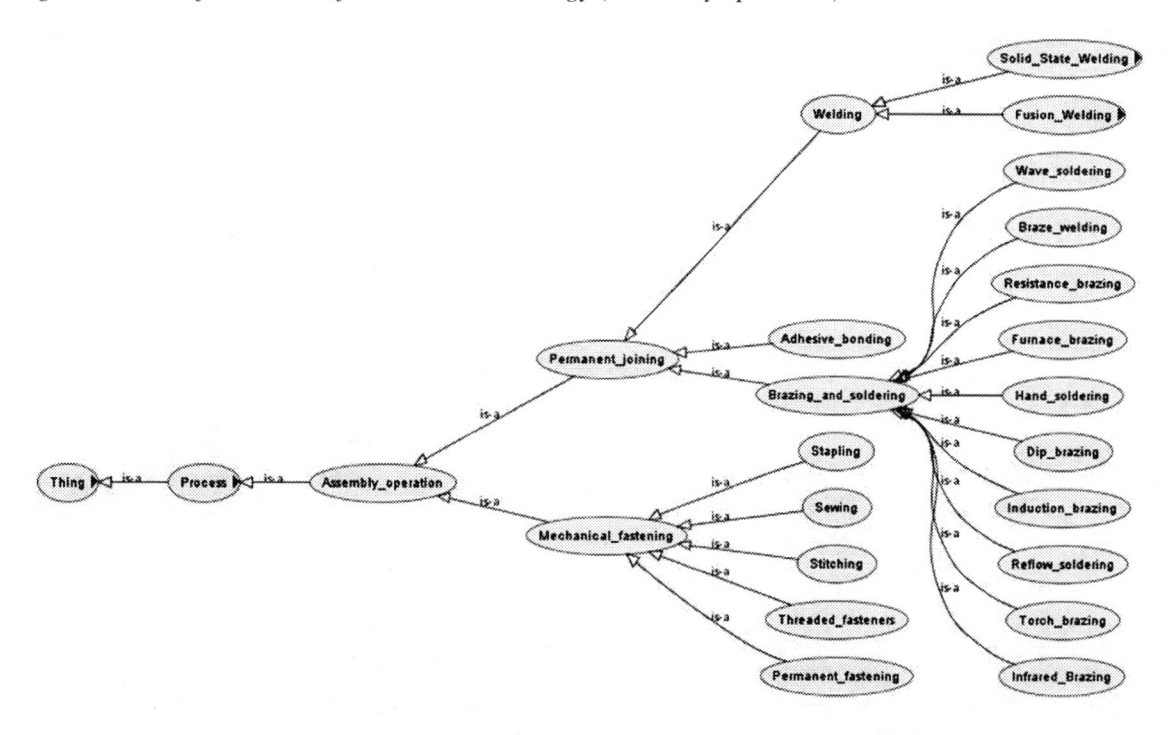

*Figure 12. Failure ontology for the telecommunication filter*

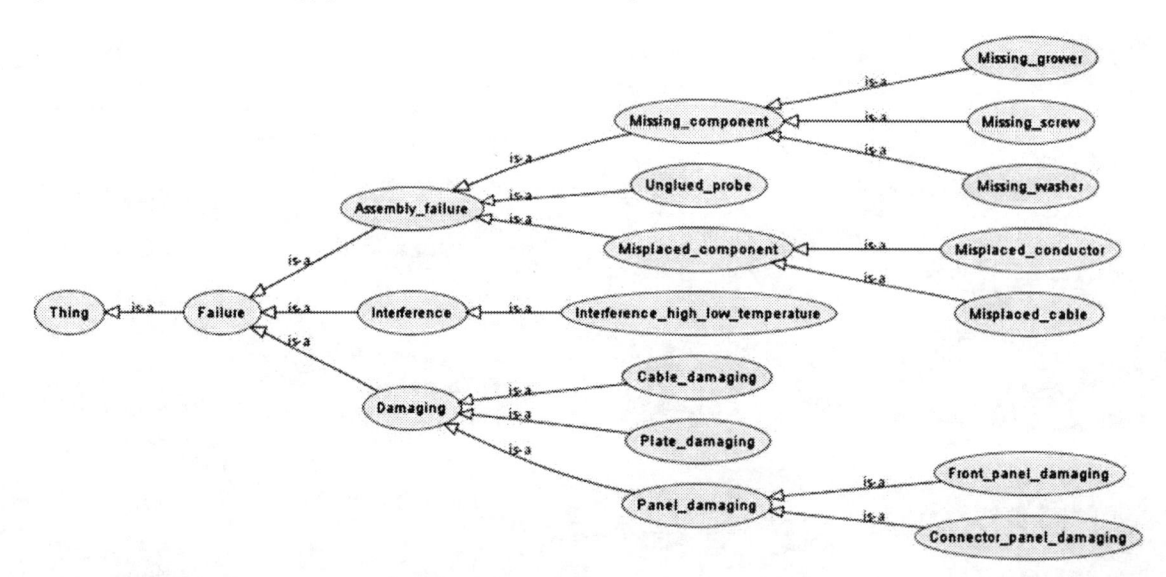

*Figure 13. Examples of BOM and working sequences files generated during the telecommunication filter lifecycle*

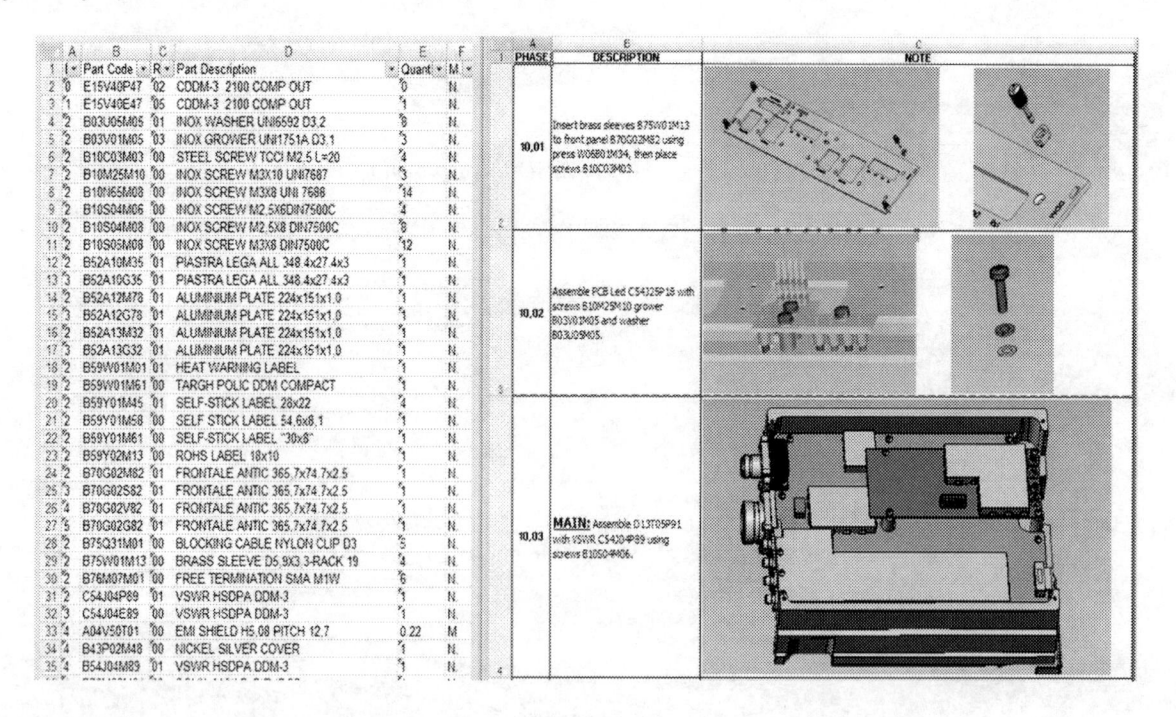

*Table 1. Example of extracted similar filters*

| SI | Product ID | Components | Failures |
|---|---|---|---|
| 1 | P5 | Termination, Front panel, Connector panel, Aluminium plate, Steel screw, Steel resonator, Capacitor, Inductor, Resistor [...] | Interference at high/low temperatures |
| 0.85 | P1 | Front panel, Connector panel, Aluminium plate, Steel screw, Steel resonator, Capacitor, Inductor, Resistor, Inox washer [...] | Interference at high/low temperatures |
| 0.62 | P2 | Termination, Front panel, FR4 plate, Steel screw, Quartz resonator, Capacitor, Inductor, Resistor [...] | Front panel damaged |
| ... | ... | ... | ... |

report is a free text. Each of these three kinds of documents are upload in the platform and analysed by performing a search in the text to retrieve the entities of the ontologies. In this way, each product is assigned to the list of its components, its operations and its failures. At the end of the semantic tagging, all the products are stored as nodes in the graph database, with the corresponding relationships with the nodes of the ontologies.

## Similarity Search

Once the database is built, it is used to retrieve information based on the similarity search. The following scenario was analysed. The designers of the Italian company designed a new variant of the telecommunication filter, named PX. They upload the corresponding BOM in the platform, so the new product is associated to its components. Before sending the order to the Romanian company, the product design manager wants to know if previous filters similar to the new one had reported some failures, in order to check if there can be a connection between the failures and the designed components.

Instead of trying to remember or manually search in the archive the products similar to the new one, the manager uses the similarity search function available in the platform, by specifying that the current product is PX and that the similarity criterion is the component similarity. The platform performs the semantic search, thus computing the similarity index between PX and all the other filters stored in the database. The list of the most similar products is then shown to the manager, in a table format as shown in Table I. In this way, the manager has the list of similar filters with the respective components and failures.

The manager sees that for the two most similar filters, there is a recurring failure, i.e., "Interference at high/low temperatures". He discovers that this failure is present in filters which have a "Steel resonator" as component, which can be the cause of the failure. He thus suggests the designers to change it with a "Quartz resonator". The designers changed the components and uploaded the new document, which in turn update the relationships in the database.

## FUTURE RESEARCH DIRECTIONS

The aim of this chapter is to advance the research in the context of knowledge management in manufacturing environments, particularly to overcome the actual issues of the meaningless and the unstructured nature of generated information.

Even if a lot of ontologies are continuously generated in literature and tested in specific contexts, having a quantitative measure of their effectiveness is not easy. Furthermore, the identification of the terminology and the hierarchies among terms is a difficult task in every domain. For this reason, a future work in this direction is to exploit more advanced methods for the automatic extraction of ontologies, e.g., by using language processing and entity recognizer tools. Also the use of folksonomies, i.e., categories without a necessary hierarchical structure and not defined a-priori but directly coming by the users will be an interesting future development of the research.

A limit of the current framework is the lack of support for decision making after the similarity search. The proposed platform is a useful tool to retrieve information, but after having extracted the similar products, the user has to discover by his own the possible correlations among data. On the contrary, having at disposal all information of interest related to products, it is possible to enrich the knowledge discovering process by exploiting data mining algorithms. For example, unsupervised data mining techniques (e.g., clustering algorithms) can be combined with the proposed similarity measure in order to automatically group products in homogeneous groups. Another future direction will be the exploitation of supervised data mining techniques (e.g., classification algorithms) to build product failure predictors or other kinds of classifiers. Finally, exploitation of association rules can suggest correlations among tags previously unknown. All these methods will suggest possible improvements in specific phases of the product lifecycle and support managers in decision making.

## CONCLUSION

In this chapter, a knowledge management platform is proposed, both to store product information by means of a semantic enrichment and to retrieve product information by means of a similarity search based on a new semantic index. This work is the first attempt to exploit a non-relational database in a manufacturing domain and the potentiality of the proposed framework is shown in an application scenario.

The application scenario reports an application in the context of filter manufacturing, but the same approach was exploited in other industrial domains, to link product data and retrieve information based on similarities. When addressing a more complicated example, the main problem is the design of the right ontology to include all the needed concepts without going at a too low level of details.

The methodology described can be applied to every lifecycle phase of the product. Due to the lack of real data covering the maintenance and the recycling phases of the telecommunication filter, the application scenario mainly covers the design and the production phases. However, given an appropriate ontology covering the concepts relevant for a lifecycle phase, it can be used to compute the similarity between products accordingly to the procedure described.

## REFERENCES

Antonelli, D., Bruno, G., Schwichtenberg, A., & Villa, A. (2013). Full exploitation of Product Lifecycle Management by integrating static and dynamic viewpoints. In *Advances in Production Management Systems. Competitive Manufacturing for Innovative Products and Services*, (pp. 176-183). Springer Berlin Heidelberg.

Baxter, D., Gao, J., Case, K., Harding, J., Young, B., Cochrane, S., & Dani, S. (2008). A framework to integrate design knowledge reuse and requirements management in engineering design. *Robotics and Computer-integrated Manufacturing*, *24*(4), 585–593. doi:10.1016/j.rcim.2007.07.010

Baxter, D., Roy, R., Doultsinou, A., Gao, J., & Kalta, M. (2009). A knowledge management framework to support product-service systems design. *International Journal of Computer Integrated Manufacturing*, *22*(12), 1073–1088. doi:10.1080/09511920903207464

Bloor, R. (2003). *The Failure of Relational Database. In The Rise of Object Technology and the Need for the Hybrid Database*. Baroudi Bloor International, Inc.

Borsato, M. (2014). Bridging the gap between product lifecycle management and sustainability in manufacturing through ontology building. *Computers in Industry*, *65*(2), 258–269. doi:10.1016/j.compind.2013.11.003

Bouzid, S., Cauvet, C., Frydman, C., & Pinaton, J. (2013). A semantic support to improve the collaborative control of manufacturing processes in industries. *IEEE International Conference on Computer Supported Cooperative Work in Design*. doi:10.1109/CSCWD.2013.6581002

Bruno, G. (2015a). Measuring product semantic similarity by exploiting a manufacturing process ontology. *IEEE International Conference on Industrial Engineering and Systems Management* (IESM'15). doi:10.1109/IESM.2015.7380313

Bruno, G. (2015b). Semantic organization of product lifecycle information through a modular ontology. *International Journal of Circuits, Systems and Signal Processing*, *9*, 16–26.

Bruno, G., Antonelli, D., Korf, R., Lentes, J., & Zimmermann, N. (2014). Exploitation of a semantic platform to store and reuse plm knowledge. In *Advances in Production Management Systems - Innovative and Knowledge-Based Production Management in a Global-Local World* (vol. 438, pp. 59–66). Springer Berlin Heidelberg.

Bruno, G., Antonelli, D., & Villa, A. (2015). A reference ontology to support product lifecycle management. *Procedia CIRP*, *33*, 41–46. doi:10.1016/j.procir.2015.06.009

Burbidge, J. L. (1996). *Production Flow Analysis For Planning Group Technology*. Oxford University Press.

Caplinskas, A., Dzemyda, G., Kiss, F., & Lupeikiené, A. (2012). Processing of Undesirable Business Events in Advanced Production Planning Systems. *Informatica*, *23*(4), 563–580.

Chen, W.-C., Wu, C.-L., Chen, Y.-H., & Fu, L.-C. (2014). An Efficient Data Storage Method of NoSQL Database for HEM Mobile Applications in IoT. *IEEE International Conference on Internet of Things, Green Computing and Communications, and Cyber-Physical-Social Computing*. doi:10.1109/iThings.2014.62

David, M., & Rowe, F. (2015). What does PLMS (product lifecycle management systems) manage: Data or documents? Complementarity and contingency for SMEs. *Computers in Industry*.

Delphi Group. (2002). *Perspectives on Information Retrieval*. Boston, MA: Delphi Group.

Efthymiou, K., Sipsas, K., Mourtzis, D., & Chryssolouris, G. (2015). On knowledge reuse for manufacturing systems design and planning: A semantic technology approach. *CIRP Journal of Manufacturing Science and Technology*, *8*, 1–11. doi:10.1016/j.cirpj.2014.10.006

Filos, E. (2006). *Smart Organizations in the Digital Age. In Integration of ICT in Smart Organizations* (pp. 1–38). IGI Global. doi:10.4018/978-1-59140-390-6.ch001

Fiorentini, X., Gambino, I., Liang, V.-C., Foufou, S., Rachuri, S., Bock, C., & Mani, M. (2007). Towards an Ontology for Open Assembly model.*Proceeding of the International Conference on Product Lifecycle Management*.

Fowler, M., & Scott, K. (2000). *UML distilled*. Addison-Wesley.

Groover, M. (2007). *Fundamentals of modern manufacturing: Materials processes, and systems*. John Wiley & Son.

Guerra-Zubiaga, D., & Young, R. (2008). Information and knowledge interrelationships within a manufacturing knowledge model. *International Journal of Advanced Manufacturing Technology*, *39*(1-2), 182–198. doi:10.1007/s00170-007-1194-6

Gunendran, A., & Young, R. (2010). Methods for the capture of manufacture best practice in product lifecycle management. *International Journal of Production Research*, *48*(20), 5885–5904. doi:10.1080/00207540903104210

Igba, J., Alemzadeh, K., Gibbons, P. M., & Henningsen, K. (2015). A framework for optimizing product performance through feedback and reuse of in-service experience. *Robotics and Computer-integrated Manufacturing*, *36*, 2–12. doi:10.1016/j.rcim.2014.12.004

Jardim-Goncalves, R., Coutinho, C., Cretan, A., Ferreira da Silva, C., & Ghodous, P. (2014). Collaborative negotiation for ontology-driven enterprise businesses. *Computers in Industry*, *65*(9), 1232–1241. doi:10.1016/j.compind.2014.01.001

Kalpakjian, S., & Schmid, S. (2013). *Manufacturing Engineering & Technology*. Prentice Hall College Di.

Laroche, F., Bordeu, F., Bernard, A., & Chinesta, F. (2012). Towards the factory of future An integrated approach of material-processes-information-human being. *ACM - Proceedings of the 2012 Virtual Reality International Conference*.

Liao, T., Warren, Z., & Claude, R. M. (1998). Similarity Measures for Retrieval in Case-Based Reasoning Systems. *Applied Artificial Intelligence*, *12*(4), 267–288. doi:10.1080/088395198117730

Liao, Y., Lezoche, M., Panetto, H., Boudjlida, N., & Rocha Loures, E. (2015). Semantic annotation for knowledge explicitation in a product lifecycle management context: A survey. *Computers in Industry*, *71*, 24–34. doi:10.1016/j.compind.2015.03.005

Liu, S., McMahon, C. A., & Culley, S. J. (2008). A review of structured document retrieval (SDR) technology to improve information access performance in engineering document management. *Computers in Industry*, *59*(1), 3–16. doi:10.1016/j.compind.2007.08.001

Loshin, D. (2013). *Big Data Analytics*. Elsevier Inc.

Lu, T., Guan, F., Gu, N., & Wang, F. (2008). Semantic classification and query of engineering drawings in the shipbuilding industry. *International Journal of Production Research*, *46*(9), 2471–2483. doi:10.1080/00207540701737922

Lupeikiene, A., Dzemyda, G., Kiss, F., & Caplinskas, A. (2014). Advanced Planning and Scheduling Systems: Modeling and Implementation Challenges. *Informatica*, *25*(4), 581–616. doi:10.15388/Informatica.2014.31

Lynn, G. S., Reilly, R. R., & Akgun, A. E. (2000). Knowledge management in new product teams: Practices and outcomes. *IEEE Transactions on Engineering Management*, *47*(2), 221–231. doi:10.1109/17.846789

Ma, K., & Sun, R. (2013). Introducing WebSocket-Based Real-Time Monitoring System for Remote Intelligent Buildings. *International Journal of Distributed Sensor Networks*, *2013*, 867693. doi:10.1155/2013/867693

Madenas, N., Tiwari, A., Turner, C. J., & Woodward, J. (2014). Information flow in supply chain management: A review across the product lifecycle. *CIRP Journal of Manufacturing Science and Technology*, *7*(4), 335–346. doi:10.1016/j.cirpj.2014.07.002

Nadoveza, D., & Kiritsis, D. (2014). Ontology-based approach for context modeling in enterprise applications. *Computers in Industry*, *65*(9), 1218–1231. doi:10.1016/j.compind.2014.07.007

*Neo4j Manual*. (n.d.). Retrieved from http://neo4j.com/docs/

Opitz, H. (1970). *A Classification System to Design Workpieces*. Pergamon Press.

Popovici, D., & Privat, G. (2015). Capturing the Structure of Internet of Things Systems with Graph Databases for Open Bidirectional Multiscale Data Mediation. *Second International Workshop on Large-scale Graph Storage and Management*.

Premkumar, V., Krishnamurty, S., Wileden, S. J., & Grosse, I. (2014). A semantic knowledge management system for laminated composites. *Advanced Engineering Informatics*, *28*(1), 91–101. doi:10.1016/j.aei.2013.12.004

PTC. (2006). *Change and Configuration Management*. Topic Sheet, Parametric Technology Corporation (PTC).

Rasmus, D. (2002). *Collaboration, Contents and Communities: An update*. Giga Information Group Inc.

Ren, J., Ma, J., Huang, R., Jin, Q., & Chen, Z. (2014). A Management System for Cyber Individuals and Heterogeneous Data. *IEEE Intl Conf on Ubiquitous Intelligence and Computing*.

Sadalage, P. J., & Fowler, M. (2013). *NoSQL Distilled*. Addison-Wesley.

Sandkuhl, K. (2009). Information logistics in networked organizations: Selected concepts and applications. *Enterp. Inf. Syst., 12*, 43–54.

Seco, N., Veale, T., & Hayes, J. (2004). An intrinsic information content metric for semantic similarity. In *WordNet, European Conference on Artificial Intelligence*.

Subrahmanian, E., Rachuri, S., Fenves, S. J., Foufou, S., & Sriram, R. D. (2005). Product lifecycle management support: A challenge in supporting product design and manufacturing in a networked economy. *Int. J. Product Lifecycle Management, 1*(1), 4–25. doi:10.1504/IJPLM.2005.007342

Teng, Z., Guo, M., Liu, X., Dai, Q., Wang, C., & Xuan, P. (2013). Measuring gene functional similarity based on group-wise comparison of GO terms. *Bioinformatics (Oxford, England), 29*(11), 1424–1432. doi:10.1093/bioinformatics/btt160 PMID:23572412

Tough, A., & Moss, M. (2003). Metadata, controlled vocabulary and directories: Electronic document management and standards for records management. *Records Management Journal, 13*(1), 24–31. doi:10.1108/09565690310465713

Wang, C., Ren, K., Lou, W., & Li, J. (2010). Toward publicly auditable secure cloud data storage services. *IEEE Network, 24*(4), 19–24. doi:10.1109/MNET.2010.5510914

Westkämper, E. (2007). Digital Manufacturing in the Global Era. Digital Enterprise Technology, (pp. 3–14). New York: Springer.

Young, R., Gunedran, A., Cutting-Decelle, A., & Gruninger, M. (2007). Manufacturing knowledge sharing in plm: A progression towards the use of heavy weight. *International Journal of Production Research, 45*(7), 1505–1519. doi:10.1080/00207540600942268

## KEY TERMS AND DEFINITIONS

**NoSQL Database:** A kind of database that provides a mechanism for storage and retrieval of data not modeled with the tabular relations used in relational databases.

**Ontology:** A set of classes and relationships between classes to represent the concepts of a specific domain.

**PLM:** Product Life cycle Management (PLM) is a process or system used to manage data and processes associated with the life of a product, from its conception through its manufacture, to its retirement and disposal.

**Product Lifecycle:** The stages of the product life from the conception trough the production to the end of life.

**RF Filter:** Radio frequency (RF) filters represent a class of electronic filter designed to operate on signals in the megahertz to gigahertz frequency ranges, used by most broadcast radio, television, wireless communication, and they are commonly used as building blocks for duplexers and diplexers to combine or separate multiple frequency bands.

**Semantic Search:** A data searching technique in a which a search query aims to not only find keywords, but to determine the intent and contextual meaning of the words a person is using for search.

**UML Sequence Diagram:** An interaction diagram that shows object interactions arranged in time sequence in a given situation, and the sequence of messages exchanged between the objects needed to carry out the functionality of the scenario.

# Chapter 9
# Knowledge of Management Tools and Systems in SMEs:
## Knowledge Transfer in Management

**Adam Pawliczek**
*Technical University of Ostrava, Czech Republic & Moravian University College Olomouc, Czech Republic*

**Miroslav Rössler**
*Moravian University College Olomouc, Czech Republic*

## ABSTRACT

*The chapter deals with knowledge management principles and their implication to knowledge in management represented by contemporary sophisticated management tools and systems. The most important management branches and methods, tools and systems, generally considered as very helpful for professional business operating, are presented. Further research results of management tools knowledge in contemporary enterprises are presented impacting the need of education and knowledge transfer in management responsible positions. The need of management knowledge for the competitiveness of enterprises is accented. Business and competitive intelligence as media for competitiveness are introduced. In the last part of the chapter, a model of the knowledge management system applicable in SMEs is suggested. The purpose of the chapter is to make the reader familiar with some of the most important management tools, methods and systems and suggest principles for an easy and effective knowledge management system in the enterprise.*

## INTRODUCTION

The entire society is constantly evolving and, recently, the fact that knowledge is arriving at the forefront is typical for it. We live no longer in an industrial society, but in a post-industrial society, sometimes referred to as information society which gradually merges into a knowledge society. Every day the amount of information increases and the need for its efficient classification and management grows. Information, however, to be useful, needs to be converted. This transformed information is called knowledge. Knowledge has some important extra over information. It is contextualized and enriched by our own experience.

DOI: 10.4018/978-1-5225-1642-2.ch009

The main goal of the chapter is to describe and discuss important interconnections of modern management tools with knowledge management principles and suggest a knowledge management model process applicable in SMEs. The chapter works with important terms of knowledge management. The partial goal is to summarize the most important modern tools used in different branches of management, which can be considered as a base of professional management knowledge. The second partial goal is to present a selection of IT support instruments (software) on the market applicable in SMEs. The reader will be familiar with different branches of modern management and tools used in them as well as with the sophisticated software support suitable for SMEs and the model of knowledge management. The acquired knowledge will improve the management skills of entrepreneurs and open new perspectives for competitiveness and prosperity.

The chapter is partially derived from an unpublished habilitation thesis concerning management methods, tools and system. Added value of the chapter is in focusing of readers on sophisticated management tools which certainly help to improve competitiveness and business results. The core contribution of the paper is in practical research results seen in part 3. The main contribution of the paper for readers is the increasing of awareness and orientation on what management knowledge to focus and adapt in order to improve business competitiveness. The chapter is dedicated mainly to students of management, entrepreneurs and SMEs managers.

The chapter layout (contents):

1. **Theory of Knowledge Management in Management:** Describing basic terms and ideas as data, information, explicit, implicit, tacit knowledge, knowledge management and knowledge in management.
2. **Knowledge in Management:** Management tools, methods and systems in particular segments of management – fields and areas of management methods, tools and systems – overview.
3. **Knowledge of Management Tools, Methods and Systems in SMEs:** Primary and secondary research results from worldwide data and the Czech Republic.
4. **Competitiveness, Innovation and Knowledge Management:** Innovation, intellectual capital and learning organization ideas, management tools, methods and systems and business performance.
5. **Business and Competitive Intelligence:** Systematic data collection and processing by the management information system.
6. **BI/CI Software Support:** Selected specific MIS software products.
7. **Solutions and Recommendations:** Design of knowledge management system for SMEs based on basic knowledge management and knowledge in management ideas.

## THEORY OF KNOWLEDGE MANAGEMENT IN MANAGEMENT

As reported by Peter Ferdinand Drucker:

*The most important and truly unique asset of the management of the twentieth century was the fifty times increased productivity of manual workers (laborers) in production. The most important asset which the management of the twenty-first century should make is the increase of the productivity of knowledge work and knowledge workers. The most important asset of companies in the twentieth century was the production equipment (machines). The most important asset of institutions (whether profit or non-profit) in the twenty-first century will be knowledge workers and their productivity (Drucker, p. 79-94, 1999).*

Knowledge and technology-based economies are performing generally better than economies based on natural resources. Knowledge can be seen as an asset to some extent, but unlike physical assets it is difficult for us to grasp and quantify. On the other hand, it has a great advantage. Knowledge can be shared with others without losing it. Knowledge sharing does not diminish its usefulness, it only reduces its value, becoming less rare (Still, pp. 8 to 9, ...).

To create knowledge in management we have to work with:

- **Data:** Can be viewed as a characteristics of a system, object, and is under the influence of chaos.
- **Information:** Usefully interpreted data can also be understood as entries on the relation of one subject to another or other.

*The mutual relationship between data, information and knowledge can be illustratively described the way that data as properly expressed symbols is considered as feedstock which is transformed into information. Knowledge defines the basic framework for thinking cognitive processes of data interpretation (Veber, p. 196, ...).*

Knowledge creates a mental system framework for evaluating and integrating new information. It is mainly the result of active learning based on own knowledge and experience, to a lesser extent the result of passively acting lessons. The process of learning and teaching classifies individual knowledge elements into certain relations. Sometimes yet another level of knowledge is featured, known as the wisdom. Knowledge is a necessary part of competent managerial decisions.

## TYPES OF KNOWLEDGE

For the purposes of knowledge management, knowledge is usually divided into the following three types:

- Explicit (explicit)
- Implicit (implicit)
- Unformulated (tacit).

*Table 1. Explicit, implicit and not-formulated knowledge*

| Types of Knowledge | | | |
|---|---|---|---|
| | **Explicit** | **Implicit** | **Tacit (Not-Formulated)** |
| Description | Formalized or documented knowledge, usually well-structured and transferable. Mostly in ICT form. | Knowledge in heads of workers which can be transferred to the explicit form any time. | Knowledge hidden in heads of workers which cannot be easily transferred to explicit form, formalized or documented. |
| Example | Documents, manuals, computers codes, etc. | Knowledge of process and its limitations in the head of the process owner. | Expert knowledge in the area, gained experience, etc. |

(Own processing, 2016)

## Definition of Knowledge Management

A large amount of definitions can be found. Three of them are presented as they are understandable and concise:

*Knowledge management can be defined e.g. as a systematic and inclusive process of management and coordination of a wide portfolio of the company activities, i.e. retrieving, creating, storing, sharing, merging, developing, evolving, and use of the knowledge of individuals and groups with the goal to achieve greater business efficiency. Knowledge in this context is certainly not a mere academic neologism, but it is a productive embodied intelligence obtained by "positive education and learning" through which the man - worker receives the amount of knowledge that allows them to orient themselves, formulate opinions, enrich their analytical and deduction skills, conclude to synthesis, fully within the meaning of the needs of the organization (Petříková, p. 115, 2010).*

Another definition says:

*Knowledge management is very difficult to define. This applies to acquiring, creating, sharing and using the knowledge. This knowledge includes both explicit and implicit knowledge. Knowledge does not only mean the know-how – to know how to, but also who knows, knows why and knows when. It does not relate to the wise books and best practices, but rather people – working communities that maintain knowledge about a topic and share what they know, build on it and adapt it for their own use. It is not a brief summary of what is known at a certain moment in time, but developing a body of knowledge maintained in its recent form by people who use it regularly (Collison, p.13, 2005).*

Arian Ward from the company Work Frontiers International defines knowledge management as follows:

*It is not creating an encyclopedia that encompasses everything that anyone has ever known. Knowledge management is more about observing those who know and develop a company culture and technology that will encourage them to speak (Collison, p.49, 2005).*

## Knowledge in Management

Knowledge pools in management can be simply divided into theory and experience (case studies). The theoretical part can be characterized by a number of management methods, tools and systems regarding to the particular branches of management and the practical one is merely dependent on the amount of professional practice.

## KNOWLEDGE IN MANAGEMENT: MANAGEMENT METHODS, TOOLS, AND SYSTEMS IN PARTICULAR SEGMENTS OF MANAGEMENT

There are many different tools, methods and systems for the effective implementation of the basic management functions such as planning, monitoring of objectives, organizing, leadership, communication, decision-making, monitoring, etc. These have been developed over more than a century of the democratic market business, particularly in Europe, North America, and Japan. Managerial methods are traditionally divided into deductive, inductive and dialectical. Another classification sees them as empirical, exact and creative approaches (Mohelská et al., 2012). These authors divide the field of the use of management methods as follows:

- Managerial decision-making,
- Risk management,
- Scheduling
- Organization
- Management of employees,
- Control and management of work activities,
- Organization performance evaluation.

## Management Methods

Management methods are procedures, methods, techniques or "ways" that lead to achieving effective negotiations and management objectives. The usual managerial objectives are financial business performance, competitiveness, growth, long-term prosperity, and sustainability. Management methods can include simple rules, more complex techniques and tools, or comprehensive management systems containing a complex of partial methods (Pearce, 1995). Descartes assumed that even the most difficult problems can be decomposed into long chains of simple steps and if their order is preserved, a solution must be found (Fajkus, 2005). The methodical approach (in contrast to intuitive management) leads to measurable results, self-reflection and the possibility of implementation of a cycle of continuous improvement. Modern trends suggest that the choice of the appropriate management methods and their implementation is the key activity to the dynamism of the enterprise performance according to the required indicators (e.g. by using the KPI). There is no clear border among the concepts of managerial methods, tools, systems, and techniques.

## Management Tools

Management tools are formalized for the performance of managerial functions in an enterprise with the aim to build a creative environment in order to increase the efficiency of managerial work. And yet, they include a wide range of management tools and techniques - from simple planning software to complex social sciences, organizational, technological, economic and social instruments which co-create the current paradigm of management. A paradigm is understood as the main idea, a given concept of managerial thinking and action. A paradigm is thus age-conditioned, based on a concept valid only for a certain era and is therefore dependent on time. Generally speaking, a paradigm is based on a system of principles (postulates) which create the particular concept of thinking.

## Management Systems

A system is a whole (1), composed of parts that interact with each other. Between the parts of the system, flows of information, matter and energy (money) can occur. A system (2) is a deliberate process, method of action and implementation of something (Klimeš, 1981). The following cases can be seen as a management systems: (A) an enterprise, logistics chain, manufacturing, project, or (B) the knowledge structure and software to support the optimal management of these activities – management information system (MIS). Management systems in the business can be regarded as open, continuous, stochastic, and dynamic. Similar properties must be also in the characteristics of the IT support means that model the actual systems themselves. The management systems can be considered as systems of processes and procedures (management methods and tools) which ensure that the organization fulfils the given tasks to achieve its goals. An important group of management systems (QMS/EMS quality management) is based on cyclical processes as Deming's PDCA.

Table 2 presents a systematic overview of management methods, tools and systems (information systems with ICT support) according to the area of management. The main reason of this table is to make the reader familiar with the most known and popular management tools according to the wide international management community at www Management Mania. Many methods, however, are universal and are used in multiple areas of management. Knowledge and implementation of an appropriate set of tools as well of their knowledge transfer through the organization is a significant condition of wise management and business prosperity.

*Table 2. Systematic overview of the selected important managerial techniques, tools, methods and systems according to the areas of management*

| Area of Management | Name of the Tool, Technique, Method, System |
|---|---|
| Strategic Management | 7 Classes of Strategic Risks (Slywotzky), **5F** (Five Forces) Analysis, **BCG** (Boston matrix), **BSC** (Balanced Scorecard), the Blue Ocean Strategy, Gap Analysis, EFE Matrix, IFE Matrix, Hierarchy of Strategies, Management by Objectives, **MOST**, **PESTLE** Analysis, the Strategy → Structure Principle, Forecasting, Scenarios Technique, **SPACE** Analysis, **SWOT** Analysis, **SMART** - Goal Design, **VRIO** Analysis, Winterling Crisis Matrix, Critical Success Factors, **KPI** (Key Performance Indicators). |
| Management Organization | **BSC** (Balanced Scorecard), ERP (Enterprise Resource Planning), MBC (Management by Competencies), **MBO** (Management by Objectives), Organizational Development, Process Management, Project Management, Change Management, SOEM (Service Oriented Enterprise Management), SOM (Service Oriented Management), 5F (Five Forces) Analysis, Boston matrix, Critical Success Factors, Pareto principle, Strategy → Structure Principle, **PESTLE** Analysis, Reengineering, **SMART** - goal design, SWOT analysis, VRIO analysis, KGI (Key Goal Indicators), **KPI** (Key Performance Indicators), Excellence Model EFQM. |
| Quality Management | APQP (Advanced Product Quality Planning), PDCA (Deming Cycle), DMAIC Improvement Cycle, Excellence Model **EFQM, Kaizen**, Quality Rings, Lean, Poka-yoke, Six Sigma, **TQM** (Total Quality Management), the 5S, DOE (Design of Experiments) Ishikawa diagram, Kano model, Pareto Principle, **FMEA** (Failure Mode and Effect Analysis), FTA (Fault Tree Analysis), QFD (Quality Function Deployment), House of quality, **G8D** (Eight Disciplines), MSA (Measurement System Analysis), PPAP (Production Part Approval Process), Quality Management Systems ISO 9001, |
| Innovation Management | Blue Ocean Strategy, **CAF** (Common Assessment Framework), **DMAIC** Improvement Cycle, **PDCA** (Deming cycle), Excellence Model **EFQM**, Kaizen, Quality Rings, Open Innovation, Six Sigma, **TQM** (Total Quality Management), User Centered Design, Brainstorming, Mindmaps, Pareto principle, SMART- goals design. |
| Change Management | Three step change (Lewin), Four step change, Eight step change, organizational development, change management by CSF (Critical Success Factors), 5F (Five Forces) Analysis, Kolb Cycle of learning, Delphi method, Pareto principle, **SMART** - goals design, **SWOT** analysis, **SWOT** analysis, Scenarios Technique, **PESTLE** analysis. |
| Production Management | ABC-D, BOA (Belastungorientiere Auftragsfreigabe), CIM (Computer Integrated Management), CRP (Capacity Resource Planning), DBR (Drum Buffer Rope), JIT (Just-in-time), MRP (Material Requirements Planning), MRP II (Manufacturing Resource Planning), ERP (Enterprise Resource Planning), KANBAN, FIFO (First In First Out), **FEFO** (First Expired, First Out), HIFO (Highest In First Out), **LIFO** (Lowest In First Out), Lean Production, BCG Matrix, Pareto principle, **VRIO** analysis, ISO 9001, ISO 14000. |

*continued on following page*

*Table 2. Continued*

| Area of Management | Name of the Tool, Technique, Method, System |
|---|---|
| Marketing and Sales | 5K Method, TLM (Total Loyalty Marketing), Branding, Blue Ocean Strategy, Holistic marketing concept, Marketing strategy, Marketing mix 3V, 4C, 4P, Positioning, **CRM** (Customer Relationship Management), Brand Management, PR (Public Relations), Market segmentation, Targeting, Product concept, Web marketing mix 4S, WOMM (Word of Mouth Marketing), 5F (Five Forces) analysis, An off matrix, **BCG** (Boston matrix), Kano model, Customer portfolio matrix, **PESTLE** analysis, **SWOT** analysis, **VRIO** analysis. |
| Process Management | BCM (Business Continuity Management), **BPM** (Business Process Management), ITIL (ICT processes management), Six Sigma, PDCA (Deming cycle), **DMAIC** improvement cycle, reengineering, Time frames, statistical methods, ISO 9001, TQM (Total Quality Management). |
| Economy and Finance Management | Pareto principle, Financial leverage, PESTLE analysis, SWOT analysis, VRIO analysis, Break Even Point Analysis, Financial statements analysis, Determination of financial indicators (liquidity, rentability, investments, indebtedness, activities, market value, productivity), TCO (Total Cost of Ownership), EBIT (Earnings before Interest and Taxes), Gross margin, Cash Flow, NOPAT (Net Operating Profit after Taxes), EVA (Economic Value Added), MVA (Market Value Added), WAAC (Weighted Average Cost of Capital), 29NPV (Net Present Value), IRR (Internal Rate of Return), Altman analysis (Altman Z-score). |
| Service Management | **BCG** matrix, Pareto principle, CorSet Framework, ITIL, ITSM (IT Service Management), SSME (Service Science, Management and Engineering), SOEM (Service Oriented Enterprise Management), SOM (Service Oriented Management), Services management system ICT ISO 20000. |
| Computer science and IT Management | SOA (Service Oriented Architecture), Code and Fix, EUP (Enterprise Unified Process), MSF (Microsoft Solutions Framework), MMDIS (Multidimensional Management and Development of Information Systems), DSDM (Dynamic System Development Method), ASD (Adaptive Software Development), BPEL (Business Process Execution Language), BPMN (Business Process Modelling Notation), ISO 8000, **ISO 9001**, ISO 15504, ISO 20000. |
| Facility Management | Process analysis, Benchmarking, Insourcing, Business Process Improvement, Outsourcing, Spatial optimization, SLA (Service Level Agreement), SLM (Service Level Management), **SWOT** analysis, Maintenance, **FMS** (Facility Management Systems), CAFM (Computer Aided Facility Management). |
| Logistics and Transport | APS (Advanced Planning & Scheduling), Benchmarking, **ERP** (Enterprise Resource Planning), JIT (Just-in-time), KANBAN, MRP (Material Requirements Planning), MRP II (Manufacturing Resource Planning), Outsourcing, SCM (Supply Chain Management), CPM (Critical Path Method), **TOC** (Theory of Constraints), Network Analysis, model SCOR (Supply Chain Operations Reference-model). |
| Project Management | Gantt chart, Project schedule, Network analysis methods, RACI and RASCI responsibility matrix, Project plan, Project-Based Management, WBS (Work Breakdown Structure), Impact Analysis, **PMBOK** (Project Management Body of Knowledge), PRINCE2 (Projects in Controlled Environment), Project management standards ISO 10006, ISO 21500. |
| Risk Management | BASEL I-III, CorIA (Core Impact Assessment), Checklist analysis, CCA (Cause-Consequence Analysis), CRI (Continuous Risk Improvement), Delphi method, **CCTA** Risk Analysis and Management Method), **CPQRA** (Chemical Process Quantitative Risk Analysis), EWRM (Enterprise-Wide Risk Management), ETA (Event Tree Analysis), FMEA (Failure Modes and Effects Analysis), FMECA (Failure Mode, Effects and Critical Analysis), FTA (Fault Tree Analysis), HAZOP (Hazard and Operability Study), HAZID (Hazard Identification Study), HRA (Human Reliability Analysis), **PHA** (Preliminary Hazard Analysis), PPAP (Production Part Approval Process), Forecasting, RIPRAN (Risk Project Analysis), **RR** (Relative Ranking), SA (Safety Audit) SR (Safety Review), VaR (Value at Risk), W-I (What-if Analysis), Winterling Crisis Matrix, Risk Management ISO 31000, OHSAS 18001. |
| Crisis Management | Crisis plan, Winterling Crisis Matrix, Pareto principle, Forecasting, SMART - objective design, Scenarios technique, |
| Knowledge Management | SECI process, Social network analysis, Sociogram, Sociometrics, Management epistemology, Learning. |
| Human Resources Management | 360° feedback, Jobs analysis, Social network analysis, BEI (Behavioral Event Interview), Jack Welch Matrix, Job description, Staff audit, Role presets, Sociogram, Sociometry, Job specification, Satisfaction Survey Methods. |

(Own processing with Management Mania data, 2015)

# KNOWLEDGE OF MANAGEMENT METHODS, TOOLS AND SYSTEMS IN SMES: SECONDARY AND PRIMARY RESEARCH RESULTS

The important question is: Which management methods, tools and systems are really worth to learn and apply? The question can be answered from two points of view:

1. Do specific management tools influence enterprise performance and how?
2. Which management tools are utilized by other successful enterprises?

The point of view (2) is answered with the help of Bain and Company, the Czech Association of SMEs and own research (primary data) research results in the world and Czech/Slovak conditions. The point of view (1) is answered later.

On the basis of the discussed basic ideas on management tools the following hypothesis was formulated: The knowledge of modern management methods, tools and systems in enterprises is generally heavily minor (under 30%).

## Management Tools Used Around the World

Bain & Company has been performing its research since 1993. The purpose of it is to provide information to managers about which management methods and tools will improve their business results and how managers of global enterprises perceive the strategic challenges and priorities. The 15th survey of Bain & Company has shown that in the year 2014, executive managers used mostly the following 10 management tools – see Table 3.

The company focuses on 25 key tools. The list can only include tools that are current, significant for senior managers, and measurable. The company approaches 13 000 respondents from more than 70 countries of America, Europe, Asia and Africa and, over the years, systematically monitors the effectiveness of managerial tools in enterprises (Bain & Company, 2015).

## Management Tools Utilized in the Czech Republic

In 2011, the Association of Small and Medium-Sized Enterprises implemented the survey no. 10 ASMEC CR "Opinions of Entrepreneurs on the Modern Methods of Management of the Company" which states that the active knowledge of modern methods of management for enterprises in the Czech Republic is at a low level (Modern management, 2011).

*Table 3. The best known management methods according to Bain & Company*

| Name of the Tool, Technique, Method, System | |
|---|---|
| • Customer relationship management (CRM), | • Balanced Scorecard, |
| • Benchmarking, | • Expression of Vision and Mission, |
| • Employee engagement survey, | • Supply Chain Management (SCM), |
| • Strategic planning, | • Change management, |
| • Outsourcing, | • Customer segmentation. |

(Own processing with Bain & Company data, 2015)

The survey focused on the following three main areas:

- Evaluation of the competitiveness of Czech enterprises and barriers to their growth as seen by entrepreneurs.
- Knowledge and attitude of Czech entrepreneurs of and towards modern methods of enterprise management.
- Knowledge and attitude of Czech entrepreneurs of and towards the EFQM model.

Target group: The segment of B2B companies with more than 25 employees with activity in manufacturing, trade and services (n = 541). Research method: CATI (Computer Assisted Telephone Interviewing). Data collection date: May 2011.

The results of the research investigation suggest that the active knowledge of modern enterprise management methods is at a relatively low level. Only 22.55% of respondents spontaneously stated some of the methods of enterprise management. A considerable part of the respondents, however, stated a non-existent method of modern management. A frequency graph shows that only very few respondents actually know any of the methods of modern business management. The awareness of modern enterprise management methods is at a low level.

When asked the question: "Do you know any modern methods of enterprise management? If so, which ones?", only 22.55% of the respondents said they knew a management tool. The best known methods are named in Table 4.

Modern methods of enterprise management are currently used by 28.1% of the surveyed enterprises. There is therefore a large space for the implementation of these procedures and methods, taking into account the fact that the management of the companies attributes this enterprise management tool great importance. Overall, 152 respondents said that they use one of the methods of business management. The most commonly used methods are:

- Lean enterprise (28,9%),
- Six Sigma (12,5%) and
- Balanced Scorecard (13,2%).

The category "Others" often named methods that are not among the modern management methods, which again highlights the ignorance of these specific management tools. It shows that the enterprises belonging to the production sector have the most extensive experience with the modern methods of management.

*Table 4. The best known management methods according to ASMEC*

| Name of the Tool, Technique, Method, System | |
|---|---|
| • Six Sigma,<br>• Lean,<br>• BSC,<br>• Kaizen,<br>• ISO norms, | • Controlling,<br>• Project management,<br>• Coaching,<br>• SWOT,<br>• Planning,<br>• Leadership. |

(Own processing with ASMEC data, 2015)

The results of the research show that only 16.9% of respondents are considering the introduction of some of the modern management methods. This group represents the potential enterprises interested in the EFQM model. The responses show that almost 80% of Czech entrepreneurs do not know of the existence of the most successful European management model (EFQM) which is used by more than 30,000 European enterprises. This is a very significant competitive disadvantage for the Czech Republic because, according to independent analyses, the EFQM model brings enterprises improvement of their business results by tens of percent.

*The survey shows that although the Czech entrepreneurs realize the importance of modern management methods, they only have minimal information about these methods and practically do not use them. Yet almost 80% of the Czech entrepreneurs in the survey said that they consider the modern management methods crucial for quality enterprise management. Moreover, 98% of the respondents considered the quality and conceptual business management important for the long-term competitiveness of the enterprise. 77% of Czech entrepreneurs actively do not know any modern management method and almost the same percentage of enterprises does not make use of any such method. One of the key elements in maintaining and increasing competitiveness is therefore among entrepreneurs neglected in such a way that this means a significant risk to the success of the Czech enterprises on the world markets. (ASMEC, 2011).*

## RESULTS OF OWN RESEARCH: PRIMARY DATA: CZECH REPUBLIC AND SLOVAKIA

The questionnaire research was realized during the spring semester 2012 by students of the Business Entrepreneurship Faculty in Karvina, Silesian University in Opava (Czech Republic). 722 companies active in the Czech and Slovak Republic in the time period 2009-2011 were subjects of interest (SMEs create 89% of the sample group in accordance with the number of employees' criterion). The interview protocol included a controlled dialogue of a student with an enterprise owner, an executive manager or a top manager, so the collected data has the character of an expert guess opinion. Company identification (10 questions) and identification of the student and their opinion on the questionnaire relevance (5 questions) was a necessary part of each form. The initial sample size of 722 companies was filtered and reduced to 677 credible items. The questionnaire form also includes the nondisclosure statement to provide business and privacy protection. Moreover, the data was analyzed anonymously and published as no-name data only. The questionnaire was focused on seven areas of interest and contained 61 questions.

The data was processed by Microsoft Excel® and IBM SPSS®. Analyses, results and discussion are presented later (Pawliczek, 2013).

## Data Structure

The analyses of the bulk sample (the all firms group including 677 enterprises) and their attitude to business strategic management brought the following information (Pawliczek, 2013).

- **Enterprise Size:** More than 51% of the questioned enterprises (the all firms group) are the so-called "micro" enterprises with no more than 10 employees, approximately 24% are "small" enterprises up to 50 employees and approximately 14% are "medium" enterprises – all together 89%

are SMEs (small and medium – incl. micro enterprises up to 250 employees). Only about 11% of the researched group are created by big enterprises with more than 250 employees.

- **Geographical Point:** From this point of view, 89,1% (603 enterprises) of the all firms group (counting 677 enterprises) are settled in the Czech Republic; 10,9% (74 enterprises) are in the Slovak Republic. 63,5% (430 enterprises) are from the Moravian-Silesian region, (34) questioned enterprises are from Prague, the capital of the Czech Republic. Overall 79,6% of enterprises are from Moravia regions and 9,5% from Bohemia regions including Prague.

- **Structure of Economic Activity:** Concerning branches according to NACE-CZ industry classification we can say that almost a quarter (24%) of the questioned enterprises were active in section C – Manufacturing. Than very closely with 23% the section G – Wholesale and retail trade; repair of motor vehicles and motorcycles is covered. On the third place, there is the section F – Construction (13%). No other sections exceed 7% and all other sections together create 40% of the all firms group.

## Selected Management Tools

Selected evaluated management methods, tools and systems:

1. **ISO 9000 Family:** (ISO 9001): A part of the family of international standards issued by the ISO (International Organization for Standardization). Standard ISO 9001 is not a management method, it is a standard or norm which serves as a reference model for setting the basic management processes in an organization that continuously helps to improve the quality of the provided products or services and customer satisfaction (that is why quality management system).

2. **ISO 14000 Family:** In the world, ISO 14001 is the most recognized and used one for environmental management systems. This standard requires the organization to identify all environmental impacts and related aspects of its business. In addition, it defines the objectives of environment and introduces measures to improve performance through process improvement in areas of high priority.

3. **EFQM Excellence Model:** (EFQM Model). The EFQM Model was developed by the EFQM Foundation as a framework for the implementation of quality management methods in the organization.

4. **TQM:** (Total Quality Management): A very complex management method that puts emphasis on the quality management in all dimensions of the organizational life. It goes beyond quality management and it is also a method of strategic management and it is a management philosophy for all of the activities of the organization. There are many different forms and interpretations of TQM.

5. **BSC:** (Balanced Scorecard) A system of management and measurement of the performance of the organization which is based on defining a balanced system of interrelated indicators of business performance. Hence the "balanced". Balanced Scorecard was developed by American consultants Robert S. Kaplan and David P. Norton in the nineties of the 20th century.

6. **KPI:** (Key Performance Indicators) A term that refers to the performance indicators/metrics associated with the process, service, organizational unit or the entire organization. KPIs reflect the desired performance (quality, efficiency or economy).

7. **EVA:** (Economic Value Added) A term that refers to the currently very important valuation measurement of the enterprise performance. The basic idea of the indicator is that the invested capital has to have a greater benefit that the cost of this capital.

8. **Porter's 5 Forces:** The work of Michael E. Porter. It is a way of analyzing the industry and its risks. The model works with the five elements (Five Forces). The principle of this method is a forecasting of the development of the competitive situation in analyzed industry, based on the estimate of the potential behavior of the subjects and objects involved in a given market and forecasting of the risk of imminent business (Porter, 1980).

9. **SWOT Analysis:** A universal analytical technique focusing on the evaluation of internal and external factors affecting the success of an organization or any other evaluated system. Most often, the SWOT analysis is used in the strategic management of an organization in the evaluation of a strategic intention. The author of the SWOT analysis is Albert Humphrey who designed it in the sixties of the 20th century.

10. **BCG Matrix:** (Growth-Share Matrix) A method that comes from the consulting company Boston Consulting Group (BCG). The name BCG matrix or Boston matrix comes from here. The BCG matrix is used for the evaluation of the product portfolio of the organization in marketing and sales planning.

11. **SMART:** An analytical technique for designing objectives in management and planning. SMART is an acronym from the initial letters of the English names of the objective attributes (Specific, Measurable, Achievable/Acceptable, Realistic/Relevant, Time Specific/Track-able).

12. **PEST(LE) Analysis:** An analytical technique used for the strategic analysis of organizational surroundings. PESTLE (sometimes also PESTEL) is an acronym and each letter represents a different type of external factors (Political, Economic, Social, Technological, Legal, Ecological).

13. **MBO:** (Management by Objectives) was designed by Peter F. Drucker as a method based on setting and mutual agreement of the objectives and evaluating the success of their achievement. The task implementers are allowed to decide which method is the most appropriate to achieve the objective. It is a delegation of responsibility for the objective to the implementer. The method is applicable in virtually all management fields.

14. **6-Sigma:** A complex method of management and, like Lean, it is known more as a philosophy that the organization (enterprise) must take. It is focused on continuous improvement (innovation) of the organization by understanding customer needs, using the process analysis and methods standardization in the measurement. It is a comprehensive, flexible management system that is based on understanding customer needs and expectations, on the disciplined use of information and data to management and decision-making.

15. **Kaizen:** A method of gradual improvement based on cultural traditions of Japan (the word itself comes from Japanese). The improvement focuses on the gradual optimizing of the processes and work practices, quality improvement and scrap reducing, material and time savings leading to cost reduction, work safety and reducing workplace accidents.

16. **Lean:** (Lean Management) is a very broad management method. The term philosophy that the organization (enterprise) must accept is most often used in the connection with Lean. Lean is based on several basic principles. Primarily it is the effort of the organization to continuously improve in all areas and to avoid unnecessary wastage. The second principle is the best possible customer needs satisfaction, no matter how. Lean is often used with different attributes; depending on what fields this philosophy is applied to (Baranov, 2011; Kotler, 2007; Management Mania, 2013).

## Research Results: Utilization of Management Tools

Research results of the original research of the author on utilization of management tools are shortly summarized in Table 5. There is well visible that the most utilized technique is the SWOT analysis (47% of enterprises are familiar with it). Further QMS and EMS systems ISO 9000 and ISO 14000 are recognized. The most of the researched methods are not recognized and used by less than 7% of the researched enterprises.

The quadratic index which results 3 can be easily calculated and it can be interpreted as follows:

18% (3) of the selected researched management tools is applied by 18% of the researched enterprises.

With the help of own original research supported by the research of ASMEC, we can approve the following hypothesis: The knowledge of modern management methods, tools and systems in enterprises is generally heavily minor (under 30%). This fact show potential for improving competitiveness by studying and adapting modern management methods, tools and systems and implement it to their knowledge management systems.

## COMPETITIVENESS, INNOVATION, AND KNOWLEDGE MANAGEMENT

Long-term adaptation of effective and progressive set of management tools, methods and systems in enterprise is the task for knowledge management. Proper knowledge management in new economy is clearly the way to improve competitiveness. Nowadays knowledge is a necessary source of the competi-

*Table 5. The percentage of management methods utilized by the examined enterprise group*

| Number | Name of the Tool, Technique, Method, System | Percentage of utilization |
|---|---|---|
| 1. | SWOT | 47% |
| 2. | ISO 9000 | 37% |
| 3. | ISO 14000 | 18% |
| 4. | TQM | 16% |
| 5. | SMART | 16% |
| 6. | EVA | 9% |
| 7. | BCG | 7% |
| 8. | BSC | 6% |
| 9. | Kaizen | 6% |
| 10. | KPI | 6% |
| 11. | MBO | 4% |
| 12. | Six Sigma | 4% |
| 13. | EFQM | 3% |
| 14. | Lean | 3% |
| 15. | PESTLE | 2% |
| 16. | 5 Forces – Porter | 2% |

(Own processing, 2016)

tive advantage. The gap between the book and the market value of the company grows in all companies regardless of their size. This difference is more pronounced in higher labor intensive sectors compared to the financial and physical means (Grublová et al., P. 39-40, 2014). One of the aspects that increase the value of the companies is the knowledge that the company possesses. Well utilized knowledge enables companies to be more successful in the market than companies that do not use their knowledge correctly.

*Innovation is the outcome of a complex (company-wide) management system of innovation activities. Information that without knowledge is elusive is important. Therefore, we are talking about the chain (transfer): Information → Knowledge → Innovation. But, even here, it holds true: "to be at the right time in the right place". Innovations are considered to be the main boosters for the economic growth. Gradually the wide economic community has increasingly focused on finding ways to manage innovations, monitor and exploit their potential to create new values. Interest was mainly in factors from which innovations arise. Innovative businesses therefore focused on developing precisely these factors. This is essentially a creation of new knowledge, application of that knowledge in the development of products and processes, and their subsequent evaluation in terms of commercial exploitation (Grublová et al., P. 1-2, 2014).*

The basic SECI model (see Figure 2) of the creation (transfer, reproduction) of knowledge is a cyclical process and therefore it is always necessary to focus on the development of knowledge, by which the organization supports its innovation potential.

*Figure 2. Model SECI: Elements of the knowledge conversion process*
*(Own processing with Pitra, 2016)*

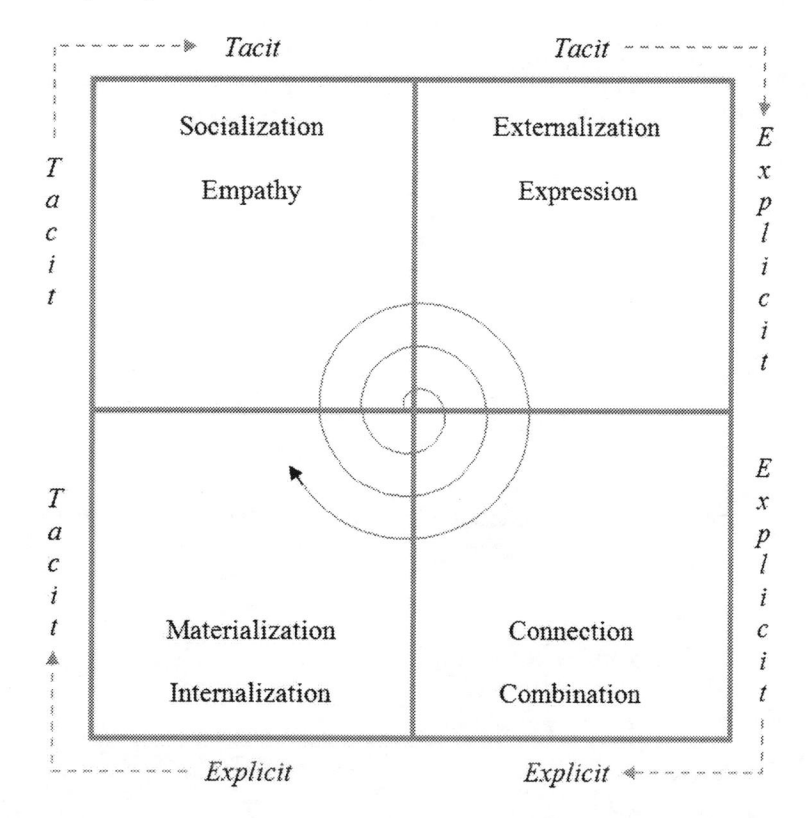

## Intellectual Capital and Learning Organization

Continuous adaptation of an effective and progressive set of management tools, methods and systems in an enterprise is a part of important intellectual capital. Intellectual capital of an organization is much more than just the sum of knowledge, skills and abilities. *Intellectual capital is a set of intangible assets that an organization possesses and can be used in the implementation of targeted changes in its business behavior through which it achieves the necessary implementation of their innovative projects. Intellectual capital of organizations therefore represents only the potential effect that, when combined with tangible assets, leads to added value and increased competitiveness of organizations offering innovative solutions (Pitra et co., P. 32, 2015).*

The chasm between the book and market value of the company is growing in all companies regardless of their size. This difference is more pronounced in more labor intensive industries in comparison to financial and physical resources. For this reason the concept of "intellectual capital" emerged which summarizes all the intangible factors contributing to the predominance of the market value of the company above its book value. These factors can include the loyalty of employees and their commitment, brand, goodwill, organizational values, customer loyalty, experience and skills of employees (Grublová et al., P. 39-40, 2014).

Composition of the intellectual capital of an organization can be seen in Figure 1. Intellectual capital consists of three basic components, namely: human capital, organizational capital and relational capital:

*Figure 1. Composition of the intellectual capital of the company*
*(Own processing with Bureš, 2016)*

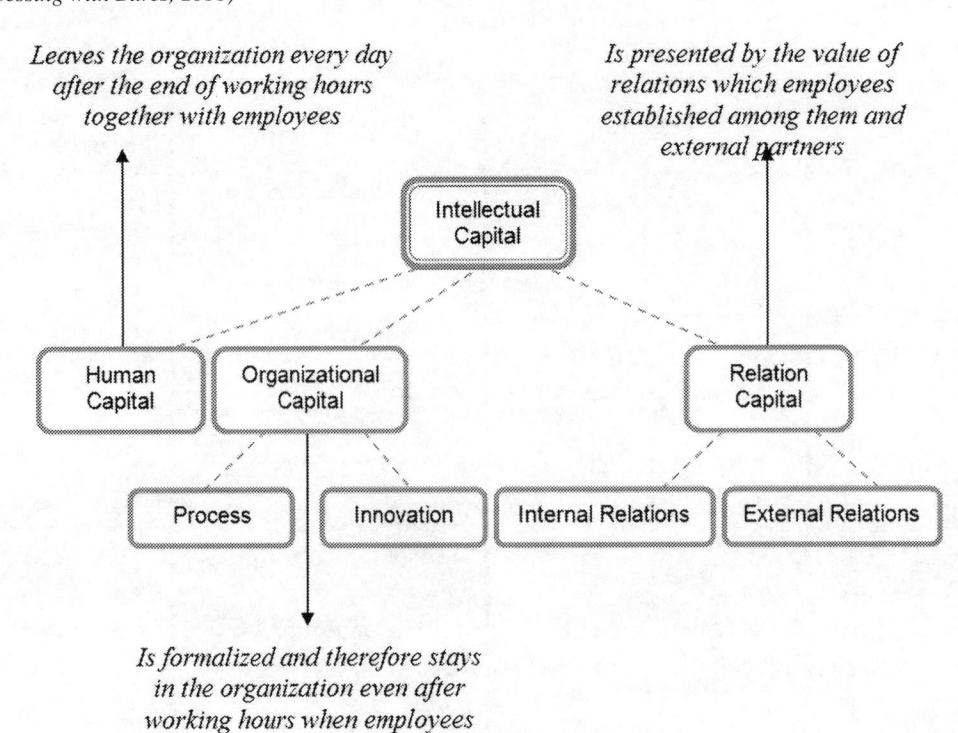

- ***Human Capital:*** *Consists of a set of knowledge, skills and abilities of individual employees of the organization and is bound on the individuality of each employee. When leaving, the staff of the organization leaves the human capital with them as well.*
- ***Organizational Capital:*** *Formalized by intangible assets, represented by purposeful linking of the contents of the database and the knowledge base of the organization. Represents the component of intellectual capital which remains in the organization even after the quitting of workers who created it.*
- ***Relational Capital:*** *Represents a set of relations that workers of the organization created with their partners within the organization and with partners who operate outside the organization. After the leaving of workers, only the formalized component (external knowledge) of the relational capital remains in the organization, the tacit component (internal knowledge) leaves along with its bearer (Pitra et co., P. 33, 2015).*

In accordance with principles of the learning organization described by one of the most important books related to knowledge management, the book The Fifth Discipline by Peter M. Senge, the following disciplines of knowledge creation and transfer must be addressed:

- **Personal Mastery:** The discipline of continuous brightening and deepening of individual personal vision, concentrating energy sources, developing patience and objective perception of reality.
- **Mental Models:** Our deeply ingrained assumptions and generalizations, affecting our world comprehension and acting in it.
- **Shaping a Common Shared Vision:** Only a true vision (not a mere declaration of a vision) is what gets people together and encourages the desire to achieve outstanding performance and learning in them – they do it because they want to, not because someone ordered them.
- **Team Learning:** Intellectual abilities of the team that can exceed the cognitive abilities of individuals (but beware, it can be vice versa).
- **Systems Thinking:** The fifth discipline, a discipline that integrates all the previous ones and creates one single associated unit.

The author accents that the basis for the success of any organization is to change its mind – the organization needs to retreat from the traditional models, have its view of itself and its surroundings changed, and begin to work on a change, a change towards a learning organization (Senge, p. 25-30, 2006).

## Management Tools, Methods and Systems and Business Performance

The previous paragraphs focused on systematic learning and the creation of intellectual capital in management aiming to successful innovativeness and competitive advance, but the point of view (a) still needs to be answered: Do specific management tools influence enterprise performance and how? Is creation and transfer of knowledge in that area meaningful?

The answer is not simple, previous research results of the authors aimed at the influence of management methods, tools and systems on different factors of enterprise performance with an impact on strategic management tools and continuous improvement tools. The research was properly documented and published (Pawliczek, 2015).

## BUSINESS AND COMPETITIVE INTELLIGENCE

Knowledge management and system thinking can be strongly supported by ICT, ensuring increase in the speed of operation, memory and sharing of results. Acronyms as MIS, BI, CI, ERP need to be clarified.

## Management Information Systems

At present, ICT support is of crucial importance for managerial decision-making. Management information systems (MIS) are systems for data processing. These systems make the information relevant for both basic as well as advanced (strategic) enterprise management decisions available. The data in MIS should include as many working systems and departments of the enterprise as possible. Currently, MIS is relevant for all medium-sized and large companies as well as for SMEs that want to be able to make decisions quickly and with confidence when dealing with everyday business problems. In order to achieve this, it is naturally necessary to have the data from many systems in one place. These systems would usually include accounting, controlling, planning, production, sales, and more. On this basis, it is possible to perform a flexible analysis of data depending on various factors and parameters, such as location (of the branch), products, time, sector of activity, customers, employees, etc. (Andersen, 2001, Pentaho, 2015).

## Business Intelligence

Business Intelligence (BI) are the skills, knowledge, know-how, technology, application, quality, risk management, security, and processes used in business to obtain a better understanding of the global context. For this purpose, enterprises undertake the collection, integration, analysis, interpretation, and presentation of business information. Business intelligence is a follow-up to MIS implementing modern management methods, tools and systems (Bartes, 2005, Lichtenthaler, 2008).

## Enterprise Resource Planning

Enterprise resource planning (enterprise information system) is an ICT assisted system whereby an enterprise (organization) manages and integrates all or most of its activity areas such as planning, inventory, purchasing, sales, marketing, finance, human resources, manufacturing, and more. The important and most popular MIS include the following (SOL, 2015):

- **Enterprise Resources Planning (ERP):** Systems for the management and planning of the resources of the enterprise.
- **Customer Relation Management (CRM):** Systems for customer relationship management.
- **Human Resources Management (HRM):** Systems for human resources management.
- **Advanced Production Systems (APS):** Systems for advanced production planning and control.
- **Computer Aided Facility Management (CFM):** Systems for the management of buildings with the support of ICT.

## Competitive Intelligence

Competitive Intelligence (CI) – competitive intelligence is one of the advanced Business Intelligence disciplines, i.e. it is an interdisciplinary field related to knowledge management. It is a systematic and ethical process of gathering, analyzing, and the use of external information which can affect the intentions of the organization, its decision-making, and behavior. CI is supposed to work as a decision-making support in order to ensure the competitiveness of the company and also as an early warning system in case of a crisis. The basis of CI is formed by the so-called news cycle using as many free Internet information resources as possible. Furthermore, the cycle uses resources of a commercial character - database centers, press agencies, etc. (Molnár, 2012). The CI should form a basis for the use of management tools which work with the obtained information (PEST, Porter 5F, SWOT, and others) for the needs of management. All of this should be linked via ICT to form a comprehensive management information system (Pawliczek, 2015).

## BI/CI SOFTWARE SUPPORT

Creating of the organizational memory for knowledge retention is connected with the implementation of the MIS software. A few examples of the MIS software with an accent to business and competitive intelligence:

- **Asseco Helios Solutions:** Provides a perfect and up-to-date overview of the market situation, the basis for strategic decision-making and automates routine operations (Helios, 2015).
- **FaMa+ CAFM:** Provides comprehensive management and maintenance of buildings and technologies, management of lease relationships (contractual relations, rental provisions and services, payments, billing, reminders), repairs, reconstruction, and related services (Tesco SW, 2015).
- **IS Karat:** Allows successful planning and decision-making, leads to the efficient use of resources. Facilitates communication and management, simplifies and accelerates the key processes in the areas of production, trade, finance, marketing, or logistics (Karat, 2015).
- **K2 Atmitec:** A comprehensive system for the management of enterprises. In its modules, the system can manage business processes, create enterprise activity overviews and provide relevant data for decision-making in a complex manner. It is divided into a number of scalable products to suit all business segments (K2 Atmitec, 2015).
- **Pentaho-Business Analytics:** A system providing an interactive visual analysis, KPI-suitable user grid, adjustable reporting, current information for management and administration, complete data integration, and predictive analysis (Pentaho, 2015).
- **Pohoda Business Intelligence:** Accounting, warehouses, documents (Stormware, 2015).
- **SAP Business Objects Business Intelligence:** Makes use of the analysis of the trade data in order to describe, predict and increase the performance of the enterprise (SAP, 2015).
- **Tovek CI:** Enables the effective processing of large amounts of unstructured data. Professional tools based on full text technology for information searching (Molnár, 2012).

## SOLUTIONS AND RECOMMENDATIONS: DESIGN OF THE KNOWLEDGE MANAGEMENT SYSTEM FOR SMES

The suggested knowledge management system is based on two interconnected phases:

- Knowledge creation,
- Knowledge continuity – interpersonal (intergenerational) transfer.

Both parts integrally include the knowledge transfer. As the knowledge transfer is intensively active, so the chance for knowledge continuity is better.

### Knowledge Creation Process

First it is necessary to realize that the process of knowledge creation is important because the development of competences (abilities to perform certain activities, use management tools) is mainly about the knowledge creation.

*The organization develops knowledge through interaction between explicit and tacit knowledge. These interactions between the two types of knowledge are referred to as the knowledge conversion. Through the process of converting, knowledge is expanding both in terms of quality and quantity. The four types of knowledge conversions include socialization, externalization, combination and internalization (Urbancová, p. 26, 2013).*

As well-known from Nonaka's theory, the knowledge creation process consists of (Bureš, p. 48-49, 2007). The spiral is shown in Figure 2.

- **Socialization:** The process of converting new tacit knowledge through experience sharing (interpersonal communication).
- **Externalization:** The process of articulation of tacit knowledge into explicit knowledge (publication).
- **Combinations:** The process of transformation of explicit knowledge into a comprehensive and systematic set of explicit knowledge (by IT software support).
- **Internalization:** The process of the embodiment of explicit knowledge into tacit knowledge (providing of products or services).

As the Figure 2 indicates, it is a cyclic process which comprises in different stages individual and group activities and the interaction of people with environment. From the process of knowledge production (a process known as SECI) and with respect to the laws of the SECI process, effective methods of managerial development should also be derived (Urbancová, p. 26, 2013).

## Knowledge Continuity

An essential part of knowledge management is the continuity of knowledge. Important reasons why the continuity of knowledge in the organization is so important (Urbancová, p. 28, 2013):

- Accelerates the training of new employees enabling them to be more productive sooner.
- Unifies knowledge and allows employees to focus on acquiring new knowledge.
- Allows increasing the productivity of the organization.
- Increases creativity, innovation, continuous improvement and organizational learning (everything depends on the knowledge of history).
- Improves decision-making, reduces errors of new workers.
- Reduces stress of employees, boosts the morale and loyalty of employees to the organization.
- Maintains knowledge networks that would otherwise be lost with leaving workers.
- Prevents the accumulation of knowledge in one person (often problem of family businesses).
- Retains organizational memory, knowledge remains in the organization.
- Reduces fluctuation and its financial implications.
- Reduces the vulnerability of organizations in the use of contingent workers (temps, etc.).

## Knowledge Management System Chart

The presented chapter focuses on knowledge in management represented by sophisticated management tools, accented by knowledge management in that area and its influence on enterprise competitiveness.

The suggested knowledge management system should content the following interconnected working components:

1. Module: Creation of knowledge in management tools supporting better knowledge of the business system and its surroundings and consequent better decision-making.
2. Module: Provide the enterprise with quality management information systems (BI/CI) to work effectively with implicit and explicit knowledge.
3. Module: Practical usages increase the amount of practical work and case studies.
4. Module: Transfer of tacit know-how (management kabbalah) from senior generation with more experience to junior generation and students by cooperation and experience.
5. Put previous activities under PDCA-SECI type cycle of continuous improvement.

Figure 3 summarizes the above mentioned modules in complex system maintaining, fortifying and increasing knowledge in an organization. The solution of the knowledge management problem lies in long-term continuously improved PDCA-SECI processes (M5) based on knowledge creation (M1) and mutual inter-employees transfer: tacit to explicit and vice versa (see Figure 2) and knowledge usage (M3). The intergeneration transfer (M4), where rare and valuable knowledge can be gained from (often undervalued) oldest and most experienced generations, is especially useful. This feature is often a very important competitive advantage of family businesses.

The knowledge management system is a part of the enterprise know-how and has to be sensitively adjusted to the specific enterprise conditions. Selection of proprietary software support (M2) is also an

*Figure 3. Knowledge management system chart*
*(Own processing, 2016)*

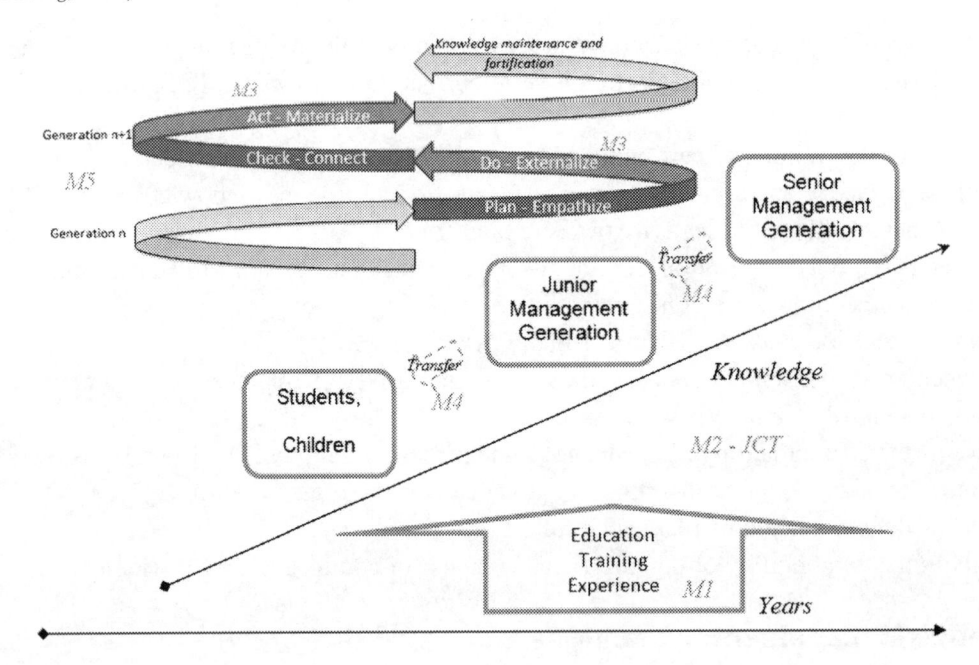

important task. As results from the previous research with other management systems (strategic management) have shown, it is certainly better to implement some knowledge management system and tune it slowly, than neglect this activity.

## FUTURE RESEARCH DIRECTIONS

Future research opportunities can be seen in:

- Deeper theoretical research of contemporary publications.
- Deeper mapping of management support software and management tools adapted in them.
- Specific characteristics of the knowledge management systems process in enterprises with relation to specific characteristics of the enterprise competitive performance.
- More detailed definition of suggested knowledge management model regarding coherent modules and their interconnection.

## CONCLUSION

The chapter discusses the issue of knowledge in management related to knowledge management where knowledge in management is represented by external, internal and tacit knowledge of sophisticated management methods, tools and systems. The empiric research (primary and secondary) indicated that the knowledge of sophisticated management methods, tools and systems on management positions in SMEs is very low. This knowledge, however, due to the increase of innovativeness and competitive advantages of enterprises has to be permanently created by tools of a learning organization and transferred, ensuring its continuity. ICT support of MIS, ERP, BI and CI for management of especially explicit knowledge is very helpful. A simple knowledge management system containing 5 modules was formulated and introduced for application.

## ACKNOWLEDGMENT

Thank you to Mgr. Jitka Lidaříková, MUCO for language corrections.

## REFERENCES

K2 Atmitec. (2015). *Informační systém K2*. Ostrava: K2 atmitec. Retrieved from: http://www.k2.cz/cz/k2software/informacni-system-k2.html

Andersen, T. J. (2001). Information technology, strategic decision making approaches and organizational performance in different industrial settings. *Journal of Strategic Information Systems, 10*(2), 101-119.

Association of Small and Medium Companies in CR (ASMEC). (2011). *Survey results no. 10.* Retrieved from: www.amsp.cz/uploads/dokumenty/AMSP _ URPruzkum_C10.pdf

Bain & Company. (2015). *Management Tools & Trends*. Retrieved from: http://www.bain.com/publications/insights/business-management-tools-andtrends.aspx

Baranov, V., Zaytsev, A., & Zaytsev, A. (2011). The Lean Production Concept and Its Influence on the Market Value of a Company. *Proceedings of the 10th International Conference Liberec Economic Forum 2011.*

Bartes, F. (2005). Inovace v podniku. Brno: Akademické nakladatelství CERM.

Bureš, V. (2007). Znalostní management a proces jeho zavádění: průvodce pro praxi. Praha: Grada Publishing.

Collison, Ch., & Parcell, G. (2005). Knowledge management: praktický management znalostí z prostředí předních světových učících se organizací. Brno: Computer Press.

Drucker, P. F. (1999). Knowledge-Worker Productivity: The Biggest Challenge. *California Management Review*. Retrieved from: http://forschungsnetzwerk.at/downloadpub/knowledge_workers_the_biggest_challenge.pdf

Fajkus, B. (2005). *Filosofie a metodologie vědy: vývoj, současnost a perspektivy*. Prague: Academia.

Grublová, E., & Frank, J. (2014). Inovace a znalosti. Olomouc: Univerzita Palackého.

Helios. (2015). *Informační systémy pro všechna odvětví*. Prague: HELIOS CR. Retrieved from: http://www.helios.eu

Karat Informační Systém. (2015). *Řešení pro výrobní firmy*. Přerov: Karat Software, a.s. Retrieved from: http://www.karatsoftware.cz/oborova-reseni/vyroba

Klimeš, L. (1981). *Slovník cizích slov, 5* (Revised Edition). Prague: SPN.

Kotler, P., & Keller, K. L. (2007). *Marketing Management*. Praha: Grada Publishing.

Lichtenthaler. (2008). Opening up strategic for. technology planning: extended roadmaps and functional markets. *Management Decision, 46*(1-2), 77-91.

*Management Mania*. (2016). Retrieved from https://managementmania.com/en

Modern Management. (2011). *Čeští podnikatelé nepoužívají moderní metody řízení*. Praha: Economia, a,s. Retrieved from: http://modernirizeni.ihned.cz/c1-52417420-cesti-podnikatele-nepouzivaji-moderni-metody-rizeni

Mohelská, H., & Pitra, Z. (2012). Manažerské metody. Prague: Professional Publishing.

Molnár, Z. (2012). Competitive intelligence aneb jak získat konkurenční výhodu. Praha: Nakladatelství Oeconomica.

Molnár, Z., & Střelka, J. (2012). Competitive Intelligence v malých a středních podnicích. *E+M Economics and Management, 15*(3), 156-170.

Pawliczek, A. (2015). *Management Methods, Tools and Systems in the Operation of Enterprises with an Accent on the Strategy, Continuous Improvement and Performance* (habilitation thesis). Zlín: Univerzita Tomáše Bati. Fakulta managementu a ekonomiky.

Pawliczek, A., & Piszczur, R. (2013). Utilization of Modern Management Methods with Special Emphasis on ISO 9000 and 14000 in Contemporary Czech and Slovak Companies. In *Proceedings of the 11th International Conference Liberec Economic Forum 2013*. Sychrov: TU of Liberec.

Pearce, D. W. (1995). *Macmillanův slovník moderní ekonomie*. Prague: Victoria Publishing.

Pentaho – A Hitachi Data Systems Company. (2015). *Pentaho Business Analytics*. Retrieved from: http://www.pentaho.com/product/business-visualization-analytics

Petříková, R. (2010). Moderní management znalostí: (principy, procesy, příklady dobré praxe). Praha: Professional Publishing.

Pitra, Z., & Mohelská, H. (2015). Management transferu znalostí: od prvního nápadu ke komerčně úspěšné inovaci. Praha: Professional Publishing.

Porter, M. E. (1980). Competitive Strategy: Techniques for Analyzing Industries and Competitors. New York: Free Press.

SAP. (2015). *Explore our analytics products*. Walldorf: SAP SE. Retrieved from: http://go.sap.com/cz/product/analytics.html

Senge, P. M. (2006). Pátá disciplína: teorie a praxe učící se organizace. Praha: Management Press.

Stormware Software Development. (2015). *POHODA Business Intelligence*. Jihlava: Stromware, s.r.o. Retrieved from: http://www.stormware.cz/pohoda/business-intelligence/reseni

Systém On Line (SOL). (2015). *Přehledy IS*. Brno: CCB, s.r.o. Retrieved from: http://www.systemonline. cz/prehled-informacnich-system

Tesco Software. (2015). *Fama+ CAFM*. Olomouc: TESCO SW, a.s. Retrieved from: http://www.tescosw. cz/facilitymanagement/fama-cafm

Tichá, I. (2005). Učící se organizace. Praha: Alfa Nakladatelství.

Urbancová, H. (2013). Kontinuita znalostí: jak uchovat znalosti klíčových pracovníků v organizaci. Praha: Nakladatelství Adart.

Veber, J. (2009). Management: základy, moderní manažerské přístupy, výkonnost a prosperita. Praha: Management Press.

## KEY TERMS AND DEFINITIONS

**Business Intelligence:** Set of skills (knowledge, know-how, technology, application, quality, risk management, security, and processes used in business) aiming better understanding of global business context.

**Competitive Intelligence:** Systematic process of gathering, analyzing, and the use of external information which can affect the intentions of the organization, its decision-making, planning and behavior.

**Competitiveness:** Ability of survival or expansion in global surrounding based on elasticity, adaptation, innovation, intellectual capital and knowledge management in a learning organization.

**Enterprise Resources Planning:** An ICT assisted system whereby an enterprise (organization) manages and integrates all or most of its activity areas such as planning, inventory, purchasing, sales, marketing, finance, human resources, manufacturing, and more.

**Knowledge Management System:** Systematic creation, classification, fortification, transfer and continuity of knowledge from senior to junior generations in organization based on PDCA and SECI cyclic processes.

**Management Information System:** Usually ICT based data processing (software) support for management by providing sophisticated structured information about an organization, processes, resources, personnel, market, etc.

**Management Tools, Techniques, Methods and Systems:** Simple, intermediate or complex analytical or creative plan activities applicable in different branches of management serving a sophisticated and effective management executive.

# Chapter 10
# From Giftedness to Compliance:
## The Best Practices in Utilizing Human Capital

**Tamás Bognár**
*Széchenyi István University, Hungary*

**Irma Rácz**
*Széchenyi István University, Hungary*

## ABSTRACT

*This chapter provides a survey of methods, utilizing the human capital that helps on one hand identify the talents or the shortage of it; specify the developmental dynamics of a skill or competence, and gives help to the prognosis of successful assessment forms by following the development progress. The authors intend to suggest best practices that provide to find and complete the best possible mission for SMEs and employees as well by taking into consideration the progressive tools of knowledge management. The chapter introduces the methods of measuring talent and capability existence or shortage, the measurement possibilities of hidden potentials and the utilization of these among SMEs' routine. Authors pay special attention to the employees maturing progress on higher levels of working experience where the talent possibly manifests as utilized knowledge. Methods will be introduced that provide this manifestation to give best practices to assessment for a better prediction.*

## INTRODUCTION

Facing of more often with the changes develop the excellent capability becoming a more natural need. As human resources plays a more and more important role in business, utilizing HR as a capital has higher and higher focus. Recognition of giftedness gave a lot of benefit to practice. Assessing the best candidates who fulfil the prospects is the top priority of recruiting. That's why it becomes very important to understand how the giftedness progress to compliance in practice. However we frequently experience the other side of the picture since the talented people always tries to initiate directions to change which

DOI: 10.4018/978-1-5225-1642-2.ch010

is not fully popular among others due to yellows and inferiority complex. Talented persons often need to confront with the resistance of the environment.

In Hungarian literature terms 'talent', 'giftedness', 'ability', 'potential' used sometimes wrongly, moreover as synonyms of each other. Among others we see ambition to differ the English giftedness and talent terms in studies of Szakács and Gaál (2008). While the previous one means a hidden skill without recognition, the latter one is identified as a result of a development program and it is a recognised ability. In this paper we would like to use these terms according to this differentiation but noticing that we think that talent is neither a manifested competence. We aim to continue to follow the development process with attention to realize what is necessary for practical manifestation.

Researching the latent skills, abilities and traits origins from the personality psychology's period when the focus was to find the factors of *personal differences* (Oláh & Gyöngyösiné, 2007). The focus of interest among some researchers was an autotelic differentiation of social comparison (Orosz & Szukics, 2012). Some others concentrated on the applying in practice. For example Barrick (Barrick & Mount, 1991) examined the compliance in five different sectors along the *"Big Five" factors of traits*:

- Extroversion,
- Emotional stability,
- Agreeableness,
- Conscientiousness, and
- Openness to Experience.

According to his results agreeableness could make a significant correlation with high performance in work. All the other factors could mean different emphasise depending on the sector, the situation, the company and a lot of other circumstances. The need of practical application increased the studies on predicting the compliance. Moreover it became required to find all the relevant factors that can provide high performance.

However, this paper intends to better light the dynamics of the competencies and talent as they progress from the incubation to manifestation in practice. That's why we didn't want only to join the row of improving a new method to assess the ideal candidate. This paper gives an overview on literature of talent and introduce an own research. At first we would like to emphasise the above mentioned limits of the current assessment paradigm. So we had to set up somehow a control group because we wondered what happens if the given competence is indicated as a potential or talent due to tests, interview or whatever selection method and it doesn't appear in manifest behaviour either.

## THEORETICAL BACKGROUND

### The Talent Approach

In Hungarian literature giftedness is identified with talent which comes from the Greek talentum term (Bőgel & Tomka, 2010). Beside the weigh and measure talentum also means a reliable skill, fortune and a gift, origins from the God (Duden, 2001, 835; Ritz & Thom, 2011, 8). Talent and talent management at first related to psychology, education and later to organisations and other economical processes as a research area. That's why we see the basic models from the view of psychology and economics. One can say talentum could be find everywhere and nowhere. The researchers are divided in the description of talent. It is also a question that managing the talent is only a new phrasing of the old terms or a new approach that could provide something different.

In the following we analyse the different approaches of giftedness and talent to be able to reach our perspective in this study.

The appreciation of giftedness was changing by eras as the social, cultural and ecological requirements were changing. Talent was considered as the gift of the God or sometimes as a demonic thing before the Enlightenment. At end of 19th century the researchers were divided in two parties. On the one hand according to Galton (1869) took a stand on giftedness is by the nature, on the other hand some experts, like Leibniz provided a new perspective by emphasising the education and the environment instead of congenital heritage, since the high level of education can exceed the performance belonging to only giftedness without any development. However, in the recent decades some human genetic research proved that the abilities comes from the talent appears as collective effect of mainly the genetic susceptibility and in a wider sense the education. So development of talent can be imagined with the existence of both variables (Czeizel, 1997).

A popular description of Gyarmathy (2006) says: "Talent is a possibility in the person which comes to surface in the interactions of internal and external factors. And it is also a behaviour and attitude, scale of value and self-perception." We talk about a special mentality and behaviour, as one can enlighten new directions and solutions, coupling with the high level of independent, genuine skills of thinking (Gyarmathy, 2006; Rácz, 2014). Petrányi (2009) has a little bit different approach with the description of talent, as it is a willingness and capability of learning, change and revival.

Let's review the elements of talent to summarize the frame of talent descriptions. We select the approaches that are related to our study from the range of talent models (Renzulli, 1979; Mönks & Boxtel, 2000; Czeizel, 1997; Gagné, 1985, 2005, 2009, 2013). Each researcher has an own aspect on the relevant factor in giftedness and talent. Renzulli (1979) separates giftedness and talent in his model. He puts forward 2 major criticisms to the definition and categories for the giftedness[1] proposed by the U.S. Office of Educaton (Marland, 1972):

- At first, "the definition does not include any reference to motivation, even though a large body of research concerning gifted or talented adults confirms the importance of this variable in this expression of creative and productive behaviours."
- At second, the six categories of giftedness referred to in the definition are not parallel (Gagné, 1985).

There are two different things meets each other in his model:

- Psychological factors, such as high level of abilities, creative outlook, commitment and motivation,
- General and specific areas where the talent can appear such as mathematics, natural science, religion and astronomy, poetry, music.

Later Mönks has completed it with the social environment factor and has created the Mönks-Renzulli model (Mönsk & Boxtel, 2000). Mönks thinks that Renzulli's model can work only if the person lives in a desert island, far from the society. He emphasises the facilitative and obstructive interaction of social environment (Mönsk & Boxtel, 2000), since the family gives the values, the schoolteachers open gates, and peers have catalytic effect. Comparing the two models, it is prominent that Renzulli's task-engagement changes to motivation in Mönks approach. Mönks want to more emphasise the importance of energetic factors.

Czeizel's 4*2+1 factored talent model (Figure 1) features three groups of factors, such as heritability, environment and fate (Czeizel, 1997).

Czeizel determines 4 intrapersonal and 4 social-environmental key-factors in the manifestation of giftedness. The intrapersonal factors are: general intellectual aptitude, specific mental aptitude, creativity, and motivation. In the case of the social-environmental factors Czeizel suggests to take into consideration the societal factor beyond family, school, and peer-relations. What is more, Czeizel suggests that an extra factor should be introduced an irrational factor, called: fate that plays an important role in unfolding of giftedness (Gyarmathy, 2006).

The above mentioned models trace out a quite complex system which is strengthened by the longitudinal research of Terman (1947, 1959). He had selected people with gifts and has been followed for 30-50 years. He found that not every of the persons with high IQ became a genius, but rather elite members of the society. So talent seems to be a complex package that could have an early representation as a giftedness (for example IQ), and evolves to different possible directions due to the interactive effects of general intelligence, creativity, motivation and external factors.

*Figure 1. 4*2+1 factor model of Czeizel*
*Source: Czeizel 1997, own edition*

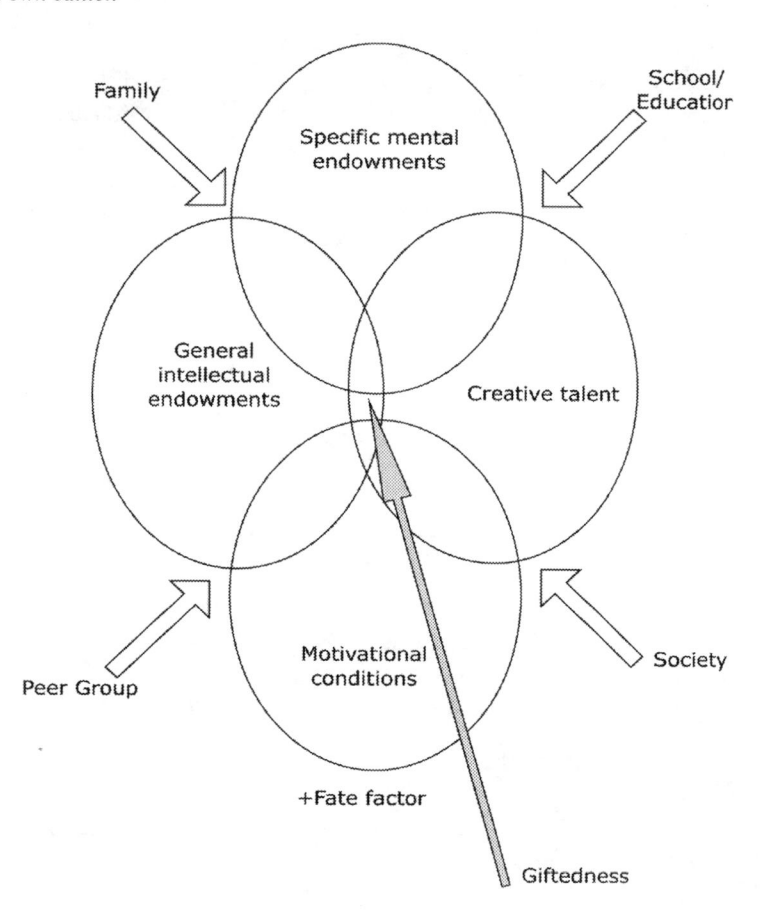

We end the range of models with mentioning Gagné's researches. In the recent decades he worked out several models (1985, 2009, 2013), which made a basis for our theory and our model. According to Gagné (2013, 1.):

- "*Giftedness* designates the possession and use of untrained and spontaneously expressed outstanding natural abilities or aptitudes (called gifts), in a least one ability domain, to a degree that places an individual at least among the top 10% of age peers."
- *Talent* designates the outstanding mastery of systematically developed competencies (knowledge and skills) in at least one field of human activity to a degree that places an individual at least among the top 10% of learning pears[2]."

Gagné (1985) introduced some specified external and internal influences as a catalyst factors which help to come giftedness to surface as a talent (Figure 2).

According to our approach this early model provides a lot of opportunity to imagine the way as elements of giftedness structures to a complex talent as a recognised and progressed ability. Our interest focused more on the catalyst factors. The latest model of Gagné (2009) represents more aspects of this catalyst factors in development process (Figure 3).

*Figure 2. Gagné´s differentiating model of giftedness and talent (1985 version)*
Source: Gagné, 1985, own edition

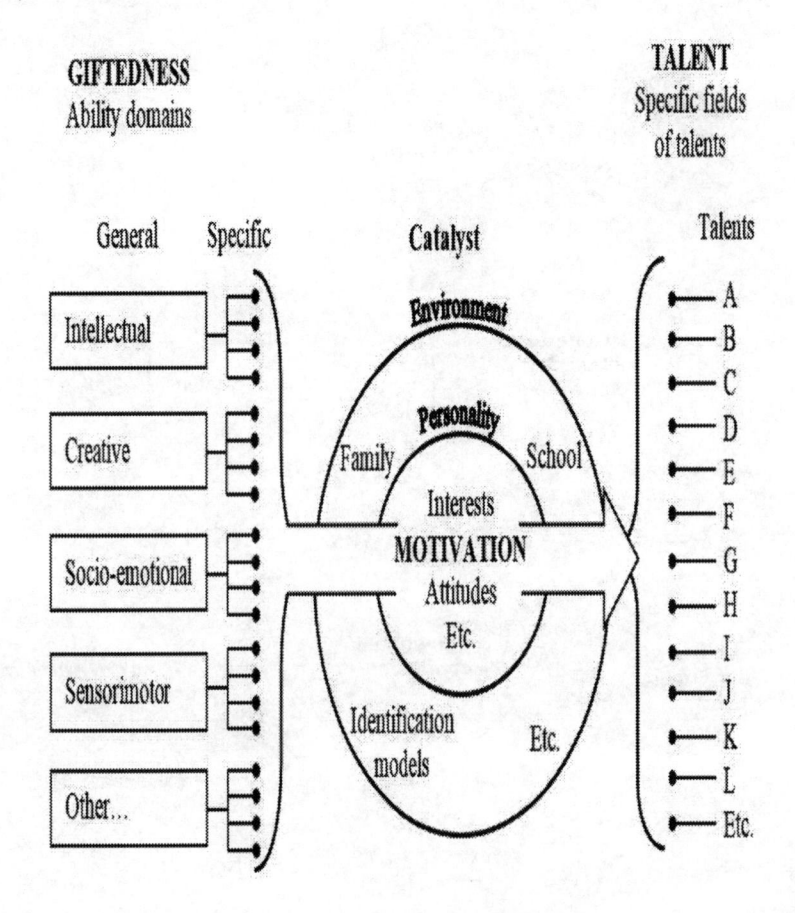

*Figure 3. Gagné´s differentiating model of giftedness and talent 2.0*
Source: Gagné, 2009, own edition

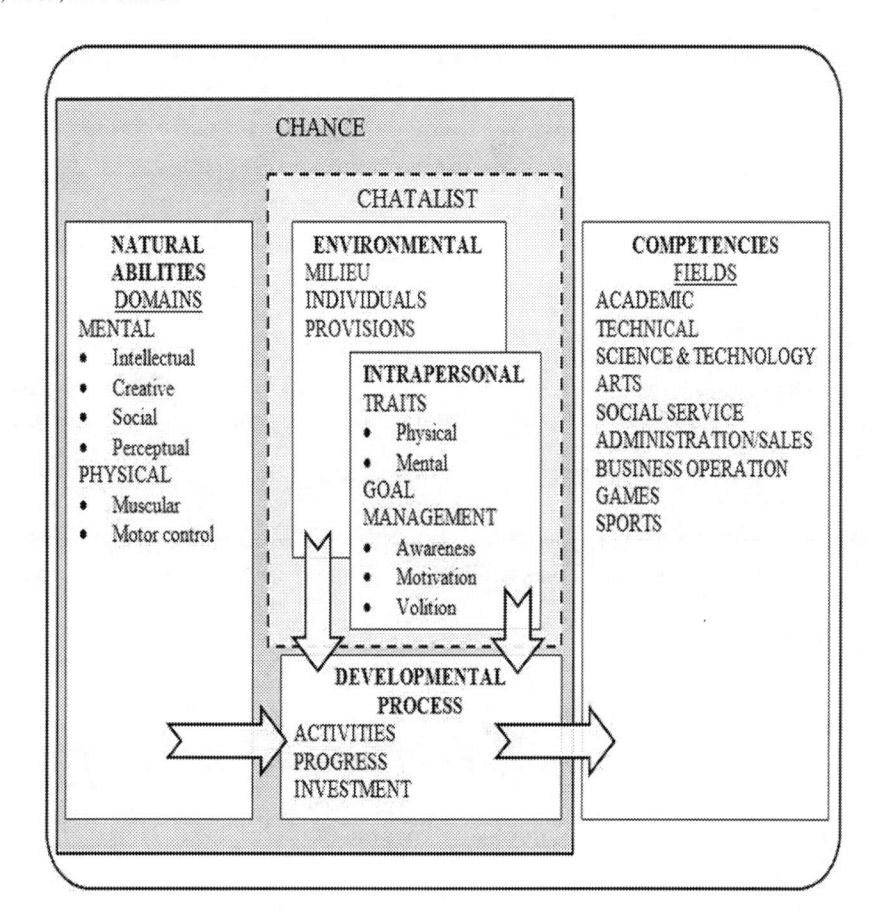

Comparing the two models raises three questions.

1.  At the first model: does recognising the talents mean the final output of development process?
2.  At the last model of Gagné: maybe the structuring result of talent can be manifold possible competencies.
3.  And finally whether is it possible that personal and environmental elements can also block the practical manifestation of talent?

Nevertheless, we focus also the external and internal catalyst processes. Our choice was not differentiating more the development process before talent, but rather we think talent is still not the end of the development so we continue the progress and find new internal and external influences that can catalyse or block the further development.

Besides the psychological description of talent it is necessary to give an economical version as well. "Better talent is worth fighting for" (Chambers et al., 1998, pp.45.) became to the most preferred epigraph for the talent focused business life of the last decade. As on the field of psychology, we cannot find a concrete definition for the concept of talent on the area of business as well.

The notion of talent and targets of talent specifications is very important step of talent management activities, but mostly rarely realized as conscious process. At this stage we should focus on the conditions which can be easily indicated in the job ads, what kind of knowledge is needed from the prospective employee. However, if organizations consciously focus on the objective of talent, their determination will happen as a result of the strategic planning, rather than an ad-hoc basis. To implement this stage successfully in terms of talent management, not only the priorities and objectives of knowledge are needed, but the interpretation of talents in the organization too (Rácz & Magyar-Stifter, 2015).

According to McKinsey:

- *The most important corporate resource over the next 20 years would be smart, sophisticated business people who are technologically literate, globally astute, and operationally agile.*
- *Talent is the sum of a person's abilities… his or her intrinsic gifts, skills, knowledge, experience, intelligence, judgment, attitude, character and drive. It also includes his or her ability to learn and grow. (Michaels et al., 2001 : xii)*

Thom (2003, 237.) describes talent as a genuine potential. He uses high potential term for a talented person. He specifies the people with abilities beyond the average with the following characteristics:

- *High education,*
- *High drive for an attracting activity, intrinsic happiness, devotion,*
- *Human oriented behaviour with colleagues and superiors,*
- *Need for personal and professional development. ( Ritz & Thom, 2011 , pp.8.)*

Ulrich (2006) takes a holistic view and published that talent is similar to competence, commitment, contribution, where:

- Competence means that "individuals have the knowledge, skills and values that are required for today and tomorrow",
- Commitment means that "employees work hard, put the time in to do what they are asked to do, giving their discretionary energy to the firm's success",
- Contribution means that "they are making a real contribution through their work — finding meaning and purpose in their work",
- Finally talent means "the drive to find, develop, and retain individuals, wherever they are located in the world, who have the competencies and commitment needed for their jobs and who can find meaning and purpose in their work."

Economically we consider high performers or above average employees as persons with a lot of experience, practical knowledge and ability to increase the competitiveness. They can reduce the budget by emphasising the quality performance and raise the income. They are motivated, competent high performers (Rácz, 2013).

Every company has to define their own concept, who will be a talent or expert of what kind of job what abilities and skills or plus endowment are needed to list them in „above average" categories. Without it, the attraction of talents to the organization is pointless and unsuccessful attempts (Rácz & Magyar–Stifter, 2015).

Martin and Schmidt (2010, pp. 15) consider the people who generates new businesses, achieves savings by introducing new methods in work, develops better partner relationships and they initiate innovation processes. Since they are the key of the future, organisations especially the companies need to recognise and utilize them (Petrány, 2009).

From the view of our practical researches we can see a huge range of talent definitions at the companies. The reason can be that every organisation is different from the other, so the ideal competencies can be different as well, which lead to specific solutions in talent management. However describing a job could mean individual competence list due to the specific requirements of company, market and culture (Ritz & Thom, 2011).

Concluding the literature of talent and giftedness we can say that there are no common definitions for the terms accepted by every researcher. However the experts are agree that the giftedness and talent itself

- Show a kind of inner power that provide the possibility of increasing social and economic performance,
- Have different models that represent the interference of complex elements.

## Measurability of Potentials

After having a global view of understanding the talent itself, we can be more interested in the manifestation of talent. Due to the dynamic model of talent we can shift our focus from the person to the profitability of the talented person from the companies view. Our first step to the final utilization of talent is to understand how it becomes unlocked. The literature of HR selection mostly focuses on the compliance of the candidate since this was the most important question for the companies to find the best candidate for a position. The researchers show a wide range of competing selection methods that anticipate the performance of the employees in an applied job. On the one hand we summarise some of them to understand the main scope of different selection approaches. On the other hand we point out that due to some practical interests the validity tests are incomplete. The reason for it is we are mostly unable to compare the winner employee with a control one, so we cannot exclude the possibility of the better performance of the not selected candidate, because he is rejected. Usually we can only measure the compliance of the winner candidate. We have another dilemma with descripting the job and the necessary skills, talents, competence, which is quite unnoticed by the researchers. That's why it is still a question if the recruiting experts should assess the maximum level of the required competencies or not. As we may suppose, if there is no development challenge in the position but the candidate seeks for the development, the position wouldn't be motivating for him. These *two dilemmas* lead to the need for examining how the potential unlocks during the career path.

- Does it give any additional information for a better prognosis?
- Are we able to help this unlocking process and the manifestation of talent with some approach?

We would like to answer these two questions by analysing some assessment processes.

Several researchers point out the notability of potentials that can be measured with tests and interviews perchance with the mixture of them (Jones et al, 1991; Goffin et al, 1996). Both experts use potential as a hidden antecedent of a certain competence. So does Carless (2009), who has found high correlation between detected potential and the compliance, but we would like to go further. If we assume that it was not sure to be able to manifest the hidden potentials in practice, the simple correlation wouldn't be enough. Certainly the lack of a necessary potential could indicate the incompetence in a job, but may be an existence is not a guarantee for the presentation of it. After having a competence list as the above mentioned researchers suggest, we intend to point out an approach that could add a few percent in validity of predicting the compliance. Moreover this method could support the development of the candidate. We suggest introducing the crisis analytic method to the selection processes, which focuses the assumption that the people go through crisis belonging to each level during the career path (Bognár, 2013a). Analysing those crises can show the attitude to the challenges of the given position. The dynamics of a crisis can indicate regression, progressive development or "won crisis" stage. While a won crisis state provides reference in manifestation of certain competencies, the progressive stage promises the actual or near outcrop of the potentials, hereby the development of the candidate can be predicted. The regressive direction of crises promises the longer term of incubation of the necessary competencies.

There is no remarkable study in the literature of selection that would have examined the performance of the rejected candidate. It is almost impossible to ensure equal circumstances to the rejected candidates at another company in the same position as he or she applied for in the examined assessment group to test his or her compliance. Certainly the reason is acceptable on the practical side. Nevertheless, to better understand the dynamics, we need to analyse some blocks or failures of a career of a person.

Let's suppose that we have a perfect competence list to a certain position, moreover an experience based list as it is suggested by Jones (Jones et al., 1991). It is not again the logic to appoint the candidates with higher scores on this list comparing with the lower scored applicants. With that we outline a static model of assessment. This method is not sensitive for two important things. At first the candidates starting immediately after the assessment may develop and they could improve the measured competencies. It was the very advantage of the selections based on tests measuring the potentials. At second if we consider the candidate who improved the required competencies to a maximum level by the time of the assessment, we ignore the possible fact that his or her ambition could drive to the direction of a higher position and the offered one could not motivates.

It is not emphasised that it is not sure that the most suitable candidate has the higher score – and consequently who is able to complete the task on the highest performance level – instead of the applicant whose career progress fits more to the challenges of the given position. If this recognition seems interesting, these anomalies of the current paradigm of selection could show a new direction because we would need a dynamic model to understand what unlocks the inner potentials. So it opens the focus of us to a new approach of research that emphasises the missing part of our knowledge about the career development. Among the models of personality development Erikson has been set up a 8-stage progress model that seems usable for career development (Erikson, 1956). Erikson says that the personality develops through these hierarchical stages which are declared with the typical crises See in Table 1.

Using his sample we emphasised the *crisis analytic method* in our other study concerning to assessment (Bognár, 2013a).

The advantage of this approach is that it focuses on mobilised skills instead of incubated potentials, however the measuring scores are not compared statically to another static standard, but we analyse the progress of the typical crises belonging to the position. The dynamics of the crises show the development and the possible regressive or progressive direction of it. The crisis analysis can identify blocks or regressions which do not predict the manifestation of the relevant competence in practice in short term even it was detected in personality tests as potential. The Figure 4 shows the *common dynamics of a crisis.*

*Table 1. Erikson's life stages*

| Stage | Psychological Crisis | Basic Virtue |
|---|---|---|
| 1 | Trust vs. mistrust | Hope |
| 2 | Autonomy vs. shame | Will |
| 3 | Initiative vs. guilt | Purpose |
| 4 | Industry vs. inferiority | Competency |
| 5 | Ego identity vs. Role confusion | Fidelity |
| 6 | Intimacy vs. isolation | Love |
| 7 | Generativity vs. stagnation | Care |
| 8 | Ego integrity vs. despair | Wisdom |

Source: Erikson (1963, cit. McLoud, 2008)

*Figure 4. The progress of crisis*
*Source: Bognár, 2013a, own edition*

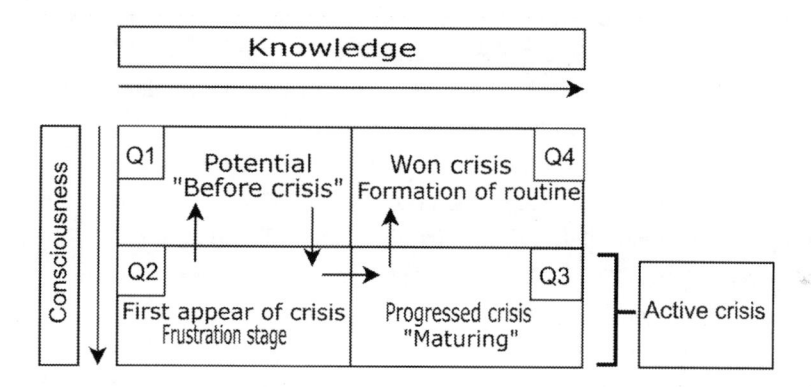

1. The first quarter (Q1) means the stage when the challenges of the crisis haven't appeared in the person's life yet. He thinks in the paradigm of the previous career stair – and he does it maybe with success but definitely without frustration.

2. The second stage (Q2) introduces blocks and regression. This quarter can determine the positive or negative prognosis of the crisis. The person meets the expectations and challenges of the career stair and the environment which are impossible to solve in the old paradigm, but he hasn't unlocked the potentials in this position. If he tries to cope with the stress by shifting the role, than he doesn't stay in the situation that provokes and induces the necessary skill. He tries to push the "solving formula" of the previous paradigm. That's the moment when he realizes the regression. In this study we examine Area Sales Managers. A possible example for this regression could be the shifting the leadership role.

3. In the third stage (Q3) the person keeps himself in the appropriate role of the position but only with an extra effort and conscious concentration. Although he may mistakes but he recognises the possibility of change and he tries to not use the out of date paradigm for the solution. Probably this is the point when he unlocks the necessary potentials belonging to the relevant paradigm of the career stair.

4.  The skills turns into routines in the fourth stage (Q4), the employee can stay in the relevant role without extra concentration; perhaps he evolves new, genuine solutions, controls the situations with gentle tools. The approach of the crisis analysis can be implemented to interviews and assessment centers, but the so far object of the examination like detecting the competences and the current appearance of them get a new dimension as analysing the crises and their dynamics.

## MAIN FOCUS OF THE CHAPTER

### Method, Pattern

We needed a complex method of assessment to be able to examine the different manifestation levels of potentials. Since the main question is the way of a talent comes to surface, we needed a qualitative approach in method. This study has examined the measuring models and the relations of them through an assessment process in a transnational corporation's Hungarian company. One of the models focused on the existing of the skills as a potential. This was a preliminary competency examination that based on the own test and an interview with the HR experts of the company. Its validity was not searched in this study; we only treated it as a variable. This meant the preliminary selection in the practice of the company that ensures to exclude candidates who doesn't have the given competency even on the level of potential. The second model was the assessment center (Krause & Gebert, 2003), that focused on detecting the mobilisation and appearance of the competences of the candidates in practice or rather in situations and comparing the candidates along this dimension. The practical use of this was to include those candidates who can prove the highest possible level of "readiness" for the given position. And finally the third model represented the most important focus for the scientific questions of the study. It was the crisis analysis of the candidates (Bognár, 2013a).

This paper analysed five AC-based selection processes at the same transnational company between 2007 and 2009. The applied position was Area Sales Manager. In three cases from the five the department was the same, the remaining two assessments was required by two similar department of the company. Due to this the competency list and the job description was quite isomorphic. Moreover only the AC had to detect this. Most of the applicants were internal candidates, which could provide a limited possibility to follow up also the rejected candidates. This was a very important think not just to present a control group for a real validation, but also to analyse the future state of the crisis progresses. We had external candidates as well in every assessment, which had a practical use but our study couldn't utilize it. All applicants in the pattern were competent on an appropriate level according to the preliminary test along the declared competence list. There 5-7 assessors on each AC, one of the authors included. The assessors didn't see the result of the preliminary tests until the end of AC. The assessors' job was to monitor the appearance the most relevant but possibly all the competencies during the situations of the AC and moreover to define the functioning of them in practice. We have set up the situations of AC to provoke the crises of the relevant career stair of the position with all the possible challenges. Two crises of the middle Managers were relevant during these selections such as "turning into operative leader from the experienced worker" and "turning into a strategic partner" (Bognár, 2013b).

We have identified the typical crises by monitoring the candidates approach. The task oriented attitudes and the signs of the disciplined in-the-box thinking were scored as earlier stages of the crises (Q1 or the regressive state of Q2) while the specific signs of sensitiveness for team dynamics and initiative participation in group problem solving showed existence of the operative leader's career stair. The future oriented thinking, the strategic viewed interpretations of the tasks represented the strategic partner's career stair. To be able to monitor all these we needed to set up the situations on the one hand with the relevant and typical challenges of the applied position. On the other hand we had to select the situations where the differences between for example the operative and strategic approaches of the people in behaviour or in communication. After identifying the stair and the belonging crisis of the candidates, the assessors had to analyse the dynamics of it. For that they had to focus on the obstructions of the team while trying to complete a team problem solving, the reactions for the frustrations and the coping strategies. 4-6 applicants participated on each AC, altogether 28 head. We have further filtered the pattern in this study and examined the candidates who still work for the company or has been worked for a long time, that's why we know their position or their performance. With that 11 people remained. So we have set up the control group to be able to examine not just the winners but also the rejected candidates.

The five assessment processes resulted five appointed employees. All of them still work for the company at the time of the study. One of them didn't meet the expectation and was moved to a Sales support department to an operative position (experienced worker career stair). The other four performs very well. One of the four works successfully as an Area Sales Manager, one was appointed to Category Sales Manager position after two years, one was appointed to Key Account Manager position, and one stepped two levels during four years to Country Business Manager position which is the head position of the product category. Five candidates from the six rejected ones still work in Sales Representative position and perform well. They haven't been appointed since the AC. One of the rejected candidates was later appointed to the Area Sales Manager position but didn't perform well so his contract was terminated in 2014.

The results of the preliminary competence measuring test are indicated in Table 2 and Table 3 on a 1 to 10 scale, where the 10 points mean the maximum. There is another 1-10 scale indicated in the table which shows the rate of the competence according the judgement of the assessors during the AC.

The two numbers are represented together (test/AC rate). The assessors evaluated the performance of the candidates during the exercises and rated the level of competencies.

*Table 2. Competence scores of selected candidates of AC on Area Sales Manager position (preliminary measured scores / scores on AC)*

| Competencies | Candidate 1 | Candidate 2 | Candidate 3 | Candidate 4 | Candidate 5 |
|---|---|---|---|---|---|
| **Preliminary Test Score / AC Score** | | | | | |
| Leading others | 7/9 | 8/8 | 9/10 | 8/7 | 9/7 |
| Negotiation skills | 8/9 | 10/9 | 9/9 | 8/9 | 9/8 |
| Problem solving | 8/9 | 9/9 | 9/8 | 8/8 | 10/8 |
| Independence | 7/10 | 8/9 | 10/9 | 8/7 | 7/8 |
| Assertiveness | 7/9 | 9/10 | 9/8 | 9/9 | 8/8 |
| Target orientation | 8/10 | 10/10 | 9/9 | 6/8 | 7/7 |
| Total | 45/56 | 54/55 | 55/53 | 47/48 | 50/46 |
| Identified career stair | Operative leader | Operative leader | Operative leader | Operative leader | Operative leader |
| Stage of crisis | Q4 | Q3 | Q4 | Q3 | Q2 |

Source: Own edition based on assessment centers between 2007 and 2008

*Table 3. Competence scores of rejected candidates of AC on Area Sales Manager position (preliminary measured scores / scores on AC)*

| Competencies | Candidate 6 | Candidate 7 | Candidate 8 | Candidate 9 | Candidate 10 | Candidate 11 |
|---|---|---|---|---|---|---|
| Preliminary Test Score / AC Score | | | | | | |
| Leading others | 9/7 | 7/3 | 10/6 | 6/6 | 6/5 | 6/5 |
| Negotiation skills | 7/7 | 8/7 | 10/10 | 7/6 | 7/5 | 7/5 |
| Problem solving | 9/9 | 8/6 | 9/8 | 8/8 | 8/7 | 7/7 |
| Independence | 8/9 | 7/8 | 8/8 | 8/6 | 8/8 | 7/6 |
| Assertiveness | 8/6 | 7/7 | 9/7 | 6/5 | 6/5 | 7/8 |
| Target orientation | 8/7 | 8/6 | 10/8 | 8/7 | 8/5 | 7/7 |
| Total | 49/45 | 45/37 | 56/47 | 43/38 | 43/35 | 41/38 |
| Identified career stair | Operative leader | Operative leader | Operative leader | Operative leader | Operative leader | Operative leader |
| Stage of crisis | Q2 | Q1 | Q2 | Q2 | Q1 | Q1 |

Source: Own edition based on assessment centers between 2007 and 2008

After the AC they had discussed the results and have brought a common decision on the competency score. There were group problem solving tasks among the blocks of AC, personal tasks represented the professional, leadership and strategic challenges of the applied position. The candidates presented their own solutions after getting the mass of relevant and irrelevant information. Furthermore there were situation and interactive tasks. The candidates played there role in these game together or with one of the assessors. Applicants were evaluated also with the third selection model such as the typical crisis of them. Setting up the thematic of the AC on the basis of the related challenges made the identifying the crises easy. For instance it is possible to approach a team problem solving situation on operative way with an individual solution but it couldn't lead to good solution because of the divided information among the participants. The task also can be approached in team. The candidates who have more routine in this crisis (Q3 and Q4 stages – Figure 1) play the appropriate leadership role with a higher credibility and during the game with fined actions due to a good timing. Candidates with a lower routine in this crisis usually try to acquire the leadership role with a bad timing or they don't even try it. Some other forms of appearance of the crises need individual interpretations. For example if a candidate recognises that his teammate leads facilitates the cooperation well not fighting for the leadership role could mean result orientation, or tactical sense, but also could mean lack of routine. It depends on the situation. And at last the given task can be approached on strategic way. It shows the future orientation. All the present actions are subordinated to that which is the third possible crisis around this position altogether with the above mentioned (experienced expert, operative leader, strategic partner crises of different career stairs).

Competency scores of the candidates (preliminary testing / AC) are represented in Table 2 and 3. As the second part of crisis analysis assessors have observed the dynamics. This has been based on the related to the specific crisis and generated by the frustration of the challenges (Törestad et al, 1990), and the possible shifting mechanism or relevant coping strategy as a response to the role and the frustration. During the analysis we had to consider the fact, that the shifting mechanisms were less represented in AC than the interviews. It is not excluded that it is due to the intention to meet the AC's expectation. The shifting mechanisms revealed themselves genuinely when the assessors were involved into situations.

We considered the regressive shifting mechanisms as bad prognosis. We concluded that the candidate may try to solve the challenges from the role of the previous position and in the previous paradigm as a reaction for the challenges instead of evolving the crises and the development itself. For example one can shuffle of the confrontation with other departments and treating the contra interests, he rather tries to work in other's stead or delegate the conflict management to his superior. Recognition of crises or rather the control of the crisis situations from the paradigm of the new position refers to a "won crisis" stage (Q4) or a progressed crisis (Q3) when although the person feels the frustration he can manage the situation in the new paradigm but he needs a special conscious effort. We can see the range of hierarchical career stairs in accordance with the dynamics shown in Figure 4, but aligned in a possible work life cycle (Figure 5). This study principally examined how candidate leave the stair of experienced expert and he turns to operative leader and strategic partner career stair.

So the AC that focused also to the crisis analysis differs to well-structured AC suggested by Jones and their colleges (Jones et al, 1991) in thematic. The reason is that we have prepared with alternative difficulty levels for each competency. We needed to give the optimal challenge that brings the crisis to surface but we also needed to have some part of the team or candidates to be able to solve the problem. For example if the team didn't throw away "accidently" an information that had been intended to seem irrelevant, the task itself was too easy for most of the candidates and the crisis didn't appear. In such cases we repeated the task with a variant on a higher difficulty level. After the tasks with the participation of the candidates the assessors discussed their scorings, comments and attributions. This paper particularly considered two outcomes from this discussion important. On the one hand the question was that had the specific competencies been appeared or not. On the other hand did it happen in the paradigm of the relevant crisis with a promising dynamic? After the AC the assessors brought their decision on the basis of all the three measuring model. The competency scores were declared as a result of a discussion and not an averaging. We tried to increase the objectivity with the consensus of diverting subjective judgements of assessors. The final part of this paper's methodology is to compare the later performance of appointed and rejected candidates with the results of the AC in 2007-2008. At first we examined if the

*Figure 5. The hierarchical career stairs with the four stages (Q1-Q4)*
*Source: Own edition, 2016*

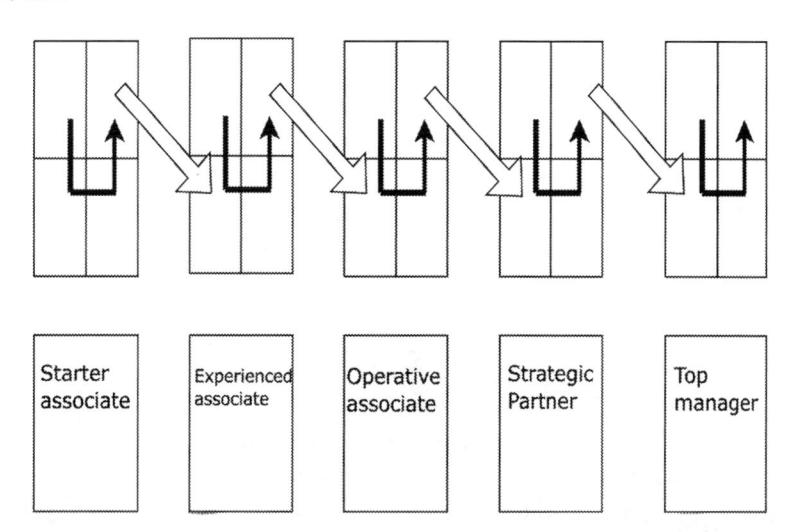

prognosis given by the assessors can be denied or not in 2015. We have compared the competence scores and the prognosis given by the assessors with the performance evaluation and personal progress and development guides recorded by the company about every employee. There were a lot of details on the examined candidates like personal objectives, advantages and disadvantages, successes and failures. We analysed again their actual crises on the relevant career stair. It was based on the personal evaluations, progress and development guides. The interpretations of these documents have been discussed with the superiors of the candidates. It was not examined in this paper if the superiors gave enough related challenges and supports them which would be one of the necessary conditions of unlocking potentials (Ritz & Thom, 2003; Martin & Schmidt, 2010).

## Hypothesises and Scientific Questions

This paper rather aim to use scientific questions instead of hypothesises work in quantitative researches because in this cases we didn't want just give a few percent to validity but we wanted to give a new value of explanation to the appearance or not appearance of competencies. This could be useful can give a new quality of prognosis. So we consider those candidates useful for this paper, who got high score of potentials according to the preliminary test and interview which indicated the potential but failed according to the analysis of assessors on AC. The preliminary test used by the company doesn't measure more than inner potentials like giftedness or talent but not even promises more. This result can use as a prognosis of compliance according to the logic that the basis of the required behaviour exists or not. If not, the rejection is reasonable, there is no question. However the AC indicated if this inner potential didn't appear in practice. We can agree the concept of divide the candidates among the appearance and not appearance of any required competence. Certainly the preliminary testing of potentials plays respectable role in process of selection, because it is easy to use in case of a numerous quantity of candidates to be able to exclude the ones who don't even have the basis of required competences. Seemingly it could be enough if a candidate with a certain high percentage of "readiness" wins the appointment. Our main point in this paper to set up common trends; however it could be examined in further detailed case studies whether a candidate with a hidden but locked potentials won his crises sooner or later in case of he is "forced" to keep in the active stages of crisis or not. If not, maybe his shifting mechanisms help him to "get off" the development. However the questions of this paper's approach:

1. What kind of dynamic causes that some candidates perform on a lower level on AC than the preliminary testing of potentials? Does this dynamic come from the progress of actual crisis?
2. Can we increase the validation of prognosis with the learning of career stairs' crises in connection with the compliance and the future development of the employees?
3. What crisis can be identified along the appointed and rejected candidates after a few years of AC from the view of crisis analysis?

## SOLUTIONS AND RECOMMENDATIONS

Generally we can say that after that few years period the rejected candidates did not falsify the decision concerning to them, although we didn't examine if they experienced the frustrating existence of the relevant crisis that would have been unlocked their potentials. We also didn't examine in details if they tried again to win the same position, tried to find new ambition, or possibly abandoned such future plans. We had six rejected candidates selected to be a part of the pattern. One of them left the company. We didn't examine if he didn't agree with the expectation for him in any position or with the evaluation belonging to his performance, or possibly the stagnation or regression due to he didn't treat the frustration well which came from the crisis (Q2 with regression). We can see a summary in Table 3. about the 1-4 candidates. Three of them have spent a few successful years in the Area Sales Manager position and then they step onto the next career stair with the active stage of the related crisis, the strategic partner's crisis. Their positions in 2015: Key Account Manager (KAM), Category Sales Manager (CSM), and Country Business Manager (CBM) positions. The fourth successful candidate still performs well in the won Area Sales Manager (ASM) position. He was not touched by the next career stair's crisis (Q1). There is an indicated ambition of the next position in his succession plan from the autumn of 2014, but the development only mean some training tool but it is not manifested in initiatives. According to his career plan he aspires to Key Account Manager (KAM) position which would mean the next career stair with its crisis of becoming a strategic partner. The candidate 5. had tried to reduce the stress coming from the crisis with shifting the appropriate leadership role according to the result of AC in 2008. According to the prognosis of crisis analysis it could block the development or turn it to regression instead of solving the crisis for a longer time. According to the crisis analysis in 2015, he is in the same stage of the same crisis (Q2). Although he tried to achieve the appropriate level of performance, the cooperation with other departments and external partners (not customers) was not successful due to the shuffling off the role. In 2015 he worked as a Sales Administrative Partner in a support department where the challenges are similar but without leadership role. The results of 1-5 candidates are summarised in Table 4.

The candidate 6. among the rejected candidates left the company from the Sales Representative position in spring of 2014. Summarisation of the analysis of rejected candidates is represented in Table 5.

According to the indications of his personal evaluation he lived the crisis of operative leader career stair, but he had been felt continuous frustration due to the shuffling off the role, the regression and respectively the unrealistic high self-esteem. The 7-11 candidates have performed well in Sales Representative position since the AC. One of them applied for an Area Sales Manager position since then. The candidate 8. lives his active crisis on either operative leader and strategic partner career stairs on theirs frustration stage(Q2). However we couldn't identify any shuffling off so his recent prognosis indicates development opportunities, but his initiatives are powerless so he often regresses to operative actions. That's why the effective time spent in the new paradigm in order to develop is consequently poor.

*Table 4. Career and crisis analysis of winner candidates of AC in 2007-2008*

|  | 1 | 2 | 3 | 4 | 5 |
|---|---|---|---|---|---|
| **Position** | KAM | CSM | CBM | ASM | **Sales Admin Partner** |
| **Career stair** | Strategic partner | Strategic partner / Top manager | Top manager | Operative leader | Operative leader |
| **Stage of crisis** | Q3 | Q3 | Q3 | Q3 | Q2 |
| **Shuffle off** | - | - | - | - | Leadership role in co-ordinate relationships |

Source: Own edition, 2016

*Table 5. Career and crisis analysis of rejected candidates of AC in 2007-2008*

| | 6 | 7 | 8 | 9 | 10 | 11 |
|---|---|---|---|---|---|---|
| **Position** | - | **Sales Repre-sentative** | **Sales Representative** | **Sales Repre-sentative** | **Sales Repre-sentative** | **Sales Repre-sentative** |
| **Career stair** | ? | Experienced associate | Operative leader Strategic partner | Experienced associate | Experienced associate | Experienced associate |
| **Stage of crisis** | ? | Q4 | Q2 | Q4 | Q4 | Q4 |
| **Shuffle off** | ? | Operative regression, shuffling off the responsibility | Powerless initiatives, regression | Operative regression, shuffling off the responsibility | Operative regression, shuffling off the responsibility | Operative regression, shuffling off the responsibility |
| **Prognosis** | - | Stays in senior sales rep. position | Cooperation with other departments would be helpful. | Stays in senior sales rep. position | Stays in senior sales rep. position | Stays in senior sales rep. position |

Source: Own edition, 2016

We can conclude the following trends from the results. Unlocking, mobilisation and bringing to surface of potentials correlate to the crisis of the concerning crisis, particularly with the 3rd and 4th stages of them (Q3 and Q4). Regression to the previous career stair could come from the reaction for the frustration described in the second stage of crisis (Q2), seemingly in case of due measure of shuffling off the role of the new paradigm. In such cases even the candidate wins the position, he aims to fit the expectation by trying to solve the tasks with the approach of the previous position, the previous career stair. This time the new competences challenged by the new situations cannot come to surface. The employee seems to fix his own frustration, which causes blockings instead of giving time for development in new paradigm, in new career stair. If the employee resigns his further ambition, he can be a successful associate in the previous position. We don't exclude that it is not easy just to renounce somebody's ambition. Certainly to keep somebody in the relevant crisis and the constructive support is not only the responsibility of selection but also the actual superior. As this study suggest crisis analysis can help to recognise the mentioned blocks, frustrations. If we can recognise the connection between these frustrations and the positions and we understand relations with the career stairs and their related crisis, we can give a better prognosis for compliance. This prognosis considers the investment risks of personnel development, although it is not excluded that the descriptions about the candidates are useful for the superiors during the training and development of them by showing the possible focus. So what kind of added value can be declared with the new aspect of career crisis analysis compared to the other used and mentioned selection methods? It is not or not just for making a "better" distinction between the candidates, but it aims to interpret the skill of bringing to surface of giftedness, mobilization of potentials, manifest the practical experience of talent. The describing dynamic of this progress is the point. It is more than feasible that the concentrated time with full of efforts people spend in the appropriate role of the position living the necessary thinking paradigm of it which helps to unlock the potentials and evolving the competence. It can happen if the employee experiences the load of the challenge. If this role is shuffled off because of a frustration reduction than the candidate tries to solve the leadership problems without leadership, the strategic tasks without future orientation with an approach of a lots of present time operative actions. One of the assessors had an expressive phrase describing this dilemma of the people: "There is no time for knitting up the shoe laces because it is time to run now!". As long as the candidate tries to meet the expectation with a wrong attitude, thinking paradigm but with another that belongs to a previous career stair, only his or her olden sills, routines and competencies are evolving, however the probable failures can even increase the frustration. This kind of frustration with the highest peak in the second stage of the crises' progress (Q2) can be a divide point because it can increase the risk of the regression but it can provoke the new paradigm. Sometimes it depends of the shifting mechanisms or the attitudes of the person as we saw in the results. Successful employees can speed up the developing their new competences by spending as much time in the challenging new position with its new role, with standing all the belonging stress where only the new competencies could help for the solution as possible. However development over the comfort zone turns into routine after a while. This stage is descripted the fourth stage of career stairs, which is called "won crisis" stage. The one who stays deep inside this comfort zone in connection with his development understandably keeps his hidden competencies on the level of potentials. The term "crisis" could lead to misunderstanding along some people because in not scientific language it contains some negative tone. However it looks like that the new challenges provoke the development but only if the employee goes deep enough into this crisis with all the dilemmas and frustrations of it. As in the personality development model of Erikson (1956) crises seem to be risky but very useful also in the career path. Trying to avoid them could lead to avoid the development itself or regression. It would be interesting from the scientific point of view that what could happen with the validation if a team measured only the competencies and this team recommended the candidate to appoint, while the crisis analytic assessment method rejected a candidate. It didn't come to that on the one hand because the economical stake of it wouldn't have endured the risk. On the other hand it would be very difficult to create clear circumstances to compare two appointed candidates (the rejected one and the recommended one according to crisis analysis), because it would need same challenge, very similar positions, same superior etc.

## FUTURE RESEARCH DIRECTIONS

Usage of results can be manifold. In selection recognising the crisis and its progress could be useful for assessing the optimal candidate and give keys for the further coaching and development. A progressed crisis can predict a good chance for paying the investment of appointing a candidate. In leadership supporting the subordinates could get some hint from crisis analysis for better improving in development and performance. The results can be useful for candidates, employees with career ambitions if they understand the nature of appearing stress instead of avoiding it. And finally all these outcomes can be utilize in a company at career and talent management programs. If the selection is working by considering the crisis analysis or without that but on the basis of manifested competence, than it could be a progressive approach to develop and challenge the talented, ambitious employees with the requirement of the aspired position before the appointment to progress the crisis and the new paradigm to an appropriate level. It can happen with the conscious support of the leader or by own initiative.

## CONCLUSION

Finally to conclude the terms of giftedness, talent, potential and competence we have introduced a new dimension that could provoke the development such as crisis and career stair. After trying to use the differentiation of mentioned researchers on giftedness and talent (Renzulli, 1979; Gagné, 1985) we have recognised that talent cannot be the end of the development process. We needed to define a middle term for a recognised and maybe trained state of a capability before bringing it to surface. That's why we agreed with Gagné (1985 to 2013), in the definition of giftedness as an inner, hidden skill. As this giftedness is being recognised there is a few opportunities to manage it to improve it to call it talent, but it seems that the talent itself can structure its element according to the development and the requirements of the environment. Considering our results we think that this term should be used for a recognised, but not manifest state of the capability. To bring this to surface something more is needed. As it is proven by our results the practical experience is a must to really unlock the talent itself. This paper tried to describe the way as it happens. We had to update the terms for that putting potential and competence to a possible place among the range of notions. The company that provided the background for the study uses the term of potential as a complex of different talent elements; and competence as a referenced, proved experience in practice. However we can fully agree with the model of Gagné (1985), but we need to point out that the catalyst process is returning again and again on different levels of career stair. Furthermore the basic unit of development – let's call it talent – changes. Potential as a seed of a competence as the companies us it in practice is a structured complex of different talents or talent elements. For example if we identify giftedness as out of box thinking without control, recognition of genuine ideas, it can develop to creative thinking according to the model of Gagné. It can further develop to creativity as a talent throw some catalyst factors. This study would like to point out that the process itself does not end with talent. To manifest it to a useful think for a company or for an own entrepreneur it has to improve to the level of innovation. Being innovative is a much more complex skill than creativity on talent level. Creativity has to face with for example the analytic and critical part of the circumstances, needs to be restructured and clog together with other talent elements such as communication, assertiveness, stress resistance, planning potentials etc. This is a kind of crisis which could have progressive or regressive outcome. Only the progressive outcome guarantees the compliance. We suggest using talent as an intermediate term between giftedness and compliance because it could be an outcome of evolving giftedness. However, the reconstruction of talent could be an input of further development process such as career development. That's the area where the potential of a practical complex competence comes to surface. The catalytic circumstances can effect on different levels which can be linked to career stairs. From that view the compliance is a continuous winning of changing crises during the career path, although only these crises bring the giftedness, talent, potential as a more complex talent to practical surface.

We need to mention the limits of this research. Large pattern would be useful to prove the results with certainty, but finding similar positions to ensure the pure variables is always difficult, moreover these are maximum similar. Due to the interest of business, setting up a correct control group always has practical limits at a company.

## REFERENCES

Barrick, M. R., & Mount, M. K. (1991). The big five personality dimensions and job performance: A meta-analysis. *Personnel Psychology*, *44*(1), 1–26. doi:10.1111/j.1744-6570.1991.tb00688.x

Bőgel, G., & Tomka, J. (2010). Tudás és tehetség. *CEO Magazine, 11*(3), 34-35.

Bognár, T. (2013a). Crisis analytic assessment methods in interviews and assessment centers. In *Proceeding of 28th Workshop on Strategic Human Resource Management*. Copenhagen, Denmark: EIASM.

Bognár, T. (2013b) Operative regression or strategic thinking – A crisis that leads to innovation or stagnation. In *Proceeding of The Economies of Balkan and Eastern Europe Countries in the changed world 2013*. Istanbul, Turkey.

Carless, S. A. (2009). Psychological testing for selection purposes: A guide to evidence-based practice for human resource professionals. *International Journal of Human Resource Management*, *20*(12), 2517–2532. doi:10.1080/09585190903363821

Chambers, E., Foulon, M., Handfield-Jones, H., Hankin, S., & Michaels, E. III. (1998). The war for talent. *The McKinsey Quarterly*, *3*, 44–57.

Czeizel, E. (1997). *Sors és Tehetség*. Budapest, Hungary: Fitt Image–Minerva Kiadó.

Duden. (2001). *Herkunftswörterbuch: Ethymologie der deutschen Sprache*. Auflage, Germany: Bibliographisches Institut.

Erikson, E. H. (1956). The Problem of Ego Identity. *Journal of the American Psychoanalytic Association*, *4*(1), 56–121. doi:10.1177/000306515600400104 PMID:13286157

Gagné, F. (1985). Giftedness and talent: Reexamining a reexamination of the definitions. *Gifted Child Quarterly*, *29*(3), 103–112. doi:10.1177/001698628502900302

Gagné, F. (2009). Building gifts into talents: Detailed overview of the DMGT 2.0. In Leadingchange in gifted education: The festschrift of Dr. Joyce VanTassel-Baska. Waco, TX: Prufrock Press.

Gagné, F. (2013). The DMGT: Changes within, beneath, and beyond. *Talent Development & Excellence*, *5*(1), 5–19.

Galton, F. (1869). *Hereditary Genius: An Inquiry into its Laws and Consequences*. London, UK: Mac-Millan. doi:10.1037/13474-000

Goffin, R. D., Rothstein, M. G., & Johnston, N. G. (1996). Personality testing and the assessment center: Incremental validity for managerial selection. *The Journal of Applied Psychology*, *81*(6), 746–756. doi:10.1037/0021-9010.81.6.746

Gyarmathy, É. (2006). *A tehetség*. Budapest, Hungary: ELTE Eötvös Kiadó.

Jones, A., P. & Long, H. B., & Drakeley, R. (1991). Attempting to improve the validity of a well-established assessment centre. *Journal of Occupational Psychology, 64*(1), 1–21.

Krause, D. E., & Gebert, D. (2003). A comparison of assessment center practices in organizations in German-speaking regions and the United States. *International Journal of Selection and Assessment*, *11*(4), 297–312. doi:10.1111/j.0965-075X.2003.00253.x

Marland, S. P. (1972). *Education of the gifted and talented: Report to the Congress of the United States by the U.S. commissioner of education*. Washington, DC: Government Printing Office.

Martin, J., & Schmidt, C. (2010). How to Keep Your Top Talent. *Harvard Business Review*, *12*(9), 6–15.

Michaels, E., Handfield- Jones, H., & Axelrod, B. (2001). *The war for talent*. Boston. MA: Harvard Business School Press.

Mihályné & Sándorné. (2008). *Tehetséggondozás*. Szarvas, Hungary: Szarvaspress Nyomda.

Mönks, F. J., & Boxtel, H. W. (2000). A Rensulli-modell kiterjesztése és alkalmazása serdülőkorban. In A tehetségfejlesztés pszichológiája (pp. 67-82). Debrecen, Hungary: Kossuth Egyetemi Kiadó.

Oláh, A., & Gyöngyösiné Kiss, E. (2007). A személyiség fogalma és vizsgálati módszerei: mérés, kutatás, elmélet. In *Vázlatok a személyiségről–A személyiség-lélektan alapvető irányzatainak tükrében*. Budapest, Hungary: Új Mandátum Könyvkiadó.

Orosz, G., & Szukics, N. (2012). A társas összehasonlítás egyéni különbségei. *Pszichológia (Budapest)*, *32*(4), 361–378. doi:10.1556/Pszicho.32.2012.4.4

Petrány, V. (2009). Versenyelőny-e a tehetségmenedzsment? Tehetséggondozás vagy tehetségvásárlás?. *Munkaügyi Szemle, 53*(1), 97-104.

Rácz, I. (2013). Business success in the mirror of talent. In *Proceedings of 2nd Workshop on Talent Management*. Brussels, Belgium: EIASM.

Rácz, I. (2014). Mentori szerep a tehetséggondozási projektekben. In XVII. Apáczai napok. Tudományos Konferencia: Mobilis in mobile. Győr, Hungary: NYME Apáczai Csere János Kar.

Rácz, I. & Magyar-Stifter, V. (2015). Knowledge Definition and Transfer by Talented Intellectual Workers. *Acta Oeconomica Universitatis Selye, 4*(2), 162-171.

Renzulli, J. S. (1979). *What makes giftedness: A reexamination of the definition of the gifted and talented*. Ventura, CA: Ventura County Superintendent of Schools Office.

Ritz, A., & Thom, N. (2011). *Talent Management*. Wiesbaden, Germany: Gabler Verlag. doi:10.1007/978-3-8349-6954-5

Terman, L. M., & Oden, M. H. (1947). *Genetic Studies of Genius. IV. The Gifted Child Groups Up*. Stanford, CA: Stanford University Press.

Terman, L. M., & Oden, M. H. (1959). *Genetic Studies of Genius. V. The Gifted Group at Mid-Life*. Stanford, CA: Stanford University Press.

Thom, N. (2003). Retention Management für High Potentials. In Jahrbuch Personalentwicklung und Weiterbildung – Praxis und Perspektivven (pp. 237-247).

Törestad, B., Magnusson, D., & Oláh, A. (1990). Coping, control, and experience of anxiety: An interactional perspective. *Anxiety Research*, *3*(1), 1–16. doi:10.1080/08917779008248737

Ulrich, D. (2006). The talent trifecta. *Workforce Management*, *10*(September), 32–33.

## KEY TERMS AND DEFINITIONS

**Competence:** A complex range of some experienced skill. Can have different meaning in companies.

**Compliance:** A candidate's success in a position both from his and the company's view.

**Crisis:** A main task to solve in a stage or a career stair. The development depends on it.

**Giftedness:** A hidden skill or ability before the recognition.

**Paradigm:** A thinking frame that provides model problems, solutions for a while until a new frame replaces it with a new scope of validity as Kuhn described in 1962 (Kuhn, 2012). In our approach the challenges in different levels provide new thinking frame and new requirement for the employees.

**Potential:** Can be interpret from the perspective of exact practical requirement. A hidden rudiment of a defined competence. Definitely a locked antecedent of a competence.

**Talent:** Recognised or managed skill but without the practical routine, a developed giftedness.

## ENDNOTES

[1]    The categories of U.S. Office of Education for Giftedness: general intellectual ability, particular scholastic aptitude, creative and productiv thinkin skills, abilities in leadership, visual and expressive arts, the psychomotor domain.

[2]    Learning peers: who have accumulated a similar amount of learning time from either current or past training. (Gagné, 2013, 1.)

# Chapter 11
# Knowledge Management and Software Development Organization:
## What Is the Challenge?

**Marcello Chedid**
*University of Aveiro, Portugal*

**Leonor Teixeira**
*University of Aveiro, Portugal*

## ABSTRACT

*Software development organization (SDO) is a kind of knowledge-intensive business and their large majority is small and medium enterprise (SME) facing similar challenges of large ones. The diversity and complexity of the SDO environment makes knowledge the fundamental element in the software development process, which strengthens the importance of an effective knowledge management process. The software development process involves multidisciplinary teams, and the various working meetings that occur during a project are conducive to generate and share a lot of knowledge, in particular tacit knowledge. The use of a knowledge management process that enables to manage tacit knowledge will define the difference between a good SDO performance and the best SDO performance. This chapter aims to present an exploratory study based on literature review, with the aim of identifying the main challenge of knowledge management in the SDO context. The authors also aim to address some new research directions.*

## INTRODUCTION

As a knowledge-intensive organization, the most valuable asset of a software development organization (SDO) is the knowledge of its employees (Lee-Kelley, Blackman, & Hurst, 2007; Walz, Elam, & Curtis, 1993). Consequently, knowledge management assumes a vital role in the software development process of any SDO.

DOI: 10.4018/978-1-5225-1642-2.ch011

Knowledge has become one of the most valuable resources for businesses, representing an important driver of strategic capability and competitive advantage (Johannenssen, Olsen, & Olaisen, 1999; Kasemsap, 2015). Nahapiet and Ghoshal (1998) added that the advantage obtained by the organizations depends largely on the ability of creating and sharing knowledge.

According to the classical division introduced by the Hungarian chemist and philosopher Polanyi (1966) and widely spread by Nonaka et al. (1996), knowledge can be explicit or tacit.

Explicit knowledge is a type of knowledge that can be easily codified, articulated, documented and archived. While tacit knowledge although being at the base of the creation of the knowledge, is complex, it is not easy to be codified, and presents some difficulty in its reproduction in a document or in a database.

Knowledge management is the process that enables the sharing, capture and application of knowledge from the individual to the group and further to organizational level (Rasmussen & Nielsen, 2011).

The current SDO environment is characterized by increased diversity and complexity in software development projects. Due to this environment, software development process involves multidisciplinary teams (Huzita et al., 2012) once a member of a team no longer has all the necessary knowledge (Desouza, 2003; Walz et al., 1993). The several working meetings that occur throughout a project are conducive to generate and share a lot of tacit knowledge.

But in the meantime, despite the importance of tacit knowledge generated in the software development process, several authors (e.g., Huzita et al., 2012; Johnson & Donnelly, 2013) pointed to the fact that due to lack of proper mechanisms that allow sharing, identification and capture of this type of knowledge, most of them is wasted resulting in unavailability for future uses or projects (Johnson & Donnelly, 2013).

However, what is the challenge of the knowledge management in SDO?

According to some authors, it is possible to suggest that the main challenge of the SDO is developing mechanisms to make the tacit knowledge more explicit as possible (Johnson & Donnelly, 2013; Shull et al., 2002).

Through a literature review on the knowledge management in SDO, the purpose of this chapter is to present an exploratory study that describes the main findings that may respond to the aforementioned question. The chapter also aims to address some further research directions.

This chapter is organized as follows. In the next section, the authors briefly introduce SDO and knowledge management. The following section, based on the literature reviewed, provides a critical discussion of the knowledge management in software development environment. Following this section, the authors discuss about the main challenges of knowledge management in the SDO context. Finally, in the remainder sections, the authors point future research directions, and conclude.

## BACKGROUND: THEORETICAL FOUNDATIONS ON SOFTWARE DEVELOPMENT ORGANIZATION AND KNOWLEDGE MANAGEMENT

In this section, the chapter outlines a brief theoretical foundation of the study. The first part covers the SDO. The second part discusses knowledge management and its processes.

### Software Development Organization

SDO is a kind of business typically based on knowledge-intensive activity (Aurum, Daneshgar, & Ward, 2008; Lee-Kelley et al., 2007; Mehta, Hall, & Byrd, 2014; Walz et al., 1993) where knowledge is the raw material (Walz et al., 1993) and the intellectual capital constitutes the major asset (Huzita et al., 2012; Peters, 1992). Due to this characteristic, according to Becerra-Fernandez and Sabherwal (2010) this kind of organization is valued at three to eight times its financial capital. Applying the "Tobin's q ratio" – relationship between a company's market value and its physical assets – Swart and Kinnie (2003) compared that whereas for the SDO the ratio is of 7.00, for the traditional companies the ratio is of nearly 1.00. Currently, SDO are distinguished as a business in increasing economic importance (Dubé & Robey, 1999; Segelod & Jordan, 2004).

The large majority of SDO is characterized as small and medium enterprise (SME) (Richardson & Von Wangenheim, 2007; Savolainen & Ahonen, 2015) and works in scenery of shortage of resources. However, small and medium SDO face similar challenges of large ones (Richardson & Von Wangenheim, 2007).

In the modern society, the software is constantly present and is widely used in several areas (Aurum et al., 2008) that makes the current environment of SDO diverse and complex (Huzita et al., 2012), causing to the SDO pressure for higher-performing products, and more frequent faster releases (Dubé & Robey, 1999).

Software development process is differently at every organization (Bogue, 2006) and represents a set of activities that occurs by processing of large amount of knowledge from different areas (Robillard, 1999), and that occurs in teams (Ryan & O'Connor, 2013). Each team member has a different expertise (Pee, Kankanhalli, & Kim, 2010) and makes a large number of decisions (Shull et al., 2002), that requires development of strong personal and team relationships (Nahapiet & Ghoshal, 1998).

The term knowledge-worker was first used by Peter Drucker in his 1959 book, "Landmarks of Tomorrow" (Drucker, 1994), and includes all these members of software development teams (Ryan & O'Connor, 2013). According to Lee-Kelley et al. (2007), the term is also frequently used to define "any employee possessing specialist knowledge or know-how who is involved in consultancy based on their specialist knowledge or know-how, or research and development work for new products, services or processes" (2007, p. 205).

In the meantime, despite this environment and the evolution of new software development organizational arrangements (e.g., outsourcing, global software development, and open source) Aurum et al. (2008) considered that software development still needs to achieve a higher level of maturity.

## Knowledge Management

There is not common knowledge definition accepted and so knowledge is defined according to the context in which it is discussed (Girard & Girard, 2015; Gloet & Terziovski, 2004; Stenmark, 2001; Stoyanov, 2014). In Rowley's (2007) opinion, there is agreement among several authors that knowledge is an elusive concept which is difficult to define. However, regardless of the concept, knowledge always brings their respective truths and beliefs, judgments and expectations, methodologies, and know-how (Prieto, Revilla, & Rodríguez-Prado, 2009).

According to the classical division introduced by the Hungarian chemist and philosopher Polanyi (1966), and widely spread by Nonaka et al. (1996) knowledge can be explicit or tacit.

Explicit knowledge is a type of knowledge that can be easily codified, articulated, documented and archived, and usually, it is stored and expressed in the form of text, data, scientific formulae, maps, manuals and books, websites, etc. (Alavi & Leidner, 2001; Iacono, Nito, Esposito, Martinez, & Moschera, 2014; Nonaka & Konno, 1998; Polanyi, 1966; Santoro & Bierly, 2006; Seidler-de Alwis & Hartmann, 2008).

Tacit knowledge is the basis of knowledge creation, it is complex and not codified, and presents some difficulty in its reproduction in document or database. Smith (2001) reported that ninety percent of the knowledge in any organization is tacit knowledge and it is embedded and synthesized in peoples' heads.

In general, the literature mentions the existence of two dimensions of tacit knowledge: (i) technical and (ii) cognitive (Alavi & Leidner, 2001; Nonaka & Konno, 1998). The technical dimension is often referred to as expertise and consist of informal personal skills and crafts that apply to a specific context. The cognitive dimension refers of mental models, beliefs, ideals, values and paradigms, which are deeply ingrained in people. Nonaka and Konno (1998) suggested that while difficult to articulate, this cognitive dimension of tacit knowledge shapes the way each one person perceives the world.

In the Figure 1, based on Nonaka (2010), the authors summarized explicit and tacit knowledge .

*Figure 1. Explicit and tacit knowledge*
*Adapted from Nonaka (2010)*

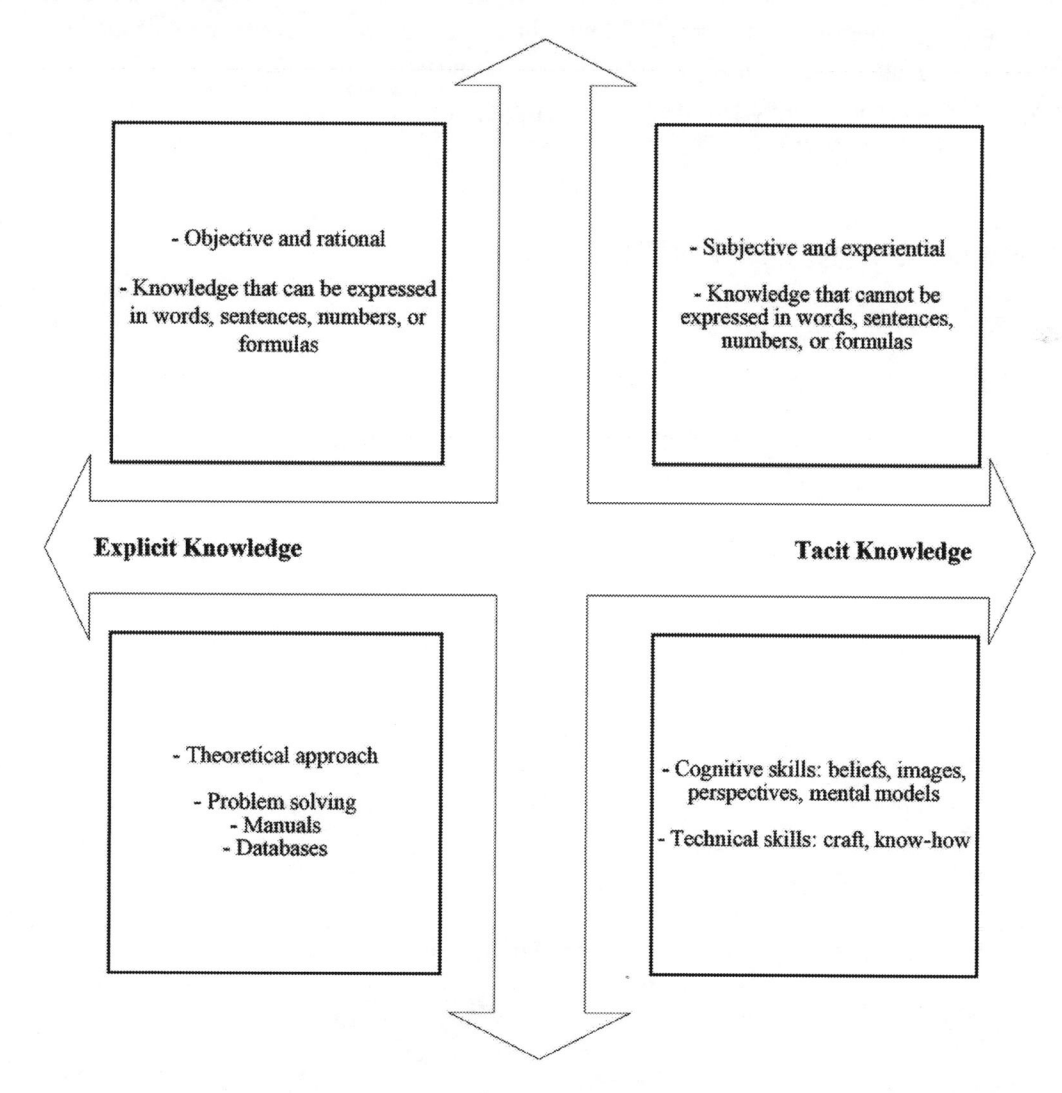

After the information management, a neutral and normative system in the organizations (Gloet & Terziovski, 2004), knowledge management emerges as a distinct area of study, establishing as a significant source of competitive advantage and as one of the most important resources in the capacity of progress of modern organizations (Mårtensson, 2000; Pekka-Economou & Hadjidema, 2011). Several authors consider that new knowledge and innovation are heavily dependent on knowledge management practices (Gloet, 2006; Inkinen, 2016). Knowledge management practices act as a key driver of innovation performance.

Knowledge management expanded rapidly in various fields such as psychology, management science, sociology, strategy, production engineering, etc. This wide diversity of areas transforms knowledge management in a complex and multi-faceted concept (Alavi & Leidner, 2001), reflecting the wide range of definitions, leading in the absence of a standard and universally accepted definition (Chen, 2006; Kakabadse, Kakabadse, & Kouzmin, 2003; Sadeghi & Salemi, 2013).

Although the absence of consensus regarding the knowledge management definition, the Davenport and Prusak's (1998) definition is one of the most cited in the literature (Metaxiotis, Ergazakis, & Psarras, 2005): "knowledge management is concerned with the exploitation and development of the knowledge assets of an organization with a view to furthering the organization's objectives."

Knowledge management is based on three main pillars:

1. Technology,
2. People, and
3. Process (Kalkan, 2008; Prieto et al., 2009) (Figure 2).

*Figure 2. Knowledge management main pillars*

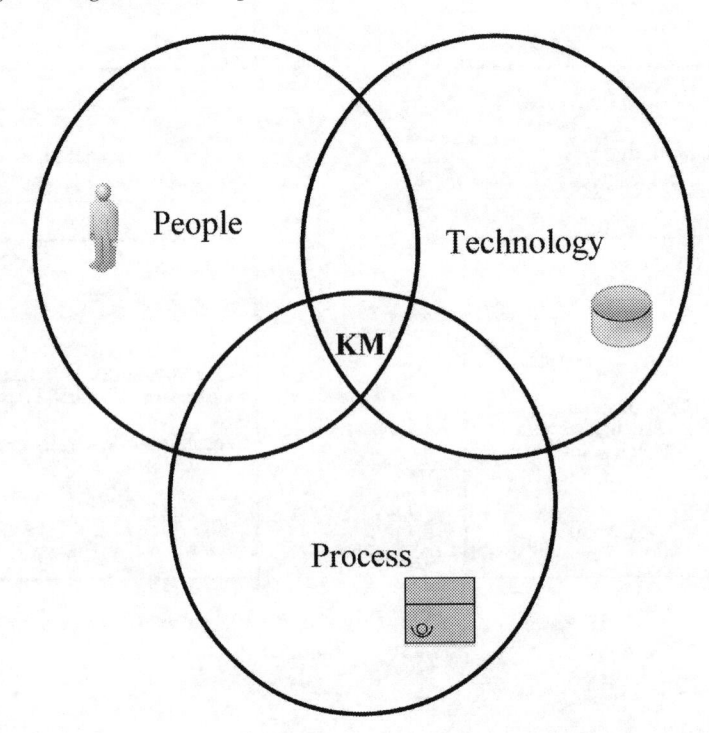

The great discussion has been about which of these pillars is the main facilitator for the knowledge management. Considering that a knowledge management system is not an automatic data processing system (Tuomi, 1999), the three mentioned pillars are important for a successful knowledge management and the focus should not be on any one element.

The strategy for developing a successful knowledge management involves a range of enabling conditions (Prieto et al., 2009) which would need to be managed to support different types of knowledge processes. In her article, Mårtensson (2000) presented a set of critical elements to develop and implement a knowledge management system, and she pointed out that in order to reach success the strategy must be taken into account both the creation and the leverage of knowledge.

As a result of the wide range of knowledge management definitions, the literature presents different sets of processes that comprise a complete knowledge management system. In general, each process is involved in creation, sharing or change of the state of knowledge. For example, Alavi and Leidner (2001) considered the processes of creating, storing/retrieving, transferring, and applying knowledge. In the standpoint of Grover and Davenport (2001), the processes are generation, codification, transfer, and realization. Nielsen (2006) identified eight key processes: creation, acquisition, capture, assembly, sharing, integration, leverage, and exploitation of (new) knowledge. Hoffman et al. (2008) indicated the processes of capture, learning, discovery, knowledge, and application. In the Nonaka et al.' (1996) opinion, the processes are socialization, externalization, combination and internalization.

In this chapter the authors consider three processes based on Rasmussen and Nielsen (2011):

1.  Knowledge sharing and transfer;
2.  Knowledge capture;
3.  Knowledge application.

## Knowledge Sharing and Transfer

As in the Kang et al.'s (2010) statement, knowledge by itself is not a useful resource that creates value and competitive advantage until it can be shared and transferred. Knowledge emerges from sharing knowledge in a social context (Jakubik, 2008) resulting of interactions between people.

Several times in the literature the terms sharing and transfer are interchangeable and appear with the same sense, or with other denominations (e.g. disseminate, distribute, exchange, translation) to identify the migration process of knowledge of a situation to another, i.e. between or within people, organizations or countries (Huzita et al., 2012).

The term sharing of knowledge has a tendency to refer more to exchanges of knowledge between people, while the transferring of knowledge expression is used more often in exchanges between units of the same organization or between other organizations (Argote & Ingram, 2000; Paulin & Suneson, 2012). The chapter's authors also suggest that sharing of knowledge is also associated to tacit knowledge and transferring of knowledge is used in the situation of explicit knowledge (Johannenssen et al., 1999).

The successful sharing and transfer of knowledge is an important factor in knowledge management performance (Wang & Noe, 2010).

## Knowledge Capture

Knowledge needs to be captured, stored and then disseminated (Huzita et al., 2012). The knowledge capture is a key process of preserving and formalizing knowledge (Becerra-Fernandez & Sabherwal, 2010) and the result is the inclusion of the knowledge into the stock of knowledge. The process of capture has various methods and the selected method depends on the type of knowledge. The process of capture must be disposed of properly, responding to the challenge of capturing only the relevant and valuable knowledge (Nielsen, 2006). Once captured, knowledge should be continuously evaluated to ensure their quality and relevance.

Although the knowledge capture is one of the primary aims of knowledge management, Hoffman et al. (2008) highlighted that some organizations have failed by applying weak methods for this process.

## Knowledge Application

This is the process of knowledge management that justifies the existence all of others. It makes no sense to create knowledge, capture it, share it and download it, if not be disseminated and applied. Starbuck (1992) argued that merely storing knowledge does not preserve it.

The importance of applied knowledge is due to be specialized knowledge (Drucker, 1994). The ability to disseminate and apply knowledge enables the opportunity of competitive advantage and becomes more important than the ability to create new knowledge (Alavi & Leidner, 2001; Nielsen, 2006).

New knowledge is disseminated through several channels available among the members of a social system (Graham et al., 2006) promoting their application (Becerra-Fernandez & Sabherwal, 2010). Social system is considered a set of interactions between people who have connection between themselves and that belong to the same context (Figure 3).

## KNOWLEDGE MANAGEMENT IN SOFTWARE DEVELOPMENT ENVIRONMENT

The current environment of SDO is of increasing diversity and complexity. Software development process is differently at every organization and may work just for a specific environment and situation (Bogue, 2006). Recently this situation has been exacerbated by the evolution of new software development organizational arrangements (e.g., outsourcing, global software development, and open source). Bresnen et al. (2003) highlighted that the need to carry out short-term projects has also caused restrictions of opportunities for innovations in the software development process.

Software development is a highly knowledge-intensive activity (Desouza, 2003) that processes large amount of knowledge from various domains (Robillard, 1999). Knowledge management assumes an important role for any SDO in providing solutions, and improving of performance (Fehér & Gábor, 2006; Meehan & Richardson, 2002; Rus & Lindvall, 2002).

According its organizational culture, and business strategy, SDO must define a strategic approach to managing knowledge (Aurum et al., 2008). Researchers have suggested some approaches, however several of them point to the codification and personalisation strategies (Desouza, 2003; Fehér & Gábor, 2006; Hansen, Nohria, & Tierney, 1999). Fehér and Gábor (2006) reinforced that typical knowledge-intensive organization, like SDO, must choose between codification and personalisation strategies.

*Figure 3. Social system*

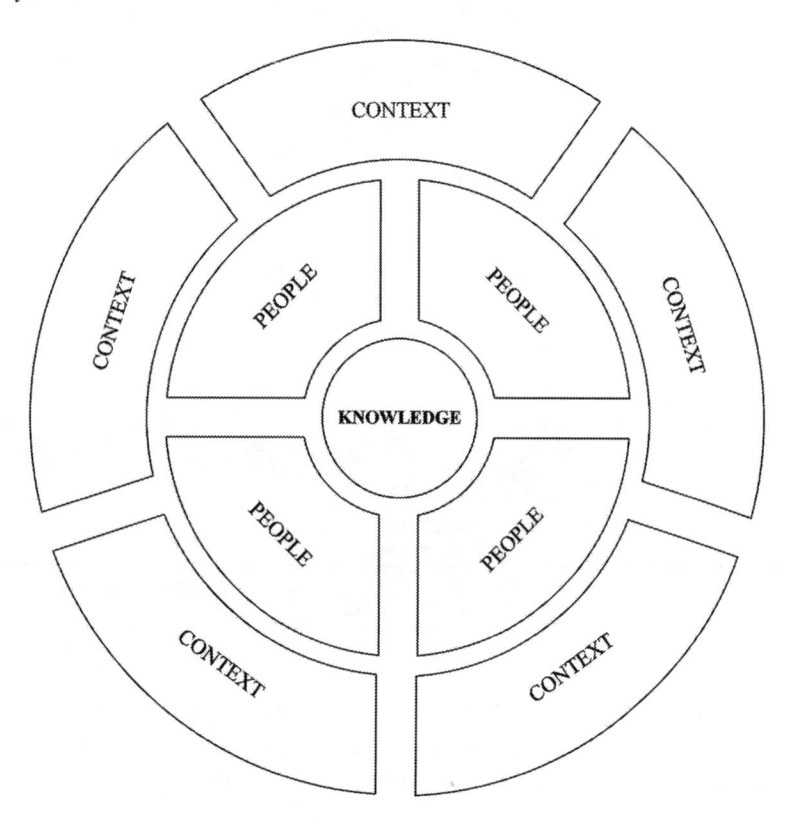

Codification strategy centers on the technology and explicit knowledge. Knowledge is codified and stored in databases, and it becomes available to be accessed and used easily by everybody (Fehér & Gábor, 2006; Hansen et al., 1999). Hansen et al. (1999, p. 2) called it "people-to-documents" strategy.

In contrast, personalization strategy is called people-to-people approach (Desouza, 2003) where tacit knowledge is the focus (Fehér & Gábor, 2006). Knowledge is shared through face-to-face interactions like brainstorming sessions, meetings and conversations, where expertise and experience have important role (Desouza, 2003; Fehér & Gábor, 2006; Hansen et al., 1999). According to Hansen et al. (1999), the most important in this strategy is a system that allows people to find the right people, in other words, a system that maps who holds the knowledge which is not fully documented in the organization. Several authors (Becerra-Fernandez & Sabherwal, 2010; Bjørnson & Dingsøyr, 2008; Erden, von Krogh, & Nonaka, 2008; Grover & Davenport, 2001) named this system as "yellow pages".

In Robillard's view "before the development of a software the knowledge have to be described and organized in a specific knowledge structure" (1999, p. 87) and he added that "software development is the processing of knowledge in a very focused way"(1999, p. 92). Robillard (1999) called knowledge-crystallization the process of transformation knowledge into a language that can be read and executed by the computer (Figure 4).

As a function of the SDO environment characteristics, Edwards (2003) argued that knowledge management in SDO is somewhat distance from mainstream. Bresnen et al. (2003) considered that knowledge management in context like existing in SDO faces many challenges due to discontinuities in methods of organization and flows of personnel, materials and information.

*Figure 4. Knowledge-crystallization*
Based on Robillard (1999)

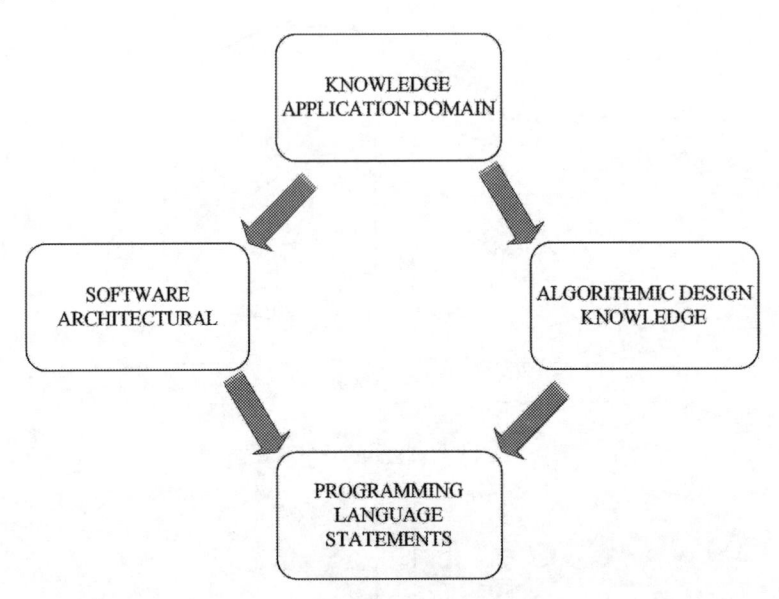

Due to the fact that just one person does not have the domain all the knowledge necessary for a project (Desouza, 2003; Walz et al., 1993) these activities are developed by multidisciplinary teams (Huzita et al., 2012). However, the composition of teams change very quickly (Edwards, 2003) as a result of the different nature of projects.

It is important to point out that SDO is a knowledge-intensive organization. According to Starbuck (1992), knowledge-intensive organizations have a stock of expertise (knowledge) which is the sum of different expertise of each team member (Pee et al., 2010). This stock has unusually complex combination of different layers (Edwards, 2003), and requires development of strong personal and team relationships (Mehta et al., 2014; Nahapiet & Ghoshal, 1998), in order to share and to leverage the expertise at the project and organization level (Shull et al., 2004).

These social interactions involve both explicit and tacit knowledge, and play an important role in sharing and creation of knowledge. These social processes in interaction with other specific mechanisms, including technology, make the knowledge more dynamic (Aurum et al., 2008; Bjørnson & Dingsøyr, 2008), requiring each team member keep up to date thus avoiding obsolescence of knowledge (Desouza, 2003).

However, the performance of the development team is affected by a number of important organizational and structural factors that act either as barriers or as facilitators for the full use of knowledge management (Bresnen et al., 2003; Ryan & O'Connor, 2013). Among the barriers or facilitators pointed out by the authors of the reviewed articles, the process of communication seems to be the most relevant, since it is the most cited (Table 1). The communication barrier is exacerbated by the utilization of multidisciplinary teams and also when occurring geographical dispersion of the sites which may difficult the actions like face-to-face (Bresnen et al., 2003), reduce the absorptive capacity (Mehta et al., 2014), introduce cultural diversity and background within the team (Schilling & Klamma, 2010) and hinder the establishment of a common vocabulary and meanings in the process of sharing (Barksdale & McCrickard, 2012).

*Table 1. Barrier / facilitator*

| Barrier / Facilitator | Issue | Reference |
|---|---|---|
| Organizational structure | Economies of scale in the use of certain mechanisms | (1) |
| Cultural context and climate for change | Continuing support across the organization whole | (1) |
| Skill and capabilities | Motivation and personal skills in development social contacts and informal networks | (1); (2); (5) |
| Communications, networks and information flows | Geographical dispersion of sites; common vocabulary and meanings | (1); (2); (3); (4); (5) |
| Technological mechanisms | Incentives and resources to use and up-date information | (1); (2) |
| Objectives and outputs | Clear set out | (1); (5) |
| **Legends:** (1) Bresnen et al. (2003); (2) Mehta et al. (2014); (3) Barksdale and McCrickard (2012) ; (4) Schilling and Klamma (2010); (5) Ryan and O'Connor (2013) | | |

This context associated with difficulty in developing and establishing stable routines, become critical success factors an effective knowledge sharing process (Aurum et al., 2008) based on a supportive culture of sharing (Edwards, 2003).

However, some authors (e.g., Aurum et al., 2008) and practioners have the opinion that the tools, techniques and methodologies currently employed by SDO are inadequate to implement an effective knowledge management model.

## Knowledge Sharing in Software Development Environment

As previously noted by the authors, in the wide literature on knowledge management is difficult to find a consensus that distinguish clearly sharing and transferring knowledge. The same is true in the software development domain with several authors diverging with regard to terminology and assumptions.

Knowledge sharing is a key process regarding to the knowledge-intensive context in general, and in particular within teams of software development (Ghobadi, 2015; Ryan & O'Connor, 2013). Considering that each team member has a different expertise (Pee et al., 2010) and that expert knowledge is mostly tacit (Ryan & O'Connor, 2013), knowledge sharing assumes increased importance in software development environment.

The Table 2 presents some relevant situations that reinforce the importance of knowledge sharing in software development environment pointed out by the authors in the literature examined.

The knowledge sharing process is not as simple and straightforward as it may seem. The process can present a number of challenges that depends on the context it happens. Shull et al. (2004) added that this situation can have impacts on the success of reuse of knowledge.

Due to the importance and complexity of knowledge sharing, Ghobadi (2015) enhanced the great and necessary effort of coordination and communication in all of software development stages.

Software is developed in teams where knowledge emerges in a social context from sharing of knowledge, resultant of several interactions within members of the team and stakeholders. The social context has an important role (Bresnen et al., 2003) in the knowledge sharing process, it is complex (Ryan & O'Connor, 2013), and needs to be encouraged and facilitated through all levels of the organization.

The social context is also very important for tacit to tacit exchange and may take place within and outside the organizations (Bresnen et al., 2003; Prieto et al., 2009)

*Table 2. The importance of knowledge sharing in SDO*

| Situation | Reference |
| --- | --- |
| Basis of the knowledge is often an individual | Edwards (2003) |
| Different projects – different teams | Edwards (2003) |
| Rapid turnover of staff | Edwards (2003) and Lee-Kelley et al. (2007) |
| Influence software development and ultimately overall | Lee-Kelley et al. (2007) |
| Eliciting both explicit and tacit knowledge | Ryan and O'Connor (2013) |
| Knowledge-intensive nature | Mehta et al. (2014) |
| Iterative development cycles | Ghobadi (2015) |
| Overcome the cultural and social challenges | Ghobadi (2015) |

Effectiveness and efficiency levels of team and consequently of organization is influenced by the extent knowledge that is shared and captured (Barksdale & McCrickard, 2012; Wang & Noe, 2010).

In recent literature review article Ghobadi (2015) has identified forty-four knowledge sharing drivers in software development teams and categorized them into four categories: people-related, structure-related, task-related, and technology-related. Nearly half of the drivers identified (twenty-one) were categorized as people-related. As people, Ghobadi (2015) considered users, managements, developers and other key stakeholders of the project.

Despite the software developers believe in the importance of knowledge sharing (Aurum et al., 2008), that process within software development team can be challenging. Knowledge sharing involves both explicit and tacit knowledge, although knowledge in software development process is almost all tacit. Tacit knowledge is an important factor in SDO, and may be situated and embedded within a social group or individuals, and context.

With the challenges of knowledge sharing in software development environment, Edwards (2003) argued that the effective process is possible and that a combination of technology, people and process-based solutions is best approach. Edwards complemented saying that the most important aspect is to develop the overall culture that encourages knowledge sharing.

## Tacit Knowledge in Software Development Environment

According to Lethbridge et al. (2005), people create software, people maintain software, people evolve software. Faced with this statement, and considering that people are rich in tacit knowledge, it is possible to complement the Segelod and Jordan's opinion (2004) and suggest that software is essentially tacit knowledge in codified form. The best use of tacit knowledge can ensure a more efficient and effective solution creation process (Bierly, Damanpour, & Santoro, 2009), having an important role in a SDO's performance (Ryan & O'Connor, 2013).

Although several researchers across several schools highlight the necessity to focus also on tacit knowledge and not exclusively on explicit knowledge (Bjørnson & Dingsøyr, 2008; Leonard & Sensiper, 1998; Rus & Lindvall, 2002), the debate is still too focused on explicit knowledge with few references on tacit knowledge (Seidler-de Alwis & Hartmann, 2008). Clark et al. (2015) alerted to the fact that massive investments that organizations have been made in systems foster the capture of explicit knowledge but shift the focus away from tacit knowledge.

Tacit knowledge is often fundamental for the interpretation of the explicit knowledge. Explicit knowledge without tacit insight quickly loses its meaning (Seidler-de Alwis & Hartmann, 2008; Shull et al., 2004), that is to say that this type of knowledge is inseparable from tacit knowledge. In general, both types of knowledge are not completely distinct and depending on the context or a specific situation each shared knowledge presents different degrees of tacitness and explicitness (Ambrosini & Bowman, 2001; Wong & Radcliffe, 2000). Wong and Radcliffe (2000) named "knowledge spectrum" the different composition of tacit and explicit knowledge of each shared knowledge, i.e., the different knowledges have different degrees of composition of both knowledges. In a similar way, Ambrosini and Bowman (2001) presented which they call "degree of tacitness", where knowledge can encompass a range of different levels of tacitness, and this range may be from deeply ingrained tacit to completely explicit. The Figure 5 shows the two models so that they can be compared.

Tacit knowledge can be shared in a number of ways, including coexistence, interactions between groups, oral communication and informal contact. According to Webber (1993), conversation is the best way for discovering what the group know, sharing what they know, and create new knowledge. Several studies have demonstrated that the contacts of the type face-to-face and informal conversations are responsible for the acquisition of up to two-thirds of knowledge, arising only a third from documents (Davenport & Prusak, 1998).

If on the one hand the multidisciplinary teams are an advantage for developing higher performance products and faster releases (Dubé & Robey, 1999), on the other hand the type of team presents barriers in the effectively sharing knowledge within the team (Barksdale & McCrickard, 2012).

Desouza (2003) in his article indicated three key issues that may inhibit knowledge sharing of tacit knowledge in development teams (Table 3).

The Agile Manifesto emphasize the importance of tacit knowledge sharing through social interaction (Ryan & O'Connor, 2013), reinforcing that the face-to-face communication is the most effective way for software development team.

*Figure 5. Knowledge spectrum and degree of tacitness*

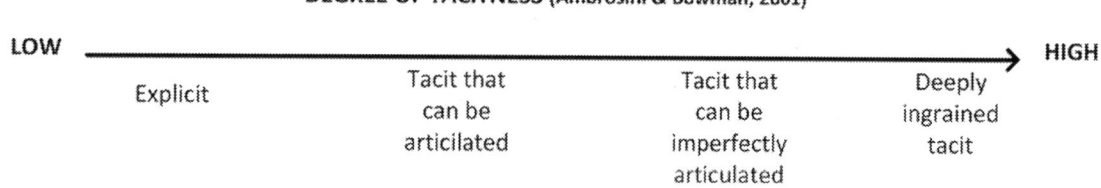

237

*Table 3. Barriers on sharing tacit knowledge*

| Issues | | Remedies |
|---|---|---|
| Resistance to be known as an expert | Once titled an expert works to one's disadvantage and hampers rather than advances one's career | Organization must encourage a knowledge-sharing culture by clearly defining incentives |
| Required knowledge cannot be captured and categorized | Knowledge is highly tacit in nature, much of which cannot be articulated well or be put in explicit format, the cost of doing so on average outweighs perceived benefits | Knowledge management system should encourage dialogue between individuals rather than just point to repositories |
| Richness of alternative knowledge exchange mediums | A key for exchange of tacit knowledge (socialization), knowledge shared surpasses knowledge in information systems | Information technology is only one means to foster knowledge and may not be a true indicator of knowledge sharing behavior |

Adapted from Desouza (2003)

Patton (2002) considered that although close collaboration is exhausting, when team finish the development process, the team's tacit knowledge is "irreplaceable". Ryan and O'Connor (2013) defined team tacit knowledge as " the aggregation of articulable tacit, individual, goal driven, expert knowledge to the team-level, where different members of the team possess different aspects of tacit knowledge" (2013, p. 1616) . In the Ryan and O'Connor's (2013) opinion the team's relationships are more associated with team performance than technical factors on successful projects.

Currently, the evolution of new software development organizational arrangements, and digital communication replacing face-to-face communication have challenged the stakeholders to effective transfer of tacit knowledge as well as forms of mitigate the effects of loss of this kind of knowledge. In Clark et al.'s opinion, "there is a lack of the role tacit knowledge plays in teams collaborating digitally" (2015, p. 113). In general, existing literature addresses tacit knowledge utilization in traditional contexts.

## WHAT IS THE CHALLENGE?

Software is developed from intensive and interactive processes within the team members and knowledge sharing is a key process in its development. Segelod and Jordan considered that software "is an intangible product consisting of nothing but pure knowledge in codified form" (2004, p. 240).

The gathering of people around a software development has the potential of sharing and leveraging different knowledges from different sources and stakeholders. The expected result is the creation of new knowledge that should be more than just the sum of the individual knowledge of each team member. The capture of new knowledge will enable its reuse with saving time, effort and cost (Hansen et al., 1999; Smith, 2001) and consequently reaching efficiency gains in future projects of development (Huzita et al., 2012; Wang & Noe, 2010).

Every form of organization has an informal organization within the formal one (Al-Rawas & Easterbrook, 1996). Knowledge can be taken during the development process but also in an informal contact (Segelod & Jordan, 2004), so it is important to encourage informal communications between different members of the team and different stakeholders.

The various working meetings that occur throughout a project are conducive to generate and share a lot of tacit knowledge. This tacit knowledge is the product of events such: discussions - whose outcome involved individuals accepting new knowledge or revising beliefs (Walz et al., 1993), parallel conversations, questions, doodles and notes on paper work, notes on blackboards, and experiences from previous projects. According to Kidwell et al. (2000), the ability to manage tacit knowledge defines the difference between a good performer and the best performer. Venkitachalam and Busch (2012) added that the desirable is discuss a way of use of tacit knowledge consistently and efficiently, so that fosters better results in SDO.

However, despite the important and large volume of tacit knowledge generated in the software development process, even if unconsciously, it is common overlook it (Shull et al., 2004). Several authors point to the fact that due to lack of proper mechanisms that allow sharing, identification and capture of this type of knowledge, most of them is wasted resulting in unavailability for future uses or projects (Al-Rawas & Easterbrook, 1996; Clark et al., 2015; Huzita et al., 2012; Johnson & Donnelly, 2013). Johnson and Donnelly (2013, p. 729) added "much of what we learn by dint of hard work is left on the room floor".

Based on the literature review and on the above discussion, it is possible to suggest that the main challenge of the SDO is the development of approaches and tools that make the tacit knowledge more explicit as possible (Johnson & Donnelly, 2013; Shull et al., 2002). Facing to the impossibility to codify the relevant tacit knowledge completely, these mechanisms should address ways of personalizing them for future use.

## FUTURE RESEARCH DIRECTIONS

After the literature review, the authors point to three possible future research directions within the domain of this chapter.

The several models of knowledge management system are limited to capture just the shared documented knowledge, neglecting undocumented face-to-face knowledge sharing (Wang & Noe, 2010). However, the intensive tacit knowledge nature of the software development process makes essential the development of research in models of knowledge management that address means of conversion of tacit knowledge into explicit or that enable register them.

Based on the new organizational SDO formats and in the practice of utilization multidisciplinary teams of software developers, future researches will benefit with a focus on understanding how cultural and background differences among the several stakeholders involved in software development may affect the ability to share and capture the tacit knowledge.

And finally, the literature concerned to the knowledge management in SDO environment is wide, which has led to increased interest in systematic reviews (Bjørnson & Dingsøyr, 2008). The revisions are important works due to the taxonomy developed, but not aims to evaluate and test the various investigated proposals. The case studies with empirical validation of models and not only with the assessment of technologies becomes a relevant direction.

## CONCLUSION

In this chapter, the aim was to highlight through the reviewed literature in the context of SDO the main challenge of knowledge management in this kind of organization.

During the review, it was possible to perceive that knowledge management in context of SDO is extremely complex, it is somewhat distanced from mainstream of knowledge management (Edwards, 2003), and still requires some special attention (Bjørnson & Dingsøyr, 2008). Although most authors (Bresnen et al., 2003; Ghobadi, 2015; Ryan & O'Connor, 2013; Shull et al., 2004) focus on the challenge in knowledge sharing, some opinions among them are divergent. For example, Shull et al. (2004) argued that there is a need for a wide range of mechanisms to permit knowledge sharing in SDO. While in Bresnen et al.'s (2003) view, interpersonal and social aspects, rather than technological or procedural mechanisms, are critical factors of a successful knowledge sharing.

The chapter's authors have the opinion that somehow knowledge sharing occurs within software development team. Actually quite encouraged by the formation and use of multidisciplinary teams in the software development process. Multidisciplinary teams have different cultures and expertise and consequently are rich in tacit knowledge. In order to find ways to reach the goal, several formal and informal meetings occur during development process. These meetings are conducive to generating and sharing a lot of tacit knowledge that team members share their perceptions, interpretations, intuitions and judgments within the group (Erden et al., 2008).

The authors also point out that the most of SDO are SME with structures more open and informal with short communications lines (Nonaka et al., 1996), that provide team members close interpersonal relationships with higher degree of trust (Erden et al., 2008). That context is extremely favorable to knowledge sharing activities. On the other hand, according to Erden et al. (2008), most SME lack the understanding of key knowledge management concepts and are slow in implementing knowledge management practices.

That context associated to the growing need to develop software in increasingly shorter periods leads each team member and also the organizations focus on solving the immediate problem and, consequently, the necessary knowledge to do so, implying in the waste of a large amount of tacit knowledge. In the Koskinen's (2001) opinion the utilization of tacit knowledge happens mainly unconsciously. The authors of the chapter tend to agree with Shull et al.'s (2004) opinion that tacit knowledge is overlooked in the context of the SDO. The process of capture or register of tacit knowledge will enable its use and reuse, in an efficient and effective manner, in the current development project and in the future.

## REFERENCES

Al-Rawas, A., & Easterbrook, S. (1996). Communication problems in requirements engineering: A field study. In *Proceedings of the First Westminster Conference on Professional Awareness in Software Engineering*.

Alavi, M., & Leidner, D. E. (2001). Review: Knowledge management and knowledge management systems: Conceptual foundations and research issues. *Management Information Systems Quarterly*, *25*(1), 107–136. doi:10.2307/3250961

Ambrosini, V., & Bowman, C. (2001). Tacit knowledge: Some suggestions for operationalization. *Journal of Management Studies*, *38*(6), 811–829. doi:10.1111/1467-6486.00260

Argote, L., & Ingram, P. (2000). Knowledge Transfer: A Basis for Competitive Advantage in Firms. *Organizational Behavior and Human Decision Processes*, *82*(1), 150–169. doi:10.1006/obhd.2000.2893

Aurum, A., Daneshgar, F., & Ward, J. (2008). Investigating knowledge management practices in software development organisations – An Australian experience. *Information and Software Technology*, *50*(6), 511–533. doi:10.1016/j.infsof.2007.05.005

Barksdale, J. T., & McCrickard, D. S. (2012). Software product innovation in agile usability teams: An analytical framework of social capital, network governance, and usability knowledge management. *International Journal of Agile and Extreme Software Development*, *1*(1), 52–77. doi:10.1504/IJAESD.2012.048302

Becerra-Fernandez, I., & Sabherwal, R. (2010). *Knowledge management: systems and processes*. Armonk, NY: M.E. Sharpe, Inc.

Bierly, P. E. III, Damanpour, F., & Santoro, M. D. (2009). The application of external knowledge: Organizational conditions for exploration and exploitation. *Journal of Management Studies*, *46*(3), 481–509. doi:10.1111/j.1467-6486.2009.00829.x

Bjørnson, F. O., & Dingsøyr, T. (2008). Knowledge management in software engineering: A systematic review of studied concepts, findings and research methods used. *Information and Software Technology*, *50*(11), 1055–1068. doi:10.1016/j.infsof.2008.03.006

Bogue, R. (2006). *Breaking down software development roles*. Retrieved from http://www.developer.com/mgmt/article.php/3490871/Cracking-the-Code-Breaking-Down-the-Software-Development-Roles.htm

Bresnen, M., Edelman, L., Newell, S., Scarbrough, H., & Swan, J. (2003). Social practices and the management of knowledge in project environments. *International Journal of Project Management*, *21*(3), 157–166. doi:10.1016/S0263-7863(02)00090-X

Chen, M.-Y. (2006). Knowledge management performance evaluation: A decade review from 1995 to 2004. *Journal of Information Science*, *32*(1), 17–38. doi:10.1177/0165551506059220

Clark, S. S., Berardy, A., Hannah, M. A., Seager, T. P., Selinger, E., & Makanda, J. V. (2015). Group Tacit Knowledge and Globally Distributed Virtual Teams: Lessons learned from using games and social media in the classroom. *Connexions - International Professional Communication Journal*, *3*(1), 113–151.

Davenport, T. H., & Prusak, L. (1998). *Working knowledge: How organizations manage what they know*. Boston, MA: Harvard Business School Press.

Desouza, K. C. (2003). Barriers to effective use of knowledge management systems in software engineering. *Communications of the ACM*, *46*(1), 99–101. doi:10.1145/602421.602458

Drucker, P. F. (1994). The age of social transformation. *Atlantic Monthly*, *274*(5), 53–80.

Dubé, L., & Robey, D. (1999). Software stories: Three cultural perspectives on the organizational practices of software development. *Accounting. Management and Information Technologies*, *9*(4), 223–259. doi:10.1016/S0959-8022(99)00010-7

Edwards, J. S. (2003). Managing Software Engineers and Their Knowledge. In *Managing Software Engineering Knowledge* (pp. 5–27). Berlin: Springer Berlin Heidelberg. doi:10.1007/978-3-662-05129-0_1

Erden, Z., von Krogh, G., & Nonaka, I. (2008). The quality of group tacit knowledge. *The Journal of Strategic Information Systems, 17*(1), 4–18. doi:10.1016/j.jsis.2008.02.002

Fehér, P., & Gábor, A. (2006). The role of knowledge management supporters in software development companies. *Software Process Improvement and Practice, 11*(3), 251–260. doi:10.1002/spip.269

Ghobadi, S. (2015). What drives knowledge sharing in software development teams: A literature review and classification framework. *Information & Management, 52*(1), 82–97. doi:10.1016/j.im.2014.10.008

Girard, J., & Girard, J. (2015). Defining knowledge management: Toward an applied compendium. *Online Journal of Applied Knowledge Management, 3*(1), 1–20.

Gloet, M. (2006). Knowledge management and the links to HRM. *Management Research News, 29*(7), 402–413. doi:10.1108/01409170610690862

Gloet, M., & Terziovski, M. (2004). Exploring the relationship between knowledge management practices and innovation performance. *Journal of Manufacturing Technology Management, 15*(5), 402–409. doi:10.1108/17410380410540390

Graham, I. D., Logan, J., Harrison, M. B., Straus, S. E., Tetroe, J., Caswell, W., & Robinson, N. (2006). Lost in knowledge translation: Time for a map? *The Journal of Continuing Education in the Health Professions, 26*(1), 13–24. doi:10.1002/chp.47 PMID:16557505

Grover, V., & Davenport, T. H. (2001). General Perspectives on Knowledge Management: Fostering a Research Agenda. *Journal of Management Information Systems, 18*(1), 5–21.

Hansen, M. T., Nohria, N., & Tierney, T. (1999). What's your strategy for managing knowledge? *Harvard Business Review, 72*(2), 106–116. PMID:10387767

Hoffman, R. R., Ziebell, D., Fiore, S. M., & Becerra-Fernandez, I. (2008). Knowledge Management Revisited. *IEEE Intelligent Systems, 23*(3), 84–88. doi:10.1109/MIS.2008.51

Huzita, E. H. M., Leal, G. C. L., Balancieri, R., Tait, T. F. C., Cardoza, E., Penteado, R. R. D. M., & Vivian, R. L. (2012). Knowledge and contextual information management in global software development: challenges and perspectives. In *2012 IEEE Seventh International Conference on Global Software Engineering Workshops* (pp. 43–48). IEEE. doi:10.1109/ICGSEW.2012.12

Iacono, M. P., De Nito, E., Esposito, V., Martinez, M., & Moschera, L. (2014). Investigating the relationship between coordination mechanisms and knowledge in a wine firm. *Knowledge and Process Management, 21*(4), 280–291. doi:10.1002/kpm.1436

Inkinen, H. (2016). Review of empirical research on knowledge management practices and firm performance. *Journal of Knowledge Management, 20*(2), 230–257. doi:10.1108/JKM-09-2015-0336

Jakubik, M. (2008). Experiencing collaborative knowledge creation processes. *The Learning Organization, 15*(1), 5–25. doi:10.1108/09696470810842475

Johannenssen, J.-A., Olsen, B., & Olaisen, J. (1999). Aspects of Innovation Theory Based on Knowledge Management. *International Journal of Information Management, 19*(2), 121–139. doi:10.1016/S0268-4012(99)00004-3

Johnson, C., & Donnelly, B. (2013). If only we knew what we know. *Chicago-Kent Law Review*, *88*(3), 729–742.

Kakabadse, N. K., Kakabadse, A., & Kouzmin, A. (2003). Reviewing the knowledge management literature: Towards a taxonomy. *Journal of Knowledge Management*, *7*(4), 75–91. doi:10.1108/13673270310492967

Kalkan, V. D. (2008). An overall view of knowledge management challenges for global business. *Business Process Management Journal*, *14*(3), 390–400. doi:10.1108/14637150810876689

Kang, J., Rhee, M., & Kang, K. H. (2010). Revisiting knowledge transfer: Effects of knowledge characteristics on organizational effort for knowledge transfer. *Expert Systems with Applications*, *37*(12), 8155–8160. doi:10.1016/j.eswa.2010.05.072

Kasemsap, K. (2015). Developing a framework of human resource management, organizational learning, knowledge management capability, and organizational performance. In P. O. de Pablos, L. J. Turró, R. D. T. Tennyson, & J. Zhao (Eds.), *Knowledge Management for Competitive Advantage During Economic Crisis* (pp. 164–193). IGI Global. doi:10.4018/978-1-4666-6457-9.ch010

Kidwell, J. J., Vander Linde, K., & Johnson, S. L. (2000). Applying corporate knowledge management practices in higher education. *EDUCAUSE Quarterly*, *23*(4), 28–33.

Koskinen, K. U. (2001). Tacit Knowledge as a Promoter of Success in Technology Firms. In *Proceedings of the 34th Hawaii International Conference on System Sciences* (pp. 1–9). doi:10.1109/HICSS.2001.926493

Lee-Kelley, L., Blackman, D. A., & Hurst, J. P. (2007). An exploration of the relationship between learning organisations and the retention of knowledge workers. *The Learning Organization*, *14*(3), 204–221. doi:10.1108/09696470710739390

Leonard, D., & Sensiper, S. (1998). The Role of Tacit Knowledge in Group Innovation. *California Management Review*, *40*(3), 112–132. doi:10.2307/41165946

Lethbridge, T. C., Sim, S. E., & Singer, J. (2005). Studying Software Engineers: Data Collection Techniques for Software Field Studies. *Empirical Software Engineering*, *10*(3), 311–341. doi:10.1007/s10664-005-1290-x

Mårtensson, M. (2000). A critical review of knowledge management as a management tool. *Journal of Knowledge Management*, *4*(3), 204–216. doi:10.1108/13673270010350002

Meehan, B., & Richardson, I. (2002). Identification of software process knowledge management. *Software Process Improvement and Practice*, *7*(2), 47–55. doi:10.1002/spip.154

Mehta, N., Hall, D., & Byrd, T. (2014). Information technology and knowledge in software development teams: The role of project uncertainty. *Information & Management*, *51*(4), 417–429. doi:10.1016/j.im.2014.02.007

Metaxiotis, K., Ergazakis, K., & Psarras, J. (2005). Exploring the world of knowledge management: Agreements and disagreements in the academic/practitioner community. *Journal of Knowledge Management*, *9*(2), 6–18. doi:10.1108/13673270510590182

Nahapiet, J., & Ghoshal, S. (1998). Social Capital, Intellectual Capital, and the Organizational Advantage. *Academy of Management Review, 23*(2), 242–266.

Nielsen, A. P. (2006). Understanding dynamic capabilities through knowledge management. *Journal of Knowledge Management, 10*(4), 59–71. doi:10.1108/13673270610679363

Nonaka, I. (2010). *Cultivating Leaders with Practical Wisdom: Scrum and Ba Building*. Retrieved October 23, 2015, from https://ai.wu.ac.at/~kaiser/birgit/Nonaka-Papers/nonaka-phronetic-leadership-folien-2010.pdf

Nonaka, I., & Konno, N. (1998). The concept of "ba": Building a foundation for knowledge creation. *California Management Review, 40*(3), 40–54. doi:10.2307/41165942

Nonaka, I., Takeuchi, H., & Umemoto, K. (1996). A theory of organizational knowledge creation. *International Journal of Technology Management, 11*(7-8), 833–845.

Patton, J. (2002). Hitting the target: Adding Interaction Design to Agile Software Development. In *OOPSLA 2002 Practitioners Reports on - OOPSLA '02* (pp. 1–7). New York: ACM Press. doi:10.1145/604251.604255

Paulin, D., & Suneson, K. (2012). Knowledge Transfer, Knowledge Sharing and Knowledge Barriers – Three Blurry Terms in KM. *Electronic Journal of Knowledge Management, 10*(1), 81–91.

Pee, L. G., Kankanhalli, A., & Kim, H. (2010). Knowledge Sharing in Information Systems Development: A Social Interdependence Perspective. *Journal of the Association for Information Systems, 11*(10), 550–575.

Pekka-Economou, V., & Hadjidema, S. (2011). Innovative organizational forms that add value to both organizations and community: The case of knowledge management. *European Research Studies, 14*(2), 81–95.

Peters, T. (1992). *Liberation Management: Necessary Disorganization for the Nanosecond Nineties* (1st ed.). New York: Alfred A. Knopf, Inc.

Polanyi, M. (1966). The logic of tacit inference. *Philosophy (London, England), 41*(155), 1–18. doi:10.1017/S0031819100066110

Prieto, I. M., Revilla, E., & Rodríguez-Prado, B. (2009). Managing the knowledge paradox in product development. *Journal of Knowledge Management, 13*(3), 157–170. doi:10.1108/13673270910962941

Rasmussen, P., & Nielsen, P. (2011). Knowledge management in the firm: Concepts and issues. *International Journal of Manpower, 32*(5/6), 479–493. doi:10.1108/01437721111158161

Richardson, I., & Von Wangenheim, C. (2007). Guest editors' introduction: Why are small software organizations different? *IEEE Software, 24*(1), 18–22. doi:10.1109/MS.2007.12

Robillard, P. N. (1999). The role of knowledge in software development. *Communications of the ACM, 42*(1), 87–92. doi:10.1145/291469.291476

Rowley, J. (2007). The wisdom hierarchy: Representations of the DIKW hierarchy. *Journal of Information Science, 33*(2), 163–180. doi:10.1177/0165551506070706

Rus, I., & Lindvall, M. (2002). Knowledge management in software engineering. *IEEE Software, 19*(3), 26–38. doi:10.1109/MS.2002.1003450

Ryan, S., & O'Connor, R. V. (2013). Acquiring and sharing tacit knowledge in software development teams: An empirical study. *Information and Software Technology, 55*(9), 1614–1624. doi:10.1016/j.infsof.2013.02.013

Sadeghi, Z., & Salemi, J. (2013). Presenting a conceptual model for innovation development in organizations. *Life Science Journal, 10*, 62–70.

Santoro, M. D., & Bierly, P. E. (2006). Facilitators of knowledge transfer in university-industry collaborations: A knowledge-based perspective. *IEEE Transactions on Engineering Management, 53*(4), 495–507. doi:10.1109/TEM.2006.883707

Savolainen, P., & Ahonen, J. J. (2015). Knowledge lost: Challenges in changing project manager between sales and implementation in software projects. *International Journal of Project Management, 33*(1), 92–102. doi:10.1016/j.ijproman.2014.04.003

Schilling, J., & Klamma, R. (2010). The difficult bridge between university and industry: A case study in computer science teaching. *Assessment & Evaluation in Higher Education, 35*(4), 367–380. doi:10.1080/02602930902795893

Segelod, E., & Jordan, G. (2004). The use and importance of external sources of knowledge in the software development process. *R & D Management, 34*(3), 239–252. doi:10.1111/j.1467-9310.2004.00336.x

Seidler-de Alwis, R., & Hartmann, E. (2008). The use of tacit knowledge within innovative companies: Knowledge management in innovative enterprises. *Journal of Knowledge Management, 12*(1), 133–147. doi:10.1108/13673270810852449

Shull, F., Basili, V., Carver, J., Maldonado, J. C., Travassos, G. H., Mendonca, M., & Fabbri, S. (2002). Replicating Software Engineering Experiments: Addressing the Tacit Knowledge Problem. In *Proceedings of the 2002 International Symposium on Empirical Software Engineering (ISESE'02)* (pp. 7–16). IEEE Comput. Soc. doi:10.1109/ISESE.2002.1166920

Shull, F., Mendonça, M. G., Basili, V., Carver, J., Maldonado, J. C., Fabbri, S., & Ferreira, M. C. et al. (2004). Knowledge-sharing issues in experimental software engineering. *Empirical Software Engineering, 9*(1/2), 111–137. doi:10.1023/B:EMSE.0000013516.80487.33

Smith, E. A. (2001). The role of tacit and explicit knowledge in the workplace. *Journal of Knowledge Management, 5*(4), 311–321. doi:10.1108/13673270110411733

Starbuck, W. H. (1992). Learning by knowledge-intensive firms. *Journal of Management Studies, 29*(6), 713–740. doi:10.1111/j.1467-6486.1992.tb00686.x

Stenmark, D. (2001). The relationship between information and knowledge. *Proceedings of IRIS, 24*, 11–14.

Stoyanov, I. (2014). Human capital and knowledge management in innovative organizations. *KSI Transactions on Knowledge Society, 7*(4), 23–29.

Swart, J., & Kinnie, N. (2003). Sharing knowledge in knowledge-intensive firms. *Human Resource Management Journal, 13*(2), 60–75. doi:10.1111/j.1748-8583.2003.tb00091.x

Tuomi, I. (1999). Data is more than knowledge: Implications of the reversed knowledge hierarchy for knowledge management and organizational memory. In *Proceedings of the 32nd Annual Hawaii International Conference on Systems Sciences. 1999. HICSS-32* (*Vol. 16*, p. 12). IEEE Comput. Soc. doi:10.1109/HICSS.1999.772795

Venkitachalam, K., & Busch, P. (2012). Tacit knowledge: Review and possible research directions. *Journal of Knowledge Management, 16*(2), 357–372. doi:10.1108/13673271211218915

Walz, D. B., Elam, J. J., & Curtis, B. (1993). Inside a software design team: Knowledge acquisition, sharing, and integration. *Communications of the ACM, 36*(10), 63–77. doi:10.1145/163430.163447

Wang, S., & Noe, R. A. (2010). Knowledge sharing: A review and directions for future research. *Human Resource Management Review, 20*(2), 115–131. doi:10.1016/j.hrmr.2009.10.001

Webber, A. M. (1993). What's so new about the new economy? *Harvard Business Review, 71*(1), 24–42.

Wong, W. L. P., & Radcliffe, D. F. (2000). The Tacit Nature of Design Knowledge. *Technology Analysis and Strategic Management, 12*(4), 493–512. doi:10.1080/713698497

## KEY TERMS AND DEFINITIONS

**Codification Approach:** A "people-to-document" approach, which knowledge is carefully codified and stored in databases where it can be accessed and used easily by anyone in the organization. Knowledge is extracted from the person who developed it, made independent of that person and reused for various purposes.

**Explicit Knowledge:** Knowledge that can be easily expressed in words, numbers, and symbols and stored in books, computers, etc...

**Knowledge Capture:** A fundamental process of preservation and formalization of knowledge.

**Knowledge Sharing:** Sharing and transfer are interchangeable, and commonly appear with the same sense in the literature. It is a key process regarding to the knowledge-intensive context in general and in particular within teams of software development.

**Knowledge-Intensive Organization:** A kind of organization that it is characterized by a high proportion of highly qualified workers, due to access to and manipulation of large quantities of knowledge.

**Multidisciplinary Team:** A group composed of members with varied but complimentary experience, qualifications, and skills that contribute to the achievement of specific objectives.

**Personalization Approach:** A "person-to-person" approach that involves ensuring that tacit knowledge is registered. The exchange is achieved by creating networks and encouraging face-to-face communication between individuals and teams by means of informal conferences, workshops, communities of practice, brainstorming and one-to-one sessions.

**Tacit Knowledge:** Knowledge that is complex, not codified, and presents some difficulty in its reproduction in a document or in a database. It can be get from experience, perceptions and individual values and depends on the context in which is inserted.

# Practical Experience (Research Results and Case Studies)

# Chapter 12
# Intercultural Knowledge Transfer in Teams

**Balzhan Orazbayeva**
*Münster University of Applied Sciences (MUAS), Germany*

**Thomas Baaken**
*Münster University of Applied Sciences (MUAS), Germany*

## ABSTRACT

*The following chapter is dedicated to knowledge management, whereby the focus is on the transfer of relevant knowledge in an intercultural team. The purpose of this study was to empirically examine, how an intercultural team deals with the cultural diversity of its members and how it influences the knowledge transfer. The research object was the intercultural team of the research institute Science-to-Business Marketing Research Centre at the Münster University of Applied Sciences (MUAS) in Germany. Ten guided interviews were conducted with ten employees of ten different nationalities. As the investigation has shown, the processes of knowledge transfer within the team of the research centre are not standardized. The actual transfer of knowledge occurs between team members on a personal level during intercultural communication in a setting of provided framework conditions. The team's cultural diversity is able not only to transfer but also to generate new knowledge. Intercultural competence in a provided framework is the crucial factor for successful cross-cultural knowledge transfer.*

## INTRODUCTION

The debate on globalization and internalisation is dominated by multinational enterprises (MNEs), while the role of small and medium-sized enterprises (SMEs) is rarely discussed. But today, globalization is a major driver that has impact on nearly every business. Due to globalisation business becomes more independent for survival and growth (Deo, 2013). In result, even smaller and locally oriented companies, which have to see themselves in a global context, meet new opportunities and confront new challenges. More often, small and medium-sized enterprises are operating in the markets that allow them to act internationally (Hutchinson et al., 2006).

DOI: 10.4018/978-1-5225-1642-2.ch012

Thus due to globalization and internationalization for all kind of businesses international activities are a matter of fact nowadays (Peng & Meyer, 2011). This process can be observed in two directions. On the one hand more and more organizations start to engage in global business expanding their activities beyond home markets (Ruzzier et al., 2006; Mohr & Shoobridge, 2011). On the other hand, due to increase – both in organizational global mobility and individual international migration – small and medium-sized enterprises now employ a multicultural workforce. Therefore, the internalization phenomenon has encouraged the exchange of human resources across borders. In a modern environment, diversity in workplace is the norm rather than exception and it is not unusual to find working teams made up of members from a number of different countries (Mohr & Shoobridge, 2011; Syfox, 2000).

Globalization has produced unprecedented volumes of trade, intercultural interactions and information flows. In such changing conditions of modern business, globalization means for SMEs, that they can only be successful if they find a sustainable competitive advantage (von Krogh & Köhne, 1998). These changing conditions manifest through increasingly intensive competition, a profound and rapid technological development and have attached a strategic value to knowledge as a success factor. Knowledge-based activities are considered nowadays to be the basis of sustainable competitive advantage in business environment (Murmann, 2003; Valkokari & Helander, 2007). The knowledge has become a key resource in organizations and companies. The increased use of a company's existing knowledge may lead to rise in productivity and quality (Hitt, 1998; Hitt et al., 1999; Argote & Ingram, 2000). Consequently, the ability of a company's competitive advantage to subsist lies on the effective transfer of available knowledge between the single business units and employees. The transfer processes are vital for organizations since an individual knowledge will not affect the units or individuals unless it is made accessible and available to others (Law & Ngai, 2008).

However, nowadays knowledge transfer is not an easy task as companies are forced to do business at an international level as a result of globalization (Khan & Khan, 2015), especially, knowledge transfer processes within SMEs, where the knowledge is typically concentrated with few key persons (Valkokari & Helander, 2007). The effective knowledge transfer is, under such conditions and the increasing internationalization of companies, one of the most difficult tasks for companies (Javidan et al., 2005; Wilkesmann et al., 2009).

Cultural differences can be easily observed in cross-cultural communication both in business and in private subjects. This is also an issue in knowledge transfer. When it comes to SMEs, whose employees due to exchange of human resources across borders, come from different countries and belong to different cultures, the process of internal knowledge transfer seems to be even more complex, because the establishment of knowledge transfer is strongly dependent on the ability of employees to access and interpret the information, they get in intercultural context (Boateng & Agyemang, 2015). Knowledge, its management, as well as its transfer become more complicated when applied in diverse intercultural environment (Bengoa & Kaufmann, 2014; Boh et al., 2013; Chen et al., 2010).

Such circumstances raise the question on how SMEs´ employees as members of working teams deal with their cultural diversity in order to overcome transfer challenges and also benefit from it. In this line, analysing the impact of national culture on the transfer of knowledge within the team is a promising area in shedding light and bringing new perspectives on the topic of cross-cultural knowledge management.

This chapter is dedicated to knowledge management, with a focus on the transfer of relevant knowledge in an intercultural team. Based on the problem definition, this chapter aims to empirically examine how the employees of a research centre, who come from different countries, deal with interculturality and to explore the impact of national culture on the knowledge transfer process.

## KNOWLEDGE

Despite the problematics of defining knowledge, because of its intangible nature, it is nonetheless agreed to understand by it an organized combination of ideas, rules, procedures, and information (Marakas, 1999). Only through the "organization" all these elements can be transformed into knowledge. Knowledge evolves in a certain context and cannot be explored isolated from it (Wöbling & Keuper, 2009). It becomes meaningful for a company only if it is appropriately and effectively utilized and thus transformed into expertise (North, 2002). In conjunction with personal experiences this knowledge is further converted into a competence, which represents a foundation for competitiveness in a corporate context (Prahalad & Hamel, 1990; Nonaka, 1994; Caiazza et al., 2015).

Team knowledge, which is increasingly recognized to be an important asset for different types of organisations, including small and medium sized enterprises as well, is defined as the collection of work- and team-related knowledge elements (Cooke et al., 2000), comprising not only knowledge held in common, but also an individual knowledge and knowledge relationships between members (Espinosa & Clark, 2014). According to Espinosa and Clark (2014: 334) "…team knowledge is inherently social construct – individuals share and exchange knowledge through communication and actions, creating relationships that help explain team dynamics, process, coordination and performance."

In terms of cross-cultural knowledge transfer, where knowledge is also seen as social construct in intercultural context, it is however crucial to identify what type of knowledge can be passed on through distribution. Decisive for the transferring are certain characteristics of knowledge, which may exert substantial influence on the knowledge dissemination processes.

Knowledge is comprised of two components: tacit and explicit. Such a distinction between types of knowledge traces back to Polanyi (1996). With his statement *"we can know more than we can tell"* Polanyi (1996) pointed out that knowledge is directly connected with personal experiences and perceptions. Polanyi indicates that person employs knowledge that cannot be fully expressed in words. Such knowledge, which is difficult to formalize and to communicate, is known as tacit or implicit knowledge. For Sternberg (1997) implicit knowledge is that what's often not easy to verbally discuss and record in writing. These features mean that such kind of knowledge is difficult to transfer, since it can be hardly codified and documented.

In contrast, explicit knowledge is formal since it can be expressed, presented and stored in form of data. Therefore, such knowledge can be easily articulated and formalized (Lehner, 2006). In a corporate context, employees can easily access explicit knowledge through the formation of a unitary structure, for example in the form of a central database.

Explicit and implicit knowledge, however, can be in interrelation with each other (Geisler & Wickramasinghe, 2015). Namely, a conversion of tacit knowledge into explicit is possible. Nonaka and Nishiguchi (2001: 14) are of the opinion that "…they interact with and change into each other in the creative activities of human being". As a result, companies can benefit from it by generating new knowledge through transformation of tacit knowledge into explicit, and by making it accessible for everyone.

This overpass concerning both types of knowledge was formulated by Nonaka together with Takeuchi (Nonaka & Takeuchi, 1995) as a fundamental problem of knowledge management in their Socialization-Externalization-Combination-Internalization (SECI) Model (Nonaka et al., 2006). Another framework, which also explores the interrelation between tacit and explicit knowledge components, is the Distribution-Interaction-Competition-Evolution (DICE) Model of Deng-Neng, Ting-Peng and Binshan (2010). From the perspective of examining knowledge transfer processes, Rivera-Vasquez, Ortiz-Fournier and Flores

(2009) describe the transfer as an exchange of both explicit and tacit elements, which consequently results a production of a new knowledge.

## Knowledge Transfer

Knowledge management is seen as an increasingly significant management concept for all types of enterprises, since its importance for the achievement of competitive advantage has been reinforced and knowledge has become a key resource within organisations (Probst et al., 2000). Although there is yet no uniform definition, the most commonly used ones have an organisational focus and are considered rather in a corporate context (Hislop, 2013; Liebl, 2015).

Basically knowledge management means that different types of organisations have to find ways to adequately manage knowledge, which help them to achieve competitive advantage (Teece, 2001). However, that can often be challenging, especially for smaller enterprises, since they normally lack the suitable resources and/or competences needed to fully utilise their available stock of knowledge (Durst & Edvardsson, 2012). Most of existing knowledge management literature focuses on large businesses neglecting smaller ones, therefore there is a need also to put more emphasis on this issue (Durst & Wilhelm, 2012; Nunes et al., 2006; Cerchione et al., 2016). Previous studies show that small businesses face unique knowledge management challenges different from those encountered by bigger ones (Edvardsson, 2009; Durst & Edvardsson, 2012; Grandinetti, 2016), therefore the application of the knowledge management instruments used in larger companies in SMEs may not be sufficient without taking into account SME´s specific features and characteristics (Wang & Yang, 2016).

An important attempt to structure and to categorize the problems in the area of knowledge management in different types of organisations belongs to Probst et al. (2000), who examine internal knowledge intensive processes. In their model, which can be applied in SMEs and small working teams too, they regard how these processes affect the management of knowledge within an organization. The model consists of eight building blocks for knowledge management and their connections. They identify six core processes of knowledge management within the organization describing and addressing operational problems, which include: knowledge identification, knowledge acquisition, knowledge development, knowledge distribution, knowledge retention, knowledge utilization. Moreover, these six operational processes are supported by two additional building blocks, knowledge goals and knowledge assessment, to complete the model.

- Knowledge identification is a creation of internal and external transparency within an organization in order to identify knowledge. Considering that, an analysis and description of the knowledge environment will be carried out. The goal is to obtain an overview of existing data, information, skills and competences.
- Knowledge acquisition. Organizations and companies import a significant portion of their knowledge needs from external sources. Here, it is about "purchasing" knowledge through relationships with clients, suppliers, competitors or partners. Sometimes, external experts and companies are recruited, since they possess an expertise on a particular field. Here it has to be clear which knowledge is required.
- Knowledge development includes the activities that help to establish new ideas, skills and abilities. Here, it comes to how the company deals with these new ideas, and how the creativity of employees is developed and applied.

- Knowledge distribution explains how to distribute the existing and acquired knowledge within an organization or a team and how knowledge can be transmitted in order to make it useful for the whole company.
- Knowledge retention is concerned with the problem of knowledge loss, since the acquired knowledge is not necessarily directly saved, and therefore cannot be available in the future. The ultimate goal of this block is the preservation of skills and competencies.
- Knowledge use is a productive and efficient deployment of the knowledge within the organisation, which is actually in fact the purpose of knowledge management. To ensure this process, potential barriers have to be overcome.
- Knowledge goals determine which layers within an organization have to be filled with which skills. Three different types of knowledge goals have to be distinguished. Normative goals relate to the knowledge management framework. They serve to build a knowledge-conscious corporate culture. Strategic goals determine the required competence and thus describe the organizational core knowledge. Operational objectives are concerned with the implementation of the entire knowledge management system within an organization.
- Knowledge measurement includes activities and indicators that help to measure normative, strategic and operative knowledge goals, which evaluate the success of the knowledge management activities within organisation.

Moreover, the building blocks concept can be used as a knowledge transfer model since it allows a clear overview on the internal knowledge transfer processes. According to Probst (1998), knowledge transfer can be seen as the central and most important block regarding knowledge management, because only through it, the potential of knowledge´s production factor can be properly utilized. Knowledge transfer, therefore, will be considered as an internal organisations area to explore in terms of cultural diversity, according to the knowledge distribution and retention blocks within working teams.

Knowledge transfer can be distinguished between an individual, an intra-organisational, and inter-organisational level (Wilkesmann et. al., 2009). This chapter focuses on knowledge transfer within the intercultural team, and therefore on the individual level. According to Haghirian (2011) knowledge is subjective, because it is personal and developed, applied, interpreted and communicated by people. Consequently, knowledge transfer is basically the process of knowledge distribution and dissemination between organizational units or, in this case, between employees. In order to share knowledge, it have to be not only communicated, but also understood, reflected and applied by team members (Hendricks, 1999; Freyens & Martin, 2007). Knowledge-intensive teamwork, which is considered as a number of collaborative activities of a certain group of individuals, includes location, dissemination, creation and application of the knowledge among team members (Chuang et al., 2016).

Therefore, the process of knowledge transferring has not to be considered only as a communication of knowledge. This process is strongly influenced by people, who interpret the knowledge and thus reconstruct it. According to Hoerem et al. (1999: 119), whose understanding of knowledge management underlies a constructivist approach, knowledge transfer is basically a learning problem. Their definition of knowledge transfer reads as follows: "We say that knowledge of a matter is transferred, when the receiver of information has gained a principally similar understanding of a matter as the transmitter." Therefore, they think that knowledge has been transferred, only if it is understood, reflected and shared by the receiver in a proper way.

In the context of this chapter, knowledge is a context-dependent collective phenomenon arising from personal interactions and effective dialogue among members coming from different countries working together in one team. Team knowledge transfer refers to activities that aid the sharing and dissemination of knowledge elements (Chuang et al., 2016; Jackson et al., 2006) among culturally diverse teams.

## CULTURE

To determine what interculturality is, firstly, the term culture should be discussed. Depending on which science it is used for, culture has a different content. Thus, different meanings and definitions of culture coexist. Culture is specific to human nature. A person forms culture himself and it is determined and marked in a certain way, as it is dictated by his certain customs and practices. Thus, humans play here, as natural beings, two roles: they are subjects of culture, because they act as cultural mediums, and at the same time they are also objects of culture, since cultural conditions exert certain influence on them.

According to Yousefi (2006), the terms nationality or religion are not sufficient to give a concrete definition to the cultural contexts; therefore, culture as a term has to be defined separately. He understands by culture a totality of life expressions of a group within a certain time and a space, which distinguishes different cultures from each other. Here, it comes to a number of abstract symbols as language, values, rules or traditions. Hofstede (1997) understands culture as the collective programming of the human mind. Therefore, culture can be seen as a program, shared by several people, which represents one common paradigm. Besides that, it allows to determine and identify the differences of one culture from another.

However, cultures are dynamic and changeable as well. They have fluid boundaries so they are unable to exist hermetically separated from each other. Therefore, they can influence each other, resulting a certain interaction and development between them (Derboven, 2009). Consequently, different foreign cultural elements can be accepted and practiced by members from different cultures, which means that culture may also be global or there may be more than one culture within certain country.

Thus, Samovar and Porter (1995: 8) also understand by the concept of culture a dynamic system, which is constantly changing and developing, and therefore they define it as "a deposit of knowledge, experiences, beliefs, values, attitudes, meanings, social hierarchies, religion, notions of time, roles, spatial relationships, concepts of the universe, and material objects acquired by a group of people in the course of generations through individual and group striving".

Culture as a collective phenomenon should be considered in terms of socialization process, which shows how an individual evolves and changes in a certain cultural environment. Basically, human nature is indissolubly related to the sense of belonging to a certain community. For individuals it is crucial to know that they are members of a group of people involved in persistent social interaction, or, in the simplest terms, that they are members of a society. Within such groups, individuals share common destiny, experience life together, follow certain norms, rules and values. In addition, they normally speak the same language and often even with a common accent or speech patterns (Bannenberg, 2010).

In summary, it can be said that culture is an orientation system, which is made of different elements and symbols. Such a system strongly affects its members' perceptions, values, traditions and actions; therefore, culture means belonging to a certain society or group, or to a certain nationality. In the present paper, culture will be regarded as a phenomenon, which represents the belonging to a particular country.

## Interculturality and Cross-Cultural Comunication

Today international or intercultural cooperation takes place all over the world through the increasing globalization. That is why international business activities increasingly result a creation of intercultural teams. Team members work together usually both as a project group or in other corporate contexts (Barmeyer & Davoine, 2006).

Interculturality is understood as the meeting of two or more cultures, in which, despite cultural differences, mutual interference arises. Thus, interculturality occurs through dialogue between and within cultures. According to Thomas (2003), "interculture" is something new resulted from interconnection between own culture and foreign culture, which is also called as a "third culture" (Adair et al., 2006; Müller & Gelbrich, 2015). In a corporate context, interculturality is seen as an integral part of human resources management within a company. Due to globalization's new changing conditions, the employees' cultural diversity has risen; therefore, an independent intercultural human resources management has to be carried out. The company's goal is here the effective application of cultural diversity in intercultural cooperation in terms of productivity and quality (Blom & Meier, 2002).

According to Marquardt and Horvath (2001), building a powerful intercultural team seems to be the biggest challenge for businesses nowadays. An intercultural team is a team composed of individuals from different national cultures, where each team member as a carrier of a certain culture belongs to different social group, coming from different national cultural spaces (Popescu et al., 2014). If team members do not have experience in intercultural cooperation, the teams' effectiveness can be substantially reduced, because they simply are not aware of how to deal with interculturality (Bronszinsky-Schwabe, 2011).

The basis for normal functioning of the teams, whose members belong to different cultures, is the cross-cultural communication, which needs to be as constructive as possible, without misunderstandings and breakdowns (Spencer-Rodgers & McGovern, 2002). By successful intercultural communication sharing and understanding set and fix the human mind-set through interpersonal social interactions, so that the mutual trust, empathy, help, opinion sharing, and a sense of togetherness can be captured. (Chua, 2002; Cavusgil et al., 2003). In this case the stronger and more trustful relationships can be built, in which cultural differences are no more seen as obstacles inhibiting intercultural communication (Nguyen & Aoyama, 2015).

However, it is often a difficult task, since during communication people have stronger emotions, or even fear. Such emotions and preliminary assumptions, which people do already have about other cultures, directly affect their reactions on "foreigners" and govern relations between communication partners. Since the actors of the communication process are carriers of different cultures, the interactions between them are complex and multi-staged. Therefore, there is an increased potential for misunderstandings in intercultural communication between communicators (Derboven, 2009). Therefore, intercultural communication searches for efficient ways to understand disputes, disagreements and challenges in personal intercultural interaction, and to produce solutions to these issues (Bennett, 1998).

According to Yousefi (2006), cross-cultural communication is a specific type of interpersonal interaction, which takes place under very special circumstances. The perception of messages during intercultural communication can be distorted because it is based on certain cultural patterns and rules, which are always different in every culture. However, not only perception depends on culture, but also the process of decoding and interpretation (Aba, 2015). Thus, the different intercultural imprints of the communication actors result that they perceive each other as foreigners.

For the knowledge transfer in an intercultural context intercultural communication is actually one of the main aspects, since the process of knowledge sharing appears to be directly dependent on it. Not only knowledge is transferred through knowledge transfer but also, to a greater or a lesser extent, culture.

## Challenges of Intercultural Knowledge Transfer

Academic literature relating to knowledge management states that national culture plays a critical role in the knowledge transfer process within cross-cultural environment (Chen et al., 2010; Nguyen & Aoyama, 2015; Khan & Khan, 2015). Members of intercultural teams do work for same organization and may have the same profession, but the fact that they do not share the same cultural background provides them, for example, with a different perception of the world, or can affect the way people negotiate and resolve disputes (Browaeys & Price, 2011).

During internalization processes, the complexity of knowledge transfer increases as well, because the establishment of knowledge transfer is strongly dependent on the ability of team members to access and interpret the information, they get in intercultural context. Cultural, language and legislation differences, among any others, are likely to be seen as factors that can inhibit the knowledge transfer in international scenario (Henriques et al., 2014; von Krogh et al., 2012). For this reason, culturally diverse teams increasingly face nowadays the challenges and complexity of intercultural knowledge transfer in teams.

Several studies have identified issue of cultural differences as one of the major challenges influencing the knowledge transfer processes in a firm or in a team (Rivera-Vasquez et al., 2009). They differ two levels of cultural issues. On the one hand there are barriers, which affect knowledge transfer at macro level, based on cultural dimensions of Hofstede (1983). On the other hand, they differ cultural issues at micro level, related to organizational culture as shaped by the national culture of citizens working in team.

Kaps (2011) implies as well, that culture has an impact on knowledge management, influencing people´s awareness of cultural differences by managing and transferring the knowledge; internal knowledge intensive processes; and systems or technologies, which are used by team members to manage or share the knowledge. She differs four different cultural challenges in knowledge transfer: communication style, power (hierarchy), language and trust.

The significant role of language in knowledge sharing process is particularly emphasized as an important factor in multicultural settings (Roos & von Krogh, 2002; Husted & Michailova, 2002; Minbaeva, 2007). Language is observed as an inherent aspect that enables the knowledge flow within the team. But in intercultural settings the language diversity may cause misunderstandings and hamper the process of knowledge transfer.

However, some authors argue that cross-cultural interactions between members of multicultural teams can help employees deal with working activities in a smoother way, at the same time also supporting team leaders and group managers in fostering and maintaining group spirit and company harmony (Nguyen & Aoyama, 2015). Nguyen & Aoyama (2015) found that the active intercultural communication enables the organisation to effectively overcome barriers and difficulties caused by cultural differences and pursue the knowledge transfer with fewer risks and conflicts.

Furthermore, some researchers even state that, nevertheless knowledge as an organisational asset is highly contextual and can be intangible in nature, it is however being created cross-culturally (Andreeva & Ikhilchik, 2011; Easa & Finchman, 2012; Hong, 2012). "This takes new significance in knowledge-oriented organizations where conflicts between groups enrich a society through gains in productivity and improved intellect, which manifests itself in innovation, problem solving, and decision making" (Khan

& Khan, 2015: 52). Therefore according to some authors interculturality can also positively affect not only knowledge transfer, but also a knowledge creation (Laitin & Jeon, 2013).

Cross-cultural communication plays a great role in international teams by transferring a knowledge among and of cultures in organization. Soley (2003) considers that any organization´s knowledge repository should include the knowledge of the culture of their workers and team members, in order to optimize the knowledge intensive processes within intercultural organizations or teams.

## METHODOLOGY

The paper deals with a case study methodology based on Gioia et al. (2013).

The research results, which will be presented in this book chapter, are based on guided interviews, which examined intercultural knowledge transfer processes through the example of an intercultural team, which consists of ten different national cultures. The main objective was to examine, if the cultural differences have an impact on internal knowledge transfer among team members, and how exactly they influence these knowledge intensive processes within the team. Based on the literature review, categories were formed, which were asked as part of each interview.

In the research institute, Science-to-Business Marketing Research Centre, ten employees (also former) each with a different culture, were interviewed. They come from Germany, Mexico, Switzerland, Vietnam, Romania, Greece, Bulgaria, Argentina, Turkey and the Netherlands. Each interview was carried out in September 2015 as a guided interview lasting 30 to 45 minutes, and take place in the Science-to-Business Marketing Research Centre office or via telephone and Skype depending on the interviewee´s preference.

The interviews, prepared in German and English, included fifteen questions referring to:

- Role of the interview partner in research centre;
- Knowledge transfer and methods and tools to share knowledge within the team members;
- Interculturality, intercultural barriers and advantages of intercultural team;
- Opportunities and risks in the intercultural knowledge transfer.

The data material, gathered through the qualitative interviews, was analysed using structured qualitative content analysis. Following an analysis of the literature certain categories were selected to filter out a specific structure and materials from the qualitative interviews (Mayring, 2010). A basic procedure for this technique based on Kuckartz's approach (2014):

**Phase 1:** Initiating text analysis: careful reading of the transcripts and highlighting the particularly interesting passages. At the end of this phase, a first case summary of each interview will be written up.
**Phase 2:** Developing main thematic categories: major themes are derived directly from the research question, literature review and guided interview (since these have already been surveyed during the interviews).
**Phase 3:** First coding process: coding of the entire data with help of the main categories. In this step, the text sections are allocated to the main categories.
**Phase 4:** Compilation of all coded text passages with the same main categories.
**Phase 5:** Inductive determination of subcategories regarding the material. These subcategories will be determined and defined according to the main topics (see Table 1).
**Phase 6:** Category-based evaluation, interpretation and presentation of results.

*Table 1. Main categories and subcategories*

| | Subcategory | Definition |
|---|---|---|
| **Role of the Interviewee** | Knowledge-intensive processes | Processes in the research centre that are directly connected with knowledge (editing, production, distribution, preservation) |
| | Expertise | Areas in which team members have expertise and in which they can be described as experts |
| **Knowledge Transfer** | Definition of knowledge transfer | The understanding of the term "knowledge transfer within the team" |
| | Type of knowledge transferred | Different types of knowledge that are transferred in the research centre. |
| | Knowledge transfer methods | Methods that team members utilize to transfer and store knowledge |
| | IT tools | IT tools or systems, that team members utilize in order to transfer and to store knowledge |
| | Rules | The extent to which a knowledge transfer process in research centre is regulated and formalized |
| **Interculturality** | Culture | The interviewee's understanding of the term "culture" |
| | Intercultural communication | The interviewee's understanding of the term "intercultural communication" |
| | Problems, barriers | All conflicts, difficulties or barriers that are caused by interculturality in team |
| | Possible solutions | Possible ways to solve problems and to overcome barriers |
| | Advantages | Benefits of an intercultural team |
| | Intercultural competence | The interviewee's understanding of "intercultural competence"; here it is also about whether the interviewee has this competence or not |
| **Intercultural Knowledge Transfer** | Intercultural knowledge transfer chances | Opportunities, advantages and positive aspects of an intercultural knowledge transfer within the team |
| | Intercultural knowledge transfer risks | Risks, potential difficulties and negative aspects of an intercultural knowledge transfer within the team |

## FINDINGS

The object was a research institute with more than fifteen team members. It is an integral part of the business faculty of a university of applied sciences in Germany. Its research concept focuses on the marketing strategies for commercialization of research competencies, capacities and services. Science-to-Business Marketing Research Centre conducts not only various academic, but also business projects in its activity fields. These range from large research projects (as for example for the European Commission) to research and consulting projects for SMEs (Baaken & Schröder, 2008; Kliewe et al., 2012). Being entrepreneurial with its marketing concept of transmitting science to business Science-to-Business Marketing Research Centre drives innovation and acts entrepreneurially.

The staff of the centre consists of an interdisciplinary team whose members being carriers of different cultures come from different countries. The term "team" is understood in the research centre, as the possibility that every team member has an opportunity to individually prioritize his or her main focus within the different fields of expertise in the research centre.

This means that all team members working together still have their own priorities and different cultural and professional backgrounds. The research team consists of academic staff and student assistants who support academic associates in research, teaching and consulting. In addition, one person in the team is responsible for business development and takes care of strategic development of the research institute and project acquisition. Moreover all team members are supported by a team assistant, who is accountable for administrative and organisational issues. Four of the interviewees are currently academic researchers; the other six team members are former student assistants, who no longer work in the research centre.

As the investigation showed, the processes of knowledge transfer and knowledge preservation are not standardized within the team. This means, that employees do not use certain methods for knowledge sharing. Knowledge is however constantly transferred between team members in the research centre, since there are always knowledge intensive processes, and all employees deal with science in all possible ways. The real knowledge transfer takes place between the employees on a personal level during everyday communication, therefore, since there are no special rules for knowledge dissemination and documentation, in particular the tacit knowledge elements are mainly transferred in this existing setting. Distribution and exchange of knowledge within small teams as well as within working SMEs´ teams may happen in corridor conversations (Wong & Aspinwall, 2004, 2005) or at team events (Durst & Wilhelm, 2012).

Thus, the knowledge distribution in the research centre is based on the building blocks model of Probst et al. (2000), which was selected as the knowledge management concept for this paper. Distribution of knowledge as part of knowledge transfer within the team runs spontaneously and is not formalized, because the team is flexible and has a certain freedom of action in everyday working life.

Knowledge retention within this team is seen as an integral part of knowledge transfer. There is, however, a lack of systematization towards it. This means, that knowledge, certain experiences, ideas or successful solutions are not uniformly stored. The knowledge does not get lost over the time though, but it is merely documented and stored separately by each of the employees.

In terms of interculturality, all employees seem to be interculturally competent in spite of the cultural differences. This depends on the fact that the team members have already gained a lot of experience in dealing with intercultural environment and therefore have a well-developed ability to be empathic and have clear expectations. There are no culture-specific problems in the team that exert a strong influence on their productivity or that lead to misunderstandings. In this team, language diversity does not play a big role as a cultural barrier, since the languages in which the team members are proficient, are spoken daily in the research centre. Nevertheless, the language, as an important communication and cultural aspect, can sometimes cause some difficulties in the understanding process. This can be easily avoided, by using direct personal communication and by clearly expressing and transferring ideas and opinions.

As the interviews have shown, the intercultural knowledge transfer within the team works efficiently, even though the process is not formalized. Cultural differences in this case do not only work as barriers but can also be seen as impulse generators. The team's cultural heterogeneity causes, as a result, a creativity and synergy potential. That means that the knowledge is not only transferred within the intercultural team, but also generated, as a result of knowledge exchange processes, which are directly affected by the cultural diversity.

Moreover, during the investigation, it was determined that in order to be successful and effective in the intercultural communication regarding knowledge transfer, one needs a particular set of skills – intercultural competence (Rathje, 2006). Such competence plays a leading role in the intercultural activity, since it makes effective communication and collaboration possible. It appears today as one of the key skills in the globalized world, since it is necessary both in the intercultural context as well as in a foreign cultural environment. Such ability is also relevant for the intercultural knowledge transfer, since smooth interactions depend on it and hence effective knowledge sharing.

Overall, since the team was able to develop its own unique working environment, which displays its own special characteristics and features that often overlap and shape the way team members act, engage and interact with each other (Howell & Annansingh, 2013; Kim & Ju, 2008), the team succeeded in intercultural knowledge transfer by having and using intercultural competence and by encouraging the interpersonal communication. Nevertheless, the actual transfer of knowledge is not standardized in terms of special dissemination and documentation rules, the exchange of knowledge elements occurs between team members on a personal level during intercultural communication within the setting of existing framework conditions. In this particular setting the team's cultural diversity is not considered as a barrier, but as a driving force, which is able both to transfer and to generate new knowledge. In this setting, when mainly the implicit knowledge is transferred, the establishment of a set of rules in terms of transfer and retention of explicit knowledge is assumed to support the intercultural knowledge transfer processes. However, it should be taken into account that intercultural competence in a provided framework is the crucial factor for successful cross-cultural knowledge sharing.

## INTERCULTURAL COMPETENCE

To be interculturally competent means, that the individual should not only follow the rules, values and norms of his/her cultural society but should also try to understand another culture. One can speak about intercultural competence, if a person has a permanent ability to effectively, culturally sensitively and tolerantly interact with carriers of other cultures and communicate with them (Yousefi, 2006).

Bennett (2004) also emphasizes that the interculturally competent individual most probably will have no conflicts in the communication with the members of other cultures. This skill can be learned, but it must be always considered that in the socialization phase, individual in all likelihood has already gained some information and certainly has experienced certain situations so that it can be determined, that there were already created certain preconditions, and that he/she might generate his own assumptions (Derboven, 2009). That is why collecting new knowledge about other cultures should always be a part of the motivation.

In other terms, intercultural competence can be named as cultural intelligence (Earley & Ang, 2003; Zander et al., 2012; Presbitero, 2016), which is defined as the capability of an individual to act effectively in situations characterized by cultural diversity and includes four factors: cognitive, metacognitive, motivational and behavioural.

By cognitive cultural intelligence is understood an individual's knowledge of different cultural environments, certain norms and rules (Earley & Ang, 2003), including the ability to understand differences and similarities across these cultural environments (Ng et al., 2012). Metacognitive cultural intelligence refers to planning, monitoring, and revising mental models of cultural norms, which are considered to be appropriate for certain societies (Ang & van Dyne, 2008). Motivational factor means that person is interested, motivated and, what is more important, confident when interacting in culturally diverse situations. Lastly, behavioural cultural intelligence includes a capacity to act and react appropriately in terms of verbal and non-verbal intercultural communication (Livermore, 2011).

Thus, it can be said that intercultural competence consists of different components and needs different skills and certain knowledge that are necessary for communication in an intercultural context. Such competence plays a leading role in the intercultural activity, since it makes effective communication and collaboration possible. Such an ability is also relevant for the intercultural knowledge transfer (Rathje, 2006), since smooth interactions depend on it and hence is able to provide an effective knowledge sharing.

## FUTURE RESEARCH DIRECTIONS

In the theoretical part of this chapter, cultural diversity in knowledge transfer was considered rather as a barrier. This classification is based on the idea that cultural differences hinder the transfer of knowledge. An important result of this study was, nevertheless, that interculturality plays a role as a driving force in knowledge transfer, and moreover is able to cause creativity and generate knowledge. Since such a consideration has not yet been made, it offers a starting point for further research focusing on cultural diversity as an advantage and a driving force.

An interesting starting point for further research would also be a consideration of the intercultural competence in knowledge transfer in an intercultural context. From this background a continuation of the cross-cultural knowledge transfer research is possible and thereby the investigation of the intercultural competence in regard of knowledge intensive processes in this context.

## CONCLUSION

Drawing on the extensive research on knowledge transfer and cultural issues and qualitative interviews, four main findings emerged from the analysis:

- Successful knowledge transfer does not necessarily have to be standardized.
- Culture matters in knowledge transfer.
- Cultural differences influence the internal knowledge transfer both in negative and positive way.
- Intercultural competence is a crucial factor of successful cross-cultural knowledge transfer.

Cultural diversity has an influence on knowledge transfer in intercultural context. Cultural differences have a very direct impact on how people share, communicate and interpret their knowledge. Intercultural communication, in terms of how explicit and precise the communication is, plays a crucial role by transferring knowledge and may cause some risks. Such aspects of cross-cultural communication as language diversity, assumptions and stereotypes, which people have about other cultures, may lead to misunderstanding, if information flows were not correctly reflected and interpreted. Cultural patterns are therefore firmly established, unconscious orientations, which have a direct impact on people´s sense making and perception.

The lack of knowledge about different cultures, the lack of soft skills and behaviours cause the ineffective transcultural communication and consequently hinder the knowledge sharing process. The intercultural competence is therefore one of the crucial factors and one of the main skills needed to operate effectively in multicultural team by sharing knowledge. It is emerging as a key competency, not only in cross-cultural communication. Intercultural competence is especially relevant to knowledge transfer processes, because the success of any knowledge intensive interaction directly depends on ability to communicate effectively, to understand others' worldviews and way of thinking. Since intercultural competence is not a naturally occurring phenomenon, it must be developed and improved to be successful both in intercultural dialog and knowledge sharing. Overall, as Bengoa and Kaufmann (2014: 11) stated, *"...the current reality of interdependent world challenges companies and human beings to develop specific intercultural skills to successfully manage the increasing level of diversity."*

Normally culturally diverse teams work either very effective or conversely very ineffective (Adler & Gundersen, 2008). In the same manner diverse national cultures of employees are likely to affect the knowledge management and transfer positively or negatively (Rivera-Vasquez et al., 2009; Peltokorpi & Vaara, 2014). However, if the team members have the appropriate competence to operate in intercultural environment, they may have no difficulties by sharing knowledge to bearers of other cultures. In order to be successful and effective in the intercultural communication regarding knowledge transfer, one needs a particular set of skills – intercultural competence (Rathje, 2006; Nguyen & Aoyama, 2015).

Moreover, the study provides the evidence that cultural diversity can have a positive impact on the transfer of knowledge (Laitin & Jeon, 2013), which is mainly implicit, since they constantly communicate personally with each other, following at the same time no formal rules. This only is successful in a setting of flexibility and freedom provided to team members. However, the establishment of a set of documents in terms of knowledge dissemination and retention could support the existing intercultural knowledge transfer processes by helping to share and to save explicit knowledge elements. Overall, cultural differences can also cause creativity, because the variety of different points of view and ways of thinking initiate a broader idea finding and solution process, and therefore generate new knowledge.

This chapter has important practical implications for SME´s that are trying to carry out internal transfer of knowledge in a cross-cultural environment, where employees being carriers of different national cultures work collaboratively as team. The findings suggest that team members as recipients or providers of knowledge should develop intercultural competence and build trustful interpersonal relationships with each other. From the practical point of view, this case study also points out the need for SMEs to create a friendly working atmosphere. Since the results show that the knowledge transfer occurs mainly informal, it is recommended to establish proper communication, both social and intercultural, and to include it as a routine in the existing working setting by encouraging face-to-face interactions between team members on an everyday basis. That can help employees to grasp and to utilise each other´s knowledge in multicultural environment.

## REFERENCES

Aba, D. (2015). Towards an intercultural communication competence tool for academic mobility purposes. *Journal of International Communication, 39*. Retrieved March 5, 2016, from http://www.immi.se/intercultural/nr39/aba.html

Adair, W. L., Tinsley, C. H., & Taylor, M. (2006). Managing the Intercultural Interface: Third Cultures, Antecedents, and Consequences. In Y.-R. Chen (Ed.), *National Culture and Groups (Research on Managing Groups and Teams)* (pp. 205–232). Bingley: Emerald Group Publishing Limited. doi:10.1016/S1534-0856(06)09009-8

Adler, N. J., & Gundersen, A. (2008). *International dimensions of organizational behavior*. Mason, OH: Thomson Higher Education.

Andreeva, I., & Ikhilchik, I. (2011). Applicability of the SECI model of knowledge creation in Russian cultural context: Theoretical analysis. *Knowledge and Process Management, 18*(1), 56–66. doi:10.1002/kpm.351

Ang, S., & van Dyne, L. (2008). *Handbook of cultural intelligence.* New York: ME Sharpe.

Argote, L., & Ingram, P. (2000). Knowledge transfer: A basis for a competitive advantage in firms. *Organizational Behavior and Human Decision Processes, 82*(1), 150–169. doi:10.1006/obhd.2000.2893

Baaken, T., & Schröder, C. (2008). The Triangle for Innovation in Technology Transfer at Münster University of Applied Sciences. In K. Laine, P. van der Sijde, M. Lähdeniemi, & J. Tarkkanen (Eds.), Higher Education Institutions and Innovation in the Knowledge Society (pp. 103-116). Helsinki: ARENE ry.

Bannenberg, A.-K. (2010). *Die Bedeutung interkultureller Kommunikation in der Wirtschaft.* Kassel: Kassel University Press GmbH.

Barmayer, I., & Davoine, E. (2006). Interkulturelle Zusammenarbeit und Führung in internationalen Teams: Das Beispiel Deutschland – Frankreich. *Zeitschrift Führung + Organisation, 75*(1), 35-39.

Bengoa, D. S., & Kaufmann, H. R. (2014). Questioning western knowledge transfer methodologies: Toward a reciprocal and intercultural transfer of knowledge. *Thunderbird International Business Review, 56*(1), 11–26. doi:10.1002/tie.21593

Bennett, M. J. (1998). Intercultural Communication: A Current Perspective. In M. J. Bennet (Ed.), *Basic Concepts of Intercultural Communication: Selected readings* (pp. 1–34). Boston, MA: Intercultural Press.

Bennett, M. J. (2004). Becoming interculturally competent. In J. Wurzel (Ed.), *Toward multiculturalism: A reader in multicultural education* (pp. 62–77). Newton, MA: Intercultural Resource Corporation.

Blom, H., & Meier, H. (2002). *Interkulturelles Management. Interkulturelle Kommunikation, internationales Personalmanagement, Diversity-Ansätze im Unternehmen.* Herne: Verlag Neue Wirtschafts-Briefe.

Boateng, H., & Agyemang, F. G. (2015). The role of culture in knowledge sharing in a public-sector organization in Ghana: Revisiting Hofstede's model. *International Journal of Public Administration, 38*(12), 486–495. doi:10.1080/01900692.2014.949743

Boh, W. F., Nguyen, T. T., & Xu, Y. (2013). Knowledge transfer across dissimilar cultures. *Journal of Knowledge Management, 17*(1), 29–46. doi:10.1108/13673271311300723

Bronszinsky-Schwabe, E. (2011). *Interkulturelle Kommunikation. Missverständnisse – Verständigung.* Wiesbaden: VS Verlag für Sozialwissenschaften. doi:10.1007/978-3-531-92764-0

Browaeys, M. J., & Price, R. (2011). *Understanding cross-cultural management.* Harlow: Pearson Financial Times.

Caiazza, R., Richardson, A., & Audretsch, D. (2015). Knowledge effects on competitiveness: From firms to regional advantage. *The Journal of Technology Transfer, 40*(6), 899–909. doi:10.1007/s10961-015-9425-8

Cavusgil, S. T., Calantone, R. J., & Zhao, Y. (2003). Tacit knowledge transfer and firm innovation capability. *Journal of Business and Industrial Marketing, 18*(1), 6–21. doi:10.1108/08858620310458615

Cerchione, R., Esposito, E., & Spadaro, M. R. (2016). A literature review on knowledge management in SMEs. *Knowledge Management Research & Practice, 14*(2), 169-177.

Chen, J., Sun, P. Y. T., & McQueen, R. J. (2010). The impact of national cultures on structured knowledge transfer. *Journal of Knowledge Management, 14*(2), 228–242. doi:10.1108/13673271011032373

Chua, N. (2002). The influence of social interaction on knowledge creation. *Journal of Intellectual Capital, 3*(4), 375–392. doi:10.1108/14691930210448297

Chuang, C.-H., Jackson, S. E., & Jiang, Y. (2016). Can knowledge-intensive teamwork be managed? Examining the roles of HRM systems, leadership, and tacit knowledge. *Journal of Management, 42*(2), 524–554. doi:10.1177/0149206313478189

Cooke, N. J., Salas, E., Cannon-Bowers, J. A., & Stout, R. J. (2000). Measuring team knowledge. *Human Factors, 42*(1), 151–173. doi:10.1518/001872000779656561 PMID:10917151

Deng-Neng, C., Ting-Peng, L., & Binshan, L. (2010). An ecological model for organizational knowledge management. *Journal of Computer Information Systems, 50*(3), 11–22.

Deo, S. (2013). *The impact of globalisation on small business enterprises (SBEs)*. Paper presented at the 26th Annual SEAANZ Conference 2013: Small Business Management in Globally Competitive Markets, Sydney, New South Wales, Australia.

Derboven, K. (2009). *Interkulturelles Training. Trainingsmanual zur Förderung interkultureller Kompetenzen in der Arbeit*. Heidelberg, Germany: Springer-Verlag.

Durst, S., & Edvardsson, I. R. (2012). Knowledge management in SMEs: A literature review. *Journal of Knowledge Management, 16*(4), 637–648.

Durst, S., & Wilhelm, S. (2012). Knowledge management and succession planning in SMEs. *Journal of Knowledge Management, 16*(6), 879–903. doi:10.1108/13673271211276173

Earley, P. C., & Ang, S. (2003). *Cultural intelligence: individual interactions across cultures*. San Francisco: Stanford University Press.

Easa, N. F., & Fincham, R. (2012). The application of the socialization, externalisation, combination and internalisation model in cross-cultural context: Theoretical analysis. *Knowledge and Process Management, 19*(2), 103–109. doi:10.1002/kpm.1385

Edvardsson, I. R. (2009). Is knowledge management losing ground? Developments among Icelandic SMEs. *Knowledge Management Research & Practice, 7*(1), 91–99. doi:10.1057/kmrp.2008.30

Espinosa, J. A., & Clark, M. A. (2014). Team knowledge-representation: A network perspective. *Human Factors, 52*(2), 333–348. doi:10.1177/0018720813494093 PMID:24689252

Freyens, B., & Martin, M. (2007). Multidisciplinary knowledge transfer in training multimedia projects. *Journal of European Industrial Training, 31*(9), 680–105. doi:10.1108/03090590710846666

Geisler, E., & Wickramasinghe, N. (2015). *Principles of knowledge management: theory, practice, and cases*. London: Routledge.

Gioia, D. A., Corley, K. G., & Hamilton, A. L. (2013). Seeking qualitative rigor in inductive research notes on the Gioia methodology. *Organizational Research Methods, 16*(1), 15–31. doi:10.1177/1094428112452151

Grandinetti, R. (2016). Absorptive capacity and knowledge management in small and medium sized enterprises. *Knowledge Management Research & Practice, 14*(2), 159-168.

Haghirian, P. (2011). *Multinationals and cross-cultural management: the transfer of knowledge within multinational corporations*. New York: Routledge.

Hendricks, P. (1999). Why share knowledge? The influence of ICT on the motivation for knowledge sharing. *Knowledge and Process Management, 6*(2), 91–100. doi:10.1002/(SICI)1099-1441(199906)6:2<91::AID-KPM54>3.0.CO;2-M

Henriques, A. C. V., Antunes, E. D. D., & Macke, J. (2014). Intercultural knowledge transfer: Processes analysis of a multinational company. *Gestão & Planejamento, 15*(3), 537–552.

Hislop, D. (2013). *Knowledge management in organizations: A critical introduction*. Oxford University Press.

Hitt, M. A. (1998). Twenty-first-century organizations: Business firms, business schools, and the academy. *Academy of Management Review, 23*(2), 218–224.

Hitt, M. A., Ireland, R. D., & Hoskisson, R. E. (1999). *Strategic Management: Competitiveness and Globalization*. Cincinnati, OH: South-Western College Publishing.

Hoerem, T., von Krogh, G., & Roos, J. (1999). Knowledge based strategic change. In G. von Krogh & J. Roos (Eds.), *Managing knowledge: perspectives on cooperation and competition* (pp. 116–136). London: SAGE Publications Inc.

Hofstede, G. (1983). The cultural relativity organizational practices and theories. *Journal of International Business Studies, 14*(2), 75–89. doi:10.1057/palgrave.jibs.8490867

Hofstede, G. (1997). *Cultures and Organizations: Software of the Mind: Intercultural Cooperation and its Importance for Survival*. New York: McGraw-Hill.

Hong, J. F. L. (2012). Glocalizing Nonaka's knowledge creation model: Issues and challenges. *Management Learning, 43*(2), 199–215. doi:10.1177/1350507611428853

Howell, K., & Annansingh, F. (2013). Knowledge generation and sharing in UK universities: A tale of two cultures? *International Journal of Information Management, 33*(1), 32–39. doi:10.1016/j.ijinfomgt.2012.05.003

Husted, K., & Michailova, S. (2002). Knowledge sharing in Russian companies with western participation. *Management International, 6*(2), 17–28.

Hutchinson, K., Quinn, B., & Alexander, N. (2006). SME retailer internationalisation: Case study evidence from British retailers. *International Marketing Review, 23*(1), 25–53. doi:10.1108/02651330610646287

Jackson, S. E., Chuang, C. H., Harden, E. E., & Jiang, Y. (2006). Toward developing human resource management system for knowledge-intensive teamwork. In J. Martocchio (Ed.), *Research in personnel and human resources management* (pp. 25–70). Oxford, UK: Elsevier. doi:10.1016/S0742-7301(06)25002-3

Javidan, M., Stahl, G. K., Brodbeck, F., & Wilderom, C. P. M. (2005). Cross-border transfer of knowledge: Cultural lessons from project GLOBE. *The Academy of Management Executive, 1*(2), 59–76. doi:10.5465/AME.2005.16962801

Kaps, I. (2011). Barriers in intercultural knowledge sharing. *Open Journal of Knowledge Management, 1*(3), 6–12.

Khan, S. R., & Khan, I. A. (2015). Understanding ethnicity and national culture: A theoretical perspective on knowledge management in the organization. *Knowledge and Process Management, 22*(10), 51–61. doi:10.1002/kpm.1440

Kim, S., & Ju, B. (2008). An analysis of faculty perceptions: Attitudes towards knowledge sharing and collaboration in an academic institution. *Library & Information Science Research, 30*(4), 282–290. doi:10.1016/j.lisr.2008.04.003

Kliewe, T., Baaken, T., & Kesting, T. (2012). Introducing a Science-to-Business Marketing Unit to University Knowledge and Technology Transfer Structures: Activities, Benefits, Success Factors. In A. Szopa, W. Karwowski, & P. Ordóñez de Pablos (Eds.), *Academic Entrepreneurship and Technological Innovation: A Business Management Perspective* (pp. 53–74). Hershey, PA: IGI Global.

Kuckartz, U. (2014). *Qualitative Inhaltsanalyse. Methoden, Praxis, Computerunterstützung*. Weinheim: Beltz Juventa.

Laitin, D. D., & Jeon, S. (2013). Exploring opportunities in cultural diversity. In R. A. Scott & S. M. Kosslyn (Eds.), *Emerging trends in the social and behavioural sciences: interdisciplinary directions* (pp. 1–17). London: SAGE Pub.

Law, C., & Ngai, E. (2008). An empirical study of the effects of knowledge sharing and learning behaviors on firm performance. *Expert Systems with Applications, 34*(4), 2342–2349. doi:10.1016/j.eswa.2007.03.004

Lehner, F. (2006). *Wissensmanagement: Grundlagen, Methoden und technische Unterstützung*. München: Carl Hanser Verlag.

Liebl, F. (2015). Knowledge management for strategic marketing. In H. E. Spotts (Ed.), *Assessing the different roles of marketing theory and practice in the jaws of economic uncertainty* (pp. 48–57). New York: Springer Cham Heidelberg.

Livermore, D. (2011). *The cultural intelligence difference: master the one skill you can't do without in today's global economy*. New York: American Management Association.

Marakas, G. M. (1999). *Decision Support Systems in the Twenty-first Century*. Englewood Cliffs, NJ: Prentice-Hall.

Marquadt, M. J., & Horvath, L. (2010). *Global Teams*. Mountain View, CA: Davies Black Publishing.

Mayring, P. (2010). *Qualitative Inhaltsanalyse: Grundlagen und Techniken*. Weinheim: Beltz Pädagogik. doi:10.1007/978-3-531-92052-8_42

Minbaeva, D. B. (2007). Knowledge transfer in multinational corporations. *Management International Review, 47*(4), 567–593. doi:10.1007/s11575-007-0030-4

Mohr, A., & Shoobridge, G. E. (2011). The role of multi-ethnic workforces in the internationalisation of SMEs. *Journal of Small Business and Enterprise Development, 18*(4), 748–763. doi:10.1108/14626001111179785

Müller, S., & Gelbrich, K. (2015). *Interkulturelles Marketing*. München: Verlag Franz Vahlen GmbH. doi:10.15358/9783800644612

Murmann, J. P. (2003). *Knowledge and competitive advantage: the coevolution of firms, technology, and national institutions (Cambridge studies in the emergence of global enterprise)*. Cambridge, UK: Cambridge University Press. doi:10.1017/CBO9780511510953

Ng, K. Y., van Dyne, L., & Ang, S. (2012). Cultural intelligence: A review, reflections, and recommendations for future research. In A. M. Ryan, F. T. Leong, & F. L. Oswald (Eds.), *Conducting multinational research: Applying organizational psychology in the workplace* (pp. 29–58). Washington, DC: American Psychological Association. doi:10.1037/13743-002

Nguyen, T. D. N., & Aoyama, A. (2015). The impact of cultural differences on technology transfer. Management practice moderation. *Journal of Manufacturing Technology Management, 27*(7), 926–954. doi:10.1108/JMTM-09-2013-0130

Nonaka, I. (1994). A dynamic theory of organizational knowledge creation. *Organization Science, 5*(1), 14–37. doi:10.1287/orsc.5.1.14

Nonaka, I., & Nishiguchi, T. (2001). *Knowledge Emergence. Social, Technical and Evolutionary Dimensions of Knowledge Creation*. New York: Oxford University Press.

Nonaka, I., & Takeuchi, H. (1995). *The Knowledge creating company*. Oxford, UK: Oxford University Press.

Nonaka, I., von Krogh, G., & Voepel, S. (2006). Organisational knowledge creation theory: Evolutionary paths and future advances. *Organization Studies, 27*(8), 1179–1208. doi:10.1177/0170840606066312

North, K. (2002). *Wissensorientierte Unternehmensführung. Wertschöpfung durch Wissen*. Wiesbaden: Gabler. doi:10.1007/978-3-322-94633-1

Nunes, M. B., Annansingh, F., Eaglestone, B., & Wakefield, R. (2006). Knowledge management issues in knowledge-intensive SMEs. *The Journal of Documentation, 62*(1), 101–119. doi:10.1108/00220410610642075

Peltokorpi, V., & Vaara, E. (2014). Knowledge transfer in multinational corporations: Productive and counterproductive effects of language sensitive recruitment. *Journal of International Business Studies, 45*(5), 600–622. doi:10.1057/jibs.2014.1

Peng, M., & Meyer, K. (2011). *International Business*. London: Cengage Learning EMEA.

Polanyi, M. (1996). *The tacit Dimension*. New York: Anchor Day Books.

Popescu, A.-D., Suciu, S., & Raoult, M.-G. (2014). *Intercultural competences in collaborative teams*. Paper presented at the 7th International Conference Interdisciplinarity in Engineering (INTER-ENG 2013). Petru Maior University of Tigru Mures, Romania.

Prahalad, C. K., & Hamel, G. (1990). The core competence of the corporation. *Harvard Business Review*, *68*(3), 79–93.

Presbitero, A. (2016). Cultural intelligence (CQ) in virtual, cross-cultural interactions: Generalizability of measure and links to personality dimensions and task performance. *International Journal of Intercultural Relations*, *50*, 29–38. doi:10.1016/j.ijintrel.2015.11.001

Probst, G., Raub, S., & Romhardt, K. (2000). *Managing knowledge: buildings blocks for success*. Chichester, UK: John Wiley & Sons Ltd.

Rathje, S. (2006). Interkulturelle Kompetenz – Zustand und Zukunft eines umstrittenen Konzepts. *Zeitschrift für Interkulturellen Fremdsprachenunterricht*, *11*(3), 1–21.

Rivera-Vazquez, J. C., Ortiz-Fournier, L. V., & Flores, F. R. (2009). Overcoming cultural barriers for innovation and knowledge sharing. *Journal of Knowledge Management*, *13*(5), 257–270. doi:10.1108/13673270910988097

Roos, J., & von Krogh, G. (2002). The new language lab. In S. Little, P. Quintas, & T. Ray (Eds.), *Managing knowledge: An essential reader* (pp. 255–263). London: SAGE Pub.

Ruzzier, M., Hisrich, R. D., & Antoncic, A. (2006). SME internationalization research: Past, present, and future. *Journal of Small Business and Enterprise Development*, *13*(4), 476–497. doi:10.1108/14626000610705705

Samovar, L. A., & Porter, R. E. (1995). *Communication between Cultures*. Belmont: Wadsworth Publishing Company.

Soley, M., & Pandaya, V. K. (2003). Culture as an issue in Knowledge Sharing: A means of Competitive Advantage. *Electronic Journal of Knowledge Management*, *1*(2), 205–212.

Spencer-Rodgers, J., & McGovern, T. (2002). Attitudes toward culturally different: The role of intercultural communication barriers, affective response, consensual stereotypes, and perceived threat. *International Journal of Intercultural Relations*, *26*(6), 609–631. doi:10.1016/S0147-1767(02)00038-X

Sternberg, R. J. (1997). Tacit Knowledge and Job Success. In N. Anderson & P. Herriot (Eds.), *International Handbook of selection and assessment* (pp. 201–213). Chichester, UK: Wiley.

Syfox, J. (2000). Globalization and cultural change in organizations. *Management Research News*, *23*(2/4), 86–87.

Teece, D. (2001). Strategies for managing knowledge assets: the role of firm structure and industrial context. In I. Nonaka & D. Teece (Eds.), *Creation, Transfer and Utilisation* (pp. 125–144). London: SAGE. doi:10.4135/9781446217573.n7

Valkokari, K., & Helander, N. (2007). Knowledge management in different types of strategic SME networks. *Management Research News*, *30*(8), 597–608. doi:10.1108/01409170710773724

von Krogh, G., & Köhne, M. (1998). Der Wissenstransfer in Unternehmen: Phasen des Wissenstransfers und wichtige Einflussfaktoren. *Die Unternehmung*, *56*(5/6), 235–252.

Wang, M.-H., & Yang, T.-Y. (2016). Investigating the success of knowledge management: An empirical study of small- and medium-sized enterprises. *Asia Pacific Management Review*, *21*(2), 79–91. doi:10.1016/j.apmrv.2015.12.003

Wilkesmann, U., Fischer, H., & Wilkesmann, M. (2009). Cultural characteristics of knowledge transfer. *Journal of Knowledge Management*, *13*(6), 464–477. doi:10.1108/13673270910997123

Wöbling, I., & Keuper, F. (2009). Produktionstheoretische Analyse der Wissensentwicklung. In F. Keuper & F. Neumann (Eds.), *Wissens- und Informationsmanagement: Strategien, Organisation und Prozesse* (pp. 33–50). Wiesbaden: Gabler Verlag. doi:10.1007/978-3-8349-6509-7_2

Wong, K. Y., & Aspinwall, E. (2004). Characterising knowledge management in small business environment. *Journal of Knowledge Management*, *8*(3), 44–61. doi:10.1108/13673270410541033

Wong, K. Y., & Aspinwall, E. (2005). An empirical study of the important factors for knowledge-management adoption in the SME sector. *Journal of Knowledge Management*, *9*(3), 64–82. doi:10.1108/13673270510602773

Yousefi, H. R. (2006). Toleranz als Weg zur interkulturellen Kommunikation und Verständigung. In H. R. Yousefi, K. Fischer, & I. Braun (Eds.), Wege zur Kommunikation. Theorie und Praxis interkultureller Toleranz (pp. 19-49). Nordhausen: Traugott Bautz.

Zander, L., Mockaitis, A. I., & Butler, C. L. (2012). Leading global teams. *Journal of World Business*, *47*(4), 592–603. doi:10.1016/j.jwb.2012.01.012

## KEY TERMS AND DEFINITIONS

**Cross-Cultural Communication:** A specific type of interpersonal interaction, where carriers of different cultures are communicating with each other.

**Cultural Intelligence:** A capability of an individual to act effectively in situations characterized by interculturality.

**Culture:** A collective phenomenon, which includes knowledge, experience, beliefs, values, attitudes, hierarchies, religion, shared by a group of people and passed through the generations.

**Explicit Knowledge:** Knowledge that can be expressed, presented and stored in form of data and is easily articulated and formalized.

**Intercultural Competence:** An ability of an individual to effectively, culturally sensitively and tolerantly interact with carriers of other cultures.

**Interculturality:** The meeting of two or more cultures through a dialogue, in which, despite cultural differences, mutual interference arises.

**Knowledge:** An organized combination of ideas, rules, procedures, and information, evolving in a certain context.

**Knowledge Transfer:** The process of knowledge distribution and dissemination between organizational units or individuals.

**Tacit Knowledge:** Knowledge that cannot be fully expressed in words and is difficult to formalize and to communicate.

# Chapter 13
# Knowledge Sharing Relation to Competence, Emotional Intelligence, and Social Media Regarding Generations

**Nora Obermayer**
*University of Pannonia, Hungary*

**Anikó Csepregi**
*University of Pannonia, Hungary*

**Edit Kővári**
*University of Pannonia, Hungary*

## ABSTRACT

*This chapter introduces the possible differences revealed of the applied methods in knowledge sharing based on generational differences. In addition the chapter investigates the relationship of knowledge sharing to competences, emotional intelligence and social media tools and presents research that were carried out between 2006-2015. The aim of this part is to enable companies, especially SMEs to learn from these research outcomes and develop strategies to trigger knowledge sharing among different generations regarding the vital competences, emotional intelligence and social media tools.*

## INTRODUCTION

Knowledge has always seen as potentially one of the key strategic resources that can be the basis for developing sustained long-term competitive advantage for organizations. Organizations that need to thrive, compete, and operate in an ever changing and evolving environment, cannot leave the development of knowledge within the organization to chance. Organizations are faced with the challenge how to get people to share their knowledge. This chapter investigates knowledge sharing related to competence, emotional intelligence and social media tools.

DOI: 10.4018/978-1-5225-1642-2.ch013

## THEORETICAL BACKGROUND

### Knowledge Management

Knowledge is becoming a strategically important resource and a very significant driver of organizational performance (Yesil & Dereli, 2013). Either located in the minds of the individuals (tacit knowledge) (Polányi, 1966), embedded in organizational routines and norms, codified in technological devices (explicit knowledge) (Nonaka & Takeuchi, 1995), knowledge enables the development of new competences (Choo, 1998). Successful companies are those that consistently create new knowledge, disseminate this knowledge throughout the organization, and embody it in technologies, products and services (Gaál et al., 2009). Knowledge management describes the processes of acquiring, developing, sharing, exploiting and protecting organizational knowledge to improve organizations' competitiveness. Organizations around the world have focused on knowledge management and have already developed knowledge management programs in order to improve their performance with varying degrees of success.

Clearly one important set of activities involves the defining knowledge and constructing the metrics to assess how effectively an organization is managing (sharing) its knowledge.

### Knowledge Sharing

To ensure the success and long-term survival of any organizations effective knowledge sharing is of critical importance (Gaál et al., 2008). Li (2010, p. 40) defines knowledge sharing as an activity, in which "participants are involved in the joint process of contributing, negotiating and utilizing knowledge". On the other hand, according to Moeller and Svahn (2004, p. 220) knowledge sharing is "sharing not only codified information"…"but also management beliefs, images, experiences, and contextualized practices". Mueller (2012, p. 436) emphasized that at least two people, groups, or organizations are involved in knowledge sharing "the sender, who is willing and able to share knowledge, and the receiver, who is willing and able to combine this new knowledge with his or her existing knowledge and use it". The two parties can also share their knowledge found in their minds or the knowledge found in electronic or traditional documents. Furthermore, the knowledge sharing process can also be simultaneous when the parties involved are all present, or consecutive when these parties make their knowledge explicit (Szabó & Csepregi, 2015). Knowledge sharing can be characterized by communication processes and information flows. In many social situations knowledge sharing is a common activity but knowledge sharing within an organization tends to be a complex and complicated issue and, as a result, needs to be actively managed. Knowledge sharing is typically focused on activities that involve providing information and knowledge to assist others in solving problems, develop new ideas, or implement processes (Cummings, 2004).

### Knowledge Sharing Behaviour

Knowledge sharing behaviour is considered as "the degree to which organizational members actually share knowledge with others" (Yang & Chen, 2007, p. 101). Focusing on an Intranet environment Masrek et al. (2011) discovered that both the length of service and the Internet experience are significant predictor of knowledge sharing behaviour. In virtual environment knowledge sharing behaviour appears as a behaviour to disseminate one member's acquired knowledge with the usage of computer mediated communication tools to other members. Since an individual cannot possess all knowledge and knowledge cannot be hoarded like gold, people should recognize that the old paradigm 'knowledge is power' is less and less relevant. One of the ways of motivating individuals to share knowledge is to introduce how knowledge sharing can support them in executing their jobs more effectively and in helping them in their personal development and achieving their personal goals (Obermayer-Kovács & Csepregi, 2007). Davenport and Prusak (1998) categorized the potential motivation behind knowledge sharing behaviour as either pure altruism, reciprocity, or reputation.

- Altruism refers to behaviour that costs an individual and benefit the other person. People donate something to other people without thinking of any returns when showing altruistic behaviour.
- Reciprocity refers to either a positive or negative response for the actions which one should treat others as one would like others to treat oneself. People share information or knowledge might expect future benefits from their present actions.
- Reputation refers to a degree of recognition and increased by information sharing among other users. People who share more knowledge receive a higher reputation.

Research works (Davenport & Prusak, 1998; Susanty & Wood, 2011) have also proved that intrinsic and extrinsic motivators influence knowledge sharing attitude. It is stated also that intrinsic motivation plays a greater role than extrinsic motivation in case of willingness to share.

- Loss of knowledge power is the perception of power and unique value lost due to knowledge contributed (Gray, 2001). Knowledge management literature reports the loss of knowledge power as a barrier to knowledge sharing. People may keep themselves out of a knowledge exchange if they feel they can benefit more by hoarding their knowledge rather than by sharing it.
- Organizational reward means the importance of economic incentives (e.g. bonuses, security, and career advancement) provided for individuals (Hall, 2001).

## Knowledge Sharing and Social Media

### Social Media Technologies

Social media has a number of definitions, such as "collaborative online applications and technologies which enable and encourage participation, conversation, openness, creation and socialization amongst a community of users" (Bowley, 2009:15), web-based tools and practices enabling participation and collaboration based on individuals' activities. Surowiecki (2005) defined that social media is to make use of the "wisdom of the crowd". Group of people are better at problem solving, fostering decision making than individuals alone.

Vuori (2011) characterises social media by considering the extent to which they support communication, collaboration, connecting, completing and combining (5C).

1. **Communication**: Social media provides new tools to share, store and publish contents, discuss and express opinions and influence:
   a. Blogs (e.g. Blogger) and microblogs (e.g. Twitter)
   b. Video sharing (e.g. YouTube)

   c.    Presentation sharing (e.g. SlideShare)

   d.    Instant messaging service (e.g. Skype)

2.   **Collaboration**: Social media enables collective content creation and edition without location and time constraints:

   a.    Wikis (e.g. Wikipedia)

   b.    Groupware/shared workspaces (e.g. GoogleDocs)

   c.    Communities of practices (e.g. MeetUp)

3.   **Connecting**: Social media offers new ways of networking with other people, socialising oneself into the community:

   a.    Social networking services (e.g. Facebook, LinkedIn):

4.   **Completing**: Social media tools are used to complete content by describing, adding or filtering information, tagging contents, and showing a connection between contents:

   a.    Visual bookmarking tool (e.g. Pinterest)

   b.    News aggregator (e.g. Digg)

5.   **Combining**: Social media tools are developed for mixing and matching contents. Combination of pre-existing web services that allow a certain user within a platform to use another application, in a specific window, without the need to get out of the initial website.

   a.    Mash-ups (e.g. Google Maps)

Social media seem a perfect way for knowledge sharing, because social activities contribute to the sharing process and collaboration. It is the success of social media that they encourage social interaction but also exploit it. People can change the contents of others, they can use (action) and respond to it (reflection). The interaction not only leads to new knowledge, it can also ensure that ties with others strengthen or weaken.

## Social Media and Knowledge Sharing

A theoretical investigation was conducted by Panahi et al. (2012) who illustrated their findings in a conceptual framework in respect of social media abilities supporting the requirements of tacit knowledge sharing. These abilities include the support of a better place for social interaction, the establishment of opportunities for experience sharing, the building of a domain of informal relationships, the support of facilities to observe, listen, and imitate best practices, and the establishment of a mutual swift trust among participants.

Sigala and Chalkiti (2015) defined a three-layer framework to measure social media's exploitation for knowledge management. On the first level the use of technological tools to search, store, categorize and link information are present. The second level represents the usage of technological tools to achieve the identification and participation in social networks in order to develop and maintain interpersonal relations that can in turn facilitate knowledge management processes as sharing, discussion and negotiation with others. Finally, the third level aims to support knowledge creation processes through synthesis and discussion. Each level also requires certain capabilities to effectively perform on the given level.

## Competence

According to Sveiby (1997, p. 38) competence "embraces factual knowledge, skill, experience, value judgments, and social networks". Skills, besides attitudes and knowledge, also appear as important elements of competence which in Stoof's (2005) viewpoint are required in jobs or tasks employees must fulfill. Gibb (1990, p. 21) describes competence being "an ability to perform certain tasks for which knowledge, skills, attitudes and motivations are necessary". Reinhardt and North (2003, p. 1374) compared to the previously presented definitions emphasize the importance of requirements by stressing that competence "describes a relation between requirements placed on a person/group or self-created requirements and these persons' skills and potentials to be able to meet these requirements". They also emphasize that competence focuses on when knowledge is applied and it can be measured when the result of actions is achieved (Reinhardt & North, 2003). Competence can be classified differently. According to Schein (1978) there are analytical, emotional and interpersonal competences, while Sternberg (1990) differentiated between objective and subjective competences. On the other hand, behavioural, core and managerial competences appear in Sparrow and Hiltrop's (1994) grouping and cognitive, functional, meta and social competences in Delamare et al.'s (2005) categorization. Social competence also appears in Forgács et al.'s (2002) grouping besides methodological, professional and personal competences. Regarding emotional intelligence Goleman et al. (2013) differentiate 18 kinds of competences which are categorized into personal and social competences. While the first determines how someone manages oneself, the later one focuses on how one manages relationships. They also emphasize that to be an effective leader one must "demonstrate strengths in at least one competence from each of the four fundamental areas of emotional intelligence" which are self-awareness and self-management belonging to personal competence, and social awareness and relationship management belonging to social competence (Goleman et al. 2013, p. 40).

## Emotional Intelligence

According to Zeidner et al (2009), emotional intelligence as science is built on three pillars: theory, measurement and applications. Higgs and Dulewicz (1999) differentiate three basic but interlinking questions concerning emotional intelligence: what is emotional intelligence; can it be measured, and can it be developed? Emotional intelligence (EI) is a concept of collection that combines social, personal, and interpersonal intelligence including capabilities, competences and non-cognitive skills which influence the ability and technique to manage external (environmental) and internal (stress) circumstances. When it comes to measurement, they suggest using the term emotional quotient (EQ) which resembles the method IQ is measured by. Bar-On (2000) by combining the predecessors' approaches uses the concept of 'emotional-social intelligence' as it is "composed of a number of intrapersonal and interpersonal competencies, skills and facilitators that combine to determine effective human behaviour" (Bar-On, 2006:2).

Emotional intelligence also bonds numerous fields of psychological science such as human cognitive abilities (brain-based skills such as problem-solving), self-regulation theory (the management of short-term desire) or the neuroscience (science study of the nervous system) of emotion (Zeidner et al, 2004).

At the turn of the 21st century, Petrides and Furnham (2001) to diminish the misconceptions of and to make a clear distinction between different theories examine the existing emotional intelligence theories and measurements. According to Pérez et al (2005) there is a clear conceptual distinction between ability (or cognitive-emotional ability) and trait (or emotional self-efficacy) emotional intelligence. The former incorporates actual emotional related cognitive abilities and is measured with maximum-performance tests, while the latter concerns emotion-related behavioural characteristics measured via self-report (Petrides, 2009).

Trait and ability distinction are not determined by the facets (elements) but the method researchers apply to measure emotional intelligence (Petrides, 2010). Mayer et al (2000) claim that the distinction is between ability and a mixed model (and not between ability and trait) whereby for the later they understand the approach that mixes abilities and personal traits also including situational, motivational, dispositional variables (MacCann et al, 2004). However, mixed theoreticians do not take methods of measurement into consideration to which Furnham (2001) calls the attention by claiming that cognitive abilities cannot be measured successfully using self-report. In the literature one can find either dividing emotional intelligence theories according to the content (ability or mixed) or to measurement (ability and trait).

Petrides (2001) argues that true trait emotional intelligence theories drive from mainstream psychological research. The Trait Emotional Intelligence Questionnaire (TEIQue) (2001, 2009) includes four factors with fifteen facets.

*Well-being* factor detects a person's level of positivity, happiness and fulfilment. It includes the following facets:

- *Happiness* which is a present oriented pleasant emotional state;
- *Optimism* is defined as a person's confidence and attitude to see the positive side of life;
- *Self-esteem* refers to personal success and confidence.

The second factor is *sociability* which considers relationship building, influence in social settings and networking. The facets are:

- *Emotional management* which is how one influences other people's feelings;
- *Assertiveness* is defined as being honest and forthright, standing up for one' right without hurting others' feelings and rights;
- *Social awareness* is the application of one's social skills and network competence.

*Emotionality* evaluates one's aptitude to recognise others' emotional states, express own emotions and develop and maintain close relationships with others. This factor includes four facets:

- *Empathy* is acknowledging and taking in someone else perspective;
- *Emotional perception* is defined as being clear and sensitive about the feelings of others;
- *Emotional expression* refers to communicating one's own feelings towards others;
- *Relationship* is the competence to fulfil personal interactions.
- The fourth factor is *self-control* which is taking control over one's impulsiveness and coping with internal pressure and stress. It includes the following facts:
- *Emotional regulation* is defined as a short, medium or long term control of one's own feelings and emotional states;
- *Impulsiveness* is the likelihood level of giving in to urges;
- *Stress management* is the capability to endure regular stress and pressure.
- In addition to the thirteen items there are two auxiliary facets that complete the model:
- *Adaptability* means one's flexibility and willingness to adapt to new situations and conditions;
- *Self-motivation* refers to one's drive and endurance of a task or activity without other's supervision.

The focus in Petrides's model is on personality traits as emotions which are undoubtedly fundamental domains of personality (Stough et al, 2009).

The TEIQue is a self-report test (see 2.5.1 and 2.5.2 for advantages of self-report test) designed to be factor analysed at a facet level on a 7-point Likert scale. Self-reporting is the most effective way to test trait emotional intelligence as it has been referred to in the Literature review (Pérez et al, 2005; Petrides, 2009). The 7-point Likert scales are argued to be the best for reliability maximisation and provide advantages over the 5-point scale alternative (Coelho & Esteves, 2007). Table 21 summarises the descriptive and internal consistence for the TEIQue variables (N=1721) (Petrides, 2009). The factors alphas (alpha measures reliability), Emotionality (0.78), Self-Control (0,79), Sociability (0,82), Well-Being (0,83) and the Global Trait EI alpha (0.90) are very strong. The TEIQue has also been proved to have high validity, especially predictive validity of job performance and organisational commitment (Van Rooy & Viswesvaran, 2004; Petrides et al, 2007; Gardner & Qualter 2010); it is the only test that covers the sampling domain of trait emotional intelligence comprehensively (Austin et al, 2004; Matthews at al, 2012) and according to Freudenthaler et al (2008) proves the universality of personality thus being culturally independent. High trait emotional intelligence was associated with lower levels of stress and higher levels of perceived job control, job satisfaction, and job commitment (Petrides & Furnham, 2006 ; Platsidou, 2010). Furthermore, high trait emotional intelligence may be conducive to entrepreneurial behaviour (Zampetakis et al, 2009), protects against burnout (Platsidou, 2010), and predicts internal work focus of control (Johnson et al, 2009). TEIQue can be used for a number of different purposes in work and life such as recruitment and selection, team building, coaching, leadership training, measuring organisational commitment, organisation change, talent development, appraisal and employee morale (Petrides, 2011).

## Emotional Intelligence and Knowledge Sharing

Abzari et al (2014) have identified that social and emotional competence have an impact on employees' knowledge sharing behaviour. Also, the effect of emotional intelligence competency has been proved to be positive and significant on knowledge sharing behaviour. Arakelian et al (2013) have conducted a structural equation modelling between emotional intelligence and knowledge sharing. Their research pinpoints a meaningful positive relationship between the two areas. Moreover, it has found positive relationships among three dimensions of emotional intelligence: self-awareness, social-awareness and relation management and knowledge sharing. Gupta (2008) after examining postgraduate students in relation to emotional stability and knowledge sharing behaviour has proved that people with higher emotional stability would be more self-confident, more secure and fear less to be involved in knowledge sharing activities. On the other hand, he has examined not only the giver but the receiver part of knowledge sharing and has found that accepting knowledge should be voluntary without forcing and with reconciliation between parties. According to Kalkan's (2004) organisation learning process model, organisational knowledge production process is based on organisational learning which is embedded in the organisational intelligence. Each group has several factors and it has to be seen that emotional intelligence builds a part of organisational intelligence and knowledge acquisition, dispersion, the interpretation of knowledge and knowledge storing, and these are forming the group of organisational learning. The third group is called organisational knowledge production process and it involves sharing tacit knowledge. So Kalkan's model shows that emotional intelligence and knowledge sharing both have place in organisational learning process and they have significant relations within this model.

Emotional intelligence plays an important role in tendency of sharing knowledge (Cote & Miners, 2006; Lindebaum, 2009). Individuals can find knowledge sharing costly and uncomfortable, so to make them feel sharing knowledge is socially good and benefits the organisation is really important. Basically, if an employee has high emotional intelligence, he or she has more tendency to share knowledge.

So emotional intelligence can be an essential aspect in influencing knowledge sharing positively (Constant et al, 1994; Karkoulian et al, 2010). Lindebaum (2009) after examining both the correlations between knowledge sharing and emotional intelligence and the influence of factors of emotional intelligence has found the following. Within the *self-awareness* factor, if an employee is aware of his/her senses and mood shifts he/she would be more likely to assess the situation when deciding about knowledge sharing. Concerning *self-management*, an employee is able to decide objectively under different circumstances. Social awareness and *relationship management* can help show empathy and stimulate knowledge sharing behaviour. In other words, the motivation of knowledge sharing can be based on emotional intelligence rate: with higher inner motivation people are more likely to share their knowledge because of altruism that is based on intrinsic motivation (Wang & Hou, 2015).

## Emotional Intelligence and Age (Generation)

Depending on the conceptualisation (trait or ability), researchers have different views on the relationship between emotional intelligence and age. The ability approach regards emotional intelligence as standard intelligence (IQ) therefore as such it would increase with age (Mayer et al, 2000; Van Rooy et al, 2005). Sliter et al (2013) argue that emotional intelligence competencies (such as understanding and regulating emotions) can be acquired through lifetime experiences. In Porter's study (2014) leaders' emotional intelligence have been found to correlate negatively with age. This means the older a leader gets, the lower the level of his/her emotional intelligence becomes. The experimental study with more than 500 participants has revealed a significant relationship between age and emotional intelligence The outcome of this result suggests that the older the employees are, the more likely they are to choose good emotional strategies that are adjusted to both individual and organisational aims (Sliter et al, 2013:476). Bar-On (in Derksen et al, 2002) and later Derksen et al (2002) replicated studies have also indicated that regarding global emotional intelligence the scores have shown a positive relationship to age up till 50 years old, but a decrease for the age of 65 and above. The trait approach, on the other hand, has found no or a minimal relationship between emotional intelligence and age (Petrides, 2009). The reason why emotional intelligence stays stable is that personality traits tend to remain constant across time as explained by Tsaousis and Kazi (2013).

## Generations

The term "generation" signifies the group of individuals, most of whom are within a similar age group, born in the same time of history and culture, having similar ideas, problems and attitudes (Weingarten, 2009). A person's age may not always be indicative of their generational characteristics, but as a common group, they are likely to have similarities. Due to the different ideologies, a generation at a certain period tends to be exposed to approximately similar generic life experiences depending on cultural background. Society is changing constantly which is likely to affect the values and experiences of different generations. Researchers have identified different generations including: Veterans, Baby Boomers, Generation X, Generation Y and Generation Z (Reeves & Oh, 2007; Weingarten, 2009; Grail Research, 2011):

- Veterans (born between 1922 and 1945) respect for authority, loyalty, hard work and sacrifice for the common good. Their motto is "live to work versus work to live".
- Baby Boomers (born between 1946 and 1964) grew up with sense that security was taken care of – this left room for exploration and protest. They place high value on youth, personal gratification, health and material wealth. They are generally optimistic, value hope and peace, and believe their generation changed the world.
- Generation X (born between 1965 and 1970) desires balance in their lives, diversity viewed as norm, motivated by money, self-reliant, value free time and having fun. Their motto is "work to live, not live to work". They assume gender equality in the workplace. This is the first generation that embraces the personal computer and Internet.
- Generation Y (born between 1981 and 1995) is the most globally oriented generation. They combine work ethic of Baby Boomers with the can-do attitude of Veterans and the technological savvy of Generation X. They are interested in health, exercise and body adornment.
- Generation Z (born from 1995 to present) is having grown up in a digital world where technology was ever present. They are more socially responsible, due to greater access to a large online information pool and always communicate through various social networking channels.

## RESEARCH SUMMARIES

In the following part studies regarding the field of knowledge sharing and emotional intelligence in different industries are summaries. These research works are good representation of a 10-year interval.

### 2006: Knowledge Management in Hungary 2005/2006 Empirical Survey

In 2004, Department of Management at the University of Pannonia joined forces with KPMG-BME Academy in order to investigate the current state of knowledge management in Hungarian profit and non-profit sectors. Therefore, a detailed survey was conducted, which examined the successfulness of knowledge management practice of organizations. In the course of the survey, answers from 130 organizations were included in the database, which was used as the basis of our research activity (KPMG-BME Academy, 2006). The organizations involved in the survey are all based in Hungary; they include SMEs, privately owned Hungarian companies, enterprises under joint foreign and Hungarian ownership, subsidiaries of global international companies, and other organizations in the fields of education, health care and public administration. The respondents are mainly upper level managers, owners and HR, strategic or IT managers. Some participants are middle level managers in the fields of economics, finances, marketing, supply, logistics or consulting. Among the organizations involved in the survey, all sectors of industry are represented with different portions. The majority of the respondents work in information technology, industrial production, business services, or retail trade. The representation of public administration is also significant in the sample. In general, knowledge management practice in Hungarian organizations is characterized by recognition of significance of the efficient management of knowledge, and the availability of the utilizable knowledge and the required infrastructure.

The results show growing awareness of knowledge management, its value to business and the benefits resulting from a systematic and holistic approach to the effective use of intangibles. In the application of knowledge, there is huge potential, which is still mostly unexploited. It indicates that the current level of knowledge management implementation is rather a challenge for the future than the reality at present. Respondents were asked whether their organization had a knowledge management strategy. The answers show that organizations in Hungary are just starting to implement knowledge management strategies. Overall, only 37% of respondent organizations have developed a comprehensive strategy in the form of a written document; however, 77% are indicating knowledge as a strategic asset. It can be seen that there is huge gap between the reality and the desire. 22% of the participants have knowledge management program and 30% are currently setting up or considering one. Nearly one third of the respondents were not aware of any, denominated knowledge management programs being conducted in the organization.

Knowledge sharing is part of knowledge management, therefore the next study in time explores this phenomenon.

## 2010: Knowledge Sharing Maturity and Competences Found Important for Knowledge Sharing Study between 2007-2010

The Strategic Management Research Group at University of Pannonia conducted a study between 2007 and 2010 investigating middle managers' knowledge sharing. Its purpose was twofold, to reveal the elements describing middle managers' knowledge sharing maturity and the competences important for knowledge sharing (Csepregi, 2012). 400 completed questionnaires, being the final sample of the study, were returned from middle managers working in various fields and organisational size (67,5% SMEs and 32,5% large-sized) having a variety of ownership ranging from being fully national and private owned (36%), fully national and state owned (14%), with a national majority and privately owned (9%), with national maturity and state owned (8%), with foreign majority (7%) and fully foreign (26%).

Knowledge sharing maturity referred to the development level of knowledge sharing and was defined by two directions and two dimensions. Recognizing the multidirectionality of middle managers relationship emphasised by Uyterhoeven (1989) the study focused on middle managers' vertical and horizontal relationships within and between different organizational units. Regarding the two dimensions „availability" and „usefulness of knowledge" were investigated. "Availability" referred to the extent to which the middle managers, their subordinates, and other middle managers are willing to spend time helping one another by sharing their knowledge, while "Usefulness of knowledge" examined whether the middle managers, their subordinates, and other middle managers possess the knowledge useful for others. The results of principal components analysis showed that knowledge sharing maturity can be described by not only middle manager - middle manager availability and middle manager - subordinate availability, but also by middle manager - middle manager usefulness of knowledge and middle manager - subordinate usefulness of knowledge.

Regarding the investigation of competences important for knowledge sharing the research study adopted Forgács et al.'s (2002) classification of competences. The investigated competences have been separated by principal component analysis into competence groups as methodological competences needed for thinking, methodological competences used for work method and style, social competences connected with communication skills, social competences connected with co-operational skills, professional competences, personal competences and intercultural competences (Szabó & Csepregi, 2011).

Focusing on SMEs and large-sized organizations the results showed there is no difference between the elements of knowledge sharing maturity based on the size of the middle managers' organizations. On the other hand, the study revealed that except professional competences, middle managers employed by SMEs and large-sized organizations found the investigated competences equally important for knowledge sharing. However the analysis of variance (sig. 0,02) showed that middle managers employed by SMEs find professional competences (working experiences gained in other special fields, experience gained by individual interests, experience at other types of organizations and experience at organizations similar to present one) more important for knowledge sharing than those employed by large-sized organizations.

The study also revealed that at methodological competences used for work method and style competence group there were differences regarding certain organizational characteristics. These differences were related primarily to customer claims fulfilled by the organizations, secondly to their activity and finally to their type. The competence group contained several competences that effect individual's performance as awareness of organizational goals, practical comprehension of tasks and result-orientation (Szabó & Csepregi, 2013).

Soft and social competences have been found as triggers of knowledge sharing, and within these emotional intelligence factors initiated major interest which inspired the next study.

## 2013: Emotional Intelligence Study at an IT Department of an Info-Communication Company

The Trait Emotional Intelligence Questionnaire (TEIQue) was selected in these studies based on its psychological theory and nearly ten years of applied research. With the head of department 29 employees worked together as a team. Out of the 29 managers 27 questionnaires were returned completed (26 managers and the head of department). The majority of the managers were between 25-35-year-old (so X and mainly Y generation), well qualified (all with BSc or MSc degrees) and could speak more than one language. The role of the managers was to direct and coordinate the work of 200 employees. The company used its own performance measurement, according to which employees' performance fell into three categories: high, stable and low. Similarly managers' potential individual performance improvement was defined by the head of department. The future performance was predicted according to present task performance and whether managers were judged to have the competencies to complete a complex task well in the future. There were two categories: a manager was capable of achieving high performance in a short time (within 3 months), or a manager needed a longer time (more than 3 months) to achieve high performance. The final analysable data to compare emotional intelligence and performance came from 22 respondents (21 managers and the head of department), out of which 3 were women and 18 were men (and the head of department was a man).

The emotional intelligence mean of the management team fell in the high emotional intelligence category. Taking performance into consideration there was an interesting result which had not been expected considering the outcomes of the previous studies. There was a reverse relationship between emotionality (as opposed to emotional intelligence) and performance. The higher the managers' performance, the lower their emotionality factor was (including empathy, relationship, emotional perception and emotional expression). Also the result showed that the higher a manager's performance was, the higher would be his/her self-control (including emotional regulation, low impulsiveness and stress management). Furthermore, the study revealed that where the head of the department saw potential in performance and the manager was deemed capable of achieving high performance within 3-month time, these members scored higher emotional intelligence levels than those for whom potential performance had been judged would take longer (more than 3 months). At factorial level similar results were observed with present performance results: those whose potential was judged would take a shorter time to achieve scored higher in self-control, sociability and well-being but not in emotionality. The main novelty of this study was that emotional intelligence factors can indicated potential high performance in a short period of time.

## 2014: Organizational Knowledge Sharing in Hungary 2013/2014 Empirical Survey

This study is a kind of longitudinal continuum of the 2006 research.

In 2013, the Strategic Management Research Group at the University of Pannonia investigated the characteristic features of knowledge sharing activities among Hungarian organizations empirically, applying quantitative research method, with questionnaire survey (KPMG Academy, 2014), which was conducted with the collaboration of the KPMG Academy, Budapest. The main objective of our research is to determine the peculiarities of using social media technologies by exploring willingness of employees' participation in knowledge sharing and investigate generational differences. In the course of the survey, answers from 299 organizations were included in the database. The participating organizations all operate in Hungary. Based on the number of employees, 55% are large companies, 45% SME. More than half of the organizations (54%) are domestic subsidiaries of foreign companies, and 46% are Hungarian-owned companies. 27% of the respondents are top managers, 42% are middle level managers and 31% are white collar workers. The participants belong to three generations; 22% from Baby Boomers, 60% from Generation X and 18% from Generation Y (KPMG Academy, 2014).

In general, due to the continuous expansion of the knowledge-based activities it can be assumed that according to the tendency of previous years, knowledge will be considered as a strategic asset characterized by the increasing proportion of organizations in the future. However, it cannot be seen that a wider range of organizations create formal knowledge management strategy. At the same time the researchers expect the growing number of projects and initiatives for knowledge sharing will continue to thrive. Respondents were asked whether their organization had a knowledge management strategy. The answers show that organizations in Hungary are just starting to implement knowledge management strategies. Overall, still only 37% of respondent organizations have developed a comprehensive strategy in the form of a written document; however, 81% states knowledge as a strategic asset. It can be seen that there is huge gap between theory and reality. Authors concluded that a formal KM strategy development is more common for large companies (45%) than for SMEs (29%). The good news is that a significant growth - from 46% to 69% of organizations - can be detected to be related to knowledge sharing programs, initiatives or projects exists in the respondents' organizations. Elaborating knowledge management strategy is still not a typical activity, but it does not mean that organizations do not try to support the dissemination of knowledge somehow.

Although individuals might recognize the importance of knowledge management practices for the success of their daily business lives, it might be presumed that the degree of the willingness of knowledge sharing depends on their personal demographic features. In the exploratory study authors examined the correlation between social media technologies - used for knowledge sharing during work – and the personal characteristics of respondents, like their age and their work position.

First of all authors examined the relationship between individual characteristics and willingness to use the internal social media technologies. A connection was found regarding presentation sharing technologies, the elder the generation the higher percentage applies (60% of Baby Boomers, 39% of Generation X, and only 35% of Generation Y). What could be the reason? How many people make presentations nowadays at all? For example, the TED talks are typically held without any presentation, some photos may be used as an illustration. Or just think about using Prezi, which is an auto-sharing application. Regarding internal social networking service we found relationship with both individual characteristics. With rise of age, the willingness to use this tool for knowledge sharing during work increases: 25% of Generation Y, 41% of Generation X, 55% of Baby Boomers. Regarding the position, only 26% of white collar workers, while nearly half (47%) of managers (middle level and top management) utilize the internal social networking service. The higher one position is the greater the need for such a tool, which facilitates to establish collaboration with colleagues working in other departments or in other countries at an international organization. Younger people choose open systems and they use such applications which has a free access anytime and anywhere and they do not use the term Intranet at all.

From the external social media technologies only one relationship was encountered. Regarding the external social networking service (e.g. Facebook, LinkedIn), the higher the position, the more frequent the work-related application is. 68% of top management, 59% of middle level managers and only almost the half (49%) of white collar workers use this tool for knowledge sharing during work. It is important to make a distinction between Facebook and LinkedIn. On Facebook less members from top managers but more from lower positions can be assumed, but on LinkedIn more and more top managers and experts appear because it is known that the executive head hunting companies often gather information from that site. The surprising result can be explained by the fact that the lower the position, the external social networking is typically not for professional usage rather than for maintaining friendship. Consequently, there is no reason to use this tool for work or for the purpose of knowledge sharing (Gaál et al., 2015).

## 2015: Knowledge Sharing Competences for Projects Study 2014-2015

The previous Emotional Intelligence study (special focus on empathy) in IT shed light on the importance of line and project managers competences in relation to knowledge sharing and generation.

Focusing on project work where the usage of social media tools also play a significant role (Jue et al., 2009; Tsay et al., 2012) the Strategic Management Research Group at University of Pannonia started a study in 2014 investigating project organizations of various sizes. The purpose of the study was to examine project work and knowledge sharing. Concerning knowledge sharing those competences were examined that could be important during project work. The survey using the 'Project management in the XXI. Century' questionnaire was conducted between 2014 and 2015. The questionnaire was available during this period and was sent out online and paper to organizations operating in Hungary. The participants of the survey were project managers involved in projects within their organization. 695 questionnaires returned were analysable. Regarding the statistics on the size of organizations the dominance of the organizations (56,3%) contained SMEs.

One of the focuses of the study was to reveal the difference in selected knowledge sharing competences used in project work regarding generation X and Y. The selected competences were related to emotional intelligence (empathy, relationship management and stress management). The importance of these competences for knowledge sharing during project work was measured on a 6-point Likert scale. The results of analysis of variance did not show any difference between the examined competences concerning the investigated 2 generations. This indicates that project managers belonging to generation X and Y find the following competences equally important for knowledge sharing: empathy (means: 4,54 at Gen X, 4,42 at Gen Y) relationship management (means: 5,34 at Gen X and Y) and stress management (means: 5,27 at Gen X, 5,31 at Gen Y). During project work not only competences related to emotional intelligence are important but also the tools needed for knowledge sharing. To use these tools certain competences can be considered required. These competences are knowledge of computer applications needed for work, usage of programs with confidence, and awareness of new technologies, developments. The results in this case also showed that all three competences related to tools needed for knowledge sharing are found important by both generations in project work.

## 2015: Emotional Intelligent and Knowledge Sharing Study (2014-2015)

Our last research took a wider range taking the previous results into consideration to extend and combine emotional intelligence and knowledge sharing research in several industries.

This research aimed to reveal the relationship between emotional intelligence and knowledge sharing of employees of Hungarian organisations. Furthermore, the emphasis is placed on identifying the specific emotional intelligence traits which enables knowledge sharing. A large-scale online survey - "Knowledge sharing and emotional intelligence in Hungary 2014/2015" - was developed, which was carried out in LimeSurvey, a web application. More than 2000 individuals received an e-mail requesting 15 minutes of their time to fill in a questionnaire. In the course of the survey, answers from 215 organizations were included in the database. The participating organizations were all operated in Hungary.

This empirical research indicated many novel outcomes. Among others, it could confirm the significant positive relationship between employees' emotional intelligence and knowledge sharing behaviour. It can be stated that those employees who had high well-being level are more willing to share their knowledge. Feeling optimist, happy and having high self-esteem level inevitably assumes a positive attitude towards knowledge sharing. Those with high emotionality and self-control level were less afraid of losing their knowledge and more willing to share it. One of the possible reasons behind it is that people with high empathy and relationship care can build more trust; therefore knowledge sharing becomes natural.

The other reason is that high stress and emotional management can make employees not fear sharing their knowledge. Sociability factor showed correlation with reputation. It can be stated that assertive communication and social awareness as part of emotional intelligence sociability factor enable employees to share their knowledge because of reputation possibilities.

Among the age groups, generation X indicated higher self-control level. Furthermore, Generation Y was the most afraid to loose knowledge but also the most willing to share knowledge for organisational reward. Generation X has the greatest value because currently it is the „sandwich-generation" between baby-boomers and Generation Y on the job market and they have to find the best ways to accommodate older and younger colleagues. Generation X is good at regulating pressure and stress (both internal and external), they can easily control their desires and urges. Baby-boomers had to learn that they can mostly prevail if they can exercise self-control. Members of Generation Y were born to the age where there are no limits. They can easily find and share almost everything in the world of internet and social media. This generation is intense, young, impulsive, the least cautious and makes decisions on the spot.

Considering organisational characteristics, no significant difference could be detected between national (Hungarian) and international companies subsidiaries. However, significant difference could be pinpointed in relation to the size: the smaller an organisation, the more afraid it was to lose knowledge. The reason could be very obvious as SMEs are specialised and that is why their knowledge is a key to success on the market.

## CONCLUSION AND RECOMMENDATIONS

Regarding the generational differences, employees from Generation Y may have no issues being asked to use a certain social media tool, a baby boomer may feel overwhelmed and frustrated by such a request and alike prefer face-to-face meetings or phone calls. Generation X and Y working in various fields do not need face-to-face meetings and would prefer to pick up the phone to send a text versus make a call. Relationship building for this group often occurs through simply "pinging" their social media networks. Implementation of a policy centred on social media can prove to be challenging with a diverse workforce. Age is often not only the basis for the issue; it's more the acceptance, readiness, and adaption to change. In fact, research has shown that the fastest-growing demographic for Facebook and other social media tools is those member of Baby boomers. They are able to quickly learn and use new devices. However, introducing a new piece of technology to this population should be different than introducing it to those who have grown up with technology from their early years. As adoption of social media tools readily grows, for both internal and external communications, it becomes important to clearly define and articulate a social media policy. While Baby boomers may be more resistant to initially using social media and accepting social media policy, Generation X and Y will almost positively grow frustrated if an organization does not use social media or fails to properly manage or recognize its use. Contrary to popular belief, social media has shown to increase productivity and employee engagement if controlled appropriately. It can also foster innovation through collaboration. As a result, more than half of the organizations using social media technology have achieved best-inclass performance (KPMG, 2012).

For organizations, mainly SMEs, that wish to enhance knowledge sharing it is becoming essential that they integrate social media tools into their daily business routines. Employees must be given easy access to such tools and be provide with appropriate training. Researchers would observe that there are numerous opportunities to use social media tools and to encourage development of competences to achieve high performance in a manner meaningful to organizations:

- **Communication between Employees can be Encouraged to Support Problem Solving:** if organization needs an expert for a specific task, a post can be placed on a blog and likely receive a response from another employee or search on LinkedIn to find a person, who can help.
- **Convert Personal Knowledge to Organisational Knowledge:** if the senior employees record videos about their work and share it with the new employees, the organization can use these videos instead of expensive training programs to explain the details.
- **Discuss Professional Problems:** with a group of people who are active practitioners in a particular area, professional communities (communities of practices – CoP) can be useful because they are neutral and can provide a way to share best practices, ask questions of and provide support for each other outside the organization.
- **Reduce Time and Money Through Integrated System:** using a "new" technology, the calendar, but not because of the calendar function, but organizing and sharing events, meetings, making appointment in a shorter time (instead of phone calls or sending lots of e-mails).
- **Focus on Competences Important for Knowledge Sharing and Enhancing Performance:** For all of the required competences to be highly developed is extremely unusual. Thus, whose competences do not meet requirements can receive relevant training. Employees knowing that the organization invests in their long-term future, allowing time for interaction with others can facilitate the acquisition of other competences leading to high level of performance and knowledge sharing.

- **Generation Difference:** young people can learn more quickly and easily which is why they realise that if they share knowledge, their organisational reward is going to grow. In this case, they also get positive feedback from the organisation. The opposite is true for older generations because they already had organisational experience and a position where they do not necessarily want to change so they do not really need organisational reward to share their knowledge. Young people are afraid of knowledge power loss due to pressure from strong competition: they may think the more knowledge they retain the more competitive advantage they gain on the job market.

In general, it is recommended that management support the introduction of social media technologies, establish the terms and conditions of their usage, communicate the benefits and provide the necessary training for their effective use. Organizations should develop a reward system to provide additional motivation to employees to use social media tools for knowledge sharing (Obermayer et al, 2016). The result of the emotional intelligence research can help SMEs, managers and HR specialists to learn how to trigger knowledge sharing behaviour according to gender and position while taking the size of the organisation into consideration.

# REFERENCES

Abzari, M., Shahin, A., & Abasaltian, A. (2014). Developing A Conceptual Framework For Knowledge Sharing Behavior By Considering Emotional, Social And Cognitive Intelligence Competencies. *Arabian Journal of Business and Management Review*, *4*(1).

Arakelian, A., Maymand, M. M., & Hosseini, M. H. (2013). Study of the relationship between Emotional Intelligence (EI) and Knowledge Sharing (KS). *European Journal of Business and Management*, *5*(32), 203–216.

Austin, E. J., Saklofske, D. H., Huang, S. H. S., & McKenney, D. (2004). Measurement of trait emotional intelligence: Testing and cross-validating a modified version of Schutte et al.'s (1998) measure. *Personality and Individual Differences*, *36*(3), 555–562. doi:10.1016/S0191-8869(03)00114-4

Bar-On, R. (2000). Emotional and social intelligence: Insights from the Emotional Quotient Inventory. In R. Bar-On & J. D. A. Parker (Eds.), *The Handbook of Emotional Intelligence*. San Francisco: Jossey-Bass.

Bar-On, R. (2006). The Bar-On model of emotional-social intelligence (ESI). *Psicothema*, *18*, 13-25.

Bowley, R. C. (2009). *A comparative case study: Examining the organizational use of social networking sites*. Hamilton: The University of Waikato.

Coelho, P. S., & Esteves, S. P. (2007). The choice between a five-point and a ten-point scale in the framework of customer satisfaction measurement. *International Journal of Market Research*, *49*, 313–340.

Constant, D., Kiesler, S., & Sproull, L. (1994). What's mine is ours, or is it? A study of attitudes about information sharing. *Information Systems Research*, *5*(4), 400–421. doi:10.1287/isre.5.4.400

Cote, S., & Miners, C. (2006). Emotional intelligence, cognitive intelligence and job performance. *Administrative Science Quarterly*, *51*(1), 1–28.

Csepregi, A. (2012). *Middle managers' knowledge sharing and their competences.* Saarbruecken: LAP Lambert Academic Publishing.

Cummings, J. N. (2004). Work groups, structural diversity, and knowledge sharing in a global organization. *Management Science, 50*(3), 352–364. doi:10.1287/mnsc.1030.0134

Davenport, T. H., & Prusak, L. (1998). *Working Knowledge: How Organizations Manage What They Know.* Boston: Harvard Business School Press.

Delamare Le Deist, F., & Winterton, J. (2005). What Is Competence? *Human Resource Development International, 8*(1), 27–46. doi:10.1080/1367886042000338227

Derksen, J., Kramer, I., & Katzko, M. (2002). Does a self-report measure for emotional intelligence assess something different than general intelligence? *Personality and Individual Differences, 32*(1), 37–48. doi:10.1016/S0191-8869(01)00004-6

Forgács,, K., Kaucsek, G., & Simon, P. (2002). A kompetens munkaerő értékelése pszichológiai teszttel és írásanalízissel. *Munkaügyi Szemle, 16*(9), 12–18.

Furnham, A. (2001). Self-estimates of intelligence: Culture and gender differences in self and other estimates of both general (g) and multiple intelligences. *Personality and Individual Differences, 31*(8), 1381–1405. doi:10.1016/S0191-8869(00)00232-4

Gaál, Z., Szabó, L., Kovács, Z., Obermayer-Kovács, N., & Csepregi, A. (2008). "Knowledge Management Profile" Maturity Model. In *Proceedings of 9th European Conference on Knowledge Management (ECKM 2008).*

Gaál, Z., Szabó, L., Kovács, Z., Obermayer-Kovács, N., & Csepregi, A. (2009). Consequence of Cultural Capital in Connection with Competitiveness. *International Journal of Knowledge. Culture and Change Management, 8*(10), 79–90.

Gaál, Z., Szabó, L., & Obermayer-Kovács, N. (2014). Personal knowledge sharing: Web 2.0 role through the lens of Generations. In *Proceedings of 15th European Conference on Knowledge Management (ECKM 2014).* School of Management and Technology - Polytechnic Institute of Santarem.

Gaál, Z., Szabó, L., Obermayer-Kovács, N., & Csepregi, A. (2015). Exploring the Role of Social Media in Knowledge Sharing. *Electronic Journal of Knowledge Management, 13*(3), 185–197.

Gardner, K. J., & Qualter, P. (2010). Concurrent and incremental validity of three trait emotional intelligence measures. *Australian Journal of Psychology*, 62–13.

Gibb, A. (1990). Training the trainers of small business. *Journal of European Industrial Training, 14*(1), 17–25. doi:10.1108/03090599010138543

Goleman, D., Boyatzis, R., & McKee, A. (2013). *Primal leadership: Unleashing the power of emotional intelligence. Boston: Massachusetts.* Boston: Harvard Business School Press.

Grail Research. (2011). *Consumers of Tomorrow Insights and Observations About Generation Z.* Retrieved March 23, 2013, from http://www.grailresearch.com/pdf/ContenPodsPdf/Consumers_of_Tomorrow_Insights_and_ Observations_About_Generation_Z.pdf

Gray, P. H. (2001). The Impact of Knowledge Repositories on Power and Control in the Workplace. *Information Technology & People*, *14*(4), 368–384. doi:10.1108/09593840110411167

Gupta, B. (2008). Role of Personality in Knowledge Sharing and Knowledge Acquisition Behaviour. *Journal of the Indian Academy of Applied Psychology*, *34*(1), 143–149.

Hall, H. (2001). Input-friendliness: Motivating Knowledge Sharing Across Intranets. *Journal of Information Science*, *27*(2), 139–146. doi:10.1177/016555150102700303

Hansen, M. T., Nohria, N. & Tierney, T. (1999, March-April). What is your strategy for managing knowledge. *Harvard Business Review*, 106-116.

Higgs, M., & Dulewicz, V. (1999). *Making sense of emotional intelligence*. Windsor: NFER-NELSON Publishing Company.

Johnson, S. J., Batey, M., & Holdsworth, L. (2009). Personality and health: The mediating role of trait emotional intelligence and work locus of control. *Personality and Individual Differences*, *47*(5), 470–475. doi:10.1016/j.paid.2009.04.025

Jue, A. L., Marr, J. A., & Kassotakis, M. E. (2009). *Social media at work: How networking tools propel organizational performance*. San Francisco, CA: John Wiley & Sons.

Kalkan, V. D. (2004). New Initiatives in Organisational Learning Studies; Organisational Intelligence and Information producing. *3rd National Information, Economics and Management Congress Final Paper*. Osmangazi University.

Karkoulian, S., Harake, N., & Messarra, L. C. (2010). Correlates of Organizational Commitment and Knowledge Sharing via Emotional Intelligence: An Empirical Investigation. *The Business Review, Cambridge*, *15*(1), 89–96.

KPMG. (2012). *Human resources and social media*. KPMG International Research report. MCGraphics.

KPMG Academy. (2014). Organizational Knowledge Sharing in Hungary 2013/2014. KPMG Academy – University of Pannonia Research Report. KPMG Akadémia Kft.

KPMG-BME Academy. (2006). *Knowledge Management in Hungary 2005/2006. KPMG-BME Academy – University of Pannonia Research Report*. Budapest: KBA Oktatási Kft.

Li, W. (2010). Virtual knowledge sharing in a cross-cultural context. *Journal of Knowledge Management*, *14*(1), 38–50. doi:10.1108/13673271011015552

MacCann, C., Matthews, G., Zeidner, M., & Roberts, R. D. (1993). Psychological assessment of emotional intelligence: A review of self-report and performance-based testing. *The International Journal of Organizational Analysis*, *11*(3), 247–274. doi:10.1108/eb028975

Masrek, M. N., Rahim, H. A., Johare, R., & Rambli, Y. R. (2011). Intranet Supported Knowledge Sharing Behavior. *Journal of Organizational Knowledge Management*, *2011*, 1–11. doi:10.5171/2011.802263

Matthews, G., Zeidner, M., & Roberts, R. D. (2012). *Emotional Intelligence 101*. New York: Springer Publishing Campany LLC.

Mayer, J. D., Salovey, P., & Caruso, D. R. (2000). Models of emotional intelligence. In R. J. Sternberg (Ed.), The handbook of intelligence (pp. 396–420). Cambridge University Press. doi:10.1017/CBO9780511807947.019

Moeller, K., & Svahn, S. (2004). Crossing East-West boundaries: Knowledge sharing in intercultural business networks. *Industrial Marketing Management, 33*(3), 219–228. doi:10.1016/j.indmarman.2003.10.011

Mueller, J. (2012). Knowledge sharing between project teams and its cultural antecedents. *Journal of Knowledge Management, 16*(3), 435–447. doi:10.1108/13673271211238751

Nonaka, I., & Takeuchi, H. (1995). *The Knowledge-creating Company*. New York: Oxford University Press.

Obermayer-Kovács, N., & Csepregi, A. (2007). Perspectives of Knowledge Management – Investigations at Hungarian Organizations. In *Proceedings of Business Scienes Symposium for Young Researchers*.

Panahi, S., Watson, J., & Partridge, H. (2012). Social Media and Tacit Knowledge Sharing: Developing a Conceptual Model. In Proceedings of World Academy of Science, Engineering and Technology. World Academy of Science, Engineering and Technology.

Pérez, J. C., Petrides, K. V., & Furnham, A. (2005). Measuring trait emotional intelligence. In R. Schulze & R. D. Roberts (Eds.), *International Handbook of Emotional Intelligence*. Cambridge: Hogrefe & Huber.

Petrides, K. V. (2009). *Technical Manual for the Trait Emotional Intelligence Questionnaires (TEIQue)*. London: Psychometric Laboratory.

Petrides, K. V. (2010). Trait emotional intelligence theory. *Industrial and Organizational Psychology: Perspectives on Science and Practice, 3*(2), 136–139. doi:10.1111/j.1754-9434.2010.01213.x

Petrides, K. V. (2011). Ability and trait emotional intelligence. In T. Chamorro-Premuzic, A. Furnham, & S. von Stumm (Eds.), *The Blackwell-Wiley Handbook of Individual Differences*. New York: Wiley. doi:10.1002/9781444343120.ch25

Petrides, K. V., & Furnham, A. (2006). The role of trait emotional intelligence in a gender-specific model of organizational variables. *Journal of Applied Social Psychology, 36*(2), 552–569. doi:10.1111/j.0021-9029.2006.00019.x

Petrides, K. V., Pérez-González, J. C., & Furnham, A. (2007). On the criterion and incremental validity of trait emotional intelligence. *Cognition and Emotion, 21*(1), 26–55. doi:10.1080/02699930601038912

Platsidou, M. (2010). Trait Emotional Intelligence of Greek Special Education Teachers in Relation to Burnout and Job Satisfaction. *School Psychology International, 31*(1), 60–76. doi:10.1177/0143034309360436

Polányi, M. (1966). *The Tacit Dimension*. London: Routledge & Kegan Paul.

Reeves, T. C., & Oh, E. J. (2007). Generation differences and educational technology research. In Handbook of research on educational communications and technology. Academic Press.

Reinhardt, K., & North, K. (2003). Transparency and transfer of individual competencies: A concept of integrative competence management. *Journal of Universal Computer Science, 9*(12), 1372–1380.

Schein, E. H. (1978). *Career Dynamics: Matching individual and organizational needs*. Reading, MA: Addison-Wesley Publishing.

Sigala, M., & Chalkiti, K. (2015). Knowledge management, social media and employee creativity. *International Journal of Hospitality Management, 45*, 44–58. doi:10.1016/j.ijhm.2014.11.003

Sliter, M., Chen, Y., Withrow, S., & Sliter, K. (2013). Older and (emotionally) smarter? Emotional intelligence as a mediator in the relationship between age and emotional labor strategies in service employees. *Experimental Aging Research, 39*(4), 466–479. doi:10.1080/0361073X.2013.808105 PMID:23875841

Sparrow, P. R., & Hiltrop, J. M. (1994). *European Human Resource Management in Transition*. London: Pretence Hall International.

Sternberg, R. J. (1990). Prototypes of competence and incompetence. In R. J. Sternberg & J. Kolligian (Eds.), *Competence Considered* (pp. 117–145). New Haven, CT: Yale University Press.

Stoof, A. (2005). *Tools for the identification and description of competencies*. (Doctoral dissertation). Open University of the Nederlands, Heerlen, Nederlands.

Stough, C., Saktofske, D. H., & Rarker, J. D. A. (2009). *Assessing Emotional Intelligence*. Theory, Research, and Applicarions, Springer Scienec and Business Media.

Surowiecki, J. (Ed.). (2005). *The Wisdom of the Crowds*. New York: Anchor Books.

Susanty, A. I., & Wood, P. C. (2011). The Motivation to Share Knowledge of the Employees in the Telecommunication Service Providers in Indonesia. *International Proceedings of Economics Development & Research, 5*(2), 2–159.

Sveiby, K. E. (1997). *The New Organizational Wealth: Managing & Measuring Knowledge-Based Assets*. San Francisco: Berrett-Koehler Publishers.

Szabó, L., & Csepregi, A. (2011). Competences found important for knowledge sharing: Investigation of middle managers working at medium- and large-sized enterprises. *The IUP Journal of Knowledge Management, 9*(3), 41–58.

Szabó, L., & Csepregi, A. (2013). Organizational characteristics and methodological competences. Management & Marketing. *Challenges for the Knowledge Society., 8*, 353–362.

Szabó, L., & Csepregi, A. (2015). Middle managers, their organization and knowledge sharing: Examination of knowledge sharing maturity. *Journal of Social Sciences Research, 7*(1), 1192–1205.

Tsaousis, I., & Kasi, S. (2013). Factorial invariance and latent mean differences of scores on trait emotional intelligence across gender and age. *Personality and Individual Differences, 54*(2), 169–173. doi:10.1016/j.paid.2012.08.016

Tsay, J. T., Dabbish, L., & Herbsleb, J. (2012). Social media and success in open source projects. In *Proceedings of the ACM 2012 conference on computer supported cooperative work companion* (pp. 223-226). New York, NY: ACM doi:10.1145/2141512.2141583

Uyterhoeven, H. (1989). General Managers in the Middle. *Harvard Business Review, 67*(5), 136–145. PMID:10295475

Van Rooy, D. L., Alonso, A., & Viswesvaran, C. (2005). Group differences in emotional intelligence scores: Theoretical and practical implications. *Personality and Individual Differences*, *38*(3), 689–700. doi:10.1016/j.paid.2004.05.023

Van Rooy, D. L., & Viswesvaran, C. (2004). Emotional intelligence: A meta-analytic investigation of predictive validity and nomological net. *Journal of Vocational Behavior*, *65*(1), 71–95. doi:10.1016/S0001-8791(03)00076-9

Vuori, V. (2011). *Social Media Changing the Competitive Intelligence Process: Elicitation of Employees' Competitive Knowledge*. Academic Dissertation. Retrieved January 10, 2014, from http://dspace.cc.tut.fi/dpub/bitstream/handle/123456789/20724/vuori.pdf

Wang, W., & Hou, Y. (2015). Motivations of employees' knowledge sharing behaviors: A self-determination perspective. *Information and Organization*, *25*(1), 1–26.

Weingarten, R. M. (2009). Four generations, one workplace: A gen x-y staff nurse's view of team building in the emergency department. *Journal of Emergency Nursing: JEN*, *35*(1), 27–30. doi:10.1016/j.jen.2008.02.017 PMID:19203677

Yang, C., & Chen, L. C. (2007). Can Organizational Knowledge Capabilities Affect Knowledge Sharing Behavior? *Journal of Information Science*, *33*(1), 95–109. doi:10.1177/0165551506068135

Yesil, S., & Dereli, S. F. (2013). An empirical investigation of organisational justice, knowledge sharing and innovation capability. *SciVerse Science Direct*, *75*, 199–208.

Zampetakis, L. A., Beldekos, P., & Moustakis, V. S. (2009). Day-to-day entrepreneurship within organisations: The role of trait emotional intelligence and perceived organisational support University of Glasgow. *European Management Journal*, *27*(3), 165–175. doi:10.1016/j.emj.2008.08.003

Zeidner, M., Matthews, G., & Roberts, R. (2009). *What we know about emotional intelligence: How it affects learning, work, relationships and our mental health*. Cambridge, MA: The MIT Press.

Zeidner, M., Matthews, G., & Roberts, R. D. (2004). Emotional intelligence in the workplace: A critical review, Applied Psychology. *International Review (Steubenville, Ohio)*, *53*(3), 371–399.

## KEY TERMS AND DEFINITIONS

**Competence:** Refers to attitudes, knowledge, skills and motivation needed to perform certain tasks within the organization.

**Generations:** The theory that people born within an approximately 20-year time period share a common set of characteristics based on the historical experiences, economic and social conditions, technological advances, and other societal changes they have in common.

**Knowledge:** The whole of information, experiences, routines, practices etc. that can be connected with people, can be found in the mind of a person or group or in electronic or paper documents and can be broadened during sharing that occurs between the knowledge giver(s) and the knowledge receiver(s).

**Knowledge Management:** Describes the processes of acquiring, developing, sharing, exploiting and protecting organizational knowledge to improve organizations' competitiveness.

**Knowledge Sharing:** A process by which knowledge is converted into a form that other individuals can understand and can collaborate to develop new ideas.

**Knowledge Sharing Behaviour:** By which an individual voluntarily provides other people with access to his/her knowledge.

**Emotional Intelligence:** A competence that enables individuals to detect and control own and perceive and handle others' emotional traits in order to improve personal well-being and private and business relationships.

**Social Media Tools:** Collaborative technologies which encourage collaboration, participation and build networks based on personal and professional interest.

# Chapter 14
# Knowledge–Sharing Is One of the Guarantees of Success in Family Businesses

**Éva Fenyvesi**
*Budapest Business School, Hungary*

**Judit Bernadett Vágány**
*Budapest Business School, Hungary*

## ABSTRACT

*In this chapter a summary of the role family businesses play in the economy will be presented along with one of the main issues of family businesses in Hungary that is succession. Innovation as one of the most important factors of successful family businesses and the organizational culture supporting innovation will also be analysed. Some of the most relevant findings of a research study conducted in Hungary in 2015 will be given. The most significant components of knowledge sharing in SMEs especially in family businesses have been identified. The research results are based on over 300 questionnaires. The following questions have been answered: 1) What is the most decisive factor of choosing between cooperation and competition? 2) Is it possible that family businesses are able to respond to changes and as a result are they innovative? and 3) Is the organizational culture necessary for tacit knowledge sharing present in family businesses?*

## INTRODUCTION

Most of the enterprises in the world are in fact family businesses. They are responsible for more than half of the total GDP and have the most employees. As a result, their activities, success or possible failure are crucially important for the national economy.

Today, in Hungary there is a large number of small-and medium sized family businesses which have gained significant market power. In Hungary, Zwack Unicum PLC. is the oldest family business and it is governed by the sixth generation of family. The average family business in Hungary has just reached the stage when the new generation should take the leadership over. It means that those who established the business will have to pass the baton to their children.

DOI: 10.4018/978-1-5225-1642-2.ch014

International cases have proved that succession is a great challenge for most of the enterprises and sometimes it even leads to the termination of an enterprise. Therefore, the success of the passing on the leadership to the potential successors is critical. The most important part of this task is to transfer years of experience, knowledge and many skills that had been compiled by the current leadership. Knowledge sharing among family members – especially tacit knowledge sharing – has its special challenges among family businesses.

## THE SIGNIFICANCE OF FAMILY BUSINESSES

Family businesses are highly relevant not only for the Hungarian economy but also for economies all over the world. As regards to their size, most of the family businesses belong to the category of small and medium sized businesses (SMEs) but there is no information about their exact number. One of the reasons for this is that there is a lack of a widely accepted definition of family businesses. Mandl, who carried out a research within the European Union found 90 different descriptions defining family businesses (Mandl, 2008).

In Europe, the percentage of family businesses is around 70 to 80% whereas in North America it is around 80 to 90% (Hnátek, 2015).

The share of family businesses by country is shown in Table 1.

In addition to small family businesses there are a considerable number of large family businesses as well. According to a survey carried out by Standard and Poor in 2015 they account for 60% of total U.S. employment, 78% of all new jobs, 65% of wages paid and 34% of these companies are listed on. With those stats as a backdrop, it's not surprising that nearly 40% of family businesses in America will be passing the reigns to the next generation over the next five years according to Businessweek News (Poza, 2003).

In Hungary there are numerous family businesses with long and successful history. One of these is Zwack Unicum which is currently lead by the 6th generation of the Zwack family.

*Table 1. Share of family businesses in European countries (as a % of total enterprise population) (Mandl, 2008)*

| Country | % | Country | % | Country | % |
|---|---|---|---|---|---|
| Austria | 80 | Greece | 52 | Poland | 70-80 |
| Belgium | 70 | Hungary | 70 | Portugal | 70-80 |
| Cyprus | 85-90 | Ireland | 75 | Romania | 50 |
| Czech Republic | 80 | Italy | 65-81 | Slovakia | 80-95 |
| Denmark | 95 | Latvia | 30 | Slovenia | 60-80 |
| Estonia | 90 | Lithuania | 38 | Spain | 85 |
| Finland | 80-85 | Luxemburg | 70 | Sweden | 54.5 |
| France | 65 | Netherlands | 22 | UK | 65 |
| Germany | 95 | | | | |

As it has been referred to previously the term family business is not an easy one to define. Neither the international nor the Hungarian literature has a commonly agreed definition. We attempt to cite the most well-known and widely used definitions.

According to Laczkó „Family businesses are founded by using family savings, work experience of family members. They fundamentally operate by relying on the daily involvement of the family members themselves." (Laczkó, 1997).

The most common definition within the European Union is the following:

1. The majority of decision-making rights are in the possession of the natural person(s) who established the firm, or in the possession of the natural person(s) who has/have acquired the share capital of the firm, or in the possession of their spouses, parents, child, or children's direct heirs;
2. Decision-making authority rights are direct or indirect;
3. At least one representative of the family or kin is formally involved in the governance of the firm;
4. Listed companies meet the definition of family enterprise if the person who established or acquired the firm (share capital) or their families or descendants possess 25 per cent of the decision-making rights mandated by their share capital (EC, 2005).

The definition created by PricewaterhouseCoopers (2015) is built on the same principles as of the definition of the EU.

Wimmer et al. claims that family businesses are those enterprises where the family or the family network play a significant role in the development and operating of the enterprise (Wimmer et al., 2004).

As the above definitions show there are several comprehensive explanation of family businesses.

Family businesses, similarly to SMEs have many positive characteristics. Several international and Hungarian researches (Szerb et al, 2014) (Mészáros and Szirmai, 2001) (Kozma and Gyenge, 2015) (Henry et al, 2013) (Antheaume and Barbelivien, 2013) (Csákné, 2012) (Bogáth, 2013) (Hnátek, 2015) (Makó et al, 2015) have dealt with the questions of SMEs and family businesses.

Based on the findings of the above researchers it can be stated that family businesses are/have:

- Able to adapt easily;
- Constantly searching for new opportunities;
- An important role in trade (the number of family businesses selling their products and/or services abroad is increasing);
- An important role in satisfying local needs;
- Long-term plans;
- Able to contribute to the diversification of economic activity and consequently encourage competition;
- Innovative and creative;
- An important role in the employment of workers with disabilities and those with a variety of disadvantages;
- Crucial in providing employment;
- Growth-oriented;
- Highly motivated; and
- Very flexible and able to respond quickly to changing market conditions.

Based on the findings of numerous international researches (e.g. Hnátek, 2015; Leach, 2011; Miller, 2014; Ruggero et al, 2014; Stamm and Lubinski, 2011) close to 70% of family businesses are terminated before the first generation change and 90% of them fail to survive into the third generation. Most of the family businesses will go through the first generation change in the near future in Hungary and most likely Hungarian family businesses will experience similar challenges to those detailed earlier.

## THE REASONS BEHIND SUCCESSFUL AND UNSUCCESSFUL LEADERSHIP SUCCESSION

Several researchers attempted to list the reasons behind success and failure of leadership succession (Leach, 2011; Ward, 2011; Konczosné, 2014; Bogdány et. al., 2015).

The most influential arguments are the followings:

- They are unable/unwilling to adapt to changes in the market environment;
- There are difficulties with financing the business;
- Leadership incompetence;
- It is easy for competitors to imitate success strategies;
- Different ideas regarding long-term goals and leadership;
- Lack of planning;
- Resentment against delegation and leadership succession;
- Decision-making based on emotion; and
- The coming generation is not interested in leading the family business or lack competence to do so etc.

Hungarian family businesses were studied by Korpás (2013) concerning their corporate culture and ways successor are found. Two fundamental components are emphasised in the study. One is the owner-manager dominance and the other is the challenges of leadership succession. The main findings of the research are summarised in Figure 1.

Figure 1. shows both those factors which slow down leadership succession (e.g. high level of centralisation, ad-hoc processes or difficulties with delegation) and those which encourage leadership succession (e.g.name and brand obligation, customer focus and commitment). It should also be mentioned that family businesses are unique because they result in a family life which is almost completely infused by the gratifications and difficulties of the family business. Family conflicts and any major changes in family life (e.g. sudden death of the head of the family, divorce or marriage) have great impact on the life of the business.

The most important factor needed for the success of a family business is to have a successful family behind it.

In order to establish a successful family communication, knowledge sharing between family members must be efficient and roles must be clearly defined.

If these are lacking there is confusion regrading roles and there is also a lot of tension both within the family and the business.

*Figure 1. Characteristics of Hungarian family owned businesses regarding their corporate culture and leadership succession*
(Korpás, 2013)

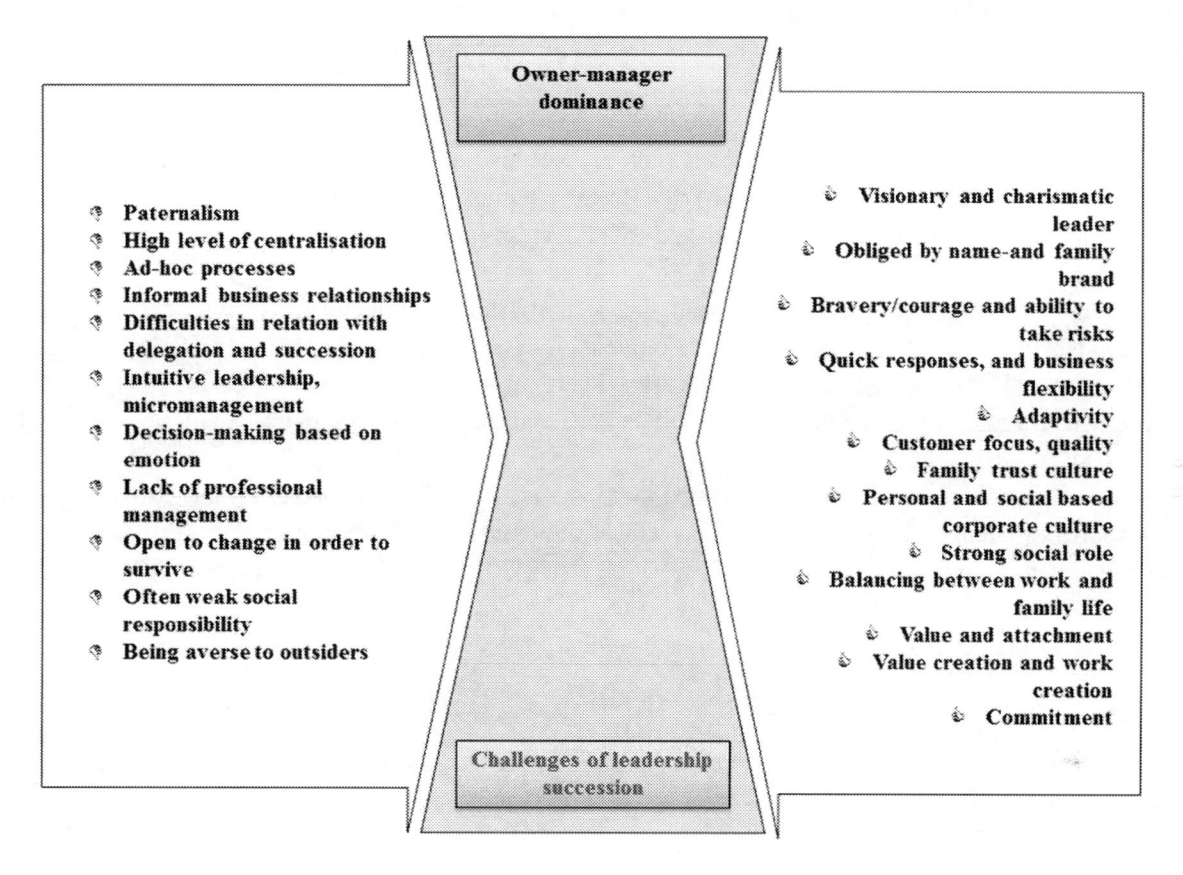

In the following section one of the crucial pillars of family businesses will be introduced: innovation. Successful innovation is of fundamental importance for family businesses as a result of factors (e.g. scarce resources, changing market requirements) explained earlier. (Vágány et al, 2015)

## ENTERPRISES AND INNOVATION

The most important factors of competitive advantage for businesses in modern economies are technological development and knowledge associated with it. The continuous broadening of available knowledge is ensured by scientific research, technological development and the scientific results of innovation processes. All of these processes have been under lot of change partly as a result of multinational companies supporting R&D as well as innovation. Several of the researchers have already recognized the significance of globalization in the 1990s (Archibugi & Michie, 1997; Howells, 1990).

This trend has reached Hungary as well and R&D expenditure (% of GDP) had increased by 30% between 2008 and 2012. In 2012 the R&D expenditure reached its highest in the last twenty years. In 2013 the total government expenditure on R&D was 1.41% of GDP which is a 5.5% increase compared to 2012 (NIH, 2013).

This ratio is quite low compared to the EU average which was 2.02% in 2013. But the Hungarian government expenditure is higher than in most of the EU 13 countries except for Slovenia, Estonia and The Czech Republic. One of the main targets of Europe 2020 is to reach a 3% increase in government expenditure on R&D. Currently there are only two countries to meet this target: Finland with 3.32% and Sweden with 3.21% (Andrejcsik et al., 2013).

R&D and innovation are both crucial to retain competitiveness in enterprises and also to promote sustainable development. Audretsch and Vivarelli (1996) claimed twenty years ago, that those small and medium sized enterprises which are involved in R&D activities and innovation are far more outstanding if they are able to build their activities related to innovation on knowledge gained from outside of the organization. Innovation activities are often capital intensive so mostly large companies are involved in innovation. Small and medium-sized businesses usually start research and development activities or enter the international scene after a long development process. Normally, bigger enterprises are involved in international or global activities from the start. There are also many small and medium-sized enterprises which never enter the international marketplace and they decide not to exceed certain company size (Csonka, 2011).

The larger a company is the more chance there is that it will be innovative. Figure 2. In Hungary one-fourth of small enterprises and close to half of large enterprises are innovative. Seven out of ten large companies carry out some form of innovation (NIH, 2013).

Other than company size the industry in which a company operates is also important. In the pharmaceutical industry (61%) and in the chemical industry (58%) innovation is much higher than in any

*Figure 2. Innovation and non-innovation companies based on company size in Hungary and in the European Union*
*NIH, 2013*

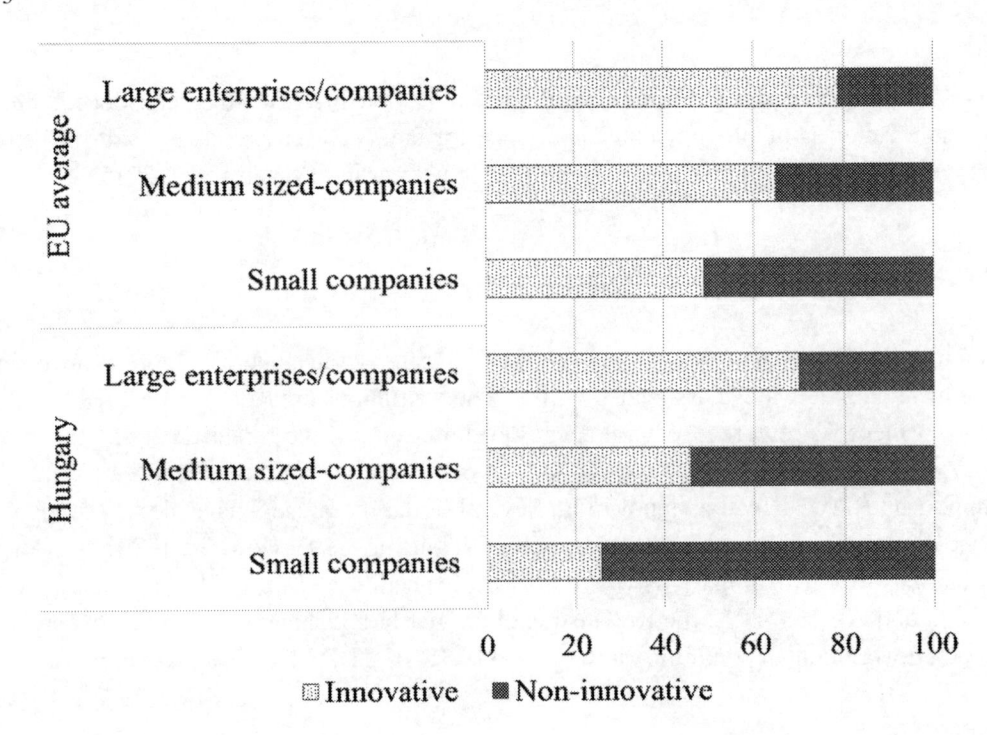

other industries. Non-innovation is the main characteristics of the textile industry, leather industry and transportation and storage. In these industries about fifth of the companies failed to introduce any kind of new technology or process at organizational level (Andrejcsik et al., 2013).

The number of R&D investments by companies first started to increase at the end of the 1990s and they have been increasing more rapidly in recent years. In 2010 large companies spent 30% more on R&D than micro, small and medium-sized enterprises altogether. Depending on company size there are huge differences as regards the financing. The smaller a company is the more government support and the less foreign support it receives for R&D in terms of finances. R&D expenditure per capita per year was 120.6 EUR in Hungary which is only one-fourth of the EU average but exceeds the average of those newly joined the EU (EU 13) (Table 2).

So, companies are able to stimulate technical development. But in order to do so highly creative atmosphere and cooperative workstyle must be encouraged. Moreover, tacit knowledge must be articulated, intellectual property must be protected and internal analysing and monitoring systems must be put in place. All in all, corporate culture needs to be continuously improved (Pakucs, 2005).

## Organizational Knowledge

Current chapter focuses on how tacit knowledge can be shared in family businesses and what decisions should be made along the way to secure success and minimize failure. Thus, the main characteristics of organizational knowledge and particularly methods of tacit knowledge sharing will be described. The relationship between knowledge sharing and corporate culture will also be examined.

## Data, Information, Knowledge, and Wisdom

There are many researches focusing on the understanding of organizational knowledge. Most of these fail to define knowledge from an epistemological perspective but rather focus on how the knowledge of organizational members contributes to the added value created by the organization itself (Polák-Weldon, 2014).

*Table 2. R&D expenditure per capita in the European Union calculated on an average exchange rate of 2011 (Eurostat, 2013)*

| Country | €/capita | Country | €/Capita | Country | €/Capita | Country | €/Capita |
|---|---|---|---|---|---|---|---|
| Sweden | 1389,0 | France | 690,6 | Czech Republic | 273,0 | Slovakia | 86,2 |
| Denmark | 1337,4 | Belgium | 690,0 | Portugal | 240,4 | Croatia | 76,2 |
| Finland | 1332,7 | Ireland | 611,8 | Hungary | 120,6 | Poland | 74,2 |
| Luxembourg | 1187,5 | United Kingdom | 495,9 | Greece | 120,1 | Latvia | 63,1 |
| Austria | 983,2 | Italy | 325,9 | Malta | 113,4 | Romania | 30,7 |
| Germany | 901,4 | Spain | 307,3 | Cyprus | 102,6 | Bulgaria | 29,3 |
| Netherlands | 738,0 | Estonia | 282,8 | Lithuania | 87,0 | EU average | 510,5 |

One of the most commonly used methods of analysing knowledge is to draw a distinction between data, information, knowledge and wisdom. „…by referring to them the real meaning of knowledge can be understood more easily. Not understanding the differences between data, information and knowledge… has caused a lot of damage already for many companies." (Davenport & Prusak, 2001, p. 17).

Data is a quantitative set of discrete, objective facts such as numbers, words, sounds and pictures. It lacks meaning or context in itself. Today, most of the companies store data in some form of technological system in order to make information retrieval fast and easy.

Data gains real meaning when it can be related to a person (Wiig, 2000). It means that "the meaning of information depends on the subject" (Noszkay, 1999). Consequently, if data is organized, grouped and classified then it becomes information. Today, these tasks are carried out by computers and as a result many organizations believe that investing in IT systems always has a good return. But investments in IT systems by themselves are not sufficient to provide information efficiently. Data collection and data handling systems are very expensive but they are not enough to make people informed (Bőgel, 1999).

Information is tangible but it is not easy to register its spreading. Knowledge is mostly in the heads of people and not only knowledge sharing is difficult to monitor but it is also difficult to find the right form to transfer it.

Several researchers have acknowledged that there are further elements as well. Apart from data, information and knowledge they add the importance of moral, wisdom, productive knowledge, experience and routine etc. Ackoff (1997). Wisdom can be found on the top of the hierarchy.

János Farkas (2001) claims that in order to have a clear picture of the relationship between knowledge and information the notion of innovation should also be introduce (Table 3). He believes that innovation as „social innovation" can be related to the notions of knowledge and information. Social innovation means that renewal is not only applied to technological processes and products but also to social structure, culture, political systems etc. Innovation provides a framework to bring information and knowledge into action.

The interdependence of data-information-knowledge-wisdom gives an opportunity to separate tacit and explicit knowledge and information and knowledge management (Figure 3).

It was Mihály Polányi, who made a clear distinction between explicit and tacit knowledge. Polányi (1997, p. 170) claims that knowledge is similar to an iceberg „We can know more than we can tell". Explicit knowledge is what can be seen and can be described with words and numbers. It can be easily

*Table 3. Characteristics of information and knowledge (Farkas 2001)*

| Information | Knowledge |
|---|---|
| Codified, indirect knowledge | Includes hidden and other types of knowledge as well. It is disposable set of expertise |
| „To know something" type of knowledge | „Knowing something" type of knowledge |
| Knowing a process in a superficial way | Knowing a process deeply and consistently |
| „Easily" only called pure information | It is considered to be systematically created, organized and verified |
| Well-formed and codified statements about the world, nature and provides algorithms of how things should be created | It includes cognitive categories, the codes of interpreting information, potential skills and problem solving and heuristic research which can be reduced to explicit algorithms |

*Figure 3. Separating information and knowledge management and tacit and explicit knowledge* (Authors' own contribution)

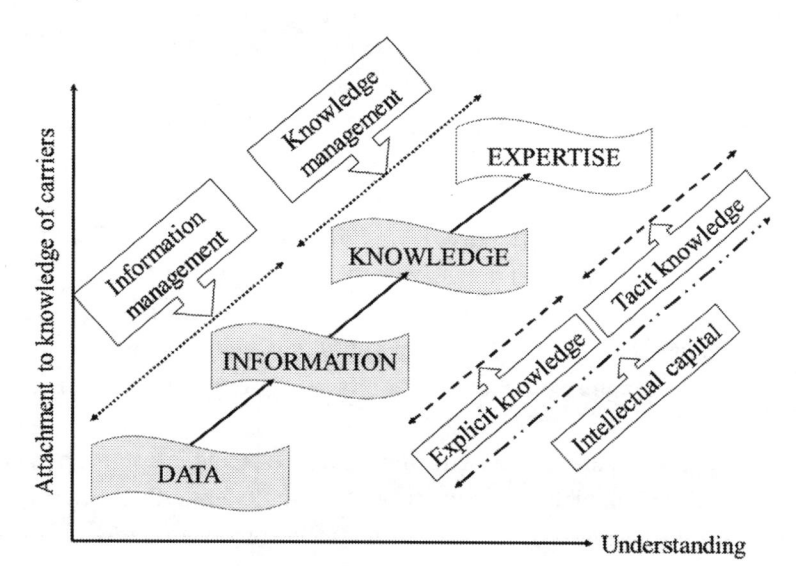

communicated and shared with others in the form of scientific formulas, coded processes or universal principles. On the other hand tacit knowledge is hidden and environment-specific. It is difficult to formulate and communicate. Tacit knowledge contains personal opinion, instincts, anticipation and cognitive as well as technical elements (Nonaka and Takeuchi, 1995, p. 56, p. 73).

Information management covers the effective planning, organising and controlling of sources of information whereas knowledge management is a business model which utilizes knowledge as a valuable organizational asset to gain competitive advantage. In order to do so tacit knowledge must be discovered and developed and some of the tacit knowledge must be transformed into explicit. The most important elements of the relationship between knowledge management and innovation is to create new knowledge and introduce it to the market.

Figure 2. illustrates that knowledge management must deal with the strong attachment of the individuals to the knowledge they possess at the same time information management doesn't have to focus on that aspect. The stronger the attachment is (vertical axis) the more difficult it will become to transfer and seize knowledge and the more monopolized it will be. Parallel to that the prospect of losing knowledge is becoming more and more real for the organization. Making people understand (horizontal axis) the importance of knowledge sharing is the best interest of all members of the organization and the organization should do its best to dismantle limitations resulting from strong attachment.

## Methods of Sharing Tacit Knowledge

- Encouraging master and apprentice relationships. According to some research the information retrieved from an average presentation is around 10%. If there are many spectacles in the presentation the information retrieval reaches 20%. „Learning by doing" increases information retrieval to 70%. Masters introduce how things work and apprentices try to imitate what they see and hear. Finally, masters review what apprentices have learned (Sveiby, 2001). Beside practice the feedback given by masters plays a very important role because details that allow apprentices to move along fast or pulls them back in the learning process can be discussed (Marczellné Szilágyi, 2012). During this process the apprentice recreates the skills and expertise of the master.

- Encouraging mentoring systems. The basic principle of mentoring is a sound and personal relationship between two people who differ in age and have different organizational and life experiences (Légrádiné, 2006). The main aim of mentoring is to convey knowledge to the next generation. Also, mentoring might be introduced to find and prepare successors or to help integration into the organization or to help individual careers. The mentoring system can support the reconciliation of organizational and personal goals. Mentoring systems are also able to encourage young entrepreneurs to start and run an enterprise. This helps them to improve their self-realization abilities (Kárpátiné Daróczi et al., 2015). Mentoring might also develop as an informal system when a more experienced colleague voluntarily supports a less experienced colleague (Arogundade, 2011).
- Constantly changing project teams. Those teams which are created as a group of constantly changing members in order to complete a certain project is usually called a task group. If these groups are formed within an organization but are different from organizational working groups then they are usually called teams or project-teams. When forming these groups it is important to keep in mind that the group should have a combination which can operate as efficiently as possible. Two outcomes must be considered in this case. One is group heterogeneity. The more heterogeneous a group is the more efficient it will be. The other is that the less similar the various characteristics of group members are the higher fluctuation will be within the group and the more conflicts will occur. As a result of these two outcomes heterogeneous groups are advised to be formed when a problem needs to be solved by the group. In order to minimise the number of conflicts the group leader needs to retain close structural and leader control. Groups formed in order to execute tasks should be more homogeneous because they are more likely to be successful (Szabó, 2011).
- Internship communities. These include people with shared interest or passion or those working jointly on a given task. Usually these community members are able to broaden their knowledge as a result of cooperation and working together and they also distribute innovation and knowledge much faster (Wenger, 1998).
- Innovative communities. These communities are mostly formed in order to create new knowledge or activities. As opposed to expert teams, innovative communities often have to deal with more stress because they are involved in many trial and error methods which rarely successful (Engestrom, 1999).

The question is whether these tools are sufficient. What are the main setbacks organizations must deal with in order to have access to more tacit knowledge of organizational members?

## Knowledge Sharing and Organizational Culture

Creating new knowledge is not possible without knowledge sharing. Similarly, the individual and organizational knowledge can only become useful if they are shared. One of the challenges of knowledge management is to help with the process of knowledge sharing. In order to succeed organizations must face many challenges such as technology, the lack of having business goals, expertise, position, mistrust, corporate culture and understanding the community thinking of the organization (Brink, 2001; Chin, 2005; Tomka, 2005; Fenyvesi, 2007).

In many cases the success or failure of a knowledge sharing system depends mostly on the culture and way of thinking of those who bring the knowledge of the community together. A shared culture is a critical factor both in case of knowledge management systems and innovation systems because it ensures sound decisions made by top management in terms of utilizing explicit and tacit knowledge. It also allows the organizations to enhance innovative ideas embodied in new products (Bencsik, 2015). There are many behavioural forms which act against knowledge sharing culture. These can be often traced among organizational members. These are:

- Knowledge sharing is selfish, and it is a tool to gain personal advantages.
- Knowledge is power, the feeling of being indispensable.
- Hiding information at the workplace in order to hold on to a job.
- Competition, be better than others no matter what.
- Fear of failure if we make a mistake.
- Passive and disinterested attitude.
- „I can only rely on myself".
- Fear that knowledge sharing is not recognized.
- It is a complete waste of time.
- Why me? Others are not doing it either.
- Communication is not trustworthy.
- We suppose that there is an inability to revive.
- Envy.

The many differences and changes between people, situations and organizations complicates the issue further (Pretorius et al., 2012)

## COOPERATION AND COMPETITION

Both during the knowledge management process and for the success of innovation processes many teams must cooperate.

Cooperation is the most relevant guiding principle of not only team formation but also shaping the society. It is an action strategy or a form of social behaviour which determines the success of the individual's work as well as personal relationships. So, if somebody is cooperative it means that working with others in harmony is self-understood. Cooperation always includes a common goal regardless of what is at stake for the participants. Competition on the other hand drives people to act in a more individualistic way. Those who compete, aim at winning over others in order to achieve a goal.

## The Fundamental Conditions of Cooperation

The fundamental conditions of cooperation are communication and trust, common goal of a culture.

- **Common Goal:** Organizational members must know the goals the organization wants to achieve and in that context how they can utilize their knowledge. Of course, employees must have the necessary knowledge that can be shared. Once the essential knowledge is available, tasks can be broken down to behavioural levels. It is the responsibility of the top management.
- **Trust:** Trust must be mutual and must be consciously built on a sense of assurance. This can be established step-by-step and under mutual control. The loss of trust can happen suddenly but to rebuilding it is a long and hard process.
- **Communication:** Those cooperating and competing both horizontal and vertical communication is needed. Common language and words increases understanding and contributes to bringing people closer together.
- **Motivations:** It is important to have an agreed on definition of performance. The direction of a decision is also paramount. The choice of cooperation or competition can be influenced by various incentives but of course the final decision depends on the individual.
- **The Relationship between Risk –Goal – and Payoff:** Cooperation has many advantages as well as disadvantages. Whenever individuals decide between different behaviours they consider the payoffs of their decisions.
- **Individual and Group Norms:** Cooperation is often obstructed by cultural differences and varying contexts. Norms are influenced by three factors: differences in the perception of a role (sustaining hierarchy or problem focussed); differences in interests; the impact of events that had happened earlier (from the aspect of cooperation the ability to forgive someone is very important because the lack of forgiveness makes cooperation impossible).

In real life purely cooperative or competitive behaviours doesn't exist. Cooperation and competition are not only opposites of each other rather they exist side-by-side. Cooperation is the prerequisite of competition because those competing must know the goals at which they aim. They should also know the rules and the sanctions of breaking the rules. If these are not clarified competition will turn into war. The opposite of that is also true because in some cases cooperation serves the sole purpose of ensuring better chance to survive. Whereas competition provokes conflicts, cooperation helps solving conflicts (Fenyvesi, 2007).

## THEORY OF STRATEGIC FAMES

If we want to think the question of cooperation further game theory of the 20th century is the appropriate theory to use. The strategic game theory examines the various combinations of cooperation and competition in social situations. The reason why this theory has the word „game" is because every game includes the main elements of conflict so it illustrates the various behaviours very well. Game theory uses the word "game" in all of those situations in which conflict is a possibility. The word strategy refers to the fact that the aim of the theory is to select the strategy out of different alternatives. The ingenuity of game theory is that highly complicated phenomena can be demonstrated with it thanks to its mathematical foundations; it is an axiomatic theory using only a few quantitative rules. The other reason why game theory is widely useful is because it can be used in general contexts and able to put the light on a number of interesting elements of conflicts. Despite the fact that data used by researchers is heavily influenced by factors such as personality (physical and emotional attitude, health conditions or different skill possessed by individuals) still the most likely behaviour of participants can be forecasted with confidence (Fenyvesi, 2007, 2010).

Early on game theory had a clear focus on competitive behavioural forms, but later turned its spotlight on cooperative strategies. One of the main findings of research on cooperation is that successful cooperation depends on two conditions. One is that participants must trust each other and they should also be aware that others trust them as well. Mutual trust has some conditions:

- Information flow should be hindered between participants,
- And they can freely search for information about their individual thoughts on the situation, the value system and whether the participants have rational thinking abilities.

The basic tool of game theory is the payoff matrix. By applying it we can design a matrix which illustrates the payoffs gained by co-workers of knowledge sharing methods are used (Table 4).

- **4:** Individual profit maximization takes place if competition is one-sided. Knowledge is power and should not be shared.
- **3:** The cooperative behaviour of co-workers puts a limit on individual profit maximization but at the same time it brings the most benefit for the organization.
- **2:** For the company the least beneficial condition is when all of the employees are competitive.
- **1:** If one of the colleagues is willing to cooperate even if the others are competitive it will bring the least benefit for the cooperative colleague.

If the compete-compete behaviour becomes the norm in a company it will collapse sooner rather than later. But those companies in which the cooperative behaviour is dominant will be able to establish a more advantageous position in market competition as opposed to those companies where co-workers are competitive.

It is most likely that the absolute „truths" explained so far appear differently in real life because in companies competition and co-operation are present parallel. Moreover, we can argue for and against both co-operation and competition. Although, looking at knowledge from a global perspective we can see that it is inexhaustible, it might become scarce at a given place and in a given time. For example, experts with exceptional expertise are usually scarce for large companies. But the scarcity of knowledge within an organization can be reduced by finding all employees the role which fits their expertise the most and

*Table 4. Payoff gained from knowledge sharing based on the generalized Prisoner's Dilemma payoff matrix (Authors' own contribution)*

| | | The Other Colleagues | |
|---|---|---|---|
| | | Cooperate | Compete |
| **One of the colleagues** | **Cooperates** | 3, 3 | 1, 4 |
| | **Competes** | 4, 1 | 2, 2 |

by motivating them to cooperate with each other. The benefits of cooperation is that it makes it possible to solve problems which otherwise couldn't be solved by only one person. It allows the organization as a whole and the individuals within the organization to have access to knowledge which normally they wouldn't have direct access to.

## ANALYSIS

The primary research presented in the previous parts of the study is based on a comprehensive questionnaire survey which took place between March and September 2015 among family businesses. The most relevant findings will be presented here.

The selection of family businesses was based on the snowball method. Professional market researchers interviewed the top or middle management or in some cases company owners who participated voluntarily.

The target was to receive a total number of 516 responds. The propensity-to-respond was 75%. The number of false of incomplete questionnaires was 54 so the final number of questionnaires to be analysed was 333.

### Introducing the Enterprises

The distribution of enterprises by size is the following: 45% of micro businesses, 26% of small businesses, 13% of medium-sized businesses, and 16% of large businesses (Figure 4).

In terms of the legal forms of the enterprises a large proportion of the sample (Figure 5) is enterprises with separate legal entity (83%). The remaining of the sample (10%) has no separate legal entity and 7% is sole proprietorship.

The longest-established family business in our sample is 150 years old. It didn't escape socialization but after the fall of communism it continued its operation as a family business. The youngest enterprise in the sample was established in 2013.

*Figure 4. The distribution of enterprises by size*
*(Authors' own contribution)*

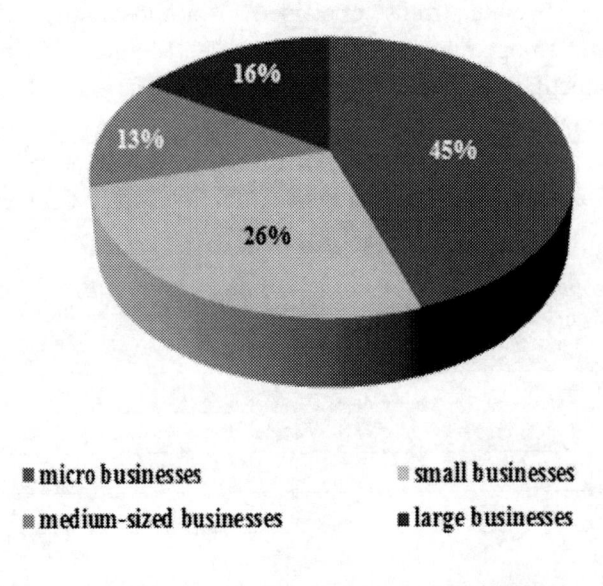

- micro businesses
- medium-sized businesses
- small businesses
- large businesses

*Figure 5. Legal forms of enterprises*
*(Authors' own contribution)*

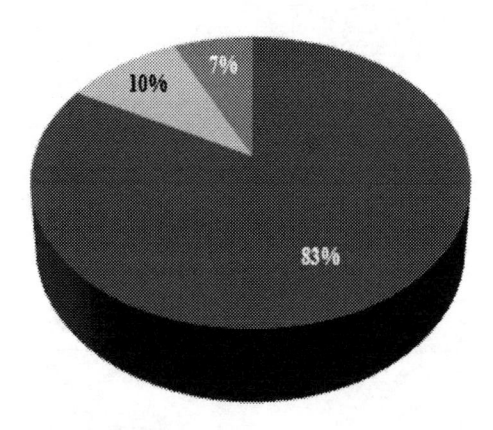

▪ enterprises with separate legal entity ▪ no separate legal entity ▪ sole proprietorship

Regarding the seat of the enterprises 45% of them are in the capital, 43% were founded in cities and 12% were founded in villages.

Regarding the scope of activities in our sample there are enterprises carrying out trading activities (29.7%), providing services (26.7%), operating in the processing industry (12%), manufacturing (10%), info-communication (7.5%) and hospitality (5.7%).

36% of the respondents were middle managers, 31% were top managers and 33% were owners.

In most parts of the questionnaire a 6-point Likert scale was used because the range captures the intensity of respondents' feelings for a given item. Yes or no type of questions would not have provided the most relevant and deep information. Responses are scored along a range between the end points of strongly disagree (minimum value) and strongly agree (maximum value) Kehl – Rappai, 2007).

In most of the cases Likert scale is odd-numbered because it gives the opportunity to the respondents to provide neutral opinion. In our experience „idle respondents" opt for the medium value on the scale which distorts research results. So, we used even-numbered scale in the questionnaire to encourage respondents to choose one of the medium values which is more representative in their opinion.

## Hypotheses Testing

In our study the following hypotheses will be tested:

**H1:** In family businesses cooperative behaviour is more typical than competitive behaviour.
**H2:** Family businesses respond to changes flexibly as a result they are innovative.
**H3:** In case of family businesses the culture of sharing tacit knowledge is more present than in case of other enterprises.

The authors relied on their previous research experiences and the contents of relevant literature in order to formulate the hypotheses. Hypotheses were tested by using the data in Table 5 and 6.

*Table 5. Summary of research results (1) (Authors' own contribution)*

| Questions | Statements and Responds in % | |
|---|---|---|
| Which is the most likely when you work together on a task with your colleagues? | Cooperation | Competition |
| | 90,7% | 9,3% |
| Colleagues… | …often hold back information necessary for my work. | … usually share information necessary for my work. |
| | 9% | 91% |
| What do you think makes (would make) your organization effective? | Outstanding individual achievement. | Outstanding team performance. |
| | 26% | 74% |
| Is it typical in your organization that knowledge can be used as an instrument of power? | Yes | No |
| | 68% | 32% |
| Do you think that your influence and power would diminish in your organization if you shared your knowledge with others? | Yes | No |
| | 92% | 8% |
| If I have an option, I usually… | …favour my interests as opposed to the company's. | …favour the interests of the company instead of mine. |
| | 89% | 11% |

*Table 6. Summary of research results (2) (Authors' own contribution)*

| Statements | Responds in % | |
|---|---|---|
| | Rather Yes (4-6) | Rather No (1-3) |
| Our organization is like a family. | 80% | 20% |
| Our organization is like a venturesome laboratory. | 76% | 24% |
| Our organization is result-oriented. Task completion has priority. | 49% | 51% |
| Our organization is highly regulated. In general formal rules determine what people should do. | 39% | 61% |
| In general, the leadership of our organization supports mentoring. | 60% | 40% |
| In general, the leadership of our organization supports innovation, risk- taking and freedom of ideas. | 80% | 20% |
| In general, the leadership of our organization supports assertive, result-oriented attitude. | 50% | 50% |
| In our organization leadership style is rather team-oriented and based on consensus. | 60% | 40% |
| In our organization leadership style is supportive of individual risk-taking and innovation. | 71% | 29% |
| In our organization leadership style is supportive of competition and result-orientation. | 68% | 32% |
| The cohesion in our organization is built on loyalty and mutual trust. | 74% | 26% |
| The cohesion in our organization is built on innovation and commitment towards development. | 72% | 28% |
| Our organization puts an emphasis on personal development. It is characterised by high level of trust and openness. | 54% | 46% |
| Our organization puts an emphasis on gaining new resources and finding new challenges. | 69% | 31% |
| Our organization puts an emphasis on competition and results. | 66% | 34% |
| The basis of organizational success is the development of human resources, team-work and employee commitment. | 60% | 40% |
| Our organization is an innovator and number one in product development. | 50% | 50% |

## Hypothesis 1

In practice, knowledge management almost works like the Prisoner's dilemma because the individuals often feel that in order to achieve maximum gain they must compete. The reason why they rather opt for competition is because cooperation results in less gain than either competing one-sided or with everyone else. It is a fact that one-sided cooperation results in a less beneficial situation. In such cases as the „Prisoner's dilemma" the organization would benefit more from one-sided competition, participants, who think in a rational way rather opt for competition.

Our earlier research results showed that 71% of organizational members choose the competing behaviour and only 6% are altruists who believe that the most appropriate behaviour is knowledge management and the rejection of competition. As for the organizations, a small number of altruists is not damaging because the main goal is not that people offer their knowledge without any conditions. What is more of a challenge for organizations is that only 14% of respondents are „Assertive" who apply both types of behaviour since they are able to make a judgment on which behaviour is more beneficial. As a result of their ability to adopt any of the behaviours they provide the most firm basis of knowledge within the organization. The most harmful group is those who are neutral (9%). These people are mostly reserved and refuse any kind of competition and have no interest in knowledge sharing either (Fenyvesi, 2007).

In case of family businesses 68% of respondents (Table 5.) believe that knowledge can be used as an instrument of power at the workplace and 92% believe that knowledge sharing leads to diminishing influence for individuals. The large number of those who have an indisposition for knowledge sharing in family businesses might seem startling but further analyses have proved that family businesses under investigation show that organizational members find sharing information necessary for work a very important factor (91%). Only 9% of respondents think that co-workers fail in passing on important information. Corresponding with that is the result that shows that 90.7% of co-workers are cooperative in case of a project in which they work together and only 9.3% is competitive in these cases. Another corresponding result is that 74% of respondents claim that a decisive factor of organizational efficiency is outstanding team-work and not outstanding individual performance.

Of course it doesn't mean that family businesses are free from the pressure of choosing between co-operation and competition. 89% of respondents would put their own interests ahead of the community if they could. The fact that in case of certain challenges finding the right solution both cooperative and competitive behaviour are present is rather useful. If the goal of the organization is to turn organizational knowledge into a significant factor of competitiveness both behaviours are needed. The aim of knowledge sharing is not to be endlessly open or to provide a platform for co-workers to pass on all information without control. But it is also impossible to hide knowledge or to improve knowledge alone. Those who are able to make a sound judgment about which behaviour to choose in a given situation provide a sound knowledge base for the organization.

But the long-term conflict of individual and community interests must be controlled because it can easily lead to the collapse of the enterprise which is obviously equal to the collapse of individual goals as well. Organizations can avoid knowledge sharing to turn into a Prisoner's dilemma type of situation because knowledge sharing has many advantages which can only be utilized for the benefit of the organization by those organizational members who apply cooperation. It is important to observe that co-workers know that organizational knowledge can be widened through its utilization, with other words through knowledge sharing. It also contributes to the reduction of the scarcity of knowledge capital.

## Hypothesis 2

Hypothesis 2 is built on the exploration of a highly debated issue. How typical is innovation to family businesses? Is it the case that the lack of resources in the SME sector (as well as in family businesses) hinders or encourages innovation? In order to answer this question it is very important to define the notion of innovation.

In our study we use the innovation definition of Christopher Freeman which talks about four different innovations:

- Gradual or modifying innovation
- Radical innovation
- Procedural changes and
- Paradigm shift (Buzás, 2003)

Based on the data in Table 6. there are four statements that we found highly relevant:

- In general, the leadership of our organization supports innovation, risk taking and freedom of ideas.
- In our organization leadership style is supportive of individual risk-taking and innovation.
- In our organization leadership style is supportive of competition and result-orientation.
- Our organization puts an emphasis on gaining new resources and finding new challenges.

The last statement of the table „Our organization is an innovator and number one in product development" is not a highly relevant comment because product development is not a characteristic of the enterprises in our research (see the scope of activities earlier).

The four statements we found highly relevant are more typical of the family businesses we studied although in varying degrees (68-80%).

71% of the small businesses in our sample are micro and small enterprises and 45% has an employee number of 0-9. In these enterprises employees have the opportunity to try their skills and abilities in different areas within the organization.

Their flexibility is mostly the result of their relatively short chain of command and flat organizational structure. This results in a very short time between reaching a decision and act on it. This leads to an advantage organizations can utilize and adapt to dynamically changing external environment.

In addition, 80% of the respondents claim that their organization is „like a family" (Table 6.) and like a „venturesome laboratory" (76%). This allows ideas to be shared freely and encourage positive synergistic effects. As G.B. Shaw put it once: „If you have an apple and I have an apple and we exchange these apples then you and I will still each have one apple. But if you have an idea and I have an idea and we exchange these ideas, then each of us will have two ideas."

## Hypothesis 3

According to János Tomka (2005) „In knowledge-oriented organizations the culture of integration or the culture of organizational traditions is in conflict with the tacit knowledge sharing culture." In Table

3. a comparison of organizational knowledge sharing culture and tacit knowledge sharing culture can be found. It is based on the THT Model (Trompenaars; Hampden-Turner) (Table 7).

*Table 7. Organizational versus community culture (Authors' own contribution)*

| | Culture of Formal Teams | Community Culture | The Characteristics of Family Businesses in the Study | Rather Yes: | Rather No: |
|---|---|---|---|---|---|
| 1. Thinking and learning approaches | Universalism: belief in the generalization of good solutions; systems, standards, rules | Particularism: emphasis on the uniqueness of circumstances; flexibility, make pragmatic exceptions | Our organization is a highly regulated place. In general formal regulations determine people's work. | 39% | 61% |
| | | | Our organization is result oriented. Finishing tasks have priority. | 76% | 24% |
| 2. Motivation and remuneration approaches | Individualism: individual freedom, independence; higher income and positions | Collectivism: individuals reach their full potential as a member of a community; the team helps the individuals but in return it expects them to integrate | The top management of our organization supports ambitious and goal-oriented attitude. | 50% | 50% |
| 3. Dealing with people | Neutral attitude: human resources, tools for achieving a goal | Emotional attitude: creative partners; work is a human matter | The top management of our organization supports mentoring in most of the cases. | 60% | 40% |
| 4. Approach to authority | Inherited status: attributed to top roles | Gained status: creativity, knowledge; attributed to the individual based on performance | In our organization leadership style is characterized by team-work and consensus. | 60% | 40% |
| 5. Relationships between co-workers | Specific: Limited to the expected behaviour; less sensitivity to criticism, it doesn't affect personal space | Diffuse: spontaneous relationships, evolved from shared creative processes | Our organization is like a family. | 80% | 20% |
| | | | The cohesion of our organization is based on loyalty and mutual trust. | 74% | 26% |
| | | | Our organization puts emphasis on individual development. It is characterised by high level of trust and openness. | 54% | 46% |
| | | | Our organization puts an emphasis on competition and results. | 63% | 34% |
| 6. Managing change | External control: try to adapt to circumstances; improvisation and coordination are important | Internal control: the rate of success is the control over the external forces; changing rules and procedures | The basis of organizational success is the development of human resources, team-work and employee commitment. | 60% | 40% |

(The first three columns: Tomka, 2005)

In real life the differences between these two cultures are not that extreme. Although in knowledge-focused organizations the traditional and the knowledge sharing organizational cultures are in some cases in conflict, for long-term organizational success both of these cultures are inevitable.

Individuals, groups and the cultural embeddedness determine the extensiveness and efficiency of organizational knowledge sharing. There are several factors responsible for the development of knowledge sharing culture: trust, shared goals, communication, commitment towards the organization, shared decision-making, internal motivation, incentive system, leading by example, leadership style, organizational climate, team learning. But organizations must meet economic as well as social requirements, so, cooperation cannot exist without competition (Konczosné, 2014; Korpás, 2013; Fenyvesi, 2007). Essentially, the traditional and the knowledge sharing organizational cultures are in some cases in conflict but both have positive and negative elements. The negative aspects of traditional organizational culture regarding knowledge are: low level of trust, not enough trans-organizational interactions, not allowed „not to know something", competition is a legitimate tool for motivation, knowledge-sharing is not rewarded. Some examples for the negative aspects of professional teams: turning into a group of friends, inbred nature, keeping a distance from other parts of the organization, ignoring individual responsibility, losing business perspective.

Therefore, instead of replacing traditional organizational culture with knowledge sharing culture the two should be synthetized in a way that the positive factors of both cultures are brought together to create a new „knowledge-oriented culture". Both of these cultures have relevant factors that can contribute to the creation a knowledge-oriented culture.

## CONCLUSION

Today, many of the Hungarian SMEs (like those enterprises in our study) has reached a critical stage. The owners of those enterprises which were founded after the fall of communism has reached the age of retirement now. So, finding a satisfying answer to the question of „how to go on" became crucially important for them.

Finding the most satisfying answer for this question is equally important for the economy because SMEs are one of the most important constituents of labour market and the economy as a whole (see the high percentage of the contribution of SMEs to the GDP).

This is clearly not a country-specific circumstance and other post-communist countries have similar SME figures to that of Hungary's.

Generation change is a huge dilemma even for those enterprises which have gone through this process at an earlier stage. Among these enterprises only about one in three survive this crisis-like situation. Hopefully, in those countries in which enterprises need to face generation-change for the first time, survival rate will be higher.

As a result our topic is important a raises more questions. Are the next generation of leaders in family businesses going to be able to follow the path established by the founders? Do the members of the new generations want to follow that path?

Last but not least it is also an important question whether the current leaders of enterprises will be able to pass on the knowledge and their contact network which in most of the cases is linked strongly to them.

Knowledge sharing will be fundamentally important issue of survival.

Our chapter has highlighted some of the most important characteristics of Hungarian family businesses. The presented research has introduced the most relevant findings of a large, more comprehensive research. The most important findings can be outlined as the following:

- In family businesses cooperation and competition are the characteristics of both the top management and employees.
- Enterprises involved in our study believe that sharing of information crucial to work is very important (91%). It leads to a more favourable situation because cooperation stimulates task completion.
- Offsetting the above research result we found that 68% of the same enterprises assume that knowledge can be used as a tool for gaining power by organizational members and 92% think that knowledge sharing leads to diminishing individual influence within the organization. In case of family businesses the high number of those who have an indisposition for knowledge sharing might seem startling because their attitude can block successful generation change.
- Family businesses respond to changes more flexibly as a result they are more innovative.
- This statement usually causes a lot of dispute among those who do research on SMEs. The starting point of the debate is whether the lack of resources in the SME sector (as well as in family businesses) hinders or encourages innovation?
- Based on our findings we firmly believe that the lack of resources can help innovation. (In relation to this statement it is important to note that the notion of innovation was applied in the full extent of the words opposed to the use of the word in the classical innovation literature for example by Schumpeter. It should also be observed that in our study sample the number of those enterprises which carry out major innovation activities such as new product development is not common and as a result of that the expenditure on R&D is quite low).
- But the innovative nature of these enterprises stems from their lack of resources. The quick respond to general problems or the continuous need to satisfy changing customer demands are conditions of their survival similar to those companies which have much more resources. Since this sector is characterised by a serious lack of resources it is "forced" to use innovative tools (using their creativity) which are reflected in their products and services.
- There are four statements that we found highly relevant and reflect the innovative approach of these enterprises. These are the followings (in order): 1) in general, the leadership of the organization supports innovation, risk taking and freedom of ideas; 2) the leadership style of the organization is supportive of individual risk-taking and innovation; 3) the leadership style of the organization is supportive of competition and result-orientation; 4) the leadership of the organization puts an emphasis on gaining new resources and finding new challenges.
- Parallel to these characteristics the flexibility of these organizations is mostly the result of their relatively short chain of command and flat organizational structure.
- In relation to knowledge sharing the following findings should be highlighted: in case of family businesses the aim is not to replace the traditional organizational culture (throughout our chapter when we talk about knowledge-oriented organizations the integration culture is called traditional culture) with knowledge sharing organizational culture but rather the two should be synthetized in a way that the positive factors of both cultures are brought together to create a new „knowledge-oriented culture". Both of these cultures have relevant factors that can contribute to the creation a knowledge-oriented culture.

# REFERENCES

Ackoff, R. L. (1997). Transformational consulting. *Management Consulting Times, 28*(6).

Andrejcsik, L., Bakos, N., Bocz, J., Tiborné, D., Herzog, T., Jávorszkyné Nagy, A., … Nagyné Pakula, U. (2015). Magyarország 2014. Budapest: Központi Statisztikai Hivatal.

Antheaume, N., Barbelivien, D., & Paulette, R. (2012). French Family Business and Longevity. Have they been conducting sustainable development policies before it became a fashion? *Business History, 2013*(September).

Archibugi, D., & Michie, J. (Eds.). (1997). *Technology, Globalisation and Economic Performance.* Cambridge, UK: Cambridge University Press.

Arogundade, D. M. (2011). Mentoring and Leadership Succession in Industries and Organizations. *Academic Journal IFE Psychologia*, (Supplement), 180–187.

Audretsch, D., & Vivarelli, M. (1996). Firm size and R&D spillovers: Evidence from Italy. *Small Business Economics, 8*(3), 249–258. doi:10.1007/BF00388651

Bencsik, A. (2015). *A tudásmenedzsment elméletben és gyakorlatban.* Budapest: Akadémia Kiadó.

Bogáth, Á. (2013). A családi vállalkozásokban megjelenő sajátosságok. In *Vállalkozásfejlesztés a XXI. Században.* Retrieved from kgk.uni-obuda.hu/sites/default/files/13_Bogath_Agnes.pdf

Bogdány, E., Balogh, Á., & Csizmadia, T. (2015). Leadership succession and the origin of successor in Hungarian SMEs. *Mangement & Marketing, 9*(3), 283–300.

Bőgel, G. (1999). Tudásmenedzsment – a láthatatlan hatalom. *Magyar Távközlés*, 3-8.

Brink, P. (2001). Measurement of Conditions for Knowledge Sharing. In D. Remenyi (Ed.), *Proceedings of the 2nd European Conference on Knowledge Management* (pp. 677-693). ECKM.

Buzás, N. (2003). A kis- és középvállalkozások innovációs tevékenysége. In Kis- és középvállalkozások a változó gazdaságban. JATE Press.

Chin, P. (2005). *Knowledge Sharing: The Facts and the Myths, Part 1.* Retrieved March 2, 2016, from http://www.paulchinonline.com/portfolio/ij/ij20050208.htm

Csonka, L. (2011). Kutatás-fejlesztés és innováció a nemzetköziesedés tükrében – a magyar információtechnológiai ágazat kis- és középvállalatainak esete. *Külgazdaság, 55*, 34–56.

Davenport, T. H., & Prusak, L. (2001). *Tudásmenedzsment.* Budapest: Kossuth Kiadó.

Engestrom, Y. (1999). Innovative learning in work teams: Analyzing cycles of knowledge creation in practice. In *Perspectives on activity theory* (pp. 377–404). Cambridge, UK: Cambridge University Press. doi:10.1017/CBO9780511812774.025

European Commission Enterprise and Industry. (2009). *Small and medium-sized enterprises (SMEs).* Retrieved January 20, 2016, from http://ec.europa.eu/enterprise/policies/sme/promoting-entrepreneurship/family-business/#h2-2

Farkas, J. (2001). Úton az ipari társadalomból az információ alapú társadalom felé. *Info-Társadalomtudomány., 53/2001*, 23–31.

Fenyvesi, É. (2007). *Együttműködés és versengés a tudásmegosztás során. PhD értekezés.* Gödöllő: Szent István Egyetem.

Fenyvesi, É. (2010). Game Theory and Knowledge Management. *Development and Finance, Quarterly Hungarian Economic Review*, 31–39.

Heidrich, B., Makó, C., Csizmadia, P., & Csákné Filep, J. (2015). *Comparative Report on Family Businesses' Succession-Intergenerational Succession in SMEs Transition.* INSIST Project.

Henry, M., Erwee, R., & Kong, E. (2013). Family Business Succession - Trust and Gender Issues in Family and Non-Family Succession. In *13th Euram Conference, Democratising Management. Galatasaray University.*

Hnátek, M. (2015). Entrepreneurial thinking as a key factor of family business success. Social and Behavior Sciences, 181. doi:10.1016/j.sbspro.2015.04.896

Howells, J. (1990). The Internationalisation of R&D and the Development of Global Research Networks. *Regional Studies, 24*(6), 495–512. doi:10.1080/00343409012331346174

Kárpátiné Daróczi, J., Fenyvesi, É., & Vágány, J. (2015). A mentorálás lehetőségei a fiatal vállalkozók számára. In Gazdálkodás és Menedzsment Tudományos Konferencia: Kecskemét, II. köt. (pp. 794-798).

Kehl, D., & Rappai, G. (2007). *Mintaelemszám tervezése Likert-skálát alkalmazó lekérdezésekben.* Retrieved January 13, 2016, from http://www.ksh.hu/statszemle_archive/2006/2006_09/2006_09_848.pdf

Konczosné Szombatelyi, M. (2014). *Családi vállalkozások generációváltásának kockázata.* Retrieved from http://kgk.sze.hu/images/dokumentumok/kautzkiadvany2014/KSZM.pdf

Korpás, Z. (2013). *Kire bízzam a ház kulcsát? Cégvezető utódkeresés a munkaerőpiacon.* Retrieved from gymskik.hu/hu/letoltes/11455/cfb06

Kozma, T., & Gyenge, B. (2015). The secret to business success after the crisis a business model in an enterprise. *Journal Of Central European Green Innovation, 3*(2), 71–82.

Laczkó, Zs. (1997). Családi vállalkozás – konfliktus és kooperáció. In *Családi vállalkozások Magyarországon, kutatási zárótanulmány.* Budapest: SEED Alapítvány.

Lakner, Légrádiné, S. (2006). Új szemlélet a fejlesztő tanácsadásban: A coaching. *Tudásmenedzsment, 7*(2), 82–92.

Leach, P. (2011). *Family Business – The Essentials.* London: Profiles Books.

Mandl, I. (2008). *Overview of family businesses relevant issues.* Final report. KMU Forschung. Retrieved January 13, 2016, from http://ec.europa.eu/enterprise/policies/sme/files/craft/family_business/doc/familybusiness_study_en.pdf

Marcellné Szilágyi, E. (2012). Az érzelmi intelligencia mint a tacit tudás része. In Átalakuló emberi erőforrás menedzsment. Budapest: CompLex Kiadó Jogi és Üzleti Tartalomszolgáltató Kft.

Mészáros, T., & Szirmai, P. (2001). Egy kutatás tanulságai – Az EU kisvállalkozáspolitikája. Pénzforrás – A pályázatok kézikönyve, 26.

Miller, S. P. (2014). *Next-generation leadership development in family businesses: the critical roles of shared vision and family climate*. Retrieved January 9, 2016, from http://journal.frontiersin.org/article/10.3389/fpsyg.2014.01335/abstract

Nemzeti Innovációs Hivatal (NIH). (2013). *Kutatás-fejlesztés és Innováció Magyarországon*. Retrieved February 10, 2016, from http://kaleidoszkop.nih.gov.hu/documents/15428/38972/Kutat%C3%A1s-fejleszt%C3%A9s%20%C3%A9s%20innov%C3%A1ci%C3%B3%20Magyarorsz%C3%A1gon

Nonaka, I., & Takuchi, H. (1995). The knowledge creating Company: How Japanese Companies Create the Dynamics por Innovation. New York: Oxford University Press.

Noszkay, E. (1999). *A gazdasági informatika helye és oktatásának sajátságos követelményei, valamint módszerei a menedzserképzésben In* . Konferencia Kiadvány I. Kötet.

Pakucs, J. (2005). Innováció és a vállalkozások. *Polgári Szemle, 1*(1). Retrieved March 1, 2016, from http://www.polgariszemle.hu/?view=v_article&ID=11&page=1

Polák-Weldon, R. (2014). Sustainable Value Creation for Employees. *BAM2014 Conference Proceedings*.

Polányi, M. (1997). *Tudomány és ember. Három tanulmány*. Budapest: Argumentum Kiadó.

Poza, E. (2003). Heirs and Graces in a Family Business. *Businessweek News*. Retrieved January 13, 2016, from http://www.bloomberg.com/news/articles/2003-08-10/heirs-and-graces-in-a-family-business

Pretorius, S., Steyn, H., & Jordaan, J. C. (2012). Project management matury and project management succes in engineering and construction. *SA Journal of Industrial Engineering, 23*(3), 1–12.

PWC. (2015). *CEE Family Business Survey, Family businesses at a crossroads*. Retrieved January 10, 2016, from http://www.pwc.com/hu/hu/kiadvanyok/assets/pdf/cee_family_survey_2015.pdf

Ruggieri, R., Pozzi, M., & Ripamonti, S. (2014). Italian Family Business Cultures Involved int he Generational Change, In: *Europe's. The Journal of Psychology, 10*(1), 79–103.

*S&P 500 Component Stocks*. (n.d.). Retrieved January 15, 2016, from https://en.wikipedia.org/wiki/List_of_S%26P_500_companies

Stamm, I., & Lubinski, C. (2011). Crossroads of family business research and firm demography – A critical assessment of family business survival rates. Journal of Family Business Strategy.

Sveiby, K. E. (2001). *Szervezetek új gazdagsága: a menedzselt tudás*. Budapest: KJK-KERSZÖV Jogi és Üzleti Kiadó Kft.

Szabó, M. (2011). *Projektmenedzsment*. Szeged: Szegedi Tudományegyetem Közoktatási Vezetőképző Intézet.

Szerb, L., Csapi, V., Deutch, N., Ulbert, J., Horváth, Á., Kruzslicz, F., … Szűcs, P. K. (2014). Mennyire versenyképesesek a magyar kisvállalatok. Marketing & Management, 48, 3-21.

Tomka, J. (2005). *A szakmai közösségek (Communities of Practice) hozzájárulása a szervezeti együttműködés fejlesztéséhez. PhD értekezés*. Budapest: BME.

Vágány, J., Kárpátiné Daróczi, J., & Fenyvesi, É. (2015). A családi vállalkozások sikere- a család sikere. Gazdálkodás és Menedzsment Tudományos Konferencia. Kecskemét.

Ward, J. L. (2011). *Keeping the Family Business Healthy: How to Plan for Continuing Growth*. Palgrave Macmillan. doi:10.1057/9780230116122

Wenger, E. (1998). *Communities of Practice: learning, meaning and identity*. Cambridge, UK: Cambridge University Press. doi:10.1017/CBO9780511803932

Wiig, K. M. (2000). *Knowledge Management: En Emerging Discipline Rooted in a long History, Knowledge Horizons: The present and promise of Knowledge Management*. Boston: Butterworth-Heinnemann.

Wimmer, R., Groth, T., & Simon, F. B. (2004). Erfolgsmuster von Mehrgenerationen-Familienunternehmen. *Wittener Diskussionspapiere. Sonderheft, Nr 5*. Retrieved from http://osb-i.com/sites/default/files/user_upload/Publikationen/Wimmer_Groth_Simon_Erfolgsmuster_von_Mehrgenerationen-FU_Juni_04.pdf

## KEY TERMS AND DEFINITIONS

**Family Business:** Economic entities of any size. They are operated and lead by at least two members of the same family of whom one is the owner. *Also, the family has a decisive share of ownership in decisions made by the owners.*

**Innovation:** It is a change which is added to the system in order to introduce a new state which is valued positive and lead to improvement of some sort. So, innovation is not a one off action but a sequence of actions which interact. It doesn't only incorporate new knowledge and abilities, new products, services, processes or finding new markets but rather all of these. It is a process which incorporates all the elements of a creative process from research to providing services and they are integrated so as to influence the achievement of a common goal.

**Knowledge:** It is a complex notion because it is intangible but has a formal structure; it is also intuitive as a result it is difficult to verbalize and impossible to understand in purely logical forms.

**Non-Technological Innovation:** As opposed to technological innovation, non-technological innovation refers to the introduction of a new marketing method or a new organizational method.

**Research Centre:** Any company, organization or organizational unit which carries out research and development activity by using their own facilities and employees.

**SMEs (Small and Medium Sized Businesses):** Those enterprises that employ less than 250 employees and the net sales revenue doesn't exceed the sum of HUF equal to EUR 50 million or a balance sheet total of the sum of HUF equal to EUR 43 million.

**Technological Innovation:** A new or a significantly improved product/service or process introduced to the everyday operation of the enterprise.

# Chapter 15
# Managing Collective Knowledge at a Small Business Group (VID Group)

**Zoltán Véry**
*Budapest Metropolitan University, Hungary*

## ABSTRACT

*Personal knowledge is the construction of the individual. It is the context of factual knowledge and experience. Collective work, thinking, writing requires adaptation, adjustment, coordination. The VID SME Group demonstrates the significance of collective knowledge, as the group is dominated by diversity, manifold ordering, but also by the maintenance and coordination of plurality. The present paper provides the framework and the praxis of the plural management of collective knowledge, hence allowing for the attainment of the approach and thinking lying therein. Following an overview of the background of the adopted systemic, pluralistic approach, the paper gives insight into the VID Group's systemically, corporally-corporately and textually ordered architecture, into its management and control praxes of collective knowledge, but it also presents the business group's principles, tasks, networks, its functional ordering and connections.*

## INTRODUCTION

Niklas Luhmann (2013) system theorist interprets knowledge as the sense context of observations. Factual knowledge, hence, knowledge as such, is construction, involving both personal and collective knowledge. Every individual and group constructs his/her/its own knowledge which evolves only throughout the engagement with objects, by way of sharing interpersonal factual knowledge, experiences and astute ideas. Signs and data are transferable, but in terms of interpretation it is unreasonable to speak of knowledge transfer, since construction is of an autopoetic (self-creating) nature the outcome of which cannot be transferred. One gains insight into the knowledge of others in the course of interpretation and understanding, always in terms of one's own context of sense. But let us turn to science. According to Dirk Baecker (1993), the constructivism of the knowledge creating process is based on three theories:

DOI: 10.4018/978-1-5225-1642-2.ch015

Spencer-Brown's difference theory, von Foerster's cybernetics of the second degree, and Maturana's theory of autopoiesis.

The multifaceted order of the organization serves as the foundation of management. Besides the orders of action and technology, we rely on social order and also on the order of language. This chapter gives insight into the system-based construction and operation of knowledge management within a small business group. It demonstrates how knowledge management cooperates with other systems of management, how collective knowledge contributes to the reaching of goals, and what significance all this bears with respect to the business group.

## BACKGROUND

Economic science belongs to the social sciences. The turn of research in the field of the social sciences, which called attention to the insufficiency of a merely technical approach, has already been noted by Cifford Geertz (1983) in his book entitled *Local Knowledge: Further Essays in Interpretative Anthropology*. Geertz formulates the insight that "the broader currents of modern thought" have brought about a turn that signals a new direction in the study of society, which "seems on the way to becoming seriously irregular. It is certainly becoming more pluralistic" (Geertz, 1983, pp. 3–4).

The social systemic approach of the organization, as an economic subsystem of society, may also seem irregular. It may seem irregular due to its demand of multiple perspectives, its claim for research results from multiple disciplines. However, such a pluralistic approach is justified and has been acknowledged by theorists of management. Its justification lies in its being necessitated by science, order and the pluralistic nature of organizations. The present paper follows such a pluralistic, multi-layered approach by way of coordinating, advocating and integrating various disciplines, orders and diversity itself.

### The Organization Is Pluralistic from a Disciplinary Point of View

In our concept of knowledge management, sociology bears great emphasis. The collective, societal nature of organizations has a decisive role in acquiring, building and sharing personal and collective knowledge, but also in its corporate application. Within the framework of sociology, the present paper follows the research directions and results presented in Niklas Luhmann's ouvre. Following Luhmann's research helps us in unfolding, understanding and building social systems. The four facets of Luhmann's system theory are general systems theory, epistemology, communication theory and evolution theory. The mentioned theories have to be applied in a combined and coordinated way in order to be of sufficient aid in the research, understanding and control of society and their institutions, such as organizations. Business, institutional and bureaucratic organizations are manifold sociotechnical entities which require a multiple-perspective approach in order to be understood adequately.

Gareth Morgan (1986) presents the pluralistic approach of the organization in his book entitled *Images of Organization* with the help of eight metaphors. Morgan explores the build-up of organizations as machines, as organisms, as brains, as cultures, as political systems, as psychic prisons, as flux and transformation, and as instruments of domination (Morgan, 1986). In this way, the work offers insight into the development of the bureaucratic organization, the unfolding of organizational needs, the organization as a thought-processing brain, the correlations of culture and organization, the organization as a system of governance, the snares involved in the hidden structures of the organization, and also into the ruling modes of organizational thinking. In addition, the book also considers the organization as a self-evolving, self-maintaining system, and its potential schemes of organizational dominance (Morgan, 1986). Hence, Morgan aims to emphasize that the organization and its complexity unfolds throughout the simultaneous application of multiple approaches and evaluations. In order to be able to unfold the organization in this way, Morgan claims, two steps have to be performed. The first is the diagnostic analysis of a given situation. Such an analysis applies various metaphors in order to reveal the key aspects of the situation. The second step involves the critical examination of the interpretations developed in line with the foregoing analysis. This critical examination also requires organizational discourse, involving all of its collectives and individuals. Moreover, it allows for the appropriate handling of organizational complexity, both in prescriptive and descriptive terms. It demonstrates the ways to interpret a situation from multiple perspectives with the help of expertise and critical thinking (Morgan, 1986). Though leaders and organization theorist often make an attempt to conceal complexity by way of hypothesizing that organizations are, after all, "rational phenomena" determined primarily by their goals, this hypothesis often proves inadequate in the course of the actual analysis of organizations and throughout the process of finding solutions to problems, according to Morgan (Morgan, 1986). Morgan's approach is also preferable from the aspect of organizational knowledge management. Acquiring, accruing, building, coordinating and applying individual and collective organizational knowledge requires that we take multiple perspectives into consideration simultaneously. The organization is not merely a value producing, value preserving, value transmitting device (which transforms inputs into outputs/results with the help of specified technologies and mechanisms), but a social (collective) system, which integrates and coordinates both the individuals and the instruments of the organization.

## The Organization Is Pluralistic from a Systemic Point of View

The question arises how the integrative order, integrating the various parts into an entirety, is formulated. The organization, as a social system, is a system of sense. Two systems of sense are to be taken into consideration in terms of the multifaceted control of the organization: two systems of sense, to be applied and reckoned with throughout the observation, interpretation, evaluation, planning, improvement and refinement of the organization itself. The perceptive, thinking and active individual (person) is one of these systems, the other is the system of communication involving the *interactions* of the members of the organization, which interactions are integrated within and delineated by the system of communication. The functional ordering of social systems follows from the differences of language use. Leaders, members (individuals) of the marketing, logistics and knowledge management functions speak and write in different languages. Such a significance of language, among the significance of other aspects of social systems (as systems of sense), will become apparent from the theoretical framework provided by Niklas Luhmann's concepts.

In his fundamental work entitled *Introduction to Systems Theory* Luhmann (2013) explicates the general theory of social systems in great detail. The three main characteristics of Luhmann's theory are the following:

1. **Society/the Organization is Made Up of Distinctions**: Systems are also distinctions in themselves, involving two sides. One of these two sides is the system, as structure, the other is its environment. When surveying the build-up of society, involving the organization, one is to think in terms of functional differentiations, since these provide the key aspects of the societal/organizational framework itself.

2. **Society/the Organization is Formulated as a System** *:* Sub-systems, distinctions and diversity make up society and organizations. The social system receives signs and data from its environment, which are perceived on the border of the system as "irritations" either received and interpreted by the system, or left entirely out of consideration. As soon as we begin to communicate we come into contact with society, with the organization. Individuals comprise the environment of the system.

3. **Society/the Organization is a System of Communication** *:* In the course of making sense and giving sense, different systems of sense (these different, autonomous systems of sense being the individual, the group and the organization) constitute the information itself. The system of communication evolves from the various interactions taking place between these distinct systems of sense.

Personally construed sense (thought, experience, knowledge) is articulated by way of communication (interactions), hence is it shared with others. The management of personal and collective organizational knowledge (acquiring, building, sharing knowledge) requires the management of communicational diversity. All forms and representations of knowledge enter the space of organizational sense by way of auditory, written and visual communication. Organizational knowledge management yields the experience and the insight that each individual possesses a personal and a public vocabulary. Such vocabularies are not always available in a written form, they are usually applied in oral language use. Not only individuals possess such a vocabulary, however. Besides individuals, organizations also have one or more vocabularies which are applied throughout communication, in the course of knowledge acquisition, knowledge codification (preparing representations of knowledge), and also during knowledge sharing.

Luhmann's general systems theory is also endowed with a vocabulary of its own, as his system theory offers a different discourse on the theories of social order, communication and the evolution of social orders as compared to former (input-output) theories. That is to say, Luhmann's theory introduces an atypical approach of the social system, and with it, hitherto unconsidered thematic aspects as well. It is essential, therefore, to give a brief and limited overview of the key concepts involved in Luhmann's theory of social systems, so as to aid the reader in understanding their working and their plurality. The knowledge management system is not only a system of action but also a system of sense. To be able to attain an understanding of systems of sense, one has to be familiar with the following key concepts: *sense, language, complexity, integration, expectation.* Our multidisciplinary approach also compels us to adapt the sociological concepts involved in general systems theory to the context of the knowledge management system:

- **Sense:** According to Luhmann's (2013) general systems theory, systems are self-referential (self-observing) systems. In self-referential systems differentiation takes place only by virtue of self-reference, self-observation. The hence created knowledge determines the context of factual knowledge, experiences, assumptions and notions. Knowledge is gained from individuals only: from ourselves and from others. As Luhmann puts it, "meaning is related to the subject" (Luhmann, 2013, p. 162). In terms of systems, the concept of the subject-relatedness of sense is articulated in the following way:

*we must apply the category of meaning to two different system types (this is my way of putting it). We have psychic systems – consciousness systems that have meaningful experiences – and we have social systems – communication systems that reproduce meaning by using it in communication. (Luhmann, 2013, p. 163)*

As before, the significance of making a difference in making sense cannot remain unnoticed: "[i] f one insisted on a definition, one might say that sense[1] is the medium that works with the difference between the actual and the potential" (Luhmann, 2013, p. 169). Organizations are not only processes of action, but also integrated systems of sense.

- **Language:** Difference acquires sense as language. "Language cannot maintain itself merely as a lexicon. […] Language, as such, […] is speaking, writing, and reading. It reproduces the possibility of creating forms, and its own condition of possibility that it is used" (Luhmann, 2013, p. 165). Linguistic difference evolves throughout the interactions between the various systems. Reaching an understanding of the hence evolved differences between the systems necessitates linguistic overlays, linguistic interpenetrations between the respective systems, so that they may establish connections of sense. In order to ensure effective knowledge management, the opportunity for fashioning the organization's autonomous linguistic order – while retaining the linguistic plurality of the systems involved – is also to be granted, besides providing possibilities for knowledge acquisition and for creating representations of knowledge. To this end, linguistic representations of individual knowledge acquisition and organizational communication have to be made available. The organization's linguistic order may be established with the help of the forms, schemes and themes of language, by aid of dictionaries and semantic ontological models. Language is the medium of shaping organizational knowledge.

- **Complexity:** Society (involving the organization) is too complex to be thoroughly comprehended and to allow for taking all its circumstances into consideration in the course of making decisions. All organizations (big and small) – besides being active, decision-making, value-creating and value-preserving "machines", mechanisms – are collective observational, sense-creating, sense-sharing corporate orders. In addition, the organization also testifies of complexity in its temporal development: "[a] system is able to realize different patterns in sequence. Elsewhere, I have called this the 'temporalization of complexity'. […] [C]ommunication systems deal with complexity in sequence." (Luhmann, 2013, p. 126). Sequentiality is the temporal dimension of systems, and in organizations it has to be handled as such. Since knowledge management is also the management of complex organizational knowledge, it is important to consider the complexity of such knowledge – which manifests itself and develops in speech, writing and visual representations (visual language) – besides studying the complexity of the organizational system and the changes taking place in the complexity of functional subsystems.

Significantly, however, social systems reduce complexity with regard to specific differences. The social system names its topic, the difference it is oriented upon, and excludes other differences with which it is not concerned in relation to a specific topic.

- **Integration:** Organizational knowledge management is concerned with integration and its multifaceted control besides the management of complexity. The social system is integrat*ed* and integrat*ive* at the same time: "[o]n the one hand, integration in respect to the action system is accomplished within the social system but, on the other hand, the social system must also be able to fulfil integrative functions by itself" (Luhmann, 2013, p. 21). The organizational cultural system lays ground for the social system, while the social system integrates the personality system – its intentions and interactions. That is to say, "[c]ulture directs the systems 'cybernetically,' as Parsons puts it, in that it influences social systems using little energy, and these then influence personal systems, which, in turn, exert their influence on their underlying organism" (Luhmann, 2013, p. 22). The events of such integrated systems require multifaceted control, but also necessitate the differentiation, integration and coordination of actions and speech (oral, written and visual). Figure 1 demonstrates the matrix of integration the cultural, social and personality systems are involved in, i.e. the "action system", adopted by Luhmann (2013) from Parsons (1978, p. 361).

- **Expectation:** The concept of expectation bears great emphasis in the management of organizational knowledge (pertaining to businesses, business groups, networks of interest). Organizational expectations are oriented upon individuals and collectives of the organization: upon designers, analysts, creative groups, working groups, project teams, etc. In terms of the various individuals, groups, roles of the organization knowledge emerges as a complex requirement, as part of a complex set of *expectations,* not as a possession. According to Luhmann, "[f]or such a theory that defines the concept of structure by means of expectations, the subject-object distinction is meaningless" (Luhmann, 2013, p. 72). Expectations are determined by the various systems involved in the build-up of the organization, hence, by the differences between the diverse systems, which have to be classified and categorized according to organizational points of view. Such points of view, in turn, are yielded by the integrated systems and functional subsystems of the organization.

*The system must be capable of creating expectations in order to see possibilities, and it must have types or schemata at its disposal in order to categorize something. This is the system's achievement that can differ greatly from one system to the next. The entire process of selection is a system-internal process and not something that in any way exists in the environment (Luhmann, 2013, pp. 91–92).*

*Figure 1. Action system (the matrix of systems of action) A = adaptation, G = goal attainment, I = integration, L = latent pattern maintenance*
*(Luhmann, 2013, p. 15.)*

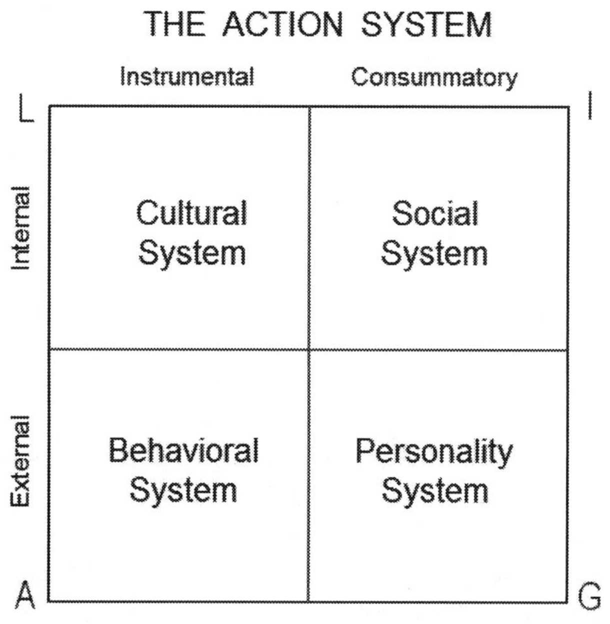

## THE ACTION SYSTEM

|  | Instrumental | Consummatory |  |
|---|---|---|---|
| L |  |  | I |
| Internal | Cultural System | Social System |  |
| External | Behavioral System | Personality System |  |
| A |  |  | G |

Knowledge management involves planning. "Expectations refer not to the past but to the future" (Luhmann, 2013, p. 241). Knowledge management planning pertains to the expectations of knowledge, their multifaceted control, refinement and synchronization in line with dependency chains (e.g. processes, mechanisms, procedures) and in accordance with the organization's externally associated interest groups. Besides operational and strategic expectations, normative expectations also subsist, the majority of which originate from the organizational environment. Among these expectations are specific *requirements*. Such are legal requirements (laws in force, government decrees), professional requirements (standards of quality, methods) and requirements of knowledge, of science. Learning is a permanent must. Organizational learning is a mode of knowledge acquisition which necessitates management, just as meeting the requirements of organizational knowledge does.

## The Organization Is Pluralistic in Its Knowledge

The need for a pluralistic approach does not manifest itself only in the disciplinary field and within the scope of various theories, or with regard to the study of social systems; it is also essential with respect to organizational knowledge.

In their work entitled *Managing Flow: A Process Theory of the Knowledge-based Firm* the authors highlight that influential management theories of the scientific world still consider firms to be stable and closed entities which function on the basis of set principles (Nonaka, Toyama & Hirata, 2008). Research based on such foundation is oriented upon making prescriptive principles more exact, more accurate. Although in these terms research findings may show the successful and unsuccessful initiatives following from the knowledge of firms' and from their modes of organizational knowledge preservation, no cues are provided regarding the ways these firms build knowledge on the basis of their own practice. According to the authors of the mentioned work, in order to understand the paradigm shift brought about by the knowledge-based society, another paradigm shift is needed in terms of thinking about knowledge and knowledge management (Nonaka et al., 2008). Traditional knowledge management has to be replaced by a knowledge-based management which stems from the complex theory of the firm. This involves the understanding of that complex process which demonstrates the creation of knowledge and also the ways the organization applies such knowledge throughout its interaction with its own environment. In establishing the theory of the knowledge-creating company, Nonaka, Toyama and Hirata (2008) apply conceptual couples bearing great significance. Such couples are the following: resource and process, objective and subjective, tacit and explicit, internal and external. Polányi differentiated tacit and explicit knowledge, but he did not separate the two. The aim of such a differentiation was to re-establish the role of the individual, i.e. the appropriate status of the thinking, acting person in the processes related to knowledge. This also demonstrates that knowledge is personal. It is rooted in the perceiving-feeling-living human organism, the individual. Tacit knowledge is not tacit because it is inarticulable, but because it is *not to be articulated,* it is *covert.* All that is covert is inherent – not to be made explicit. The sense making, active individual is imbued with tacit knowledge. Hence, in our consideration, Nonaka's, Toyama's and Hirata's conceptual couple involving tacit and explicit is inappropriate, just as the one in which subjective and objective are opposites. Thinking in terms of differences and distinctions, systems, subsystems and environments, in terms of language and sense shows that the "object" is never independent from the "subject", i.e. the individual and the "objects" of its concerns are inseparably entwined within the threads of perception and interpretation, therefore, their distinction is not only inappropriate but is also without use.

From this follows that the present study does not find the Nonaka–Takeuchi SECI model a suitable representation of the knowledge creating process either. The SECI model conceives a spiral process which serves as the transformation of knowledge taking place in four steps, four phases. These four phases are socialization, externalization, combination and internalization (Nonaka, Toyama & Hirata, 2008). Nonaka and Takeuchi hold the view that in the course of socialization and externalization individual knowledge becomes explicit, to be shared with others and thus, to be enriched (combined). The hence created, enriched "subjective knowledge" can be reinternalized. This time, however, internalization ensues with respect to more individuals, i.e. more people acquire the surfaced and enriched "subjective knowledge", which, hence, serves as the foundation of a new cycle of knowledge creation for several people. In our view, knowledge creation is not a process of succession, as presented in the SECI model, but one of simultaneous plurality. In this sense do we apply Michel Foucault's term "discursive ferment" (Foucault, 1999, p. 20)[2], representing a process during which knowledge is developed, multiplied and shared by virtue of its rootedness in speech and through its multi-aspected reinterpretation.

Professor Erzsébet Noszkay made an attempt at understanding the phenomenon of the "discursive ferment" by conducting researches related to the issue. The "capillary model" devised by professor Noszkay presents the processes involving the permeation and the spreading of knowledge in an organizational context. The name of the model derives from the analogy with the phenomenon of capillarity[3:]

*The analogy was based on a simple consideration. Organizational islands, hubs, communities endowed with an aptitude and sensitivity for knowledge management had to be found, which promised to be of use in transmitting the appropriate solutions devised by the experts of knowledge management, the initiators of the sustainment of knowledge management, through [...] the capillaries, ensuring thereby the development of knowledge management besides providing the requirements and factors which aid such a development. (Noszkay, 2013, p. 70)[4]*

The "capillary model", as a metaphor, is also of great aid in demonstrating that knowledge-sharing organizational culture may be built and shaped in a "natural", self-organizing way. It also validates the claim and makes it easy to see that personal and collective knowledge are not spread in a circular or spiralled way, as Nonaka's and Takeuchi's SECI model maintains, but by way of the "discursive ferment". "Discursive ferment" means that organizational communication transpires through personal and collective connections and communication (oral, written and visual). The "capillary model" encourages collectives and individuals to establish natural connections, to become engaged in dialogues and to be involved in actions according to the *sense* and *themes of speech,* corresponding to the *relational conditions* and to the *logic* of the *compositions of speech.* None of this may take place outside the functional circles (units) and the multifaceted linguistic order of the organization, however. Particularly by way of its approach, the "capillary model" helps one reach an understanding of the "ferment" of organizational sense, supports the shaping of the organizational knowledge management system, but also provides aid in establishing a framework for and regulating the behavioural requirements of sharing knowledge. The "capillary model" reveals that not all approaches and praxes are spiralled. Sufficient attention has to be dedicated to the capillary "mechanisms" of organizational knowledge management, for these are the mechanisms to be actually understood.

## THE BUSINESS GROUP AS A LOCALITY

The VID Group is situated in Hungary, operating on the northern shore of Lake Balaton called the Balaton Uplands. The VID Group is a local group of enterprises. Twelve small enterprises and a holding belong to the business group. Their knowledge of locality is essential to their functioning. Besides their individual ties, these small enterprises were brought together by their accumulated factual knowledge and experience concerning the Balaton Uplands. Hence, besides expertise it is collective knowledge which maintains the business group. In the course of planning, problem solving, control and decision-making, the following questions always arise: "Where is it?", "Where does it operate?", "What is it close to?" The following thoughts formulated by Arjun Appadurai, researcher, may highlight the significance of these questions:

*[m]uch that has been considered local knowledge is actually knowledge of how to produce and reproduce locality under conditions of anxiety and entropy, social wear and flux, ecological uncertainty and cosmic volatility, and the always present quirkiness of kinsmen, enemies, spirits, and quarks of all sorts. The locality of local knowledge is not only, or even mainly, its embeddedness in a nonnegotiable here and now [...]. (Appadurai, 1998, p. 181)*

The VID Group is a business enterprise group that acquires, contextualizes and applies "local knowledge". Building industry and facilities maintenance operate in the Balaton Uplands. The holding of the group is situated in Budapest. It manages the business group's subsidiary enterprises, building enterprises, enterprises of facilities maintenance and its local employees both financially and strategically. Tasks in finance, investment planning, infocommunicational-technological development, knowledge management and strategic planning, hence, are undertaken in the capital.

## The Architecture of the Business Group

Architecture is structure, building and the self-building (self-construing) of a system. Architecture involves overground construction, civil engineering, landscaping and interior design, but also the construction and realization of business models, the elevation and delineation of structures. As such, architecture encompasses boundaries of sense, but also marks the limits that organizational personal and collective knowledge testify of. Architecture also entails the communication of structural changes and the embedding of these changes into the discourse of the enterprise. Structures are also to be discussed, not only to be built.

At a small business group, buildings, equipment, technologies and their structure are designed and built by owners of knowledge such as building, mechanical, electrical engineers, economists, lawyers, informaticians, IT operatives and communication experts. The owners of knowledge constitute a multidisciplinary and versatile creative team, who have to infiltrate and create overlaps in each other's knowledge, just like a chamber orchestra whose members are dependent upon one another's knowledge and performance. The control of architecture means primarily the validation of architectural knowledge whereby the observers overview and approve the design, while also monitoring the processes and the compliance of realization. Observers also detect mistakes and the sources of mistakes, which entail the lack of knowledge and false knowledge.

*Figure 2. The architecture of the VID Group*

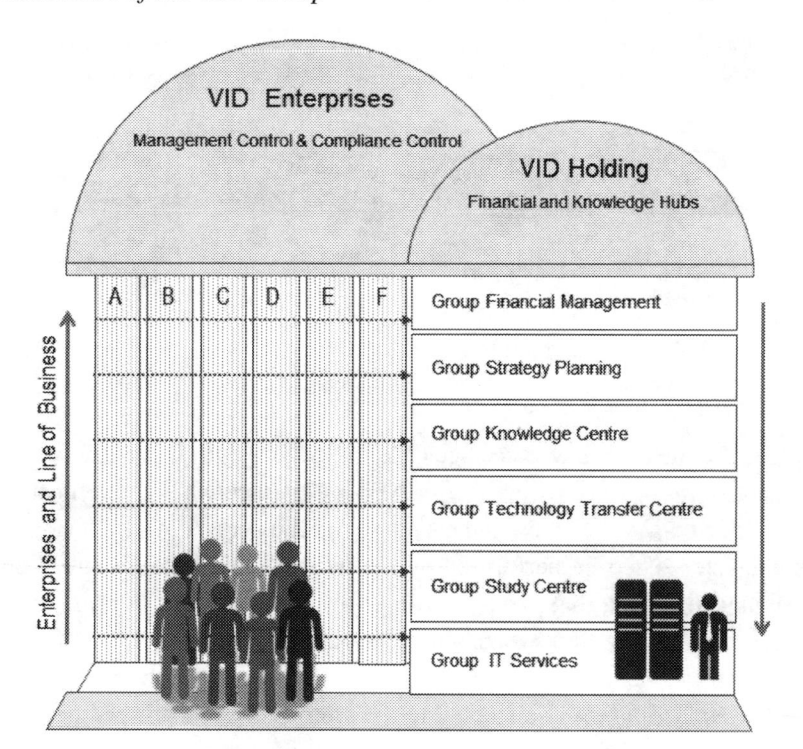

## The Business Group as a System

The VID Group is a pluralistic system. Personal and collective knowledge embracing the organization has to be built, updated and developed within this plural order. It has to be actual and connectible to strategic and operative aims. This is a challenge to leaders – to all leaders of the organization, as they assign particular significance to the requirements (expectations) of knowledge necessary for action, besides paying attention to personal and collective activities, achievement and turnout. All knowledge is knowing how to act. Managing the personal and the collective knowledge of the organization means managing the knowledge to act, which is a phenomenon loaded with factual knowledge, experiences and praxes. This also implies that managing the knowledge to act involves the management of the lack of knowledge, which always accompanies knowledge. The lack of knowledge is usually understood as false knowledge, inaccurate knowledge, misunderstanding, non-understanding, flawed praxis and mistakes arising from inexperience.

The VID Group applies the following system types in operating the organizational system, which involves the knowledge management system. We introduce system types with the help of metaphors, in line with Gareth Morgan's principle of plurality.

### Personal System

The "organizational being" is a person. The person, as an individual, cannot exist without its cultural and societal being. If we consider and think of organizational knowledge as a requirement (expectation),

*Figure 3. Types of subsystems within the organizational system*

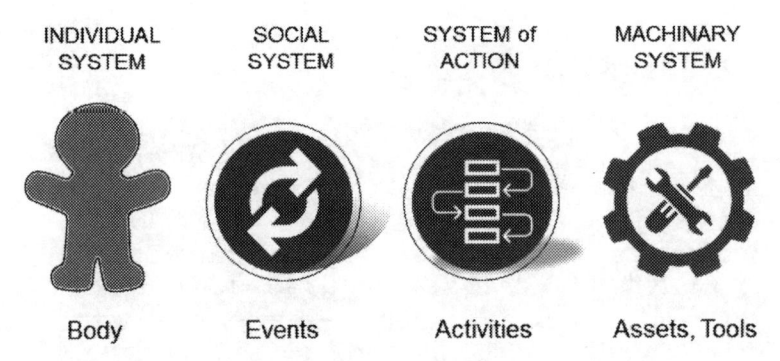

we speak of and describe the person as a collage of knowledge requirements (expectations). The word *persona* used to denote a mask worn by actors during performances in ancient theatres, later referring to a particular role performed by the actor, and eventually to the actor himself, performing the role. The *persona* is a role character. The role performed by the person within the organization establishes the link between the organization and that person. In order to understand the relations stemming from the bond between person and organization, we also have to consider what the sense of the personal system in an organization is. Persons/individuals are cognitive systems observed by other cognitive systems or by social systems. The concept of the personal system therefore involves the perspective of observation. When observational perspectives are actualized by the personal system, cognitive and personal systems come to be almost of the same sense. Within an organization the personal system is an assortment of *persona*s, i.e. of organizational roles. The choice of roles takes place each time as an interaction of the communication system. In this way, throughout the process of communication within the social system, selections are connected to selections, which connections function as points of reference for persons/ individuals. By way of the interactions taking place within the social system, cognitive systems become individuals. The social system is built of personal relations and interactions, but is not limited to these. Apparently, social systems have to be separated clearly from personal systems, as they are two different types of system: the organization as a social system consists of communicative interactions, while personal systems are made up of cognitive events. The knowledge management system, being a social system itself, observes individuals and other social systems.

## Social System

Social systems are communication systems. Social systems create connections within the organization and favour these connections as opposed to the ones found within the environment. Social systems are systems of sense. This concept refers to the mode of constitution systems testify of: systems differentiate themselves on the basis of sense relations, not on the basis of objects. Social systems are organizational functions interpenetrating one another, and are delineated by virtue of their sense, thus also on the basis of their speech. That is to say, social systems are not made up of individuals, but of communicative interactions which also maintain them. Knowledge management is one of the organizational functions. It plans, communicates and coordinates the organization's collective and personal requirements (expectations) of knowledge besides monitoring their performance and compliance. Moreover, knowledge management also makes thematic suggestions, since an individual can communicate and share experiences, factual knowledge only if (s)he is related to specific topics, alternating between them and making diverse remarks upon or related to them. Personal and collective organizational knowledge can be managed by way of planning the requirements (expectations) of knowledge, providing its descriptions and monitoring its compliance control. In addition, personal and collective organizational knowledge may also be managed through setting expectations concerning topics. The question is, how the social system serves the integration of actions. Let us see:

## System of Action

Action is related to individuals and to established connections. The action system is made up of actions and processes. As Luhmann highlights, according to Parsons (as cited in Luhmann, 2013), an action becomes possible if tools and aims can be differentiated, if collective prescriptions of value exist, and if an actor is available to perform the action, or a chain of actors and actions subsists, which we regard as a process. Social integration is the interpretative integration of actions. Social systems fulfil the integrative and coordinating functions of action systems, which functions involve the integration and the coordination of actions, action relations, requirements of knowledge and praxes. Moreover, social systems have to be able to recognize and handle the problems, standstills, obstacles and faults appearing throughout the processes. The knowledge of processes does not cover mere routine: the knowledge of processes concerns the ways to act, which implies coordination. Furthermore, the social system integrates action and actor through observation, by way of providing opportunity for communication and by maintaining the connection between communicative events. The network of speech overlaps with action chains. Almost all activities and cooperations are preceded, accompanied or followed by speech (oral, written, visual). Communication is a circular process separate from actions, but creating, following, controlling and interpreting these. Communication is not an action itself, but an event of sense and of making sense. Knowledge management pertains to the ways of action which create, transmit and give sense to values. It is also important to bear in mind though that apart from individuals, machines are also capable of action.

## Machinery System

Human knowledge is binding. It binds associations, groups, projects, undertakings, processes, tools and machines. However, human knowledge separates too. It separates professions, experts, areas of knowledge and technologies. Tools in themselves present a mere potential which necessitates the ability to utilize them – to be able to apply machines and technologies effectively – and also requires praxis in such utilization. In addition, the application of technology requires knowledge: the know-how of making, using and utilizing things. Such knowledge broadens the area of available human abilities. Utilization means being oriented upon a goal. Technology (machinery) makes one capable. Personal and collective organizational knowledge praxes acquire sense and significance in sync with the abilities to apply specific tools in specific situations. Knowledge management monitors, regulates and retains the control of the organizational application, development and extension of smart technology. If it fails to do so, the continued operation of the enterprise and its system of sense are put to risk.

## INTERPRETING COLLECTIVE KNOWLEDGE WITHIN THE VID GROUP

Regarding the creation of organizational values, it is not the knowledge of the members of the organization (individuals) that bears primary significance, but the knowledge of collectives (organizational units, processes, project teams). Collective knowledge is a self-created social system brought about by communicative events (interactions). Knowledge management has to take three dimensions of individual abilities into consideration, which are the following: intellect, imagination, memory. For example, strategic and operative planning relies upon fantasy, realization necessitates long and short term memory, problem solving counts upon astuteness. The knowledge triangle of the members also sets the dimension of the collective's knowledge space. The members of the collective do not react to the irritations of the collective as individuals, but as a system, i.e. as a corpus of sense. The collective sense corpus of dynamic bodies, as a closed system, fits into the entire plural order of the organization. We have to think in terms of individuals and knowledge accruing, knowledge-sharing collective corpora, not in terms of human resource.

The organizations (enterprises) of the VID Group are based upon team work. This is not due to the frequency of building projects only, but also to the demand of involving multiple perspectives in planning, working, problem solving and decision making. This bears particular significance in relation to the embodiment of collective wisdom within the business group, which builds and utilizes its personal relationships, connections and shared knowledge – briefly, its social and intellectual capital. Business and social power lie with the comprehensive plural approach, thinking and connections.

## THE STRUCTURE OF THE VID GROUP'S PLURAL SYSTEM

In an organization organizational language predominantly means linguistic order and discourse (language use). Knowledge acquisition, the accrual and the sharing of knowledge, thus, codified (written) knowledge

*Figure 4. A three-dimensional model of collective knowledge*

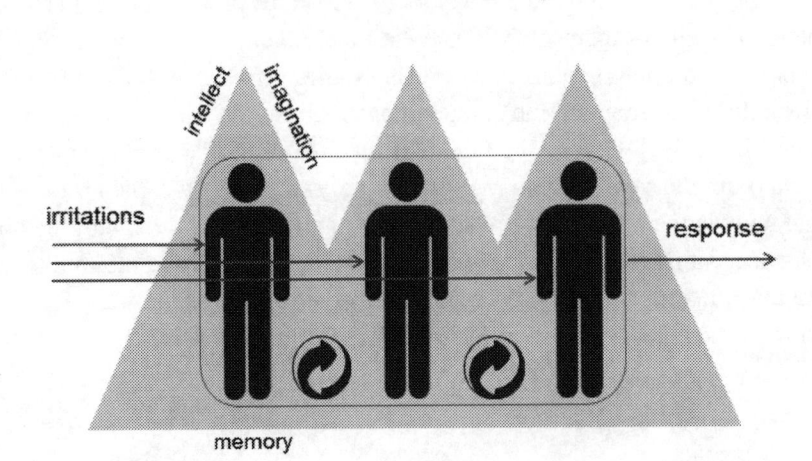

also has to be handled linguistically, which necessity arises mainly from the need to understand and to make others understand something.

Within the VID Group knowledge is considered a cognitive requirement (expectation), while knowledge management is regarded as a function. Every organizational function involves more activities, and represents, maintains, operates something which others functions do not. The concordance of functional connections and the agreement between functional wholes and parts sustain the entire organization. The fundamental functions and the systemic structure of the VID Group is demonstrated in Figure 5.

Building operations and facilities maintenance also mean systemic thinking, creative design and establishment, which implies the marking of a territory, its spatialization and population. This, again, requires a multifaceted (pluralistic) approach and a pluralistic system in case of every enterprise that is part of the business group. We have created the model entitled *Mindmill & Technology Systems* (see Figure 5) and applied it to the enterprises of the group in order to demonstrate the structure, the plurality and the complexity of the system. The model shows that the system is not only open (input-output) and technologically determined (machinery oriented), but is also closed, meaning that it is made up of social subsystems. All organizations of the business group are sociocultural technology systems. The circles denote the fundamental social subsystems, the organizational functions, while the arrow shape represents the technological subsystems. The entire figure demonstrates the integral and plural system, structure.

The knowledge system is a social system performing the observation of organizational and inter-organizational topics. However, the knowledge system performs other tasks as well, for example, it is related to and cooperates with the quality management system. Knowledge management itself fulfils the function of continual coordination, development, improvement and refinement of knowledge. If necessary, it standardizes the individual and collective modes of knowledge acquisition, accrual, sharing and application. In this, the PDCA and SDCA cycles of quality management show striking similarities

*Figure 5. A model of the sociocultural technology system*

**Mindmill & Technology Systems**

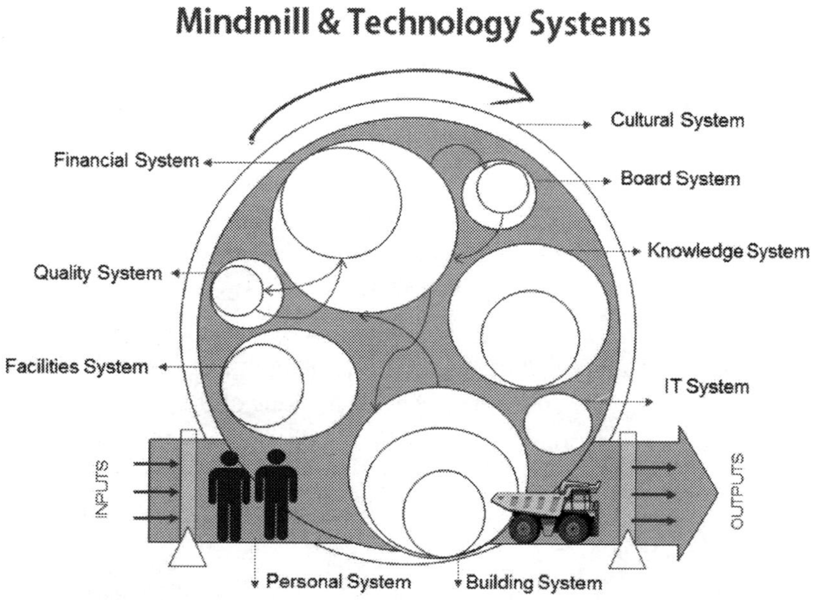

*Figure 6. Quality cycles. SDCA = routine work and PDCA = improvement work*
*(Shiba & Walden, 2001, p. 289)*

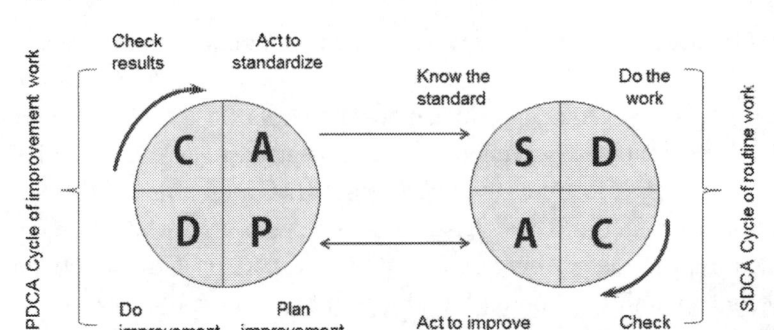

to knowledge management. The mentioned quality management cycles, for example, do not plan but standardize routine tasks. Figure 6 demonstrates the connection set up between the two quality cycles.

Let us now consider another cycle, related to quality cycles.

## THE VID KNOWLEDGE MANAGEMENT CYCLE

From the very beginning, the VID Group laid down, communicated and made comprehensible for every organizational actor what personal and collective knowledge stood for in the operation and development of the member enterprises and the business group as such. The organizational requirements of knowledge (expectations), organizationally accessible knowledge and the scope of potential organizational knowledge – to be reckoned with by the actors of the organization – was made clear. The function was thought over in the course of a collective effort, the result of which was the POCA cycle, a knowledge management cycle, demonstrated in Figure 7.

Knowledge management within the VID Group is of a systemic approach. Knowledge management is a system created in order to observe the whole of the business group and also its parts. As such, knowledge management is focussed on planning, observing and controlling knowledge-based activities, processes and transactions. Moreover, it may also intervene and initiate interventions in the field of knowledge acquisition and knowledge accrual, just as in the sharing and the application of knowledge. The POCA cycle involves sections of planning, controlling, observation and intervention. Observation is not directed upon the environment only (in which other systems are situated), but also upon the knowledge management cycle itself, becoming an observer and a self-observer at the same time. It cooperates with strategic and operative planning, but it also observes itself. The cycle observes all it has to learn and improve, all its knowledge and lack of knowledge in the field of planning. Planning the requirements (expectations) pertaining to skills itself, the cycle monitors and controls planning and compliance on the one hand, and the appropriacy of expectations on the other. The fourth circle of the knowledge management cycle is the circle of interpretations and actions, involving the standardization, the change, the correction and the refinement of recognized plans and observations. Providing feedback to the actors and feedforward to the learning system may also prove to be a necessity. The circle is hence closed, the next cycle may commence. The POCA cycle is in motion.

*Figure 7. An iterative knowledge management cycle: the POCA cycle*

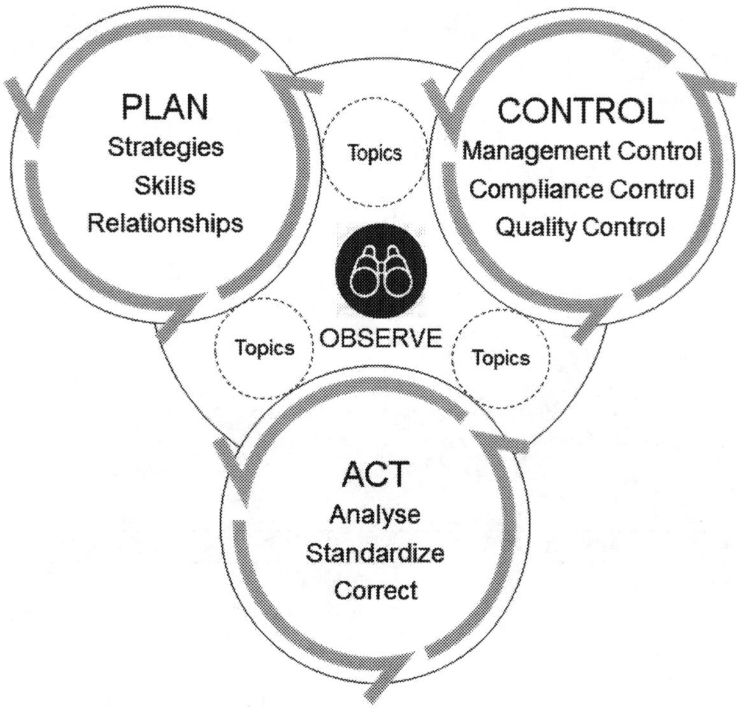

## THE TASKS OF VID KNOWLEDGE MANGEMENT

The VID Group is made up of goal directed enterprises. Centralized knowledge management undertakes singular tasks, contributing hence to the accomplishment of the following strategic and operative aims:

1. Knowledge management is a strategic function, therefore, it penetrates the entire business group.
2. Knowledge management provides internal service available on the Intranet.
3. Knowledge management plans, coordinates and controls expectations regarding praxes in a manifold way.
4. Knowledge management supports the interpersonal discursive ferment by way of fostering spaces of discourse.
5. Knowledge management ensures that the space of sense encompassed by the Body of Knowledge Library is always adapted to the knowledge praxis of the business group.
6. Knowledge management edits, updates and makes the VID KMBok Guide available.
7. Knowledge management edits, updates and makes the VID KMBok Ethical Code available.
8. Knowledge management creates and sustains the various semantic models of the business group.
9. Knowledge management is accountable for the validation of the business group's knowledge technologies and knowledge contents.
10. Knowledge management performs the linguistic and professional revision of knowledge contents.
11. Knowledge management plans and monitors collective organizational education.
12. Knowledge management cooperates with other systems of management.

*Table 1. Body of Knowledge (BoK) Library*

| | Group Level | Building Division | Facility Division |
|---|---|---|---|
| 1. | Strategy Managament BoK | | |
| 2. | Quality Management BoK | | |
| 3. | Risk Management BoK | | |
| 4. | Knowledge Management BoK | | |
| 5. | | Project Management BoK | |
| 6. | | | Facility Management BoK |
| 7. | Finance Management BoK (IFRS) | | |
| 8. | IT Infrastructure Library (ITIL) | | |

*Table 2. Thematic connections (structural coupling) between the knowledge management system and other systems of management*

| | Other Systems of Management | Thematic Connection |
|---|---|---|
| Knowledge management | Strategic management | a) taking part in strategic planning<br>b) breaking down skill gaps into educational programmes<br>c) linguistic revision of the written strategy |
| | Quality management | a) mutual problem solving, if necessary<br>b) giving feedback regarding mistakes originating from the lack of knowledge<br>c) creating and validating quality ontologies |
| | Risk management | a) taking part in risk analysis<br>b) uncovering and analysing the reasons of the non-occurrence of knowledge |
| | Project management | a) mutual problem solving, if necessary<br>b) providing projects with technologies of knowledge<br>b) giving feedback regarding anomalies originating from the lack of knowldege |
| | Financial management | a) knowledge management cost controlling and investment controlling<br>c) taking part in planning the enterprise's output, determining the nature of its expenses, its cost centres and its cost bearers |
| | IT management | a) mutual problem solving, if necessary<br>b) collective planning and supervising knowledge management investments<br>c) supervising knowledge management developments<br>d) applying technology supervising systems<br>e) handling the eligibility of knowledge management applications' use<br>f) supervising the accessibility of digital objects |

## THE PRINCIPLES OF VID KNOWLEDGE MANAGEMENT

Knowledge management – besides observation and action – is regulation. It provides a base of coordinated rules which permeate actions, processes, plans, controls and decisions in the realm of knowledge management. The professional units within an organization follow diverse principles, even when working simultaneously. Personal and collective knowledge are to exhibit a unified view, however. The various disciplines, despite their differences, have to be based upon common principles. The VID Group works in line with the following principles of knowledge management:

1. We plan knowledge as an expectation regarding roles and control the compliance of realization.
2. We adjust requirements (expectations) of knowledge to strategic goals.
3. We respect each other's knowledge.
4. We learn everything available within the business group from each other's knowledge praxis.
5. We perform the codification of factual knowledge and experience in a differentiated way, according to preferred structures.
6. We give preference to personal, face-to-face modes of sharing knowledge.
7. We support the collective acquisition, accrual and sharing of knowledge with smart technologies.
8. We keep to the valid ethical code of knowledge management.

These principles fit well into the culture of the business group and serve as a basis for the establishment of the body of principles pertaining to knowledge management, which provides detailed regulation of the activities and processes related to the acquisition, sharing, application, updating and validation of knowledge. With the help of such a body of principles, the employees may perform their tasks in line with the accepted code of conduct, in keeping with the common orientation and with regard to the pluralistic structure of the business group.

## THE NETWORK CENTRES OF VID KNOWLEDGE MANAGEMENT

"We build ourselves and others according to modern, systematized, coordinated requirements of knowledge" – this is the slogan of the business group. Being modern means conforming to the latest achievements of scientific, technical progress and business innovations. Being systematized means that order prevails in every field: within the group, the enterprises, with regard to technologies, contents and connections, within and between the systems of management. Being coordinated means that despite the spatial, technological and interpretative fragmentariness of the business group, it is built and operated integrally. With the help of such systemacity and expertise does the business group build its own knowledge, buildings and other facilities for its customers. The business group is also a plural, complex system. Knowledge management is a subsystem within the business group's entire system, which subsystem undertakes the comprehension, taxonomization, planning, observation and the multifaceted control of organizational sense, all in line with the possibilities and forms of language. These tasks are performed in *three centres of competence,* via the internal network (Intranet) of the business group.

### VID Knowledge Centre

Knowledge is built, formed within the context of sense. Without such self-building collective knowledge, the business group is at a loss. Mere actions do not take us far. The self-construction of collective knowledge requires the development and maintenance of a regulated space of knowledge. The accrual and the updating of collective knowledge is the social and intellectual capability and responsibility of collectives. The VID Knowledge Centre was called into being as a service centre. Just as in the case of every other business factor, collective knowledge is also monitored by a competence centre. Order and regulation prevails in every field. As one of the centres of the business group's Intranet, the knowledge centre controls the order and the regulation of knowledge. It provides planning, controlling, observational and transformational services (procurement, taking a stance, standardization, generating further knowledge acquisition, integration, differentiation) for every enterprise, i.e. to the whole of the business group. Mechanisms of iteration and improvement operate the whole of the group. The connections and services provided by the VID Knowledge Centre is demonstrated in Figure 8.

## The Observation of Knowledge Praxis

Knowledge management creates a multifaceted order, as it is a plural order in itself. The knowledge management system is a planning, analysing, controlling, engineering and observational system. Second-order observation means that second-order observers observe the actions and distinctions of first-order observers (actors, planners, leaders) and detect their blind spots. After making sense of these blind spots some of them are selected according to given criteria, and the deficiencies arising from these selected blind spots are incorporated into the thinking (speech and writing) of leaders, so that everyone may learn from them and introduce changes, if necessary. Buildings are constructions of knowledge. Such knowledge involves knowing how to act, read, write, speak and understand each other; how to differentiate differences. Differentiation is a necessity also in the field of organizational knowledge, involving auditory and written differentiation, self-building, delineation and structures. As the researcher notes: "[w]riting […] initiates a structural development because it strengthens the basis for such development, the difference between action and observation" (Luhmann, 1995, p. 302). In order to be able to perform our tasks efficiently and effectively, we have to observe the activities, events and connections regarding processes, projects, teams and other collectives of knowledge within the business group. This pertains especially to knowledge flows, obstructions of knowledge, hesitations and knowledge gaps. Knowledge sharing in meeting rooms taking place face to face, and the creation and sharing of objects of digital knowledge also have to be observed. The observation and control of written speech is the responsibility

*Figure 8. The organization and activities of the VID Knowledge Centre*

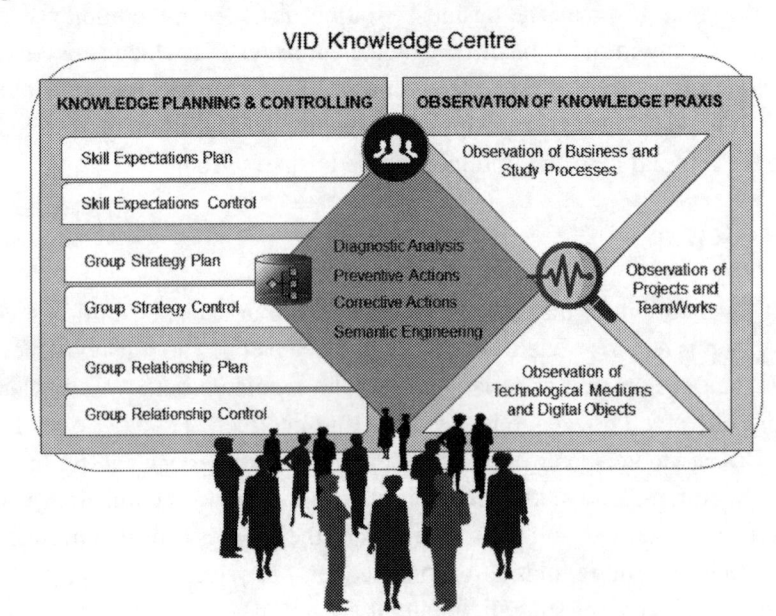

and the task of the knowledge management collective. Besides observation, this collective is also occupied with planning, controlling and developing knowledge. Hence, much is to be done.

## Planning and Controlling Knowledge

What does knowledge planning mean for the VID Group? The short answer is: it means three things. To be more explicit, it primarily means planning the knowledge management strategy and the requirements (expectations) of knowledge specified in the strategies. Secondly, it means the expectations of knowledge praxes with regard to VID collectives and concerning the individuals belonging to these collectives. Last but not least, it means the internally and externally oriented connections involved in the strategies; the actors, the collectives and the themes of planned connections (for example new CRM, new processes). That is to say, knowledge planning encompasses all we have to provide information about, all we have to speak about. Collective knowledge is made up of dynamic relations, collective themes and understanding. Collective sense is embedded into themes, themes are entailed in events and remarks. We have to plan what and with whom we have to discuss, but also the technological medium or form in which our discussions are to take place. Moreover, we have to decide what we are to share before, during and after our tasks and cooperations. Figure 9 exhibits the structure of our proposed knowledge planning, knowledge observing and knowledge sharing mechanism. The mechanisms of the strategic circle, the knowledge management circle and the process circle are connected to each other by way of double coupling, operating whenever necessary.

Building and managing collective knowledge is a strategic task for the VID Group. The group is well aware – for they experience it – that cooperation requires coordinated work, collective knowledge and synchronized actions. In creating and planning strategy, knowledge management represents knowledge

*Figure 9. The dynamic knowledge planning, knowledge observing and knowledge sharing mechanism within collectives*

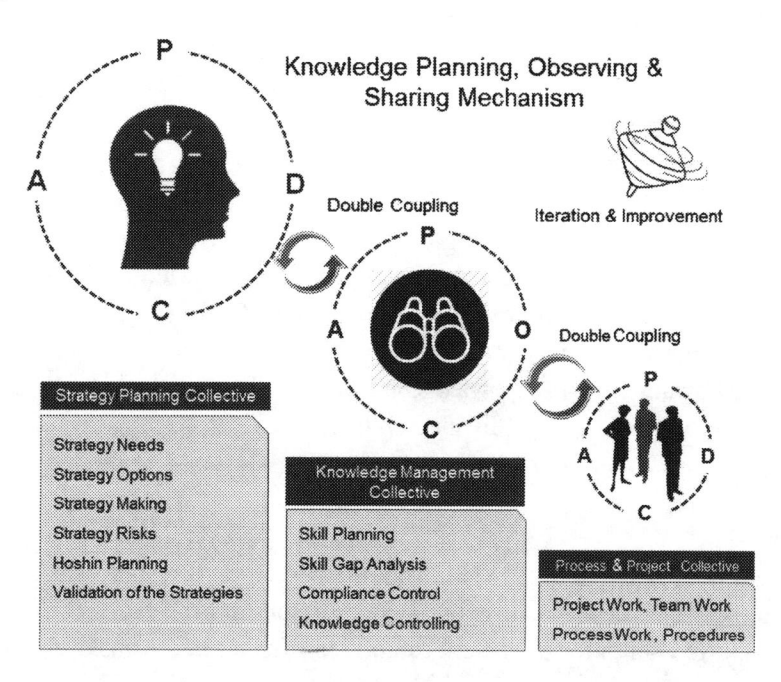

strategy. It adjusts future requirements (expectations) of knowledge to strategic aims and objectives. Moreover, it follows and monitors the realization of the strategy, the compliance of its realization, but also checks the aspect of individual and collective skills. One of VID Group's knowledge management strategies is the following:

Strategic incentives:

1. A new order and comprehensive regulation of collective knowledge praxis
2. The redevelopment of knowledge codification and knowledge sharing
3. The redevelopment and maintenance of the plural order
    - **GOAL 1:** Reorganization of the plural (social, linguistic) order at every enterprise belonging to the group:

**Objective 1.1:** Rethinking, codifying and regulating knowledge management in terms of the business group.

**Objective 1.2:** Creating and introducing the social order.

**Objective 1.3:** Creating and introducing the linguistic, semantic order.

- **GOAL 2:** The modernization, centralization and introduction of business group knowledge technologies:

**Objective 2.1:** Creating and introducing the Knowledge Management Body of Knowledge Guide.

**Objective 2.2:** Creating and sharing the Knowledge Management Ethical Code.

**Objective 2.3:** Installing, applying and introducing recreated technologies of knowledge.

The VID Group applies the Hoshin Planning method and the Plan Base application in strategic planning. Hence is the knowledge planning and knowledge sharing mechanism called into being (see Figure 9). The circles bound by double coupling are of two types. The circular process of PDCA is an iterative process of improvement, while POCA is one of observation, controlling and development. This mechanism serves as a tool for realizing the discursive ferment, since collectives (systems) are permanently available, connectible and disconnectible, therefore their rotation is reliable for all entitled to establish knowledge connections.

## Knowledge Engineering

Knowledge and knowledge management also require continual engineering which necessitates economic, educational, but also legal, regulatory and linguistic work and support. The multidisciplinary view is the basic orientation of knowledge engineering. The plurality of knowledge management is embodied predominantly in the multifaceted, multidisciplinary collective of knowledge management, be it within or outside the business group. External contributors (counsellors, supporters) also belong to the knowledge collective of the business group. Knowledge engineering is the core of knowledge management, constituting its source of renewal and its semantic engine.

## VID Study Centre

The leader of the business group held the view from the beginning that the organizational institutionalization of learning is necessary, since it is the pledge of constant renewal. Internal education is not provided for the employees in order to present them a certificate, but to make them understand new tasks, expectations, and also, to enable their compliance with these expectations. Internal training may be supported by brief curricula. Mistakes may also be furthering the process of learning. The repeated appearance of the same mistakes signals that something is amiss within the system. The error might stem from the lack of understanding and/or a lack of knowledge. The effectiveness of the internal training system will be sufficient only if the yet unknown may be learnt in a personalized, rapid way, with the help of internal and/or external tutors. Smart technologies and knowledge technologies are also of considerable help. Classroom study serves the purposes of study groups. The organizational network of knowledge is the space of sharing knowledge between working groups and creative collectives, in which space colleagues acquire ways to learn from each other.

## VID Technology Transfer Centre

All technologies of knowledge are constructions created by individuals and collectives. It is a machinery system applied extensively throughout the business group. Hence, not only the tools of the business group change constantly, but also the world of employees within the business group. Knowledge technology introduces change. VID knowledge technologies and its tools have changed the sense and the meaning of the context of objects, encompassing both physical and digital objects. Change, therefore, has affected electronic and technical media (drives, sensors), interpersonal equipment and gadgets (computer, smart phones, smart applications), but also electronic texts, images, film and audio data; differently put, all

*Figure 10. The structure and activities of the VID Study Centre*

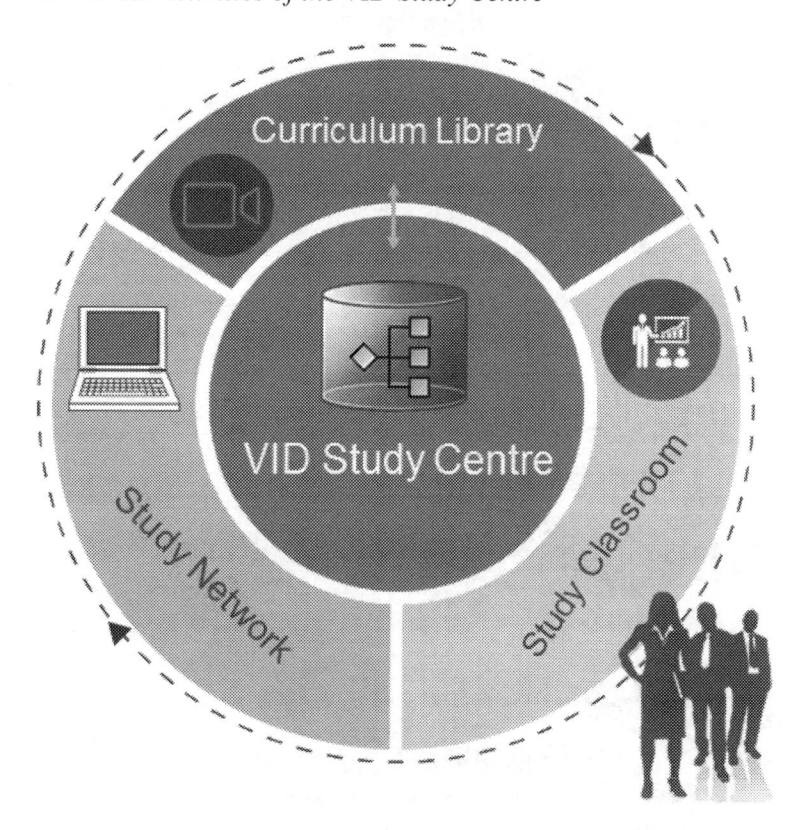

digital representations of knowledge and experience. In our view, the technology of knowledge considers technical objects (physical and digital objects) to be the *components, containers of action*. It is by way of these components, containers of action that organizational actors are able comply with expectations. They connect and disconnect one promptly with another, save and make written and visual factual knowledge, data and signals accessible, hence opening horizons and extending our world: our world of sense, our world of relations and our world of situations. The basic strategy involved in the application of VID knowledge management technology is that by way of the utilization, adjustment and integration of open source softwares client server and smart phone applications are planned and constructed in order to manage the business group's knowledge. Thus, a solution has been created which ensures that the operation and the development of the business group become and remain sufficient.

## CONCLUSION

The present paper created an overview of the knowledge management approach, thinking and praxis characterizing the VID Group. Particular emphasis was given to the plural system, the self-building mechanisms and the functions of the VID Group, but also to its modes of cooperation. The establishment of a social, semantic and technological order required collective work undertaken as a collective effort of research and engineering groups, in a cooperative and multidisciplinary framework. This collective effort delivered a complex, plural, multi-layered solution. That is to say, not only a digital and technological, but also a social and semantic solution was brought forth, where signs and their usage, the handling of applied distinctions and meanings was incorporated into the knowledge management system. The various representations of collective knowledge – prints and digital objects – are made accessible with the help of technical tools unconstrained in terms of time and space. The establishment of a multi-layered sociotechnical network leads to a new sense of time and space. The business group's Intranet constitutes the virtual space of factual knowledge, experiences, concepts and rules. Written, auditory and visual signs are also part of this virtual space. The application of mediating and storage tools involved within the scope of visual media are among the prospective plans of the business group. Letters, words and sentences are increasingly complemented by icons, drawings, images and video foot-

*Figure 11. VID Technology Transfer Centre*

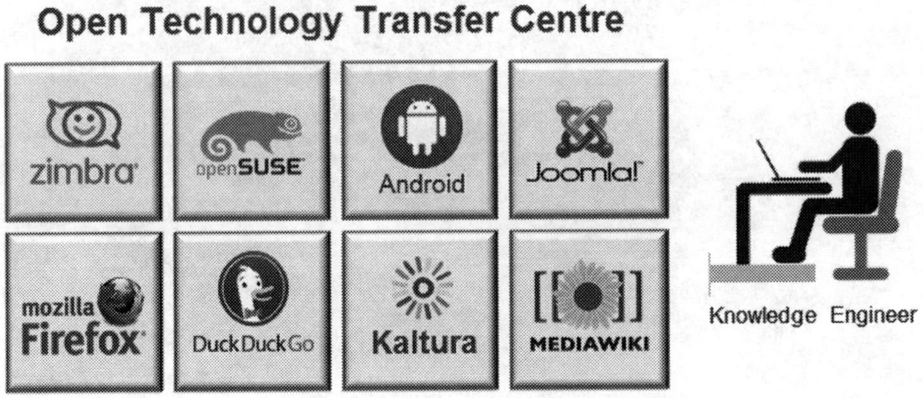

338

*Figure 12. The layering of the VID organizational system from the perspective of knowledge management*

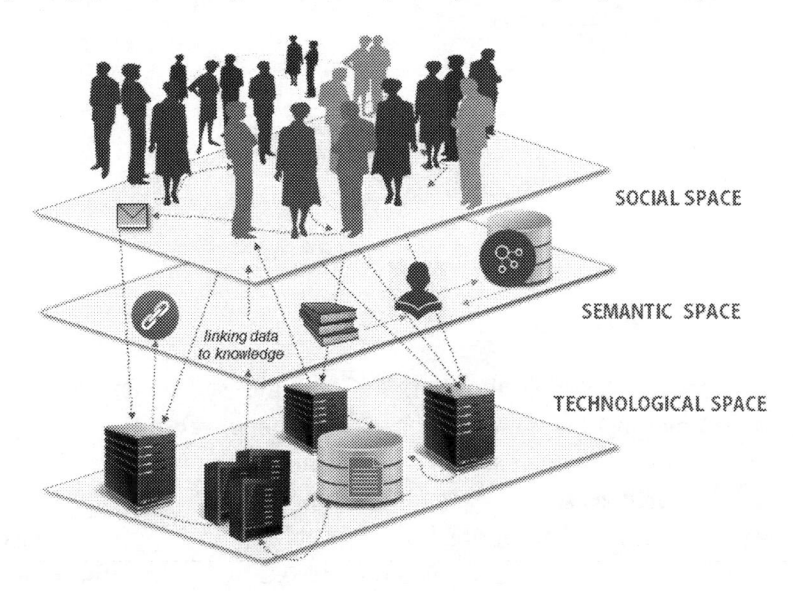

age, which are particularly suitable for the purposes of giving insight and sharing knowledge. Endowing the business group with a semantic technology is a task of the near future. Figure 12 shows the layering of the entire system.

## REFERENCES

Appadurai, A. (1998). *Modernity at Large: Cultural Dimensions of Globalization*. Minneapolis, MN: University of Minnesota Press.

Baecker, D. (1993). *Die Form des Unternehmens* [The Form of the Enterprise]. Frankfurt am Main: Suhrkamp.

Capillarity. (2016). In *Encyclopaedia Britannica*. Retrieved January 13, 2016, from http://www.britannica.com/science/capillarity

Foucault, M. (1999). A szexualitás története: A tudás akarása. [The History of Sexuality: The Will to Knowledge] Budapest: Atlantisz.

Geertz, C. (1983). *Local Knowledge: Further Essays in Interpretative Anthropology*. New York: Basic Books.

Luhmann, N. (1995). *Social Systems*. Stanford, CA: Stanford University Press.

Luhmann, N. (2013). *Introduction to Systems Theory*. Cambridge, MA: Polity Press.

Morgan, G. (1986). Images of Organization. Beverly Hills, CA: Sage Publications.

Nonaka, I., Toyama, R., & Hirata, T. (2008). *Managing Flow: A Process Theory of the Knowledge-Based Firm*. Houndmills, UK: Palgrave Macmillan.

Noszkay, E. (2013). *A rendszerszemléletű tudásmenedzsment.* [System-based Knowledge Management] Harlow: Pearson Education Limited.

Parsons, T. (1978). *Action Theory and the Human Condition.* Free Press.

Shiba, S., & Walden, D. (2001). *Four Practical Revolutions in Management: Systems for Creating Unique Organizational Capability.* New York: Productivity Press.

## KEY TERMS AND DEFINITIONS

**Autopoietic Organization:** Autopoiesis means self-building, self-organization. The organization is a social system, which, by way of communication, as a system of sense, creates itself exclusively by way of its own operations (binding interactions). The organization is made up of diverse subsystems, endowed with autopoietic (circular) structures.

**Collective Knowledge:** The members of organizational collectives (groups, teams) create, establish, operate with the help of their relations, bonds and cooperation. In this way, the application of factual knowledge and values, the initiation of activities becomes possible only for a collective, not for individual members, however. The members of a collective are mutually dependent upon one another, assuming the possession of knowledge, experience and expecting a particular performance on one another's part while cooperating in the framework of these.

**Compliance Control:** Monitoring compliance to organizational expectations and interpreting, analysing the differences between planned and actual results.

**Knowledge Praxis:** Knowledge praxis does not rely and build exclusively upon scientific knowledge but also upon practical experiences and their common context. In collective action, construction, and in the creation of values the most important is knowing how to act.

**Knowledge Triangle:** Knowledge is the linguistic articulation of human knowledge, its context. The forms of knowledge constitute the unity of three related abilities: intellect, imagination and memory. These weave the textures of knowledge.

**Quality-Driven Knowledge Management:** Knowledge is not an asset, but an expectation and the compliance to this expectation (requirement). We have to keep our colleagues' mistakes, errors, lack of knowledge and false knowledge under close scrutiny and learn from them. The same pertains to misunderstandings and imperfections. Hence, continuous iteration and improvement is required in the knowledge management area.

**Observing Organizations:** All our knowledge stems from observation and observers. Observation does not involve perception and interpretation only, but also differentiation. Without differentiation, observation does not take place. Organizational observation necessitates a systemic approach, order and systems themselves, but also second-order and third-order observers, who perform multidirectional and self-observational surveillance.

**Social System:** Organizations are made up of closed, social subsystems. Social systems are not constituted by people but by communicative interactions. They are endowed with the ability to establish connections for their own purposes, refining these connections as opposed to the connections set up in their environment.

## ENDNOTES

[1]   Translation slightly modified. We translate the German word *der Sinn* as 'sense', properly to its lexically determined use, as opposed to 'meaning' (Ger. *die Bedeutung*), applied by the cited translation.

[2]   Adopted from the Hungarian translation of Michel Foucault's work.

[3]   Capillarity „is the rise or depression of a liquid in a small passage such as a tube of small cross-sectional area, like the spaces between the fibres of a towel or the openings in a porous material. Capillarity is not limited to the vertical direction. Water is drawn into the fibres of a towel, no matter how the towel is oriented. […] Capillarity is the result of surface, or interfacial, forces. The rise of water in a thin tube inserted in water is caused by forces of attraction between the molecules of water and the glass walls and among the molecules of water themselves." (*Encyclopaedia Britannica,* 2016, para 1 and 3)

[4]   Translated from Hungarian.

# Chapter 16
# The Practice of Mentoring:
## Based on Empirical Research Carried Out at Hungarian Companies

**Timea Juhasz**
*Hostlogic Ltd., Hungary*

**Horvath-Csikós Gabriella**
*Szent Istvan University, Hungary*

## ABSTRACT

*This abstract deals with mentoring as one of the most popular forms of knowledge-sharing nowadays. On one hand the authors give a theoretical introduction about the protocol, the types, and the participants and about the realization of mentoring; while on the other hand some results of a complex research are also shown. The research was carried out with the participation of Hungarian companies and employees, both in qualitative and in quantitative way. Although the researches cannot be considered representative, the authors of the chapter reckon that a clear view can be obtained about the Hungarian mentoring practice. In light of the results it can be stated that the respondents basically consider this form of knowledge-sharing useful, which provides a good base and support for the operation of a consistent knowledge-management system and mentoring should represent positive values and practice in this process.*

## INTRODUCTION

Different organisations, institutions and companies are made up of individuals who try their best to operate in the most effective and most reasonable way. Those institutions, which split the big problems into smaller problems and manage them as smaller ones, will become severe and rigorous, especially when the organisation is in the process of undergoing a quick change.

The *'knowledge management'* means corporate policy, practice and tools, which make it possible for the individuals to understand and to get a clear view about how their job contributes to the whole of the company, what benefits they might have and how they can contribute to the more effective and more successful operation of their companies. The most important value and product of a given company is

DOI: 10.4018/978-1-5225-1642-2.ch016

the knowledge itself. The employees have to be encouraged to acquire, to keep and to transfer knowledge. (Nemirowsky and Solomon, 2000). The employees have to learn and apply different techniques in order to be able to convert their know-how systematically into an important knowledge-source for the organisation. (Choo, 1996, Reich-Czeglédi-Fonger, 2015).

The leaders have to support the establishment of a corporate culture, where knowledge is value, where knowledge-transfer is supported and where innovation and development is considered important. However, there can be some obstacles of effective knowledge-management, such as lack of self-confidence, lack of time, lack of possibilities, and intolerance towards errors. The appreciation/rewarding solely affect those who possess the knowledge or it is simply the lack of capacity from the receiving party towards receiving the new knowledge (Davenport, 1997). It also frequently happens that the employees of the organisation acquire the offered knowledge, but later they do not utilize that knowledge (Elmore, 1990).

The effective knowledge-management requires new roles and responsibility from the leaders and from the employees as well. It is necessary that the participants of the process can observe their own work from multiple perspectives, they can phrase their opinions, they are able to make and receive critical remarks and they have to be suitable and willing to share their knowledge with each other. Its success depends on several factors, such as trust, cultural indifference, lack of reception, communicational problems and the attitudes of the participants, etc. (Bencsik, 2009).

Although at the same time, a study, which was carried out in 2014 (Bencsik-Juhász-Kovács, 2014) studied the openness of the respondents with regard to their knowledge-sharing showed that the knowledge-sharing willingness of that survey was basically average and they did not really welcome the idea to share their practical knowledge with others. The respondents were less interest-centred and expectation-oriented with their friends, acquaintances and with strangers in return of their knowledge-sharing than with acquaintances of formal relationships. (Bencsik-Juhász-Kovács, 2014).

There are several forms of knowledge sharing in corporate practice, which can become corporate protocol with more or less success or can be created spontaneously. Mentoring is one form of knowledge-transfer, which is becoming more and more popular nowadays.

## BACKGROUND

The practice of mentoring is not new. The phrase 'mentor' comes from the ancient Greek writings. Mentor was the son of Alcumus, who was good friend of Odyssey when he was old. When Ulysses left for the Trojan War, he asked Mentor to take care of his young son, Telemachus and his palace. (Homer: Odyssey). Mentor acted as a person in charge of the boy, he also put in a word for the boy at the Ithaca assembly, when his father was far from him. When Pallas Athena, the goddess of wisdom gave pieces of good advice to Telemachus, she appeared to the boy in the form of Mentor. She encouraged the boy to travel around and ask about his father.

Mentoring as a tool for knowledge-sharing had an important role in the life and artistic development of several artists and scientists. We can mention Alexander, the Great whose mentor was Aristotle or also Leonardo, who learnt from Verrocchio.

Mentoring as such is a professional term, which is quite difficult to conceive and has several definitions. Researchers have not found common grounds so far to create the functional and professional definition of mentoring.

In the field of mentoring and in connection with its participants, there were two studies carried out in the 1970's. These studies served as the base for later researches. One of the two studies is the paper of Kanter, Levinson, Darrow and Klein (1977, 1978); while the authors of the other study are Levinson and McKee (1978). The authors in both studies emphasized that from the aspect of a mentored/protégée it is very beneficial to have a mentor in his career. Furthermore, the authors pointed also to the fact that mentoring as such is also advantageous for the mentor, because on one hand it can support the renewal of his own career and on the other hand the mentor can also develop by helping others.

In the study 'Men and Women of the Corporation' (1977) Kanter emphasized that being a mentored does not only mean that the most advantageous and the most preferred job can be his, but it also means that he receives opportunity and chance to map the power relations within the company and to understand them well.

*Levinson* and his team detailed in their work *'Seasons of a Man's Life'* (1978) that mentoring is not only a patronage or sponsorship, as *Kanter* characterized it in 1977, but rather it is a very important developmental process of adulthood. The mentoring process was characterized as a strong and very complex relationship, where the mentor plays the role of 'partner or parent' and above this he can take the role of a teacher, counsellor or a friend as well.

The definition of mentor is quite similar to the original meaning of mentor, that is -starting from the work of Homer-, where the mentor was an experienced supporter, who appeared as a father-figure and gives advice and guidance to his mentored regarding his private life and his professional career.

There were interesting papers and studies (Jarnagin, lea Marie, 2010; Dougherty, Dreher, Vaoram, Wilbank, 2013) published with regard to possible differences between a female and a male mentor and with regard to the typical personality and characteristic features of those who do not choose mentor for themselves specifically. The non-specific approach emphasizes that basically it is the personal features, which decide whether to get into a mentoring position or not, thus for example the qualification, competition- and career-orientedness and/or work experience. In contrast with this, the theories concentrating on the operation of the organisations do not explain it with the differences of individual features, but with the basic operational features of the organisation. The most well-known paper is the theory of Kanter (1977), which says that the groups being in minority, for instance female-mentors within an organisation are always in the limelight, as their number is small. The majority of the group continuously observe them censoriously and their activities are often attributed to their group-affiliation and not to their individual characteristics.

According to Kanter (1977) however the inclination to similarity simply originates from the intense insecurity of the corporate environment, which results in the fact that in order to solve the tasks more efficiently, the participants of the organisation will primarily get in touch with people who are similar to them; thus male participants will create relationship with male, while female participants will create informal relationship with female and they imagine mentoring relationship with them.

The research of Ibarra (1992) pointed out that men and women develop their corporate relations differently. While men rather choose male for their expressive and instrumental relationships, women tend to choose male as instrumental relationship (counselling, influencing) in order to maximize their emotional and instrumental power resources, while they choose women as their expressive contacts (friendship), although at the same time men and women are in an equal rate in their communicational net.

The importance of the mentor's person is emphasized by Kanter. According to him, the mobility (sponsored mobility) is determined by the selecting mechanisms controlled by the corporate elite within the organisation and it is not the winning individuals who can step forward (contest mobility). The supporters help the individuals to get out of the crowd; they stand by him at various platforms, thus giving them promising opportunities to use with their support.

Researchers dealing with organisations have been studying the role of supporters/mentors for more decades. One of the earliest writings is the work of Kram (1985), with the title Mentoring at Work. Increased interest was observed towards the topic in the 1970's, more and more new territories were involved in the research. After the launch of the formal mentoring processes at the majority of the American companies, there were opportunities opened to compare the informal and formal mentoring systems and to revel the accidental differences (Ragins–Cotton 1999).

Shapiro and his colleagues (1978) noted that mentors are at the end of the wild-scale loss of supporters; therefore researches should rather focus on getting to know the other forms of patronizing relationships.

The researches of Bencsik-Juhász (2014) also justified that the personality characters of the mentors and mentored can be decisive factors in the implementation of a successful mentoring.

In their article, Catling and Davies (2008) collected the characteristic features, which can promote a successful cooperation between a mentor and a mentored. Therefore, the authors mention humility, where encouraging, accepting and using criticism is vital. It is also essential to be open-minded, which means there are no preconceptions with regard to the process. The authors deal with willingness, which refers to the task of the mentored to pay attention to the counsellor and to accept what he says. Curiosity is also essential, as it is always important to know where, when and how things are happening. Parallel thinking means that we have to take into consideration what we hear and we need to think it over where we can utilize it. Calmness is necessary in order to create a well-developed mentoring relationship. Toughness is also important in the mentor-mentored relationship. By integrity, trustworthiness and acceptance of the other's rights are observed from the beginning. The importance of time factor has to be noted, because the time spent in the relationship is considered investment not only for the mentored, but also for the mentor and for the organisations.

Mentoring has become in the centre of attention in the last decade again. Mentoring can be characterized as a very strong and effective tool in the business environment and processes with the purpose of long-term personality-development.

Mentoring is a relationship between two individuals, where the common aim of the participants is to reach their career-goals. Therefore, the long-term personality-development affects all the participants of the process. This relationship does not substitute any corporate protocol. Moreover, it supplements them with on-the-job training and coaching or any other workplace training/education.

Rhodes' (2002) definition about mentoring entrants is one of the most well-known definitions in professional literature. According to Rhodes caring relationship may develop among youth and experienced family friends, teachers, where the older party continuously gives advice, provides guidance to the younger one for the sake of the development of the mentored with regard to his personality and competency. During the time the two parties spend together, a relationship is developed, which is based on mutual respect, loyalty and trust and can later help the younger one to get to adulthood.

David L. DuBois (2005) conceived that mentoring is a rather structured and trustworthy relationship, which connect young people with supporters/mentors who encourage them, give them support and guidance, consequently the competency and personality of the mentored will develop. Mentoring is a vigorously emotional relationship between an elder and a younger person, in which the elder one is a responsible, reliable and loveable participant and he is more experienced in guiding the young ones (Budavári-Takács-Csehné Papp-Jekkel, 2015).

Ehigie-Koang-Ibode (2011) stated that mentoring is an informal relationship, which primary output is the development of the mentored. However, the principle aim of mentoring is educating. The three authors at the same time emphasized that this process affects several features of the organisation, for example among others it affects leadership, corporate culture and work capacity.

Bell (2002) phrased that a mentor is a teacher, a leader, with the help of who the mentored could widen and develop his skills and his knowledge. It is also a fact that in the process of a successful mentoring both participants will win from the other's knowledge and interactions. (Goodbar- Lewis 2015).

Mcshane and Glinow (2000, with reference to Arogundade) consider mentoring as a learning process, during which the mentored learns the habits of the corporate life from his mentor. The mentor is an experienced and influential person, who is working at the organisation and gives personal advice to the mentored with regard to his career. The mentor provides the mentored work, which help him to develop and he also provides opportunities for the mentored to get to know as many experienced people at the company as it is possible.

After examining the definitions in professional literature, the following consensus can be drawn:

1.  The mentor is an experienced counsellor and teacher;
2.  The mentor guides the mentored and supports his development;
3.  The mentor and the mentored develop a relationship, which is based on mutual trust.

Mentoring is sometimes mixed up with coaching, although the aims of the two developmental forms are completely different. While in case of coaching, the relationship can be developed between any leaders, colleagues or an outsider coach; the mentoring is a so-called non-reporting relationship usually with an outsider leader. Examining the two processes from the aspect of expertise, it can be stated that in case of coaching, the coach is the expert of one given field; while in case of mentoring the mentor is a man of great learning with extensive net of connections. While the coach concentrates on the given problem/task (short-term needs); the mentor has long-term plans for the sake of development.

In case of coaching, it is the coach, who determines the direction of interaction, while in case of mentoring it is the mentored (student) who defines the direction and the space of the relationship. Only the coach gives feedback to the employer, while in case of mentoring both the mentor and the mentored participate in the process of common knowledge sharing giving/receiving feedback.

Kram identified 4 phases of the mentoring process itself (1985, with reference of Arogundade, 2011). The first phase is the introduction, which can take for 12 months. This period is the time to get to know each other, and from the side of the protégé it involves the identification of senior management competencies, which might give him guidance and support on one hand. On the other hand, the mentor also maps the skills of the mentee and examines the field of teaching opportunities. The second phase is the phase for practicing, which might take from 2 years to 5 years. During this period, the mentor helps, supports and guides his mentored, who is enriched with new impressions, values and working styles by the new challenges. In the third phase -called separation phase- the mentored experiences self-dependence and independence, which is a kind of separation from the mentor and this phase can usually be full of discomfort for the mentored. Finally, in the phase of recontextualizing mentoring turns into a kind of friendship, where the senior mentor further supports his 'student 'and is very proud of his mentored. The mentored is grateful for the mentor for the common work, but at the same time he cannot become the assistant or the subordinate of the mentor.

To know the functions and the roles of mentoring helps a lot in understanding the process of mentoring. Several researches have been published since the 1980's, which classified the roles and functions of the mentor into two groups: career and psychosocial support. Career support by the mentors involves coaching, protecting, finding career and challenging workplace (Kram, 1983). As far as the psychosocial support is concerned, encouraging, counselling, feedback and developing competency and efficiency can be mentioned. (Kram, 1983).

Fajana and Gbajumo-Sheriff in their work (2011) classified career function into further 5 categories, which were the following: support, visualization, coaching, patronage and task-challenge. Within the psycho-social classification, the authors mentioned further 5 categories, such as modelling, acceptance, affirmation, counselling and friendship.

Professional literature examined mentoring functions in two dimensions (career and psychosocial psychosocial functions) (Wanberg-Welsh-Hezlett, 2003), while from the mentor's aspect most of the studies examined what the mentor's advantages are during the process (Haggard-Turban, 2012).

Byrne (1991) grouped mentoring in three simple, but very clear categories. The three groups are the following: traditional mentoring, professional mentoring and formal mentoring.

## Traditional Mentoring

Traditional mentoring is the oldest form of mentoring (Byrne, 1991), and it has been applied by several patrons of arts and sciences throughout history. In the traditional sense, mentors are people who use their knowledge, power and status to assist their mentored and assist their careers.

Its most significant feature and the same time the major disadvantage of it is that its selective and elitist nature. (Byrne, 1991). It is usually the senior member, who is responsible for recognizing the potential future talent and to initiate relationship with him. Odiorne (1985, 63-70p) in his work stated that some mentors are quite biased towards people who come from the same cultural background. This might be favouritism or simply a factor of human nature, which means that people feel closer to those who share similar values and interest. Or it might be considered a kind of discrimination if the mentor chooses his mentored because he has similar qualities, competencies, experience or values, etc.

There were several reasons why mentoring programs became more and more formal at the end of the 1970's by public and private organisations. The fact that mentoring is beneficial for the mentor, the mentored and for the organisation as well was accepted without doubt. (Zey, 1988). But there was another reason for the mentoring's becoming more formal, which was to reveal the problem of 'homosocial reproduction'. Kanter (1977) coined the expression 'homosocial reproduction', which describe the informal processes how males help and sponsor males in their career development within the organisation. Kanter said that this happens because people tend to support people of their own gender, especially when they share common opinion. Researches indicate that women get much less opportunities in the field of sciences, education (Patterson, 1994) and managerial contexts (Noe, 1988, Kanter 1977) to participate in mentoring processes. The previously mentioned 'homosocial reproduction 'can be one reason why women rarely participate in traditional mentoring.

According to Beam-Chen-Greenberger (2002) in case of adult mentors, there can be certain factors observed in the mentoring relationship, which can be noticed in the relationship with parents and fellows:

- The social situations and recreational activities with the mentor can have beneficial effect on the mentoree's emotional well-being and in his social relations.

- Cognitive development is supported by common learning, intellectually challenging situations and conversations.
- The role-model offered by the mentor can have a positive influence on developing the identity. (Rhodes, Spencer, Keller, Liang and Noam 2006)

## Professional Mentoring

Unlike traditional mentoring, professional mentoring is not established on personal choice of the individual mentor, but on the contrary it is established by the encouragement and proposal of the leader. It is not an indispensable part of the operation of the organisation, but it can be a very effective tool of it. (Byrne, 1991). One of the most important advantages of professional mentoring is that it is not compulsory, but voluntary; thus success is not guaranteed.

## Formal Mentoring

While professional mentoring means a step towards the direction where mentoring is a consciously applied process in the life of organisations; formal and institutionalized mentoring goes one step further by making mentoring a standard part of management practice. Therefore it can become a compulsory and core part of it. In organisations, which have formal mentoring, a small group of elder staff and younger staff work together. According to Douglas (1997:1) the formal programs are guided and supervised by the organisation. The advantage of formal mentoring is without doubt the fact that anybody can participate in this program, even if they did to have the opportunity to get into the previously mentioned two mentoring categories.

The participants of the mentoring process are the mentor, the mentored and the organisation. All the participants undergo a certain development in the process of mentoring. As far as the advantages of mentoring are concerned, the benefits of it can be different, mainly because the mentoring as such can have various forms. The role of the mentor as well can be various. For instance, the intensity of the emotional relationship between the mentor and the mentored is not a feature, which can be characterized in case of formal mentoring (Levinson, 1978), where a senior mentor is assigned to support a junior mentee for a short period of time. It is also worth mentioning that there is a dynamic relationship between the mentor and his mentee, they work together and they have to discover together what he mentee needs (Holden, 2014).

New forms of mentoring have appeared in the last ten years.

One form is when it is not the senior, experienced managers who teach, but on the contrary the junior employees act as mentors in order to teach their elder colleagues something new, especially when they teach them new technologies (Harvey-McIntyre-Heames-Moeller, 2009). The so-called reversed or reciprocal mentoring came to life basically because of globalization, quick technological development and market requirements. Harvey-McIntyre-Heames-Moeller (2009) summarized that students graduating from colleges and universities have high knowledge of internet, computer studies and other web-based technologies and they are very enthusiastic to share their knowledge with others. This form of mentoring has positive effects on both of its participants.

David Clutterbuck (2002) introduced the concept of structured developing mentoring in Europe. According to Clutterbuck we talk about mentoring when somebody uses his own wisdom to build the other's wisdom. This shows and expects a really high level of intellectual and emotional intelligence from the members of the relationship. In the followings the authors collected the characteristic features of mentoring – primarily regarding mentors and mentees-without attempting to be comprehensive

The features of mentoring are summarized in Table 1.

The question about the benefits of mentoring can arise. Several researches were studying the positive output of the mentoring process. Payne and Huffman (2005) collected numerous advantages of mentoring referring to the results of empirical researches carried out in this field. According to the authors there were at least three explanations for the existence of the connection between emotional commitment and mentoring. Therefore mentoring inspires the reception of corporate values. In the second place, the mentored will be able to manage workplace stress and to cope with them, and it will help him to become a person of more positive attitude and to become more committed to his workplace. Finally, mentors act as a kind of role-models, which result in a certain respect between mentor and his mentored and it can easily be turned into a positive work attitude.

According to Harvey-McIntyre-Heames-Moeller (2009), mentoring can have several positive career effects for the mentored, such as promotion, bigger career-satisfaction, higher salary and greater mobility opportunities.

In the followings, the advantages of mentoring are enumerated from the aspect of all the participants:

*Table 1. The features of mentoring*

| Feature | | Mentoring |
|---|---|---|
| 1. Primary location | | Internal, corporate |
| 2. Primary role | Mentor | Scope of authority or professionalism within company. Staying at the company for effectively long. A person, who is interested in coaching or is dealing with management and is able to find the new talents and opportunities for his company. |
| | Mentored | A person who is flexible and open to new ideas. A person who has goals and plans with regard to mentoring and who is ready to give and get common feedback. |
| 3. Necessary experience and knowledge | Mentor | Extensive knowledge about the structure, the policy and the processes of the company. Similar career goals in the future. Widespread work experience and field of interest. |
| | Mentored | Open-minded, communicative person who has goals and expectations, and tries to develop confidential relationship with the mentor. Should be flexible and should be able to keep secret. |
| 4. Aims | Mentor | Supporting success and progress. Supporting career building and counselling. Mediation in favour of the mentored. Counselling: how to move on the political scene of the organisation and how to find the possible opportunities, what strategies should be used to reach the workplace goals in the most effective way, how to meet the demands of the organisation in the most appropriate way. |
| | Mentored | Accepts support, applies the suggested ideas and strategies. Flexible. |
| 5. Methods | | Discussion without involving others. Developing a comfortable, trustworthy atmosphere. One-and two-way knowledge-sharing. Communicating, suggesting, counselling, teaching, listening, accepting. |
| 6. Involvement of others | | In order to solve the task the mentored can be oriented to others. |
| 7. Scope | | Vertical and horizontal movement within the organisation by taking the future career opportunities, the present job and further perspectives into account. |

(own table)

Mentoring can provide the following key benefits to the mentored:

- Gets a clear view about his own career and personal goals,
- Helps him to get a better understanding of the organisation's culture and unspoken rules,
- He is exposed to new ideas and ways of thinking,
- Provides networking contact for the mentored,
- Gets access to new resources,
- Gets the opportunity to develop new skills and knowledge,
- Will more likely be successful in his career,
- Increases his self-confidence,
- Teaches him how to speak up and be heard,
- His skills will develop in the field of interpersonal relationships, and
- Learns how to manage feedbacks.

During the process the mentor has the possibility to develop his management abilities and to lift them to a higher level by:

- Seeing the business from a leader's point of view,
- Facing challenges, as he has to apply his knowledge in real situation,
- Getting to know the new members of the organization,
- Reminds him how to listen actively rather than passively,
- Helps re-energize his career,
- He is exposed to fresh perspectives and ideas,
- Encourages him to share knowledge, which will increase his sense of self-worth,
- Strengthens his interpersonal skills, and
- Leads to a more personal satisfaction on his behalf.

When a certain employee decides to be a mentor, there are some questions he has to ask from himself, such as:

- Am I happy to accept the role of a mentor?
- Do I have enough time for this?
- Is it the right time to mentor that person?
- What advantages will I have to be a mentor?
- Am I able to commit myself for this time in the long-term?
- Am I aware of the functions and methods of mentoring?
- Am I provided enough support to be a mentor? (e.g. trainings)

Of course, the answer of the would-be mentor depend on the given situation, how much he is loaded at his workplace and how much time he has for the future work.

Besides the fact that the process is beneficial for both parties, the organisation can enjoy several advantages as well. Mentoring contributes to the continuous transfer of talent/knowledge and it provides the opportunity for the today-leaders to transfer their knowledge to the future-leaders, which might result in the followings:

- Employees will get a more self-confident knowledge about business life and about the organization,
- Retention of staff,
- A more effective, a more successful organization,
- A more developed communication within the organization,
- Shows the outside world that the organisation values its employees,
- Results is a more positive work environment,
- Fosters leadership skills in mentors,
- Supports a sense of cooperation and harmony within the organization,
- Increases the loyalty of employees towards the organisation –which can save money on recruitment and training costs, and
- Encourages the mentoree's growth from junior level members to future leader.

Finally, it is worth examining what factors obstruct the mentoring process in its operation. According to Burke and Mckeen (1989) a typical problem during formal mentoring is when there is an idealized picture about mentoring and about the mentored, the mentor and the boss. Although it sometimes happens that the mentor and his mentored cannot function well with each other. This might easily cause anger, suspicion, dissatisfaction and offense among the participants, which can ruin the common work of the mentor and mentored (Scandura, 1998).

## THE RESEARCH CONNECTED TO MENTORING PRACTICE

The authors carried out an extensive study in 2014-2015 in order to map what mentoring practices are applied at Hungarian organisations. The basic principle of the research was to get to know the present knowledge-transfer methods of the participating people and organisations and to reveal what synergy exists between mentoring and the other forms of knowledge-management system. The research was carried out in two forms. On one hand there were qualitative researches that are in-depth interviews; while on the other hand there were quantitative researches based on questionnaires on the internet.

In case of the two types of researches, both the employees and the employers were examined.

Table 2. shows the matrix of the research methods.

*Table 2. The methods of the research*

|  | **Qualitative Research** | **Quantitative Research** |
|---|---|---|
| Aim | To get to know the Hungarian practice, descriptive analysis | To focus on connections and its systems |
| Tools | In-depth interviews | Questionnaires on the internet |
| Sample | Employees<br>Employers | Employees<br>Employers |
| Evaluation | Analysis of the responses (text-analysis) | With one-or two variant statistic methods |

(own table)

In the followings the authors detail the results of the qualitative and quantitative researches separately. Choosing the sample from the side of the employees and employers was not accidental, although it can provide a view about the Hungarian practice.

## Qualitative Researches

## Corporate Research

From the side of the corporate, 15 big companies were asked in in-depth interviews. The number of staff at those companies was above 250 people. With regard to their field of operation, the companies were of different sectors. The majority of them operate in service sector (financial, IT sector, transportation, strategy), but there were also some companies from the agricultural industry or from car-industry or from trading. Only one company was state-owned.

The interviews with the companies were made after getting in touch with them and based on previously prepared, structured questions. The questions can be classified into different groups. Therefore, the first group of questions involved questions about the organisation, about its profile, its employment structure and about the company's knowledge-base and knowledge-management protocol.

The second group of questions focused on mentoring practice. The questions wanted to reveal what initiations brought mentoring action of the organization, how spontaneous is its realization and whether it happened by guided protocol. Furthermore, there were questions regarding the fields where mentoring practice could basically appear and strengthen; who will become mentors or mentees in the organization and what tasks the participants of the process have. Another field of study was to examine how mentoring system can be built into knowledge-management, and to what extent it supplements or obstructs the other processes of the system.

Answering the final group of questions, the respondents had to give a complex evaluation about their own practice, about its positive and negative elements and about future plans regarding development.

Considering the interviews carried out with big companies, the authors could conclude the following statements:

- Human capital and its knowledge were considered one of the most important values and success factors at companies. The knowledge of the workers was also determined as part of the entrance requirements, which is the acceptance of qualified workers, was aimed on one hand. While on the other hand the preservation of knowledge, development according market needs and actualization were also taken into consideration.
- The mentoring system was generally considered as useful and important mode of knowledge transfer within the organization. According to the respondents it supports the mutual development of the participants and it can have a favourable effect on the operation of the whole organization and on its sub-processes.
- Besides the fact that mentoring is explained as a type of knowledge-transfer by the organization, according to the companies it can be seen as an independent and unbiased communicational channel, with the help of which it is possible to reveal the accidental problems in an early phase and to analyse it from different aspects and finally to provide possible solutions. According to the respondents it can help the organisations to elaborate their own preventive systems as early as possible in order to handle the problems properly and to manage them in unit and to connect it to the other units of the whole system of knowledge-management.

- In case of the examined companies, formal mentoring programs were operating, which were mainly initialized by middle- or by senior officials. The aim of mentoring practice was –among others- to support the employment and social inclusion of new entrants into corporate culture, to provide them the necessary information for their independent work and for their development and to educate the future leaders with the patronage of an experienced leader, who is working for the company.

- The description of mentoring work and the documentation of the process was missing at the majority of companies. There were only few companies, which represented mentoring program consciously documented as well. Its implementation form was the talent-program, where the representative of the mentoring program was in charge; while there were cases when the HR department was responsible for the documentation. The aim of these documentation procedures was to summarize the different materials and supplements and also to evaluate the mentoring work, thus both the mentors and the mentees can make use of it.

- In case of almost half of the participating companies, there was no knowledge-management system at all; therefore mentoring practice could not become part of it. However, in case of companies, which had knowledge-management system, the mentoring practice either could not become a content element or could not totally adapt to the knowledge management system and management practice. Several companies were aware of the lack of integrated system-approach, therefore knowledge management and especially many elements of mentoring remained unexploited without the synergy.

## Research Regarding the Employees

The examination of the side of the employees was preceded by a study, which was carried out in 2014 (Bencsik-Juhász-Kovács), where knowledge-transferring willingness was examined. The results of the research showed that the knowledge-transferring willingness among the participants of the sample was medium and the requirements for sharing the information were differentiated. Significant differences were primarily shown in genders, qualification and age with regard to knowledge-transfer. The results showed that women were basically more unselfish than men (although it is true that the size of the sample was rather different), and by increasing the age, the knowledge-transfer willingness was more dynamic, while qualification did not show any significant influence in the sample.

Taking this research into account, the authors carried out in-depth interviews among employees who already participated in mentoring processes as mentored. Choosing the given technology was justified by the fact that the authors wanted to reveal deeper explanations and views from the interviewees. The questions of the in-depth interview could be classified into three basic groups.

The first group of questions contained the features of the organization, such as the size of the company, its profile, the role of knowledge within the operation of the company and the tools for knowledge development.

The second group of questions included questions about the characteristic features of mentoring practice, such as its definition, the skills of the participants and the appearance of this method of knowledge transfer within the system of the corporate activity.

The final group of questions reviewed the place and position of mentoring practice in the company's knowledge-management processes from the aspect of mentored, that is it detailed the relational dimensions

*Table 3. The structure of the questionnaire*

| Corporate Features | Characteristics of Mentoring Practice in the Organization | Mentoring Practice in the Knowledge-Management Process of the Corporate |
|---|---|---|
| Corporate size<br>Field of activity<br>Role of knowledge in corporate<br>Tools of developing knowledge within the organization | Definition of mentoring practice<br>Characterizing the participants of the mentoring process<br>Appearance of mentoring process in the corporate's systems of activity | Characteristics of corporate's knowledge-management system<br>Connectional dimensions between the mentoring process and knowledge-management processes<br>Role of mentoring process in the corporate's value-creating system |

between mentoring and other processes of knowledge-management, furthermore it discussed the role of a mentor in the company. The structure of the questionnaire was similar to the questionnaire in Table 3.

The sample number of the participants in the research was 30 people, who really participated and acted as mentored in the mentoring process and valued the process successful. Half of the respondents worked for big companies and almost a quarter of them worked for middle-sized companies. The companies employing them were of different sectors, such as IT, security technology, finance, energetic sector, etc. Based on the age-factor, the majority of the respondents were represented from the age-group under 41. The followings were uncovered from the interviews:

- The respondents set a high value on tacit knowledge beyond the necessary professional knowledge, which -according to them- the employees can acquire by experience. Moreover they considered the effect and role of emotional intelligence also very important.
- Mentoring protocol was understood to be a process, when an experienced colleague shares his knowledge with a newcomer or with somebody who is less competent. Mentoring promotes knowledge-sharing and a quicker integration of the new entrants. Knowledge-acquisition, trust, giving help, teaching and patronage was also emphasized in the process.
- Most of the respondents agreed that the implementation of mentoring process can happen at any field and it can be useful for anybody. It is basically the mentor who can help his mentored at any phase of the process either being active or remaining in the background. Recognizing the latter is a very important pillar of successful mentoring. In this case they said the mentor only fulfilled the task of a controller or a counsellor.
- The respondents revealed it also that the mentor has to know when to step back and let the mentored evolve. Splitting is not good if it happens too early or too late.
- Finally the respondents agreed that mentoring practice could strengthen the value-developing processes at the company. It can influence and can be an active part of establishing, preserving and transferring knowledge-management and the successful process has serious efficiency- and capacity increasing influence, it increases flexibility and multi-aspect problem-solving; therefore it can have a value-increasing effect for the corporate.

The basic aim of the qualitative research was to get to know the situation, then later the authors carried out the quantitate researches based on the previous statements. Similarly to the previous researches, both parties were asked. The results of the quantitative research will be shown in the followings:

## Quantitative Researches

## Corporate Research

69 organisations participated in the corporate research, whose managers filled in a questionnaire on the internet. The procedure for sample-collection was the snowball-method, thus the research cannot be considered neither based on the procedure, nor on the several of the samples. Similarly to the qualitative research 3 groups of questions were asked; the first group of questions wanted to reveal the characteristic features of the corporate, the second one was dealing with the operating mentoring practice, while the third group of questions included the relational examination of mentoring practice with the knowledge-management system. As far as the industrial sectors of the examined companies are concerned, there were companies dealing with trade, repairing or even with finance or agriculture. Regarding the size of them, nearly 40% of them were big companies, one fifth of them were middle-company, one-fourth of them were small enterprise and the rest was micro organization. The following results could be justified with the one-or more variable statistical methods:

- At the examined companies it was difficult to substitute the knowledge of the leaving employees, while it was only rarely typical that the corporate-specific knowledge was documented. However, it was also revealed that this knowledge could not only be acquired at trainings, thus tacit knowledge has significant role as well.
- The field of application of mentoring system could make the knowledge-transfer and integration of the entrants quicker. Using mentoring as rising new generation of managers was less typical at the companies.
- It was clear from the responses that both the formal and the informal form could have been widespread at companies, but the documentation of the formal form is still rare.
- The examined companies considered the integration of new entrants, a more efficient work and multi-sided knowledge-transfer as the advantages of mentoring process; while they agreed on that the individual development of the mentored as a secondary aspect was a disadvantage compared to his professional development.
- The work of the mentors was usually used by the employees; while the smallest proportion of mentored come from the chief management.
- At the majority of companies there was no knowledge-management system; therefore they could not talk about the effect of synergy between mentoring and knowledge-management. It was typical at Hungarian companies; although every third company judged that the two processes could have a positive effect on each other.
- A more developed and a much structured mentoring process were still missing at many companies, because the mentoring system has not been operating at them for a long time and it has no developed protocol.

## Research on Employees

279 respondents participated in the sample on the employees, who filled in an online questionnaire. The method of asking was the snowball method. As regards their Hungarian location, the majority of the sample was mainly from the central-Hungarian, west-and central Transdanubium, which are considered

to be the three most developed regions of Hungary (75% of the sample). Men and women participated in the research in a similar proportion. Nearly half of the respondents worked for big companies and the majority of them had university degree.

The group of questions were similar to the sample regarding the corporate sample.

The first group of questions examined the knowledge and the fields in connection with its importance and application from the respondents' point of view. The second group involved the mentoring processes; while the third one wanted to reveal the connection and synergy between mentoring and knowledge-management. The following statements can be made based on the research:

- In the examined sample, the knowledge required by the companies was mainly the special, professional knowledge, language use and IT knowledge. Having previous work experience was extremely valuable. Consequently it was not by coincidence that one third of the respondents felt that he could hardly be substituted if he left the company.
- The majority of the respondents participated voluntarily in the mentoring processes and they used the opportunity mainly for acquiring new knowledge and making their integration easier and faster. Every second respondent mentioned the opportunity of mutual learning between mentors and mentored, that is they were talking about the existence of higher level mentoring processes even if it was not always a conscious process.
- The respondents agreed that it was mainly the knowledge from experience and emotional intelligence, which the mentor could not share with his mentored.
- Among others, the strengthening of confidential values within the corporate culture, the development of self-confidence on both sides, the multi-sided knowledge-transfer, a more effective work and a more open flow of information were highlighted as advantages of mentoring processes.
- The respondents considered the costs, the constant work-supervision, and the lack of knowledge-transfer, professional jealousy and the laziness of the mentored to be the obstacles of mentoring processes.
- Based on the opinion of the majority, the mentoring process has positive effect on other processes of knowledge-management.

On the whole the response was in harmony with the results of the corporate side, which showed that with regard to the examined Hungarian companies, the mentoring processes had basically classical mentoring features, however they give the chance to other higher-level practices to develop, to the two-sided flow- and transfer of information. Although the mentoring systems represent additive value in the knowledge-management system of the company, they cannot be considered as functional part of the structure, therefore the positive effects originating from the synergy are yet unexploited.

## CONCLUSION

Although the researches of the authors are not representative, they are able to provide a clear view about the mentoring processes implemented at Hungarian organisations. In the light of the researches, it was justified that the classical mentoring practice –with the characteristic features defined by Kram (Kram, 1985) - was applied at these companies. The respondents basically agreed that these processes of knowledge transfer was useful, which has positive impact on all the participants and on the company as well (Harvey-McIntyre-Heames-Moeller, 2009Arogundade, 2011).

Based on the results of the researches carried out by the authors we can state that mentoring is basically productive, but it is also true that sometimes it had unproductive practice. The corporate practices basically supported the integration of the company's new or junior staff; they supported their career opportunities, therefore these processes indirectly affected the elements of the corporate culture, they could offer and strengthen new values or could weaken old ones in the corporate culture (Bencsik-Juhász- Machova, 2014, Bencsik, 2015, Payne and Huffman, 2005). The activity of the mentor was particularly important for the employer when new employees entered the company. With the help of the mentor the integration of the employee was not spontaneous, but rather it happened with support and the company receives feedback about the opinion of the employees, how they observe the company and what problems they encountered. This rather long process has several stations; this is why it is important to continuously evaluate performances. If it does not happen or happens scantly, then this might set back the work of the mentored.

The basic elements of the successful processes are trust, acceptance of the others, respect, mutual listening and a partner-like relation, which was in harmony with the results of a previous research (Catling and Davies, 2008). The requirements set towards the mentor were quite multiple. Some requirements –among others- are professional knowledge, enough practice, knowledge of place, loyalty towards the company, good communicational skills and respect and weigh with the employees. It was also determining that a good human- and working relationship should be established between the mentor and the mentored. In their free time the mentors usually give advice or talk to the mentored, which is in itself respectful.

Unfortunately it is still typical in Hungary that employers expect the entrants –on entering the company- to possess the knowledge and skills the company requires. If the entrants cannot gain enough experience, then later this can be an obstacle for them to find job. At present it would also be practical that the mentors provide support in organizing trainings, in preparing the workers for the job and also in finding the workplaces (Holden, 2014). Mentoring is often the missing link, which connects the new employees with his future workplace successes (Levinson and McKee, 1978). If he previous does not exist, the latter should also be missing. Yet there are only few Hungarian companies, which invest money and energy into developing a mentoring program of their own.

However, it was noticed that the elements and practice of reciprocal mentoring have already appeared at the Hungarian organisations, either unwittingly or not. It was when the participants discover the opportunity of mutual information transfer and learning. Even if this process was not realized consciously, it was mentioned as a requirement in most cases, which promote the motivation towards mentoring processes and towards developing the protocol. The corporate mentoring activity is a long-term supporting process, of which target is to help the mentored develop and advance. Although at multinational companies mentoring is often a formally developed program and the support may also come via informal talks and independendently from this.

As a developed knowledge-management system was mainly missing at the given organisations, it was rather difficult to examine and catch the mutual influence and dependence of its elements. At the same time the respondents already realized that they could use the synergies, but for this at present and in the future they would still need the development and strengthening of certain parts of the system. The positively operating mentoring systems by all means can create a good base for the operation of a well-structured, documented and complex knowledge-management system and mentoring should fulfil an active and additive role and task for the organisations and for its workers.

# REFERENCES

Arogundade, O. (2011). Mentoring and leadership succesion in industries and organizations. *IFE PsychlogIA*, (Supplement), 180–187.

Beam, M. R., Chen, C., & Greenberger, E. (2002). The nature of the relationships between adolescents and their "very important" nonparental adults. *American Journal of Community Psychology*, 305–325. doi:10.1023/A:1014641213440 PMID:12002248

Bell, C. R. (2002). *Manager as mentors* (2nd ed.). San Francisco, CA: Berrettkoehler.

Bencsik, A. (2009). *A tudásmenedzsment emberi oldala*. Győr: Z-Press Kiadó Kft.

Bencsik, A. (2015). *A tudásmenedzsment elméletben és gyakorlatban*. Akadémiai Kiadó.

Bencsik, A., & Juhász, T. (2014). *Mentori gyakorlat a magyarországi szervezeteknél*. Under publishing.

Bencsik, A., Juhász, T., & Kovács, S. (2014). A tudásmegosztási hajlandóság aktuális kérdései, avagy jobb adni, mint kapni (empirikus vizsgálat alapján). *Alkalmazott tudományok Fóruma I. konferenciakötet*, 55-61.

Bencsik, A., Juhász, T., & Machova, R. (2014). Mentor system/practice on the behalf of knowledge sharing. *Acta Politechnica Hungarica*, *11*(9), 95-114.

Budavári-Takács, I., Csehné Papp, I., & Jekkel, O. (2015). Karrier építési tudatosság vizsgálata fiatal felnőttek körében. In Innováció – növekedés – fenntarthatóság.

Burke, R. J., & McKeen, C. A. (1989). Developing formal mentoring programs in organizations. *Business Quarterly*, *53*, 76–79.

Byrne, E. (1991). *Mentorship in human resource and career development: a policy approach*. Unpublished paper.

Catling, T., & Davies, M. (2008). Mentoring the objective support that managers need. *British Journal of Adiministrative Management*, 22-23.

Choo, C. W. (1996). The knowing organization: How organzations use information to construct meaning, create knowledge and make decision. *International Journal of Information Management*, *16*(5), 23–40. doi:10.1016/0268-4012(96)00020-5

Clutterbuck, D. (2002). *Mentoring and diversity: an international perspective*. Butterworth Heinemann.

Davenport, T. H. (1997). *Information ecology: mastering the information and knowledge environment*. Oxford University Press.

Dougherty, T. W., Dreher, G. F., Vaoram, A., & Wilbank, J. E. (2013). *Mentor status, occupational context, and protégé career outcomes: differential returns for males and females*. Elsiever Inc.

Douglas, C.A. (1997). *Formal mentoring programsin organisations: an annotated bibliography*. Centre for Creative Leadership.

DuBois, D. L., & Karcher, M. J. (2005). *Handbook of Youth Mentoring*. London: Sage Publication.

Ehigie, B. O., Koang, G. O., & Ibode, F. O. (2011). Mentoring and organisational behavior. *IFE PsychlogIA*, (Supplement), 398–419.

Elmore, R. (1990). On changing the structure of public schools. Restructuring Schools.

Fajana, S., & Gbajumo-Sheriff, M. (2011). Mentoring: A human resource tool for acheiving organisational effectiveness. *IFE PsychlogIA*, (Supplement), 420–432.

Goodbar, N.H. & Lewis, K.F. (2015). Finding and working with mentors. *American of Health-System Pharmacy*, 921-922.

Haggard, D. L., & Turban, D. B. (2012). The mentoring relationship as a context for psychological contract development. *Journal of Applied Social Psychology*, *42*(8), 1904–1931. doi:10.1111/j.1559-1816.2012.00924.x

Harvey, M., McIntyre, N., Heames, J. T., & Moeller, M. (2009). Mentoring global female managers in the global marketplace: Traditional, reverse and reciprocal mentoring. *International Journal of Human Resource Management*, *20*(6), 1344–1361. doi:10.1080/09585190902909863

Holden, D. (2014). *The Lost Art of Inspired Mentoring*. Retrieved from http://www.iienet2.org/details.aspx?id=38250

Ibarra, H. (1992). Homophily and differential returns: Sex differences in network structure and access in an advertising firm. *Administrative Science Quarterly*, *37*(3), 422–447. doi:10.2307/2393451

Jarnagin, L. M. (2010). *Mentors are from Venus and Mars: exploring the benefits of homogeneous and heterogeneous gender pairings in the mentoring relationships of female senior student affairs officers*. ProQuest LLC, Ed.D. Dissertation, University of California, Los Angeles.

Kanter, R. M. (1977). *Men and women of the corporation*. New York: Basic Books.

Kram, K. E. (1983). Phases of the mentor relationship. *Academy of Management Journal*, *26*(4), 608–625. doi:10.2307/255910

Kram, K. E. (1985). *Mentoring at work*. Boston: Scott. Foresman.

Levinson, D. J., Darrow, C. N., Klein, E. B., Levinson, M. H., & McKee, B. (1978). *The seasons of a man's life*. New York: Balantine Books.

Nemirovsky, R., & Solomon, J. (2000). *"This is crazy. Difference of differences!" On the flow of ideas in a mathematical conversation*. Paper prepared for Videopapers in Mathematics Education Conference, Dedham, MA.

Noe, R. A. (1988). Women and mentoring: A review and research agenda. *Academy of Management Review*, *13*(1), 65–77.

Odiorne, G. S. (1985). Mentoring- an American management innovation. *The Personnel Administrator*, *30*(5), 63–70. PMID:10270460

Patterson, J. A. (1994). Shattering the glass ceiling: women in school administration. Chapel Hill, NC: Academic Press.

Payne, S. C., & Huffman, A. H. (2005). A longitudinal examintation of the influence of mentoring on commitment and turnover. *Academy of Management Journal*, *48*(1), 158–168. doi:10.5465/AMJ.2005.15993166

Ragins, B. R., & Cotton, J. L. (1999). Mentor functions and outcomes: A comaprison of men and women in formal and informal mentoring relationships. *The Journal of Applied Psychology*, *84*(4), 529–550. doi:10.1037/0021-9010.84.4.529 PMID:10504893

Reich, M., Czeglédi, C., & Fonger, J. (2015). Expectations of employees on the effects of workplace health management as a part of an internal diversity management-explorative study. *Trendy v podnikání*, 49-58.

Rhodes, J. E. (2002). *Stand by me: the risk and rewards of mentoring today`s youth*. Cambridge, MA: Harvard University Press.

Rhodes, J. E., Spencer, R., Keller, T. E., Liang, B., & Noam, G. (2006). A model for the influence of mentoring relationships on youth development. *Journal of Community Psychology*, *6*(6), 691–707. doi:10.1002/jcop.20124

Scandura, T. A. (1998). Dysfunctional mentoring relationships and outcomes. *Journal of Management*, *24*(3), 449–467. doi:10.1177/014920639802400307

Shapiro, E. C., Haseltine, F. P., & Rowe, M. P. (1978). Moving up: Role models, mentors and the patron system. *Sloan Management Review*, 51–58.

Wanberg, C.R., Welsh, E.T., & Hezlett, S.A. (2003). Mentoring research: a review and dynamic process model. *Research in Personnel and Human Resources Management*, 39-124.

Zey, M. (1988). A mentor for all. *The Personnel Journal*, *67*(2), 46–51.

## KEY TERMS AND DEFINITIONS

**Corporate Culture Supporting Mentoring:** Corporate culture, of which main principles are trust, open and frank communication, supporting knowledge acquisition and respect towards other members of the organisation.

**Formal Mentoring:** Mentoring programs supported and guided by organisations.

**Informal Mentoring:** A spontaneous, voluntary form of mentoring, which is not organized by organisations.

**Mentor:** An experienced, highly-qualified person in the organisation, who shares his knowledge (professional knowledge, management style, corporate culture, values) with the mentored, and at the same time he has influence on the professional and psycho-social development of the mentored.

**Mentored:** A rather inexperienced person in the organisation, who needs mentoring for the sake of his quick integration, professional development or for his career.

**Mentoring Practice:** Mentoring is a type of knowledge-transferring process, where the participants receive information from each other and both parties expand and develop their knowledge.

**Traditional Mentoring:** It is usually an elder member of the organisation, who teaches, educates and supports a talented young one.

# Chapter 17
# The Transfer of Knowledge and University–Firm Tensions:
## Contributions from S&T Studies to the Understanding of a New Institutional Paradigm

**Hugo Pinto**
*University of Coimbra, Portugal*

## ABSTRACT

*Innovation is transformed in an encompassing domain where different types of actors are connected and interrelated. Nevertheless, academic science often feels threatened by the new emerging institutional paradigm characterized by the economic exploitation of public research results. This chapter explores university-firm relations and tensions, discussing the increased relevance of knowledge transfer. The ideas of Ludwik Fleck, intellectual precursor of Social Studies of S&T, contribute to the understanding of the difficulties of communication between different collectives, their styles of thought and the importance of 'marginal individuals' in connecting different institutional spheres. Based on a qualitative approach to the case study of a Portuguese university attempting to create bridges with the business world, the text illustrates differences between the 'academic science' and the firm, the recent institutionalization of commercialization of research, and findings for policy-making and management of knowledge transfer activities.*

## INTRODUCTION

The 'third mission' of the university is related with the emergence of a new mode of knowledge production, the importance of science in innovation systems, and triple helix relations, underlining the focus given to a variety of organizations and institutions related to innovation. A different logic has emerged where the role of knowledge networks is underlined with various actors interacting in the public and private sectors. Recent decades witnessed the growing difficulty in separating between public good and

DOI: 10.4018/978-1-5225-1642-2.ch017

industrial property. These two spheres were initially distant but are now closer, which has led to the emergence of 'academic enterprise' with new regulatory and normative schemes and cognitive values centered in a systematic effort to strengthen the short-term economic value of research and facilitate commercialization of inventions (Larsen, 2011). The emergence of 'academic enterprise' results largely from dissatisfaction with the direct and measurable benefits of public science. This fact, noted by Pavitt (2001) as the search for greater relevance of public science, was the first justification for the university to seek the firm. The second justification for this new relationship has been the sharp decline in public funding for academic research associated with the increasing costs of research.

These topics are normally analyzed using quantitative approaches (Bergman, 2010). It is common for studies on university-industry relations to focus certain metrics and use econometric approaches to ascertain the determinants and effectiveness of this relationship, both from the perspective of firms and public science actors (Larsen, 2011). However, the study of university-firm interactions would benefit of incorporating concepts and approaches from areas such as the Science and Technology Studies (STS) that have also given attention to these phenomena, yielding important policy implications for science and technology (S&T).

This chapter seeks to deepen the debate on knowledge transfer and university-firm relations. The text is organized as follows. The first section discusses the notions of knowledge transfer and its emergence as a central aspect of contemporary change in the role of science. The second section presents the main ideas of Fleck, the precursor of STS, emphasizing relevant aspects to the understanding of knowledge transfer. Then, it presents an empirical study analyzing the specific case of the interaction of the University of Algarve (UAlg) in Portugal[1] and the regional economic fabric, the attempts to understand differences between the collectives of thought of researchers and firms, namely small and medium enterprises (SMEs) that represent the large majority of firms in this region, and how these groups comprise the role of university's knowledge transfer office in mediating the relationship between these two institutional spheres. The chapter concludes with solutions and recommendations for the limits of knowledge transfer and presents future research directions.

## BACKGROUND

### The New Role of the University and the Importance of Knowledge Transfer

The intense attention over the last half-century that innovation policies had as a development tool, particularly in developed countries, gave central importance to scientific knowledge for economic progress (Lundvall, 2007). Characterizing contemporary societies as being organized around knowledge generated through scientific research and technological development brought to the center of discussion the importance of knowledge and its impacts, as well as emphasizing notions such as a knowledge society, knowledge economy and risk society (Estanque & Nunes, 2003). The role of universities became more relevant than in the traditional view of innovation where the firm was the main target of attention. Several theories highlighted the new role of knowledge and the university as the Mode 2 of knowledge production (Gibbons et al., 1994), the triple helix (Etzkowitz & Leydesdorff, 1997) or the regional innovation systems (Cooke, 1998) emphasizing that the university is currently characterized by a new mission of its effective participation in territorial dynamics. In this 'third mission', transferring knowledge is assumed to be a central aspect for competitiveness and cohesion of territories, particularly in the explicit and structured interconnections between actors within innovation systems.

The idea of knowledge transfer is distinguished from other similar activities such as the dissemination of technology or the diffusion of innovation. It is based on an active and predominantly formal process of voluntary engagement, between a diversity of actors (research centers, universities, businesses, governments or communities) to the appropriation of new knowledge for mutual benefit in order to improve material, human, and environmental well-being (Pinto, 2012). This broad definition, inspired by Bozeman (2000) and Molas-Gallart et al. (2002), is different from others commonly used that limit the transfer of knowledge to a sub-group of activities with financial goals and business benefits.

The formal character of the transfer of knowledge is embedded in protocols, agreements, payments that originate contracts, patents and technology-based companies. Several authors (inter alia, D'Este & Patel, 2007; Debackere & Veugelers, 2005; Bercovitz & Feldman, 2005) identify the formal mechanisms of knowledge transfer: the creation of start-ups and spin-offs, the development and exploitation of industrial property rights, research and development projects, and other channels, such as cooperation in education and training, advanced training to business staff, or student internships. In addition, formal relations are based on personal networks, which increase the likelihood of knowledge exchanges. These informal relationships are difficult to quantify but central to the future formalization of the transfer (Pinto, 2012). Only a minority of university-industry relations are directly connected to commercialization; however, the mobility of human resources, consulting services, collaborative projects and informal contacts have less attention than patent licensing or spinning-off, commonly referred to as the most important channels, because of their potential in attracting additional revenues for the university in times of economic downturn.

## Dilemmas in University-Firm Relations

Several new tensions emerge with the change in the reality of science, which are illustrated by the ongoing debate between the costs and the benefits from knowledge commercialization. There are obvious benefits in terms of profits, incentives and recognition, which can be directed to other research projects, even of a fundamental nature. The existence of patents and applied R&D projects may lead, for example, to new products and processes that improve the range of availabilities for individuals and firms, enhancing consumer society and improving productivity. But there are less positive aspects, considered by Bok (2003) among others, as costs, often speculative and intangible, that result in breaches of academic standards.

The emergence of a patenting culture as a way of marketing knowledge also created limits for scientific credibility (Packer & Webster, 1996). The conversion of academic science to patenting raises new questions for researchers in the recognition of their knowledge networks, as they are increasingly moving between different social worlds to be rewarded for their academic achievements and patenting results. There are important limits to the behavior of the scientist, in particular, when we recall the Mertonian ethos with the principles of universalism, communalism, disinterestedness and organized skepticism, which guaranteed the 'good science'. The vision of Nelson (2004) and Santos (2008) underlines the dangers of patenting, a process that has been particularly intense in the last decade in the scientific areas with the greatest economic potential, such as biotechnology; this has changed relationships within the academy, often blocking free discussion and open results, jeopardizing the production of new knowledge and distorting the research agenda setting (Jaffe & Lerner, 2004).

Shapin (2008) enters this discussion with another perspective. There is a great moral heterogeneity, and there is room to think that there is more than only one location, the university, where the good scientific life can be found. The business environment can also be adequate for freethinking leading to the generation of scientific knowledge transferable to the market.

Several types of organizations have emerged in the boundary areas of science and business, functioning as intermediary structures: technology centers, laboratories and certification testing, technology parks, science parks, services to support research and innovation, technology platforms, patent centers, and business incubators. Knowledge transfer offices (KTOs) in universities are an example of this type of entity that tries to suppress communication gaps to approach the market and technology expertise with business demand. Guston (1999) showed how these organisms are boundary organizations that characterize the view advocated by the principal-agent theory. A boundary organization runs a stabilization mechanism that internalizes the contingent nature of science in their everyday practice, creating boundary objects for cooperation between principals and agents. These offices are organizations that provide common ground, legitimizing the creation and use of boundary objects (Gieryn, 1983), such as patents, and originating the participation of key actors where they appear as expert mediators. Siegel et al. (2003) summarize the main stakeholders and their organizational cultures in knowledge transfer overlapping areas:

- Scientists with an academic organizational culture attempt to produce new scientific knowledge, motivated by peer recognition, for additional financial gains and funding for research;
- The KTOs, which have a bureaucratic organizational culture, work with universities and industry to structure cooperation, protect and commercialize intellectual property of the university, facilitate communication, ensure technological diffusion, and secure additional funding for research.
- The companies/entrepreneurs with an entrepreneurial organizational culture expect to commercialize new technology, benefit financially, and maintain ownership of knowledge and technology.

It is important to underline that even if we consider only companies a variety of organizational cultures does exist. These cultures influence innovative behavior and are connected with the absorptive capacity of the firm (Cohen & Levinthal, 1990). Innovative companies tend to present a strong specific culture (Büschgens et al., 2013).

## CONTRIBUTIONS FROM STS TO KNOWLEDGE TRANSFER

### The Interest in Ludwik Fleck within STS

Since its almost random discovery, the monograph "Entsehung und Entwicklung einer wissenschaftelichen Tatsache", translated as "Genesis and Development of a Scientific Fact" (Fleck, 1935|1979) and written in 1935, has been the subject of much academic interest. Robert Merton, the great instigator of this translation, found in Ludwik Fleck clues about his personal interest in the influence of the social structure in the production of scientific knowledge. Fleck wrote texts that were largely ignored. In 1935, he wrote an essay about scientific observation and perception in which introduced the idea of style of thought; he then extended the discussion of collectives of thought with his 1936 essay "On the Crisis of 'Reality'". However, most of his ideas are well presented in the monograph. In 1960, Fleck wrote "Crisis in Science" that is considered his last writing and was rejected by the journal Science.

Fleck remained forgotten until the seventies of the twentieth century when his work was translated into English reaching a much wider audience than the German edition allowed. Fleck (1896-1961) devoted himself to medicine and bacteriology, and he became interested in science as a subject of research in the interdisciplinary environment at the University of Lwów, then part of Poland and now Ukraine, where he participated in various scientific circles. Fleck, a Polish Jew imprisoned during World War II in concentration camps, was obliged to create vaccines for Nazi forces, which allegedly were tested on other prisoners. This mysterious character of Fleck's biography has boosted interest in not only exploring his theoretical contributions but also his life.

Despite the late discovery, the influence and impact of Fleck in STS have been enormous. Fleck is currently presented as a thinker ahead of his time, a forerunner of the constructivist approach that blended practical knowledge with academic reflection. Kuhn was one of the first to recognize the importance of Fleck. In the preface to the first edition of the book "The Structure of Scientific Revolutions" in 1962 (Kuhn, 1962), he wrote "[through] random exploration [...] I have encountered almost unknown Fleck's monograph [...] an essay that anticipates many of my own ideas." In the prologue to the English translation of this monograph (Fleck, 1935|1979), Kuhn explains his story with Fleck and how a footnote in another book aroused the interest of reading a book with a title so suggestive for his own research interests Kuhn was particularly stimulated by the difficulties of transmission of ideas between collectives and the possibilities and limitations of participation in different communities.

With great importance in the School of Edinburgh, Fleck currently attracts increasing interest from researchers who focus their work in laboratory and discursive practices (Lowy, 1994). The reception of Fleck and his influence on STS, as underlined by Nunes (2007), ranges from the epistemographic readings of Dear and praxiographic readings of Mol, social studies of biomedicine, and the issue of co-existence and articulation of incommensurable styles and collectives to "thinking with eyes and hands" (Latour, 1986), the inscriptions and the materiality of science (Latour & Woolgar, 1979), the biomedical platforms, the enactment of biomedical entities and their ontology, boundary concepts and objects (Star, 1989), and the elaboration of the concept of style in philosophy and history of science and the question of the disunity of science (Galison & Stump, 1996).

For example, Bruno Latour, one of the instigators of Actor-Network-Theory (ANT), presents Fleck as the founder of the sociology of science (Latour, 2005). The conceptual framework proposed by Actor-Network-Theory, which benefits from the ideas of Fleck, appears to understand other dimensions of knowledge transfer. Several authors think that ANT is an appropriate approach to analyze 'black-boxing' in the innovation process (eg, McMaster et al., 1997; Oliveira, 2008; Pinto et al., 2015). The idea of transfer easily connects with the central notion of ANT, translation, the process in which actors constantly engage to transfer their languages, problems, identities and interests to others (Callon, 1999). "Translating is transferring": transferring interests, purposes, devices, applications. The transfer allows the consideration of a set of practices that produce change (Corcuff, 2001). The notion of network points to an incomplete stabilization among different types of actors, individuals, groups or objects in ANT. The network is the result of a relatively stable balance of power in the translation process. Actors, people, and objects are not fixed and only achieve meaning through relationships with other actors. It is the network that allows players to increase power and influence. At the beginning of translation the worlds of the university and the firm are separate without communication; in the end there is a discourse about shared objectives and common activities (Colyvas & Powell, 2006; Berman, 2008).

The comparative epistemology of Fleck offers a unique set of tools to look at the production and circulation of knowledge in contemporary societies, allowing the construction of a geography of intellectual fields, describing not only the people and places but also the change happening (Rochel of Camargo, 2002). The approach to science and Fleck's philosophical concepts are rooted in practical experience as a medical bacteriologist. The interest in Fleck also lies in its ability to study various types of communities and their interactions with knowledge. The fact that Fleck comes from the Health sector makes it particularly attractive for application in this field of science, in particular the use of the concepts of style of thought, in order to understand the community, its connection to practice and instruments used. By underlining the differences between styles of different groups, his ideas reveal the centrality of 'marginal individuals' and may contribute to an explanation of relevant processes of knowledge transfer between universities and firms.

## Main Contributions from Fleck's Monograph

In his monograph, Fleck describes the evolution of the concept of syphilis, stressing that science must be seen as a historically bounded activity by the existence of different collectives. Fleck shows how a disease can be seen as a social construction and how physicians find it impossible to describe an infection, an event of great complexity involving the interaction of at least two complex systems, parasite and host, by a simple causality. This type of causality is only meaningful when framed by a common style of thought. The style of thought not only determines how the object is observed but highlights certain elements while neglecting others. The scientific facts have a genesis and development and are the result of scientific activity in the context of specific thinking frameworks. The relevance of social and cultural dynamics originates the need for a comparative historical epistemology. The present and past knowledge is the starting point for the genesis and development of new knowledge. The distinction between truth and error can only make sense in the context of styles of thought and certain collective thinking. There are continuities between common sense, scientific thinking and their languages that cannot be neglected, such as the heuristic nature of proto-ideas. The study of science should be understood in a relativistic way taking into account social and axiological assumptions.

The construction of knowledge should not only be considered a bilateral relationship; rather, the subject should also still consider the state of latent knowledge in the collective as a way to connect object and subject. A quote from the Descriptive Analysis of the English translation of Fleck's monograph, a summary of an unpublished work in 1961 "Towards a Free and More Human Science", refers that "[b]etween the subject and the object there exists a third thing, the community. It is creative like the subject, refractory like the object, and dangerous like an elemental power." Cognition is thus a function of these three components: the subject, the object and the collective thinking in which the subject acts.

Fleck (1935|1979) states that each style of thought characterizes a certain collective. The style of thought is a collective function that fits the historical development of a field of thought and leads to a specific stock of knowledge and cultural characteristics. The style of a group is the result of the theoretical and practical education of a particular individual, the transfers between teachers and students, and the relationships with the community. Importantly, it is not an optional process but rather an imposition that happens during the process of socialization (Rochel de Camargo, 2002). Individuals with the same references belong to the same collective of thought. Fleck interconnects the relationship between observation, theory and construction of scientific fact. The scientific fact is understood within the style of thought, linked to the concepts of observation and experience, giving diversity to collectives of thought. Fleck argues that there is a connection between styles and relevant concepts existing at a particular time, so there is a constraint on the historical development of thought. The different styles of thought can coexist but are restrictions to the understanding of each new scientific discovery. Fleck (1936|1986) notes that the technical terms of a collective of thought not only express the meaning assigned to them by the members but also assume a symbolic, almost "sacred" connotation for practitioners, unreachable for the uninitiated, that transmits a specific power. A collective of thought can thus be understood as a community of people exchanging ideas and maintaining an intellectual interaction within the same style of thought. In each collective there is an esoteric circle, experts who produce knowledge, and an exoteric circle, educated amateurs, where Fleck sometimes includes the general public. There is tension between the two circles, as members of the esoteric circle tend to repel non-members (Rochel de Camargo, 2002). However, advances in science are often a result of contacts between the circles. Acceptance into the group occurs after a learning period in which power and authority play a relevant role. In this process, the increased ability to recognize certain phenomena accompanies a reduction in the ability to recognize and use certain other, technical capabilities (Lowy, 1994).

There is a limited ability to communicate between groups, but there are some styles that are closer to each other than others, which facilitate communication between collectives, e.g., between physicians and biologists or between economists and managers. Therefore, varieties of styles and varieties of collectives exist and vary in degrees of closeness with each other. A particular style of thought determines the perception and the creation of tools and techniques, as well as the interpretation of results. The determination of the phenomena incorporating a common classification depends on the beliefs and practices in each historic period. Communication between collectives depends on the circulation of facts and concepts. The facts do not exist, per se; they only make sense as they adapt to style. Events produced by a particular group are assimilated by other collectives through translation processes to their own styles. Translation is always damaging, modifying facts and ignoring and emphasizing certain aspects in order to adapt to the style of the receiver. The relationship between collectives is carried out by 'marginal individuals' who belong to more than one collective and move at the intersections between different groups, favoring the creation of new ways of thinking, and increasing the generation of proto-ideas, the genesis of inventions (Figure 1).

*Figure 1. The 'Marginal individual' between collectives of thought*
*Source: Pinto (2012)*

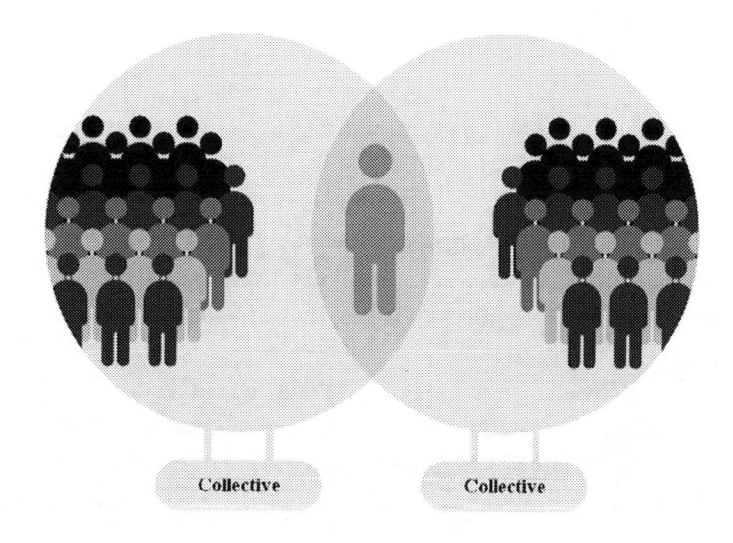

Many scientific facts are born from these initial ideas. This complex process of interaction between collectives leads to deterioration of the systems view; the change in styles of thought opens up new possibilities for the creation of new facts. In Fleck's framework, there are two phases in the development of the ideas: the first, classicism, in which all the facts agree and adapt to the existing theory, and the second, reinterpretation, where theory becomes increasingly inappropriate and facts lack reinterpretation in light of new theories. In this process, there are two types of observation: the confused observation, an inaccurate look at the phenomenon, and the formative and direct observation, requiring scientific training and constituting the basis of styles of thought.

This short insight into the ideas through which Ludwik Fleck emphasized the importance of combining theory and practice reveal the fallacies that occur when these elements in science are lacking (Pfuetzenreiter, 2003). The "mythology" of Fleck was challenged by Hedfors (2008, 2007, 2006) and answered by Amsterdamka et al. (2008). The subject of the debate was that this first author indicated that there was no reason for so much attention to the ideas of Fleck. The argument is based on the assumption that their epistemological ideas were not ignored but rejected by their peers. The aim of Fleck's arguments was, according to Eva Hedfors, to legitimize his questionable scientific practices. The author also raised questions about the ethical dimension of Fleck's research, suggesting that he was involved in different criminal experiments during his imprisonment in Nazi concentration camps in World War II. Despite this controversy, Fleck is an author of great importance; he is a pioneer in the way he formulated debates with depth that remain central to STS, implicitly arguing that scientific knowledge is a result of a collective process of construction, reproduction, socialization and learning.

## SYNTHETIC PRESENTATION OF THE CASE STUDY: KNOWLEDGE TRANSFER IN THE ALGARVE

The Portuguese region of the Algarve is certainly not known nationally and internationally for its innovative capacity or its scientific and technological profile (Pinto, 2009). It is a tourism destination that has benefited much in terms of economic development from its particularly productive specialization, transforming from a region considered poor on the European scene to one of the most developed in national standards (Guerreiro, 2008). For the European structural and investment funds allocation in the period of 2007-2013, the region abandoned the group of convergence regions; and, for 2014-2020, it maintains this status, now designated as a 'region in transition'.

The concentration of resources and investments in tourism caused some lack of attention to other activities; but, from the standpoint of strategy, regional actors have tried to engage in efforts to diversify the regional economy (Barreira, 2009). Note, for example, the attention given by the Regional Strategy 2007-13 (CCDR Algarve, 2006) or the Regional Innovation Plan (UAlg, 2007a), or more recently the RIS3 - Research and Innovation Strategy for Smart Specialization (CCDR, 2014), where it is assumed that the challenge is to transform the Algarve into a knowledge-based region. This path is not easy because several obstacles need to be overcome for the consolidation of regional innovation dynamics (Pinto & Guerreiro, 2010).

In this vision of a more innovative region, the UAlg is a central actor (Pinto et al., 2012). UAlg is the only public higher education institution in the region. Despite its short existence, created in 1979, the University assumes a role not only as a center of qualification of human capital but also as the most important research institution in this region. An evaluation of UAlg performance in R&D and cooperation in services between 2000 and 2006 (Cruz, 2006) highlighted that the expertise is concentrated in the fields of natural sciences, particularly in marine sciences, an area in which the University presents a significant critical mass in terms of the existence of excellence centers, training of human resources and market linkages. The merit in this field was one of the main drivers for UAlg demonstrating a good capacity of knowledge production measured by international scientific publications (Sousa Lobo, 2005). In parallel, the coexistence in the same institution of the university and polytechnic subsystems have also been identified as important for the strong relationship with the region itself (UAlg, 2007b). This regional "monopoly" assured to UAlg a relationship with the firms that tried to invest in knowledge and innovation in recent years.

Since 2003, the UAlg has structured a KTO, the Regional Center for Innovation of the Algarve (CRIA). It was a device for participating in various networks underpinning the national level, e.g., the offices for industrial property promotion (GAPI) and the technology transfer and knowledge offices (OTIC), with the aim of consolidating relations between the university and industry, while supporting and promoting the use of mechanisms for protecting intellectual property. The intervention of this office was recognized by relevant regional and national partners, with their participation in several networks and the preparation of strategic studies on the topic of innovation. The low density of innovation actors in this region gave this KTO excessive relevance, broader than in comparable cases of academic intermediation bodies (Pinto, 2012). It has assumed a central role in the connectivity of the entire innovation system (CCDR, 2006). Figure 2 outlines the workflows, the role of the actor in the innovation system, and the relative attention to certain activities. The comparison between this and other innovation intermediation actors can be found in Pinto (2012). The analysis of the knowledge transfer activities for linking the university to the firm, facilitate the understanding of the four main channels used by this KTO:

- The implementation of initiatives to increase the levels of entrepreneurship inside the academia;
- Direct support to business consolidation based on scientific knowledge;
- The support for the establishment of partnerships with firms seeking the university; and,
- The support to researchers seeking solutions to transfer R&D results to firms.

The focus of the KTO connects with academic entrepreneurship, where the office has collected relevant expertise particularly linked to the sciences and technologies of the Sea, creating a diversity of 'boundary objects'. These artefacts reside across borders of different 'social worlds', allowing a more effective communication among groups with differing perspectives (Star, 1989) as the support to spin-offs, the creation of pre-incubation services, seeking funding, and competition of ideas. The office, hierarchically dependent on the Rectory, seeks to connect university research with companies; however, the reverse also occurs, as companies try to meet the demand for knowledge from regional firms, assuming a role of connection in the regional innovation system, in particular for the creation of advanced enterprises.

The dependence on structuring partnerships in the context of European cooperation programmes was a distinguishing factor from other national offices, including even the leadership of a project focused on knowledge transfer in the maritime clusters. In January 2010, with the changes introduced by the creation of new Statutes of the University to respond to the new legal framework of higher education institutions, UAlg absorbed the KTO into its functional structure. CRIA was then established as a formal division of the University, the Division of Entrepreneurship and Technology Transfer, inside the UAIC - Support Unit of the Scientific Research and Postgraduate Training.

*Figure 2. The Organization of Knowledge Transfer in the KTO*
Source: Pinto (2012)

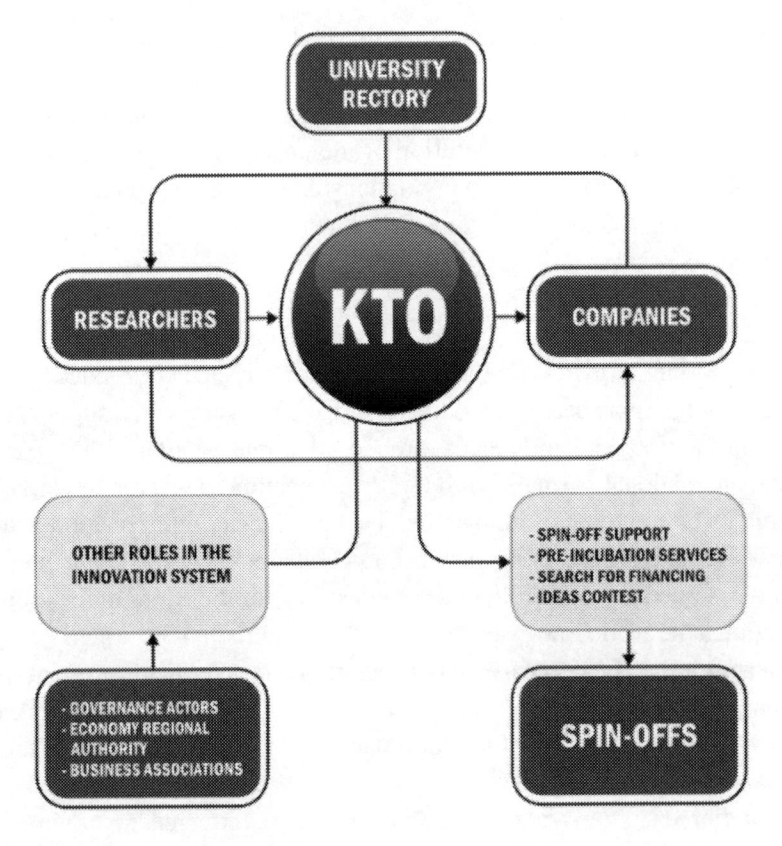

## TENSION IN UNIVERSITY-FIRM RELATIONS: PERCEPTIONS FROM THE BOUNDARY AREA

### Methodological Notes

The literature review allows, at this point, the emphasis of two central aspects: i) the transfer of knowledge between universities and companies is a central process in the dynamics of innovation, and ii) the contact between collectives is made more effective by 'marginal individuals', which facilitates the translation process.

The innovative profile of the Algarve, synthetically presented in the previous section, showed contrasts between the collectives of thought of the thirty-year-old university and the regional firms based on tourism-related activities and often characterized by the low intensity of scientific knowledge and limited value added. Thus, this case can be considered a 'strategic research site' (Merton, 1987). The 'strategic research materials' are places, objects, or events which present the phenomena to be explained or interpreted with such an advantage and in an affordable way that allows the research to understand problems previously inaccessible. It is assumed that the characteristics of the regional structure of the Algarve provide clear evidence of the tensions between academia and enterprise. This section frames a applied empirical study, seeking to understand the problems that emanate directly from reality and proposing concrete action (Fernández-Esquinas, 2006). The empirical study seeks to highlight the importance of approaches grounded in STS to understand the transfer of knowledge. The analysis discusses two critical issues. The first is whether the differences between entrepreneurs and researchers shape different collectives of thought in Fleck's perspective. The second question refers to the findings of the importance of 'marginal individuals'. For this, the section presents the vision of these groups about the KTOs. To analyze these issues there were different moments for gathering information, based on formal attempts of the UAlg, to create a stable platform between both groups to increase the effectiveness of transfer.

The first moment of data collection was through participant observation in Faro in June 2007 at a workshop on financing opportunities for SMEs in R&D, which sought the creation of consortium research projects. This event brought together about one hundred and twenty people, of whom about two-thirds came from the business world.

In December 2007, the University organized the INOVA 2007 - Exhibition and Conference on Innovation and Technology Transfer in the Algarve. This event tried to address issues related to creating a more favourable environment for innovation. The special session of agro-food technologies was the second moment of collecting information through observation. The event involved a moment of extended exchange of ideas and multilateral meetings, which sought to strengthen personal contacts and informal knowledge creation to facilitate an understanding of the convergent interests of the participants.

Finally, one final moment for data collection was a work session on the connection between the university and companies in the region, inserted in the meetings of the Institute for Competitiveness Support to Small and Medium Enterprises and Innovation (IAPMEI), held in Faro in December 2009. This event brought together twenty-seven participants, nineteen companies and even more facilitators (researchers and technicians from the University, as well as representatives of relevant agencies in the region). The organizers prepared a report with the main results (IAPMEI, 2009). There were three working groups, one of which focused explicitly on "Strategies for Leveraging Technology and Knowledge Transfer for Companies". A focus group methodology was employed with two moderators, one of whom was the author of this chapter, essentially looking to confirm the problems of the university-firm identified above, highlighting critical factors of these problems and making proposals to overcome them. The results were eminently confirmatory of previous collection moments.

## Dimensions of Tension between Collectives of Thought

The analysis shows the misaligned positions and allows the highlighting of central topics to the relationship of the business world and academia. Based on the notes taken at these meetings, it was possible to systematize the positions on some issues for both groups. The empirical analysis carried out allows the emphasizing of four main dimensions of tension between entrepreneurs and researchers with contrasting styles of thought.

## University-Firm Relations

There is a general mistrust between the two collectives. Entrepreneurs think that researchers approach companies only when they do not have resources to fund their research. In the context of economic downturn, the constantly repeated statement is that the approach of the universities to the business world is due only to the precarious financial situation of public scientific research in Portugal, in particular with universities, something that seems to be a small part of what actually occurs. On the contrary, however, researchers find that when their research arouses interest in business, it is because its value is clearly superior to what the company is offering to pay to fund R&D. Often, speculatively, their activities become more expensive, leading to shrinkage of the initial private interest.

It was noted that the university often promotes research that the local firms or market do not demand. There is a gap between what researchers want to investigate and what companies actually need. According to the general opinion of the participants in the focus group, this gap between what is sought by companies and the provision of advanced services was usually related to a lower sophistication of companies, which originated the lack of interest by the university in conducting research to the regional business fabric. On the other hand, many researchers believe that focusing research on the needs of companies does not allow them to engage in scientific production of an excellence level required on international terms, the main criteria of their current assessment exercises. Universities also have few channels to detect what firms need. An improvement of enterprises' capacities can come through collaborative projects with the university, in particular applied research that may favour the creation and definition of strategic innovation. The university should strengthen itself organizationally for a professionalized and consistent approach to knowledge transfer.

However, both groups consider it important to boost university-firm relations, as there are very positive aspects that can result from this. Companies referred mainly to their ability to access the expertise, infrastructure and equipment to which they would otherwise not have access. This allows them to participate in interesting projects for their productive activity, enabling them to have an image in the market of innovation and differentiating them from their competitors, obtaining competitive advantages. The aspect most highlighted by the researchers was that collaboration with companies helps to approach the empirical reality, giving them a greater capacity to understand basic science, discovering clues and directions for research, and enabling the entry of additional financial resources which can be directed towards new research.

Even with the accumulated knowledge and the geographical proximity of the university with companies, a limited threshold of protocols and partnerships between research units and companies continues to exist. The criticisms from researchers and entrepreneurs supported by intermediary organizations, such as KTOs, are weaker. Usually, those who obtain support from these entities are members of overlapping areas from each of the groups, with interest in working together. This frequently occurs in repeated cooperation, and these experiences can gradually generate trust and social capital throughout the collectives of the organizations. Both researchers and firms showed appreciation of the existence of an intermediate body. Value is placed on the emergence of a new actor focused not on specific objectives for any of the collectives but on targets linked with the success of the interconnection between the two groups.

## The Role of Science

There are doubts about the relationship between the 'academic science' and the activities of the 'academic enterprise'. Starting with the academic world, there is no consensus about the definition and role of science in society. Professors have difficulty realizing what is required from them in adapting education, particularly the first cycle of Bologna (undergraduate level), with the basic research activities that they must perform. Professors, when involved in projects, are often burdened with administrative and financial issues that affect time availability, eliminating the possibility of knowledge being applied in tasks that were more important. The university is fractured. On the one hand, some argue that the importance of research and 'academic science' is the main mission of the university and the basis and reference for all the knowledge either applied or not applied. On the other hand, many argue that science has to approach the problems of empirical reality by engaging with companies and that the study of "transcendent" phenomena should not monopolize the time of researchers.

The first group sees applied research as a distortion of the role of 'academic science' in which disinterest is necessary, while the latter thinks that science only moves forward with its application and only makes sense when generating economic and social returns. For the latter, the test in applied fields allows access to more robust responses, confrontation of theoretical models with empirical reality, finding errors in the theories formulated or new problems that require new solutions. These extreme views of science are in agreement with the proposal of Lam (2010). In the view of entrepreneurs, the role of science is "to advance knowledge". However, there are major questions about the behaviour of scientists. Entrepreneurs do not understand the reason why researchers have so much freedom at work. Many entrepreneurs pointed out that this flexibility generated no need to deliver results. In parallel, even those who were presenting results produced it in a form that was not understandable to laymen, usually as scientific articles with no effort of translation to the public understanding. Entrepreneurs do not understand why researchers travel so much, why they go to conferences, seminars and workshops, why they give lessons at other universities and why they remain different lengths of time in R&D centers abroad. The 'academic science' is viewed with great suspicion, because it often "serves no purpose". They consider that research should be more focused on the problems that exist in firms' day-to-day life and the search to overcome these issues. Some entrepreneurs consider themselves the human component that creates value in society, revealing a suspicion for members of the academy who are characterized with a more passive behavior.

## Profit, Times, and Deadlines

Profit from research activities remains difficult to understand for some members in the academy. Even if a steady change seems to be occurring, professors that engage in entrepreneurial projects, applied R&D and consulting remain easy targets of criticism from their peers. This criticism regards the provision of services, in which the analysis is oriented to the conclusions that the contracting entity wants to reach. Professors allocated to research can be accused of forgetting their teaching responsibilities and focusing on their "private" business. This was previously enhanced by the absence of reference frameworks in Portugal, and in Europe in general, something that begins to be limited with the creation of internal regulations for external services, intellectual property rights (IPR) codes of conduct, and guidelines for the creation of spin-offs and start-ups.

Entrepreneurs have a focus on profit; however, it is too often focused on a short-term profit, limiting horizons and the dynamics of creating added value. A businesswoman quoted Milton Friedman ["The Social Responsibility of Business is to Increase its Profits" by Milton Friedman in The New York Times Magazine, September 13, 1970], stressing that corporate social responsibility is only about making profit, paying wages to workers and fulfilling commitments to suppliers. She was giving less relevance to the role of the company in contributing to qualified employment and sustainable economic growth at an aggregate level.

Another problem mentioned by entrepreneurs about researchers is that their response time is often considered too long. In parallel, researchers suggest that entrepreneurs who have an immediate interest are much less concerned with the overall validation of the results of research. Researchers believe to be focused on the positive understanding, gradually permitting the building of economic advantages to be appropriated by the company. According to the information from the firms, in addition to the researchers' difficulties in meeting deadlines, the functioning of the university and other public research organizations presents itself with a very high amount of negative bureaucracy, which slows and threatens all collaborative processes.

## Human Resources Training

The essential role of the university remains the training of human resources. This is a central channel for transferring knowledge because the inclusion of qualified personnel improves not only the competitiveness of the company, in particular in SMEs, but also its 'absorption capacity' of new knowledge. Furthermore, in the opinion of the participants, the fact that a company employs former university students creates a cognitive proximity that induces additional contacts with the research. Many collaborative relationships are based on these previous, informal contacts.

However, participants on the business side stressed that the university does not train students for specific regional companies limiting their preparation for working life. The lack of students for the business fabric of the region remains high. The insertion of students is limited, despite being an essential mechanism for the increased absorption capacity in companies, restricting the existence of qualified people who can interact with advanced knowledge.

The university as a source of recruitment continues to fail, missing the connection paths with business. The creation of mechanisms to support student recruitment and entry into employment is important, emphasizing the relevance of professional internships, extinguished at undergraduate level with the implementation of the Bologna process. The link between employability and knowledge transfer mechanisms should be a target for additional attention.

## SOLUTIONS AND RECOMMENDATIONS

Overcoming these dimensions of tension requires some action such as the examples that the group suggested. University-firm relations need a more effective dissemination of the knowledge supply and existing technology and a deeper understanding of business needs. Researchers should be encouraged to establish agreements and partnerships between the university, research centers and skills and the local business.

Within the university, it is crucial to set up offices or cells within each school and/or faculty to assess the knowledge developed and related business demand. This can be very useful for identifying companies' skills to stimulate the sophistication of their strategies, in particular innovative activities, thereby enhancing competitiveness. Regularly translating scientific research developed and published in specialty magazines for non-expert audiences is fundamental in order for knowledge to be detected by the entrepreneurial system and seized by citizens in general. The successful communication of science can have positive impacts on the absorption capacity of individuals and firms, in particular SMEs.

To promote the university as a source of recruitment, an emphasis should be placed on the technical component, which has been more sought by companies with greater connection to practice. Another aspect is to focus on a greater involvement of firms in education pathways, participation in training events, internships for students and re-structuring of curricula.

Unanimously, there is a required action for organizational strengthening within the university regarding the transfer of knowledge. It is very important to develop regulations and standards for creating relationships with start-ups and academic spin-offs, for the adaptation to the teaching service of these activities, for the new role of the university and for the protection, management and licensing of IPRs. In parallel, the autonomy and professionalism of knowledge transfer services must be guaranteed. According to the vision of the participants and with the support of the university, particularly in the financial aspect, the KTOs should be free of project perspectives, stabilizing and qualifying their staff to ensure higher decisional autonomy. The office should institutionalize its activities. This issue conditions all the success of the new role of the university in the perspective of participants.

Finally, KTOs, as mediators that focus both collectives, must contain elements in their staff who can understand different styles of thought, specifically the university and the firm, in order to facilitate an effective translation. Members of staff of these intermediate bodies require increasingly new types of entrepreneurial skills and a mix of business people from the academy with a new type of researcher. These individuals need to maintain a quasi-firm activity based on highly competitive R&D and should be more concerned with the issues of transfer while being able to translate their own interests.

## FUTURE RESEARCH DIRECTIONS

Knowledge transfer and university-firm interactions are important topics to be studied by future research. Management, Economics, Sociology and a variety of social sciences will be interested in looking to these phenomena as scientific knowledge increases its contribution to the generation of innovation and the creation of competitive advantage in firms.

Knowledge management initiatives within firms need to pay attention to cooperation and the linkages to external actors, such as universities and other public research organizations, which are important sources of information. The crucial knowledge for the production is becoming more dispersed, and firms need to create the tools that facilitate its capture in external environments. Stabilizing a strong innovation network, with diverse and solid relations with the research system is an opportunity for firms to absorb new knowledge and improve products and processes. For SMEs the challenge is even bigger as they are limited by resources, physical and financial, to develop the necessary R&D efforts to be innovative. In this way, universities may play a crucial role to SMEs by providing knowledge intensive services that are not available in the market at an affordable price to more fragile companies.

From the current chapter three future research opportunities can be suggested: the study of organizational cultures in different types of innovation actors; the functioning of intermediary organizations in the creation of bridges between collectives of thought, and the tools to improve communication between different types of actors, with emphasis in the specific constraints that SMEs face to obtain and manage knowledge. We suggest that studies in this subject should use theoretical-methodological models that are able to both understand the explicit dimensions that are easily quantifiable, as knowledge transfer results, patents, spin-offs, and those dimensions that are incommensurable and are qualitative in nature, such as the organizational culture or the style of thought. In this way it seems reasonable that empirical studies on knowledge transfer and university-firm interactions begin to use more regularly methodological approaches mixing quantitative and qualitative traditions.

## CONCLUSION

Knowledge transfer and university-firm interactions have had the attention of decision makers in stimulating regional development on different scales of intervention, from the regional strategies to the European Policy. This chapter underlined that the transfer of knowledge deserves a closer look from other approaches. The contributions from the STS can be crucial to understand what goes on inside these 'black boxes' that we have come to see just like indicators and, increasingly, as goals: a created new product, a new technology-based company, a licensed patent, or a collaborative research project. It is crucial to understand what happens until the transfer goes ahead. It is this attempt to realize the transfer process, the role of the actors and the structure of the networks that may be enriched by the contributions of the STS to create more satisfactory knowledge about what conditions enhance a successful, university-firm relationship.

The discussion highlighted the contributions of Fleck to the understanding of the current context of the scientific world where the production, dissemination and transfer of knowledge encompasses a broad range of actors. These actors belong to distinct collectives of thought characterized by specific styles, as proved to be the case for individuals from academia and the business world. The transfer of knowledge requires an effective translation between these collectives that is neither easy nor free from lapses.

The empirical analysis of the Algarve in Portugal helped to emphasize the importance of 'marginal individuals' in the contact, migration and cross-fertilization of concepts between collectives of thought and reinforced the role that interface organizations assume as mediators in the process of knowledge transfer. Tensions illustrated with the styles of thought, of the firm and the university, tend to be overcome with the emergence of hybrid actors, 'marginal' in the designing of Fleck, who can talk with the various groups.

## REFERENCES

Algarve, C. C. D. R. (2006). *Estratégia de Desenvolvimento Regional 2007-13 Algarve*. Faro: Comissão de Coordenação e Desenvolvimento Regional do Algarve.

Algarve, C. C. D. R. (2014). *Estratégia de Especialização Inteligente RIS3 Algarve*. Faro: Comissão de Coordenação e Desenvolvimento Regional do Algarve.

Amsterdamska, O., Bonah, C., Borck, C., Fehr, J., Hagner, M., Klingberg, M., & Zittel, C. et al. (2008). Medical Science in the Light of a Flawed Study of the Holocaust: A Comment on Eva Hedfors' Paper on Ludwik Fleck. *Social Studies of Science*, *38*(6), 937–944. doi:10.1177/0306312708098609

Barreira, A. P. (2009). The Regional Profile of Algarve in Innovation, *Spatial and Organizational Dynamics Discussion Papers*, CIEO-Research Centre for Spatial and Organizational Dynamics. *University of Algarve*, *0*, 58–75.

Bercovitz, J., & Feldman, M. (2005). Entrepreneurial Universities and Technology Transfer: A Conceptual Framework for Understanding Knowledge-Based Economic Development. *The Journal of Technology Transfer*, *31*(1), 175–188. doi:10.1007/s10961-005-5029-z

Bergman, E. (2010). Knowledge links between European universities and firms: A review. *Papers in Regional Science*, *89*(2), 311–334. doi:10.1111/j.1435-5957.2010.00310.x

Berman, E. P. (2008). Why Did Universities Start Patenting? Institution-Building and the Road to the Bayh-Dole Act. *Social Studies of Science*, *38*(6), 835–871. doi:10.1177/0306312708098605 PMID:19227798

Bok, D. (2003). *Universities in the Marketplace – The commercialization of Higher Education*. Princeton University Press.

Bozeman, B. (2000). Technology transfer and public policy: A review of research and theory. *Research Policy*, *29*(4-5), 627–655. doi:10.1016/S0048-7333(99)00093-1

Büschgens, T., Bausch, A., & Balkin, D. B. (2013). Organizational Culture and Innovation: A Meta-Analytic Review. *Journal of Product Innovation Management*, *30*(4), 763–781. doi:10.1111/jpim.12021

Callon, M. (1999). Some Elements of a Sociology of Translation. In M. Biagiolli (Ed.), *The Science Studies Reader* (pp. 67–83). New York: Routledge.

Colyvas, J., & Powell, W. (2006). Roads to Institutionalization: The Remaking of Boundaries between Public and Private Science. *Research in Organizational Behavior*, *27*, 305–353. doi:10.1016/S0191-3085(06)27008-4

Cooke, P. (1998). Introduction: Origins of the Concept. In H.-J. Braczyc, P. Cooke, & M. Heideinrech (Eds.), *Regional Innovation Systems* (pp. 2–27). London: UCL Press.

Corcuff, P. (2001). *As Novas Sociologias (2nd ed.)*. Sintra: Editora Vral.

Cruz, A. R. (2006). *Redes de Investigação: A Relação da Universidade do Algarve com Organismos Nacionais, Europeus e Internacionais*. Faro: Universidade do Algarve.

D'Este, P., & Patel, P. (2007). University-industry linkages in the UK: What are the factors underlying the variety of interactions with industry? *Research Policy*, *36*(9), 1295–1313. doi:10.1016/j.respol.2007.05.002

Debackere, K., & Veugelers, R. (2005). The role of academic transfer organizations in improving industry science links. *Research Policy*, *34*(3), 321–342. doi:10.1016/j.respol.2004.12.003

Estanque, E., & Nunes, J. A. (2003). Dilemas e desafios da Universidade: Recomposição social e expectativas dos estudantes na Universidade de Coimbra. *Revista Critica de Ciencias Sociais*, *66*(66), 5–44. doi:10.4000/rccs.1139

Etzkowitz, H., & Leydesdorff, L. (1997). *Universities and the Global Knowledge Economy – A Triple Helix of University-Industry-Government Relations*. Londres: Continuum.

Fernández-Esquinas, M. (2006). La sociologia aplicada. *Revista Espanola de Investigaciones Sociologicas*, *115*(115), 11–40. doi:10.2307/40184765

Fleck, L. (1979). *Genesis and Development of a Scientific Fact*. Chicago: Chicago University Press. (Original work published 1935)

Fleck, L. (1986). The Problem of Epistemology. In R. S. Cohen & T. Schnelle (Eds.), *Cognition and Fact* (pp. 79–112). Dordrecht: Reitel Publishing Company. (Original work published 1936) doi:10.1007/978-94-009-4498-5_5

Galison, P., & Stump, D. J. (1996). *The Disunity of Science: Boundaries, Contexts, and Power*. Stanford, CA: Stanford University Press.

Gibbons, M., Limoges, C., Nowotny, H., Schwartzman, S., Scott, P., & Trow, M. (1994). *The New Production of Knowledge: The Dynamics of Science and Research in Contemporary Societies*. Londres: Sage.

Gieryn, T. (1983). Boundary work and the Demarcation of Science from Non-science: Strains and Interests in Professional Ideologies of Scientists. *American Sociological Review*, *48*(6), 781–795. doi:10.2307/2095325

Guerreiro, J. (2008). *Caracterização da Estrutura Económica do Algarve*. Loulé: NERA.

Guston, D. H. (1999). Stabilizing the Boundary Between US Politics and Science: The Rôle of the Office of Technology Transfer as a Boundary Organization. *Social Studies of Science*, *29*(1), 87–111. doi:10.1177/030631299029001004 PMID:11623653

Hedfords, E. (2007). Fleck in Context. *Perspectives on Sciences*, *15*(1).

Hedfors, E. (2006). *Reading Fleck: Questions on Philosophy and Science*. (PhD Dissertation). KTH, Stockholm, Sweden.

Hedfors, E. (2008). Medical Science in the Light of Holocaust: Departing from a Postwar Paper by Ludwik Fleck. *Social Studies of Science*, *38*(2), 259–283. doi:10.1177/0306312707082953 PMID:18831133

IAPMEI. (2009). *1ª Sessão de Trabalho entre a Universidade do Algarve e as Empresas da Região*. Retrieved from www.cria.pt

Jaffe, A. B., & Lerner, J. (2004). *Innovation and Its Discontents: How Our Broken Patent System Is Endangering Innovation and Progress, and What to Do about It*. Princeton, NJ: Princeton University Press.

Kuhn, T. S. (1962). *The Structure of Scientific Revolutions*. Chicago: The University of Chicago Press.

Lam, A. (2010). From 'Ivory Tower Traditionalists' to 'entrepreneurial Scientists'?: Academic Scientists in Fuzzy University-Industry Boundaries. *Social Studies of Science*, *40*(2), 307–340. doi:10.1177/0306312709349963

Larsen, M. T. (2011). The implications of academic enterprise for public science: An overview of the empirical evidence. *Research Policy*, *40*(1), 6–19. doi:10.1016/j.respol.2010.09.013

Latour, B. (1986). Visualization and Cognition: Thinking with Eyes and Hands. *Knowledge in Society*, *6*, 1–40.

Latour, B. (2005). *Reassembling the Social: An Introduction to Actor-Network-Theory*. New York: Oxford University Press.

Latour, B., & Woolgar, S. (1979). *Laboratory Life: the Social Construction of Scientific Facts*. Los Angeles, CA: EUA.

Löwy, I. (1994). Ludwik Fleck e a Presente História das Ciências. *Manguinhos, I*(1), 7–18. PMID:11624967

Lundvall, B. A. (2007). National Innovation Systems – Analytical Concept and Development Tool. *Industry and Innovation, 14*(1), 95–119. doi:10.1080/13662710601130863

McMaster, T., Vidgen, R. T., & Wastell, D. G. (1997). Technology Transfer: Diffusion or Translation? In T. McMaster et al. (Eds.), *Facilitating Technology Transfer through Partnership*. London: Chapman & Hall. doi:10.1007/978-0-387-35092-9_4

Merton, R. K. (1987). Three Fragments from a Sociologist's Notebook: Establishing the Phenomenon, Specified Ignorance and Strategic Research Materials. *Annual Review of Sociology, 13*(1), 1–28. doi:10.1146/annurev.so.13.080187.000245

Molas-Gallart, J., Salter, A., Patel, P., Scott, A., & Duran, X. (2002). *Measuring Third Stream Activities: Final Report to the Russell Group of Universities*. Science and Technology Policy Research Unit, University of Sussex.

Nelson, R. (2004). The market economy, and the scientific commons. *Research Policy, 33*(3), 455–471. doi:10.1016/j.respol.2003.09.008

Nunes, J. A. (2007). *Discurso(s) sobre as Ciência(s) e as Tecnologia(s). Presentation of the Doctoral Programme in "Governação, Conhecimento e Inovação"*. Centro de Estudos Sociais, Faculdade de Economia da Universidade de Coimbra.

Oliveira, L. (2008). *Sociologia da Inovação – A Construção Social das Técnicas e dos Mercados*. Oeiras: Celta Editora.

Packer, K., & Webster, A. (1996). Patenting Culture in Science: Reinventing the Scientific Wheel of Credibility. *Science, Technology & Human Values, 21*(4), 427–453. doi:10.1177/016224399602100403

Pavitt, K. (2001). Public Policies to Support Basic Research: What Can the Rest of the World Learn from US Theory and Practice? (And What They Should Not Learn). *Industrial and Corporate Change, 10*(3), 761–779. doi:10.1093/icc/10.3.761

Pfuetzenreiter, M. R. (2003). *Epistemologia de Ludwik Fleck como Referencial para a Pesquisa nas Ciências Aplicadas*. Porto Alegre: Episteme.

Pinto, H. (2009). Challenges for Innovation in the Algarve: contributions to understand the regional innovation system, Spatial and Organizational Dynamics Discussion 2009-00. CIEO-Research Centre for Spatial and Organizational Dynamics, University of Algarve.

Pinto, H. (2012). *Transferência do conhecimento em Portugal. Mudança e institucionalização das relações universidade-empresa*. (Doctoral Thesis). Faculdade de Economia da Universidade de Coimbra.

Pinto, H., Cruz, A. R., & Almeida, H. (2015). Academic Entrepreneurship and Knowledge Transfer Networks: Translation Process and Boundary Organizations. In L. Carvalho (Ed.), *Handbook of Research on Entrepreneurial Success and its Impact on Regional Development*. Hershey, PA: IGI Global.

Pinto, H., & Guerreiro, J. (2010). Innovation regional planning and latent dimensions: The case of the Algarve region. *The Annals of Regional Science, 44*(2), 315–329. doi:10.1007/s00168-008-0264-5

Pinto, H., Guerreiro, J., & Uyarra, E. (2012). Diversidades de Sistemas de Inovação e Implicações nas Políticas Regionais: Comparação das Regiões do Algarve e da Andaluzia. *Revista Portuguesa de Estudos Regionais, 29*, 3–14.

Rochel de Camargo, K. J. (2002). The Thought Style of Physicians: Strategies for Keeping up with Medical Knowledge. *Social Studies of Science, 32*(5-6), 827–855. doi:10.1177/030631270203200501

Santos, B. S. (2008). *A universidade no século XXI: Para uma universidade nova.* Coimbra: Edições Almedina.

Shapin, S. (2008). *The Scientific Life: A Moral History of a Late Modern Vocation.* Chicago: The University of Chicago Press. doi:10.7208/chicago/9780226750170.001.0001

Siegel, D. S., Waldman, D., & Link, A. (2003). Assessing the impact of organizational practices on the relative productivity of university technology transfer offices: An exploratory study. *Research Policy, 32*(1), 27–48. doi:10.1016/S0048-7333(01)00196-2

Sousa Lobo, L. (2005). *Publicações Internacionais.* Ranking das Universidades Portuguesas.

Star, S. L. (1989). The structure of ill-structured solutions: boundary objects and heterogeneous distributed problem solving. In Distributed artificial intelligence. Pitman.

UAlg. (2007a). *Plano Regional de Inovação do Algarve.* Faro: Universidade do Algarve.

UAlg. (2007b). *Horizonte 2010, Princípios Estratégicos para a Universidade do Algarve.* Faro: Universidade do Algarve.

## KEY TERMS AND DEFINITIONS

**Academic Enterprise:** The efforts generated by academic actors, in particular universities and other public research organizations, in pursuing the economic valorization of academic science, with commercialization of research, research contracts, licensing intellectual property, or creating new knowledge spin-offs.

**Academic Science:** The efforts generated by academic actors, in particular universities and other public research organizations, in pursuing the generation of new knowledge with basic and applied research.

**Actor-Network-Theory:** A methodological framework from the STS that pays attention to the associations and interactions among different types of actors in the creation of common goals. The actors translate their interests into others stabilizing a network with a common purpose.

**Boundary Object:** An object that facilitates the interaction between different social worlds, such as science and business, by creating intermediary platforms that facilitate the translation of vocabularies, cultures and interests of diverse types of actors and create points of contact between them.

**Collective of Thought:** A specific group of individuals that shares the same style of thought. Communication among different collectives requires additional efforts of translation and mediation.

**Knowledge Transfer:** A process of transfer of knowledge between two actors, one recipient and one absorber. Often it regards the transfer of knowledge from academic science to firms. It is commonly associated with a formal dimension, embodied in patents, protocols, contracts, but has an informal dimension, that is very important to the effectiveness and long term success of the collaborations.

**Knowledge Transfer Office:** An intermediary organization that is focused in the transfer of knowledge. They are especially prominent has a tool in the public research system to transfer research results to the economic fabric. Today the majority of universities has developed dedicated KTOs.

**Marginal Individual:** A person or organization that lies between two or more collectives of thought. This means that this marginal individual has a style of thought that is a hybrid and in this way is able to function as a translator to different collectives.

**Mode 2:** The emergent knowledge production model in the 21st century where the crucial role is not limited to academic science but transversally distributed to a variety of actors and types of knowledge.

**Style of Thought:** Socialization forms the cognitive maps for individuals to understand and interact with the real world. The socialization processes involve a variety of domains, including scientific specialization or professional areas, generating diversity of styles of thought. When individuals share the same style of thought they create a collective of thought where their communication and interaction is facilitated by trust and mutual understanding.

**Third Mission:** The role of universities is not limited to human capital training and to knowledge production. The third mission refers to the efforts of universities to transfer results of Education and Research to the economic dynamics and regional environment.

**Triple Helix:** The innovation dynamics depends on the collective efforts of three different institutional spheres with growing overlapping areas: industry, university and government. Currently, a quadruple helix is suggested, incorporating the relevance of users and beneficiaries in the generation of innovation.

## ENDNOTE

[1]    The research presented in this chapter benefited from the support of FCT – Portuguese Foundation for Science and Technology (SFRH/BD/35887/2007) financed by POPH - NSRF - Type 4.1 - Advanced Training, subsidized by the European Social Fund and national funds of Ministry of Science, Higher Education and Technology. Currently the author benefits from a post-doctoral grant from the same source (SFRH/BPD/84038/2012). A preliminary version of this article was published in the CIEO discussion papers (working paper series).

382

# Compilation of References

Aba, D. (2015). Towards an intercultural communication competence tool for academic mobility purposes. *Journal of International Communication, 39*. Retrieved March 5, 2016, from http://www.immi.se/intercultural/nr39/aba.html

Abel, M. H. (2015). Knowledge map-based web platform to facilitate organizational learning return of experiences. *Computers in Human Behavior, 51*, 960–966. doi:10.1016/j.chb.2014.10.012

Abzari, M., Shahin, A., & Abasaltian, A. (2014). Developing A Conceptual Framework For Knowledge Sharing Behavior By Considering Emotional, Social And Cognitive Intelligence Competencies. *Arabian Journal of Business and Management Review, 4*(1).

Ackoff, R. L. (1997). Transformational consulting. *Management Consulting Times, 28*(6).

Adair, W. L., Tinsley, C. H., & Taylor, M. (2006). Managing the Intercultural Interface: Third Cultures, Antecedents, and Consequences. In Y.-R. Chen (Ed.), *National Culture and Groups (Research on Managing Groups and Teams)* (pp. 205–232). Bingley: Emerald Group Publishing Limited. doi:10.1016/S1534-0856(06)09009-8

Adler, N. J., & Gundersen, A. (2008). *International dimensions of organizational behavior.* Mason, OH: Thomson Higher Education.

Agarwal, N., & Brem, A. (2012). Frugal and reverse innovation - Literature overview and case study insights from a German MNC in India and China. In *Proceedings of Engineering, Technology and Innovation (ICE),18th International ICE Conference.* Munich, Germany: IEEE.

Aidemark, J. E. (2009). Knowledge Management Paradoxes. *Electronic Journal of Knowledge Management, 7*(1), 1–10.

Aizpurúa, L. I., Saldaña, P. E. Z., & Saldaña, A. Z. (2011). Learning for sharing: An empirical analysis of organizational learning and knowledge sharing. *The International Entrepreneurship and Management Journal, 7*(4), 509–518. doi:10.1007/s11365-011-0206-z

Akerman, N. (2014). An international learning typology: Strategies and outcomes for internationalizing firms. *Baltic Journal of Management, 9*(4), 382–402. doi:10.1108/BJM-12-2013-0176

Alavi, M., & Leidner, D. E. (1999). Knowledge management systems: Issues, challenges, and benefits. *Communications of the AIS, 1*(2es), 1.

Alavi, M., & Leidner, D. E. (2001). Review: Knowledge management and knowledge management systems: Conceptual foundations and research issues. *Management Information Systems Quarterly, 25*(1), 107–136. doi:10.2307/3250961

Alegre, J., & Chiva, R. (2013). Linking entrepreneurial orientation and firm performance: The role of organizational learning capability and innovation performance. *Journal of Small Business Management, 51*(4), 491–507. doi:10.1111/jsbm.12005

Algarve, C. C. D. R. (2006). *Estratégia de Desenvolvimento Regional 2007-13 Algarve*. Faro: Comissão de Coordenação e Desenvolvimento Regional do Algarve.

Algarve, C. C. D. R. (2014). *Estratégia de Especialização Inteligente RIS3 Algarve*. Faro: Comissão de Coordenação e Desenvolvimento Regional do Algarve.

Al-Rawas, A., & Easterbrook, S. (1996). Communication problems in requirements engineering: A field study. In *Proceedings of the First Westminster Conference on Professional Awareness in Software Engineering*.

Ambrosini, V., & Bowman, C. (2001). Tacit knowledge: Some suggestions for operationalization. *Journal of Management Studies*, *38*(6), 811–829. doi:10.1111/1467-6486.00260

Amoako-Gyampah, K., & Salam, A. F. (2004). An extension of the technology acceptance model in an ERP implementation environment. *Information & Management*, *41*(6), 731–745. doi:10.1016/j.im.2003.08.010

Amsterdamska, O., Bonah, C., Borck, C., Fehr, J., Hagner, M., Klingberg, M., & Zittel, C. et al. (2008). Medical Science in the Light of a Flawed Study of the Holocaust: A Comment on Eva Hedfors' Paper on Ludwik Fleck. *Social Studies of Science*, *38*(6), 937–944. doi:10.1177/0306312708098609

Andersen, T. J. (2001). Information technology, strategic decision making approaches and organizational performance in different industrial settings. *Journal of Strategic Information Systems*, *10*(2), 101-119.

Anderson, C. (2010). *Free: The Future of a Radical Price*. New York, NY: Random House.

Andreeva, I., & Ikhilchik, I. (2011). Applicability of the SECI model of knowledge creation in Russian cultural context: Theoretical analysis. *Knowledge and Process Management*, *18*(1), 56–66. doi:10.1002/kpm.351

Andrejcsik, L., Bakos, N., Bocz, J., Tiborné, D., Herzog, T., Jávorszkyné Nagy, A., … Nagyné Pakula, U. (2015). Magyarország 2014. Budapest: Központi Statisztikai Hivatal.

Ang, S., & van Dyne, L. (2008). *Handbook of cultural intelligence*. New York: ME Sharpe.

Anklam, P. (2002). Knowledge Management. The Collaboration Thread. *Bulletin of the American Society for Information Science and Technology*, *28*(6), 8–11. doi:10.1002/bult.254

Antheaume, N., Barbelivien, D., & Paulette, R. (2012). French Family Business and Longevity. Have they been conducting sustainable development policies before it became a fashion? *Business History*, *2013*(September).

Antonelli, D., Bruno, G., Schwichtenberg, A., & Villa, A. (2013). Full exploitation of Product Lifecycle Management by integrating static and dynamic viewpoints. In *Advances in Production Management Systems. Competitive Manufacturing for Innovative Products and Services*, (pp. 176-183). Springer Berlin Heidelberg.

Antonova, A., & Gourova, E. (2009). Business Patterns for Knowledge audit implementation within SMEs. 14th EuroPLoP, Irsee, Germany.

Appadurai, A. (1996). *Modernity at Large. Cultural Dimensions of Globalization*. Minneapolis, MN: University of Minnesota Press.

Appadurai, A. (1998). *Modernity at Large: Cultural Dimensions of Globalization*. Minneapolis, MN: University of Minnesota Press.

Aragón, M. I. B., Jiménez, D. J., & Valle, R. S. (2014). Training and performance: The mediating role of organizational learning. *BRQ Business Research Quarterly*, *17*(3), 161–173. doi:10.1016/j.cede.2013.05.003

Arakelian, A., Maymand, M. M., & Hosseini, M. H. (2013). Study of the relationship between Emotional Intelligence (EI) and Knowledge Sharing (KS). *European Journal of Business and Management, 5*(32), 203–216.

Archibugi, D., & Michie, J. (Eds.). (1997). *Technology, Globalisation and Economic Performance*. Cambridge, UK: Cambridge University Press.

Argote, L., & Ingram, P. (2000). Knowledge Transfer: A Basis for Competitive Advantage in Firms. *Organizational Behavior and Human Decision Processes, 82*(1), 150–169. doi:10.1006/obhd.2000.2893

Argyris, C., & Schön, D. A. (1978). *Organizational Learning, A Theory of Action Perspective*. Boston: Addison-Westley.

Argyris, C., & Schön, D. A. (1996). *Organisational learning II: Theory, method and practice*. Reading, MA: Addison–Wesley.

Arogundade, D. M. (2011). Mentoring and Leadership Succession in Industries and Organizations. *Academic Journal IFE Psychologia*, (Supplement), 180–187.

Arogundade, O. (2011). Mentoring and leadership succesion in industries and organizations. *IFE PsychlogIA*, (Supplement), 180–187.

Arundel, A., Colecchia, A., & Wyckoff, A. (2006). Rethinking science and technology indicators for innovation policy in the 21st century. In L. Earl & F. Gault (Eds.), *Innovation and Impacts: The Next Decade* (pp. 167–198). Cheltenham: Edward Elgar.

Association of Small and Medium Companies in CR (ASMEC). (2011). *Survey results no. 10*. Retrieved from: www.amsp.cz/uploads/dokumenty/AMSP _ URPruzkum_C10.pdf

Audretsch, D., & Vivarelli, M. (1996). Firm size and R&D spillovers: Evidence from Italy. *Small Business Economics, 8*(3), 249–258. doi:10.1007/BF00388651

Aurum, A., Daneshgar, F., & Ward, J. (2008). Investigating knowledge management practices in software development organisations – An Australian experience. *Information and Software Technology, 50*(6), 511–533. doi:10.1016/j.infsof.2007.05.005

Austin, E. J., Saklofske, D. H., Huang, S. H. S., & McKenney, D. (2004). Measurement of trait emotional intelligence: Testing and cross-validating a modified version of Schutte et al.'s (1998) measure. *Personality and Individual Differences, 36*(3), 555–562. doi:10.1016/S0191-8869(03)00114-4

Avnet, M. S. (2015). A network-based approach to organizational culture and learning in system safety. *Procedia Computer Science, 44*, 588–598. doi:10.1016/j.procs.2015.03.061

Baaken, T., & Schröder, C. (2008). The Triangle for Innovation in Technology Transfer at Münster University of Applied Sciences. In K. Laine, P. van der Sijde, M. Lähdeniemi, & J. Tarkkanen (Eds.), Higher Education Institutions and Innovation in the Knowledge Society (pp. 103-116). Helsinki: ARENE ry.

Baas, L. (2007). To make zero emissions technologies and strategies become a reality, the lessons learned of cleaner production dissemination have to be known. *Journal of Cleaner Production, 15*(13/14), 1205–1216. doi:10.1016/j.jclepro.2006.07.017

Baecker, D. (1993). *Die Form des Unternehmens* [The Form of the Enterprise]. Frankfurt am Main: Suhrkamp.

Bain & Company. (2015). *Management Tools & Trends*. Retrieved from: http://www.bain.com/publications/insights/business-management-tools-andtrends.aspx

Bakacsi, G., Bokor, A., Császár, C., Gelei, A., Kováts, K., & Takács, S. (2000). *Stratégiai emberi erőforrás menedzsment*. Budapest: KJK-Kerszöv Jogi és Üzleti Kiadó Kft.

Balabanis, G., Theodosiou, M., & Katsikea, E. (2004). Export marketing: Developments and a research agenda. *International Marketing Review, 21*(4/5), 353–377. doi:10.1108/02651330410547081

Balkrishna, C. R. (2013). How disruptive is frugal? *Technology in Society, 35*(1), 65–73. doi:10.1016/j.techsoc.2013.03.003

Ballesteros, J. L., de Saá, P., & Domínguez, C. (2012). The role of organizational culture and HRM on training success: Evidence from the Canarian restaurant industry. *International Journal of Human Resource Management, 23*(15), 3225–3242. doi:10.1080/09585192.2011.637071

Banerjee, P. M. (2013). *The 'Frugal' in Frugal Innovation. Evolution of Innovation Management: Trends in an International Context*. London: Palgrave Macmillan.

Bannenberg, A.-K. (2010). *Die Bedeutung interkultureller Kommunikation in der Wirtschaft*. Kassel: Kassel University Press GmbH.

Bañón-Gomis, A. J. (2015). Ethical healthiness: A key factor in building learning organizations. In D. Palmer (Ed.), Handbook of research on business ethics and corporate responsibilities (pp. 356–372). Hershey, PA: IGI Global. doi:10.4018/978-1-4666-7476-9.ch017

Baracskai Z., & Velencei J. (2015). Smart or Wise. *Svarog, Naučno-stručni časopis, 10*(1), 29-32.

Baracskai, Z., Dörfler, V., & Velencei, J. (2007). The ES Could Probably Know More - But Man Would Not Make Better Business Decisions. VIPSI 2007, Bled, Slovenia.

Baracskai, Z., Velencei, J., & Dörfler, V. (2005). Reductive Reasoning, *Montenegrin. Journal of Economics, 1*(1), 59–66.

Baracskai, Z., Velencei, J., Dörfler, V., & Szendrey, J. (2014). The Tunnel of Doctus KBS The Deeper You Get the Darker It Is. In *Proceedings of the 2nd International OFEL Conference on Governance, Management and Entrepreneurship* (vol. 2, pp. 397-407). Dubrovnik, Croatia: Governance Research and Development Center

Barakonyi, K., & Lorange, P. (2000). *Stratégiai menedzsment*. Budapest: KJK.

Baranov, V., Zaytsev, A., & Zaytsev, A. (2011). The Lean Production Concept and Its Influence on the Market Value of a Company. *Proceedings of the 10th International Conference Liberec Economic Forum 2011*.

Barbrook, R. (1995). *Media Freedom: The Contradictions of Communication in the Age of Modernity*. Macmillan.

Barbrook, R. (2007). *Imaginary Futures: From Thinking Machines to the Global Village*. London: Pluto Press.

Barksdale, J. T., & McCrickard, D. S. (2012). Software product innovation in agile usability teams: An analytical framework of social capital, network governance, and usability knowledge management. *International Journal of Agile and Extreme Software Development, 1*(1), 52–77. doi:10.1504/IJAESD.2012.048302

Barmayer, I., & Davoine, E. (2006). Interkulturelle Zusammenarbeit und Führung in internationalen Teams: Das Beispiel Deutschland – Frankreich. *Zeitschrift Führung + Organisation, 75*(1), 35-39.

Barnes, S., & Milton, N. (2015). *Designing a Successful KM Strategy: A Guide for the Knowledge Management Professional*. Medford, NJ: Information Today Inc.

Bar-On, R. (2006). The Bar-On model of emotional-social intelligence (ESI). *Psicothema, 18*, 13-25.

Bar-On, R. (2000). Emotional and social intelligence: Insights from the Emotional Quotient Inventory. In R. Bar-On & J. D. A. Parker (Eds.), *The Handbook of Emotional Intelligence*. San Francisco: Jossey-Bass.

Barreira, A. P. (2009). The Regional Profile of Algarve in Innovation, *Spatial and Organizational Dynamics Discussion Papers*, CIEO-Research Centre for Spatial and Organizational Dynamics. *University of Algarve, 0*, 58–75.

Barrick, M. R., & Mount, M. K. (1991). The big five personality dimensions and job performance: A meta-analysis. *Personnel Psychology, 44*(1), 1–26. doi:10.1111/j.1744-6570.1991.tb00688.x

Bartes, F. (2005). Inovace v podniku. Brno: Akademické nakladatelství CERM.

Bass, B. M. (1999). Two decades of research and development in transformational leadership. *European Journal of Work and Organizational Psychology, 8*(1), 9–32. doi:10.1080/135943299398410

Basu, R., Preeta, M. B., & Sweeny, E. G. (2013). Frugal Innovation. *Core Competencies to Address Global Sustainability Journal of Management for Global Sustainability, 1*(2), 63–82. doi:10.13185/JM2013.01204

Baxter, D., Gao, J., Case, K., Harding, J., Young, B., Cochrane, S., & Dani, S. (2008). A framework to integrate design knowledge reuse and requirements management in engineering design. *Robotics and Computer-integrated Manufacturing, 24*(4), 585–593. doi:10.1016/j.rcim.2007.07.010

Baxter, D., Roy, R., Doultsinou, A., Gao, J., & Kalta, M. (2009). A knowledge management framework to support product-service systems design. *International Journal of Computer Integrated Manufacturing, 22*(12), 1073–1088. doi:10.1080/09511920903207464

Beam, M. R., Chen, C., & Greenberger, E. (2002). The nature of the relationships between adolescents and their "very important" nonparental adults. *American Journal of Community Psychology*, 305–325. doi:10.1023/A:1014641213440 PMID:12002248

Becerra-Fernandez, I., & Sabherwal, R. (2010). *Knowledge management: systems and processes*. Armonk, NY: M.E. Sharpe, Inc.

Beenen, G., & Goodman, P. S. (2014). Too little of a good thing? How organizational learning contracts can refocus B-schools on the business of learning. *The International Journal of Management Education, 12*(3), 248–259. doi:10.1016/j.ijme.2014.05.011

Bell, C. R. (2002). *Manager as mentors* (2nd ed.). San Francisco, CA: Berrettkoehler.

Bencsik, A. (2013). *Best practice a tudásmenedzsment rendszer kiépítésében*. Bungay: Longman Addison Wesley.

Bencsik, A., & Juhász, T. (2012). Chance of Success at Hungarian Small and Medium Sized Enterprises. *Problems of Management in the 21st Century, 5*, 16-30.

Bencsik, A., Boda, G., Klimkó, G, Kő, A., & Noszkay, E. (2010). Tudásmenedzsment. In Menedzsment tanácsadási kézikönyv. Budapest, Hungary: Akadémiai Kiadó.

Bencsik, A., Juhász, T., & Kovács, S. (2014). A tudásmegosztási hajlandóság aktuális kérdései, avagy jobb adni, mint kapni (empirikus vizsgálat alapján). *Alkalmazott tudományok Fóruma I. konferenciakötet*, 55-61.

Bencsik, A., Juhász, T., & Machova, R. (2014). Mentor system/practice on the behalf of knowledge sharing. *Acta Politechnica Hungarica, 11*(9), 95-114.

Bencsik, A. (2003). Csoportfejlődés és csoportszerepek érvényesülése a tanulószervezetben. *Matrix (Stuttgart, Germany), 4*, 13–27.

Bencsik, A. (2005). Dolgozói elégedettség - a szervezeti versenyképességet befolyásoló tényező. *Vezetéstudomány, 6*, 41–47.

Bencsik, A. (2009). *A tudásmenedzsment emberi oldala*. Győr: Z-Press Kiadó Kft.

Bencsik, A. (2015). *A tudásmenedzsment elméletben és gyakorlatban*. Budapest: Akadémia Kiadó.

Bencsik, A. (2015). *A tudásmenedzsment elmélete és gyakorlata*. Budapest: Akadémiai Kiadó.

Bencsik, A., & Juhász, T. (2014). *Mentori gyakorlat a magyarországi szervezeteknél*. Under publishing.

Bengoa, D. S., & Kaufmann, H. R. (2014). Questioning western knowledge transfer methodologies: Toward a reciprocal and intercultural transfer of knowledge. *Thunderbird International Business Review, 56*(1), 11–26. doi:10.1002/tie.21593

Bengtsson, L. (2004). Explaining born globals: An organisational learning perspective on the internationalisation process. *International Journal of Globalisation and Small Business, 1*(1), 28–41. doi:10.1504/IJGSB.2004.005616

Bennett, M. J. (1998). Intercultural Communication: A Current Perspective. In M. J. Bennet (Ed.), *Basic Concepts of Intercultural Communication: Selected readings* (pp. 1–34). Boston, MA: Intercultural Press.

Bennett, M. J. (2004). Becoming interculturally competent. In J. Wurzel (Ed.), *Toward multiculturalism: A reader in multicultural education* (pp. 62–77). Newton, MA: Intercultural Resource Corporation.

Bercovitz, J., & Feldman, M. (2005). Entrepreneurial Universities and Technology Transfer: A Conceptual Framework for Understanding Knowledge-Based Economic Development. *The Journal of Technology Transfer, 31*(1), 175–188. doi:10.1007/s10961-005-5029-z

Bergman, E. (2010). Knowledge links between European universities and firms: A review. *Papers in Regional Science, 89*(2), 311–334. doi:10.1111/j.1435-5957.2010.00310.x

Berman, E. P. (2008). Why Did Universities Start Patenting? Institution-Building and the Road to the Bayh-Dole Act. *Social Studies of Science, 38*(6), 835–871. doi:10.1177/0306312708098605 PMID:19227798

Bhatti, Y. A. (2012). *What is Frugal, What is Innovation? Towards a Theory of Frugal Innovation*. Retrieved May 02, 2014, from http://ssrn.com/abstract=2005910

Bierly, P. E. III, Damanpour, F., & Santoro, M. D. (2009). The application of external knowledge: Organizational conditions for exploration and exploitation. *Journal of Management Studies, 46*(3), 481–509. doi:10.1111/j.1467-6486.2009.00829.x

Birenbaum, M., Kimron, H., & Shilton, H. (2011). Nested contexts that shape assessment for learning: School-based professional learning community and classroom culture. *Studies in Educational Evaluation, 37*(1), 35–48. doi:10.1016/j.stueduc.2011.04.001

Bjørnson, F. O., & Dingsøyr, T. (2008). Knowledge management in software engineering: A systematic review of studied concepts, findings and research methods used. *Information and Software Technology, 50*(11), 1055–1068. doi:10.1016/j.infsof.2008.03.006

Blom, H., & Meier, H. (2002). *Interkulturelles Management. Interkulturelle Kommunikation, internationales Personalmanagement, Diversity-Ansätze im Unternehmen*. Herne: Verlag Neue Wirtschafts-Briefe.

Blomme, R. J. (2015). Self-organization as a perspective for organizational learning: A new role for learning practitioners. In P. Ordoñez de Pablos, L. Turró, R. Tennyson, & J. Zhao (Eds.), *Knowledge management for competitive advantage during economic crisis* (pp. 56–68). Hershey, PA: IGI Global. doi:10.4018/978-1-4666-6457-9.ch004

Bloor, R. (2003). *The Failure of Relational Database. In The Rise of Object Technology and the Need for the Hybrid Database*. Baroudi Bloor International, Inc.

Boateng, H., & Agyemang, F. G. (2015). The role of culture in knowledge sharing in a public-sector organization in Ghana: Revisiting Hofstede's model. *International Journal of Public Administration, 38*(12), 486–495. doi:10.1080/01900692.2014.949743

Boda, G. (2003). A láthatatlan tőkét is lehet és kell mérni. *Menedzsment Fórum*. Retrieved from www.mfor.hu

Boda, G. (2008). *A tudástőke mérési módszerei és használhatóságuk. CEO Magazin, 9(3)*. Appendix.

Bogáth, Á. (2013). A családi vállalkozásokban megjelenő sajátosságok. In *Vállalkozásfejlesztés a XXI. Században*. Retrieved from kgk.uni-obuda.hu/sites/default/files/13_Bogath_Agnes.pdf

Bogdány, E., Balogh, Á., & Csizmadia, T. (2015). Leadership succession and the origin of successor in Hungarian SMEs. *Mangement & Marketing, 9*(3), 283–300.

Bőgel, G. (1999). Tudásmenedzsment – a láthatatlan hatalom. *Magyar Távközlés*, 3-8.

Bőgel, G. (2005). Tudás, pénz, hatalom I.-II. *CEO, 6*(1-2), 8-15, 27-33.

Bőgel, G., & Tomka, J. (2010). Tudás és tehetség. *CEO Magazine, 11*(3), 34-35.

Bognár, T. (2013a). Crisis analytic assessment methods in interviews and assessment centers. In *Proceeding of28th Workshop on Strategic Human Resource Management*. Copenhagen, Denmark: EIASM.

Bognár, T. (2013b) Operative regression or strategic thinking – A crisis that leads to innovation or stagnation. In *Proceeding of The Economies of Balkan and Eastern Europe Countries in the changed world 2013*. Istanbul, Turkey.

Bogue, R. (2006). *Breaking down software development roles*. Retrieved from http://www.developer.com/mgmt/article.php/3490871/Cracking-the-Code-Breaking-Down-the-Software-Development-Roles.htm

Boh, W. F., Nguyen, T. T., & Xu, Y. (2013). Knowledge transfer across dissimilar cultures. *Journal of Knowledge Management, 17*(1), 29–46. doi:10.1108/13673271311300723

Bok, D. (2003). *Universities in the Marketplace – The commercialization of Higher Education*. Princeton University Press.

Borsato, M. (2014). Bridging the gap between product lifecycle management and sustainability in manufacturing through ontology building. *Computers in Industry, 65*(2), 258–269. doi:10.1016/j.compind.2013.11.003

Boulding, K. E. (1985). *The World as a Total System*. Beverly Hills, CA: Sage Publications.

Boutellier, R., Gassmann, O., & Zedtwitz, M. (2009). Managing Global Innovation. *R & D Management, 3*(2), 225–226.

Bouzid, S., Cauvet, C., Frydman, C., & Pinaton, J. (2013). A semantic support to improve the collaborative control of manufacturing processes in industries. *IEEE International Conference on Computer Supported Cooperative Work in Design*. doi:10.1109/CSCWD.2013.6581002

Bowley, R. C. (2009). *A comparative case study: Examining the organizational use of social networking sites*. Hamilton: The University of Waikato.

Bozeman, B. (2000). Technology transfer and public policy: A review of research and theory. *Research Policy, 29*(4-5), 627–655. doi:10.1016/S0048-7333(99)00093-1

Bradford, M., & Florin, J. (2003). Examining the role of innovation diffusion factors on the implementation success of enterprise resource planning systems. *International Journal of Accounting Information Systems, 4*(3), 205–225. doi:10.1016/S1467-0895(03)00026-5

Bresnen, M., Edelman, L., Newell, S., Scarbrough, H., & Swan, J. (2003). Social practices and the management of knowledge in project environments. *International Journal of Project Management, 21*(3), 157–166. doi:10.1016/S0263-7863(02)00090-X

Brink, P. (2001). Measurement of Conditions for Knowledge Sharing. In D. Remenyi (Ed.), *Proceedings of the 2nd European Conference on Knowledge Management* (pp. 677-693). ECKM.

Bronszinsky-Schwabe, E. (2011). *Interkulturelle Kommunikation. Missverständnisse – Verständigung.* Wiesbaden: VS Verlag für Sozialwissenschaften. doi:10.1007/978-3-531-92764-0

Brouthers, L. E., Nakos, G., Hadjimarcou, J., & Brouthers, K. D. (2009). Key success factors for successful export performance for small firms. *Journal of International Marketing, 17*(3), 21–38. doi:10.1509/jimk.17.3.21

Browaeys, M. J., & Price, R. (2011). *Understanding cross-cultural management.* Harlow: Pearson Financial Times.

Bruno, G. (2015a). Measuring product semantic similarity by exploiting a manufacturing process ontology. *IEEE International Conference on Industrial Engineering and Systems Management* (IESM'15). doi:10.1109/IESM.2015.7380313

Bruno, G., Antonelli, D., Korf, R., Lentes, J., & Zimmermann, N. (2014). Exploitation of a semantic platform to store and reuse plm knowledge. In *Advances in Production Management Systems - Innovative and Knowledge-Based Production Management in a Global-Local World* (vol. 438, pp. 59–66). Springer Berlin Heidelberg.

Bruno, G. (2015b). Semantic organization of product lifecycle information through a modular ontology. *International Journal of Circuits, Systems and Signal Processing, 9*, 16–26.

Bruno, G., Antonelli, D., & Villa, A. (2015). A reference ontology to support product lifecycle management. *Procedia CIRP, 33*, 41–46. doi:10.1016/j.procir.2015.06.009

Bucsy, L. (1976). *Az innovációk rendszere és a vállalati fejlődés.* Budapest: Közgazdasági és Jogi Könyvkiadó.

Budavári-Takács, I., Csehné Papp, I., & Jekkel, O. (2015). Karrier építési tudatosság vizsgálata fiatal felnőttek körében. In Innováció – növekedés – fenntarthatóság.

Burbidge, J. L. (1996). *Production Flow Analysis For Planning Group Technology.* Oxford University Press.

Bureš, V. (2007). Znalostní management a proces jeho zavádění: průvodce pro praxi. Praha: Grada Publishing.

Burke, R. J., & McKeen, C. A. (1989). Developing formal mentoring programs in organizations. *Business Quarterly, 53*, 76–79.

Burlton, R. (2001). *Business process management; profiting from process; Principles of process management.* Indianapolis: Pearson Education-SAMS Publishing.

Büschgens, T., Bausch, A., & Balkin, D. B. (2013). Organizational Culture and Innovation: A Meta-Analytic Review. *Journal of Product Innovation Management, 30*(4), 763–781. doi:10.1111/jpim.12021

Buzás, N. (2003). A kis- és középvállalkozások innovációs tevékenysége. In Kis- és középvállalkozások a változó gazdaságban. JATE Press.

Byrne, E. (1991). *Mentorship in human resource and career development: a policy approach.* Unpublished paper.

Cabrera, E., & Cabrera, A. (2005). Fostering knowledge sharing through people management practices. *International Journal of Human Resource Management, 16*(5), 720–735. doi:10.1080/09585190500083020

Caiazza, R., Richardson, A., & Audretsch, D. (2015). Knowledge effects on competitiveness: From firms to regional advantage. *The Journal of Technology Transfer, 40*(6), 899–909. doi:10.1007/s10961-015-9425-8

Calhoun, J., & Douglas, A. (2015). An analysis of hospitality and tourism research: Learning organization's (LO) influence on sustainability practices. In A. Camillo (Ed.), Handbook of research on global hospitality and tourism management (pp. 359–381). Hershey, PA: IGI Global. doi:10.4018/978-1-4666-8606-9.ch019

Callon, M. (1999). Some Elements of a Sociology of Translation. In M. Biagiolli (Ed.), *The Science Studies Reader* (pp. 67–83). New York: Routledge.

Camps, J., & Luna-Aroca, R. (2012). A matter of learning: How human resources affect organizational performance. *British Journal of Management*, *23*(1), 1–21. doi:10.1111/j.1467-8551.2010.00714.x

Capillarity. (2016). In *Encyclopaedia Britannica.* Retrieved January 13, 2016, from http://www.britannica.com/science/capillarity

Caplinskas, A., Dzemyda, G., Kiss, F., & Lupeikiené, A. (2012). Processing of Undesirable Business Events in Advanced Production Planning Systems. *Informatica*, *23*(4), 563–580.

Cappetta, R., & Paolino, C. (2015). Is it always worth waiting? The effect of autonomy-supportive teaching on short-term and long-term learning outcomes. *British Journal of Management*, *26*(1), 93–108. doi:10.1111/1467-8551.12065

Carless, S. A. (2009). Psychological testing for selection purposes: A guide to evidence-based practice for human resource professionals. *International Journal of Human Resource Management*, *20*(12), 2517–2532. doi:10.1080/09585190903363821

Carlstedt, G. (1997). Quotation. In E. Oakley & D. Krug (Eds.), *Korszerű változásmenedzselés*. Budapest: Bagolyvár Könyvkiadó.

Carr, N. (2010). *The Shallows: What the Internet Is Doing to Our Brains*. New York, NY: Norton & Company.

Carroll, J. S., & Edmondson, A. C. (2002). Leading organisational learning in health care. *Quality & Safety in Health Care*, *11*(1), 51–56. doi:10.1136/qhc.11.1.51

Catling, T., & Davies, M. (2008). Mentoring the objective support that managers need. *British Journal of Adiministrative Management*, 22-23.

Cavusgil, S. T., Calantone, R. J., & Zhao, Y. (2003). Tacit knowledge transfer and firm innovation capability. *Journal of Business and Industrial Marketing*, *18*(1), 6–21. doi:10.1108/08858620310458615

Cegarra-Navarro, J. G., & Sánchez-Polo, M. T. (2011). Influence of the open-mindedness culture on organizational memory: An empirical investigation of Spanish SMEs. *International Journal of Human Resource Management*, *22*(1), 1–18. doi:10.1080/09585192.2011.538963

Cepeda-Carrion, G., Cegarra-Navarro, J. G., & Jimenez-Jimenez, D. (2012). The effect of absorptive capacity on innovativeness: Context and information systems capability as catalysts. *British Journal of Management*, *23*(1), 110–129. doi:10.1111/j.1467-8551.2010.00725.x

Cerchione, R., Esposito, E., & Spadaro, M. R. (2016). A literature review on knowledge management in SMEs. *Knowledge Management Research & Practice*, *14*(2), 169-177.

Chalmers, A. (1982). *What is this thing Called Science?* Queensland, Australia: University of Queensland Press.

Chambers, E., Foulon, M., Handfield-Jones, H., Hankin, S., & Michaels, E. III. (1998). The war for talent. *The McKinsey Quarterly*, *3*, 44–57.

Chan, K. (2013). *Frugal Innovation: A Groundbreaking Business Strategy.* Retrieved from http://www.onedesk.com/2013/04/frugal-innovation-a-groundbreaking-business-strategy/

Chang, D. R., & Cho, H. (2008). Organizational memory influences new product success. *Journal of Business Research*, *61*(1), 13–23. doi:10.1016/j.jbusres.2006.05.005

Chen, C. J., & Huang, J. W. (2009). Strategic human resource practices and innovation performance: The mediating role of knowledge management capacity. *Journal of Business Research*, *62*(1), 104–114. doi:10.1016/j.jbusres.2007.11.016

Chen, G., Tjosvold, D., Zhao, H., Ning, N., & Fu, Y. (2011). Constructive controversy for learning and team effectiveness in China. *Asia Pacific Journal of Human Resources*, *49*(1), 88–104. doi:10.1177/1038411110391708

Chen, J., Sun, P. Y. T., & McQueen, R. J. (2010). The impact of national cultures on structured knowledge transfer. *Journal of Knowledge Management*, *14*(2), 228–242. doi:10.1108/13673271011032373

Chen, M.-Y. (2006). Knowledge management performance evaluation: A decade review from 1995 to 2004. *Journal of Information Science*, *32*(1), 17–38. doi:10.1177/0165551506059220

Chen, W.-C., Wu, C.-L., Chen, Y.-H., & Fu, L.-C. (2014). An Efficient Data Storage Method of NoSQL Database for HEM Mobile Applications in IoT. *IEEE International Conference on Internet of Things, Green Computing and Communications, and Cyber-Physical-Social Computing*. doi:10.1109/iThings.2014.62

Chesbrough, H. (2006). *Open business models: How to thrive in the new innovation landscape*. Boston, MA: Harvard Business School Press.

Chesbrourg, H., Vanhaverbeke, W., & West, J. (Eds.). (2014). *New frontiers in Open Innovation*. Oxford University Press. doi:10.1093/acprof:oso/9780199682461.001.0001

Chiaburu, D. S., van Dam, K., & Hutchins, H. M. (2010). Social support in the workplace and training transfer: A longitudinal analysis. *International Journal of Selection and Assessment*, *18*(2), 187–200. doi:10.1111/j.1468-2389.2010.00500.x

Chin, P. (2005). *Knowledge Sharing: The Facts and the Myths, Part 1*. Retrieved March 2, 2016, from http://www.paulchinonline.com/portfolio/ij/ij20050208.htm

Chiva, R., & Alegre, J. (2009). Organizational learning capability and job satisfaction: An empirical assessment in the ceramic tile industry. *British Journal of Management*, *20*(3), 323–340. doi:10.1111/j.1467-8551.2008.00586.x

Choo, C. W. (1996). The knowing organization: How organzations use information to construct meaning, create knowledge and make decision. *International Journal of Information Management*, *16*(5), 23–40. doi:10.1016/0268-4012(96)00020-5

Chouseinoglou, O., Iren, D., Karagoz, N. A., & Bilgen, S. (2013). AiOLoS: A model for assessing organizational learning in software development organizations. *Information and Software Technology*, *55*(11), 1904–1924. doi:10.1016/j.infsof.2013.05.004

Cho, V. (2007). A study of the impact of organizational learning on information system effectiveness. *International Journal of Business and Information*, *2*(1), 127–158.

Chua, N. (2002). The influence of social interaction on knowledge creation. *Journal of Intellectual Capital*, *3*(4), 375–392. doi:10.1108/14691930210448297

Chuang, C.-H., Jackson, S. E., & Jiang, Y. (2016). Can knowledge-intensive teamwork be managed? Examining the roles of HRM systems, leadership, and tacit knowledge. *Journal of Management*, *42*(2), 524–554. doi:10.1177/0149206313478189

Chung, H. F. L., Yang, Z., & Huang, P. H. (2015). How does organizational learning matter in strategic business performance? The contingency role of guanxi networking. *Journal of Business Research*, *68*(6), 1216–1224. doi:10.1016/j.jbusres.2014.11.016

Chung, T. R., Liang, T., Peng, C., & Chen, D. (2014). How knowledge creation capabilities lead to competitive advantage. In M. Chilton & J. Bloodgood (Eds.), *Knowledge management and competitive advantage: Issues and potential solutions* (pp. 36–52). Hershey, PA: IGI Global. doi:10.4018/978-1-4666-4679-7.ch003

Clark, S. S., Berardy, A., Hannah, M. A., Seager, T. P., Selinger, E., & Makanda, J. V. (2015). Group Tacit Knowledge and Globally Distributed Virtual Teams: Lessons learned from using games and social media in the classroom. *Connexions - International Professional Communication Journal, 3*(1), 113–151.

Clutterbuck, D. (2002). *Mentoring and diversity: an international perspective*. Butterworth Heinemann.

Coelho, P. S., & Esteves, S. P. (2007). The choice between a five-point and a ten-point scale in the framework of customer satisfaction measurement. *International Journal of Market Research, 49*, 313–340.

Cohen, W. M., & Levinthal, D. A. (1990). Absorptive capacity: A new perspective on learning and innovation. *Administrative Science Quarterly, 35*(1), 128–152. doi:10.2307/2393553

Collison, Ch., & Parcell, G. (2005). Knowledge management: praktický management znalostí z prostředí předních světových učících se organizací. Brno: Computer Press.

Colyvas, J., & Powell, W. (2006). Roads to Institutionalization: The Remaking of Boundaries between Public and Private Science. *Research in Organizational Behavior, 27*, 305–353. doi:10.1016/S0191-3085(06)27008-4

Constant, D., Kiesler, S., & Sproull, L. (1994). What's mine is ours, or is it? A study of attitudes about information sharing. *Information Systems Research, 5*(4), 400–421. doi:10.1287/isre.5.4.400

Consulting, I. Q. (2003). *Versenyképesség az Európai Unióban – A vezetők által közvetlenül befolyásolható szervezeti dimenziók 9*. Retrieved from www.iqconsulting.hu

Cooke, N. J., Salas, E., Cannon-Bowers, J. A., & Stout, R. J. (2000). Measuring team knowledge. *Human Factors, 42*(1), 151–173. doi:10.1518/001872000779656561 PMID:10917151

Cooke, P. (1998). Introduction: Origins of the Concept. In H.-J. Braczyc, P. Cooke, & M. Heideinrech (Eds.), *Regional Innovation Systems* (pp. 2–27). London: UCL Press.

Corcuff, P. (2001). *As Novas Sociologias (2ⁿᵈ ed.)*. Sintra: Editora Vral.

Costello, J. T., & McNaughton, R. B. (2016). Can dynamic capabilities be developed using workplace e-learning processes? *Knowledge and Process Management, 23*(1), 73–87. doi:10.1002/kpm.1500

Cote, S., & Miners, C. (2006). Emotional intelligence, cognitive intelligence and job performance. *Administrative Science Quarterly, 51*(1), 1–28.

Cruz, A. R. (2006). *Redes de Investigação: A Relação da Universidade do Algarve com Organismos Nacionais, Europeus e Internacionais*. Faro: Universidade do Algarve.

Csepregi, A. (2012). *Middle managers' knowledge sharing and their competences*. Saarbruecken: LAP Lambert Academic Publishing.

Cser, L., & Fajszi, B. (2004). *Üzleti tudás az adatok mélyén – Adatbányászat alkalmazói szemmel*. Budapest, Hungary: BMGE GTK Információ- és Tudásmenedzsment Tanszék.

Csonka, L. (2011). Kutatás-fejlesztés és innováció a nemzetköziesedés tükrében – a magyar információtechnológiai ágazat kis- és középvállalatainak esete. *Külgazdaság, 55*, 34–56.

Cummings, J. N. (2004). Work groups, structural diversity, and knowledge sharing in a global organization. *Management Science, 50*(3), 352–364. doi:10.1287/mnsc.1030.0134

Cummings, T., & Worley, Ch. (2013). *Organization Development and Change*. Singapore: Cengage Learning.

Curley, K., & Kivowitz, B. (2001). *The manager's pocket guide to knowledge management and organizational learning*. Los Angeles: HRD Press.

Czeizel, E. (1997). *Sors és Tehetség*. Budapest, Hungary: Fitt Image–Minerva Kiadó.

D'Este, P., & Patel, P. (2007). University-industry linkages in the UK: What are the factors underlying the variety of interactions with industry? *Research Policy, 36*(9), 1295–1313. doi:10.1016/j.respol.2007.05.002

Dalkir, K. (2011). *Knowledge Management in Theory and Practice*. Cambridge, MA: The MIT Press.

Damanpour, F. (1991). Organizational innovation: A meta-analysis of effects of determinants and moderators. *Academy of Management Journal, 34*(3), 555–590. doi:10.2307/256406

Davenport, T. H. (1997). If only HP knew what HP knows…. *Perspectives on Business Innovation, 1*, 20–25.

Davenport, T. H. (1997). *Information ecology: mastering the information and knowledge environment*. Oxford University Press.

Davenport, T. H., & Prusak, L. (1998). *Working Knowledge*. Boston: Harvard Business School Press.

Davenport, T. H., & Prusak, L. (1998). *Working Knowledge. Managing What Your Organization Knows*. Boston, MA: Harvard Business School Press.

Davenport, T. H., & Prusak, L. (1998). *Working knowledge: How organizations manage what they know*. Boston, MA: Harvard Business School Press.

Davenport, T. H., & Prusak, L. (1998). *Working Knowledge: How Organizations Manage What They Know*. Boston: Harvard Business School Press.

Davenport, T. H., & Prusak, L. (2001). *Tudásmenedzsment*. Budapest: Kossuth Kiadó.

David, M., & Rowe, F. (2015). What does PLMS (product lifecycle management systems) manage: Data or documents? Complementarity and contingency for SMEs. *Computers in Industry*.

Davila, T., Epstein, M., & Shelton, R. (2012). *Making Innovation Work: How to Manage It, Measure It, and Profit from It*. Pearson FT Press.

Davis, D. C., & Lopuch, V. S. (2016). Learning organizations: Connections between diversity and innovation. In J. Prescott (Ed.), *Handbook of research on race, gender, and the fight for equality* (pp. 267–297). Hershey, PA: IGI Global. doi:10.4018/978-1-5225-0047-6.ch012

Dayaram, K., & Fung, L. (2014). Organizational learning in the Philippines: How do team and individual learning contribute? *Asia Pacific Journal of Human Resources, 52*(4), 420–442. doi:10.1111/1744-7941.12039

De Long, D. W., & Fahey, L. (2000). Diagnosing Cultural Barriers to Knowledge Management. *The Academy of Management Executive, 14*, 113–127. doi:10.5465/AME.2000.3979820

Debackere, K., & Veugelers, R. (2005). The role of academic transfer organizations in improving industry science links. *Research Policy, 34*(3), 321–342. doi:10.1016/j.respol.2004.12.003

Delamare Le Deist, F., & Winterton, J. (2005). What Is Competence? *Human Resource Development International, 8*(1), 27–46. doi:10.1080/1367886042000338227

Delphi Group. (2002). *Perspectives on Information Retrieval*. Boston, MA: Delphi Group.

Demirel, Y., Arzova, B., Ardic, K., & Bas, T. (2013). Organizational learning on coopetition strategy: An exploratory research on a Turkish private banks credit card application. *Procedia: Social and Behavioral Sciences*, *99*, 902–910. doi:10.1016/j.sbspro.2013.10.563

Deng-Neng, C., Ting-Peng, L., & Binshan, L. (2010). An ecological model for organizational knowledge management. *Journal of Computer Information Systems*, *50*(3), 11–22.

Deo, S. (2013). *The impact of globalisation on small business enterprises (SBEs)*. Paper presented at the 26th Annual SEAANZ Conference 2013: Small Business Management in Globally Competitive Markets, Sydney, New South Wales, Australia.

Derboven, K. (2009). *Interkulturelles Training. Trainingsmanual zur Förderung interkultureller Kompetenzen in der Arbeit*. Heidelberg, Germany: Springer-Verlag.

Derksen, J., Kramer, I., & Katzko, M. (2002). Does a self-report measure for emotional intelligence assess something different than general intelligence? *Personality and Individual Differences*, *32*(1), 37–48. doi:10.1016/S0191-8869(01)00004-6

Desouza, K. C. (2003). Barriers to effective use of knowledge management systems in software engineering. *Communications of the ACM*, *46*(1), 99–101. doi:10.1145/602421.602458

Deutsch, K. (1983). Soziale und politische Aspekte der Informationsgesellschaft. In Die Zukunft der Informationsgesellschaft (pp. 68-88). Frankfurt/Main: Haag & Herchen.

Dodgson, M. (1993). Organizational learning: A review of some literatures. *Organization Studies*, *14*(3), 375–394. doi:10.1177/017084069301400303

Dong, J. Q., & Yang, C. H. (2015). Information technology and organizational learning in knowledge alliances and networks: Evidence from U.S. pharmaceutical industry. *Information & Management*, *52*(1), 111–122. doi:10.1016/j.im.2014.10.010

Döös, M., Johansson, P., & Wilhelmson, L. (2015). Organizational learning as an analogy to individual learning? A case of augmented interaction intensity. *Vocations and Learning*, *8*(1), 55–73. doi:10.1007/s12186-014-9125-9

Dörfler, V., & Ackermann, F. (2012). Understanding Intuition: The Case for Two Forms of Intuition. *Management Learning*, *43*(5), 545–564. doi:10.1177/1350507611434686

Dougherty, T. W., Dreher, G. F., Vaoram, A., & Wilbank, J. E. (2013). *Mentor status, occupational context, and protégé career outcomes: differential returns for males and females*. Elsiever Inc.

Douglas, C.A. (1997). *Formal mentoring programsin organisations: an annotated bibliography*. Centre for Creative Leadership.

Dreyfus, H. L., & Dreyfus, S. E. (1986). *Mind over Machine. The Power of Human Intuition and Expertise in the era of Computer*. London, UK: Macmillan Publishers.

Drucker, P. F. (1999). Knowledge-Worker Productivity: The Biggest Challenge. *California Management Review*. Retrieved from: http://forschungsnetzwerk.at/downloadpub/knowledge_workers_the_biggest_challenge.pdf

Drucker, P. (1993). *Post-Capitalist Society*. New York: Harper Business.

Drucker, P. (2003). Az innováció lehetőségei. *Harvard Business Manager*, *5-6*, 28–34.

Drucker, P. (2003). *The Essential Drucker by Peter F. Drucker*. New York, NY: Regan Books.

Drucker, P. F. (1992). *The Age of Discontinuity: Guidelines to Our Changing Society*. New Brunswick: Transaction Publishers.

Drucker, P. F. (1994). The age of social transformation. *Atlantic Monthly, 274*(5), 53–80.

Dubé, L., & Robey, D. (1999). Software stories: Three cultural perspectives on the organizational practices of software development. *Accounting. Management and Information Technologies, 9*(4), 223–259. doi:10.1016/S0959-8022(99)00010-7

DuBois, D. L., & Karcher, M. J. (2005). *Handbook of Youth Mentoring*. London: Sage Publication.

Duden. (2001). *Herkunftswörterbuch: Ethymologie der deutschen Sprache*. Auflage, Germany: Bibliographisches Institut.

Duffield, S., & Whitty, S. J. (2015). Developing a systemic lessons learned knowledge model for organisational learning through projects. *International Journal of Project Management, 33*(2), 311–324. doi:10.1016/j.ijproman.2014.07.004

Durst, S., & Edvardsson, I. R. (2012). Knowledge management in SMEs: A literature review. *Journal of Knowledge Management, 16*(4), 637–648.

Durst, S., & Wilhelm, S. (2012). Knowledge management and succession planning in SMEs. *Journal of Knowledge Management, 16*(6), 879–903. doi:10.1108/13673271211276173

Dvans, M., Dalkir, K., & Bidian, C. (2014). Holistic View of the Knowledge Life Cycle: The Knowledge Management Cycle (KMC). *Model Electronic Journal of Knowledge Management, 12*(2), 148.

Dyer, J. H., & Singh, H. (1998). The relational view: Cooperative strategy and sources of interorganizational competitive advantage. *Academy of Management Review, 23*(4), 660–679. doi:10.2307/259056

Eagar, R., van Oene, F., Boulton, Ch., Roos, D., & Dekeyseret, C. (2011). The Future of Innovation Management: The Next 10 Years. London: Arthur D. Little.

Earley, P. C., & Ang, S. (2003). *Cultural intelligence: individual interactions across cultures*. San Francisco: Stanford University Press.

Easa, N. F., & Fincham, R. (2012). The application of the socialization, externalisation, combination and internalisation model in cross-cultural context: Theoretical analysis. *Knowledge and Process Management, 19*(2), 103–109. doi:10.1002/kpm.1385

Edvardsson, I. R. (2009). Is knowledge management losing ground? Developments among Icelandic SMEs. *Knowledge Management Research & Practice, 7*(1), 91–99. doi:10.1057/kmrp.2008.30

Edwards, J. S. (2003). Managing Software Engineers and Their Knowledge. In *Managing Software Engineering Knowledge* (pp. 5–27). Berlin: Springer Berlin Heidelberg. doi:10.1007/978-3-662-05129-0_1

Efthymiou, K., Sipsas, K., Mourtzis, D., & Chryssolouris, G. (2015). On knowledge reuse for manufacturing systems design and planning: A semantic technology approach. *CIRP Journal of Manufacturing Science and Technology, 8*, 1–11. doi:10.1016/j.cirpj.2014.10.006

Egan, T. M., Yong, B., & Bartlett, K. R. (2004). The effects of organizational learning culture and job satisfaction on motivation to transfer learning and turnover intention. *Human Resource Development Quarterly, 15*(3), 279–301. doi:10.1002/hrdq.1104

Ehigie, B. O., Koang, G. O., & Ibode, F. O. (2011). Mentoring and organisational behavior. *IFE PsychlogIA*, (Supplement), 398–419.

Elliott, J. (1991). Action research educational. Open University Press.

Elmore, R. (1990). On changing the structure of public schools. Restructuring Schools.

Engestrom, Y. (1999). Innovative learning in work teams: Analyzing cycles of knowledge creation in practice. In *Perspectives on activity theory* (pp. 377–404). Cambridge, UK: Cambridge University Press. doi:10.1017/CBO9780511812774.025

Erden, Z., von Krogh, G., & Nonaka, I. (2008). The quality of group tacit knowledge. *The Journal of Strategic Information Systems, 17*(1), 4–18. doi:10.1016/j.jsis.2008.02.002

Erikson, E. H. (1956). The Problem of Ego Identity. *Journal of the American Psychoanalytic Association, 4*(1), 56–121. doi:10.1177/000306515600400104 PMID:13286157

Erkelens, R., van den Hooff, B., Huysman, M., & Vlaar, P. (2015). Learning from locally embedded knowledge: Facilitating organizational learning in geographically dispersed settings. *Global Strategy Journal, 5*(2), 177–197. doi:10.1002/gsj.1092

Espinosa, J. A., & Clark, M. A. (2014). Team knowledge-representation: A network perspective. *Human Factors, 52*(2), 333–348. doi:10.1177/0018720813494093 PMID:24689252

Estanque, E., & Nunes, J. A. (2003). Dilemas e desafios da Universidade: Recomposição social e expectativas dos estudantes na Universidade de Coimbra. *Revista Critica de Ciencias Sociais, 66*(66), 5–44. doi:10.4000/rccs.1139

Etzkowitz, H., & Leydesdorff, L. (1997). *Universities and the Global Knowledge Economy – A Triple Helix of University-Industry-Government Relations*. Londres: Continuum.

European Commission Enterprise and Industry. (2009). *Small and medium-sized enterprises (SMEs)*. Retrieved January 20, 2016, from http://ec.europa.eu/enterprise/policies/sme/promoting-entrepreneurship/family-business/#h2-2

Fahey, L., & Prusak, L. (1998). The eleven deadliest sins of knowledge management. *California Management Review, 40*(3), 265–276. doi:10.2307/41165954

Fajana, S., & Gbajumo-Sheriff, M. (2011). Mentoring: A human resource tool for acheiving organisational effectiveness. *IFE PsychlogIA*, (Supplement), 420–432.

Fajkus, B. (2005). *Filosofie a metodologie vědy: vývoj, současnost a perspektivy*. Prague: Academia.

Farkas, J. (2001). Úton az ipari társadalomból az információ alapú társadalom felé. *Info-Társadalomtudomány., 53/2001*, 23–31.

Farsani, J. J., Bidmeshgipour, M., Habibi, M., & Rashidi, M. M. (2012). Intellectual capital and organizational learning capability in Iranian active companies of petrochemical industry. *Procedia: Social and Behavioral Sciences, 62*, 1297–1302. doi:10.1016/j.sbspro.2012.09.222

Fehér, P. (2002). Tudásmenedzsment: Problémák és Veszélyek. *Vezetéstudomány, 34*(4), 36–45.

Fehér, P., & Gábor, A. (2006). The role of knowledge management supporters in software development companies. *Software Process Improvement and Practice, 11*(3), 251–260. doi:10.1002/spip.269

Fenyvesi, É. (2007). *Együttműködés és versengés a tudásmegosztás során. PhD értekezés*. Gödöllő: Szent István Egyetem.

Fenyvesi, É. (2010). Game Theory and Knowledge Management. *Development and Finance, Quarterly Hungarian Economic Review*, 31–39.

Fernández-Esquinas, M. (2006). La sociologia aplicada. *Revista Espanola de Investigaciones Sociologicas, 115*(115), 11–40. doi:10.2307/40184765

Fernandez-Mesa, A., & Alegre, J. (2015). Entrepreneurial orientation and export intensity: Examining the interplay of organizational learning and innovation. *International Business Review, 24*(1), 148–156. doi:10.1016/j.ibusrev.2014.07.004

Filep, B. (2008). The economic regional cooperation and management of Universities and in particular the Széchenyi István University. In *Proceedings of Integrating perspectives on performance management*. Prague: University of Economics.

Filos, E. (2006). *Smart Organizations in the Digital Age. In Integration of ICT in Smart Organizations* (pp. 1–38). IGI Global. doi:10.4018/978-1-59140-390-6.ch001

Fiorentini, X., Gambino, I., Liang, V.-C., Foufou, S., Rachuri, S., Bock, C., & Mani, M. (2007). Towards an Ontology for Open Assembly model. *Proceeding of the International Conference on Product Lifecycle Management.*

Fioretti, G. (2007). A connectionist model of the organizational learning curve. *Computational & Mathematical Organization Theory, 13*(1), 1–16. doi:10.1007/s10588-006-9003-6

Fleck, L. (1979). *Genesis and Development of a Scientific Fact.* Chicago: Chicago University Press. (Original work published 1935)

Fleck, L. (1986). The Problem of Epistemology. In R. S. Cohen & T. Schnelle (Eds.), *Cognition and Fact* (pp. 79–112). Dordrecht: Reitel Publishing Company. (Original work published 1936) doi:10.1007/978-94-009-4498-5_5

Fletcher, M., & Prashantham, S. (2011). Knowledge assimilation processes of rapidly internationalising firms: Longitudinal case studies of Scottish SMEs. *Journal of Small Business and Enterprise Development, 18*(3), 475–501. doi:10.1108/14626001111155673

Floyde, A., Lawson, G., Shalloe, S., Eastgate, R., & D'Cruz, M. (2013). The design and implementation of knowledge management systems and e-learning for improved occupational health and safety in small to medium sized enterprises. *Safety Science, 60*, 69–76. doi:10.1016/j.ssci.2013.06.012

Fong, C. Y., Ooi, K. B., Tan, B. I., Lee, V. H., & Yee-Loong Chong, A. (2011). HRM practices and knowledge sharing: An empirical study. *International Journal of Manpower, 32*(5/6), 704–723. doi:10.1108/01437721111158288

Forgács,, K., Kaucsek, G., & Simon, P. (2002). A kompetens munkaerő értékelése pszichológiai teszttel és írásanalízissel. *Munkaügyi Szemle, 16*(9), 12–18.

Foucault, M. (1999). A szexualitás története: A tudás akarása. [The History of Sexuality: The Will to Knowledge] Budapest: Atlantisz.

Foucault, M. (1971). *L'Ordre du discours*. Paris: Gallimard.

Fowler, M., & Scott, K. (2000). *UML distilled*. Addison-Wesley.

Freyens, B., & Martin, M. (2007). Multidisciplinary knowledge transfer in training multimedia projects. *Journal of European Industrial Training, 31*(9), 680–105. doi:10.1108/03090590710846666

Froehlich, D., Segers, M., & van den Bossche, P. (2014). Informal workplace learning in Austrian banks: The influence of learning approach, leadership style, and organizational learning culture on managers' learning outcomes. *Human Resource Development Quarterly, 25*(1), 29–57. doi:10.1002/hrdq.21173

Frost, A. (2014). *Knowledge Management Systems*. Retrieved March 29, 2016, from http://www.knowledge-management-tools.net/knowledge-management-systems.html

Furnham, A. (2001). Self-estimates of intelligence: Culture and gender differences in self and other estimates of both general (g) and multiple intelligences. *Personality and Individual Differences, 31*(8), 1381–1405. doi:10.1016/S0191-8869(00)00232-4

Gaál, Z., Szabó, L., Kovács, Z., Obermayer-Kovács, N., & Csepregi, A. (2008). "Knowledge Management Profile" Maturity Model. In *Proceedings of 9th European Conference on Knowledge Management (ECKM 2008).*

Gaál, Z., Szabó, L., Kovács, Z., Obermayer-Kovács, N., & Csepregi, A. (2009). Consequence of Cultural Capital in Connection with Competitiveness. *International Journal of Knowledge. Culture and Change Management, 8*(10), 79–90.

Gaál, Z., Szabó, L., & Obermayer-Kovács, N. (2014). Personal knowledge sharing: Web 2.0 role through the lens of Generations. In *Proceedings of 15th European Conference on Knowledge Management (ECKM 2014)*. School of Management and Technology - Polytechnic Institute of Santarem.

Gaál, Z., Szabó, L., Obermayer-Kovács, N., & Csepregi, A. (2015). Exploring the Role of Social Media in Knowledge Sharing. *Electronic Journal of Knowledge Management, 13*(3), 185–197.

Gagné, F. (2009). Building gifts into talents: Detailed overview of the DMGT 2.0. In Leadingchange in gifted education: The festschrift of Dr. Joyce VanTassel-Baska. Waco, TX: Prufrock Press.

Gagné, F. (2013). The DMGT: Changes within, beneath, and beyond. *Talent Development & Excellence, 5*(1), 5–19.

Gagné, F. (1985). Giftedness and talent: Reexamining a reexamination of the definitions. *Gifted Child Quarterly, 29*(3), 103–112. doi:10.1177/001698628502900302

Gagné, M. (2009). A model of knowledge-sharing motivation. *Human Resource Management, 48*(4), 571–589. doi:10.1002/hrm.20298

Galison, P., & Stump, D. J. (1996). *The Disunity of Science: Boundaries, Contexts, and Power*. Stanford, CA: Stanford University Press.

Galton, F. (1869). *Hereditary Genius: An Inquiry into its Laws and Consequences*. London, UK: MacMillan. doi:10.1037/13474-000

García-Morales, V. J., Jiménez-Barrionuevo, M. M., & Gutiérrez-Gutiérrez, L. (2012). Transformational leadership influence on organizational performance through organizational learning and innovation. *Journal of Business Research, 65*(7), 1040–1050. doi:10.1016/j.jbusres.2011.03.005

Gardiner, B. (2013). Jugaad' innovation: the businesses getting creative in the face of scarcity. *The Guardian*. Retrieved September 12, 2014, from http://www.theguardian.com/sustainable-business/jugaad-innovation-business-creativity-scarcity

Gardner, K. J., & Qualter, P. (2010). Concurrent and incremental validity of three trait emotional intelligence measures. *Australian Journal of Psychology*, 62–13.

Garrido, M. J., & Camarero, C. (2010). Assessing the impact of organizational learning and innovation on performance in cultural organizations. *International Journal of Nonprofit and Voluntary Sector Marketing, 15*(3), 215–232.

Garvin, D. A. (1993). Building a learning organization. *Harvard Business Review, 71*(4), 78–91. PMID:10127041

Gáthy, A. (2004). Egyetemisták ismeretszintje a fenntartható fejlődés fogalomköréről. *Acta Agraria Debreceniensis, 13*, 232–241.

Geertz, C. (1983). *Local Knowledge: Further Essays in Interpretative Anthropology*. New York: Basic Books.

Geisler, E., & Wickramasinghe, N. (2015). *Principles of knowledge management: theory, practice, and cases*. London: Routledge.

George, G., McGahan, A. M., & Prabhu, J. (2012). Innovation for Inclusive Growth: Towards a Theoretical Framework and a Research Agenda. *Journal of Management Studies, 49*(4), 661–683. doi:10.1111/j.1467-6486.2012.01048.x

Ghobadi, S. (2015). What drives knowledge sharing in software development teams: A literature review and classification framework. *Information & Management, 52*(1), 82–97. doi:10.1016/j.im.2014.10.008

Gibb, A. (1990). Training the trainers of small business. *Journal of European Industrial Training, 14*(1), 17–25. doi:10.1108/03090599010138543

Gibbons, M., Limoges, C., Nowotny, H., Schwartzman, S., Scott, P., & Trow, M. (1994). *The New Production of Knowledge: The Dynamics of Science and Research in Contemporary Societies.* Londres: Sage.

Gieryn, T. (1983). Boundary work and the Demarcation of Science from Non-science: Strains and Interests in Professional Ideologies of Scientists. *American Sociological Review, 48*(6), 781–795. doi:10.2307/2095325

Gioia, D. A., Corley, K. G., & Hamilton, A. L. (2013). Seeking qualitative rigor in inductive research notes on the Gioia methodology. *Organizational Research Methods, 16*(1), 15–31. doi:10.1177/1094428112452151

Girard, J., & Girard, J. (2015). Defining knowledge management: Toward an applied compendium. *Online Journal of Applied Knowledge Management, 3*(1), 1–20.

Gladwell, M. (2007). *Blink: The Power of Thinking Without Thinking.* Boston, MA: Little, Brown and Company.

Gloet, M. (2006). Knowledge management and the links to HRM. *Management Research News, 29*(7), 402–413. doi:10.1108/01409170610690862

Gloet, M., & Terziovski, M. (2004). Exploring the relationship between knowledge management practices and innovation performance. *Journal of Manufacturing Technology Management, 15*(5), 402–409. doi:10.1108/17410380410540390

Goffin, R. D., Rothstein, M. G., & Johnston, N. G. (1996). Personality testing and the assessment center: Incremental validity for managerial selection. *The Journal of Applied Psychology, 81*(6), 746–756. doi:10.1037/0021-9010.81.6.746

Goh, S. C. (2003). Improving organizational learning capability: Lessons from two case studies. *The Learning Organization, 10*(4), 216–227. doi:10.1108/09696470310476981

Goleman, D. (2002). *Érzelmi intelligencia a munkahelyen.* Budapest: SHL Edge 2000. Kft.

Goleman. (2003). *A természetes vezető.* Budapest: Vince Kiadó.

Goleman, D. (1995). *Emotional Intelligence: Why it can matter more than IQ.* New York: Bantam.

Goleman, D. (1997). *Érzelmi intelligencia.* Budapest: Háttér Kiadó.

Goleman, D. (2003). *A természetes vezető.* Budapest: Vince Kiadó.

Goleman, D., Boyatzis, R., & McKee, A. (2013). *Primal leadership: Unleashing the power of emotional intelligence. Boston: Massachusetts.* Boston: Harvard Business School Press.

Golovko, E., & Valentini, G. (2011). Exploring the complementarity between innovation and export for SMEs growth. *Journal of International Business Studies, 42*(3), 362–380. doi:10.1057/jibs.2011.2

Gomes, L. (2013). IBM's 'Frugal Innovation' Takes Root in Africa - Combining high and low tech, IBM's famous R&D lab tackles the challenges of a rapidly urbanizing continent. *Operations, Information & Technology Global Business Africa, 3*. Retrieved from https://www.gsb.stanford.edu/insights/ibms-frugal-innovation-takes-root-africa

Goodbar, N.H. & Lewis, K.F. (2015). Finding and working with mentors. *American of Health-System Pharmacy,* 921-922.

Gourova, E., Antonova, A., & Todorova, Y. (2009). Knowledge audit concepts, processes and practice. *WSEAS Transactions on Business and Economics, 6*(12), 605 – 619.

Govindarajan, V., & Trimble, C. (2012). *Reverse Innovation: Create Far from Home, Win Everywhere.* Boston: Harvard Business Review Press.

Govindarajan, V., & Trimble, C. (2014). Reverse Innovation. *Management International Review*, *54*(2), 277–282.

Graham, I. D., Logan, J., Harrison, M. B., Straus, S. E., Tetroe, J., Caswell, W., & Robinson, N. (2006). Lost in knowledge translation: Time for a map? *The Journal of Continuing Education in the Health Professions*, *26*(1), 13–24. doi:10.1002/chp.47 PMID:16557505

Grail Research. (2011). *Consumers of Tomorrow Insights and Observations About Generation Z*. Retrieved March 23, 2013, from http://www.grailresearch.com/pdf/ContenPodsPdf/Consumers_of_Tomorrow_Insights_and_ Observations_About_Generation_Z.pdf

Grandinetti, R. (2016). Absorptive capacity and knowledge management in small and medium sized enterprises. *Knowledge Management Research & Practice*, *14*(2), 159-168.

Gray, P. H. (2001). The Impact of Knowledge Repositories on Power and Control in the Workplace. *Information Technology & People*, *14*(4), 368–384. doi:10.1108/09593840110411167

Groover, M. (2007). *Fundamentals of modern manufacturing: Materials processes, and systems*. John Wiley & Son.

Grover, V., & Davenport, T. H. (2001). General Perspectives on Knowledge Management: Fostering a Research Agenda. *Journal of Management Information Systems*, *18*(1), 5–21.

Grublová, E., & Frank, J. (2014). Inovace a znalosti. Olomouc: Univerzita Palackého.

Guerra-Zubiaga, D., & Young, R. (2008). Information and knowledge interrelationships within a manufacturing knowledge model. *International Journal of Advanced Manufacturing Technology*, *39*(1-2), 182–198. doi:10.1007/s00170-007-1194-6

Guerreiro, J. (2008). *Caracterização da Estrutura Económica do Algarve*. Loulé: NERA.

Gumusluoglu, L., & İlsev, A. (2009). Transformational leadership, creativity, and organizational innovation. *Journal of Business Research*, *62*(4), 461–473. doi:10.1016/j.jbusres.2007.07.032

Gunendran, A., & Young, R. (2010). Methods for the capture of manufacture best practice in product lifecycle management. *International Journal of Production Research*, *48*(20), 5885–5904. doi:10.1080/00207540903104210

Gupta, B. (2008). Role of Personality in Knowledge Sharing and Knowledge Acquisition Behaviour. *Journal of the Indian Academy of Applied Psychology*, *34*(1), 143–149.

Guston, D. H. (1999). Stabilizing the Boundary Between US Politics and Science: The Rôle of the Office of Technology Transfer as a Boundary Organization. *Social Studies of Science*, *29*(1), 87–111. doi:10.1177/030631299029001004 PMID:11623653

Gyarmathy, É. (2006). *A tehetség*. Budapest, Hungary: ELTE Eötvös Kiadó.

Haggard, D. L., & Turban, D. B. (2012). The mentoring relationship as a context for psychological contract development. *Journal of Applied Social Psychology*, *42*(8), 1904–1931. doi:10.1111/j.1559-1816.2012.00924.x

Haghirian, P. (2011). *Multinationals and cross-cultural management: the transfer of knowledge within multinational corporations*. New York: Routledge.

Hall, H. (2001). Input-friendliness: Motivating Knowledge Sharing Across Intranets. *Journal of Information Science*, *27*(2), 139–146. doi:10.1177/016555150102700303

Hámosi, B., & Szabó, K. (Eds.). (2012). *Innovációs verseny - esélyek és korlátok*. Budapest: Aula Kiadó.

Handy, C. (2002). *Empty Raincoat. Making Sense of the Future*. New York, NY: Random House.

Hansen, M. T., Nohria, N. & Tierney, T. (1999, March-April). What is your strategy for managing knowledge. *Harvard Business Review*, 106-116.

Hansen, M. T., Nohria, N., & Tierney, T. (1999). What's your strategy for managing knowledge. *Harvard Business Review*, *77*(2), 109–122. PMID:10387767

Hansen, M. T., Nohria, N., & Tierney, T. (1999). What's your strategy for managing knowledge? *Harvard Business Review*, *72*(2), 106–116. PMID:10387767

Hansen, M. T., Nohria, N., & Tierney, T. (1999). What's Your Strategy For Managing Knowledge? *Harvard Business Review*, *77*(2), 106–116.

Hartley, J. (2014). New development: Eight and a half propositions to stimulate frugal innovation. *Public Money & Management*, *34*(3), 227–232. doi:10.1080/09540962.2014.908034

Harvey, M., McIntyre, N., Heames, J. T., & Moeller, M. (2009). Mentoring global female managers in the global marketplace: Traditional, reverse and reciprocal mentoring. *International Journal of Human Resource Management*, *20*(6), 1344–1361. doi:10.1080/09585190902909863

Hay Group. (2008). *Making the leap: Encouraging innovation.* Retrieved March 24, 2014, from http://www.haygroup.com/downloads/au/au_icm_innovation_low_res.pdf

Hedfords, E. (2007). Fleck in Context. *Perspectives on Sciences*, *15*(1).

Hedfors, E. (2006). *Reading Fleck: Questions on Philosophy and Science.* (PhD Dissertation). KTH, Stockholm, Sweden.

Hedfors, E. (2008). Medical Science in the Light of Holocaust: Departing from a Postwar Paper by Ludwik Fleck. *Social Studies of Science*, *38*(2), 259–283. doi:10.1177/0306312707082953 PMID:18831133

Hedlund, E., & Österberg, J. (2013). Team Training, Team Learning, Leadership and Psychology Safety: A Study of Team Training and Team Learning Behavior during a Swedish Military Staff Exercise. *Sociology Mind*, *3*(1), 89-98. Retrieved from http://www.scirp.org/journal

Heeks, R., Foster, Ch., & Nugroho, Y. (2014). New models of inclusive innovation for development. *Innovation and Development*, *4*(2), 175–185. doi:10.1080/2157930X.2014.928982

Heidrich, B., Makó, C., Csizmadia, P., & Csákné Filep, J. (2015). *Comparative Report on Family Businesses' Succession-Intergenerational Succession in SMEs Transition.* INSIST Project.

Helios. (2015). *Informační systémy pro všechna odvětví.* Prague: HELIOS CR. Retrieved from: http://www.helios.eu

Hendricks, P. (1999). Why share knowledge? The influence of ICT on the motivation for knowledge sharing. *Knowledge and Process Management*, *6*(2), 91–100. doi:10.1002/(SICI)1099-1441(199906)6:2<91::AID-KPM54>3.0.CO;2-M

Henriques, A. C. V., Antunes, E. D. D., & Macke, J. (2014). Intercultural knowledge transfer: Processes analysis of a multinational company. *Gestão & Planejamento*, *15*(3), 537–552.

Henry, M., Erwee, R., & Kong, E. (2013). Family Business Succession - Trust and Gender Issues in Family and Non-Family Succession. In *13th Euram Conference, Democratising Management. Galatasaray University.*

Hídvégi, P. (2003). E-learning megoldások. In J. Mayer & P. Singer (Eds.), *A tanulás kora.* Országos Közoktatási Intézet.

Higgs, M., & Dulewicz, V. (1999). *Making sense of emotional intelligence.* Windsor: NFER-NELSON Publishing Company.

Hislop, D. (2013). *Knowledge management in organizations: A critical introduction.* Oxford University Press.

Hitt, M. A. (1998). Twenty-first-century organizations: Business firms, business schools, and the academy. *Academy of Management Review, 23*(2), 218–224.

Hitt, M. A., Ireland, R. D., & Hoskisson, R. E. (1999). *Strategic Management: Competitiveness and Globalization.* Cincinnati, OH: South-Western College Publishing.

Hnátek, M. (2015). Entrepreneurial thinking as a key factor of family business success. Social and Behavior Sciences, 181. doi:10.1016/j.sbspro.2015.04.896

Hoang, H., & Rothaermel, F. T. (2005). The effect of general and partner-specific alliance experience of joint R&D project performance. *Academy of Management Journal, 48*(2), 332–345. doi:10.5465/AMJ.2005.16928417

Hoerem, T., von Krogh, G., & Roos, J. (1999). Knowledge based strategic change. In G. von Krogh & J. Roos (Eds.), *Managing knowledge: perspectives on cooperation and competition* (pp. 116–136). London: SAGE Publications Inc.

Hoffman, R. R., Ziebell, D., Fiore, S. M., & Becerra-Fernandez, I. (2008). Knowledge Management Revisited. *IEEE Intelligent Systems, 23*(3), 84–88. doi:10.1109/MIS.2008.51

Hofstede, G. (1983). The cultural relativity organizational practices and theories. *Journal of International Business Studies, 14*(2), 75–89. doi:10.1057/palgrave.jibs.8490867

Hofstede, G. (1997). *Cultures and Organizations: Software of the Mind: Intercultural Cooperation and its Importance for Survival.* New York: McGraw-Hill.

Holden, D. (2014). *The Lost Art of Inspired Mentoring.* Retrieved from http://www.iienet2.org/details.aspx?id=38250

Holt, L., Beard, J., & Lee, D. S. (2013). Use of information technology in organizational learning: Effective practices of award-winning organizations. In V. Bryan & V. Wang (Eds.), *Technology use and research approaches for community education and professional development* (pp. 24–39). Hershey, PA: IGI Global. doi:10.4018/978-1-4666-2955-4.ch002

Hong, J. F. L. (2012). Glocalizing Nonaka's knowledge creation model: Issues and challenges. *Management Learning, 43*(2), 199–215. doi:10.1177/1350507611428853

Hotho, J. J., Lyles, M. A., & Easterby-Smith, M. (2015). The mutual impact of global strategy and organizational learning: Current themes and future directions. *Global Strategy Journal, 5*(2), 85–112. doi:10.1002/gsj.1097

Howell, K., & Annansingh, F. (2013). Knowledge generation and sharing in UK universities: A tale of two cultures? *International Journal of Information Management, 33*(1), 32–39. doi:10.1016/j.ijinfomgt.2012.05.003

Howells, J. (1990). The Internationalisation of R&D and the Development of Global Research Networks. *Regional Studies, 24*(6), 495–512. doi:10.1080/00343409012331346174

Hsiao, H. C., Chang, J. C., & Chen, S. C. (2014). The influence of support for innovation on organizational innovation: Taking organizational learning as a mediator. *The Asia-Pacific Education Researcher, 23*(3), 463–472. doi:10.1007/s40299-013-0121-x

Hu, B. (2014). Linking business models with technological innovation performance through organizational learning. *European Management Journal, 32*(4), 587–595. doi:10.1016/j.emj.2013.10.009

Hughes, M., Morgan, R. E., Ireland, R. D., & Hughes, P. (2014). Social capital and learning advantages: A problem of absorptive capacity. *Strategic Entrepreneurship Journal, 8*(3), 214–233. doi:10.1002/sej.1162

Husted, K., & Michailova, S. (2002). Knowledge sharing in Russian companies with western participation. *Management International, 6*(2), 17–28.

Hutchinson, K., Quinn, B., & Alexander, N. (2006). SME retailer internationalisation: Case study evidence from British retailers. *International Marketing Review, 23*(1), 25–53. doi:10.1108/02651330610646287

Huzita, E. H. M., Leal, G. C. L., Balancieri, R., Tait, T. F. C., Cardoza, E., Penteado, R. R. D. M., & Vivian, R. L. (2012). Knowledge and contextual information management in global software development: challenges and perspectives. In *2012 IEEE Seventh International Conference on Global Software Engineering Workshops* (pp. 43–48). IEEE. doi:10.1109/ICGSEW.2012.12

Iacono, M. P., De Nito, E., Esposito, V., Martinez, M., & Moschera, L. (2014). Investigating the relationship between coordination mechanisms and knowledge in a wine firm. *Knowledge and Process Management, 21*(4), 280–291. doi:10.1002/kpm.1436

IAPMEI. (2009). *1ª Sessão de Trabalho entre a Universidade do Algarve e as Empresas da Região*. Retrieved from www.cria.pt

Ibarra, H. (1992). Homophily and differential returns: Sex differences in network structure and access in an advertising firm. *Administrative Science Quarterly, 37*(3), 422–447. doi:10.2307/2393451

Igba, J., Alemzadeh, K., Gibbons, P. M., & Henningsen, K. (2015). A framework for optimizing product performance through feedback and reuse of in-service experience. *Robotics and Computer-integrated Manufacturing, 36*, 2–12. doi:10.1016/j.rcim.2014.12.004

Inkinen, H. (2016). Review of empirical research on knowledge management practices and firm performance. *Journal of Knowledge Management, 20*(2), 230–257. doi:10.1108/JKM-09-2015-0336

Iyengar, S. (2010). *The Art of Choosing*. New York, NY: Hachette Book Group.

Jackson, S. E., Chuang, C. H., Harden, E. E., & Jiang, Y. (2006). Toward developing human resource management system for knowledge-intensive teamwork. In J. Martocchio (Ed.), *Research in personnel and human resources management* (pp. 25–70). Oxford, UK: Elsevier. doi:10.1016/S0742-7301(06)25002-3

Jaffe, A. B., & Lerner, J. (2004). *Innovation and Its Discontents: How Our Broken Patent System Is Endangering Innovation and Progress, and What to Do about It*. Princeton, NJ: Princeton University Press.

Jakubik, M. (2008). Experiencing collaborative knowledge creation processes. *The Learning Organization, 15*(1), 5–25. doi:10.1108/09696470810842475

Jardim-Goncalves, R., Coutinho, C., Cretan, A., Ferreira da Silva, C., & Ghodous, P. (2014). Collaborative negotiation for ontology-driven enterprise businesses. *Computers in Industry, 65*(9), 1232–1241. doi:10.1016/j.compind.2014.01.001

Jarnagin, L. M. (2010). *Mentors are from Venus and Mars: exploring the benefits of homogeneous and heterogeneous gender pairings in the mentoring relationships of female senior student affairs officers*. ProQuest LLC, Ed.D. Dissertation, University of California, Los Angeles.

Javidan, M., Stahl, G. K., Brodbeck, F., & Wilderom, C. P. M. (2005). Cross-border transfer of knowledge: Cultural lessons from project GLOBE. *The Academy of Management Executive, 1*(2), 59–76. doi:10.5465/AME.2005.16962801

Jaw, B. S., & Liu, W. (2003). Promoting organizational learning and self-renewal in Taiwanese companies: The role of HRM. *Human Resource Management, 42*(3), 223–241. doi:10.1002/hrm.10082

Jerez-Gomez, P., Cespedes-Lorente, J., & Valle-Cabrera, R. (2005). Organizational learning capability: A proposal of measurement. *Journal of Business Research, 58*(6), 715–725. doi:10.1016/j.jbusres.2003.11.002

Jiao, H., Wei, J., & Cui, Y. (2010). An empirical study on paths to develop dynamic capabilities: From the perspectives of entrepreneurial orientation and organizational learning. *Frontiers of Business Research in China*, *4*(1), 47–72. doi:10.1007/s11782-010-0003-5

Johannenssen, J.-A., Olsen, B., & Olaisen, J. (1999). Aspects of Innovation Theory Based on Knowledge Management. *International Journal of Information Management*, *19*(2), 121–139. doi:10.1016/S0268-4012(99)00004-3

Johnson, C., & Donnelly, B. (2013). If only we knew what we know. *Chicago-Kent Law Review*, *88*(3), 729–742.

Johnson, S. J., Batey, M., & Holdsworth, L. (2009). Personality and health: The mediating role of trait emotional intelligence and work locus of control. *Personality and Individual Differences*, *47*(5), 470–475. doi:10.1016/j.paid.2009.04.025

Jones, A., P. & Long, H. B., & Drakeley, R. (1991). Attempting to improve the validity of a well-established assessment centre. *Journal of Occupational Psychology, 64*(1), 1–21.

Jones, M. C., Zmud, R. W., & Thomas, D. C. (2008). ERP in practice: A snapshot of post-installation perception and behaviors. *Communications of the Association for Information Systems*, *23*(1), 437–462.

Joo, Y. J., Lim, K. Y., & Park, S. Y. (2011). Investigating the structural relationships among organisational support, learning flow, learners' satisfaction and learning transfer in corporate e-learning. *British Journal of Educational Technology*, *42*(6), 973–984. doi:10.1111/j.1467-8535.2010.01116.x

Jue, A. L., Marr, J. A., & Kassotakis, M. E. (2009). *Social media at work: How networking tools propel organizational performance*. San Francisco, CA: John Wiley & Sons.

K2 Atmitec. (2015). *Informační systém K2*. Ostrava: K2 atmitec. Retrieved from: http://www.k2.cz/cz/k2software/informacni-system-k2.html

Kahneman, D. (2011). *Thinking, Fast and Slow*. New York, NY: Farrar, Straus and Giroux.

Kakabadse, N. K., Kakabadse, A., & Kouzmin, A. (2003). Reviewing the knowledge management literature: Towards a taxonomy. *Journal of Knowledge Management*, *7*(4), 75–91. doi:10.1108/13673270310492967

Kalkan, V. D. (2004). New Initiatives in Organisational Learning Studies; Organisational Intelligence and Information producing. *3rd National Information, Economics and Management Congress Final Paper*. Osmangazi University.

Kalkan, V. D. (2008). An overall view of knowledge management challenges for global business. *Business Process Management Journal*, *14*(3), 390–400. doi:10.1108/14637150810876689

Kalpakjian, S., & Schmid, S. (2013). *Manufacturing Engineering & Technology*. Prentice Hall College Di.

Kamp, B. (2012). Reverse innovation: inversing the international product life cycle model and lead market theory [Innovación inversa: invirtiendo el modelo internacional de ciclo de vida del producto y la teoría del mercado líder]. *Boletín de estudios económicos*, *207*(6-7), 481.

Kane, G. G., & Alavi, M. (2007). Information technology and organizational learning: An investigation of exploration and exploitation processes. *Organization Science*, *18*(5), 796–812. doi:10.1287/orsc.1070.0286

Kang, J., Rhee, M., & Kang, K. H. (2010). Revisiting knowledge transfer: Effects of knowledge characteristics on organizational effort for knowledge transfer. *Expert Systems with Applications*, *37*(12), 8155–8160. doi:10.1016/j.eswa.2010.05.072

Kanter, R. M. (1977). *Men and women of the corporation*. New York: Basic Books.

Kaplan, R. S., & David, P. (1996). Linking the Balanced Scorecard to Strategy. *California Management Review*, *39*(1), 53–79. doi:10.2307/41165876

Kaps, I. (2011). Barriers in intercultural knowledge sharing. *Open Journal of Knowledge Management, 1*(3), 6–12.

Karat Informační Systém. (2015). *Řešení pro výrobní firmy.* Přerov: Karat Software, a.s. Retrieved from: http://www. karatsoftware.cz/oborova-reseni/vyroba

Karkoulian, S., Harake, N., & Messarra, L. C. (2010). Correlates of Organizational Commitment and Knowledge Sharing via Emotional Intelligence: An Empirical Investigation. *The Business Review, Cambridge, 15*(1), 89–96.

Kárpátiné Daróczi, J., Fenyvesi, É., & Vágány, J. (2015). A mentorálás lehetőségei a fiatal vállalkozók számára. In Gazdálkodás és Menedzsment Tudományos Konferencia: Kecskemét, II. köt. (pp. 794-798).

Kasemsap, K. (2013). Practical framework: Creation of causal model of job involvement, career commitment, learning motivation, and learning transfer. *International Journal of the Computer, the Internet and Management, 21*(1), 29–35.

Kasemsap, K. (2014a). Strategic innovation management: An integrative framework and causal model of knowledge management, strategic orientation, organizational innovation, and organizational performance. In P. Ordóñez de Pablos & R. Tennyson (Eds.), *Strategic approaches for human capital management and development in a turbulent economy* (pp. 102–116). Hershey, PA: IGI Global. doi:10.4018/978-1-4666-4530-1.ch007

Kasemsap, K. (2014b). Developing a unified framework and a causal model of transformational leadership, empowerment, innovation support, and organizational innovation. In N. Erbe (Ed.), *Approaches to managing organizational diversity and innovation* (pp. 280–303). Hershey, PA: IGI Global. doi:10.4018/978-1-4666-6006-9.ch014

Kasemsap, K. (2014c). The role of social media in the knowledge-based organizations. In I. Lee (Ed.), *Integrating social media into business practice, applications, management, and models* (pp. 254–275). Hershey, PA: IGI Global. doi:10.4018/978-1-4666-6182-0.ch013

Kasemsap, K. (2014d). Constructing a unified framework and a causal model of occupational satisfaction, trainee reactions, perception of learning, and perceived training transfer. In S. Hai-Jew (Ed.), *Remote workforce training: Effective technologies and strategies* (pp. 28–52). Hershey, PA: IGI Global. doi:10.4018/978-1-4666-5137-1.ch003

Kasemsap, K. (2015). Developing a framework of human resource management, organizational learning, knowledge management capability, and organizational performance. In P. O. de Pablos, L. J. Turró, R. D. T. Tennyson, & J. Zhao (Eds.), *Knowledge Management for Competitive Advantage During Economic Crisis* (pp. 164–193). IGI Global. doi:10.4018/978-1-4666-6457-9.ch010

Kasemsap, K. (2015a). The roles of international entrepreneurship and organizational innovation in SMEs. In L. Carmo Farinha, J. Ferreira, H. Smith, & S. Bagchi-Sen (Eds.), *Handbook of research on global competitive advantage through innovation and entrepreneurship* (pp. 410–438). Hershey, PA: IGI Global. doi:10.4018/978-1-4666-8348-8.ch024

Kasemsap, K. (2015b). Implementing enterprise resource planning. In M. Khosrow-Pour (Ed.), *Encyclopedia of information science and technology* (3rd ed.; pp. 798–807). Hershey, PA: IGI Global. doi:10.4018/978-1-4666-5888-2.ch076

Kasemsap, K. (2015c). The role of cultural dynamics in the digital age. In B. Christiansen & J. Koeman (Eds.), *Nationalism, cultural indoctrination, and economic prosperity in the digital age* (pp. 295–312). Hershey, PA: IGI Global. doi:10.4018/978-1-4666-7492-9.ch014

Kasemsap, K. (2016a). Promoting leadership development and talent management in modern organizations. In U. Aung & P. Ordoñez de Pablos (Eds.), *Managerial strategies and practice in the Asian business sector* (pp. 238–266). Hershey, PA: IGI Global. doi:10.4018/978-1-4666-9758-4.ch013

Kasemsap, K. (2016b). The roles of knowledge management and organizational innovation in global business. In G. Jamil, J. Poças-Rascão, F. Ribeiro, & A. Malheiro da Silva (Eds.), *Handbook of research on information architecture and management in modern organizations* (pp. 130–153). Hershey, PA: IGI Global. doi:10.4018/978-1-4666-8637-3.ch006

Kasemsap, K. (2016c). The roles of e-learning, organizational learning, and knowledge management in the learning organizations. In E. Railean, G. Walker, A. Elçi, & L. Jackson (Eds.), *Handbook of research on applied learning theory and design in modern education* (pp. 786–816). Hershey, PA: IGI Global. doi:10.4018/978-1-4666-9634-1.ch039

Kasemsap, K. (2016d). Analyzing the roles of human capital and competency in global business. In S. Sen, A. Bhattacharya, & R. Sen (Eds.), *International perspectives on socio-economic development in the era of globalization* (pp. 1–29). Hershey, PA: IGI Global. doi:10.4018/978-1-4666-9908-3.ch001

Kasemsap, K. (2016e). Utilizing communities of practice to facilitate knowledge sharing in the digital age. In S. Buckley, G. Majewski, & A. Giannakopoulos (Eds.), *Organizational knowledge facilitation through communities of practice in emerging markets* (pp. 198–224). Hershey, PA: IGI Global. doi:10.4018/978-1-5225-0013-1.ch011

Kehl, D., & Rappai, G. (2007). *Mintaelemszám tervezése Likert-skálát alkalmazó lekérdezésekben*. Retrieved January 13, 2016, from http://www.ksh.hu/statszemle_archive/2006/2006_09/2006_09_848.pdf

Khan, S. R., & Khan, I. A. (2015). Understanding ethnicity and national culture: A theoretical perspective on knowledge management in the organization. *Knowledge and Process Management, 22*(10), 51–61. doi:10.1002/kpm.1440

Kidwell, J. J., Vander Linde, K., & Johnson, S. L. (2000). Applying corporate knowledge management practices in higher education. *EDUCAUSE Quarterly, 23*(4), 28–33.

Kim, D. D. (1993). The link between individual and organizational learning. *MIT Sloan Management Review, 35*(1), 37–50.

Kim, M. K., Kim, S. M., & Bilir, M. K. (2014). Investigation of the dimensions of workplace learning environments (WLEs): Development of the WLE measure. *Performance Improvement Quarterly, 27*(2), 35–57. doi:10.1002/piq.21170

Kim, N., & Atuahene-Gima, K. (2010). Using exploratory and exploitative market learning for new product development. *Product Development & Management Association, 27*(4), 519–536. doi:10.1111/j.1540-5885.2010.00733.x

Kim, S., & Ju, B. (2008). An analysis of faculty perceptions: Attitudes towards knowledge sharing and collaboration in an academic institution. *Library & Information Science Research, 30*(4), 282–290. doi:10.1016/j.lisr.2008.04.003

King, W. (2001). *Strategies for creating a learning organization Korszerű Vezetés 10*. Budapest: BME-OMIKK.

Kliewe, T., Baaken, T., & Kesting, T. (2012). Introducing a Science-to-Business Marketing Unit to University Knowledge and Technology Transfer Structures: Activities, Benefits, Success Factors. In A. Szopa, W. Karwowski, & P. Ordóñez de Pablos (Eds.), *Academic Entrepreneurship and Technological Innovation: A Business Management Perspective* (pp. 53–74). Hershey, PA: IGI Global.

Klimeš, L. (1981). *Slovník cizích slov, 5* (Revised Edition). Prague: SPN.

Klimkó, G., & Tóth, R. (2007). Tudásmenedzsment az üzleti stratégia szolgálatában. *Vezetéstudományi szemle, 38*(7-8), 6-10.

Knight, L. (2002). Network learning: Exploring learning by interorganizational networks. *Human Relations, 55*(4), 427–454. doi:10.1177/0018726702554003

Kő, A. (2007). Üzleti intelligencia, in Döntéstámogató rendszerek. Panem Gazdaságinformatika sorozat. Budapest, Hungary: Panem Kiadó.

Konczosné Szombatelyi, M. (2014). *Családi vállalkozások generációváltásának kockázata*. Retrieved from http://kgk. sze.hu/images/dokumentumok/kautzkiadvany2014/KSZM.pdf

Korpás, Z. (2013). *Kire bízzam a ház kulcsát? Cégvezető utódkeresés a munkaerőpiacon*. Retrieved from gymskik.hu/ hu/letoltes/11455/cfb06

Koskinen, K. U. (2001). Tacit Knowledge as a Promoter of Success in Technology Firms. In *Proceedings of the 34th Hawaii International Conference on System Sciences* (pp. 1–9). doi:10.1109/HICSS.2001.926493

Koskinen, K. U. (2012). Organizational learning in project-based companies: A process thinking approach. *Project Management Journal, 43*(3), 40–49. doi:10.1002/pmj.21266

Kotler, P., & Keller, K. L. (2007). *Marketing Management*. Praha: Grada Publishing.

Kotter, J., & Rathgeber, H. (2005). *Our Iceberg Is Melting: Changing and Succeeding Under Any Con-ditions*. New York, NY: St. Martin's Press.

Kovács, I. (2008). A hagyományostól eltérő tanulási-tanítási formák. In L. Szabados (Ed.), *Pedagógia és/vagy andragógia Jászberény* (pp. 219–237). Szent István Egyetem Alkalmazott Bölcsészeti Kar.

Kozma, T., & Gyenge, B. (2015). The secret to business success after the crisis a business model in an enterprise. *Journal Of Central European Green Innovation, 3*(2), 71–82.

KPMG Academy. (2014). Organizational Knowledge Sharing in Hungary 2013/2014. KPMG Academy – University of Pannonia Research Report. KPMG Akadémia Kft.

KPMG. (2012). *Human resources and social media*. KPMG International Research report. MCGraphics.

KPMG-BME Academy. (2006). *Knowledge Management in Hungary 2005/2006. KPMG-BME Academy – University of Pannonia Research Report*. Budapest: KBA Oktatási Kft.

Kram, K. E. (1983). Phases of the mentor relationship. *Academy of Management Journal, 26*(4), 608–625. doi:10.2307/255910

Kram, K. E. (1985). *Mentoring at work*. Boston: Scott. Foresman.

Krause, D. E., & Gebert, D. (2003). A comparison of assessment center practices in organizations in German-speaking regions and the United States. *International Journal of Selection and Assessment, 11*(4), 297–312. doi:10.1111/j.0965-075X.2003.00253.x

Krogh, G., & Nonaka, I. (2000). Enabling Knowledge Creation. Oxford University Press. doi:10.1093/acprof:o so/9780195126167.001.0001

Krogh, G., Roos, J., & Slocum, K. (1994). An essay on Corporate Epistemology. Strategic Management Journal, 15, 53-72. doi:10.1002/smj.4250151005

Kuckartz, U. (2014). *Qualitative Inhaltsanalyse. Methoden, Praxis, Computerunterstützung*. Weinheim: Beltz Juventa.

Kuhn, T. S. (1962). *The Structure of Scientific Revolutions*. Chicago: The University of Chicago Press.

Laczkó, Zs. (1997). Családi vállalkozás – konfliktus és kooperáció. In *Családi vállalkozások Magyarországon, kutatási zárótanulmány*. Budapest: SEED Alapítvány.

Laitin, D. D., & Jeon, S. (2013). Exploring opportunities in cultural diversity. In R. A. Scott & S. M. Kosslyn (Eds.), *Emerging trends in the social and behavioural sciences: interdisciplinary directions* (pp. 1–17). London: SAGE Pub.

Lakner, Légrádiné, S. (2006). Új szemlélet a fejlesztő tanácsadásban: A coaching. *Tudásmenedzsment, 7*(2), 82–92.

Lam, A. (2004). Organizational innovation. In J. Fagerberg, D. Mowery, & R. R. Nelson (Eds.), *The Oxford Handbook of Innovation*. Oxford, UK: Oxford University Press.

Lam, A. (2010). From 'Ivory Tower Traditionalists' to 'entrepreneurial Scientists'?: Academic Scientists in Fuzzy University-Industry Boundaries. *Social Studies of Science, 40*(2), 307–340. doi:10.1177/0306312709349963

Laperrière, A., & Spence, M. (2015). Enacting international opportunities: The role of organizational learning in knowledge-intensive business services. *Journal of International Entrepreneurship, 13*(3), 212–241. doi:10.1007/s10843-015-0151-y

Laroche, F., Bordeu, F., Bernard, A., & Chinesta, F. (2012). Towards the factory of future An integrated approach of material-processes-information-human being. *ACM - Proceedings of the 2012 Virtual Reality International Conference*.

Larsen, M. T. (2011). The implications of academic enterprise for public science: An overview of the empirical evidence. *Research Policy, 40*(1), 6–19. doi:10.1016/j.respol.2010.09.013

Latour, B. (1986). Visualization and Cognition: Thinking with Eyes and Hands. *Knowledge in Society, 6*, 1–40.

Latour, B. (2005). *Reassembling the Social: An Introduction to Actor-Network-Theory*. New York: Oxford University Press.

Latour, B., & Woolgar, S. (1979). *Laboratory Life: the Social Construction of Scientific Facts*. Los Angeles, CA: EUA.

Law, C., & Ngai, E. (2008). An empirical study of the effects of knowledge sharing and learning behaviors on firm performance. *Expert Systems with Applications, 34*(4), 2342–2349. doi:10.1016/j.eswa.2007.03.004

Lazarová, B., Pol, M., Hloušková, L., Novotný, P., & Sedláček, M. (2013). Support for organizational learning in Czech basic schools. *Procedia: Social and Behavioral Sciences, 93*, 302–307. doi:10.1016/j.sbspro.2013.09.194

Leach, P. (2011). *Family Business – The Essentials*. London: Profiles Books.

Lee, C. C., Lin, S. P., Yang, S. L., Tsou, M. Y., & Chang, K. Y. (2013). Evaluating the influence of perceived organizational learning capability on user acceptance of information technology among operating room nurse staff. *Acta Anaesthesiologica Taiwanica, 51*(1), 22–27. doi:10.1016/j.aat.2013.03.013

Lee, K. C., Lee, S., & Kang, I. W. (2005). KMPI: Measuring knowledge management performance. *Information & Management, 42*(3), 469–482. doi:10.1016/j.im.2004.02.003

Lee-Kelley, L., Blackman, D. A., & Hurst, J. P. (2007). An exploration of the relationship between learning organisations and the retention of knowledge workers. *The Learning Organization, 14*(3), 204–221. doi:10.1108/09696470710739390

Lehner, F. (2006). *Wissensmanagement: Grundlagen, Methoden und technische Unterstützung*. München: Carl Hanser Verlag.

Lengyel, B. (2004). A tudásteremtés lokalitása: hallgatólagos tudás és helyi tudástranszfer. *Tér és Társadalom, 18*(2), 51-71.

Leonard, D., & Sensiper, S. (1998). The Role of Tacit Knowledge in Group Innovation. *California Management Review, 40*(3), 112–132. doi:10.2307/41165946

Lethbridge, T. C., Sim, S. E., & Singer, J. (2005). Studying Software Engineers: Data Collection Techniques for Software Field Studies. *Empirical Software Engineering, 10*(3), 311–341. doi:10.1007/s10664-005-1290-x

Letmathe, L., Scweitzer, M., & Zielinski, M. (2011). How to Learn New Tasks: Shop Floor Performance Effects of Knowledge Transfer and Performance Feedback. *Journal of Operations Management, 30*(3), 221–236. doi:10.1016/j.jom.2011.11.001

Levinson, D. J., Darrow, C. N., Klein, E. B., Levinson, M. H., & McKee, B. (1978). *The seasons of a man's life*. New York: Balantine Books.

Levitt, B., & March, J. G. (1988). Organizational learning. *Annual Review of Sociology, 14*(1), 319–340. doi:10.1146/annurev.so.14.080188.001535

Lewin, K. (1946). Action Research and Minority Problems. *Journal of Social Issues*, (3).

Liao, T., Warren, Z., & Claude, R. M. (1998). Similarity Measures for Retrieval in Case-Based Reasoning Systems. *Applied Artificial Intelligence, 12*(4), 267–288. doi:10.1080/088395198117730

Liao, Y., Lezoche, M., Panetto, H., Boudjlida, N., & Rocha Loures, E. (2015). Semantic annotation for knowledge explicitation in a product lifecycle management context: A survey. *Computers in Industry, 71*, 24–34. doi:10.1016/j.compind.2015.03.005

Lichtenthaler. (2008). Opening up strategic for. technology planning: extended roadmaps and functional markets. *Management Decision, 46*(1-2), 77-91.

Lichtenthaler, U. (2009). Absorptive capacity, environmental turbulence, and the complementarity of organizational learning processes. *Academy of Management Journal, 52*(4), 822–846. doi:10.5465/AMJ.2009.43670902

Liebl, F. (2015). Knowledge management for strategic marketing. In H. E. Spotts (Ed.), *Assessing the different roles of marketing theory and practice in the jaws of economic uncertainty* (pp. 48–57). New York: Springer Cham Heidelberg.

Liebowicz, J. (2012). *Knowledge Management Handbook: Collaboration and Social Networking.* CRC Press. doi:10.1201/b12285

Li, S., & Lin, B. (2006). Accessing information sharing and information quality in supply chain management. *Decision Support Systems, 42*(3), 1641–1656. doi:10.1016/j.dss.2006.02.011

Liu, S., McMahon, C. A., & Culley, S. J. (2008). A review of structured document retrieval (SDR) technology to improve information access performance in engineering document management. *Computers in Industry, 59*(1), 3–16. doi:10.1016/j.compind.2007.08.001

Liu, X., Xu, G., & Hu, B. (2010). Relational embeddedness, exploratory learning and firm technological innovation performance. *International Journal of Technology, Policy and Management, 10*(4), 343–359. doi:10.1504/IJTPM.2010.036921

Livermore, D. (2011). *The cultural intelligence difference: master the one skill you can't do without in today's global economy*. New York: American Management Association.

Li, W. (2010). Virtual knowledge sharing in a cross-cultural context. *Journal of Knowledge Management, 14*(1), 38–50. doi:10.1108/13673271011015552

Lloria, M. B., & Moreno-Luzon, M. D. (2014). Organizational learning: Proposal of an integrative scale and research instrument. *Journal of Business Research, 67*(5), 692–697. doi:10.1016/j.jbusres.2013.11.029

Lopuch, V. S., & Davis, D. C. (2014). The role and value of diversity to learning organizations and innovation. In N. Erbe (Ed.), Approaches to managing organizational diversity and innovation (pp. 213–236). Hershey, PA: IGI Global. doi:10.4018/978-1-4666-6006-9.ch011

Loshin, D. (2013). *Big Data Analytics*. Elsevier Inc.

Löwy, I. (1994). Ludwik Fleck e a Presente História das Ciências. *Manguinhos, I*(1), 7–18. PMID:11624967

Lozano, R. (2013). Are companies planning their organisational changes for corporate sustainability? An analysis of three case studies on resistance to change and their strategies to overcome it. *Corporate Social Responsibility and Environmental Management, 20*(5), 275–295. doi:10.1002/csr.1290

Lozano, R. (2014). Creativity and organizational learning as means to foster sustainability. *Sustainable Development, 22*(3), 205–216. doi:10.1002/sd.540

Lucier, C. E., & Torsilieri, J. D. (1997). *Why Knowledge Programs Fail: A CEO's Guide to Managing Learning.* Strategy & Business.

Luhmann, N. (1995). *Social Systems.* Stanford, CA: Stanford University Press.

Luhmann, N. (2013). *Introduction to Systems Theory.* Cambridge, MA: Polity Press.

Lundvall, B. A. (2007). National Innovation Systems – Analytical Concept and Development Tool. *Industry and Innovation, 14*(1), 95–119. doi:10.1080/13662710601130863

Lupeikiene, A., Dzemyda, G., Kiss, F., & Caplinskas, A. (2014). Advanced Planning and Scheduling Systems: Modeling and Implementation Challenges. *Informatica, 25*(4), 581–616. doi:10.15388/Informatica.2014.31

Lu, T., Guan, F., Gu, N., & Wang, F. (2008). Semantic classification and query of engineering drawings in the ship-building industry. *International Journal of Production Research, 46*(9), 2471–2483. doi:10.1080/00207540701737922

Luzwick, P. (1999). *What's a pound of your information worth? Constructs for collaboration and consistency.* Unpublished white paper. Author.

Lyles, M. A. (2014). Organizational learning, knowledge creation, problem formulation and innovation in messy problems. *European Management Journal, 32*(1), 132–136. doi:10.1016/j.emj.2013.05.003

Lynn, G. S., Reilly, R. R., & Akgun, A. E. (2000). Knowledge management in new product teams: Practices and outcomes. *IEEE Transactions on Engineering Management, 47*(2), 221–231. doi:10.1109/17.846789

MacCann, C., Matthews, G., Zeidner, M., & Roberts, R. D. (1993). Psychological assessment of emotional intelligence: A review of self-report and performance-based testing. *The International Journal of Organizational Analysis, 11*(3), 247–274. doi:10.1108/eb028975

Machlup, F. (1962). *The Production and Distribution of Knowledge in the United States.* Princeton University Press.

Madenas, N., Tiwari, A., Turner, C. J., & Woodward, J. (2014). Information flow in supply chain management: A review across the product lifecycle. *CIRP Journal of Manufacturing Science and Technology, 7*(4), 335–346. doi:10.1016/j.cirpj.2014.07.002

Mahindra & Mahindra Ltd. (2014). *The Mahindra Group.* Retrieved February 11, 2014, from http://www.mahindra.com/Who-We-Are

Mahindra Group USA. (2014). *Mahindra USA.* Retrieved October 14, 2014, from http://mahindrausa.com/news/mahindra-usa-celebrates-20-years-growth-north-america

Ma, K., & Sun, R. (2013). Introducing WebSocket-Based Real-Time Monitoring System for Remote Intelligent Buildings. *International Journal of Distributed Sensor Networks, 2013*, 867693. doi:10.1155/2013/867693

Malhotra, A., Gosain, S., & El Sawy, O. A. (2007). Leveraging standard electronic business interfaces to enable adaptive supply chain partnerships. *Information Systems Research, 18*(3), 260–279. doi:10.1287/isre.1070.0132

*Management Mania.* (2016). Retrieved from https://managementmania.com/en

Mandal, S. (2014). Frugal Innovations for Global Health — Perspectives for Students. *IEEE Pulse, 5*(1), 11–13.

Mandl, I. (2008). *Overview of family businesses relevant issues.* Final report. KMU Forschung. Retrieved January 13, 2016, from http://ec.europa.eu/enterprise/policies/sme/files/craft/family_business/doc/familybusiness_study_en.pdf

Manuti, A., Pastore, S., Scardigno, A. F., Giancaspro, M. L., & Morciano, D. (2015). Formal and informal learning in the workplace: A research review. *International Journal of Training and Development, 19*(1), 1–17. doi:10.1111/ijtd.12044

Marakas, G. M. (1999). *Decision Support Systems in the Twenty-first Century*. Englewood Cliffs, NJ: Prentice-Hall.

Marcellné Szilágyi, E. (2012). Az érzelmi intelligencia mint a tacit tudás része. In Átalakuló emberi erőforrás menedzsment. Budapest: CompLex Kiadó Jogi és Üzleti Tartalomszolgáltató Kft.

March, J. G. (1991). Exploration and exploitation in organizational learning. *Organization Science, 2*(1), 71–87. doi:10.1287/orsc.2.1.71

March, J. G. (1994). *A Primer on Decision Making: How Decisions Happen*. New York, NY: Free Press.

Marland, S. P. (1972). *Education of the gifted and talented: Report to the Congress of the United States by the U.S. commissioner of education*. Washington, DC: Government Printing Office.

Marquadt, M. J., & Horvath, L. (2010). *Global Teams*. Mountain View, CA: Davies Black Publishing.

Mårtensson, M. (2000). A critical review of knowledge management as a management tool. *Journal of Knowledge Management, 4*(3), 204–216. doi:10.1108/13673270010350002

Martin, J., & Schmidt, C. (2010). How to Keep Your Top Talent. *Harvard Business Review, 12*(9), 6–15.

Martin, R. L. (2009). *The Design of Business: Why Design Thinking is the Next Competitive Ad-vantage*. Cambridge, MA: Harvard University Press.

Masrek, M. N., Rahim, H. A., Johare, R., & Rambli, Y. R. (2011). Intranet Supported Knowledge Sharing Behavior. *Journal of Organizational Knowledge Management, 2011*, 1–11. doi:10.5171/2011.802263

Matthews, G., Zeidner, M., & Roberts, R. D. (2012). *Emotional Intelligence 101*. New York: Springer Publishing Campany LLC.

Mayer, J. D., Salovey, P., & Caruso, D. R. (2000). Models of emotional intelligence. In R. J. Sternberg (Ed.), The handbook of intelligence (pp. 396–420). Cambridge University Press. doi:10.1017/CBO9780511807947.019

May, M. E. (2006). *The Elegant Solution: Toyota's Formula for Mastering Innovation*. New York, NY: Free Press.

Mayring, P. (2010). *Qualitative Inhaltsanalyse: Grundlagen und Techniken*. Weinheim: Beltz Pädagogik. doi:10.1007/978-3-531-92052-8_42

McAdam, R., Moffett, S., Hazlett, S. A., & Shevlin, M. (2010). Developing a model of innovation implementation for UK SMEs: A path analysis and explanatory case analysis. *International Small Business Journal, 28*(3), 195–215. doi:10.1177/0266242609360610

Mcdermott, R., & O'dell, C. (2001). Overcoming cultural barriers to sharing knowledge. *Journal of Knowledge Management, 5*(1), 76–85. doi:10.1108/13673270110384428

McLuhan, M., & Powers, B. (1989). *The Global Village: Transformations in World Life and Media in the 21st Century*. Oxford, UK: Oxford University Press.

McMaster, T., Vidgen, R. T., & Wastell, D. G. (1997). Technology Transfer: Diffusion or Translation? In T. McMaster et al. (Eds.), *Facilitating Technology Transfer through Partnership*. London: Chapman & Hall. doi:10.1007/978-0-387-35092-9_4

Meehan, B., & Richardson, I. (2002). Identification of software process knowledge management. *Software Process Improvement and Practice, 7*(2), 47–55. doi:10.1002/spip.154

Mehta, N., Hall, D., & Byrd, T. (2014). Information technology and knowledge in software development teams: The role of project uncertainty. *Information & Management*, *51*(4), 417–429. doi:10.1016/j.im.2014.02.007

Melo, S., & Beck, M. (2015). Intra and interorganizational learning networks and the implementation of quality improvement initiatives: The case of a Portuguese teaching hospital. *Human Resource Development Quarterly*, *26*(2), 155–183. doi:10.1002/hrdq.21207

Menguc, B., Auh, S., & Shih, E. (2007). Transformational leadership and market orientation: Implications for the implementation of competitive strategies and business unit performance. *Journal of Business Research*, *60*(4), 314–321. doi:10.1016/j.jbusres.2006.12.008

Merad, M., Dechy, N., & Marcel, F. (2014). A pragmatic way of achieving highly sustainable organisation: Governance and organisational learning in action in the public French sector. *Safety Science*, *69*, 18–28. doi:10.1016/j.ssci.2014.01.002

Merton, R. K. (1987). Three Fragments from a Sociologist's Notebook: Establishing the Phenomenon, Specified Ignorance and Strategic Research Materials. *Annual Review of Sociology*, *13*(1), 1–28. doi:10.1146/annurev.so.13.080187.000245

Mészáros, T., & Szirmai, P. (2001). Egy kutatás tanulságai – Az EU kisvállalkozáspolitikája. Pénzforrás – A pályázatok kézikönyve, 26.

Metaxiotis, K., Ergazakis, K., & Psarras, J. (2005). Exploring the world of knowledge management: Agreements and disagreements in the academic/practitioner community. *Journal of Knowledge Management*, *9*(2), 6–18. doi:10.1108/13673270510590182

Michaels, E., Handfield-Jones, H., & Axelrod, B. (2001). *The war for talent*. Boston. MA: Harvard Business School Press.

Mihályné & Sándorné. (2008). *Tehetséggondozás*. Szarvas, Hungary: Szarvaspress Nyomda.

Miles, R. E., & Snow, C. C. (1978). Organisational Strategy, Structure and Process. New York: McGraw-Hill.

Miller, S. P. (2014). *Next-generation leadership development in family businesses: the critical roles of shared vision and family climate*. Retrieved January 9, 2016, from http://journal.frontiersin.org/article/10.3389/fpsyg.2014.01335/abstract

Minbaeva, D. B. (2007). Knowledge transfer in multinational corporations. *Management International Review*, *47*(4), 567–593. doi:10.1007/s11575-007-0030-4

Mintzberg, H., Ahlstrand, B., & Lampel, J. (1998). *Strategy Safari: A Guided Tour through the Wilds of Strategic Management*. New York, NY: Free Press.

Minzberg, H. (2009). *Managing*. Oakland, CA: Berrett-Koehler Publishers.

Modern Management. (2011). *Čeští podnikatelé nepoužívají moderní metody řízení*. Praha: Economia, a,s. Retrieved from: http://modernirizeni.ihned.cz/c1-52417420-cesti-podnikatele-nepouzivaji-moderni-metody-rizeni

Moeller, K., & Svahn, S. (2004). Crossing East-West boundaries: Knowledge sharing in intercultural business networks. *Industrial Marketing Management*, *33*(3), 219–228. doi:10.1016/j.indmarman.2003.10.011

Mohelská, H., & Pitra, Z. (2012). Manažerské metody. Prague: Professional Publishing.

Mohr, A., & Shoobridge, G. E. (2011). The role of multi-ethnic workforces in the internationalisation of SMEs. *Journal of Small Business and Enterprise Development*, *18*(4), 748–763. doi:10.1108/14626001111179785

Molas-Gallart, J., Salter, A., Patel, P., Scott, A., & Duran, X. (2002). *Measuring Third Stream Activities: Final Report to the Russell Group of Universities*. Science and Technology Policy Research Unit, University of Sussex.

Molnár, Z. (2012). Competitive intelligence aneb jak získat konkurenční výhodu. Praha: Nakladatelství Oeconomica.

Molnár, Z., & Střelka, J. (2012). Competitive Intelligence v malých a středních podnicích. *E+M Economics and Management, 15*(3), 156-170.

Mönks, F. J., & Boxtel, H. W. (2000). A Rensulli-modell kiterjesztése és alkalmazása serdülőkorban. In A tehetségfejlesztés pszichológiája (pp. 67-82). Debrecen, Hungary: Kossuth Egyetemi Kiadó.

Montalvo, C. (2006). What triggers change and innovation? *Technovation, 26*(3), 312–323. doi:10.1016/j.technovation.2004.09.003

Moreno-Luzon, M. D., & Lloria, M. B. (2008). The role of non-structural and informal mechanisms of integration and coordination as forces in knowledge creation. *British Journal of Management, 19*(3), 250–276. doi:10.1111/j.1467-8551.2007.00544.x

Morgan, G. (1986). Images of Organization. Beverly Hills, CA: Sage Publications.

Morgan, N. A., Katsikeas, C. S., & Vorhies, D. W. (2012). Export marketing strategy implementation, export marketing capabilities, and export venture performance. *Journal of the Academy of Marketing Science, 40*(2), 271–289. doi:10.1007/s11747-011-0275-0

Mueller, J. (2012). Knowledge sharing between project teams and its cultural antecedents. *Journal of Knowledge Management, 16*(3), 435–447. doi:10.1108/13673271211238751

Mukerjee, K. (2012). Frugal innovation: The key to penetrating emerging markets. *Ivey Business Journal.* Retrieved September 20, 2014, from http://iveybusinessjournal.com/uncategorized/frugal-innovation-the-key-to-penetrating-emerging-markets#.VE4P5hZCw5A

Müller, S., & Gelbrich, K. (2015). *Interkulturelles Marketing.* München: Verlag Franz Vahlen GmbH. doi:10.15358/9783800644612

Mura, L., & Rózsa, Z. (2013). The Impact of Networking on the Innovation Performance of SMEs. In *Proceedings of MSED The 7th International Days of Statistics and Economics.* Praha: University of Economics.

Mura, L., Žuľová, J., & Madleňák, A. (2016). Strategic management and management of personnel costs: Employing young people in the Slovak Republic. *Problems and Perspectives in Management, 14*(1), 79–84.

Murmann, J. P. (2003). *Knowledge and competitive advantage: the coevolution of firms, technology, and national institutions (Cambridge studies in the emergence of global enterprise).* Cambridge, UK: Cambridge University Press. doi:10.1017/CBO9780511510953

Nadoveza, D., & Kiritsis, D. (2014). Ontology-based approach for context modeling in enterprise applications. *Computers in Industry, 65*(9), 1218–1231. doi:10.1016/j.compind.2014.07.007

Naghi, A. A., Gholamrez, J., Mehdi, A. S., Reza, H., & Majid, R. (2010). Increasing the intellectual capital in organization: Examining the role of organizational learning. *European Journal of Social Sciences, 14*(1/2), 98–112.

Nahapiet, J., & Ghoshal, S. (1998). Social Capital, Intellectual Capital, and the Organizational Advantage. *Academy of Management Review, 23*(2), 242–266.

Negroponte, N. (1996). *Being Digital.* New York: Vintage.

Nelson, R. (2004). The market economy, and the scientific commons. *Research Policy, 33*(3), 455–471. doi:10.1016/j.respol.2003.09.008

Nemirovsky, R., & Solomon, J. (2000). *"This is crazy. Difference of differences!" On the flow of ideas in a mathematical conversation.* Paper prepared for Videopapers in Mathematics Education Conference, Dedham, MA.

Nemzeti Innovációs Hivatal (NIH). (2013). *Kutatás-fejlesztés és Innováció Magyarországon.* Retrieved February 10, 2016, from http://kaleidoszkop.nih.gov.hu/documents/15428/38972/Kutat%C3%A1s-fejleszt%C3%A9s%20%C3%A9s%20 innov%C3%A1ci%C3%B3%20Magyarorsz%C3%A1gon

*Neo4j Manual.* (n.d.). Retrieved from http://neo4j.com/docs/

Nevis, E. C., DiBella, A. J., & Gould, J. M. (1995). Understanding organizations as learning systems. *MIT Sloan Management Review, 36*(2), 73–85.

Ng, K. Y., van Dyne, L., & Ang, S. (2012). Cultural intelligence: A review, reflections, and recommendations for future research. In A. M. Ryan, F. T. Leong, & F. L. Oswald (Eds.), *Conducting multinational research: Applying organizational psychology in the workplace* (pp. 29–58). Washington, DC: American Psychological Association. doi:10.1037/13743-002

Nguyen, T. D. N., & Aoyama, A. (2015). The impact of cultural differences on technology transfer. Management practice moderation. *Journal of Manufacturing Technology Management, 27*(7), 926–954. doi:10.1108/JMTM-09-2013-0130

Nielsen, A. P. (2006). Understanding dynamic capabilities through knowledge management. *Journal of Knowledge Management, 10*(4), 59–71. doi:10.1108/13673270610679363

Noe, R. A. (1988). Women and mentoring: A review and research agenda. *Academy of Management Review, 13*(1), 65–77.

Noe, R. A. (2002). *Employee training and development.* New York, NY: McGraw–Hill.

Nonaka, I. (2010). *Cultivating Leaders with Practical Wisdom: Scrum and Ba Building.* Retrieved October 23, 2015, from https://ai.wu.ac.at/~kaiser/birgit/Nonaka-Papers/nonaka-phronetic-leadership-folien-2010.pdf

Nonaka, I., & Takuchi, H. (1995). The knowledge creating Company: How Japanese Companies Create the Dynamics por Innovation. New York: Oxford University Press.

Nonaka, I., Takeuchi, H., & Umemoto, K. (1996). A theory of organizational knowledge creation. *International Journal of Technology Management, 11*(7-8), 833–845.

Nonaka, I., Toyama, R., & Hirata, T. (2008). *Managing Flow: A Process Theory of the Knowledge-Based Firm.* Houndmills, UK: Palgrave Macmillan.

Nonaka, I. (1994). A dynamic theory of organizational knowledge creation. *Organization Science, 5*(1), 14–37. doi:10.1287/orsc.5.1.14

Nonaka, I., Kodama, M., Hirose, A., & Kohlbacher, F. (2014). Dynamic fractal organizations for promoting knowledge-based transformation – A new paradigm for organizational theory. *European Management Journal, 32*(1), 137–146. doi:10.1016/j.emj.2013.02.003

Nonaka, I., & Konno, N. (1998). The concept of "ba": Building a foundation for knowledge creation. *California Management Review, 40*(3), 40–54. doi:10.2307/41165942

Nonaka, I., & Nishiguchi, T. (2001). *Knowledge Emergence. Social, Technical and Evolutionary Dimensions of Knowledge Creation.* New York: Oxford University Press.

Nonaka, I., & Takeuchi, H. (1995). *The Knowledge creating company.* Oxford, UK: Oxford University Press.

Nonaka, I., & Takeuchi, H. (1995). *The Knowledge-creating Company.* New York: Oxford University Press.

Nonaka, I., & Takeuchi, H. (1995). *The Knowledge-Creating Company.* Oxford: Oxford University Press.

Nonaka, I., & Takeuchi, H. (1995). *The knowledge-creating company: How Japanese companies create the dynamics of innovation.* New York, NY: Oxford University Press.

Nonaka, I., & Takeuchi, H. (1995). *The Knowledge-Creating Company: How Japanese Companies Create the Dynamics of Innovation.* New York: Oxford University Press.

Nonaka, I., von Krogh, G., & Voepel, S. (2006). Organisational knowledge creation theory: Evolutionary paths and future advances. *Organization Studies, 27*(8), 1179–1208. doi:10.1177/0170840606066312

North, K. (2002). *Wissensorientierte Unternehmensführung. Wertschöpfung durch Wissen.* Wiesbaden: Gabler. doi:10.1007/978-3-322-94633-1

Noszkay, E. (2013). A rendszerszemléletű tudásmenedzsment. [System-based Knowledge Management] Harlow: Pearson Education Limited.

Noszkay, E. (2013). A rendszerszemléletű tudásmenedzsment. Pearson Publishing.

Noszkay, E. (2013). A rendszerszemléletű tudásmenedzsment. Pearson.

Noszkay, E. (2013). *Tudásmenedzsment – módszertani megközelítésben.* Paper presented at Vezetéstudományi Konferencia "Vezetésésszervezetek Taylor után 102 évvel", Szeged, Hungary

Noszkay, E., & Balogh, A. (2015). Operational Characteristics of Knowledge-Intensive Service Companies and Knowledge-Intensive Business Services (KIBS). In Tudásteremtés és - alkalmazás a modern társadalomban. Tanulmánykötet.

Noszkay, E. (1999). *A gazdasági informatika helye és oktatásának sajátságos követelményei, valamint módszerei a menedzserképzésben In* . Konferencia Kiadvány I. Kötet.

Noszkay, E. (2012). *Tudásmenedzsment … és ahogyan fejlődik.* Budapest: Poziteam.

Noszkay, E. (2013). *A rendszerszemléletű tudásmenedzsment.* Pearson.

Noszkay, E., & Balogh, A. (2015). Tudásigényes vállalatok és tudásigényes szolgáltatások működési jellegzetességeik tükrében. In B. Norbert & P. Szabolcs (Eds.), *Tudásteremtés és -alkalmazás a modern társadalomban Tanulmánykötet* (pp. 146–157). Szegedi Tudományegyetem.

Nunes, J. A. (2007). *Discurso(s) sobre as Ciência(s) e as Tecnologia(s). Presentation of the Doctoral Programme in "Governação, Conhecimento e Inovação".* Centro de Estudos Sociais, Faculdade de Economia da Universidade de Coimbra.

Nunes, M. B., Annansingh, F., Eaglestone, B., & Wakefield, R. (2006). Knowledge management issues in knowledge-intensive SMEs. *The Journal of Documentation, 62*(1), 101–119. doi:10.1108/00220410610642075

Nwankpa, J., & Roumani, Y. (2014). Understanding the link between organizational learning capability and ERP system usage: An empirical examination. *Computers in Human Behavior, 33*, 224–234. doi:10.1016/j.chb.2014.01.030

Oakley, E., & Krug, D. (1997). *Korszerű változásmenedzselés.* Budapest: Bagolyvár Könyvkiadó.

Obermayer-Kovács, N., & Csepregi, A. (2007). Perspectives of Knowledge Management – Investigations at Hungarian Organizations. In *Proceedings of Business Scienes Symposium for Young Researchers.*

Odiorne, G. S. (1985). Mentoring- an American management innovation. *The Personnel Administrator, 30*(5), 63–70. PMID:10270460

Oláh, A., & Gyöngyösiné Kiss, E. (2007). A személyiség fogalma és vizsgálati módszerei: mérés, kutatás, elmélet. In *Vázlatok a személyiségről–A személyiség-lélektan alapvető irányzatainak tükrében.* Budapest, Hungary: Új Mandátum Könyvkiadó.

Oliveira, L. (2008). *Sociologia da Inovação – A Construção Social das Técnicas e dos Mercados.* Oeiras: Celta Editora.

Olšovská, A., Mura, L., & Švec, M. (2015). The most recent legislative changes and their impact on interest by enterprises in agency employment: What is next in human resource management? *Problems and Perspectives in Management, 13*(3), 47–54.

Opfer, V. D., Pedder, D., & Lavicza, Z. (2011). The influence of school orientation to learning on teachers' professional learning change. *School Effectiveness and School Improvement, 22*(2), 193–214. doi:10.1080/09243453.2011.572078

Opitz, H. (1970). *A Classification System to Design Workpieces*. Pergamon Press.

Orosz, G., & Szukics, N. (2012). A társas összehasonlítás egyéni különbségei. *Pszichológia (Budapest), 32*(4), 361–378. doi:10.1556/Pszicho.32.2012.4.4

Packer, K., & Webster, A. (1996). Patenting Culture in Science: Reinventing the Scientific Wheel of Credibility. *Science, Technology & Human Values, 21*(4), 427–453. doi:10.1177/016224399602100403

Pakucs, J. (2005). Innováció és a vállalkozások. *Polgári Szemle, 1*(1). Retrieved March 1, 2016, from http://www.polgariszemle.hu/?view=v_article&ID=11&page=1

Panahi, S., Watson, J., & Partridge, H. (2012). Social Media and Tacit Knowledge Sharing: Developing a Conceptual Model. In Proceedings of World Academy of Science, Engineering and Technology. World Academy of Science, Engineering and Technology.

Pansera, M., & Richard, O. (2014). Eco-Innovation at the 'Bottom of the Pyramid'. In Collaboration for Sustainability and Innovation: A Role For Sustainability Driven by the Global South? (pp. 293-313). Springer.

Parsons, T. (1978). *Action Theory and the Human Condition*. Free Press.

Patterson, J. A. (1994). Shattering the glass ceiling: women in school administration. Chapel Hill, NC: Academic Press.

Patton, J. (2002). Hitting the target: Adding Interaction Design to Agile Software Development. In *OOPSLA 2002 Practitioners Reports on - OOPSLA '02* (pp. 1–7). New York: ACM Press. doi:10.1145/604251.604255

Paulin, D., & Suneson, K. (2012). Knowledge Transfer, Knowledge Sharing and Knowledge Barriers – Three Blurry Terms in KM. *Electronic Journal of Knowledge Management, 10*(1), 81–91.

Pavitt, K. (2001). Public Policies to Support Basic Research: What Can the Rest of the World Learn from US Theory and Practice? (And What They Should Not Learn). *Industrial and Corporate Change, 10*(3), 761–779. doi:10.1093/icc/10.3.761

Pawliczek, A. (2015). *Management Methods, Tools and Systems in the Operation of Enterprises with an Accent on the Strategy, Continuous Improvement and Performance* (habilitation thesis). Zlín: Univerzita Tomáše Bati. Fakulta managementu a ekonomiky.

Pawliczek, A., & Piszczur, R. (2013). Utilization of Modern Management Methods with Special Emphasis on ISO 9000 and 14000 in Contemporary Czech and Slovak Companies. In *Proceedings of the 11th International Conference Liberec Economic Forum 2013*. Sychrov: TU of Liberec.

Payne, S. C., & Huffman, A. H. (2005). A longitudinal examination of the influence of mentoring on commitment and turnover. *Academy of Management Journal, 48*(1), 158–168. doi:10.5465/AMJ.2005.15993166

Pearce, D. W. (1995). *Macmillanův slovník moderní ekonomie*. Prague: Victoria Publishing.

Pee, L. G., Kankanhalli, A., & Kim, H. (2010). Knowledge Sharing in Information Systems Development: A Social Interdependence Perspective. *Journal of the Association for Information Systems, 11*(10), 550–575.

Pekka-Economou, V., & Hadjidema, S. (2011). Innovative organizational forms that add value to both organizations and community: The case of knowledge management. *European Research Studies, 14*(2), 81–95.

Peltier, J. W., Schibrowsky, J. A., Schultz, D. E., & Zahay, D. (2006). Interactive IMC: The relational-transactional continuum and the synergistic use of customer data. *Journal of Advertising Research, 46*(2), 146–159. doi:10.2501/S0021849906060193

Peltier, J. W., Zahay, D., & Lehmann, D. R. (2013). Organizational learning and CRM success: A model for linking organizational practices, customer data quality, and performance. *Journal of Interactive Marketing, 27*(1), 1–13. doi:10.1016/j.intmar.2012.05.001

Peltokorpi, V., & Vaara, E. (2014). Knowledge transfer in multinational corporations: Productive and counterproductive effects of language sensitive recruitment. *Journal of International Business Studies, 45*(5), 600–622. doi:10.1057/jibs.2014.1

Peng, M., & Meyer, K. (2011). *International Business*. London: Cengage Learning EMEA.

Pentaho – A Hitachi Data Systems Company. (2015). *Pentaho Business Analytics*. Retrieved from: http://www.pentaho.com/product/business-visualization-analytics

Pérez, J. C., Petrides, K. V., & Furnham, A. (2005). Measuring trait emotional intelligence. In R. Schulze & R. D. Roberts (Eds.), *International Handbook of Emotional Intelligence*. Cambridge: Hogrefe & Huber.

Perez-Soltero, A., Zavala-Guerrero, A. G., Barcelo-Valenzuela, M., Sanchez-Schmitz, G., & Meroño-Cerdan, A. L. (2015). A Methodology for the Development and Implementation of Knowledge Management Strategy in a Mexican SME Trading Company. *The IUP Journal of Knowledge Management, 13*(2), 25–44.

Peters, T. (1992). *Liberation Management: Necessary Disorganization for the Nanosecond Nineties* (1st ed.). New York: Alfred A. Knopf, Inc.

Petrány, V. (2009). Versenyelőny-e a tehetségmenedzsment? Tehetséggondozás vagy tehetségvásárlás?. *Munkaügyi Szemle, 53*(1), 97-104.

Petrides, K. V. (2009). *Technical Manual for the Trait Emotional Intelligence Questionnaires (TEIQue)*. London: Psychometric Laboratory.

Petrides, K. V. (2010). Trait emotional intelligence theory. *Industrial and Organizational Psychology: Perspectives on Science and Practice, 3*(2), 136–139. doi:10.1111/j.1754-9434.2010.01213.x

Petrides, K. V. (2011). Ability and trait emotional intelligence. In T. Chamorro-Premuzic, A. Furnham, & S. von Stumm (Eds.), *The Blackwell-Wiley Handbook of Individual Differences*. New York: Wiley. doi:10.1002/9781444343120.ch25

Petrides, K. V., & Furnham, A. (2006). The role of trait emotional intelligence in a gender-specific model of organizational variables. *Journal of Applied Social Psychology, 36*(2), 552–569. doi:10.1111/j.0021-9029.2006.00019.x

Petrides, K. V., Pérez-González, J. C., & Furnham, A. (2007). On the criterion and incremental validity of trait emotional intelligence. *Cognition and Emotion, 21*(1), 26–55. doi:10.1080/02699930601038912

Petříková, R. (2010). Moderní management znalostí: (principy, procesy, příklady dobré praxe). Praha: Professional Publishing.

Pfuetzenreiter, M. R. (2003). *Epistemologia de Ludwik Fleck como Referencial para a Pesquisa nas Ciências Aplicadas*. Porto Alegre: Episteme.

Piazza, R. (2010). The learning region between pedagogy and economy. *European Journal of Education, 45*(3), 402–418. doi:10.1111/j.1465-3435.2010.01437.x

Pinto, H. (2009). Challenges for Innovation in the Algarve: contributions to understand the regional innovation system, Spatial and Organizational Dynamics Discussion 2009-00. CIEO-Research Centre for Spatial and Organizational Dynamics, University of Algarve.

Pinto, H. (2012). *Transferência do conhecimento em Portugal. Mudança e institucionalização das relações universidade-empresa.* (Doctoral Thesis). Faculdade de Economia da Universidade de Coimbra.

Pinto, H., Cruz, A. R., & Almeida, H. (2015). Academic Entrepreneurship and Knowledge Transfer Networks: Translation Process and Boundary Organizations. In L. Carvalho (Ed.), *Handbook of Research on Entrepreneurial Success and its Impact on Regional Development.* Hershey, PA: IGI Global.

Pinto, H., & Guerreiro, J. (2010). Innovation regional planning and latent dimensions: The case of the Algarve region. *The Annals of Regional Science, 44*(2), 315–329. doi:10.1007/s00168-008-0264-5

Pinto, H., Guerreiro, J., & Uyarra, E. (2012). Diversidades de Sistemas de Inovação e Implicações nas Políticas Regionais: Comparação das Regiões do Algarve e da Andaluzia. *Revista Portuguesa de Estudos Regionais, 29,* 3–14.

Pirsig, R. (1991). *LILA: An Inquiry into Morals.* New York, NY: Bantam Book.

Pitra, Z., & Mohelská, H. (2015). Management transferu znalostí: od prvního nápadu ke komerčně úspěšné inovaci. Praha: Professional Publishing.

Platsidou, M. (2010). Trait Emotional Intelligence of Greek Special Education Teachers in Relation to Burnout and Job Satisfaction. *School Psychology International, 31*(1), 60–76. doi:10.1177/0143034309360436

Polák-Weldon, R. (2014). Sustainable Value Creation for Employees. *BAM2014 Conference Proceedings.*

Polanyi, M. (1996). *The tacit Dimension.* New York: Anchor Day Books.

Polányi, M. (1962). Tacit Knowing. Its Bearing on Some Problems of Philosophy. *Reviews of Modern Physics, 34*(4), 601–616. doi:10.1103/RevModPhys.34.601

Polanyi, M. (1964). *Personal Knowledge. Towards A Post-Critical Philosophy.* London: Routledge & Kegan Paul Ltd.

Polanyi, M. (1966). The logic of tacit inference. *Philosophy (London, England), 41*(155), 1–18. doi:10.1017/S0031819100066110

Polányi, M. (1966). *The Tacit Dimension.* Garden City, NY: Doubleday & Co.

Polányi, M. (1997). *Tudomány és ember. Három tanulmány.* Budapest: Argumentum Kiadó.

Popescu, A.-D., Suciu, S., & Raoult, M.-G. (2014). *Intercultural competences in collaborative teams.* Paper presented at the 7th International Conference Interdisciplinarity in Engineering (INTER-ENG 2013). Petru Maior University of Tigru Mures, Romania.

Popovici, D., & Privat, G. (2015). Capturing the Structure of Internet of Things Systems with Graph Databases for Open Bidirectional Multiscale Data Mediation. *Second International Workshop on Large-scale Graph Storage and Management.*

Popper, K. (1998). *Unended Quest: An Intellectual Autobiography.* Chicago, IL: Carus Publishing Company.

Popper, M., & Lipshitz, R. (1998). Organizational learning mechanisms: A structural and cultural approach to organizational learning. *The Journal of Applied Behavioral Science, 34*(2), 161–179. doi:10.1177/0021886398342003

Porat, M. U. (1977). *The Information Economy: Definition and Measurement.* Retrieved March 29, 2016 from http://eric.ed.gov/?id=ED142205

Porter, M. (1980). Competitive Strategy. New York: The Free Press.

Porter, M. E. (1980). Competitive Strategy: Techniques for Analyzing Industries and Competitors. New York: Free Press.

Poza, E. (2003). Heirs and Graces in a Family Business. *Businessweek News*. Retrieved January 13, 2016, from http://www.bloomberg.com/news/articles/2003-08-10/heirs-and-graces-in-a-family-business

Prahalad, C. K., & Ramaswamy, V. (2003). *The New Frontier of Experience Innovation.* Retrieved January 29, 2016, from http://sloanreview.mit.edu/article/the-new-frontier-of-experience-innovation/

Prahalad, C. K., & Hamel, G. (1990). The core competence of the corporation. *Harvard Business Review, 68*(3), 79–93.

Premkumar, V., Krishnamurty, S., Wileden, S. J., & Grosse, I. (2014). A semantic knowledge management system for laminated composites. *Advanced Engineering Informatics, 28*(1), 91–101. doi:10.1016/j.aei.2013.12.004

Presbitero, A. (2016). Cultural intelligence (CQ) in virtual, cross-cultural interactions: Generalizability of measure and links to personality dimensions and task performance. *International Journal of Intercultural Relations, 50*, 29–38. doi:10.1016/j.ijintrel.2015.11.001

Pretorius, S., Steyn, H., & Jordaan, J. C. (2012). Project management matury and project management succes in engineering and construction. *SA Journal of Industrial Engineering, 23*(3), 1–12.

Prieto, I. M., Revilla, E., & Rodríguez-Prado, B. (2009). Managing the knowledge paradox in product development. *Journal of Knowledge Management, 13*(3), 157–170. doi:10.1108/13673270910962941

Probst, G. (1998). Practical Knowledge Management: A Model that Works. *Prism, 2*, 17–29.

Probst, G., Raub, S., & Romhardt, K. (2000). *Managing knowledge: buildings blocks for success.* Chichester, UK: John Wiley & Sons Ltd.

Probst, G., Raub, S., & Romhardt, K. (2006). *Wissen Managen Wie Unternehmen ihre wertvollste Ressource optimal nutzen.* Wiesbaden: Gabler GmbH.

Probst, G., Raub, S., & Romhardt, K. (2006). *Wissen Managen, Wie Unternehmen ihre wertvollste Ressource optimal nutzen.* Wiesbaden: Gabler GmbH.

Probst, G., Romhardt, K., & Raub, S. (2000). *Managing Knowledge. Building Blocks For Success.* New York: John Wiley & Sons.

PTC. (2006). *Change and Configuration Management.* Topic Sheet, Parametric Technology Corporation (PTC).

PWC. (2015). *CEE Family Business Survey, Family businesses at a crossroads.* Retrieved January 10, 2016, from http://www.pwc.com/hu/hu/kiadvanyok/assets/pdf/cee_family_survey_2015.pdf

Pyrko, I., Dörfler, V., & Eden, C. (2015). Thinking Together: Making Communities of Practice Work. Academy of Management Best Paper Proceedings, 2015(1).

Rácz, I. & Magyar-Stifter, V. (2015). Knowledge Definition and Transfer by Talented Intellectual Workers. *Acta Oeconomica Universitatis Selye, 4*(2), 162-171.

Rácz, I. (2013). Business success in the mirror of talent. In *Proceedings of 2nd Workshop on Talent Management.* Brussels, Belgium: EIASM.

Rácz, I. (2014). Mentori szerep a tehetséggondozási projektekben. In XVII. Apáczai napok. Tudományos Konferencia: Mobilis in mobile. Győr, Hungary: NYME Apáczai Csere János Kar.

Radjou, N. (2014). *NaviRadjou*. Retrieved October 10, 2014, from http://naviradjou.com/

Radjou, N., & Prabhu, J. (2013). *Frugal Innovation: A New Business Paradigm*. Instead Knowledge. Retrieved May 15, 2014, from http://knowledge.insead.edu/innovation/frugal-innovation-a-new-business-paradigm-2375

Radjou, N., Prabhu, J., & Ahuja, S. (2012). *Jugaad Innovation: Think Frugal, Be Flexible, Generate Breakthrough Growth*. San Francisco: Jossey-Bass.

Ragins, B. R., & Cotton, J. L. (1999). Mentor functions and outcomes: A comaprison of men and women in formal and informal mentoring relationships. *The Journal of Applied Psychology*, *84*(4), 529–550. doi:10.1037/0021-9010.84.4.529 PMID:10504893

Rasmus, D. (2002). *Collaboration, Contents and Communities: An update*. Giga Information Group Inc.

Rasmussen, P., & Nielsen, P. (2011). Knowledge management in the firm: Concepts and issues. *International Journal of Manpower*, *32*(5/6), 479–493. doi:10.1108/01437721111158161

Rathje, S. (2006). Interkulturelle Kompetenz – Zustand und Zukunft eines umstrittenen Konzepts. *Zeitschrift für Interkulturellen Fremdsprachenunterricht*, *11*(3), 1–21.

Real, J. C., Roldán, J. L., & Leal, A. (2014). From entrepreneurial orientation and learning orientation to business performance: Analysing the mediating role of organizational learning and the moderating effects of organizational size. *British Journal of Management*, *25*(2), 186–208. doi:10.1111/j.1467-8551.2012.00848.x

Reeves, T. C., & Oh, E. J. (2007). Generation differences and educational technology research. In Handbook of research on educational communications and technology. Academic Press.

Reich, M., Czeglédi, C., & Fonger, J. (2015). Expectations of employees on the effects of workplace health management as a part of an internal diversity management-explorative study. *Trendy v podnikání*, 49-58.

Reinhardt, K., & North, K. (2003). Transparency and transfer of individual competencies: A concept of integrative competence management. *Journal of Universal Computer Science*, *9*(12), 1372–1380.

Ren, J., Ma, J., Huang, R., Jin, Q., & Chen, Z. (2014). A Management System for Cyber Individuals and Heterogeneous Data. *IEEE Intl Conf on Ubiquitous Intelligence and Computing*.

Renzulli, J. S. (1979). *What makes giftedness: A reexamination of the definition of the gifted and talented*. Ventura, CA: Ventura County Superintendent of Schools Office.

Rhodes, J. E. (2002). *Stand by me: the risk and rewards of mentoring today`s youth*. Cambridge, MA: Harvard University Press.

Rhodes, J. E., Spencer, R., Keller, T. E., Liang, B., & Noam, G. (2006). A model for the influence of mentoring relationships on youth development. *Journal of Community Psychology*, *6*(6), 691–707. doi:10.1002/jcop.20124

Richardson, I., & Von Wangenheim, C. (2007). Guest editors' introduction: Why are small software organizations different? *IEEE Software*, *24*(1), 18–22. doi:10.1109/MS.2007.12

Ridderstråle, J., & Nordström, K. A. (2005). *Karaoke Capitalism Management for mankind*. Harlow, UK: Pearson Education Limited.

Ritz, A., & Thom, N. (2011). *Talent Management*. Wiesbaden, Germany: Gabler Verlag. doi:10.1007/978-3-8349-6954-5

Rivera-Vazquez, J. C., Ortiz-Fournier, L. V., & Flores, F. R. (2009). Overcoming cultural barriers for innovation and knowledge sharing. *Journal of Knowledge Management*, *13*(5), 257–270. doi:10.1108/13673270910988097

Roberts, N., Galluch, P. S., Dinger, M., & Grover, V. (2012). Absorptive capacity and information systems research: Review, synthesis and directions for future research. *Management Information Systems Quarterly, 36*(2), 625–648.

Robertson, J. (2007). *There are no "KM systems"*. Retrieved March 29, 2016 from http://www.steptwo.com.au/papers/cmb_kmsystems/

Robillard, P. N. (1999). The role of knowledge in software development. *Communications of the ACM, 42*(1), 87–92. doi:10.1145/291469.291476

Rochel de Camargo, K. J. (2002). The Thought Style of Physicians: Strategies for Keeping up with Medical Knowledge. *Social Studies of Science, 32*(5-6), 827–855. doi:10.1177/030631270203200501

Roos, J., & von Krogh, G. (2002). The new language lab. In S. Little, P. Quintas, & T. Ray (Eds.), *Managing knowledge: An essential reader* (pp. 255–263). London: SAGE Pub.

Ross, A. (2009). Nice Work If You Can Get It: Life and Labor in Precarious Times. New York: New York University Press.

Rothwell, R. (1994). Towards the Fifth-generation Innovation Process. *International Marketing Review, 11*(1), 7–31. doi:10.1108/02651339410057491

Routson, J. (2011). Embracing a Way to Change the World. *Entrepreneurship, Health Care, Social Innovation, 5*(1). Retrieved from https://www.gsb.stanford.edu/insights/embracing-way-change-world

Rowley, J. (2007). The wisdom hierarchy: Representations of the DIKW hierarchy. *Journal of Information Science, 33*(2), 163–180. doi:10.1177/0165551506070706

Ruggieri, R., Pozzi, M., & Ripamonti, S. (2014). Italian Family Business Cultures Involved in the Generational Change, In: *Europe's. The Journal of Psychology, 10*(1), 79–103.

Rus, I., & Lindvall, M. (2002). Knowledge management in software engineering. *IEEE Software, 19*(3), 26–38. doi:10.1109/MS.2002.1003450

Ruzzier, M., Hisrich, R. D., & Antoncic, A. (2006). SME internationalization research: Past, present, and future. *Journal of Small Business and Enterprise Development, 13*(4), 476–497. doi:10.1108/14626000610705705

Ryan, S., & O'Connor, R. V. (2013). Acquiring and sharing tacit knowledge in software development teams: An empirical study. *Information and Software Technology, 55*(9), 1614–1624. doi:10.1016/j.infsof.2013.02.013

Rylková, Ž. (2013). Innovative Business and the Czech Republic. In *Proceedings of the 11th International Conference Liberec Economic Forum.* Liberec: Technical University of Liberec.

*S&P 500 Component Stocks.* (n.d.). Retrieved January 15, 2016, from https://en.wikipedia.org/wiki/List_of_S%26P_500_companies

Sabir, H. M., & Kalyar, M. N. (2013). Firm's innovativeness and employee job satisfaction: The role of organizational learning culture. *Interdisciplinary Journal of Contemporary Research in Business, 4*(9), 670–686.

Sadalage, P. J., & Fowler, M. (2013). *NoSQL Distilled*. Addison-Wesley.

Sadeghi, Z., & Salemi, J. (2013). Presenting a conceptual model for innovation development in organizations. *Life Science Journal, 10*, 62–70.

Saini, R. (2013). Model development for key enablers in the implementation of knowledge management. *IUP Journal of Knowledge Management, 11*(2), 46.

Saito, M. (2012). Managing knowledge for enhancing the participants through organizational learning and leadership. In *Organizational learning and knowledge: Concepts, methodologies, tools and applications* (pp. 1749–1759). Hershey, PA: IGI Global. doi:10.4018/978-1-60960-783-8.ch507

Salim, I., & Sulaiman, M. (2011). Organizational learning, innovation and performance: A study of Malaysian small and medium sized enterprises. *International Journal of Business and Management, 6*(12), 118–126. doi:10.5539/ijbm.v6n12p118

Samovar, L. A., & Porter, R. E. (1995). *Communication between Cultures*. Belmont: Wadsworth Publishing Company.

Sandkuhl, K. (2009). Information logistics in networked organizations: Selected concepts and applications. *Enterp. Inf. Syst., 12*, 43–54.

Santander, C. (2013). *Frugal forward-thinking*. Santander Corporate & Commercial. Retrieved October 07, 2014, from http://www.santandercb.co.uk/knowledge-hub/frugal-forward-thinking

Santoro, M. D., & Bierly, P. E. (2006). Facilitators of knowledge transfer in university-industry collaborations: A knowledge-based perspective. *IEEE Transactions on Engineering Management, 53*(4), 495–507. doi:10.1109/TEM.2006.883707

Santos, B. S. (2008). *A universidade no século XXI: Para uma universidade nova*. Coimbra: Edições Almedina.

Santos, N. (2014). Organizational learning and Web 2.0 technologies: Improving the planning and organization of a software development process. In M. Cruz-Cunha, F. Moreira, & J. Varajão (Eds.), *Handbook of research on enterprise 2.0: Technological, social, and organizational dimensions* (pp. 512–528). Hershey, PA: IGI Global. doi:10.4018/978-1-4666-4373-4.ch027

SAP. (2015). *Explore our analytics products*. Walldorf: SAP SE. Retrieved from: http://go.sap.com/cz/product/analytics.html

Saraf, N., Langdon, C. S., & Gosain, S. (2007). IS application capabilities and relational value in interfirm partnerships. *Information Systems Research, 18*(3), 320–339. doi:10.1287/isre.1070.0133

Savolainen, P., & Ahonen, J. J. (2015). Knowledge lost: Challenges in changing project manager between sales and implementation in software projects. *International Journal of Project Management, 33*(1), 92–102. doi:10.1016/j.ijproman.2014.04.003

Scandura, T. A. (1998). Dysfunctional mentoring relationships and outcomes. *Journal of Management, 24*(3), 449–467. doi:10.1177/014920639802400307

Schein, E. H. (1978). *Career Dynamics: Matching individual and organizational needs*. Reading, MA: Addison-Wesley Publishing.

Schienstock, G. (2009). *Organisational Innovations: Some Reflections on the Concept*. Research Unit for Technology, Science and Innovation Studies (TaSTI) University of Tampere IAREG Working Paper 1.2.

Schilling, J., & Klamma, R. (2010). The difficult bridge between university and industry: A case study in computer science teaching. *Assessment & Evaluation in Higher Education, 35*(4), 367–380. doi:10.1080/02602930902795893

Schilling, M. A. (2012). *Strategic management of technological innovation*. New York, NY: McGraw–Hill.

Schilling, M. A., & Fang, C. (2014). When hubs forget, lie, and play favorites: Interpersonal network structure, information distortion, and organizational learning. *Strategic Management Journal, 35*(7), 974–994. doi:10.1002/smj.2142

Schlosser, F., Templer, A., & Ghanam, D. (2006). How human resource outsourcing affects organizational learning in the knowledge economy. *Journal of Labor Research, 27*(3), 291–303. doi:10.1007/s12122-006-1024-x

Schumpeter, J. A. (1980). *A gazdasági fejlődés elmélete*. Budapest: Közgazdasági és Jogi Könyvkiadó.

Schumpeter, J. A. (2012): Asian innovation. *The Economist*. Retrieved September 03, 2014, from http://www.economist.com/node/21551028

Seco, N., Veale, T., & Hayes, J. (2004). An intrinsic information content metric for semantic similarity. In *WordNet, European Conference on Artificial Intelligence*.

Sedighi, M., & Zand, F. (2012). Knowledge Management: Review of the Critical Success Factors and Development of a Conceptual Classification Model. *10th International Conference on ICT and Knowledge Engineering*. doi:10.1109/ICTKE.2012.6408553

Sedlacek, T. (2013). *Economics of Good and Evil: The Quest for Economic Meaning from Gilgamesh to Wall Street*. Oxford, UK: Oxford University Press.

Segelod, E., & Jordan, G. (2004). The use and importance of external sources of knowledge in the software development process. *R & D Management, 34*(3), 239–252. doi:10.1111/j.1467-9310.2004.00336.x

Seidler-de Alwis, R., & Hartmann, E. (2008). The use of tacit knowledge within innovative companies: Knowledge management in innovative enterprises. *Journal of Knowledge Management, 12*(1), 133–147. doi:10.1108/13673270810852449

Senge, P. M. (2006). Pátá disciplína: teorie a praxe učící se organizace. Praha: Management Press.

Senge, P. (1990). *The fifth discipline: The art and practice of the learning organization*. New York, NY: Doubleday.

Senge, P. (1998). *5. alapelv. A tanuló szervezet kialakításának elmélete és gyakorlata*. Budapest HVG Rt.

Serinkan, C., Enli, P., Akcit, V., & Kiziloglu, M. (2014). Evaluation of knowledge level of cargo companies about their organizational learning and team management: An empirical research in cargo companies in Turkey. *Procedia: Social and Behavioral Sciences, 116*, 4170–4174. doi:10.1016/j.sbspro.2014.01.911

Shapin, S. (2008). *The Scientific Life: A Moral History of a Late Modern Vocation*. Chicago: The University of Chicago Press. doi:10.7208/chicago/9780226750170.001.0001

Shapiro, S. (2013). *Innovation for Innovators*. Retrieved December 12, 2014, from http://stephenshapiro.com/speaking/

Shapiro, S. (2014). *Innovation Philosophies*. Retrieved February 13, 2015, from www.stephenshapiro.com

Shapiro, E. C., Haseltine, F. P., & Rowe, M. P. (1978). Moving up: Role models, mentors and the patron system. *Sloan Management Review*, 51–58.

Shapiro, S. (2011). *Best Practices Are Stupid: 40 Ways to Out-Innovate the Competition*. London: Portfolio Penguin.

Shiba, S., & Walden, D. (2001). *Four Practical Revolutions in Management: Systems for Creating Unique Organizational Capability*. New York: Productivity Press.

Shull, F., Basili, V., Carver, J., Maldonado, J. C., Travassos, G. H., Mendonca, M., & Fabbri, S. (2002). Replicating Software Engineering Experiments: Addressing the Tacit Knowledge Problem. In *Proceedings of the 2002 International Symposium on Empirical Software Engineering (ISESE'02)* (pp. 7–16). IEEE Comput. Soc. doi:10.1109/ISESE.2002.1166920

Shull, F., Mendonça, M. G., Basili, V., Carver, J., Maldonado, J. C., Fabbri, S., & Ferreira, M. C. et al. (2004). Knowledge-sharing issues in experimental software engineering. *Empirical Software Engineering, 9*(1/2), 111–137. doi:10.1023/B:EMSE.0000013516.80487.33

Sicilia, M. A., & Lytras, M. D. (2005). The semantic learning organization. *The Learning Organization, 12*(5), 402–410. doi:10.1108/09696470510611375

Siegel, D. S., Waldman, D., & Link, A. (2003). Assessing the impact of organizational practices on the relative productivity of university technology transfer offices: An exploratory study. *Research Policy*, *32*(1), 27–48. doi:10.1016/S0048-7333(01)00196-2

Sigala, M., & Chalkiti, K. (2015). Knowledge management, social media and employee creativity. *International Journal of Hospitality Management*, *45*, 44–58. doi:10.1016/j.ijhm.2014.11.003

Simon, H. (1997). *Models of Bounded Rationality*. Cambridge, MA: MIT Press.

Simonyi, Á. (2004). Jóléti politika a munkahelyeken és a munkaadók társadalmi felelőssége. *Esély*, *1*, 26-37. Retrieved from http://www.esely.org/kiadvanyok/2004_1/SIMONYI.pdf

Singh, S., Gambhir, A., Sotiropoulos, A., & Duckworth, S. (2012). *Frugal Innovation: Learning from Social Enterpreneurs in India*. Serco Institute. Retrieved April 22, 2014, from http://www.serco.com/Images/FrugalInnovation_tcm3-39462.pdf

Skyrme, D., & Amidon, D. (1998). The Knowledge Agenda. In J. W. Cortada & J. A. Woods (Eds.), *The Knowledge Management Yearbook 1999-2000*. Boston: Butterworth-Heinemann.

Slater, S. F., & Narver, J. C. (1995). Market orientation and the learning organization. *Journal of Marketing*, *59*(3), 63–74. doi:10.2307/1252120

Sliter, M., Chen, Y., Withrow, S., & Sliter, K. (2013). Older and (emotionally) smarter? Emotional intelligence as a mediator in the relationship between age and emotional labor strategies in service employees. *Experimental Aging Research*, *39*(4), 466–479. doi:10.1080/0361073X.2013.808105 PMID:23875841

Smith, E. A. (2001). The role of tacit and explicit knowledge in the workplace. *Journal of Knowledge Management*, *5*(4), 311–321. doi:10.1108/13673270110411733

Snowdon, B., & Stonehouse, G. (2006). Competitiveness in a globalised world: Michael Porter on the microeconomic foundations of the competitiveness of nations, regions, and firms. *Journal of International Business Studies*, *37*(2), 163–175. doi:10.1057/palgrave.jibs.8400190

Soley, M., & Pandaya, V. K. (2003). Culture as an issue in Knowledge Sharing: A means of Competitive Advantage. *Electronic Journal of Knowledge Management*, *1*(2), 205–212.

Sousa Lobo, L. (2005). *Publicações Internacionais*. Ranking das Universidades Portuguesas.

Sparrow, P. R., & Hiltrop, J. M. (1994). *European Human Resource Management in Transition*. London: Pretence Hall International.

Spencer-Rodgers, J., & McGovern, T. (2002). Attitudes toward culturally different: The role of intercultural communication barriers, affective response, consensual stereotypes, and perceived threat. *International Journal of Intercultural Relations*, *26*(6), 609–631. doi:10.1016/S0147-1767(02)00038-X

Stamm, I., & Lubinski, C. (2011). Crossroads of family business research and firm demography – A critical assessment of family business survival rates. Journal of Family Business Strategy.

Stankosky, M., & Baldanza, C. (2000). *A systems approach to engineering a knowledge management system*. White paper. The George Washington University.

Star, S. L. (1989). The structure of ill-structured solutions: boundary objects and heterogeneous distributed problem solving. In Distributed artificial intelligence. Pitman.

Starbuck, W. H. (1992). Learning by knowledge-intensive firms. *Journal of Management Studies*, *29*(6), 713–740. doi:10.1111/j.1467-6486.1992.tb00686.x

Stenmark, D. (2001). The relationship between information and knowledge. *Proceedings of IRIS, 24*, 11–14.

Sternberg, R. J. (1990). Prototypes of competence and incompetence. In R. J. Sternberg & J. Kolligian (Eds.), *Competence Considered* (pp. 117–145). New Haven, CT: Yale University Press.

Sternberg, R. J. (1997). Tacit Knowledge and Job Success. In N. Anderson & P. Herriot (Eds.), *International Handbook of selection and assessment* (pp. 201–213). Chichester, UK: Wiley.

Stocker, M. (2010). *Tudásszervezetek értékteremtésének anomáliái*. Tudásmenedzsment Workshop. Budapest: Budapesti Kommunikációs Főiskola.

Stoian, M. C., Rialp, A., & Rialp, J. (2011). Export performance under the microscope: A glance through Spanish lenses. *International Business Review, 20*(2), 117–135. doi:10.1016/j.ibusrev.2010.07.002

Stoof, A. (2005). *Tools for the identification and description of competencies*. (Doctoral dissertation). Open University of the Nederlands, Heerlen, Nederlands.

Stormware Software Development. (2015). *POHODA Business Intelligence*. Jihlava: Stromware, s.r.o. Retrieved from: http://www.stormware.cz/pohoda/business-intelligence/reseni

Stough, C., Saktofske, D. H., & Rarker, J. D. A. (2009). *Assessing Emotional Intelligence*. Theory, Research, and Applicarions, Springer Scienec and Business Media.

Stoyanov, I. (2014). Human capital and knowledge management in innovative organizations. *KSI Transactions on Knowledge Society, 7*(4), 23–29.

Subrahmanian, E., Rachuri, S., Fenves, S. J., Foufou, S., & Sriram, R. D. (2005). Product lifecycle management support: A challenge in supporting product design and manufacturing in a networked economy. *Int. J. Product Lifecycle Management, 1*(1), 4–25. doi:10.1504/IJPLM.2005.007342

Subramaniam, M., & Youndt, M. A. (2005). The influence of intellectual capital on the types of innovative capabilities. *Academy of Management Journal, 48*(3), 450–463. doi:10.5465/AMJ.2005.17407911

Sujan, M. (2015). An organisation without a memory: A qualitative study of hospital staff perceptions on reporting and organisational learning for patient safety. *Reliability Engineering & System Safety, 144*, 45–52. doi:10.1016/j.ress.2015.07.011

Sung, S. Y., & Choi, J. N. (2014). Do organizations spend wisely on employees? Effects of training and development investments on learning and innovation in organizations. *Journal of Organizational Behavior, 35*(3), 393–412. doi:10.1002/job.1897

Sun, P. Y. T., & Anderson, M. H. (2010). An examination of the relationship between absorptive capacity and organizational learning, and a proposed integration. *International Journal of Management Reviews, 12*(2), 130–150. doi:10.1111/j.1468-2370.2008.00256.x

Surowiecki, J. (Ed.). (2005). *The Wisdom of the Crowds*. New York: Anchor Books.

Susanty, A. I., & Wood, P. C. (2011). The Motivation to Share Knowledge of the Employees in the Telecommunication Service Providers in Indonesia. *International Proceedings of Economics Development & Research, 5*(2), 2–159.

Sveiby, K. (2001). *Szervezetek új gazdasága: a menedzselt tudás*. Budapest: Kjk - Kerszöv Jogi és Üzleti Kiadó Kft.

Sveiby, K. E. (1997). *The new organizational wealth: Managing & measuring knowledge-based assets*. San Francisco: Berrett-Koehler Publishers.

Sveiby, K. E. (2001). *Szervezetek új gazdagsága: a menedzselt tudás*. Budapest: KJK-KERSZÖV Jogi és Üzleti Kiadó Kft.

Sveiby, K. E. (1996). Transfer of knowledge and the information processing professions. *European Management Journal, 14*(4), 379–388. doi:10.1016/0263-2373(96)00025-4

Sveiby, K. E. (1997). *The New Organizational Wealth: Managing & Measuring Knowledge-Based Assets*. San Francisco: Berrett-Koehler Publishers.

Swart, J., & Kinnie, N. (2003). Sharing knowledge in knowledge-intensive firms. *Human Resource Management Journal, 13*(2), 60–75. doi:10.1111/j.1748-8583.2003.tb00091.x

Syfox, J. (2000). Globalization and cultural change in organizations. *Management Research News, 23*(2/4), 86–87.

Systém On Line (SOL). (2015). *Přehledy IS*. Brno: CCB, s.r.o. Retrieved from: http://www.systemonline.cz/prehled-informacnich-system

Szabó, L., & Csepregi, A. (2011). Competences found important for knowledge sharing: Investigation of middle managers working at medium- and large-sized enterprises. *The IUP Journal of Knowledge Management, 9*(3), 41–58.

Szabó, L., & Csepregi, A. (2013). Organizational characteristics and methodological competences. Management & Marketing. *Challenges for the Knowledge Society., 8*, 353–362.

Szabó, L., & Csepregi, A. (2015). Middle managers, their organization and knowledge sharing: Examination of knowledge sharing maturity. *Journal of Social Sciences Research, 7*(1), 1192–1205.

Szabó, M. (2011). *Projektmenedzsment*. Szeged: Szegedi Tudományegyetem Közoktatási Vezetőképző Intézet.

Szerb, L., Csapi, V., Deutch, N., Ulbert, J., Horváth, Á., Kruzslicz, F., … Szűcs, P. K. (2014). Mennyire versenyképesesek a magyar kisvállalatok. Marketing & Management, 48, 3-21.

Taleb, N. N. (2007). *The Black Swan: The Impact of the Highly Improbable*. New York, NY: Random House.

Taleb, N. N. (2012). *Antifragile: Things That Gain from Disorder*. London, UK: Penguin Books.

Taylor, G. S., Templeton, G. F., & Baker, L. T. (2010). Factors influencing the success of organizational learning implementation: A policy facet perspective. *International Journal of Management Reviews, 12*(4), 353–364. doi:10.1111/j.1468-2370.2009.00268.x

Teece, D. (2001). Strategies for managing knowledge assets: the role of firm structure and industrial context. In I. Nonaka & D. Teece (Eds.), *Creation, Transfer and Utilisation* (pp. 125–144). London: SAGE. doi:10.4135/9781446217573.n7

Teng, Z., Guo, M., Liu, X., Dai, Q., Wang, C., & Xuan, P. (2013). Measuring gene functional similarity based on group-wise comparison of GO terms. *Bioinformatics (Oxford, England), 29*(11), 1424–1432. doi:10.1093/bioinformatics/btt160 PMID:23572412

Terman, L. M., & Oden, M. H. (1947). *Genetic Studies of Genius. IV. The Gifted Child Groups Up*. Stanford, CA: Stanford University Press.

Terman, L. M., & Oden, M. H. (1959). *Genetic Studies of Genius. V. The Gifted Group at Mid-Life*. Stanford, CA: Stanford University Press.

Ternes, C. D. (2011). *Confirming the Stankosky Knowledge Management Framework*. The George Washington University.

Tesco Software. (2015). *Fama+ CAFM*. Olomouc: TESCO SW, a.s. Retrieved from: http://www.tescosw.cz/facility-management/fama-cafm

Thakor, A. (2013). *Innovation and Growth – What Do We Know?* Singapore: Word Scientific Publishing. doi:10.1142/8115

Thom, N. (2003). Retention Management für High Potentials. In Jahrbuch Personalentwicklung und Weiterbildung – Praxis und Perspektivven (pp. 237-247).

Tichá, I. (2005). Učící se organizace. Praha: Alfa Nakladatelství.

Tippins, M. J., & Sohi, R. S. (2003). IT competency and firm performance: Is organizational learning a missing link? *Strategic Management Journal*, 24(8), 745–761. doi:10.1002/smj.337

Tiwari, R. & Herstatt, C. (2012c). Frugal Innovation: A Global Networks' Perspective; Die Unternehmung. *Swiss Journal of Business Research and Practice*, 66(3), 245-274.

Tiwari, R., & Herstatt, C. (2012a). *Open global innovation networks as enablers of frugal innovation: Propositions based on evidence from India.* Hamburg, Germany: Hamburg University of Technology, Technology and Innovation Management, Working Paper 72.

Tiwari, R., & Herstatt, C. (2012b). *India - a lead market for frugal innovations? Extending the lead market theory to emerging economies.* TIM/TUHH Working Paper 67.

Tohidi, H., Seyedaliakbar, S. M., & Mandegari, M. (2012). Organizational learning measurement and the effect on firm innovation. *Journal of Enterprise Information Management*, 25(3), 219–245. doi:10.1108/17410391211224390

Tomka, J., & Bőgel, G. (2014). *Megéri jónak lenni? – A Biblia és a menedzsment II.* Budapest: Nemzeti Tankönyvkiadó.

Tomka, J. (2005). *A szakmai közösségek (Communities of Practice) hozzájárulása a szervezeti együttműködés fejlesztéséhez. PhD értekezés.* Budapest: BME.

Törestad, B., Magnusson, D., & Oláh, A. (1990). Coping, control, and experience of anxiety: An interactional perspective. *Anxiety Research*, 3(1), 1–16. doi:10.1080/08917779008248737

Tough, A., & Moss, M. (2003). Metadata, controlled vocabulary and directories: Electronic document management and standards for records management. *Records Management Journal*, 13(1), 24–31. doi:10.1108/09565690310465713

Truch, E., & Bridger, D. (2002). The importance of strategic fit in Knowledge Management. In *Proceedings of the 10th European Conference on Information Systems: Information Systems and the Future of the Digital Economy.*

Tsai, W., & Ghoshal, S. (1998). Social capital and value creation: The role of intrafirm networks. *Academy of Management Journal*, 41(4), 464–476. doi:10.2307/257085

Tsaousis, I., & Kasi, S. (2013). Factorial invariance and latent mean differences of scores on trait emotional intelligence across gender and age. *Personality and Individual Differences*, 54(2), 169–173. doi:10.1016/j.paid.2012.08.016

Tsay, J. T., Dabbish, L., & Herbsleb, J. (2012). Social media and success in open source projects. In *Proceedings of the ACM 2012 conference on computer supported cooperative work companion* (pp. 223-226). New York, NY: ACM doi:10.1145/2141512.2141583

Tuomi, I. (1999). Data is more than knowledge: Implications of the reversed knowledge hierarchy for knowledge management and organizational memory. In *Proceedings of the 32nd Annual Hawaii International Conference on Systems Sciences. 1999. HICSS-32* (Vol. 16, p. 12). IEEE Comput. Soc. doi:10.1109/HICSS.1999.772795

Tushman, M. L., & Nadler, D. A. (1986). Organizing for innovation. *California Management Review*, 28(3), 74–92. doi:10.2307/41165203

UAlg. (2007a). *Plano Regional de Inovação do Algarve.* Faro: Universidade do Algarve.

UAlg. (2007b). *Horizonte 2010, Princípios Estratégicos para a Universidade do Algarve*. Faro: Universidade do Algarve.

Ulrich, D. (2006). The talent trifecta. *Workforce Management, 10*(September), 32–33.

United Nations. (2014). *World Investment Report, Investing in the SDGs: An Action Plan*. New York: United Nations.

Urbancová, H. (2013). Kontinuita znalostí: jak uchovat znalosti klíčových pracovníků v organizaci. Praha: Nakladatelství Adart.

Uyterhoeven, H. (1989). General Managers in the Middle. *Harvard Business Review, 67*(5), 136–145. PMID:10295475

Uzzi, B. (1997). Social structure and competition in interfirm networks: The paradox of embeddedness. *Administrative Science Quarterly, 42*(1), 35–67. doi:10.2307/2393808

Vágány, J., Kárpátiné Daróczi, J., & Fenyvesi, É. (2015). A családi vállalkozások sikere- a család sikere. Gazdálkodás és Menedzsment Tudományos Konferencia. Kecskemét.

Valkokari, K., & Helander, N. (2007). Knowledge management in different types of strategic SME networks. *Management Research News, 30*(8), 597–608. doi:10.1108/01409170710773724

Van Aalst, H. F. (2003). Networking in Society. Organisations and Education. In *Networks of Innovation for Schools and Systems*. Paris: OECD.

van Hoof, B. (2014). Organizational learning in cleaner production among Mexican supply networks. *Journal of Cleaner Production, 64*, 115–124. doi:10.1016/j.jclepro.2013.07.041

van Puijenbroek, T., Poell, R. F., Kroon, B., & Timmerman, V. (2014). The effect of social media use on work-related learning. *Journal of Computer Assisted Learning, 30*(2), 159–172. doi:10.1111/jcal.12037

Van Rooy, D. L., Alonso, A., & Viswesvaran, C. (2005). Group differences in emotional intelligence scores: Theoretical and practical implications. *Personality and Individual Differences, 38*(3), 689–700. doi:10.1016/j.paid.2004.05.023

Van Rooy, D. L., & Viswesvaran, C. (2004). Emotional intelligence: A meta-analytic investigation of predictive validity and nomological net. *Journal of Vocational Behavior, 65*(1), 71–95. doi:10.1016/S0001-8791(03)00076-9

Varga, K. (1988). *Az emberi és szervezeti erőforrás fejlesztése*. Budapest: Akadémiai Kiadó.

Vargas, M. I. R. (2015). Determinant factors for small business to achieve innovation, high performance and competitiveness: Organizational learning and leadership style. *Procedia: Social and Behavioral Sciences, 169*, 43–52. doi:10.1016/j.sbspro.2015.01.284

Veber, J. (2009). Management: základy, moderní manažerské přístupy, výkonnost a prosperita. Praha: Management Press.

Velencei, J., Baracskai, Z., & Dörfler, V. (2015a, May). Supporting the Competent Practitioner: Transdisciplinary Coaching with Knowledge-Based Expert System. *MakeLearn, 2015*, 27–29.

Velencei, J., Dörfler, V., Baracskai, Z., & Szendrey, J. (2015b). Prelude for Experience Mining (Re-)Using Relevant Experience for Smart Decision Support. *International OFEL Conference on Governance, Management and Entrepreneurship*.

Venkitachalam, K., & Busch, P. (2012). Tacit knowledge: Review and possible research directions. *Journal of Knowledge Management, 16*(2), 357–372. doi:10.1108/13673271211218915

Villar, C., Alegre, J., & Pla-Barber, J. (2014). Exploring the role of knowledge management practices on exports: A dynamic capabilities view. *International Business Review, 23*(1), 38–44. doi:10.1016/j.ibusrev.2013.08.008

von Krogh, G., & Köhne, M. (1998). Der Wissenstransfer in Unternehmen: Phasen des Wissenstransfers und wichtige Einflussfaktoren. *Die Unternehmung*, *56*(5/6), 235–252.

Vuori, V. (2011). *Social Media Changing the Competitive Intelligence Process: Elicitation of Employees' Competitive Knowledge*. Academic Dissertation. Retrieved January 10, 2014, from http://dspace.cc.tut.fi/dpub/bitstream/handle/123456789/20724/vuori.pdf

Waight, C. L. (2015). Learning during the integration phase of mergers and acquisitions: Perspectives from learning and development professionals. *Performance Improvement Quarterly*, *28*(1), 7–26. doi:10.1002/piq.21184

Walz, D. B., Elam, J. J., & Curtis, B. (1993). Inside a software design team: Knowledge acquisition, sharing, and integration. *Communications of the ACM*, *36*(10), 63–77. doi:10.1145/163430.163447

Wanberg, C.R., Welsh, E.T., & Hezlett, S.A. (2003). Mentoring research: a review and dynamic process model. *Research in Personnel and Human Resources Management*, 39-124.

Wang, C. L. (2008). Entrepreneurial orientation, learning orientation, and firm performance. *Entrepreneurship Theory and Practice*, *32*(4), 635–657. doi:10.1111/j.1540-6520.2008.00246.x

Wang, C., Ren, K., Lou, W., & Li, J. (2010). Toward publicly auditable secure cloud data storage services. *IEEE Network*, *24*(4), 19–24. doi:10.1109/MNET.2010.5510914

Wang, J. (2012). Organizational learning and technology. In V. Wang (Ed.), *Technology and its impact on educational leadership: Innovation and change* (pp. 217–233). Hershey, PA: IGI Global. doi:10.4018/978-1-4666-0062-1.ch017

Wang, M.-H., & Yang, T.-Y. (2016). Investigating the success of knowledge management: An empirical study of small- and medium-sized enterprises. *Asia Pacific Management Review*, *21*(2), 79–91. doi:10.1016/j.apmrv.2015.12.003

Wang, S., & Noe, R. A. (2010). Knowledge sharing: A review and directions for future research. *Human Resource Management Review*, *20*(2), 115–131. doi:10.1016/j.hrmr.2009.10.001

Wang, W., & Hou, Y. (2015). Motivations of employees' knowledge sharing behaviors: A self-determination perspective. *Information and Organization*, *25*(1), 1–26.

Ward, J. L. (2011). *Keeping the Family Business Healthy: How to Plan for Continuing Growth*. Palgrave Macmillan. doi:10.1057/9780230116122

Webber, A. M. (1993). What's so new about the new economy? *Harvard Business Review*, *71*(1), 24–42.

Weingarten, R. M. (2009). Four generations, one workplace: A gen x-y staff nurse's view of team building in the emergency department. *Journal of Emergency Nursing: JEN*, *35*(1), 27–30. doi:10.1016/j.jen.2008.02.017 PMID:19203677

Wenger, E., & Snyder, W. (2000, January-February). Communities of Practice: The Organizational Frontier. *Harvard Business Review*.

Wenger, E. (1998). *Communities of Practice: learning, meaning and identity*. Cambridge, UK: Cambridge University Press. doi:10.1017/CBO9780511803932

Westkämper, E. (2007). Digital Manufacturing in the Global Era. Digital Enterprise Technology, (pp. 3–14). New York: Springer.

Wieneke, S., & Phlypo-Price, K. (2003). *The knowledge management domain – a knowledge management approach to knowledge management*. White paper. General Motors Corporation.

Wiig, K. M. (1993). *Knowledge Management Foundations. Thinking About Thinking-How People and Organizations Create, Represent, and Use Knowledge.* Arlington: Schema Press.

Wiig, K. M. (2000). *Knowledge Management: En Emerging Discipline Rooted in a long History, Knowledge Horizons: The present and promise of Knowledge Management.* Boston: Butterworth-Heinnemann.

Wilkesmann, U., Fischer, H., & Wilkesmann, M. (2009). Cultural characteristics of knowledge transfer. *Journal of Knowledge Management, 13*(6), 464–477. doi:10.1108/13673270910997123

Wimmer, R., Groth, T., & Simon, F. B. (2004). Erfolgsmuster von Mehrgenerationen-Familienunternehmen. *Wittener Diskussionspapiere. Sonderheft, Nr 5.* Retrieved from http://osb-i.com/sites/default/files/user_upload/Publikationen/Wimmer_Groth_Simon_Erfolgsmuster_von_Mehrgenerationen-FU_Juni_04.pdf

Wöbling, I., & Keuper, F. (2009). Produktionstheoretische Analyse der Wissensentwicklung. In F. Keuper & F. Neumann (Eds.), *Wissens- und Informationsmanagement: Strategien, Organisation und Prozesse* (pp. 33–50). Wiesbaden: Gabler Verlag. doi:10.1007/978-3-8349-6509-7_2

Wong, K. Y. (2005). Critical success factors for implementing knowledge management in small and medium enterprises. *Industrial Management & Data Systems, 105*(3), 261–279. doi:10.1108/02635570510590101

Wong, K. Y., & Aspinwall, E. (2004). Characterising knowledge management in small business environment. *Journal of Knowledge Management, 8*(3), 44–61. doi:10.1108/13673270410541033

Wong, W. L. P., & Radcliffe, D. F. (2000). The Tacit Nature of Design Knowledge. *Technology Analysis and Strategic Management, 12*(4), 493–512. doi:10.1080/713698497

Xue, L., Ray, G., & Sambamurthy, V. (2012). Efficiency or innovation: How do industry environments moderate the effects of firms' IT asset portfolios? *Management Information Systems Quarterly, 36*(2), 509–528.

Yang, C., & Chen, L. C. (2007). Can Organizational Knowledge Capabilities Affect Knowledge Sharing Behavior? *Journal of Information Science, 33*(1), 95–109. doi:10.1177/0165551506068135

Yesil, S., & Dereli, S. F. (2013). An empirical investigation of organisational justice, knowledge sharing and innovation capability. *SciVerse Science Direct, 75*, 199–208.

Yew Wong, K., & Aspinwall, E. (2005). An empirical study of the important factors for knowledge-management adoption in the SME sector. *Journal of Knowledge Management, 9*(3), 64–82. doi:10.1108/13673270510602773

Yli-Renko, H., Autio, E., & Sapienza, H. J. (2001). Social capital, knowledge acquisition, and knowledge exploitation in young technology-based firms. *Strategic Management Journal, 22*(6/7), 587–613. doi:10.1002/smj.183

Young, R., Gunedran, A., Cutting-Decelle, A., & Gruninger, M. (2007). Manufacturing knowledge sharing in plm: A progression towards the use of heavy weight. *International Journal of Production Research, 45*(7), 1505–1519. doi:10.1080/00207540600942268

Yousefi, H. R. (2006). Toleranz als Weg zur interkulturellen Kommunikation und Verständigung. In H. R. Yousefi, K. Fischer, & I. Braun (Eds.), Wege zur Kommunikation. Theorie und Praxis interkultureller Toleranz (pp. 19-49). Nordhausen: Traugott Bautz.

Yu, H., Fang, L., & Ling, W. (2009). An empirical study on the construct and effective mechanism of organizational learning. *Frontiers of Business Research in China, 3*(2), 242–270. doi:10.1007/s11782-009-0013-3

Yu, Y., Dong, X. Y., Shen, K. N., Khalifa, M., & Hao, J. X. (2013). Strategies, technologies, and organizational learning for developing organizational innovativeness in emerging economies. *Journal of Business Research, 66*(12), 2507–2514. doi:10.1016/j.jbusres.2013.05.042

Zack, M. H. (1999). Developing a Knowledge Strategy. *California Management Review, 41*(3), 125–145. doi:10.2307/41166000

Zack, M. H. (2000). Developing a Knowledge Strategy: Epilogue. In N. Bontis & C. W. Choo (Eds.), *The Strategic Management of Intellectual Capital and Organisational Knowledge: A Collection of Readings*. Oxford University Press.

Zahra, S. A. (2012). Organizational learning and entrepreneurship in family firms: Exploring the moderating effect of ownership and cohesion. *Small Business Economics, 38*(1), 51–65. doi:10.1007/s11187-010-9266-7

Zampetakis, L. A., Beldekos, P., & Moustakis, V. S. (2009). Day-to-day entrepreneurship within organisations: The role of trait emotional intelligence and perceived organisational support University of Glasgow. *European Management Journal, 27*(3), 165–175. doi:10.1016/j.emj.2008.08.003

Zander, L., Mockaitis, A. I., & Butler, C. L. (2012). Leading global teams. *Journal of World Business, 47*(4), 592–603. doi:10.1016/j.jwb.2012.01.012

Za, S., Spagnoletti, P., & North-Samardzic, A. (2014). Organisational learning as an emerging process: The generative role of digital tools in informal learning practices. *British Journal of Educational Technology, 45*(6), 1023–1035. doi:10.1111/bjet.12211

Zeidner, M., Matthews, G., & Roberts, R. (2009). *What we know about emotional intelligence: How it affects learning, work, relationships and our mental health*. Cambridge, MA: The MIT Press.

Zeidner, M., Matthews, G., & Roberts, R. D. (2004). Emotional intelligence in the workplace: A critical review, Applied Psychology. *International Review (Steubenville, Ohio), 53*(3), 371–399.

Zeschky, M. B., Winterhalter, S., & Gassmann, O. (2014). From Cost to Frugal and Reverse Innovation. *Mapping the Field and Implications for Global Competitiveness Research-Technology Management, 57*(4), 20–27.

Zey, M. (1988). A mentor for all. *The Personnel Journal, 67*(2), 46–51.

Zhou, K. Z., Yim, C. K., & Tse, D. K. (2005). The effects of strategic orientations on technology- and market-based breakthrough innovations. *Journal of Marketing, 69*(2), 42–60. doi:10.1509/jmkg.69.2.42.60756

Zott, C., & Amit, R. (2007). Business model design and the performance of entrepreneurial firms. *Organization Science, 18*(2), 181–199. doi:10.1287/orsc.1060.0232

# About the Contributors

**Andrea Bencsik** MSc. Industrial Engineer of Chemistry (1984), Doctor univ.(1986), CSc. on Economics (1992), PhD on Organization and Economics Science (2004), habilitation in HR (2008) is a professor of economic and management science at Széchenyi István University of Győr in Hungary and in J. Selye University in Komarno in Slovakia. She is doing research in the fields of knowledge- change- human- and project management and teaching these disciplines at the same time. She is the author of a number of scientific publications as well as a member of some international scientific committees.

\*\*\*

**Thomas Baaken** holds a position as Tenure Professor in Marketing at the Münster University of Applied Sciences (MUAS) since 1992. 1998-2003 he served as Vice President Research and TechTransfer at MUAS and was responsible for Research Strategies, Industrial Liaison, Entrepreneurial Activities, links to the European Commission, Technology Transfer, and the Marketing of the University's Research. In 2002 he founded the "Science-to-Business Marketing Research Centre" (www.science-marketing.com), which is creating Marketing Strategies for Research. The Centre itself and the University have been awarded by the Government and the Initiative of German Industry for Sciences (Stifterverband für die Deutsche Wissenschaft) as best practice for its unique and most successful University-Industry Interaction approach. Thomas Baaken was Visiting Professor at the ECIC University of Adelaide in Australia in 2003/2004 for 16 months and sequentially was appointed Adjunct Professor with the ECIC until today. Besides this Adjunct Position, Thomas Baaken holds International Fellowships at VU Vrije Universiteit Amsterdam, The Netherlands, IHI Zittau of Technical University Dresden, Germany and at Satakunta University of Applied Sciences in Finland. Thomas Baaken was responsible for a major study on "University-Business Cooperation in Europe" for the European Commission (www.ub-cooperation.eu). He published a number of papers in international journals, book chapters and reports and his records of presentations are listing more 40 countries in the world.

**Anikó Balogh** is a teacher both at Central European University, and Eötvös Loránd University on the subjects of Information Technology, Knowledge Management, eLearning, Information Society and Organisational Behaviour. She is a public member of the Hungarian Academy of Sciences, Hungarian Economic Association and John von Neumann Computer Society. She is also an active participant of the Hungarian Academy of Sciences Working Committee of Knowledge Management. She regularly lectures on the topic of eLearning and Knowledge Management at conferences, publishes in national and international journals, co-author of the E-Learning 2005 manual. Since 2006 she works as an independent expert at the European Commission for programs related to information and communication technologies (ICT) in Luxembourg and Brussels.

**Zoltán Baracskai** a Doctor of Economic Sciences since 1983. He was a Professor in Decision Making at some universities in Bosnia and Herczegovina, Croatia and Hungary. Now he holds a Visiting Professor of Decision Making at the Babeş-Bolyai University, Cluj-Napoca, Romania. Author of 16 books and over 120 conference papers. He developed Doctus, a knowledge-based expert system, and he created 160 knowledge-bases in different companies.

**Tamás Bognár** runs an own consultant company on organization development, works for multinational companies. He's doing his PhD studies at Széchenyi István University of Győr in Hungary. He is doing research in the fields of career development, HR selection and assessment. He is an author of some scientific publications on career management.

**Giulia Bruno** holds a Ph.D. in Information and System Engineering from Politecnico di Torino and currently she is a post-doc researcher in the same University. Her research activity is focused on data mining, semantic ontologies and system modeling and analysis. She was involved in several national and European projects on data analysis and product lifecycle management. She is also working in collaboration with the healthcare sanitary agencies for clinical and biological data analysis.

**Marcello Chedid** is a PhD student at the Department of Economics, Management and Industrial Engineering at the University of Aveiro (Portugal). He graduated in Economics from the Rio de Janeiro State University (Brazil), in 1980. Currently he is pursuing the PhD in Management and Industrial Engineering. Previously, he developed an executive career characterized by innovative actions and creativity. He accumulated great experience in implementation of computerized systems and in development of operational processes and of reengineering in large enterprises and varied segments. His current research interests include knowledge management applied to university-industry collaboration.

**Anikó Csepregi** is an Assistant Professor at the Department of Management, University of Pannonia, Veszprém. She obtained her Ph.D. (The Knowledge Sharing and Competences of Middle Managers) at the Doctoral School of Management Sciences and Business Administration in 2011 at University of Pannonia, Hungary. Anikó has been teaching a variety of bachelor and master courses including Management, Competence and Incentive Management, Project Management, Project Planning and Controlling, Labor Connections Controlling Personnel Processes, Professional Socialization Training. Since 2006 she has worked as a researcher: research team member of "International Mapping of Knowledge Sharing Excellence" (2006-2009: focusing on Hungary, Serbia, and Bulgaria), "Middle Managers' Knowledge Sharing and Knowledge Sharing Competences" (2009-2013: Hungary), "Project Management in the XXI. Century" (2014-present: Hungary) research. She is a full member of IAKM (International Association for Knowledge Management). She has been an editorial board member of Management & Marketing and a reviewer of Knowledge Management Research and Practice and for several international management journals. She was also a conference committee member of international conferences: European Conference on Knowledge Management in 2012, 2013, 2014, and 2015, 2016 and International Conference on Knowledge Management in 2015. Her main fields of interest are organizational culture, knowledge, competence, and project management. She has published numerous papers and has presented her research results at national and international conferences.

**Éva Fenyvesi** is a professor and head of the Institute of Economics and Social Sciences at Budapest Business School Faculty of Commerce, Catering and Turism. Her research focus is on knowledge management, economics and corruption economic analysis of excise goods' consumption.

**Bálint Filep** received his university degree in economics from the Széchenyi István University, Győr, Hungary, in 2004. He finished his doctoral studies in the same institution in the field of business and administration sciences in 2009. In 2005 he was hired at the Rector's Office as administrator expert. In 2014 he became the chancellor of the Széchenyi István University. Besides that he gained the associate professor classification. His main research areas are the regional competitiveness and the role of higher education institutions.

**Gabriella-Horváth Csikós** has been in the field of higher education for 15 years. At present she is teaching technical and professional language at Szent István University. Her PhD is in progress at Eötvös Lorand University.

**Tímea Juhász** has 18-years business experience primarily in the field of logistics, human resources and finance. She obtained her doctorate at the Doctoral School of Regional - and Economic Sciences at Széchenyi István University in 2010. At present she is working as a counsellor and teaches management studies at several Hungarian universities. Her research field: knowledge-management and human resource management. Author and co-author of several Hungarian and international articles and books.

**Kijpokin Kasemsap** received his BEng degree in Mechanical Engineering from King Mongkut's University of Technology, Thonburi, his MBA degree from Ramkhamhaeng University, and his DBA degree in Human Resource Management from Suan Sunandha Rajabhat University. He is a Special Lecturer in the Faculty of Management Sciences, Suan Sunandha Rajabhat University, based in Bangkok, Thailand. He is a Member of the International Association of Engineers (IAENG), the International Association of Engineers and Scientists (IAEST), the International Economics Development and Research Center (IEDRC), the International Association of Computer Science and Information Technology (IACSIT), the International Foundation for Research and Development (IFRD), and the International Innovative Scientific and Research Organization (IISRO). He also serves on the International Advisory Committee (IAC) for International Association of Academicians and Researchers (INAAR). He has had numerous original research articles in top international journals, conference proceedings, and books on the topics of business management, human resource management, and knowledge management, published internationally.

**Edit Kővári** is a lecturer at the Institute of Management, University of Pannonia, Veszprém, Hungary, and a finishing Ph.D. candidate at the Business School, University of Derby, UK. Her thesis concerns emotional intelligence of practicing managers and their relation to individual performance within organisational culture. Edit has been involved in a variety of undergraduate, master and MBA courses, numerous national and international, research, cooperation and projects and have been a visiting lecturer and trainer in several European countries.

**Erzsébet Noszkay**, Professor Emerita, expert and executive teacher at Budapest Metropolitan University, leader of Management and Organization Sciences Knowledge Center, head of MBA Turnaround management department, supervisor and teacher in two doctoral schools at Szent István University. ICMCI Academic Fellow, and the owner of more Hungarian awards in business advisory and management consulting. She is a very well recognized character in the Hungarian management and leadership: Member of the Committee on Business Administration of the Hungarian Academy of Sciences. President of Committee on Business Administration Hungarian Academy of Sciences of Knowledge Management Working Committee. Vice-president of Department of Professional Counseling at the Chamber of Trade and Commerce of Budapest. President of the National Association of Change and Turnaround Managers. She is the author of many specialized textbooks and publications.

**Nóra Obermayer** is an Associate Professor at the Department of Management, University of Pannonia, Veszprém. She obtained her Ph.D. (Conscious knowledge management in knowledge economy) in Economics and Management in 2008. She won the Best Young Researcher and Scientist Paper Award and received most prestigious Winner of Elsevier Scopus Young Researcher Awards in Engineering category. Nóra has been teaching a variety of management master courses including Strategic Human Resource Management, Globalization and Organizational Culture and Competence Management. She has gained international teaching experience as a participant in the Erasmus Teacher's Mobility Program. In 2013 she was a visiting lecturer at Fontys University of Applied Sciences in Eindhoven (The Netherlands) and had seminar focused on strategic human resource management and leadership. This year she is going to give lectures at the University of Lapland, Faculty of Social Science in Rovaniemi (Finland) in the field of Knowledge Management. Since 2004 she has worked as a researcher; as co-leader at "Knowledge Management in Hungary 2005/2006", „Organizational Knowledge Sharing in Hungary, 2013/2014", Knowledge sharing and emotional intelligence 2014/2015" national research and as recipient at international „Global Knowledge Survey 2012/2013" research. She is member of Hungarian Academy of Sciences (MTA), Section of Economics and Law (Committee on Economics – Knowledge Management) and the Program Committee of the European Conference on Knowledge Management. She has published numerous papers and presented at national and international conferences.

**Balzhan Orazbayeva** is affiliated with the Science-to-Business Marketing Research Centre (S2BM-RC) at Münster University of Applied Sciences (MUAS) in Germany, Balzhan Orazbayeva researches university-business collaboration and knowledge transfer processes. She is a researcher in the consulting project for the European Commission (DG Education and Culture), implementing the largest European study in the area of university-business collaboration. Balzhan also coordinates industry projects executed by students as part of International Marketing and Strategic Marketing modules at MUAS. Combining thinking in political terms with the willingness to understand how cross-cultural differences affect human´s behaviour on different levels, Balzhan is not only passionate about how higher educational institutions build relationships with the private sector in different countries, but also how interaction process between carriers of different cultures on individual level takes place. Her research interests include university-industry relationships, knowledge management and transfer, cross-cultural communication and intercultural competence. Balzhan is also a doctoral candidate and focuses in her PhD on cultural differences across different countries in terms of university-business collaboration. She holds a Bachelor degree on International Relations in a field of political and social sciences from German-Kazakh University (DKU) in Almaty, Kazakhstan. In addition, she holds a Master degree on Integrative Project

Management from International Institute (IHI) Zittau, a central academic unit of Dresden University of Technology (TUD) in Germany.

**Adam Pawliczek** currently works as a senior lecturer at the Institute of Economics and Control Systems at VŠB – Technical University of Ostrava and as a senior lecturer at the Department of Management and Marketing at Moravian University College Olomouc. After technic and economic degrees he obtained more than 12 years of experience as a project manager and as a researcher and over 7 years of experience as a university teacher. During his work experience he has published more than 40 scientific and educational publications on different topics concerning management, entrepreneurship, sustainability issues, SMEs performance and other. He has plenty of experience with the management of a small research team and with research and development projects.

**Hugo Pinto** has a PhD in Economics - Knowledge and Innovation (University of Coimbra). He was project manager in several R&D institutions in Portugal (BIC Algarve-Huelva, CRIA – University of Algarve, Centre of Marine Sciences, and University of Aveiro). Currently he is a research fellow at Centre for Social Studies, University of Coimbra. He lectures in the Faculty of Economics - University of Algarve and he is an associate member of the Research Centre for Spatial and Organizational Dynamics. His research interests are resilience of innovation systems, emergence of maritime clusters, knowledge production and transfer, and the role of universities in regional development. He is also interested in the discussion of Economics as a science. Hugo Pinto has participated in the preparation of several strategic documents, being the most recent the Algarve's RIS3 - Research and Innovation Strategy for Smart Specialization. Recent published research includes articles in Regional Studies, European Planning Studies, Technological Forecasting & Social Change or Marine Policy. He has edited "Resilient territories: Innovation and Creativity for New Modes for Regional Governance" (Cambridge Scholars Publishing).

**Irma Rácz** is an Assistant Professor of economic and management sciences and she's doing her PhD studies at Széchenyi István University in Hungary. Her research and teaching fields are knowledge- talent - change- human management. She is the author of some scientific publications on knowledge and talent management.

**Miroslav Rössler** is the Head of the Department of Management and Marketing at MUCO. He has 11 years of experience as a university teacher in the field of management and economics and 9 years of experience in scientific and research projects in university education. In the past, he worked at Palacký University in Olomouc. He has also large experience with managing a hospital and with scientific and research projects at universities.

**Leonor Teixeira** graduated in Industrial Engineering and Management, received a M.Sc. degree in Information Management, and a PhD in Industrial Management (Information Systems area), in 2008, from the University of Aveiro, Portugal. She is currently an Assistant Professor of the Department of Economics, Management and Industrial Engineering at the University of Aveiro and teaching subjects related to Information Systems, Information Technologies to undergraduate and post-graduate studies. She is also a researcher at the Institute of Electronics and Telematics Engineering (IEETA) of University of Aveiro. She has published in several peer-reviewed journals, book chapters and proceedings, and participated in several international scientific conferences, some of which as invited speaker. She serves as a member of Program Board and Organizing Committees for several Scientific Committees of International Conferences. She is associated with IIIS, IEEE and EMBS.

**Judit Bernadett Vágány** has a PhD in Management and Business Administration Sciences. She is a professor at Institute of Economics and Social Sciences at Budapest Business School Faculty of Commerce, Catering and Turism. Her research fields are general management, SME's and family businesses.

**Jolán Velencei** received her PhD in Economics and Management from the Budapest University of Technology and Economics in 2008. She received the Habilitation degree in 2016 for her thesis entitled "Decision makers vary". She is currently an Associate Professor at Keleti Faculty of Business and Management of Óbuda University, Budapest, Hungary. Her research is focused on modelling personal knowledge supported by building knowledge bases and drawing concept maps. Recently she has developed two Massive Open Online Course (MOOC) titled "Decision Support Systems" and "Innovation for Entrepreneurs" which are delivered in Hungary. Author of 5 books and over 70 scholarly articles in management science.

**Zoltán Véry** is a management professional, economist, titular associate professor. He worked as a business controller, later as a business development manager at knowledge-based enterprises. Currently, he teaches communication management in the framework of an MA program at the Budapest Metropolitan University, Hungary. His areas of expertise encompass the autopoietic organization and the versatile observation, management of small business enterprises. He is in close cooperation with the Budapest Chapter of the Hungarian Project Management Institute. He is also the author of numerous articles, studies and reviews in the field of management.

# Index

## A

Absorptive Capacity 42, 44, 47-48, 51, 234, 364
Academic Enterprise 362, 372, 380
Academic Science 361, 363, 372-373, 380-381
Actor-Network-Theory 365, 380
Altruism 271, 276
Assessment 9, 19, 125, 134-135, 204-205, 211-212, 214-215, 221, 239, 251, 372
Autopoietic Organization 340

## B

Balanced ScoreCard 7, 18, 120
Balanced ScoreCard-Assisted Learning-Development 132
Body of Knowledge 183, 336
Boundary Object 380
Business and Competitive Intelligence 180, 196-197
Business Intelligence 12, 129, 196-197, 203
Business Model 45, 72-73, 82, 84-86, 90, 299

## C

Capillary Model 137, 146-147, 149, 323
Coach 38, 346
Codification 8-9, 23, 231-233, 246, 319
Codification Approach 246
Collective Knowledge 50, 104, 316-317, 323-325, 328, 330, 332-333, 335, 338, 340
Collective of Thought 366-367, 380-381
Communities of Practice 50, 95, 112, 144-145, 153, 246
Competence 16, 20, 47-48, 68, 75, 83, 86, 91, 96, 99, 101-102, 109, 112-113, 121, 125, 127, 142, 204-205, 210-212, 214-215, 217-218, 220-222, 225, 248, 250, 257-258, 261, 268-269, 272-273, 275-276, 278-279, 289-290, 333, 346-347
Competition 28, 31-32, 36, 43, 68-69, 99, 114-115, 249, 291, 301-303, 307, 310, 369

Competitive Intelligence 180, 196-197, 203
Competitiveness 39, 42, 44, 48, 51, 68-69, 75, 91-92, 96, 98-99, 104-106, 108, 180-181, 184, 189, 192, 194, 197, 199, 203, 210, 250, 270, 289, 296, 307, 363, 371, 374
Compliance 125, 204-205, 211-212, 218, 220, 222, 225, 324, 326-327, 330, 336-337, 340
Compliance Control 327, 340
Controlling 81, 196, 299, 327, 330, 333-336
Cooperation 46, 70, 72-73, 75, 84, 98, 142-144, 153-154, 216, 219, 254, 291, 301-304, 307, 310, 335, 338, 340, 345, 363-364, 368-369, 372, 375
Corporate Culture Supporting Mentoring 360
Corporate Strategy 113-116, 118-121, 125, 132, 141
Crisis 146, 197, 212-222, 225, 364
Cross-Cultural Communication 249, 254, 256, 260, 268
Cultural Diversity 234, 248-249, 252, 254, 258-261
Cultural Intelligence 259, 268
Culture 3, 14, 26, 28, 39, 48, 50-51, 68-71, 73-76, 81, 83-84, 86, 90-97, 99, 101, 104, 106, 109, 112, 120, 123, 125, 130, 132, 137-138, 142-144, 147, 149, 183, 211, 232, 235-236, 249, 253-256, 259, 268, 276, 291, 294-295, 297-298, 300-302, 308-310, 317, 323, 333, 343, 346, 357, 360, 363-364, 375
Czech Republic 187, 189, 296

## D

Data 2-3, 12, 23, 30, 36-38, 45, 67, 122, 127-129, 132, 157-166, 174, 178-179, 182, 187-189, 196, 203, 228, 231, 250, 256, 268, 279, 297-298, 303, 305, 308, 316, 337-338, 371
Digital Economy 2, 158, 160
DoctuS Knowledge-Based System 41

## E

E-Learning 11, 14, 19-20, 23, 50, 127
Emotional Intelligence 96, 98-99, 101, 112, 269, 273-

## F

## G

## H

## I

## K